ANALYZING GENDER

ANALYZING GENDER

A Handbook of Social Science Research

EDITORS
Beth B. Hess
AND
Myra Marx Ferree

SAGE PUBLICATIONS
The Publishers of Professional Social Science
Newbury Park   Beverly Hills   London   New Delhi

For information address:

SAGE Publications, Inc.
2111 West Hillcrest Drive
Newbury Park, California 91320

SAGE Publications Inc.      SAGE Publications Ltd.
275 South Beverly Drive   28 Banner Street
Beverly Hills   London EC1Y 8QE
California 90212   England

SAGE PUBLICATIONS India Pvt. Ltd.
M-32 Market
Greater Kailash I
New Delhi 110 048 India

Printed in the United States of America

Library of Congress Cataloging-in-Publication Data

Analyzing gender.

Bibliography: p.
Includes indexes.
1. Women--History.   2. Sex role.   3. Feminism.
I. Hess, Beth B., 1928-   . II. Ferree, Myra Marx.
HQ1154.A685   1987   305.4'09   87-23439
ISBN 0-8039-2719-3

CONTENTS

DEDICATION

This book is dedicated to the memory of Richard Hess, husband of Beth and cousin to Myra. It was this family connection that brought the editors of *Analysing Gender* together as colleagues many years ago, even though we are as different from one another as any two feminist sociologists can be. Our shared family bond soon led to successful collaboration on a number of projects, of which this volume is the most recent.

Dick Hess has been a marvelous example of the capacity to adapt and change. Socialized to traditional norms, he became a strong supporter of civil rights, the antiwar movement, and feminism—not in rebellion against his upbringing, but because he was also raised to care about justice, fairness, and ethical conduct. He would most certainly have become a feminist even without Beth's influence!

No one could have been more supportive of a spouse's career: sharing childcare during graduate student days, encouraging scholarly production, assisting with the tasks of professional office. He will be greatly missed.

B.B.H.
M.M.F.

Introduction

MYRA MARX FERREE
University of Connecticut

BETH B. HESS
County College of Morris

O NE way of dating the feminist revolution in the social sciences is to begin from the publication of Marcia Millman and Rosabeth Kanter's *Another Voice* in 1975. This was hardly the first feminist contribution to the social sciences of recent years, nor was it the first collection of feminist essays provoked by the reemergence of an organized women's movement in the 1960s. Nonetheless, it marked the beginning of an era of feminist social science.

Before *Another Voice* the many daring and original articles that connected feminist concerns to the practices and issues of social science appeared primarily in movement publications. These essays were only gradually collected into books aimed at a mass market (e.g., Morgan, 1970; Gornick and Moran, 1971). Relatively little of this early intellectual ferment appeared in established academic sources or was directed to specifically academic audiences. By the early 1970s, researchers influenced by the burgeoning women's movement began to frame their questions about the status of women in social scientific terms. The first notable collection of such work, *Changing Women in a Changing Society* (1973), edited by Joan Huber, originally appeared as a special issue of the *American Journal of Sociology*. The first edition of Jo Freeman's *Women: A Feminist Perspective* (1975) also brought together original synthesizing essays that challenged traditional theories and conclusions about women. *Another Voice,* however, more than these or other early collections, began to move in the direction of developing feminist theory. The volume provided integrated and comprehensive critiques of the social sciences from a feminist perspective, pushing the field beyond the simple "add-women-and-stir" formula for incorporating women into existing paradigms of research.

Another Voice made clear that there were feminist questions that had not yet been imagined and that the answers would demand a fundamental transformation of the social sciences. Provocative problems were posed in that volume including many that remain unresolved: What class position do women hold? Why is deviance for women equated with sexuality? What kind of work is housework and whom does it benefit? What does male-centered education do to women? By asking searching questions of all the major institutional areas studied by the social sciences, *Another Voice* was a revolutionary book. As a pioneering work, it was also seriously limited by existing gaps in theory and research. Nonetheless, the essays stimulated an entire generation of feminist social scientists to realize that the questions existed and the answers were significant.

In the years since *Another Voice* the work of feminist social scientists directed to these issues has become impressive in its scope, quality, and significance. Major journals in all the social sciences regularly publish studies focusing on women, if not typically ones that challenge presuppositions of the field. Journals with a specific focus on gender issues have been establishing this concern as a significant speciality. The literature on gender continues to grow exponentially until it is now a double-edged sword: The sweep and richness of this work are exciting to scholars already in the area, but may be daunting to newcomers, be they graduate students or faculty.

The present volume is an attempt to provide an overview of feminist perspectives in the social sciences today. Like any survey of a rapidly changing field, it cannot claim to be definitive. It is an effort, however, to move out and away from questions toward answers. Collections that pose feminist challenges to the standard paradigms of the social sciences have become common (e.g. Sherman and Beck, 1979; Spender, 1981; Roberts, 1981; Bowles and Duelli-Klein, 1983). It is our premise that feminist research has now multiplied and matured sufficiently to allow a self-reflective examination of what has been accomplished and where further work is needed. While the chapters of this volume vary in scope and in style, they share a common concern with articulating what we know and what we need to know about the significance of gender in social organization. Because this book is intended as a compendium in the social sciences of feminist research on gender, it is important to clarify what is meant by each of these terms.

THE DOMAIN OF SOCIAL SCIENCE

The interdisciplinary focus of women's studies is central to its self-definition. The journals of this field, such as *Signs* or *Feminist Studies*, make deliberate and largely successful efforts to cross the boundaries of traditional disciplines and to develop new knowledge that fits women better than it fits the traditional pigeonholes of academic discourse. In this context, it would be impossible to present an overview of feminist research that confined itself to the territory of any one conventional discipline. Scholars trained to respect the boundaries of academic departments tend to ask, "Is it economics?" or "Is it psychology?" before considering whether a research question is important and to whom. This sort of disciplinary fencing is not really feasible for the feminist research surveyed here. Although authors were chosen who hold positions in a variety of social science departments and whose disciplinary training is also diverse, the areas they cover spread across traditional lines. They incorporate perspectives more characteristic of the fundamentally interdisciplinary nature of women's studies than of their own fields.

At the same time, the authors are not representative of all of women's studies either, as they share a focus and perspective that distinguishes them as social scientists. The perspective can loosely be called "structural": Attention is directed outward from the individual to the social structures that shape experience and meaning, that give people a location in the social world, and that define and allocate economic and social rewards. This type of analysis is quite different from that appropriate for self-referential symbol systems such as literary texts or from other types of scientific endeavor. Even within the social sciences a structural perspective is not always applied; some scholars take the individual as the basic unit, with social organization added on. From a structural perspective, however, individuality itself is a social product.

Because most research within the social sciences has suffered from systematic biases regarding women, feminists see a need for correction on several levels. The most elementary is the recognition of absence—that women have been excluded from consideration, and that many of the most meaningful issues have not been addressed. The process of filling these voids has moved rapidly enough in most disciplines that it is now evident that these omissions were there for a reason. Recognition of the systematic nature of these gaps demands a rethinking of basic conceptual frameworks, including a reexamination of how women and men are differentiated. The emergent feminist perspective represented in this book defines this difference in social structural, rather than individual, terms.

Feminist critics have also described a number of biases within the social sciences that go beyond the simple exclusion of women from entire areas of study and the failure to explore the social origins of differences between men and women. The choice of different concepts, interpretations, and even language for describing women's experience has often been made in the context of a tendency to devalue the female as an expression of an intrinsically lesser nature. Because social scientific thought has been formulated by men, placing men at the center, and with men as the intended audience, women have been transformed into objects without consciousness, existing only in relation to men. As Dorothy Smith explained it, the social sciences constitute a community of discourse with a momentum of its own, a landscape in which even the most accomplished women scholars are in part strangers because it fails to incorporate their experience of reality, even as an African child brought up on British books finds a division between the mental and physical worlds of experience (1979: 138-139).

Moreover, there has been an inclination to press an abstract dichotomization by sex on the natural diversity of humanity, ignoring variation within each group and reifying group differences as an attribute of persons. Male and female have been taken as opposite ends of a continuum, as discrete and non-overlapping categories, and as biologically defined traits rather than as socially constructed labels that carry a situationally variable degree of significance (Lopata and Thorne, 1978). For example, sociologists understood "being blind" as a social construct before being able to recognize "being male" as similarly socially defined (see Scott, 1969), despite the ubiquity of rituals for establishing and asserting "manhood."

Because of these biases, the structural perspective characteristic of the social sciences has not yet been consistently and coherently applied to men and women as such. The feminist project demands reconceptualization of what "male" and "female" mean in terms of the social systems that organize perception, identity, action, and the allocation of costs and benefits for all people. "Maleness" and "femaleness" are then perceived consequences of the operation of these social systems on the variability provided by nature rather than as the property of individuals abstracted from their culture. This is a perspective that is as distinctively social as it is feminist.

DOING FEMINIST RESEARCH

There is today, also, an expanding literature on feminist methodology in the social sciences that attempts systematically to consider how to do research that is more consistent with this theoretical approach (see the annotated bibliography in Bowles and Duelli-Klein, 1983). There are several premises central to the practice of feminist research that inform many of the chapters of this book.

First, there is a fundamental rejection of the ideal of value-free research in favor of a conscious partiality. The increased visibility of the once unconscious bias toward a male-defined, male-centered world in the supposedly value-free research of the past has exposed this ideal as a political myth. There is also a theoretical objection to the idea that any significant work can be done without a perspective or theory behind it; any choice of perspective is by definition political because it defines both a community of knowers and objects to be known. The "generalizing impersonal mode" obscures but does not eliminate the reality of a perspective rooted in the experience of a specific, limited community and concrete, everyday activity (Smith, 1979).

This critique is a self-reflective one. It does not suffice to recognize the biases hidden in the generalizing impersonal language of male-defined social science without taking the next step—to uncover and reject the generalizing impersonal when used by white, middle-class feminists to speak of all women (Joseph and Lewis, 1981; Bell-Scott, 1982). Thus feminist methodology interprets conscious partiality as a mandate for deliberately inclusive research designs and for awareness of the significance of gender, race, and class in constituting the social scientific community of discourse. The various chapters of this book strive to reflect this conscious attention to the diversity of women's voices.

Second, feminist methodology rejects the positivist division between theory and practice, between the researcher and the "object" of research (Mies, 1983; Stacey and Thorne, 1985). The image of science as establishing mastery over subjects, as demanding the absence of feeling, and as enforcing separateness of the knower from the known, all under the guise of "objectivity," has been carefully critiqued even in reference to the physical sciences (e.g., Keller, 1982). Elements that are present in scientific knowing but devalued because they are associated with femaleness—intuition, empathy, and passion—are ignored in the positivist account and eventually distort the actual process of doing science. Yet it is this masculinized image of science, rather than the more complex reality, that the social sciences embraced in their drive to attain academic credibility (Ross, 1979). Feminist social scientists, reclaiming the value of the female, legitimate these very elements that have been denied and repressed in science itself (e.g., Elshtain, 1979; Westcott, 1979).

Commitment to these more inclusive forms of knowing discredits the image of the uninvolved spectator as the ideal social scientist. The feminist view encourages research based on engagement in struggle as a means of becoming conscious of social relationships and structures that might otherwise remain obscure (e.g., Reinharz, 1979). The original essays collected here express different sorts of political orientations but share a willingness to make these commitments visible and to use them reflexively as a conceptual tool. This also makes the chapters less static than most reviews of literature tend to be. The authors are empathetic and passionate in their scholarship and thus attuned to the currents of change in society at large as well as in the research literature.

Third, the emerging feminist methodology that is developing is profoundly anti-functionalist, whether this comes in a conventional or Marxist guise (e.g., Stanley and Wise, 1983). There is a desire to accommodate a holistic view of social structural arrangements as defining situations and limiting the range of possible actions with a recognition of individuals as agents of change. Social structures are viewed as having contradictory impulses rather than as promoting a smooth and satisfactory accommodation between individual needs and social demands. Attention is directed to the conflicts within experience, to the reality of guilt and ambivalence rather than either simple accommodation or resistance to structures that oppress people (Stacey and Thorne, 1985; Stanley and Wise, 1983).

Consequently, the structural perspective in feminist research and in this volume is less deterministic than commonly found in the social sciences. By insisting on beginning from and remaining true to personal experience, feminist researchers preserve the distinction between knowing what is expected and doing it (e.g. Gerson, 1985). Resistance, ambivalence, conflict, and struggle are key concepts for feminist theory and methodology because of the centrality of the distinction between what is and what ought to be. The view of women as agents of change rather than as merely passive victims of circumstances animates research into how women themselves interpret and respond to structures of opportunity and constraint, but also forces recognition of the limited alternatives for action facing women who wish to resist oppression (Westcott, 1979; Smith, 1979).

The awareness of change and inconsistency within individuals as well as between them has rendered traditional theories of socialization based on assumptions of internalization and compliance obviously inadequate (Stacey and Thorne, 1985; Stanley and Wise, 1983; Weitzman, 1984). Recognition of how people do not become what they are expected to be has produced growing criticism of functionalist ideas embedded in the concepts of "sex role" and "socialization" (Lopata and Thorne, 1978). This critique has been sufficiently expanded to present a profoundly different perspective on female and male as categories of persons, one that centers on the concept of gender.

ANALYZING GENDER

The study of men and women as such has moved through three distinct stages in just the past twenty years, from an emphasis on sex differences through preoccupation with sex roles to the centrality of gender. The sex differences perspective is, of course, the most traditional. It holds that maleness and femaleness are biologically given properties of individuals with clear implications for social behavior of one sort or another. Within this perspective, the egalitarian view is that such sex differences are small relative to intrasex variation, that they are rarely relevant for important behaviors, and that the differences are as likely to be instances of female superiority as male. Historically, a nonegalitarian view of sex differences has been more prevalent; these differences are used to explain male dominance by assuming that they are large, socially significant, and consistently favor men. In both cases, the source of sex differences is either sought among specific biological features or assumed to be known, and is not considered to need social scientific explanation. Within this perspective, the egalitarians have always found themselves on the defensive, trying to demonstrate that the intrinsic differences between men and women are not large or meaningful enough to account for the degree and ubiquity of male domination observed in society.

Politically and conceptually, the move to a sex role socialization model was a great improvement. From this perspective, the biological determinants of maleness and femaleness could be combined with social determination via upbringing in any proportion of nature and nurture that seemed appropriate. Sex differences were no longer intrinsically important issues, since both large and small differences could be explained by socialization. Egalitarians could not be distinguished from sexists on the matter of magnitude, but rather in the amount of attention they gave to specific socialization practices, especially those of early childhood. If the socialization of very young children was demonstrably different for boys than for girls, then such differences of nurture would be sufficient to account for sex differences in personality or behavior in adulthood.

Given the assumption that socialization practices are more susceptible to change than are biological features, the sex roles debate often confounded questions about the desirability or feasibility of altering relationships between men and women with questions about whether a particular difference could be attributed to nature or to nurture. In fact, as shown in the case of transsexuals, some biological features are more readily altered than social ones. It is also easy to imagine social arrangements that accommodate or compensate for biological differences (e.g., eyeglasses for astigmatism) as well as those that reflect and reinforce biological differences that have been endowed with social significance (e.g., shunning short men or tall women).

A second problem in the literature on sex roles involves the presumption of continuity throughout the life course. Advocates of nurture accepted the premise that early learning was one of the most influential determinants of later behavior and assumed consistency between the behaviors and expectations typical of children (e.g., playing with dolls or trucks) and those of adults (e.g., male or female sex-typed careers). This perspective not only trivializes the consequences of adult learning and change throughout life, but also rests on the idea of an abstract female role that exists apart from any specific interpersonal relationship and without concrete behavioral content. The focus is on personality traits that are presumed to be constant across situations and over the life cycle and that can supposedly be used to predict a wide range of behaviors. As Lopata and Thorne (1978) argue, this is neither the way that sociologists have usually theorized roles nor is it a plausible model of female behavior. The absurdity of speaking of "race roles" or "the black role" brings home the contrast between the structural and situational perspective used for race and class, on the one hand, and the individualized, essentialist view inherent in the sex roles approach on the other.

Just as the awareness of cross-cultural differences in what constituted maleness and femaleness was an important step in moving from a biologically determined view of sex differences to a socialization determined view of sex roles, the increasing evidence of inconsistency of any one individual's behavior across time and in different situations now casts doubt on both of these determinist views. So-called sex roles as personality traits or characteristics of individuals (as in the Bem Sex Role Inventory) are notoriously poor predictors of behaviors. While the naive view or "natural attitude" supposes people to have a stable and consistent personality developed in infancy, the absence of predictability of behavior from one context to another has long made this essentialist assumption scientifically dubious. Moreover, the only trait that links behaviors as diverse as sewing, nursing, and scrubbing floors is the sex-typing done by the perceiver. The fact that each characteristic could in theory be separately socialized into little girls does not begin to explain why they are packaged together conceptually. The label "female" is itself an abstract categorization that links an incredible diversity of unrelated and frequently inconsistent behavioral expectations and outcomes. To describe anything that receives the label "female" as part of a supposed sex role is to grant it a coherence, consistency, and constancy that the evidence does not justify (see Gerson, 1985).

As a result, recent years have seen the emergence of an entirely new perspective on maleness and femaleness. The key concept in this view is gender, seen as a principle organizing social arrangements, behavior, and even cognition. One of the central elements in gender systems is the taboo against the sameness of male and female, "a taboo which exacerbates the biological differences between the sexes and thereby *creates* gender"(Rubin, 1975: 178). Because the gender system insists on and rewards difference, men and women are created who have an interest in presenting themselves and being perceived as "real" men and "real" women—that is, without elements socially defined as belonging in the other category. As Gayle Rubin put it, "from the standpoint of nature, men and women are closer to each other than either is to anything else—for instance, mountains, kangaroos, or coconut palms . . . the idea that men and women are two mutually exclusive categories must arise out of something other than a non-existent 'natural' opposition. Far from being an expression of natural differences, exclusive gender identity is the suppression of natural similarities" (1975: 179-180) for social purposes and by social means.

The division of labor by sex, whatever it might be in any given society, is then understood to be also an outgrowth of that fundamental taboo rather than the cause of the differences between men and women. Doing gender-specific work is part of what defines "real" men and women as such; so too are gender-specific sexual relations. Gender is not a trait but a system for dividing people into distinct, nonoverlapping categories despite their natural variability on any particular characteristic and regardless of the inconsistency between features that are all supposed to be definitive.

Because the gender system is not a reflection of natural differences, creating gender is a struggle. We all bear "the traces of conscription" into a system that represses parts of our potential and no one ever fully conforms to it. On the other hand, even those individuals who deliberately refuse to take their allotted place in the system cannot escape knowing what it is (Rubin, 1975). Unlike the socialization account of sex roles, the psychic processes central to the gender model include ambivalence, conflict, and rebellion. Indeed, there can be no such thing as the well-socialized individual who smoothly accommodates all of society's demands because the demands themselves are inconsistent and even contradictory.

Moreover, like other power relations, gender is constantly being renegotiated and reconstituted (Margolis, 1985) and it is particularly visible at boundaries and points of change (Gerson and Peiss, 1985). Because gender is relational rather than essential, structural rather than individual, analyzing gender requires consideration of changes in systems over time. The alteration in social structures themselves as well as variation in individual relations within these gender systems demand attention to both macro and micro levels of structure and of change.

The editors and authors of this volume adopt the gender perspective and analyze its implications for the social sciences. The basic assumption is that gender is a property of systems rather than people, but that it is also important to trace the experiences of people within a gendered social structure. The first part, "Gender and Ideology," examines the meaning of gender and the ways in which gender ideology has been used as an organizing principle for social systems, for knowledge, and for perception itself. The next two sections explore the dynamics of gender understood as a property of social systems: Part II, "Social Control of Female Sexuality," deals with the social construction and organization of sexuality and reproduction; and Part III develops perspectives on "Gender Stratification" in economic relations. The chapters in Part IV, "Gendered Worlds," investigate the consequences of gender for women's lives in selected areas of civil society. The final section, "Gender and the State," considers the significance of gender in relationship to political systems and processes.

PART I: GENDER AND IDEOLOGY

The book opens with anthropologist Christine Ward Gailey's analysis of how and why gender has been constructed in the transition from kinship to state societies. Beginning with an overview of kinship societies, Gailey notes that gender must clearly be distinguished from biological sex in that it is possible to acknowledge at least four "genders": children, for whom reproduction is not relevant; adult males and females of reproductive age; and elders, who occupy a status defined by age rather than reproductive capacity. Because our society emphasizes gender differentiation from cradle to grave, we overlook the significance of cultures that use only one term for children or elders of both sexes. Gailey also distinguishes patriarchy—male dominance through specific kin roles—from other forms of male supremacist society. She draws an interesting parallel between Western industrial societies and Inca culture, where abstract maleness was equated with power, so that women of the ruling group could be "honorary males" while people of conquered nations were defined as female. The only universals about gender, Gailey finds, are that it is defined in part independently of biological sex—as when *berdaches* or other transsexuals cross gender lines in a culturally acceptable manner—and that it provides a basis for division of labor in all societies.

Gailey then critically examines existing theories of gender hierarchy and the origins of male supremacy—not only the biological determinism of the myth of "man the hunter" and its most recent apotheosis in sociobiology, but also several of the culturally universalistic schemas proposed by feminist scholars. Gailey finds flaws in arguments based on such dichotomies as public/private or culture/nature, and on structuralist principles of exchange. Eschewing global explanations of women's subordination, Gailey locates the origins of gender inequality in the history of other forms of stratification, primarily the emergence of the organized state, both precapitalist and capitalist. She argues that especially in class societies women come to be defined solely in terms of membership in this abstract gender category rather than through particular kin-defined identities. As the gender hierarchy is intertwined with these other bases of stratification, Gailey proposes that the agenda for change must challenge all sources of inequality: race, ethnicity, and class, as well as gender.

The significance of beliefs in the inevitability and importance of difference in constructing gender is a starting point for social psychologist Janet Sayers in her analysis of science and feminism. She shows how existing ideas of women as embodiments of domesticity and morality were adapted by the scientific "experts" who replaced religious authorities in the early nineteenth century. Where evangelical beliefs placed women closer to God, the ideology guiding science defined women as closer to nature. As religious orthodoxy lost its power to justify social relations, science emerged as the idiom of debate for social and political questions.

Sayers demonstrates how both feminists and antifeminists sought to bend these ideas to their own purposes. The nineteenth-century scientific investigation of menstruation, brain size, and instincts has parallels in twentieth-century studies of endocrinology and brain lateralization, both in the political agenda guiding such research and in the contrasting interpretations applied to findings. While it is easy to recognize the distortions introduced into nineteenth-century science by the overriding commitment to find some sort of natural difference to account for inequality, it is much more difficult to expose the ideology underlying contemporary science. Unlike earlier efforts, current scientific practice has not yet had its premises disproved by women's actual success in overcoming the inequities that such science is being used to justify. Convictions about gender not born of data continue to influence priorities, methodologies, interpretations, and the likelihood of publication in the sciences.

Yet Sayers cautions us not to abandon science because it has failed to meet the test of objectivity; rather, feminists can and must enter these fields in order to correct such biases and to apply the insights and prestige of scientific research toward the goal of transforming power relationships in the wider society. Thus she is as critical of feminist equations of femaleness with nature, the innocent victim of science, as she is of the antifeminist variants of this theme. Sayers also questions whether some feminist reactions to male-defined science might not also rely on the dominant gender ideology that assigns women the moral obligation of tempering male brutality.

The scientific search for sex differences has perhaps nowhere been more feverishly pursued than in psychology, some branches of which have been built precisely on the assumption of such basic differences. Psychologists Kay Deaux and Mary F. Kite begin by examining research on sex similarities and differences in cognitive functioning and personality dispositions, showing once again how gender preconceptions are so deeply entrenched that every aspect of the enterprise is questionable: the assumptions, the instruments, the selection of samples, the disregard of findings of no difference, and the persistence of a gender belief system in the face of disconfirming evidence. The motivation for this intense search for sex differences in traits and attitudes seems to lie in the researchers' gender beliefs, which posit the necessity of basic sex differences to account for gender inequality.

Deaux and Kite then contrast this approach to that implied by the gender perspective, in which the gender belief system *itself* becomes the object of study. The perceiver, whether psychologist or subject, holds certain beliefs, evaluations, judgments, and attitudes toward women and men. Inherent differences between women and men are thought to be expressed in characteristic behaviors, types of dress and appearance, occupations, and roles. Such essentialist views have directed disproportionate research attention to individual personality measures as defining maleness and femaleness, as basic traits with global consequences, ignoring statistical variability.

Deaux and Kite's gender analysis sees all these perceptions—of traits, of behaviors, of one's self and others—as organized by the underlying ideology of the observer. The authors seek to uncover the interrelation of these diverse views and their connections to actual behaviors of women and men in specific situations. This perceiver-focused analysis of gender beliefs highlights the significance of context, especially in those situations where beliefs and behaviors diverge. This perspective leads to a dynamic analysis that not only describes the stereotypes that people hold but also the effects of such stereotypes and the ways in which they change.

PART II: SOCIAL CONTROL OF FEMALE SEXUALITY

If the search for sex differences in brains and psyches has been largely chimerical, one distinction appears ineluctable: sexuality itself. The study of sexuality is a pivotal element in linking gender-based preconceptions to the social construction of inequality. Questions of power—Who defines sexuality and divides acceptable from unacceptable behaviors? What is the nature of erotic power? How is gender inequality expressed in sexual relationships?— are central to the chapter by sociologists Beth E. Schneider and Meredith Gould. These authors have been pioneers in the emerging sociology of sexuality and its challenge to masculinist definitions of what women ought to feel and how they should achieve "true" sexual pleasure (e.g., vaginal orgasm in a heterosexual relationship) and to the traditional social science methods for gathering and interpreting "data." The starting point for this new area of study is the realization that "social actors possess genitals rather than the other way around"—that is, that sexuality is socially structured, not biologically driven, and that gender is perhaps the most crucial principle around which sexuality is organized. Schneider and Gould argue that the most accurate way to study female sexuality is to pay attention to what women actually say about their experiences. While this has been ignored in the past, women today are reclaiming the power to name what is happening to them in sexual as well as nonsexual relationships.

Schneider and Gould trace the ways in which contemporary women are changing their sexual scripts, noting dilemmas posed by the equation of heterosexuality with violence and domination in much of the feminist literature and by the counterattack on sexuality from the political right. They thus set the stage for a theory of female sexuality that transcends the crippling constraints of heterosexist, reproduction-oriented views of women.

Female reproduction, so central to feminist analysis and antifeminist organizing, is the focus of sociologist Barbara Katz Rothman's analysis. She notes that although individual women may have conflicting or ambiguous feelings about motherhood, the "feminist position" on the issue has been relatively unproblematic: The key to equality is control over reproductive choice. But today's questions are not quite as clear-cut, and choice alone will not resolve key ethical dilemmas confronting women who have the power to choose. Control over such choices may also gradually be slipping into the hands of reproductive technicians. Rothman reviews the position of mini- malist and maximalist feminists (i.e., those who view sex differences as basically inconsequential, and those who claim that there is a unique female essence associated with birthing/mothering) and concludes that either viewpoint can be used *against* women in patriarchal society. Women need to articulate their own experiences of childbirth but also to subject these personal feelings to critical examination for they are produced in a particular social context that includes some very powerful prescriptions for what mothers should feel.

One very disturbing element of the present social context is the develop- ment of reproductive technologies that alienate mother from child, so that the fetus is perceived as the patient—sometimes coequal with the women in whose womb it resides, but increasingly as an entity whose rights can conflict with those of the mother (e.g., in the case of court-ordered caesarean sections or fetal surgery). Other dilemmas confront women faced with choices about abortion of "defective" fetuses. In a society that defines female, black, and handicapped children as lacking in value, how can women make a "free" choice? Ultimately, the questions raised by Rothman's analysis are designed to provoke "the articulation of a feminist ideology that can embrace the feelings of women as mothers, the technology of reproduction, and the social context in which both develop."

As the first two chapters in Part II indicate, not only is female sexuality socially constructed, it is also socially controlled. Political scientist Carole J. Sheffield examines the use of violence or threats of violence—"sexual terrorism"—as a mechanism for keeping women in their place. Sheffield delineates the ideological supports for female subordination, their expression in pornography and such acts of amoral violence as rape, wife assault, the sexual abuse of children, sexual harassment, and sexual slavery. Scholars do not yet know how these various manifestations of anti-female violence are linked to one another or whether their apparent recent increase is a direct response to the new feminist activism. Still there can be no doubt that a growing awareness of their vulnerability has affected millions of American women. The perceptions of victims and their attempts to overcome intimidation are briefly described; but as Sheffield notes at the beginning and end of her chapter, however far we may have moved toward equality, these steps are relatively meaningless if girls and women cannot walk the streets in safety or live in their homes without fear.

Sheffield remarks on the role of the mass media in perpetuating the image of women as victim and in reinforcing stereotypes of masculine power and "honor" that justify sexual terrorism. In the following chapter, sociologist Muriel Cantor details how gender is built into every aspect of mass communications but especially focuses on portrayals of men and women in media primarily directed to female consumers: magazines, romance fiction, and television soap operas. Across the media, over time, regardless of social class and despite enormous changes in the society and culture, one theme remains dominant: the supreme importance of romance in the life of a woman. This is particularly true for the portrayal of sexuality.

Cantor also discusses how such items of popular culture are created and who controls the productive process, as well as the effects of audiences on the content of the material they are offered. For all its modern veneer, women's fiction continues to construct women's sexual and social needs in ways that reinforce dependence on men and that perpetuate gender inequality. Cantor notes that women accept these constructions because they provide substitute satisfactions for other, less attainable ideals. Women's actual subordination creates the demand for fantasies to obscure this reality, while producers of media products for this market are shaping their wares to meet this demand.

PART III: GENDER STRATIFICATION

The imposition of an ideology of two genders and the differential evaluation of these differences has one universal outcome: systems of gender stratification in which males have greater claims on and access to the scarce resources—power, prestige, and property—of a society than do females. The first chapter in this section, by sociologist Susan Tiano, provides an overview of the socioeconomic status of women in developing societies. Using the framework of a critique of three explanatory schema—integration, marginalization, and exploitation—Tiano documents the failure of the world capitalist system to bring prosperity to the vast majority of Third World peoples. Rather, existing stratification hierarchies have been reinforced by the move toward cash/market economies, rapid population growth, and the exclusion of most women from the limited formal work sector, except as poorly paid assemblers.

Throughout the Third World, as the local subsistence economy is replaced by cash crops or assembly-line work for multinational corporations and as men migrate to urban shanty towns, it is poor rural women who have borne the brunt of recent changes. But even women of the small middle-class stratum lose power relative to their husbands. Tiano concludes that both "marginality and exploitation are the twin faces of women's subordinate status" in the developing nations of Asia, Africa, and Central and South America. Women rendered economically vulnerable in a cash economy can be readily exploited by multinational firms seeking a docile labor force.

Faced with the need to supplement household income through paid employment but still burdened with full responsibility for child care, Third World women drift between the formal and informal work sectors, further eroding their economic position. Nonetheless, Tiano notes the liberating potential of development particularly in the areas of health care and communications. But the obstacles are enormous: imperialism, which oppresses all Third World people; capitalism, which oppresses all wage workers; and partriarchy, which oppresses all women. It is not enough, then, to resist only one of these interlocking systems of power.

Shifting their gaze to the more developed nations, economists Penelope Ciancanelli and Bettina Berch examine systems of gender inequality in industrial society as these have been rationalized by mainstream economic models. Standard economic theory focuses on the individual who is assumed to make rational choices on the basis of a personal calculus of costs and benefits. Thus women's location in low-paying jobs and their unequal pay scales are explained in terms of choices that workers make in the light of competing demands and perceived opportunity costs. But the tractability of these positivist models is bought at the cost of a narrow perspective that systematically excludes the consideration of power and inequality, so that stratification is rendered invisible.

Ciancanelli and Berch show how the application of these models to the division of labor at both the societal and household levels has serious inconsistencies. For example, income and work that are essential to making the micro-level models work have to be hidden in order to make the macro-level models usable. Since the work and income that are thus obscured are women's, it appears that women continue to create anomalies in the paradigm constructed around male labor.

These models are also scientifically dubious as they cannot be disproved: Any choice is *post facto* assumed to reflect the values that a given woman places on leisure, household labor, or paid employment. Like the biological and psychological theories examined by Sayers and by Deaux and Kite, the very premise of orthodox economics rests on the need to discover innate differences in order to rationalize inequality. In discussions of discrimination and comparable worth, mainstream economists revert to political assertions about the invisible hand of the market that they would scarcely take seriously in any context other than sex differences in jobs and pay.

The authors also discuss the work of economists outside the mainstream—primarily feminists and marxists—who have sought to introduce structural elements (including capitalism and patriarchy) into the analysis of labor force segregation and inequitable pay scales. In this perspective, the division of labor in the economy and household are "not simply efficient allocations of tastes, but simultaneously a gendered and hierarchical distribution of status and income."

Ciancanelli and Berch then examine several scenarios for the future, and find little about which to be sanguine. For example, it is doubtful that free market forces will ultimately reduce male-female labor disparities, or that the electronic cottage will enhance women's economic power, or that the high-tech revolution will provide women with high status jobs. There are, however, promising "feminist interventionist" strategies to be pursued, such as the current fight for pay equity. Systems of "difference," whether based on race, gender, or ethnicity, claim the authors, will not automatically fade away. Stratification is not the outcome of neutral allocation processes but the very method of allocation itself.

Despite the many differences between developing and industrial nations, these two chapters reach very similar conclusions, largely because in all societies most women carry a double burden: productive labor within or outside the household, on the one hand, and exclusive responsibility for homemaking and child care on the other. Yet a cloud of gender assumptions regarding work continues to obscure this reality. Sociologist Christine E. Bose represents a needed corrective to most sociohistorical accounts of the ideal and reality of "dual spheres"—that is, the presumed split between a male world of work outside the home and a woman's world confined to household and family, as an inevitable outcome of the industrial revolution in Western societies.

Such a formulation neatly excludes the experience of women of color, immigrant "girls," and working-class women in general, most of whom have always maintained some form of paid work. Bose explores the ideological bases of this belief, its functions in maintaining racial, class, and gender stratification systems, and the ways in which U.S. census definitions reinforced the inaccurate classification of women's work in the period of transition from an agricultural to an industrial labor force. Forms of women's paid work that took place in the home were particularly likely to be invisible to census takers. Even when women contributed cash earnings to the household, they still defined themselves primarily as housewives so that their labor was never enumerated. From an analysis of trends in women's employment in this century as well, Bose concludes that the traditional view of dual spheres is being preserved even while currently being adapted to take account of women's segregation within the paid labor force.

The theme of gender inequality in today's work place is further examined by sociologist/economists Paula England and Lori McCreary. The authors carefully review the data on sex segregation in jobs, earnings differentials, and possible differences in nonmonetary rewards, applying various explanatory factors—socialization, human capital characteristics, discrimination in hiring and promotion, and the existence of structured mobility ladders. The authors conclude that no single model is sufficient to explain sex differentials in jobs and pay, but that all these elements interact in a reciprocal feedback loop that has historically tended to reinforce sex discrimination and its long-range effects, but which also has the potential for magnifying a spiral of change once reverse momentum is generated. Such a reversal appears unlikely, however, without more rigorous government enforcement of antidiscrimination statutes in the work place or without greater sharing of household and child-care responsibilities in the home. And neither of these shifts appears imminent so long as Americans continue to believe that paid work is central to manhood and that women would prefer to stay home if it were economically feasible. But this may be an area in which women will create far-reaching change through political struggle as they experience job segregation and pay inequity.

PART IV: GENDERED WORLDS

The themes of conflict and struggle are central to Myra Marx Ferree's analysis of women in paid employment. Ferree explores the meaning of women's expanded labor force participation for the great majority who work in nonelite jobs. Arguing that unconventional behavior by women is not new, and hence hardly nontraditional, Ferree examines the variety of forms of women's resistance to gender stereotypes and restrictions. She argues that a description of gender based on the lives of white middle-class women understates the traditions of resistance found among most women workers.

The first section of Ferree's chapter provides an overview of the types of jobs occupied by most women workers today and contrasts this reality to the myth of the "liberated" woman professional. Yet even if paid work is not as rewarding or emancipating as is sometimes claimed, it is not without important positive value. The second part of this chapter explores the meanings and rewards of work—paid and unpaid—for women in male-sex-typed and female-sex-typed jobs.

Women's experience in factory, clerical, and service jobs shows class and race to be interrelated structures that produce exclusionary and demeaning behaviors between women as well as solidarity and celebration. The commonalities among woman can be used to overcome differences, as indicated in studies of cross-ethnic solidarity in factories, but can also be used to oppress, as illustrated by studies of male harassment of both black and white women in male-typed occupations. Evidence of white women's abuse of nonwhite domestic employees, in contrast, indicates that women's work culture does not automatically arise from the experience of working in a female-typed job. Class and race differences are used in domestic labor to obscure the reality of women's common responsibility for housework. Gender solidarity, when it arises, is actively created by participants as a form of resistance to a shared oppression. Ferree argues that conflicts between workers of the same class but different genders, or same gender but different class, are not inevitable, even if structurally induced. The essay highlights the ways in which workers as active agents make gender, race, and class variably significant within an occupational structure that depends on these divisions and in which employers can exploit their salience.

Resisting exploitation is often linked to fighting for a better chance in life for one's children. For women, resistance can mean struggle to preserve their families as well as an attempt to escape limits that their families impose on them. Family life can be a source of essential gratification, and also an iron cage. The centrality of family and its gendered nature are the subject of chapters by Evelyn Nakano Glenn and Helena Z. Lopata.

Glenn examines three major themes in the feminist reconstruction of family studies. First, she offers an in-depth critique of the androcentrism of leading sociological perspectives on the family. Not only functional analysis but exchange theory and interactionist models fail to appreciate the influence of emotions, power inequality, and conflict on family outcomes. In contrast to the relatively "benign" view of contemporary paradigms, says Glenn, we must continue "to focus consciously on how gender and structures of gender subordination systematically affect interaction and shape definitions of reality."

Second, we must also recognize that the family is not necessarily an entity with unitary interests. Rather, the family must be *deconstructed* into its constituent parts or subsystems, always remaining aware of actual and potential conflicts between and among its members. Glenn also notes the many links between family and outside institutions, and the overlap of public and private production.

The third focus of a feminist revisioning of the family involves bringing race and class into the center of the analysis. The family that is perceived as oppressive by white middle-class women is often a crucial support system for nonwhite and ethnic working-class women. Indeed, in Barrie Thorne's (1982) words, the family is "a tangle of love and domination" so that women located differently in the stratification system may see only one side of the contradictory position of women in the family. They may experience the family primarily as a source of collective resistance to the atomizing demands of employers or state bureaucrats, or they may perceive the family primarily as a coercive institution that threatens their own individuality and represses their real needs.

The family is such a protean topic that there are a number of ways in which women's familial relationships can be approached. Helena Z. Lopata writes from the life-course perspective currently emerging in social.gerontology, as she follows the transformations in role sets—in rights and duties between a person and her social circles—that accompany the journey from girlhood to widowhood in old age. Lopata's multitextured model examines the ways in which gender expectations and sexual stratification constrain choices and shape identities at all ages, despite considerable variation within the female population. She highlights the variability between expectations at different moments in the life course, as American women adopt different family roles from daughter to grandmother and including stepmother and mother-in-law. Even when the ideology of "femininity" or "sex role" would define these divergent roles as identical or at least continuous, the gender perspective that Lopata adopts makes their inconsistency visible and significant.

The relationship of women to religion and religious structures in the United States has been somewhat ambiguous, to say the least. Although women account for the majority of worshipers, and although American churches have, over time, become feminized in the sense that they are perceived as instruments of succor, these established religious bodies also represent the essence of male dominance in their leadership, doctrine, and language. Theologian Sheila Briggs details the feminist critique of Western religions as bulwarks of patriarchy. Briggs describes the struggle of religious feminists to claim full participation in governance and ritual, while also trying to express a distinctive female voice. These two thrusts—exemplified in the debates over ordination and over nonsexist discourse—are fully examined for both mainstream and Afro-American churches.

Briggs's description of the experiences of women in the Afro-American religious tradition provides many important and often overlooked insights.

For example, the way in which women in the congregation direct the style and content of male preaching is explored.

Another societal sphere in which women predominate as receivers of services is the health care system, which shares many of the structural properties of the religious system: controlled almost exclusively by men, built on gendered assumptions about sex differences, and practiced primarily on women. As in the case of religion, the gender hierarchy of the medical establishment became an early target of feminist revisioning. That the doctor-patient relationship reflected the power inequities of the larger system was galling enough, but critics also objected to the content and quality of the health care being provided to women by physicians (of either sex) trained in the American medical tradition.

Mary K. Zimmerman's chapter analyzes both the causes of dissatisfaction among female patients and the attempts to create an alternative system of health care. She describes how the women's health movement emerged in the 1960s to deal with problems of health and illness that were either ignored or misinterpreted by the existing system and then began to move beyond criticism to the actual delivery of health care in nonhierarchical settings. Sympathetically but critically, Zimmerman delineates the successes and failures of various facets of the movement. Alternative health care systems remain subordinate to the legal and political power of the medical establishment while efforts to integrate medicine and to transform it from within often fail to resist cooptation. The paradox is illustrated by the divergent paths chosen by Florence Nightingale and Elizabeth Blackwell; while neither route separately has proved successful, the potential of a combined assault on the medical establishment has yet to be fully tested.

PART V: GENDER AND THE STATE

The final three chapters bring us back to a consideration of the state as product and producer of gender inequality. Ava Baron's discussion of feminist legal strategies embodies many of the major threads woven through this volume. First, there is the law as reification of gender ideology, its manifest support for patriarchal relationships, and its treatment of women as "Other." Second, American legal efforts to extend the rights of women reflect the same tension between formal equality (based on the assumption of sameness) and recognition of women's unique biological role as mother (the assumption of difference) that is evident in most of the other chapters.

Laws designed to protect privacy—reflecting a "hands off" policy—fail to protect women from abuse and exploitation, but when the patriarchal state does intervene, the effects are also frequently harmful to women. Baron traces the contradictory outcomes of legal strategies in such crucial areas as family relationships, violence against women, reproductive control, and work and earnings, noting in each instance the limitations of pursuing legal equality as an end in itself.

Despite such shortcomings, Baron also sees the legal system as a viable area for resistance, conflict, and basic change. The essay concludes with an outline of a feminist jurisprudence capable of attacking the structural sources of inequality. Two immediate goals are (1) to recognize the interlocking nature of public and private spheres for women, and (2) to clarify the intersections of class, race, and gender, as these are currently obscured in the law. So enormous a task cannot be accomplished by any single strategy, and consensus is not necessarily desirable. As with the medical system, the legal system may be most susceptible to change when it is challenged from many angles simultaneously.

The dual themes of public versus private spheres and the sameness versus difference debate appear once more in the chapter by political scientists Irene Diamond and Martha Ackelsberg. They find that feminist rethinking in political science, as in so many other disciplines, has taken three forms: (1) critiques of the conventional (male) views of women in both classic texts and empirical studies; (2) "reading" women into traditional paradigms; and (3) transforming the paradigms. Relegating women to the private (read "nonpolitical") sphere is a defining characteristic of political philosophy from Plato to Podhoretz. Consequently, only public displays of power have been studied as "politics," ignoring completely the private realm as an arena of political behavior or the possibility that sex differences in political behavior do not reflect innate biological traits. The gender perspective, in contrast, emphasizes the *social construction* of such differences and identifies the beneficiaries of traditional interpretations.

Feminist scholars in political science seek to revise and correct the basic models of their field through studies of women as political actors and as objects of public policy, most particularly as clients of the welfare state. The role of the state is itself subject to debate between those who see intervention as buffering the impact of capitalism and patriarchy and those who are more skeptical about the efficacy of state policy.

The effort to restructure political theory has centered around the issue of dealing with women's "difference" without reviving the public/private dichotomy and without erasing recognition of the differences among women. Diamond and Ackelsberg review the most recent writings in this ongoing debate, concluding that both mainstream individualism in political theory and the emphasis on class divisions of Marxism fail to appreciate the fact that women's political involvement has long been contingent on their experiences as members of primary groups—families, friendship networks, and neighborhoods. Politics, therefore, is best reconceptualized not as the study of power but of communities in action.

The book closes with a chapter that links the personal to the global and forces us to consider the worldwide consequences of gendered and stratified modes of knowledge and control. Political scientist Cynthia Enloe presents a feminist analysis of militarization as a social process in part fueled by the concept of masculinity as something distinct from femininity, thus explaining its existence in societies at different stages of economic and political development and across the range of human history. By thus placing gender at the heart of the issue, Enloe also points to the possibility of a feminist analysis that could reverse this deadly process by showing how militarization "is a surface symptom of more basic assumptions in the culture about marriage, property, reproduction, and heterosexuality—all of which are essential to the maintenance of male privilege." At the same time, Enloe argues that militarization is not merely masculinity writ large, as evidenced by the considerable efforts required to inculcate military attitudes and behaviors in men and by the active roles women play in military activities in most societies, including our own. While dichotomous gender ideology obscures the participation of women in militarization, the conceptual categories of war and peace also mask the reality of militarization as an ongoing and spiraling process.

Further, a focus on the connections between masculinity and militarization brings us closer to the thinking and theorizing of Third World women, who cannot separate fears for their survival into neat categories of national security or domestic violence. Finally, militarization also injures men, in open and hidden ways, so that they too may come to realize that they have as much to lose as to gain from patriarchal structures and assumptions of masculinity and femininity.

In the course of bringing gender analysis to bear on the salient issues of contemporary social science, the authors have inevitably raised new questions, further stimulating the dialectic that makes this such an exciting and fruitful field of study today. We hope that a new generation of scholars will see this volume as another milestone in the emerging discourse on gender and society. The primary task ahead, as implied by so many of our authors and forcefully stated by Diamond and Ackelsberg, is not to replace a disembodied "masculine" rationalism with some sort of "feminine" irrationality, but rather to transform our ways of seeing and knowing in order to give an expanded and integrated account of reason *and* emotion, thought *and* experience, individuality *and* connectedness in our daily lives and beyond.

REFERENCES

BELL-SCOTT, P. (1982) "Debunking sapphire: Toward a non-racist and non-sexist social science," pp. 85-92 in G. T. Hull et al. (eds.) Some of Us Are Brave. Old Westbury, NY: Feminist Press.

BOWLES, G. and R. DUELLI-KLEIN (1983) Theories of Women's Studies. London: Routledge & Kegan Paul.

ELSHTAIN, J. B. (1979) "Methodological sophistication and conceptual confusion: A critique of mainstream political science," pp. 229-252 in J. Sherman and E. T. Beck (eds.) The Prism of Sex: Essays in the Sociology of Knowledge. Madison: University of Wisconsin Press.

FREEMAN, J. (1975) Women: A Feminist Perspective. Palo Alto, CA: Mayfield.

GERSON, K. (1985) Hard Choices. Berkeley: University of California Press.

GERSON, J. and K. PEISS (1985) "Boundaries, negotiation, consciousness: Reconceptualizing gender relations." Social Problems 32, 4: 317-331.

GORNICK, V. and B. K. MORAN (1971) Women in Sexist Society. New York: New American Library.

HUBER, J. (1973) Changing Women in a Changing Society. Chicago: University of Chicago Press.

JOSEPH, G. and J. LEWIS (1981) Common Differences: Conflicts in Black and White Feminist Perspectives. Garden City, NY: Doubleday/Anchor.

KANTER, R. and M. MILLMAN (1975) Another Voice: Feminist Perspectives on Social Life and Social Science. Garden City, NY: Doubleday/Anchor.

KELLER, E. F. (1982) "Feminism and science." Signs 7, 3: 589-602.

LOPATA, H. and B. THORNE (1978) "On the term sex roles." Signs 3, 3: 718-721.

MARGOLIS, D. (1985) "Redefining the situation: Negotiations on the meaning of 'women.'" Social Problems 32, 4: 332-347.

MIES, M. (1983) "Towards a methodology for feminist research," pp. 117-139 in G. Bowles and R. Duelli-Klein (eds.) Theories of Women's Studies. London: Routledge & Kegan Paul.

MORGAN, R. (1970) [Ed.] Sisterhood is Powerful: An Anthology of Writing from the Women's Liberation Movement. New York: Random House.

REINHARZ, S. (1979) On Becoming a Social Scientist. San Francisco: Jossey-Bass.

ROBERTS, H. (1981) Doing Feminist Research. London: Routledge & Kegan Paul.

ROSS, D. (1979) "The development of the social sciences," pp. 107-137 in A. Olson and J. Voss (eds.) The Organization of Knowledge in Modern America. Baltimore, MD: Johns Hopkins University Press.

RUBIN, G. (1975) "The traffic in women: Notes on the political economy of sex," pp. 157-120 in R. Reiter (ed.) Toward an Anthropology of Women. New York: Monthly Review Press.

SCOTT, R. (1969) The Making of Blind Men. New York: Russell Sage Foundation.

SHERMAN, J. and E. T. BECK (1979) The Prism of Sex: Essays in the Sociology of Knowledge. Madison: University of Wisconsin Press.

SMITH, D. (1979) "A sociology for women," pp. 135-188 in J. Sherman and E. T. Beck (eds.) The Prism of Sex: Essays in the Sociology of Knowledge. Madison: University of Wisconsin Press.

SPENDER, D. (1981) Men's Studies Modified: The Impact of Feminism on the Academic Disciplines. New York: Pergamon.

STACEY, J. and B. THORNE (1985) "The missing feminist revolution in sociology." Social Problems 32, 4: 301-316.

STANLEY, L. and S. WISE (1983) Breaking Out: Feminist Consciousness and Feminist Research. London: Routledge & Kegan Paul.

THORNE, B. (1982) "Feminist rethinking of the family: an overview," pp. 1-24 in B. Thorne and M. Yalom (eds.) Rethinking the Family: Some Feminist Issues. New York: Longman.

WEITZMAN, L. (1984) "Sex role socialization," pp. 157-237 in J. Freeman (ed.) Women: A Feminist Perspective. Palo Alto, CA: Mayfield.

WESTCOTT, M. (1979) "Feminist criticism of the social sciences." Harvard Educational Review 49, 4: 422-430.

I

GENDER AND IDEOLOGY

1 Evolutionary Perspectives on Gender Hierarchy

CHRISTINE WARD GAILEY
Northeastern University

G ENDER hierarchy describes a situation where social power and control over labor, resources, and products are associated with masculinity (Gailey, 1985a). Patriarchy is one form of gender hierarchy, but not the only form. In a patriarchal society, effective social authority over women is exercised through the roles of father and husband. Under patriarchal conditions, women sometimes exercise authority through the role of mother, as opposed to other kin roles, such as wife, daughter, sister, or aunt (Sacks, 1979).

Until recently,[1] patriarchy was the prevailing form of gender hierarchy in Western civilization. Today, however, the form is different. Social power now is identified with attributes considered to be masculine; male or female people may fill roles through which power is exercised, but they hold masculine roles. Because the roles are symbolically masculine, discrimination against women filling those roles receives ideological reinforcement.

Another nonpatriarchal form of gender hierarchy can be seen in an earlier civilization, the Inca empire. The Inca were an ethnic group that conquered a number of other peoples in the Andean region. The relationship of the Inca elite to the conquered groups was presented symbolically as one of male to female. The Inca presented themselves as male, and the conquered communities were seen by them as female (Silverblatt, 1978, 1980). Incaic civilization was by no means patriarchal. Women in the Inca elite exercised considerable social power—a kind of parallel rulership (Silverblatt, 1987). But gender hierarchy existed: Maleness was associated with social power, femaleness with subservience.

All civilizations present divine, customary, or natural origins for social hierarchies. The prevailing thread in contemporary Western civilization is to propose natural reasons for the existing social order. In our society, this tendency can be seen in widespread beliefs that resources have been scarce since the dawn of human existence; that intelligence is inherited and can be measured accurately; and that although race and sex discrimination may be objectionable, they are rooted in natural inferiority or superiority. These notions are paralleled in some religious circles by divinely ordained reasons for existing race and sex inequities (Wolf and Gray, 1981).

Many people in our society assume that men are naturally more aggressive. Women are sometimes urged to develop assertiveness, but men are told to channel what is assumed to be a natural resource, presumably linked to the Y chromosome. Discussions about discrimination against women tend to leap from "Women are not equal" to "Women have never been equal" and beyond that to "Women's status must be due to sex differences."

Alternative theories argue that males and females are basically similar, at least with regard to intellectual and emotional potentials. In this view, differences between women and men reflect cultural factors, the expectations placed on males that differ from those placed on females (Mead, 1935; Oakley, 1972). These theorists are then left with the problem of explaining how women became "the second sex."

To pursue this line of research, we need the work of anthropologists. Fortunately, our sources of information are better than they were even thirty years ago, when studying women's status and women's roles in anthropology was the fast lane to professional obscurity.[2] Cross-cultural studies of gender now have a respected place in the field of scientific inquiry, due primarily to the growth and influence of women's movements throughout the world (Rapp, 1978a). We will examine a range of theories of women's subordination, which are grouped according to their causes: biological, cultural and universal, or cultural and historical.

The position taken here is that whatever the similarities and differences between males and females as sexes, political and economic subordination is a cultural phenomenon and had best be examined from that basis first. If we find universal patterns in what different societies consider appropriate behavior for men and women, then we can start talking about natural bases for cultural features. Our task is to seek an adequate historical or cultural explanation for the status of women in the range of human societies. If we cannot find a cultural explanation, then we should by all means look to biological origins. To make this argument, we first need to establish what we are investigating. Many social scientists have assumed that to investigate sex differences is to investigate gender. A body of anthropological literature on gender argues that sex and gender are not identical, even in our own society.

SEX AND GENDER

Sex differences are not gender differences. Few people would say that being a female means being womanly or being a male means being manly. Sex differences are physiological features related to procreation, to biological reproduction. The sex division of labor in reproduction is well understood. Males produce sperm, females produce eggs; females bear young. Sex differences are found in all mammals. However, humans from their very origins have interpreted and reshaped their physical and social environment through symbolizing (Leakey and Lewin, 1977b). Humans are self-reflective, culture-creating animals. Humans have sex differences, but like all other aspects of physical differentiation, they are experienced symbolically. In human societies, sex differences are experienced as gender.

While sex differences are physical, gender differences are socially constructed. Concepts of gender are cultural interpretations of sex differences (Oakley, 1972). Gender is related to sex differences but not necessarily to the physiological differences as we see them in our society. Gender depends on how society views the relationship of male to man and female to woman. Every culture has prevailing images of what men and women are "supposed" to be like. What does maleness mean? What does femaleness involve? How are women and men supposed to relate to each other?

Variation in Gender Across Cultures

Investigating gender differences opens us up to the tremendous variety of cultures in the world. In some societies, the gender division of labor is one of the key ways in which all economic tasks are organized. In others, the gender division of labor is found primarily in a domestic (or reproductive) sphere. Differences between societies where gender is central to economic production and those where it is secondary parallel differences in the overall authority structures.

Stratification will be discussed in a later section. For now, the focus will be on *kinship societies,* where gender is central to production, distribution, exchange, and consumption. This form of society, usually called "primitive,"[3] has characterized by far the longest period in human history. The term "kinship societies" refers to those social formations where property is held communally, with rights to use resources being allocated to every person through his or her affiliation to the group. In such societies, relations that organize production, distribution, consumption, and reproduction are all constituted through sociological kinship. Although kin societies vary in terms of social authority—egalitarian, ranked, or stratified (but not class-stratified)— what all share in common is an absence of separate public and private (or public and domestic) spheres: All activities are ordered through kin or kin-modeled connections. They are thus distinct from societies with impeded access to resources and civilly held or privately held property and those where the relations of production/reproduction are determined primarily by permanent social hierarchies, especially class or caste. A number of societies organized along kinship lines exist today, and many more are known to us through historical documents and archaeological research. Most scholars writing about the origins of women's subordination have turned to contemporary or historically known kinship societies for evidence.

Most kinship societies have two genders, derived from the sexes. But not all. There is another logical way of approaching sex differences. In physical terms, secondary sexual characteristics are not pronounced until puberty; in some populations, secondary sexual characteristics are never as pronounced or as culturally enhanced as they are in our experience. If gender is based loosely on physical features related to biological reproduction, in theory there can be four genders, depending on when a culture determines the onset and termination of reproductive activity. Maturation, culturally defined, is inextricably bound to gender. Children, in other words, could be considered *as a separate gender,* "those who cannot reproduce."

Logically also, some kin societies define a period of life that is supposed to end engagement in reproduction. This may be related to menopause in females, but it can be defined generationally and thus apply to men as well as women on life status grounds. For instance, people whose children have children may pass into another life status—elders, who are not expected to reproduce. With age, secondary sexual characteristics diminish and people (in the absence of hormonal stimulants) begin to look similar again. In theory, then, at least four genders are possible, related directly to biological reproduction. One can reinterpret ethnographic reports in this light, particularly for those societies that have no gender-linked terms for boys and girls, or for older people.

Alternatively, there may be two genders, but they may be effective—influential on activities—only during what is defined as one's reproductive years. There also are cultural variants on adult gender, where sexual preference can create other gender roles or people can cross genders, even adopting the other gender's procreative roles. To focus solely on sex differences is to ignore cultural creativity. Our society typecasts women and men from birth through death—pink and blue from baby clothes to caskets—but other societies exist where gender differences are not extended beyond adult reproductive roles.

The Hua society, in the highlands of Papua New Guinea, have a two-gender system, men and women. Meigs (1976) points out that for the Hua, gender is a process. People with large quantities of femaleness are invulnerable, but polluted, and thus dangerous; people with maleness have high status, but they are vulnerable and must take burdensome precautions about their diets and hygiene. All children are born at least partially female and polluted. Male children are given more masculine substance through growth rituals conducted by adult men. Girl children are seen as healthier and faster growing because they are female and less vulnerable. As a person matures, he or she loses in-born gender and gradually becomes the other gender. The Hua are extremely attentive to the disposal of bodily excretions: sweat, mucous, sexual fluids, urine, and feces. These excretions contain the gender substance and can harm others if one is not careful.

Women lose their female substance through menstruation and childbirth. The Hua say men become pregnant if they eat certain red-colored foods or anything that has been touched by a menstruating woman. But men are vulnerable: Women can give birth safely; pregnancy in a man is fatal. In childbirth, some of her female substance is transferred to the infant. By the time a woman has born three children, she is effectively no longer polluted and is inducted into the men's society. She can then live in the men's house, take part in men's discussions and rituals, but she also must become careful about her diet and sanitary habits, being masculine. Men lose their masculine substance through time, in the process of helping boys acquire masculinity. Older men become female, invulnerable but polluted. Older men work with the young married women in the fields, but they have little social authority. Older women have considerable say in social arrangements, and spend much of their day talking in the men's house.

Among the Hua, then, gender is only tangentially related to sex differences; it is mutable, and flows from person to person. The process of engendering is lifelong, and through it males and females shed the gender they were born with and acquire the opposite characteristics. However, even young adult women exercise control over the products of their labor and have claims to the labor of various male relatives, so gender hierarchy as we have defined it does not exist. The Hua have a hierarchy of maleness and femaleness, but women as a group are not subordinate. Both women and men exercise social authority, although at different points in their life cycles.

The more stratified but still kin-based Lovedu people of Zambia, prior to British colonization, provide an example of how gender roles are decidedly different from sex roles (Poewe, 1980). Among the Lovedu, a woman arranged the marriages of her brothers' children. Often, this paternal aunt would arrange a marriage between her son and her brother's daughter. However, a high-ranking or ambitious woman might elect to marry her brother's daughter herself. The young woman would live in her husband/paternal aunt's compound and any children born to the young wife (sired by lovers of her choice) would have a female father. At least some Lovedu women were simultaneously wives and mothers, and husbands and fathers. They absorbed both genders in a range of masculine and feminine kin roles.

In other societies, crossing genders appears to have been possible without long-term loss of social standing. The *berdaches* of the Crow Indians of the Great Plains of North America were males who had chosen to adopt womanhood as an identity. They did the work of women, dressed as women, married men and could adopt children as their own. The berdache provided a viable status alternative to warriorhood for pubescent males. Berdaches sometimes were ridiculed for their choice, but not if they took womanhood seriously. Regardless of temporary ridicule, berdaches were considered essential for the success of any warfare as well as any marriage ceremonies.

Activities we associate with feminine roles—nurturance, domestic chores, child care—are not limited to women in a number of societies. In the ranked Tongan Islands society prior to European influence, for example, men did virtually all the cooking (Gailey, 1980). Care of infants is primarily associated with women, but not necessarily the mother, and in a number of kin-based societies men routinely care for and play with infants (Lee, 1984; Shostak, 1981; Mead, 1935). In addition, childhood typically involves much less dependency than in our society (Sorenson, 1978). In most kin societies, toddlers begin to spend considerable time with their peers and nonparental adults. In many cases, children around the age of six begin to accompany adults of the child's sex on their daily rounds. In other words, children are more autonomous and child-care responsibilities are widely shared.

We also know that women have been responsible for activities we associate with men. Iroquois women, through their control of the food supply, decided whether or not the men would go to war and the duration of the warfare (Brown, 1975). Lest we think of women as pacifists by nature, Iroquois women also conducted the torture of male war captives (Leacock, 1977). Women engage in hunting activities among the !Kung, and Australian aboriginal women use what anthropologists have dubbed a "digging stick" to extract roots and stab small animals. When men carry such multipurpose implements, anthropologists have considered them spears.

Social decision making is not an exclusively male realm in a range of societies less stratified than our own. The Igbo of southeastern Nigeria, prior to British subversion of the system, were organized in a network of related villages. Van Allen (1972) investigated the role of women as in-marrying wives in patrilineal Igbo villages prior to and during the early years of British colonial rule. In every village there was an association of all the wives of lineage men. This named association was responsible for setting prices for marketing and for protecting the interests of in-marrying women. Men who challenged the women's marketing activities, who disrupted their travels to or from the marketplace, or who allowed their animals to get into the women's crops faced collective retaliation. The response would be decided consensually by the association and was carried out collectively. The responses varied from fines to a strike by all wives until the husbands relented and compensated them to a form of warfare called "sitting on" a man. To "sit on" an offender, the women dressed as for war; they encircled the offender's house, sat down and sang scurrilous songs about him until he repented. If he refused they could burn his house down and beat him up. No other man would dare to intervene. The system operated as an effective check on the potential power of a group of patrilineally related men vis-à-vis a group of unrelated women. Colonial repression effectively eliminated these lineage wives' associations.

There thus appear to be two universals about gender: (1) It is not identical with sex differences, and (2) it provides a basis for a division of labor in all societies. There simply is no global content to gender roles. How women and men are conceptualized varies enormously. In some societies, males or females have options of adopting the work and life roles of people of the opposite sex. The gender division of labor would include these people in their adoptive role, not by their sex (Clastres, 1977). In some cases, women and men have antagonistic views of each other—competing gender ideologies. In other cases, there is a shared view that women have less power, even though decision making, personal autonomy, labor, and property claims are not necessarily skewed in favor of men (Murphy and Murphy, 1974). How, then, can we gauge whether women are subordinate? The first step is to clarify what we mean by subordination.

Subordination

Subordination can be defined as relative powerlessness. In terms of social authority, a subordinated group has little or no control over decision making that affects the future of that group. Workers, for instance, have no effective veto if a corporation decides to close a factory and relocate abroad. We can talk about gender subordination in this country because women are not in control of the institutions that determine policy affecting women, such as reproductive rights or parity in employment practices.

In economic terms, for the subordinated group to subsist, services or products must be provided to another group without comparable return. Discrimination in hiring practices, pay scales, job security, and promotion schedules is one example of women's economic subordination in this society. In other types of societies, subordination may involve the need for women to marry in order to survive, coupled with two other conditions: The role of wife must be inferior in authority to the role of husband, and other adult gender role pairs important for subsistence in which the woman has effective authority (as brother/sister or mother-in-law/son-in-law roles in some kin settings) must be ineffectual. In short, subordination involves systematic dependency, whether or not the subordinated group is active in productive activities. The position of most peasant women derives from this set of conditions (Friedl, 1978; Pruitt, 1967; Wolf, 1972).

Subordination is more difficult to determine if one focuses solely on attitudes. Expressed attitudes can change relatively quickly, since they are sensitive to rapid changes in the political climate. People may think they are equal, believing that they are as good as any other group; they may in fact be subordinated, regardless of their beliefs. People have the symbolic capacity to create beliefs that cloak existing conditions and therefore bolster the system as constituted. Symbolically, subordination often is expressed as a complementary relationship. Workers need employers and employers need workers, "it takes two to tango," and so on. The power aspect of the relationship is denied. For that reason, it is more reliable to focus on political and economic relations than on attitudes.

How groups are treated by other groups in a society can give us evidence of subordination. Rape in our society, for example, usually is done by a man to a woman. Despite claims to the contrary—without ethnographic evidence—by sociobiologists, rape is unknown in some kin-based societies (Benderly, 1982). Rape is found in some kinship societies and all class societies. Relative powerlessness can be seen in both the frequency of rape in a society and the degree to which women are victims. Widespread violence in the form of beatings or physical torture is another gauge of subordination.

The problem confronting feminist scholars is whether subordination of women is timeless or whether it has developed during human history. A number of theories hold that subordination is either natural or cultural, and universal. Let us consider these theories first.

THEORIES OF GENDER HIERARCHY: FROM THE BEGINNING

Some scholars contend that women have always been subordinate. They link male dominance to human origins, sexual reproduction, or human adaptations to supposedly natural laws. Women's subordination has been attributed variously to inherent passivity, to physical weakness of various sorts, or to an incapacity to function as an equal because of the demands of procreation. Four groups of universal and timeless subordination theories can be identified: early adaptation, technical-environmental, sociobiological, and structuralist. While all propose primordial patriarchy, they have little else in common.

Man the Hunter: Subordination Rooted in Human Origins

The first of the universal and natural theories concerns early human adaptation as a basis for a sex division of labor and female subordination. Although criticized roundly, the "hunting hypothesis" (Ardrey, 1976) continues to capture a prominent place in the popular media. For hunting origins theorists, female subordination has prehuman or proto-human roots (see Tiger, 1969, 1971; Lee and DeVore, 1968; Washburn and Lancaster, 1968; Laughlin, 1968). According to this argument, our hominid ancestors relied on hunting for survival in the savannas of eastern and southern Africa between 1 and 2 million years ago. "Man the hunter" theorists assumed the following: 1) Hunting was important to our hominid ancestors' survival; 2) males did most of the hunting; 3) females were dependent on males for meat; 4) males shared hunted meat primarily with their own females and offspring; and 5) once imprinted, the early hunting adaptation set a pattern of sex roles that persists to this day.

The reason given for males hunting is that females were supposedly "homebound" or less mobile due to the burdens of childbearing and nursing. Females, then, were unable to develop the aggressiveness, attention to detail, planning, and group loyalty and cooperation ostensibly linked to hunting as an activity. This subsistence adaptation imprinted humankind with a sex division of labor whereby men became more aggressive and more able to work closely in groups, while women became more passive and more fixated on homemaking and child care.

A deluge of contradictory evidence has overwhelmed man-the-hunter assumptions over the past fifteen years, and yet hunting as a primordial activity continues to dominate the popular media. Many critics have shown the male bias inherent in these hypotheses (Slocum, 1975; Rohrlich-Leavitt et al., 1975). For instance, the emphasis on hunting as essential for the development of culture is dubious at best. In fact there is absolutely no evidence that hunting was practiced by our hominid ancestors, let alone hunting by males (Leakey and Lewin, 1977a, 1977b). Hominids ate meat, but butchering sites indicate that scavenging from predators or gathering dead or dying animals may well have provided the bulk of the meat in the diet (Shipman, 1986). Scavenging or killing weak or immature animals could be done by virtually anyone. Although our hominid ancestors were omnivorous, most of their diet was vegetarian and, as Liebowitz (1978) has suggested, juveniles may have been important scavengers and foragers. Reliable evidence of deliberate hunting, as opposed to meat eating, occurs much later in human history. It appears to take the form of drive-hunts—forcing animals into swamps or off cliffs, where they could be killed easily. In contemporary practice, drive-hunts are not an exclusively male domain (Turnbull, 1962).

The primary importance of gathered foods is found in all known gatherer-hunter peoples, excepting some Inuit (Eskimo) groups (Lee, 1979). Among today's foraging peoples, men do most of the hunting and women do most of the gathering, but there is a wide range of meat acquisition techniques in addition to all-male group hunts. The Mbuti people of Zaïre, for example, conduct drive-hunts involving every willing person in the local camp—women, men, and children (Turnbull, 1978). Inuit women know how to fish and to hunt seals and do both routinely. Estioko-Griffin (1986) reports from the Philippines that Agta women often hunt, using knives or bows and arrows. In most foraging societies, women hunt small game while they are out gathering in groups. Men also collect edible plants while they are afield. In any case, women are not dependent homebodies; gathering expeditions involve groups of cooperating women who may walk up to ten miles in search of a suitable variety of edible plants (Lee, 1979).

Another problem lies in situating nuclear families at the dawn of humanity. There is no evidence of nucleation in hominid groups. The sparse evidence we have supports a model of flexible local foraging groups: adult females, infants, fewer (perhaps transient) adult males, and a preponderance of juveniles of both sexes (Liebowitz, 1978).

In contemporary foraging societies, family forms are varied. Food is shared with others in the local camp and with nearby camps. The lines of sharing are rarely, if ever, restricted to husband-wife-children. Typically food is shared throughout the local group. This pattern of food sharing permits people who are infirm to rest in camp; arrangements for pregnant and lactating women vary, but generally there are enough people who for whatever reasons remain in the camp to look after young children. As for meat, sharing patterns extend far beyond the conjugal unit. Among the Tiwi of northern Australia, a husband hunts not for his wife but for his mother-in-law (Goodale, 1971), and among the !Kung of the Kalahari desert in southern Africa young husbands provide meat for their in-laws (Draper, 1975). For the Sharanahua of the upper Amazonian region, meat belongs to the eldest woman in the household; if there is a special hunt, meat belongs to the hunter's current lover (Siskind, 1973). In all cases, meat is divided and shared out several times, both before and after cooking. The effective unit of consumption is rarely the nuclear family, and wives are not dependent on their husbands for a meat supply.

The third major problem with the primordial hunting theory is how it overlooks the skills and respect accorded gathering. If the hunting hypothesis is accurate, one has to wonder how humans evolved at all, given that only half of them learned to cooperate, share, and plan, while the other half was presumably socializing infants in other directions (Slocum, 1975). A number of scholars have pointed out that parallel skills are involved in gathering and hunting. The earliest tools found—choppers and scrapers—could be used either for meat or plant preparation (Leakey and Lewin, 1977b). It is our androcentric bias that sees them as hunting weapons and their makers as male.

The !Kung do value meat and are excited when a large kill is made. But people returning to camp from either gathering or hunting are greeted with excitement. One man explained that he "harvested" meat, revealing in his choice of words that the distinction between hunting and gathering is not so clear-cut as we make it. Conceptually, gathering, hunting, and fishing are all forms of appropriating foodstuffs. To assume that one form is prestigious while another is "drudge work" is ethnocentric. To make the male activity the driving force of human evolution interprets the paleontological data with tunnel vision and simply ignores the role of *both* gathering and hunting in known foraging societies.

"Male Supremacist Complex":
Warfare and Population Control

Technical-environmental explanations take what is claimed to be a natural law (scarcity of resources, population pressure) and argue that cultural features emerge to meet the challenge, to help the society adapt to the strictures of natural laws (Nonini, 1985). One of these theories purports to explain "why men dominate women" (Harris, 1977). It asserts that population control has been a problem in human societies from time immemorial, and that societies developed cultural means of limiting reproduction through offering sexual rewards for male aggressiveness in warfare and socializing females to be passive (Divale and Harris, 1976).

Male dominance is presented, as in man-the-hunter theories, as adaptive in human history. The complex—said to be superfluous now because of new birth control devices—ostensibly helped to prevent the "misery and annihilation implicit in women's reproductive potential" (Harris, 1977). Significantly, the theorists assume that women are untrustworthy in the development of population planning: Only male-important institutions are invested with social responsibility.

Women's subordination is thus held to be derived from their role in childbearing. The argument is based on the theory of Thomas Malthus, who held that populations increase exponentially until a crisis of overpopulation reduces numbers and the cycle begins anew. Although this thesis has been debunked for human populations (Nell, 1979; Cowgill, 1975), it continues to influence theories of economic development (Boserup, 1965, 1970). Implicitly, such arguments hold women responsible for population growth rather than point to increasing economic insecurity as a cause (Lappé and Collins, 1977). Solutions, therefore, are phrased in terms of controlling women's role in biological reproduction.

Divale and Harris (1976) state, accurately, that for most of human history—spent in kinship-ordered societies—populations have been relatively stable. They then go on to attribute this stability to cultural "mechanisms." In kin societies, they claim, birth control technology is unreliable, so to avert Malthusian population pressure cultural institutions emerged, including the "male supremacist complex." This complex involves male dominance through warfare, coupled with (hetero-) sexual rewards for successful warriors. This argument is presented in a series of assertions: (1) that women are excluded from warfare in kinship societies and intimidated by other exclusively male activities; (2) that female infanticide is the basic means of birth control in kinship societies; (3) that polygyny is an indication of male dominance; and (4) that polygyny increases the scarcity of women and thus enhances sexual rewards for male aggressiveness.

Technical-environmental theories have been criticized by a number of scholars for their ethnocentrism, inaccuracies, and curious logic (see Diener et al., 1978; Slocum, 1975; Leacock, 1981; Gailey, 1984; Poewe, 1980; Sacks, 1979). The first problem is that not all kinship societies engage in warfare (Turnbull, 1978; Lee, 1984). The second is that in many of the societies that do have ritual warfare, women are active participants and sometimes have pivotal roles in determining the onset of hostilities and their duration (Brown, 1975; Muller, 1985). Women may perform needed rituals to make the warfare successful (Harner, 1972). They may also have a combat role, as among the Kapauku (Pospisil, 1963). Part of the problem has been male-biased reporting, which denies women's participation even while describing it (Gailey, 1984). Another problem is the identification of warfare with combat instead of the range of rituals involved in deciding on a raid or confrontation, preparing for it, ensuring the safety of warriors during it, and rituals concluding the warfare for the benefit of the community. The male supremacist complex focuses exclusively on combat, and even there relies on distorted reports for evidence.[4]

Similarly, there is negative evidence for the assertion that female infanticide is the prevalent means of birth control in kin societies. All societies practice birth control techniques; some practice occasional, not routine, infanticide (Shostak, 1981).[5] But the only cases in kinship societies—as opposed to peasant or other class societies—where the female infanticide rate is known to be higher than that for males is among some Polar Eskimo groups, where the adult mortality rate for men is far greater than that for women, so that to achieve a balanced adult sex ratio some female infants are put away at birth. There is no reliable information for any other groups, but most scholars concur that infanticide in all cases is rare. More common means of population planning include postpartum sexual abstinence for women, periodic sexual abstinence for adults, delayed onset of sexual intercourse, and abortion (see Gailey, 1980; Thomas, 1958; Cowgill, 1975).

Third, there is little evidence from any kinship society for women being used as sexual rewards for warriors. The implication in Divale and Harris (1976) is that warriors have dominant positions in their societies, but this is not the case in almost every kin society known. For Native Americans, even the militarized Plains cultures during the U.S. conquest, the highest leadership positions were reserved for nonwarriors.

Examples to the contrary are almost always cited from groups in severe crisis and dislocation, such as Yanomamö groups in the Amazon Basin, who have been subject to a range of outside influences, including epidemics that skewed local sex ratios and encroachment on their lands (Kellman, 1982). The most widely read study of the Yanomamö (Chagnon, 1968) fails to mention elevated mortality rates, especially of lactating women, as a result of periodic measles epidemics following contact with the white society, which, in turn, intensified raiding other villages for wives. Other anthropologists (Smole, 1976; Lizot, 1976) have documented nonviolent relationships between men and women in the villages further from the ravages of such epidemics and from the ethnocidal impact of white traders, labor contractors, and missionaries. In other words, Chagnon's description of the Yanomamö uncritically accepted by those seeking proof of "man's" essential warlike nature, does not faithfully represent what these people were like in the last century—*before* their way of life was profoundly disturbed by whites.

Divale and Harris's (1976) argument that polygyny means male dominance and restricts sexual access to women is contradicted by the plethora of adultery claims or de facto divorces through abandonment in kin societies that practice polygyny (e.g., Hart and Pilling, 1960). Polygyny in class societies often is associated with gender hierarchy, but so is monogamy in such societies. Polygyny in kin societies often involves co-wives who are close relatives and who form a cooperative work group. In other cases the wives may be unrelated, but their authority relations are regulated by seniority.

Either way, one cannot conclude that male dominance is associated with plural marriage. Even in those cases where husbands have considerable authority over wives, it does not mean that men wield social authority over women. In the Tongan Islands of Polynesia, for example, men of high rank were polygynous and wives were supposed to defer to husbands. But women exercised social authority in their roles as sisters and father's sisters (Gailey, 1980). In other words, the conjugal relationship may not be central in the exercise of women's social authority (Etienne and Leacock, 1980; Paulmé, 1971; Leacock, 1977; Sacks, 1979).

Sociobiology: Subordination
Increases Fitness

Man-the-hunter and male supremacist complex theories differ from recent sociobiological works (Wilson, 1975; Barash, 1979; Symons, 1979) in their proposals for cultural solutions to women's subordination. At least some hunting hypothesis proponents have argued that social institutions can redirect or sublimate our "hominid heritage" of male aggressiveness; technical-environmental arguments favor technological innovations to release women from bondage to households and child care. For sociobiologists, cultural institutions also can help human survival—social change is desirable—but only when it is in keeping with what is asserted to be natural sex inequality.

Harkening back, via Darwin, to earlier theories of sex-based inequality, sociobiologists such as Wilson (1975, 1978) attribute male dominance to the workings of natural selection and especially of inclusive fitness. Attempts to alter sexist practices thus contradict natural law and can only lead to long-term disorder. Sociobiologists hold that males and females are predisposed to have different degrees of "investment" in their young: Males produce millions of sperm, while females produce a relatively small number of eggs. Therefore, the argument runs, males maximize their reproductive success by impregnating as many females as possible, while for a female to maximize the number of her eggs that become offspring, and for those offspring to reach reproductive maturity, she must somehow attract and convince a male to increase his investment in his offspring by her. Culturally specific human practices, such as sexual teasing by unmarried women, are provided with analogues from animal research. More seriously, violent practices, such as rape, found in some human societies but asserted to be universal, are presented as parallel with certain animals' mating behavior. It needs only to be pointed out that rape is not a universal practice, being rare or unreported in the vast majority of kinship societies (Benderly, 1982).

Wilson (1978: 134, 137) claims that women are naturally inclined to child care; and since men are assumed not to be, women must try to find and hold a man who will provide "parental investment." Men are said to be physically aggressive and assertive, and women are held not to be (1978: 128). Against the evidence of variation in human cultures, Wilson presents sex roles as universally male-important and stable, being based on sex-linked dimorphism of temperament and physique (Kreniske, 1984: 173).

In general, critics agree that the sociobiological undertaking is ideology rather than science (Gould, 1982; Leacock, 1981; Wolf and Gray, 1981). Despite a ream of contradictory evidence (see, e.g., Hubbard and Lowe, 1979; Leacock, 1981, 1954; Lee, 1982; Shostak, 1981; Friedl, 1978), Wilson (1978) claims that women are "objects of exchange" in "primitive" societies and have low status even in gatherer-hunter societies. He confuses historical with biological facts and uses labeling in lieu of evidence. In one case, he applies the cultural term "rape" to an animal pattern—duck mating behavior. Naming deer mating groups "harems" enhances our understanding neither of the intricacies of deer reproduction nor of polygyny and concubinage in certain archaic state societies. The appropriation of "natural selection" and other terms from population genetics and evolutionary theory is not accompanied by the same meaning that those terms have in their original fields of inquiry (Kreniske, 1984).

Cultural But Universal Theories

A second set of theories holds that women's subordination is cultural but also universal. The major proponents of this view are open to charges of biological determinism, although they disclaim it. One group of these theories considers women to have both lower status and less authority because women are associated with a domestic realm while men are associated with a public domain (Rosaldo, 1974). This split, which is held to be universal, is said to derive from women's childbearing and child-care responsibilities (Firestone, 1971). The relative status of women, therefore, depends on the degree to which they are involved in the public sphere and men in the domestic sphere.

A split between public and private matters certainly characterizes all class societies, past and present (Lamphere, 1974; Rapp, 1978a). A growing association of women with domestic work often is tied to declining authority (Sacks, 1975, 1976, 1979). But the existence of such a division in uncolonized kin societies is questionable. Capitalist colonization has been cited in many cases as spawning the domestication of women and women's tasks (Etienne and Leacock, 1980). If the same considerations—kin connections, gender, and life status—organize both production and the reproduction of the society as a whole, there can be no neat division between private and public relations. Where kin groups perform social production and embody social continuity, roles are simultaneously public and private.

Childbearing and child care do not isolate mothers the way they can in our own society. The tasks are absorbed by a broader range of people, and children are more incorporated into public activities than they are in middle-class, nuclear family systems (Leacock, 1977). Moreover, motherhood (either through childbirth, adoption, or fosterage) often conveys an *increase* in status, giving women a greater say in matters than when they were not fully adult (Etienne, 1979). In patrilineal, polygynous situations, a mother may become the ancestress/founder of a new lineage. In other societies, motherhood is not as authoritative a role for women as, for instance, that of sister or father's sister, roles that persist throughout life (Sacks, 1979; Gailey, 1980). In any case, childbearing and child care do not necessarily diminish women's social authority.

Other anthropologists argue that women's subordination is cultural but rooted in the gender division of labor (Godelier, 1981; Ortner, 1974, 1981). They argue that the division of labor by gender in kinship societies grows out of a universal, symbolic association of women with nature and men with culture, where culture is superior to nature. There are protestations to the contrary, that such a structuralist approach is a form of biological determinism, centering women's subordination at a neurological level of brain functions (Lévi-Strauss, 1969; see Diamond, 1974).

Several of the scholars who argue for cultural and aboriginal subordination consider themselves to be feminists (Rosaldo, 1974; Ortner, 1974; Rubin, 1975). The division of labor by gender is said to make marriage a necessity in kinship societies (Rubin, 1975). Following Lévi-Strauss, they contend that the primary cultural rule is the incest taboo, being at once a prohibition (cultural) and universal (natural). Marriage "out"—that is, to a group apart from one's natal unit—derives from this convergence of culture and nature. Kinship relations develop out of nodal pairs of relatives: parents, children, and siblings. Out-marriage depends, it is said, on the availability of men as fathers and brothers to create alliances with other men, using their daughters and sisters as gifts to establish ongoing relations. Men, it is asserted, exchange women in marriage: thus women are a medium through which men communicate with one another (Lévi-Strauss, 1969). Women may have high status in kin societies, but their brothers or fathers control the disposition of their potential fecundity, their ability to produce other humans (Ortner, 1974, 1981).

Structuralist formulations freeze nuclear family relations as central throughout history (other family forms are said to derive from the "elementary structures" of husband-wife, parent-child, and brother-sister). Structuralist models present oppositions such as nature/culture as if these were universal and timeless, yet there is abundant evidence to the contrary. In nineteenth-century England, for example, regardless of childbirth functions women were associated with culture (training children to behave, a civilizing influence on men, etc.) and men with animal nature, a theme still found in our popular culture. In addition, a split between nature and culture cannot be demonstrated for a range of kinship societies (Leacock and Nash, 1977). For kin-organized people, nature as an abstract entity does not exist: Animal, vegetable, or mineral, the world is a kin-defined universe. Culture and nature may be seen as in flux, as dialectically related, rather than as opposed or polarized categories (Radin, 1971). There is no reason to suppose that the impressive variety of family forms develops out of a core concept that is a conjugal pair and their children (Gough, 1968). Nuclear families often emerge as a consequence of colonial impositions of various kinds, including religious conversion (Leacock, 1977; Gailey, 1981).

Do men exchange women in kinship societies? Is marriage a mechanism for men's communication? Logically, a gender division of labor does not make marriage necessary: Siblings or other relatives could serve as well. The structuralist emphasis on conjugal relations as the basis of production is not supported for all societies; indeed, in many, wider kin groupings are more important (Leacock, 1977). In Dobu (South Pacific), for instance, people marry and have children, but the marriage is not the basis of the household. Instead, a man lives with his sister and her children; he is primarily responsible for the men's part of provisioning (Fortune, 1963). In the Tongan Islands, a woman could freely appropriate the goods of her brother and his children, and so was not dependent on her husband for men's goods (Gailey, 1980).

Similarly, in many kin societies women are exchanged, but the character of the exchange is not one of women's subordination. It may reflect the claims that older people have in younger people. In the Tongan Islands, for instance, women arranged the marriages of their brothers' children (Gailey, 1980). And although among the Warlpiri of Australia it is men who announce marriages, the initiative and arrangements are in the hands of the prospective mothers-in-law (Bell, 1980). In the Trobriand Islands (South Pacific), women are exchanged in marriage, but this does not limit their authority. Instead, marriage expands a woman's kin network and claims to others' labor: A married woman can embark on building her reputation and influence. Because of the gifts her brother provides to her husband in her name, her husband must convert men's wealth to women's wealth to assist her (Weiner, 1976). The receipt of bridewealth in some herding societies activates the newly married woman's labor claims in her natal kin group. Her brothers, who will use the bridewealth for their own marriages, owe their adult status to her and therefore must aid her when requested (Goody and Tambiah, 1973).

In addition, structuralists overemphasize first marriages as the most prestigious form of marriage. In most uncolonized kin societies, people marry more than once in the course of their lives. For the Warlpiri of Australia, Bell (1980) found that while the first marriage was arranged, subsequent ones were contracted through personal preference. She also found that each camp included a group of women who preferred not to remarry or not to live with their husbands. Gough (1971) found that the elaborate marriage arrangements reported for the Sudanese Nuer actually described only one form of socially acceptable marriage.

In sum, the problem is not the existence of a division of labor by gender or that marriage of some sort is a universal institution, but the content of those forms. Do women control strategic products? Is marriage critical for production and social authority? If so, is women's authority exercised primarily through the role of wife or mother, or are there other roles that carry more weight? We can find similarities of form everywhere, if we ignore the meaning and dynamics of the relationships for the particular society or type of society. The gender division of labor in industrial capitalist societies *is* oppressive to women, whose work in the public arena is considered either an intrusion on male territory or an addition to their "real" work—domestic service and child care. It does not follow, however, that all divisions of labor by gender involve such a public/domestic division or relegate women's work to a lesser status. In the Tongan Islands, for example, men's work was considered inferior to women's work; the high-status, necessary items made by women were critical in the maintenance of kin connections among people throughout their lives. Moreover, women controlled the disposition of these valuables (Gailey, 1980).

Similarly, marriage in kin societies does involve exchange, but men are not the sole transactors, and young men as well as women are exchanged. To understand the character of marriage as an institution, we need to understand who seals the exchange, the relative ease of divorce, and what marital status conveys in the way of additional authority and claims to products or labor. If we consider the content of marriage, the content of exchange, and the content of kinship relations, then universal patterns dissolve. Where there are patterns to the content, these are tied to historical dynamics, which need to be investigated.

SUBORDINATION AS A HISTORICAL PROCESS

If natural or global explanations are unacceptable, the problem of origins remains. A growing number of feminist scholars have turned to historical and archaeological research for evidence that links gender subordination to other forms of social hierarchy. This task involves understanding the kinds of social stratification that exist or have existed, and the relationships of those forms of stratification to the division of labor and property relations. A brief guide to types of human political economies and authority structures is essential.

Stratification in Human Societies

Our experience of gender and women's status comes from living in a class-stratified society with a capitalist economy. Not all societies share these features. In the past there have been class-stratified societies with decidedly different economic structures (such as feudal Europe; tribute-based civilizations in many parts of the ancient world; the slave-based Greek and Roman civilizations). In the contemporary world, there still are societies organized entirely along kinship lines. Since political and economic patterns are well described, we can use a *political economy* framework for comparative and historical research on women's status and gender relations. The dynamics of each type of political economy are intricate, as indicated by a brief summary of the key features of kinship societies and a particularly widespread type of precapitalist state society.

Kinship societies have no governmental structures and no permanent occupational specialization. The difficulty in using kinship societies for comparative and historical research lies in the political and economic upheaval of the last four centuries. Most kin societies known today have lost their sovereignty to state societies. The colonial expansion of capitalist countries around the world accelerated conquest to a degree unprecedented in the ancient world. Some kin peoples were exterminated, and most surviving kin societies have experienced severe dislocation (Bodley, 1982). State-sponsored capitalist development often has forced kinspeople into debt-related or wage labor, formal education, conversion to Christianity, private property ownership, Western models of gender roles, production for a world market, and so on. Careful use of early documents about kin societies can help make our use of contemporary field studies more accurate (Leacock, 1954). Unfortunately, many researchers have simply ignored the dramatic and deleterious impact of colonialism on kinship peoples when it comes to gender relations (Etienne and Leacock, 1980).

With that cautionary note, we will describe several key features of societies organized along kin and quasi-kin lines (Diamond, 1974). Property in kinship societies typically is "owned" by the group as a whole. Resources needed for subsistence are made available to everyone who is considered a member of the group, according to kinship connections by birth, adoption, or marriage. Labor is organized along the same lines: gender, stage of maturity (age), kin roles, and personal skills together determine what one will be doing, with whom, when, and for whom.

Production of goods and provision of services is always for use (Sahlins, 1972). Exchanges within the society are governed by kinship or fictive kinship relations among the exchangers and typically take the form of gifts. Goods also may be traded with unrelated peoples, but here again exchanges are organized through fictive kin connections (sometimes called trade-friendships) or marital connections. Even with long-distance trade, the goods received are destined for consumption, for use rather than for reinvestment or accumulation. Prestige can come through trade, but only if one distributes rather than hoards the goods received.

Some kin-communal societies are egalitarian, especially those involved in gathering and hunting or fishing. In egalitarian societies there is no appreciable social stratification; leadership in one activity does not entitle anyone to leadership in any other activity. Leadership tends to follow the division of labor: A combination of gender, age, kin role, and skills, as well as personality factors determines the arenas in which a person may be accorded special respect (Fried, 1967). Leadership does not convey the right to order or command anyone, which is widely viewed as an assault on the individual's autonomy (Lee, 1984). In egalitarian societies, in the absence of threats from the outside, the gender division of labor is central in subsistence pursuits and gender relations are reported to be amicable (Dentan, 1978; Turnbull, 1978; Rohrlich-Leavitt et al., 1975; Lee, 1984).

Other kin societies rank people according to how close they are to the group's designated ancestor or ancestress, as well as by achievement. In most cases, subsistence techniques include horticulture, combined with fishing, hunting, or animal husbandry. The gender division of labor remains key to subsistence. If hunting is part of the subsistence strategy, men usually are responsible for it. But there is no universal rule about which gender does the gardening, fishing, or care of any domesticated animals.

In such ranked societies, leadership positions are achieved mostly through demonstrated skills at persuasion, personal maturity, and generosity (Fried, 1967). There may be a limited number of leaders, but the genealogical requirements are usually ambiguous so there is a pool of potential leaders large enough to make the other factors more important (Gailey, 1981). In such societies the only compulsion is custom, understood by everyone. Leaders do not make law; they interpret custom. But if people do not agree in general with the interpretation, there is no means of enforcement (Diamond, 1974).

Some kin societies were stratified, but not along class lines. In precolonial Polynesia and along the Northwest Coast of North America, there were societies that had ranking in combination with hereditary orders, namely, chiefly and nonchiefly (Rousseau, 1978). While official leadership positions existed and titled chiefs were selected from the chiefly order, most chiefly people were untitled. Informal leadership also existed, similar to the achieved positions described for ranked kinship societies. These orders were not classes, however, and there were no governmental structures. Property remained communal, and although titled chiefs, as superior men and women, distributed the rights to use the land and other resources, they could not deny local kin groups access without incurring rebellion (Gailey, 1983). Labor relations were organized along kin lines as well. Higher-ranking people had claims to some of the labor or products of their lower-ranking kin. Chiefly people as a group remained involved in making the goods and providing the services needed to maintain the society. Nonchiefly people did more work, and titled chiefs sometimes did not work. Gender relations in stratified settings are ambivalent. Generally, women retained high status, but the sexual behavior of the highest-ranking women was controlled—by other high-ranking women. Women typically exercised considerable social authority over women and men through a combination of kin roles and rank (Gailey, 1980).

Class-stratified societies have emerged only in the past 6,000 or 7,000 years. Class societies have greater and more consistent social inequality, backed by a state structure. The *state* can be defined briefly as *a set of related institutions—at least taxation, draft, and legal-judicial—that act to reproduce class-based labor and property arrangements* (Diamond, 1951). The politically dominant class (or classes) as a whole is not involved directly in subsistence production. Members of dominant classes may act as administrators, managers, overseers, or contractors, but they do no productive labor. Peasants and artisans create the goods and services that fuel the government, support the nonproducing class or classes, and supply their own subsistence needs.

For our purposes, one form of precapitalist state was more important than most: The tribute-based state extracted goods and labor from a predominantly peasant population; the dominant class was supported immediately through the appropriated labor and revenues (Amin, 1976). The major empires that were taken over by expanding capitalist societies in the last few centuries were almost all tribute based (India, China, Aztec, Inca, Near East, East and West African kingdoms, etc.). In tribute-based societies, the state claimed all land and other resources and levied taxes and rents for using them. State-associated officials or nobles received estates to use, had the obligation to collect and transfer tax-rents and laborers (tribute) as requested by the state, and to provide military support on demand. In most cases, local kin-organized communities were annexed as groups into state societies. To use traditional lands, they then had to pay tribute in labor or products (Marx, 1965). Local kin communities might be left intact to a degree, subject to the labor and product demands of state officials (Krader, 1975).

In the formation of tribute-based states, a split developed for the first time in human history between the needs of the direct producers—peasants or artisans—and production for the state-associated class or classes (tribute production). In general, peasant needs were subordinated, relegated to a domestic sphere. Within the domestic sphere—still predominantly kin-organized and still oriented toward production for use—the gender division of labor found in kinship settings remained crucial. In the civil or "public" sphere—oriented toward tribute production—a gender division of labor also was important (Gailey, 1985b; Silverblatt, 1978).

These two types of societies provide a framework for examining gender relations historically and across cultures. There are patterns to the range of political and economic structures in societies. Gender roles and women's status follow these variations, if one traces the influence of conquest by other precapitalist states and capitalist expansions throughout the world. In short, women's status and authority are highest where economic and political stratification are the least developed; colonial influences can be shown to lower the status and authority of women even in kinship societies; and all state societies involve some form of gender hierarchy, often patriarchy. Since the transitions from kinship to class involve a twin process—class and state formation—we will consider gender relations in this process.

Stratification and Gender

Some feminists hold that women's subordination is a necessary prerequisite to class stratification. MacKinnon (1982, 1983) concurs with earlier Marxist-feminist theory in stating that state formation involves increasing oppression for women and is intrinsically patriarchal. But in agreement with structuralists, she argues that women are subordinate in kinship societies as well through marriage exchanges. Rohrlich (1980), on the other hand, uses evidence from Sumer in early Mesopotamia to postulate that a patriarchal civilization replaced a prior, more beneficent, matriarchal civilization. The criticism of universal subordination through marriage exchange has been given previously. Although the importance of women in pre-state Mesopotamia is undisputed, the claim of matriarchy seems unfounded. Rather, gender relations appear similar to those of other stratified but kin-organized societies.

If increasing stratification affects women's status, it either enhances or diminishes women's options. Some structuralist-feminists hold that in stratified societies, the gender division of labor is less important than other differences and thus, from a structuralist perspective, women have enhanced opportunities for status mobility (Ortner, 1978, 1981). Ortner (1981) argues that status mobility for women in "hierarchical" societies is tied to continued male control over women's reproductive potential and continued male dominance in political affairs. In other words, women can have more power in hierarchical settings than in kin-defined settings through their sexual potential.

Criticism of Ortner's position centers on her focus on a rather vaguely defined notion of status rather than on arenas of authority. While anthropologists generally agree that status mobility is possible in state societies, many point out that status mobility is far more pronounced in kinship settings; they also question the assumption that males control women's reproductive potential and political affairs in kinship societies. Critics of Ortner's thesis focus on social authority and relative control over products and labor, including, but not restricted to, reproductive labor. From this perspective, there is a clear *decline* in women's authority with class and state formation. Some women do indeed change status and may even enjoy exalted rank, but only as they are denied influence in their natal communities and as they shift allegiance and their reproductive potential to the state—but not necessarily to men (Silverblatt, 1978; Gailey, 1984). Such loss of control contrasts with women's authority over reproductive matters in less stratified settings.

The position that women's authority and status decline with class stratification and the origins of state societies was argued in the late nineteenth century by Engels, who based his work on Marx's last writings (Engels, 1972; Marx, 1974). Engels identified several related processes that together resulted in women's subordination: the creation of commodities—goods made as private property to trade for a profit; the restriction of people's rights to use subsistence resources; the transformation of goods and resources into private property; and the founding of institutions to support these changing social and economic relations (i.e., the state). In the process, kinship rights became constrained, marriage rights of wives restricted, and the family as a patriarchal, property-transmitting unit came into being.

The resurgence of feminism in the 1960s and 1970s found anthropologists reading Engels, correcting his faulty data, and abandoning the linear evolution of his argument (Leacock, 1972; Sacks, 1975). One corrective was that a transition to socialism did not remove gender hierarchy, although in general, economic security and political rights of women in socialist societies were greater than in capitalist ones. Gender hierarchy appeared linked to state formation rather than to property relations alone.

The new synthesis of feminism and Marxism argues that increasing stratification constrains women's social authority (see, for example, Lamphere, 1974; Leacock, 1983; Rapp, 1978a; Sacks, 1979). They argue that class and gender hierarchies are intertwined with state formation, and should be examined as interrelated processes. The factors attracting most of their attention are commodity production or production of tribute, and the restriction of kin-connected use-rights and labor claims (Gailey, 1980, 1984, 1985b; Leacock, 1983; Muller, 1977, 1985; Silverblatt, 1978, 1987).

There are disagreements within the Marxist-feminist group about women's status in ranked kin societies (e.g., Lamphere, 1974, vs. Etienne and Leacock, 1980), reflecting the degree of structuralist influence on Marxist scholarship (Edholm et al., 1977; Godelier, 1981). Despite agreement that women are subordinate in some surviving kin societies (as among the Yanomamö studied by Chagnon), many hold that investigating the effects of indirect colonization (ranging from commodity production and trade to epidemic-linked depopulation) or of defense against annexation by encroaching state societies can explain some of women's loss of authority (Leacock, 1983; Sacks, 1979; Klein, 1983). Others point out the problems with how anthropologists have conceptualized gender relations and authority relations in contemporary kin societies (Edholm et al., 1977; Rapp, 1978b; Gailey, 1985a).

Structuralist and modernization theorists consider kinship and state societies as categories, and kin societies as unchanging except through outside influence. The view here is that class and state formation are *processes,* not essences. Class and state formation are long-term, often inconclusive processes that can occur through internal dynamics or in combination with introduced factors. Most modern states have emerged from colonially imposed conditions in conjunction with internal tensions in previously class-based or kinship-based societies. The types of societies described in the previous section contain social tensions that tend toward and against increasing stratification. The reproduction of a society as a whole, then, includes the reproduction of tensions. Kinship societies are dynamic, not static, and the re-creation of kin-based property and labor relations means rejection of the potential for class relations. Kinship societies thus have histories, histories that involve actively sustaining less hierarchical relations (see Clastres, 1977).

Most of the theorists who look at gender hierarchy as a historical process linked with class and state formation search for the origins of exploitation in general and for the dynamics that create and support exploitative inequalities. Typically, state formation theorists who are not feminists ignore issues of gender and relegate gender hierarchy to a kind of fallout from the overall process (Claessen and Skalnik, 1979, 1981). The position taken here is that gender relations are crucial to understanding class and state formation as a related process, and thus a "women's issue" is part and parcel of scientific understanding (Diamond, 1951; Gailey, 1985a; Leacock, 1983; Sacks, 1979). Nevertheless, since they hold that gender hierarchy emerges with class and state formation, these scholars must address a knotty problem: If biology is not destiny, then why should women, rather than men, become the subordinate gender?

STATE FORMATION AND WOMEN'S AUTHORITY

In state formation women's authority is undercut in both elite and producing classes. We understand from the preceding sections that women in kinship societies are engaged simultaneously in productive and reproductive activities. In no way can their reproductive involvement be reduced to their role in biological reproduction. Women's social status and authority are an amalgam of rank, life stage, and kin-role considerations. In many kin societies, women are associated symbolically with kin group continuity. In the Trobriand Islands, for instance, women restore people's lineage identity when death threatens to end it: The mortuary exchanges of women's products, viewed as wealth objects, reassemble the identity that transition through various life stages (including death) has fragmented; women thus reproduce the lineage through generations (Weiner, 1976). In the Tongan Islands, women made goods, also seen as wealth, and distributed them during major life transitions. The presentation of these valuables validated the person's new status, both in terms of maturation—at birth, marriage, death—and social achievement—acquisition of names or chiefly titles (Gailey, 1980). These roles in social reproduction, as distinct from sexual reproduction, paralleled women's productive roles.

In state formation, however, kin-based production and reproduction are challenged by those seeking to reproduce class relations. State formation allows at least one group to become permanently disengaged from subsistence production. To ensure the continuity of class relations, the meaning of kinship as reciprocal claims to labor and products must be subordinated to class-based, unilateral claims (Gailey, 1985b). Kinship remains an important organizing principle within each of the developing classes, but the claims derived from kinship no longer determine the access one has to resources, labor, and goods (Rapp, 1978a). In the struggle between kin communities and the emerging civil sphere, kin-based authority and kin-organized production, distribution, and consumption patterns are undercut; but kin communities cannot be eliminated altogether, for two reasons. First, the emerging state is too weak to do it, and second, class relations depend on features of the division of labor by gender, age, and kin role to organize tribute production. The maintenance of the labor force also depends on survival of aspects of the kin-defined universe.

For class relations to stabilize, kin groups must cease to be autonomous: They must provide products and labor to support a nonproducing elite, regardless of local determination of need.[6] Therefore, the kin-based communities stand opposed in structural terms to incorporation into a larger, class-based society. Reproduction in this general sense of social continuity, becomes increasingly politicized (Gailey, 1985a). *In this crisis of social reproduction lie the origins of gender hierarchy.*

Kin communities must survive in some manner since they form the backbone of the production scheme, but they cannot be allowed autonomy. One common form of limiting local autonomy has been to prevent communities from reproducing without state intervention. The relatively unsubtle means used in some archaic states to determine local reproduction have included extraction of women from communities for service to the state (Inca, Dahomey). Rebellious groups in many archaic states were dispersed or exterminated, denying social continuity. In other cases, such as the Aztec, women from rebellious communities were put to work by their captors while the men were sacrificed. In the ancient Babylonian empire, states claimed the right to determine community reproduction through the regulation of marriages. State agents intervened in bridewealth arrangements and conducted collective wedding ceremonies.

Reproduction of class relations, then, involves replication of the existing labor force, replacement through conquest, or a combination of both means. State-sponsored religious, military, or other non-kin-based institutions act in different ways to promote reproduction of the hierarchical relations. Religious institutions promote notions of obedience, acceptance, controlled sexuality, and kinship along state-sanctioned (as opposed to customary) lines.

These efforts to regulate reproduction at home are echoed in efforts to subject neighboring peoples (Diamond, 1951). In Andean communities prior to Inca takeover, warfare entailed a ritual hierarchy of conqueror and conquered, but no control of the conquered by the conqueror group (Silverblatt, 1978). The Inca, however, injected this form of "conquest hierarchy" with new meaning. Men and women in conquered communities were considered symbolically female and thus subject to the disposal of the "male" state elite (Silverblatt, 1978). Among the Germanic peoples, living in the shadow of the Roman empire, temporary non-kin-based military retinues developed for a new purpose, raiding and acquisition of captives. For the first time, women were excluded from warfare, and these non-kin retinues gradually became permanent forces, creating discrepancies in men's and women's economic and political power (Muller, 1977, 1985). The militarization typical of state formation decreases women's authority as it transforms the nature of warfare (Gailey, 1984).

Why Women?

To discover why women's status and authority suffer more than men's in state formation, we must return to women's role in production and social reproduction. Control over labor (and through labor, goods) is the primary political issue in state formation. The existence of a sphere of tribute production destined for the civil authorities and the partial continuance of kin-oriented production initiates the fragmentation of the kinship division of labor. The split between public/civil and kinship/domestic spheres also shatters the unity of kinspeople's social identity. The new, class-based division of labor—operating in the tribute sphere—calls people into labor service according to categories of gender and age, but these aspects are divorced from the integrating influence of kin roles. In other words, at least in the civil sphere people can have abstract identities: an adult man, an adult woman. In the kin-defined sphere, they remain simultaneously men, brothers, husbands, fathers, mother's brothers, or women, sisters, wives, mothers, father's sisters, and so on. *The civil sphere creates a situation in which people can be considered solely in terms of their sex.* Their kin-defined social personhood is secondary, just as the kinship sphere is subordinate to the civil one.

Where work groups are defined according to one or two abstract qualities, the stage is set for biological reductionism. Constituents of the particular work group (e.g., peasants, men or women, war captives or members of conquered communities) tend to be defined in physical terms. Exploitative labor relations—the extraction of goods and services to support nonproducing peoples, without consensual agreement by the producers—give rise to class, sex, and racial stereotypes. These stereotypes vary with each state society, but each state society has created an ideology justifying class, sex, and racial inequality on the basis of innate differences.

Engagement in direct production is a gauge of subordination; removal from it, a gauge of superiority. In general, those who do "mental labor" are presented as purer or more cultured, and manual workers as rough and animalistic; those who are captives are described in ways said to be physically distinctive—color, facial configuration, or stature; those who are members of a gender become defined as members of a sex. Race, class, and sex stereotypes emerge alongside a division of labor that privileges uselessness and the institutions of state that enforce the class relations. People who fit more than one category, such as foreign women captives, tend to receive a combination of projections from the dominant ideology: As a rule, they are seen as simultaneously less civilized, more sexual, and stronger, and thus more appropriate for drudge work. The exact configurations vary widely, but the overall tendency is to imbue the exploitative division of labor in the civil sphere with supernatural and natural sanctions.

Why women should receive extreme ideological debasement is related to the abstraction of women in the civil division of labor and the suppression of kin group autonomy in reproduction. Leacock (1983) points out that women not only work but are capable of producing other laborers. As such, producing class women become a major focus of state control.

In archaic states producing women are involved in tribute work, but they also remain involved in the production and reproduction activities of their natal and marital kin groups. The domestic/kin sphere is downgraded in state ideologies, as are the people whose authority resides in kin connections. Kinswomen are defined in the civil division of labor as females. In the eyes of the state, as females, they are associated with childbearing and thus more closely than their kinsmen with the ability of communities to reproduce autonomously.

MacKinnon (1982, 1983) holds that state patriarchy necessarily involves control over women's sexuality, although she does not relate control efforts as a process to the reduction of kin group autonomy or changing production. But certainly state formation entails efforts to use women's reproductive potential and, at the same time, assert state control over local reproduction. The situation of concubines and female slaves is typical. In the kingdom of Zazzau in West Africa, for instance, state officials were the predominant slave holders; a slave woman was freed if she bore a child to her male owner (Smith, 1960).

The Inca periodically selected young women from local communities and trained them as state officiants. These women were married in name to the king and permanently alienated from their natal kindreds. They were to remain virgins while in state service. These *aclla* produced cloth, corn beer, and other items for elite use. In time, they could be given as secondary wives to elite men, or remain in service to state religious institutions until their death (Silverblatt, 1978). Their elevated social status was tied to state control over their reproductive potential. In the kin communities, women enjoyed sexual freedom prior to marriage, use-rights independent of their husbands, and control over the fruits of their labor. The aclla enjoyed no such autonomy or authority.

In Dahomey, some of the women convicted of state-defined crimes or nominated as wives of the king were stationed in local communities. They were supposed to entice men into having intercourse, prosecute them for rape (of a king's wife!), and receive fines in compensation; they were taxed annually. Men found guilty were conscripted into the army (Diamond, 1951). The prostitutes owed their living (their lives in the case of convicts) to their attachment to the state; the state received revenues and conscripts through the arrangement.

Every three years, a new crop of pubescent girls was selected by state agents from kin communities, escorted to the capital city, where some were chosen as wives to the king and the rest sent home to resume their kin-defined roles. Those chosen women who did not become prostitutes became the chaste warriors that formed the core of the Dahomeyan army. These "amazons" also enjoyed high status. Again, the women were alienated from their kin communities and their reproductive potential was entirely at the disposal of the king. Once defined in terms of their sexual potential, they lost all control over their own sexuality, fecundity, and labor, a situation unknown for women in the kin communities (Diamond, 1951). Thus Ortner's position (1981) that stratification increases women's status mobility receives partial support, but in fact most women's status falls. And even those whose status rises experience a precipitous decline in their authority and relative autonomy.

State ideologies may demean women but, at the same time, exalt certain categories of females who serve state interests and whose destinies are controlled by the state. State ideologies, often religious, emphasize the childbearing function of women, although the female deities of archaic states often show sexual as well as maternal aspects. Alternatively, some female deities display dualistic aspects, such as sex and death, or have complementary male components (Friedrich, 1978). The point is that sexuality and fecundity in women are presented in state-sponsored ideologies as requiring external control if they are not to become destructive.[7]

State efforts to restrict women's reproductive potential have serious consequences for the kin communities. Threats to kin group continuity, in the form of taxes and labor drafts, produce a heightened awareness of group continuity on the local level. Restriction of use-rights, interruption of rituals of renewal, and so on may lead to greater emphasis on control over remaining kin claims within the local community. Customs regulating access to lands may be interpreted narrowly to strengthen control over resources. The reinterpretation must take into account state demands; in many cases, the dynamic results in a restriction of women's claims to land and other resources. The kin community, in short, may become more defensive, more rigid in consolidating its position.

As the reproduction of the civil sphere becomes entrenched, kin groups become more marginal, more in danger of dissolution. In many cases, pressures emerge within the kin community for regulating the allocation of women as simultaneously productive workers and bearers of children. For example, loose kin claims to lands come to be strictly patrilineal, effectively shifting women's access primarily to the role of wife or daughter. Inheritance of use-rights becomes an issue: with it, legitimacy, chastity, and other aspects of sexual life are charged with new-found importance. State penetration makes reproduction of the kin group an omnipresent crisis; in the kin-civil conflict (Diamond, 1951), the range and content of women's kin roles may decline and the remaining roles become oppressive. The relative strength of the state will be reflected in the relative weakness of producing women's authority in both kin and civil spheres. Kin structures are most oppressive to women in areas that have the longest experience of state penetration. It is no accident that almost every known peasant revolutionary movement has included condemnation of women's subordination.

Elite Women

The consolidation of class domination politicizes ruling class kinship and reproduction as well. Like all ruling class people, elite women are unproductive. As such, they and elite men have solely reproductive functions—the reproduction of themselves and of class relations in general. But the kin relations they help to reproduce are not those of the producing people. It is a kinship devoid of all but political functions. Kinship in the elite is related to political alliances and inheritance—of wealth, of high office, of rank. It is no wonder the elites of precapitalist states are mired in intrigue, in hypertrophy of genealogical manipulation, and in jockeying for position. More so than nonelite women, who retain productive importance, high-ranking women are associated solely with the reproduction of their class. Typically their sexuality and marital alliances are far more closely supervised than those of the peasantry. Out-of-place fertility can cause political turmoil, as the plethora of succession disputes in early states attest. In all precapitalist state societies, the elite attempts to limit the ambiguities of kinship, to make succession orderly. Either the sexuality of the highest-ranking women must be controlled so a definitive heir can be produced, or succession must have nothing to do with kinship. In either case, the biological dimensions of sexuality and kinship are politicized.

In Dahomey, for example, the next king could never be the son of one of the king's wives; he had to be a son of a concubine, thus undercutting the influence of high-ranking women. Royal marriages became institutionalized as political alliances or as expressions of state relations (military or prostitute-revenues) rather than related to the continuity of a royal lineage (Diamond, 1951). In this setting, women clearly were exchanged by men in marriage, but Dahomey was hardly a kin society.

In most early states, elite women exercise considerable social authority. The dominant classes are still kin-ordered themselves, and thus gender remains an important organizing principle within the ruling circles as well. Often rulership in states emerging out of kin societies involves parallel lines of authority for women and men. Drawing on the authority linked to gender roles in the prestate society, a married couple, a mother-son pair, or a brother-sister dyad exercises gender-linked lines of social power. This phase in state formation is often what researchers have confused with matriarchy. Ruling class women had considerable political power, as in ancient Crete and Mycenaean Greece, but they were not solitary rulers.

The tendency in state formation, however, is for kinship in general to be demeaned. With the relegation of kinship to a domestic sphere, the political power of women within the elite declines, although their class position continues to afford them power vis-à-vis producing peoples. In short, *gender hierarchy is born of kin-civil conflict, set in motion during class and state formation.* At first, the abstraction of femaleness and the reduction of women's social identity to their reproductive potential is confined to tribute production. The "biology as destiny" tendency centers on producing class women vis-à-vis the elite. If state formation continues, the gender hierarchy that first characterized the relations between the elite and the producing classes filters into the internal dynamics of both elites and kin communities. Producing class women to absorb the brunt of the changes, for they have no effective social power. Elite women participate in the subordination process, for whether or not they have political parity within the elite, they exercise social power.

In nonstate settings, biology is not destiny. In state formation, however, reproductive potential has unprecedented political implications, because political domination rests on control over both the reproduction of producing communities and the emerging elite. Within the elite, reproductive issues are paramount because of the succession and inheritance issues characteristic of nonproducing classes. On the community level, the threats to the integrity and use-rights of kin foster efforts to control the allocation of women and their reproductive potential, but for opposite reasons: to try to preserve kin group autonomy rather than destroy it. Whatever the reasons, however, the dynamics of state formation are inimical to women's authority.

THEORY AND SOCIAL CHANGE

The theories of gender hierarchy outlined in this chapter provide different possibilities for social change. As a proponent of the class and state formation/gender hierarchy link, I would argue that this process-oriented approach accounts for more of the existing cultural variation and historical changes than do the other theories. As every social theory includes a political agenda, so also do theories of women's subordination.

The sociobiological approaches suggest that movements for women's equality are senseless, even destructive, because they fly in the face of inclusive fitness and sexual selection as natural laws. Social change that allows a sex division of labor more in keeping with what are purported to be universal laws would be desirable. As such, some sociobiologists (Wilson, 1975) even call for the end of discrimination against people of color and nonheterosexual preferences, although their reasons seem also to constitute discrimination.[8] However, sex discrimination remains justified, indeed necessary.

Technico-environmentalists would offer technological solutions, such as reducing women's subordination through birth control and population planning. For the middle class, declining fertility has been associated with expanded opportunities for women, but the correlation should not be confused with causation: What *else* is associated with expanded opportunities, and what—in addition to child care and childbearing—has restricted the opportunities of women in other classes? The worrisome aspects of a technical-environmental approach are that it does not address the control issue: Who decides if fertility is the central problem, and who develops population policy? Who controls the means and availability of birth control? Top-down approaches present elite solutions to purportedly natural problems. The greater availability of birth control devices in contemporary industrial societies has not produced dramatic rises in women's political or economic power. If anything, the causal link is reversed: An active women's movement creates political and economic pressure for effective birth control and reproductive choices.

If gender hierarchy derives from our hominid subsistence adaptations, routes to greater equality require finding cultural means to redirect hominid patterns. Men would need outlets for killing or hunting aggressiveness; women would need social means of combining their childbearing and child-care proclivities with more public activities. The dependency of females and children—assumed to be primal—could be redirected to the state, presumably, instead of to husbands or fathers. Man-the-hunter solutions point to the capitalist welfare state, with appended male-oriented contact sports and all-male clubs. In a situation such as our own, where women are associated with child rearing and where social services are being curtailed, the expansion of state-sponsored services for child care and child support would be ameliorative of women's economic binds. But the extension of such services should not be linked with the promotion of innate differences in temperament or the continuance of societywide sexism.

If gender hierarchy is rooted in our capacity to create symbols, there is no solution. Any change is epiphenomenal. If, as some structuralists argue, it is rooted in the gender division of labor, then equality demands an eradication of gender-linked tasks. This also implies the right to transform kinship societies, where gender divisions of labor are central to production; put politely, it means ethnocide based on an assertion that because *our* gender division of labor is oppressive, so also is everyone else's. Domestically, the solution is one of modern reform liberalism: If gender barriers are removed from occupations, and if men perform domestic tasks, women become equal.

While such changes are desirable, they do not address more fundamental gender hierarchy issues. Gender hierarchy itself could continue: The men and women of the dominant class could be symbolically male, as in the Incaic civilization. Margaret Thatcher becomes the "Iron Lady," symbolically a powerful man. More profoundly, if women and men have parity as stockbrokers, bankers, lawyers, politicians, capitalists, and so on, other forms of discrimination could easily continue, particularly those based on race, class, and sexual preference. The structuralist solution disregards the historical interconnections among race, class, and gender as forms of stratification. Simply put, one alone cannot be eliminated. They developed together out of the same set of circumstances. Either none goes or they all go.

The class and state formation theory implies fundamental social change. The theory does not demand the destruction of a gender division of labor, but it does imply that all persons should be simultaneously involved in both productive and reproductive work. Moreover, it denies the superiority of mental versus manual labor. Women's capacity to bear children is not seen as inimical to equivalent social security and authority, and every economic and political change that works toward the removal of restricted use-rights to social resources and undemocratic social decision making would help. The goal is the reconstruction, with the technological capacity at hand, of the conditions that allow women equivalent social power in kinship societies. These conditions include ready access to subsistence resources, reciprocal labor claims, support services during life crises such as childbirth, social responsibility for child care, and sharing of social products with all according to need. In political terms, it entails the empowerment of all women, in whatever fields of endeavor, in the making and implementation of policy concerning their interests. Such conditions would also ameliorate the oppressions of class and race as well. Kinship societies are the only truly democratic societies on this planet; for women to share social power again, we must learn from them.

NOTES

1. The dissolution of kinship is one of the hallmarks of capitalist relations. Today we experience it as a burgeoning number of single-parent families and the "feminization of poverty." Patriarchy is opposed to the destruction of at least the nuclear family: The "moral majority" and other right-wing movements embrace the patriarchal family as a bulwark against the destruction of kinship. But patriarchy is an anachronism in capitalist societies.

For capitalist relations to emerge, people have to be defined as legally free individuals: The solidarity of even a minimal kin group—the nuclear family, for instance—is called into question. Where people are defined as individuals, a growing contradiction emerges between patriarchal authority (kinship groups legally defined as microcosms of state authority vis-à-vis local communities) and economic relations. The form of gender hierarchy shifts to accommodate the fragmentation of the patriarchal family. Women remain subordinate, but as abstract individuals, not as members of patriarchal households. Patriarchy in its classic sense can remain a powerful ideological force, as fundamentalist "New Right" movements attest, but the impact is a general repression of women's rights, not the reconstruction of the patriarchal family. Patriarchal relations can persist, but only in marginal sectors of the society.

Within the capitalist class—as opposed to those sectors that enjoy large salaries but own little income-producing property—familism remains strong as a means of keeping property consolidated, but the family form is rarely patriarchal. Marriages typically involve intricate property arrangements, with provisions for potential divorce and inheritance problems: Wives and husbands do not necessarily merge property as happens typically in middle-class marriages. Women remain holders of property, conduits for heirs, but they are not legally under the aegis of their fathers and husbands.

2. There were very few exceptions to this rule. The only famous exception was Margaret Mead, whose field research in New Guinea (now Papua New Guinea) and Samoa led her to state that personality differences between women and men were not the same in all cultures (Mead, 1928, 1935). There are methodological and conceptual problems with her work, but there are more profound problems with that of her sociobiological critic, Derek Freeman (1983). The prominent place of Mead in the public eye is related to her writing for a popular audience and her enthusiasm for speaking out on issues of public concern. She and a number of other female graduate students were encouraged by Franz Boas, the "father" of American anthropology, but as anthropology became a profession, fewer women were encouraged to pursue it as a career. The pattern did not begin to change until the late 1960s, when the women's movement sparked renewed interest in cross-cultural studies—and collective demands by women in graduate education to be taken seriously.

3. The pejorative connotations of "primitive" make it an unfortunate label. I prefer to use the term "kinship society" because in this form of society property, labor, and social reproduction are organized through relations of descent, adoption, and marriage. There are a number of kinship societies in the world today, and the term "primitive," while it accurately contrasts with state-level societies (civilizations), implies that these people are somehow backward. They are not.

4. Divale and Harris (1976) base their theory on information in the Human Relations Area Files (HRAF). These ethnographic reports, coded for specific topics, are notorious for their lack of attention to historical change and to social process, as opposed to categories. For example, in the case of the Lovedu father's sister-brother's daughter marriage, where the young wife moved to her paternal aunt's compound after marriage, the HRAF reports the postmarital residential pattern as "virilocal," that is, residence with the husband. This is technically correct, but to call the Lovedu virilocal misses the range of marriage types, including "amitalocality"—residence with the aunt (father's sister)—which Divale and Harris deny as a possibility (Poewe, 1980).

5. In one incident described in Shostak's biography of a !Kung woman, a mother considers infanticide because her young daughter may not have sufficient food if the new baby is kept. She is persuaded not to kill the infant by the daughter, according to the daughter as a grown woman. The baby in question was a son (Shostak, 1981).

6. As a rule, elites try to justify surplus production and extraction through ideological means, but force is invoked if more subtle measures fail.

7. Development ideology, holding women as responsible for the so-called "population bomb," is a modern variant.

8. Obviously, not all sociobiologists press for such change. Those who urge the acceptability of homosexuality base their position on the notion of inclusive fitness—a situation where altruistic behavior helps in the reproductive success of biologically close relatives. It is not a particularly compelling argument, since it reduces kinship to biology. The metaphoric association of homosexual men and sterile drones is also inappropriate (Wilson, 1975). It recapitulates the discrimination at another level: Since homosexuality is not "real" sexuality, homosexual persons should be tolerated insofar as their actions assist those who reproduce sexually. This hardly constitutes acceptance.

The racial discrimination argument is imbued with notions of innate intelligence. Sociobiologists are inclined to see intelligence as largely inherited and differential in individuals (Wilson, 1975; see Herrnstein, 1971). These differences are said to be comparably distributed across all human populations. The catch is that I.Q. testing is said to indicate the meritorious individuals within each population. The claim that intelligence is an inherited trait, and scientifically measurable, has been challenged by a range of researchers (e.g., Gould, 1981; Goldfarb et al., 1980). The removal of official barriers, then, would merely shift the level of discrimination to the level of test-creation and class or cultural assumptions.

REFERENCES

AMIN, S. (1976) Unequal Development. New York: Monthly Review.

ARDREY, R. (1976) The Hunting Hypothesis. New York: Atheneum.

BARASH, D. (1979) The Whispering Within. New York: Harper & Row.

BELL, D. (1980) "Desert politics: Choices in the marriage market," pp. 239-269 in M. Etienne and E. B. Leacock (eds.) Women and Colonization. New York: Bergin and Garvey/Praeger.

BENDERLY, B. (1982) "Rape free or rape prone." Science 82, 3: 40-43.

BODLEY, J. (1982) Victims of Progress. Palo Alto, CA: Mayfield Press.

BOSERUP, E. (1965) The Conditions for Agricultural Growth. Chicago: Aldine.

BOSERUP, E. (1970) Women's Role in Economic Development. New York: Allen & Unwin.

BROWN, J. (1975) "Iroquois women: An ethnohistoric note," pp. 235-251 in R. R. Reiter (ed.) Toward an Anthropology of Women. New York: Monthly Review.

BROWN, J. (1981) "Women's life cycle in cross-cultural perspective." Presented at the Canadian Ethnological Society (CESCE) Annual Meetings, Ottawa, March.

CARROLL, V. [ed.] (1970) Adoption in Polynesia. Honolulu: University of Hawaii Press.

CHAGNON, N. (1968) Yanomamö: The Fierce People. New York: Holt, Rinehart and Winston.

CLAESSEN, H.J.M. and P. SKALNÍK [eds.] (1981) The Study of the State. The Hague: Mouton.

CLAESSEN, H.J.M. and P. SKALNÍK [eds.] (1979) The Early State. The Hague: Mouton.

CLASTRES, P. (1977) "The bow and the basket," pp. 83-107 in Society Against the State. New York: Urizen Books.

COWGILL, G. (1975) "On causes and consequences of ancient and modern population changes." American Anthropologist 77, 3: 505-525.

DENTAN, R. (1978) "Notes on childhood in a non-violent context: The Semai case," pp. 94-143 in A. Montagu (ed.) Learning Non-Aggression. New York: Oxford University Press.

DIAMOND, S. (1951) Dahomey: A Proto-State in West Africa. Ann Arbor, MI: University Microfilms.

DIAMOND, S. (1974) In Search of the Primitive: A Critique of Civilization. New Brunswick, NJ: Transaction.

DIENER, P., E. ROBKIN, and D. NONINI (1978) "The dialectics of the sacred cow in India." Dialectical Anthropology 3, 3: 221-241.

DIVALE, W. and M. HARRIS (1976) "Population, warfare, and the male supremacist complex." American Anthropologist 78, 3: 521-538.

DOUGLAS, M. (1966) Purity and Danger. London: Routledge & Kegan Paul.

DOUGLAS, M. (1973) Natural Symbols. New York: Random House.

DRAPER, P. (1975) "!Kung women," pp. 77-109 in R. R. Reiter (ed.) Toward an Anthropology of Women. New York: Monthly Review.

EDHOLM, F., O. HARRIS, and K. YOUNG (1977) "Conceptualising women." Critique of Anthropology 3, 9-10: 101-130.

ENGELS, F. (1972) The Origin of the Family, Private Property, and the State (E. B. Leacock, ed.). New York: International Publishers.

ESTIOKO-GRIFFIN, A. (1986) "Daughters of the forest." Natural History, 95, 5 (May).

ETIENNE, M. (1979) "The case for social maternity: Adoption of children by urban Baulé women." Dialectical Anthropology 4: 237-242.

ETIENNE, M. and E. B. LEACOCK (1980) "Introduction," pp. 1-24 in M. Etienne and E. Leacock (eds.) Women and Colonization. New York: Bergin and Garvey/Praeger.

FIRESTONE, S. (1971) The Dialectic of Sex. New York: Bantam Books.

FORTUNE, R. (1963) Sorcerers of Dobu. New York: E. P. Dutton.

FREEMAN, D. (1983) Margaret Mead and Samoa: The Making and Unmaking of an Anthropological Myth. Cambridge, MA: Harvard University Press.

FRIED, M. (1967) The Evolution of Political Society. New York: Random House.

FRIEDL, E. (1978) "Society and sex roles." Human Nature 1 (April): 68.

FRIEDRICH, P. (1978) The Meaning of Aphrodite. Chicago: University of Chicago Press.

GAILEY, C. W. (1980) "Putting down sisters and wives: Tongan women and colonization," pp. 294-322 in M. Etienne and E. B. Leacock (eds.) Women and Colonization. New York: Bergin and Garvey/Praeger.

GAILEY, C. W. (1981) "Our History Is Written . . . in Our Mats": State Formation and the Status of Women in the Tongan Islands. Ann Arbor, MI: University Microfilms.

GAILEY, C. W. (1983) "Categories without culture: Structuralism, ethnohistory and ethnocide." Dialectical Anthropology 8, 3: 241-250.

GAILEY, C. W. (1984) "Women and warfare: Shifting status in precapitalist state formation." Culture (Journal of the Canadian Ethnological Society/Société canadienne d'ethnologie) 4, 1: 61-70.

GAILEY, C. W. (1985a) "The state of the state in anthropology." Dialectical Anthropology 9, 1-2: 65-89.

GAILEY, C. W. (1985b) "The kindness of strangers: Transformation of kinship in precapitalist class and state formation." Culture (Journal of the Canadian Ethnological Society/Société canadienne d'ethnologie) 5, 2.

GODELIER, M. (1981) "The origins of male domination." New Left Review 127 (May/June): 3-17.

GOLDFARB, M., L. SCHWARTZ, and M. SCHWARTZ (1980) "Recent developments in IQ research: Implications for policymakers." Clearinghouse for Civil Rights Research VI 1, 1-2: 3-19.

GOODALE, J. (1971) Tiwi Wives. Seattle: University of Washington Press.

GOODY, J. and S. J. TAMBIAH (1973) Bridewealth and Dowry. Cambridge: Cambridge University Press.

GOUGH, K. (1968) "The Nayars and the definition of marriage," pp. 49-73 in P. Bohannan and J. Middleton (eds.). Marriage, Family and Residence. Garden City, NY: Natural History Press.

GOUGH, K. (1971) "Nuer kinship: A re-examination," pp. 79-122 in T. Beidleman (ed.) The Translation of Culture. London: Tavistock.

GOULD, S. J. (1981) The Mismeasure of Man. New York: Norton.

GOULD, S. J. (1982) The Panda's Thumb. New York: Norton.

HARNER, M. J. (1972) The Jivaro. New York: Doubleday/Natural History Museum.

HARRIS, M. (1977) "Why men dominate women." New York Times Magazine, November 13.

HART, C. W. and A. R. PILLING (1960) The Tiwi of Northern Australia. New York: Holt.

HERRNSTEIN, R. (1971) "I.Q." Atlantic Monthly 228, 3: 44-64.

HUBBARD, R. and M. LOWE. [eds.] (1979) Genes and Gender II: Pitfalls in Research on Sex and Gender. New York: Gordian Press.

KELLMAN, S. (1982) "The Yanomami—their battle for survival." Journal of International Affairs 36, 1: 15-42.

KLEIN, A. (1983) "The Plains truth: The impact of colonialism on Indian women." Dialectical Anthropology 7, 2: 299-313.

KRADER, L. (1975) The Asiatic Mode of Production. Assen, Neth.: Van Gorcum.

KRENISKE, J. (1984) "Sociobiology: The runcible science." Ph.D. dissertation, Columbia University, New York.

LAMPHERE, L. (1974) "Strategies, cooperation, and conflict among women in domestic groups," pp. 97-112 in M. Rosaldo and L. Lamphere (eds.) Women, Culture and Society. Stanford, CA: Stanford University Press.

LANDES, R. (1971) The Ojibwa Women. New York: Norton.

LAPPE, F. M. and COLLINS, J. (1977) Food First: Beyond the Myth of Scarcity. New York: Random House.

LAUGHLIN, W. (1968) "Hunting: An integrating biobehavioral system and its evolutionary importance," pp. 304-320 in R. B. Lee and I. DeVore (eds.) Man the Hunter. Chicago: Aldine.

LEACH, E. (1966) "The structural implications of cross-cousin marriage," pp. 54-104 in Rethinking Anthropology. New York: Humanities Press.

LEACOCK, E. B. (1954) "The Montagnais 'hunting territory' and the fur trade." American Anthropological Association Memoir No. 78.

LEACOCK, E. B. (1972) "Introduction," pp. 7-67 in F. Engels, The Origin of the Family, Private Property, and the State. New York: International Publishers.

LEACOCK, E. B. (1977) "The changing family and Lévi-Strauss, or whatever happened to fathers?" Social Research 44, 2: 235-259.

LEACOCK, E. B. (1981) Myths of Male Dominance. New York: Monthly Review.

LEACOCK, E. B. (1983) "The origins of gender inequality: Conceptual and historical problems." Dialectical Anthropology 7, 4: 263-284.

LEACOCK, E. B. and R. B. LEE [eds.] (1982) Politics and History in Band Societies. Cambridge: Cambridge University Press.

LEACOCK, E. B. and J. NASH (1977) "Ideology of sex: Archetypes and stereotypes." Annals, New York Academy of Sciences, No. 285.

LEAKEY, R. and R. LEWIN (1977a) "Is it our culture, not our genes, that makes us killers?" Smithsonian (November): 56-66.

LEAKEY, R. (1977b) Origins. New York: E. P. Dutton.

LEE, R. B. (1979) The !Kung San: Men, Women and Work in a Foraging Society. Cambridge: Cambridge University Press.

LEE, R. B. (1982) "Politics, sexual and non-sexual, in an egalitarian society," pp. 37-60 in E. B. Leacock and R. Lee (eds.) Politics and History in Band Societies. Cambridge: Cambridge University Press.

LEE, R. B. (1984) The Dobe !Kung. New York: Holt, Rinehart & Winston.

LEE, R. B. and I. DEVORE [eds.] (1968) Man the Hunter. Chicago: Aldine.

LÉVI-STRAUSS, C. (1969) The Elementary Structures of Kinship. Boston: Beacon.

LIEBOWITZ, L. (1975) "Perspectives on the evolution of sex differences," pp. 20-35 in R. R. Reiter (ed.) Toward an Anthropology of Women. New York: Monthly Review.

LIEBOWITZ, L. (1978) Females, Males, Families: A Biosocial Approach. North Scituate, MA: Duxbury Press.

LIZOT, J. (1976) The Yanomami in the Face of Ethnocide. IWGIA Document 22. Copenhagen: IWGIA.

MACKINNON, C. (1982) "Feminism, marxism, method and the state: Part 1." Signs 7, 3: 515-544.

MACKINNON, C. (1983) "Feminism, marxism, method and the state: Part 2." Signs 8, 4: 635-658.

MARX, K. (1965) Pre-Capitalist Economic Formations (Eric Hobsbawm, ed.). New York: International Publishers.

MARX, K. (1974) The Ethnological Notebooks (L. Krader, trans.) (1881). Assen, Neth.: Van Gorcum.

MEAD, M. (1928) Coming of Age in Samoa. New York: Natural History Museum Press/William Morrow.

MEAD, M. (1935) Sex and Temperament. New York: William Morrow.

MEIGS, A. (1976) "Male pregnancy and the reduction of sexual opposition in a New Guinea highlands society." Ethnology 15, 4: 393-408.

MONTAGU, A. (1968) The Natural Superiority of Women. New York: Macmillan.

MONTAGU, A. (1980) Sociobiology Examined. Oxford: Oxford University Press.

MULLER, V. (1977) "The formation of the state and the oppression of women: A case study in England and Wales." Review of Radical Political Economics 9, 3: 7-21.

MULLER, V. (1985) "Origins of class and gender stratification in Northwest Europe." Dialectical Anthropology 9, 3-4: 93-105.

MURPHY, R. and Y. MURPHY (1974) Women of the Forest. New York: Columbia University Press.

NELL, E. (1979) "Population pressure and methods of cultivation: A critique of classless theory," pp. 457-468 in S. Diamond (ed.) Toward a Marxist Anthropology. The Hague: Mouton.

NONINI, D. (1985) "Varieties of materialism." Dialectical Anthropology 9, 1-2.

OAKLEY, A. (1972) Sex, Gender and Society. New York: Harper & Row.

ORTNER, S. (1974) "Is female to male as nature is to culture?" pp. 67-88 in R. Rosaldo and L. Lamphere (eds.) Women, Culture and Society. Stanford, CA: Stanford University Press.

ORTNER, S. (1978) "The virgin and the state." Feminist Studies 4, 3: 19-36.

ORTNER, S. (1981) "Gender and sexuality in hierarchical societies," pp. 359-409 in S. Ortner and H. Whitehead (eds.) Sexual Meanings. New York: Cambridge University Press.

PAULMÉ, D. [ed.] (1971) Women of Tropical Africa. Berkeley: University of California Press.

POEWE, K. (1980) "Universal male dominance: An ethnological illusion." Dialectical Anthropology 5: 110-125.

PROSPISIL, L. (1963) The Kapauku Papuans. New York: Holt, Rinehart & Winston.

PRUITT, I. (1967) A Daughter of Han. Stanford, CA: Stanford University Press.

RADIN, P. (1971) The World of Primitive Man. New York: E.P. Dutton.

RAPP, R. (1978a) "Gender and class: An archeology of knowledge concerning the origin of the state." Dialectical Anthropology 2, 4: 309-316.

RAPP, R. (1978) "Andean women in the Inca empire." Feminist Studies 4, 3: 37-61.

SHIPMAN, P. (1986) "Scavenging or hunting in early hominids: Theoretical framework and tests." American Anthropologist, 88(1): 27-43.

SILVERBLATT, I. (1978) "Andean women in the Incan empire." Feminist Studies, 4, 3: 37-61.

SILVERBLATT, I. (1980) " 'The universe is turned inside out . . . there is no justice for us here': Andean women under Spanish rule," pp. 149-187 in M. Etienne and E. B. Leacock (eds.) Women and Colonization. New York: Bergin and Garvey/Praeger.

SILVERBLATT, I. (1987) Moon, Sun, and Witches: Gender Ideologies and Class in Inca and Colonial Peru. Princeton, NJ: Princeton University Press.

SISKIND, J. (1973) To Hunt in the Morning. London: Oxford University Press.

SLOCUM, S. (1975) "Woman the gatherer: Male bias in anthropology," pp. 36-50 in R. R. Reiter (ed.) Toward an Anthropology of Women. New York: Monthly Review Press.

SMITH, M. G. (1960) Government in Zazzau, 1800-1950. London: Oxford University Press.

SMOLE, W. J. (1976) The Yanomamö Indians. Austin: University of Texas Press.

SORENSON, E. R. (1978) "Cooperation and freedom among the Fore of New Guinea," pp. 12-30 in A. Montagu (ed.) Learning Non-Aggression. New York: Oxford University Press.

SYMONS, D. (1979) The Evolution of Human Sexuality. New York: Oxford University Press.

THOMAS, E. M. (1958) The Harmless People. New York: Random House.

TIGER, L. (1969) Men in Groups. New York: Random House.

TIGER, L. (1971) The Imperial Animal. New York: Holt, Rinehart & Winston.

TURNBULL, C. (1962) The Forest People. New York: Simon & Schuster.

TURNBULL, C. (1978) "The politics of non-aggression," pp. 161-221 in A. Montagu (ed.) Learning Non-Aggression. New York: Oxford University Press.

VAN ALLEN, J. (1972) "'Sitting on a man': Colonialism and the lost political institutions of Igbo women." Canadian Journal of African Studies 6: 165-181.

WASHBURN, S. and C. S. LANCASTER (1968) "The evolution of hunting," pp. 293-303 in R. B. Lee and I. DeVore (eds.) Man the Hunter. Chicago: Aldine.

WEINER, A. (1976) Women of Value, Men of Renown. Austin: University of Texas Press.

WILSON, E. O. (1975) Sociobiology: The New Synthesis. Cambridge, MA: Belknap Press/Harvard University Press.

WILSON, E. O. (1978) On Human Nature. Cambridge, MA: Harvard University Press.

WOLF, L. D. and J. P. GRAY (1981) "Creationism and popular sociobiology as myths." The Humanist 41: 43-48.

WOLF, M. (1972) Women and the Family in Rural Taiwan. Stanford, CA: Stanford University Press.

2 Science, Sexual Difference, and Feminism

JANET SAYERS
University of Kent, England

T HE relation of science to society is nothing if not contradictory. It has contributed to the enhancement and to the degradation of our quality of life, using nature to both constructive and destructive effect. Science is truly a force for life and death, presenting us with the nightmare of nuclear holocaust even as it makes possible a standard of living undreamt of by our forebears.

It is therefore little wonder that feminists should be ambivalent about science. In this chapter I shall explore this ambivalence. First I shall sketch out how feminists, like their opponents, have increasingly come to use science in place of morality and religion in the debate over sexual difference and its implications for prevailing social inequalities between the sexes. I shall then deal with the recent rejection of science by feminism—a rejection that to some extent replaces with pantheism the religious account of sexual difference outlined in the introduction to the first section of this chapter. This rejection has in large measure been provoked by the failure of science to attend to women's needs and interests as it should. I shall conclude by arguing that this, science's present bias against women's interests, can only be overcome by achieving the sexual equality sought both by feminists opposed and sympathetic to science.

IDEOLOGIES OF SEXUAL DIFFERENCE

Preoccupation with sexual difference and inequality has tended to be particularly intense at those time when prevailing differences between the sexes seem most likely to be eroded. This happened at the time of the French Revolution, when women as well as men demanded that they be freed from

---

AUTHOR'S NOTE: My thanks to the following for their extremely helpful comments and suggestions on earlier drafts of this chapter: Robyn Cooper, Myra Ferree, Beth Hess, Anne Seller, and Shirley Toulson.

feudal bondage. Inspired by the revolution, Mary Wollstonecraft argued that women were essentially the same as men in their powers of reason, that the path of virtue lay in these capacities being developed in both sexes so that they might equally become independent and free citizens. By contrast, those who were fearful lest a similar revolution occur in England opposed this philosophy of equal rights. For example, leading evangelical Hannah More stated that social harmony would be best served by women and men conforming with the "respective appropriate qualifications" she believed to differentiate the sexes (More, 1778: 3). Refusing to read Wollstonecraft's *Vindication of the Rights of Women,* More took issue with its Englightenment morality as follows: "Each sex has its proper excellencies," she wrote, "which would be lost were they melted down into the common character by the fusion of the new philosophy" (More, 1799: 21). Men, she asserted, are made for "deep and daring scenes of action and of council; in government, in arms, in science, in commerce, and in those professions which demand a higher reach, and a wider range of powers." Woman, she maintained, "has other requisites better adapted to answer the purposes of her being, by 'Him who does all things well'" (More, 1799: 24). While men, claimed More, are all too often alienated by science from religion, women are more receptive to religion for which their domestic situation gives them the necessary "leisure and tranquility" (More, 1799: 34-35).

This ideology of sexual difference—of men involved in "the tumult of a bustling world" and of women smoothing and polishing the "harshness and asperities" of men (More, 1799: 21, 35)—was to be further elaborated and reiterated in the early decades of the nineteenth century. This was again due to the way social developments then threatened to "turn upside down" previous gender distinctions (Alexander, 1984). The changeover to factory production made possible by the scientific and technological advances of the Industrial Revolution gave women an opportunity to become independent wage-earners (Gardiner, 1974; Gittins, 1983). Alarmed at the way women now gained jobs at men's expense, thus undermining patriarchal authority in the home, labor movement organizers of the period joined middle-class philanthropists in condemning this trend. In doing so they drew on earlier evangelical ideas about sexual difference—of woman as closer than men to God. They condemned women's work in the mines (Humphries, 1981) and in the factories (Engels, 1958) on the grounds that it ruined women morally for their task as mothers, as "angels of the hearth," as moral guardians of society and its future. Thus began a process, continued to our day, whereby women and their failure to conform to the moral and ethical ideals assumed to differentiate them from men have regularly been blamed for social ills that are in fact more often due to inequalities of sex, race, and class (Shields, 1984).

Although industrialization undermined earlier ideals of sexual difference, it also secured them on a new footing. Women were never able to command the same factory wages as men. Men's wages, unlike those of women, were supposed to cover both their upkeep and that of their families. Men's "family wages" both reflected and cemented their authority in the home (Hartmann, 1979; Barrett and McIntosh, 1980). Unable to contribute as men could to the financial upkeep of their families, women found themselves, and still find themselves, deferring to men on this account (Kerr, 1985).

Nor were middle-class women freed from sexual inequality by industrialization. Instead, industrialization consolidated rather than abolished sexual inequalities and differences in both the middle and working classes. The expansion of trade and industry made possible by the Industrial Revolution resulted in business being established away from its original household base. Middle-class women accordingly found themselves no longer involved in the day-to-day supervision of their families' business, as they once had been. Instead, their work was reduced to that of running the home and supervising any servants they could afford (Branca, 1974). The development of the railways enabled the middle classes to move from the cities to the suburbs (Davison, 1978). As a result, the already established identification of women with the home as "carriers of morality" was now supplemented with the idea of the home and of women as closer to nature, an attitude in which the "'unnatural' world of the market place was counterposed to a nostalgic Arcadian ideal of home in a rural community" (Davidoff and Hall, 1983: 329).

But however blissful this ideal—and it was celebrated in literature (Tennyson, 1847; Dickens, 1865), folktales (Zipes, 1982), and culture generally—its effects were disastrous for those women who had no means to realize this ideal in practice. Brought up to a life of domesticity, middle-class women lacked the education necessary for gaining respectable jobs when, like the fictional *Jane Eyre* (1847), they had no one else to support them. It was this—the plight of unsupported middle-class women—that above all led to the feminist campaigns of the mid-nineteenth century for higher education and increased job opportunities for women (Strachey, 1979).

THE RISE OF SCIENTIFIC AUTHORITY

Science now came into its own in the ensuing debate about women's rights. Science had earned its authority in such matters largely from its proven effectiveness in bringing about social and technological progress during the early phases of the Industrial Revolution. Science had thereby not only helped free women from patriarchal authority, but also released the mercantile and industrial classes from subordination to the aristocracy and the church. Ideologically, science offered these emergent classes a means of founding social relations less on religious orthodoxy than on a "secular, empirically based knowledge of the natural and social world" (Jordanova, 1980: 45). As historian of science Elizabeth Fee (1983) puts it, "The older aristocratic classes had depended on religious authority to legitimize social hierarchy and thus maintain social order; the new bourgeois and petit-bourgeois classes turned instead to science as the new source of authority" (1983: 12). Nietzsche heralded this change thus: "Science is power, God is dead" (Irigaray, 1982: 960).

In an earlier decade, as we have seen, Wollstonecraft and More imported Enlightenment and evangelical morality to justify their opposing views as to the sameness and difference of the sexes (see also Lewin, 1984). Now science became the idiom of debate on this issue. Feminists and antifeminists alike drew on contemporary scientific theory—its ideas about menstruation, the brain, and instincts, for example.

As regards *menstruation,* some authorities continued to argue in religious or quasi-religious terms that women should not become doctors, for instance, because menstruation rendered them ritually unclean (Storer, 1868). Increasingly, however, such claims drew on the scientific theory of the conservation of energy, a theory that had proved most serviceable in the design of factory machinery. Those opposed to women having the same university education as men argued that university study would deplete the energy necessary to women's menstrual and reproductive functions and so prevent them from becoming mothers (Maudsley, 1874). By contrast, those favoring women's university education insisted that the expenditure of energy in study would not prevent later childbearing (Anderson, 1874). Only as women increasingly gained access to university education did it become possible for them empirically to demonstrate that academic work had no ill-effects on their health (Jacobi, 1877).

Just as it was the proven efficacy of science that had earned its ascendancy over religion as a vehicle of debate about social issues, so the downfall of its assertions about these issues came about when they proved wrong in practice, in this case because university study patently did not prevent women becoming mothers as scientists had predicted. As Lee Holcombe (1973) puts it, "The foundations of the Victorian patriarchy did not crumble because of the feminists' verbal assaults, but because the patriarchal ideal departed so far from reality" (1973: 10).

A similar fate befell *brain size* arguments about sexual inequality. These arguments drew on the science of craniology that in the latter half of the nineteenth century displaced the mumbo jumbo of phrenology. Those opposed to women's higher education argued in terms of craniological theory that women's small brains made it impossible for them to equal men intellectually whether or not they had the same education as men, so that the campaign to attain this end was therefore misguided and futile (Allan, 1869). Conversely, proponents of higher education for women claimed that if, as craniology held, the small size of women's brains was an effect of their social inferiority, this should be remedied so that women's brains could develop fully (Distant, 1874).

As with the conservation of energy debate, this argument was not so much decided by the greater cogency of either the feminist or antifeminist version of it but by its proving mistaken in practice. As women gained access to higher education and thereby showed themselves to be intellectually equal to men it became absurd to accept craniological measures of intelligence that implied this to be impossible.

A third "scientific explanation" of female inferiority was couched in terms of *instinct theory*. It was in these terms that Darwin, in his *Descent of Man,* cast his generation's belief in woman as "angel of the hearth." "Parental instinct," claimed Darwin, made women naturally more tender and less selfish than men. On this basis those opposed to the women's rights movement of the day argued that, although women's parental or maternal instincts might fit them well for the private sphere of home and hearth, these instincts would be a liability in the public sphere. Maternal instincts would result in the indulgence of the poor, who, in the natural course of social evolution, should die out so that only the fittest would survive (Spencer, 1873). Supporters of women's rights, however, used Darwinian theory to argue that if women's instincts made them naturally more caring than men, this was ample reason for giving women greater say in public life so as to further the general well-being of society in the cause of peace rather than war (Addams, 1907, 1922).

In time, the instinct argument too was overtaken by social and practical events rather than by developments within scientific theory, which itself was affected by these events. The increasing automation of industry at the turn of the century and the demand for an ever more efficient work force generated the theory that, whatever their instinctual endowment, women could be trained through suitable environmental manipulation to be maximally efficient workers. In turn this theory—Taylor's principles of scientific management—was applied to the domestic sphere. Thus the behaviorist John Watson (1925) argued that women should be trained for motherhood, that their instincts were an untrustworthy guide to maternal success. As environmentalism came to displace instinct theory in psychology, it consolidated a process already underway even in the heyday of instinct theory when the Victorian *pater familias* had still been able to oversee his wife's moral guardianship of his children's spiritual and educational welfare. Over time this patriarchal role was eroded by the demands on men's time of their work outside the home (Davidoff and Hall, 1983; Harris, 1984). The result was not that matriarchal authority came to replace patriarchy, as some have claimed (Contratto, 1984). Rather, women's role as mother now came to be increasingly supervised by science-educated experts and other representatives of the state (Donzelot, 1980; Ehrenreich and English, 1979).

SCIENCE AND SEX DIFFERENCES
IN THE TWENTIETH CENTURY

By the early decades of this century, controversy about sexual inequality and differences had diminished somewhat only to reemerge with full force in the wake of the U.S. civil rights, antiwar, and general student movements of the 1960s. And once again scientific theory has been invoked by both sides of this controversy. It should be pointed out, however, that science-based arguments about sexual inequality and difference have wider currency in the United States than in England, where science is treated with the same snobbery as earlier generations treated retail trade. And even in the United States, science is losing its authority as arbiter of such issues now that its destructive character is so much more evident in its contribution to unemployment—particularly women's unemployment (Arnold and Faulkner, 1985)—and in the threat of nuclear annihilation. Films and television, for instance, now more often depict scientists as harmful than as helpful (Comstock, 1985). Nevertheless, science continues to be appealed to by feminists and antifeminists alike in current discussions about sexual inequality. I shall briefly outline three examples that draw on evolutionary theory, endocrinology, and neurology, respectively.

Evolutionary theory has recently been reformulated by sociobiology. Sociobiology holds "the selfish gene" to be the main motor of evolution (Dawkins, 1976). The model assumes that genes operate to maximize their reproductive success and to maximize the genetic information they transmit from one generation to the next. Sociobiology thus grafts onto biology the central tenet of monetarism, that business operates to maximize the circulation of currency. Sociobiology also reflects our society's preoccupation with information technology—a preoccupation that feminist historian of science Donna Haraway (1979) traces to military needs in World War II for developing sophisticated tracking and communication devices. Whatever its genesis, modern sociobiology has been used both to justify and to question existing inequalities between the sexes. Some claim that, since pregnant women invest so much of themselves in nurturing the developing embryo, they can realize maximum reproductive success of their own genes by continuing to invest time and effort in caring for their offspring once they are born. Reproductive success for men's genes, however, is best served by leaving their children in the care of their mother while they go off to impregnate other women. According to these writers, thousands of years of evolutionary history have selected for nurturance in women and for philandering in men, so that the current unequal division of child care between the sexes is genetically determined and, therefore, irreversible. Feminist scholars, by contrast, have used sociobiological reasoning to advance the opposite thesis—that evolution has selected for equality between the sexes in child care. They claim that the reproductive success of men's genes is best served by men contributing equally with women to child care because men thereby increase their children's chances of surviving to reproductive maturity and so avoid the cost of competing for other mates (Tanner and Zihlman, 1976).

A second argument draws on *endocrinology*. Women's hormones, it is held, make them more responsive than men to infants and hence better fitted for motherhood. In an echo of the nineteenth-century instinct debate, some have claimed on this hormonal basis that women should not therefore seek for "equal participation of women and men in the workplace" (Rossi, 1977: 25). Conversely, others hold that if women's hormones make them more caring than men, then women should be encouraged to participate more in the public sphere where their caring attributes, whether hormonally or socially determined, would enrich the quality of life (Gilligan, 1982).

If women's hormones are said to make them more caring, men's are presumed to make them the more aggressive sex, and therefore the sex most suited to the rat race of occupational life. It is accordingly argued that it is futile for feminists to hope to achieve sex equality in work and public life (Goldberg, 1977). Others maintain that if men's hormones make them naturally aggressive then the cause of peace and progress would best be served by women having increased influence in public and world affairs (Holliday, 1978).

A third argument draws on recent *neurological research* that suggests that while women process verbal and visual-spatial information with either hemisphere of the brain, men usually process verbal information with the left and visual-spatial information with the right cerebral hemisphere. This sex difference was not apparent while brain research was confined to studies of the war-wounded, an all-male population (given the exclusion of women from armed combat), but emerged after the war when developments in the surgical treatment of epilepsy provided data on both males and females. It had already been noted by psychologists that girls on average are verbally more fluent than boys. Now this superiority could be attributed to sex differences in the brain's processing of verbal information. Not surprisingly, this argument has been used to suggest that women are better fitted for child care than are men, especially for teaching children to speak (Gray and Buffery, 1971). Yet it can also be contended that if women's brains make them verbally more adept than men, there should be more women in jobs requiring verbal facility—jobs such as politics, law, and management (Ardener, 1978).

CLAIMS TO SCIENTIFIC OBJECTIVITY

The authority of science in adjudicating such issues derives not only from its contribution to technological and social progress, but also from its claim to neutrality and objectivity—a claim rendered all the more plausible by the fact that it studies objects, physical objects. How have feminists used science and its canons of objectivity and neutrality to challenge science-based claims that the existing social inequalities between the sexes are inevitable? This has involved exposing the lack of neutrality in the priorities, methods, description, interpretation, and publication of research on sex differences.

First, as to *priorities*, feminists have pointed out that the assumption that the source of sexual inequality lies in individuals—in the biology and/or psychology of women and men—leads to undue emphasis on the biological and psychological concomitants of sexual inequality, to the neglect of its historical and social genesis. Caroline Sherif (1979) points out that feminism's detractors regularly derogate the latter type of research as "soft," not "hard," science—as not really science. And this often seems a convincing refutation. For as a result of the development of social relations under capitalism, whereby people have become increasingly free to sell their labor as individuals, the destiny of women and men does indeed appear to be determined more by their individual capacity, whether given by biology or psychology, than by social and historical factors. The latter are therefore easily caricatured as merely transient epiphenomena, as "soft" rather than "hard" data (Sève, 1968). Furthermore, the belief that individual biology or psychology is the real source of sexual inequality biases researchers toward investigating sex differences rather than the wide range of similarities between the sexes in their biology and psychology. The outcome, as chemist Marion Lowe points out, is that "scientists attempt to find tools to measure the differences that are assumed to be there, rather than examine whether or not the differences actually exist" (Lowe, 1983: 49).

Second, as regards research *methodology*, feminists have shown that the assumption that sexual inequality is biologically determined and hence inevitable biases researchers toward treating the biological basis of behavior as fixed. Therefore they control for the effects on their result of only environmental, not biological, variation (Birke, forthcoming). Yet there is now much evidence to indicate that biology is not fixed but also varies just as the environment does. Specialization of the brain for visual-spatial function, for instance, might well be affected by education (Sherman, 1977). And it is clear that "male" hormone levels in animals vary as an effect of social factors, such as changes in their position in dominance hierarchies with their cage mates (Lowe, 1983).

Champions of sex equality over the centuries have regularly drawn attention to the way research into men's and women's character fails to control for effects of men's social dominance and women's social subordination (Alaya, 1977). Today behavioral scientists sympathetic to the feminist cause continue to stress the need for research methods that take account of the historical, social, and cultural factors affecting observed differences between the sexes (Weisstein, 1982). Psychologist Anne Anastasi (1981), for example, draws attention to the need for well-designed cohort studies of psychological sex differences that span critical periods of societal change. Biologists Jon Beckwith and John Durkin (1981) urge researchers investigating sex differences in mathematics ability to take account of the social factors impeding this ability in girls, as, for example, when parents are much less likely to equip their daughters than their sons with computers.

Another way in which research methodology is skewed by the assumption that sexual inequality is biologically determined is that it assumes, as did our evangelical forbearers, that this inequality is an effect of men being naturally aggressive and women naturally nurturant. Researchers accordingly often use only male subjects when studying aggression, only female subjects when studying nurturance (McKenna and Kessler, 1977). Fathers are not observed to see if they too speak the "motherese," for example, that supposedly facilitates child language development. In addition, researchers tend to investigate the effects of the "male" hormones on aggression to the neglect of the role of the "female" hormones in activating this behavior (Bleier, 1978).

Feminists have also drawn attention to the way the assumption of biological determinism biases the *interpretation* of research data. For example, by describing as "tomboyish" the fighting behavior of girls fetally exposed to excess androgens, researchers prejudge the issue of whether such behavior is inherently male (Longino and Doell, 1983). Feminists have highlighted instances where researchers have overextrapolated from the evidence in the interests of proving the biological inevitability of patriarchy. One example is the way scientists selectively report data on animal societies in which male dominance occurs without pointing out that such dominance is only found in some species and then only under certain conditions (see e.g., Bleier, 1978). Another example of overextrapolation from the data involves arguing on the basis of observed sex differences in aggression that male dominance is inevitable, while adducing no evidence to show any link between aggression and dominance (Sayers, 1982). In fact, the evidence suggests that aggression is negatively associated with dominance at least in human societies (Nicholson, 1984). Similarly, overextrapolation from the data mars interpretation of research on sex differences in visual-spatial ability where these differences are taken to explain the underrepresentation of women in science and engineering despite the fact that the sex differences in these professions are vast whereas the differences between the sexes in visual-spatial ability are small (Kimball, 1981) or nonexistent (Caplan et al., 1985). Even if women were innately less capable than men, this is no reason to conclude that sexual inequality is inevitable (Lambert, 1978) for that is "like saying we must accept near-sightedness because it is genetic and forget about developing eye glasses" (Beckwith and Durkin, 1981: 34). Indeed, scientists are rightly proud of the ways they have succeeded in transforming and improving on nature and biology (Hubbard, 1983a: 6).

The interpretation of research data is further perverted by the assumption of the inevitability of sexual inequality when results inconsistent with this belief do not lead to the revision of this assumption. As feminists have shown, all too often "results that do not come out as expected are blamed on faulty methodology or bad data and rejected" (Lowe, 1983: 49). A nice example of this tendency may be found in nineteenth-century brain research. Presuming that the lack of eminent women in public life was due to their being naturally less intelligent than men, scientists who found that women's frontal lobes were relatively larger than men's concluded that the seat of the intellect must not be in the frontal lobes, as previously thought, but in the parietal lobes as these were relatively larger in men (Shields, 1975). Similarly the conviction that the underrepresentation of women in science reflects a lack of natural aptitude has led to one attempt after another to locate this supposed deficiency in women's biology—in their genes, hormones, and brains—despite the fact that these attempts have all proved singularly unsuccessful (Saraga and Griffiths, 1981).

Last, feminists and their supporters have exposed how *publication* of research in both scientific and popular journals and magazines has been warped by assumptions about the inevitability of sexual inequality and difference. Results reinforcing these beliefs are more readily accepted for publication than are those that throw these opinions into doubt. Until recently findings of no sex difference were rarely published in the most prestigious academic journals (Maccoby and Jacklin, 1974; Lloyd, 1976). And the popular press devotes far more space to research, however spurious, that ascribes psychological sex differences to biology than it gives to research demonstrating the environmental and social determinants of these differences (Messing, 1983; Beckwith, 1984).

THE REACTION AGAINST SCIENCE

Faced with the ways in which science has been used against their cause, feminists nevertheless remain generally sympathetic to its project of criticizing in theory and testing in practice our understanding of the world. Some believe that science can be fairly easily purged of its antifeminist bias (Stark-Adamec and Kimball, 1984). Others are more skeptical, given how easily findings inconsistent with prevailing ideas about sexual difference are so regularly discounted and ignored by the scientific community.

It has been pointed out for instance that although psychologist Helen Thompson empirically demonstrated in 1903 the lack of any significant psychological differences between the sexes, attempts to show such differences continue unabated today (Rosenberg, 1982). Similarly, feminists have shown that although Thompson's contemporary Leta Hollingworth found that menstruation did not impair women psychologically, such data have not stopped researchers from seeking to show that it does (Sherif, 1979). Carol Rosenberg (1982) likewise points out that in the 1930s Margaret Mead's evidence of the cultural determination of temperamental differences between the sexes was discounted while her detractors' claim about the biological determinants of these differences flourished. And this despite the fact that their research methodology was typically much more flawed than Mead's. For instance, Lewis Terman's (Terman & Miles, 1936) masculinity-femininity (M-F) test, which he claimed proved the innateness of existing psychological sex differences, remained in use long after Mead's research was dismissed as methodologically suspect even though it has never been shown that women and men actually embody the traditional notions of sexual difference incorporated, wittingly or unwittingly, in Terman's M-F test (Lewin, 1984). Lois Hoffman (1984) similarly shows that in the 1950s and 1960s research demonstrating that women's paid work did not have a deleterious effect on their children was suppressed, so prevalent was the belief that women should stay home rather than go out to work. And Stephanie Shields (1982) documents the fact that some scientists still maintain that men are the more progressive force in evolution despite a century of evidence disconfirming this thesis.

These examples clearly demonstrate that, contrary to the implications of the Popperian image of science as abandoning its hypotheses when they are falsified in practice, received wisdom about sexual difference has not been revised when it has been falsified by scientific data. Research on sexual differences is of a piece with science generally in that the discovery of "anomalies," of evidence inconsistent with its prevailing beliefs—"paradigms" as Kuhn (1970) terms them—seldom if ever is sufficient to overturn those beliefs. This has led philosophers of science such as Imre Lakatos (1970) to argue that science is more accurately characterized in terms of its programs of research, which are defined by a coherent and relatively fixed set of theories and research methods and which are then tested in practice in terms of whether they generate new discoveries. Some have gone on to argue that since different, competing, and often opposing paradigms or programs are treated as equally scientific, there are therefore no limits to what counts as science. In science, writes Paul Feyerabend (1984) "anything goes."

Many feminists take issue with this viewpoint, claiming that it is not true that anything counts as science. Rather, they argue, the paradigms and programs of science are all essentially masculinist in character. French psychoanalyst and philosopher Luce Irigaray (1982) puts this point thus: "It is always men who have spoken and above all written in science, philosophy, religion, and politics. What have been the main features of this discourse? Production, property order, form, unity, visibility, erection" (1982: 964-965). She and other like-minded feminists have claimed that science, like language, is essentially male. Science, it is argued, silences women and alienates them from the truth of their experience, cutting us off—women and men alike—from nature so that we forget our unity with it and the fact that we are part of the nature studied by science (Gearhart, 1983).

On the other hand, some writers also maintain that because science and society are essentially male-dominated, women do not share our society's general divorce from nature. Women, it is said, have a greater sense of the unity of mental and manual labor (Hartsock, 1983). They "know this earth is made from our bodies," that "we are nature" (Griffin, 1980: 226.).

Not for nothing, it is sometimes claimed, is science's investigation of nature so often identified with men's sexual and social control of women, as when Francis Bacon wrote of science as "leading to you nature with all her children to bind her to your service and make her your slave" (Merchant, 1980: 170).

Feminist historians have drawn attention to the way in which science is regularly understood as involving penetration, through investigation and reason, of nature understood as female—an understanding immortalized at the Paris medical faculty by the statue of a woman bearing the inscription "Nature unveils herself before Science" (Jordanova, 1980: 54).

Many feminists have unremittingly focused on the negative and destructive aspects of science's control of nature, forgetting that women, like men, have also benefitted from science's productive investigation, control, and use of nature, which Marx (1970) and others have shown to distinguish our species from others. They have overlooked the fact that women have also contributed to the negative aspects of science's control over nature and that it is not only men who are destructive in this sense (as Andrea Dworkin, 1980, and others imply). Women may not have invented and made as many weapons of death and destruction as men, but they have contributed to their manufacture and use (Amram, 1984; Wainwright, 1983). Nonetheless, many feminists equate science and industry's destructiveness with maleness and men's social control and dominance over women (Merchant, 1980: King, 1983). As Ruth Bleier (1984) puts it, "Science is the male intellect: the active, knowing subject; its relationship to nature—the passive object of knowledge, the untamed—is one of manipulation, control, and domination; it is the relationship of man to woman, of culture to nature" (1984: 196).

An often cited example of the way in which science is at one with the general social control of women and men is the case of obstetrics. Feminists have described the history of this medical specialty as involving the appropriation by men of women's traditional role as birth attendant, defining their practice as scientific while labeling midwifery superstitious hocus pocus (Oakley, 1976; Faulkner, 1985). Adrienne Rich (1977) argues that men's wresting of the control and management of childbirth from women is another instance of their general appropriation of women's power as mothers.

In this Rich, like many others, uncritically accepts the ideology of sexual difference that equates women essentially with mothering (see also de Beauvoir, 1972)—an ideology that, as we have seen, has come to involve treating woman as closer to nature, as less scientific, as the carriers of a new morality through which the artificiality of civilization might be transcended (Jordanova, 1980). Instead of challenging "the idea of nature that has been established" for women (Wittig, 1979: 70), some feminists take women's experience of themselves as closer to nature to constitute the whole truth of their being. They reiterate rather than question our society's belief that women are closer to nature, that they are more instinctive, intuitive, expressive, and emotional, that they embody softness and things of the heart, whereas men embody hardness and things of the brain—reason, instrumentality, and science (Rose, 1983). Some even go so far as to argue that we should entirely dispense with theory, with science, and with technology, so baneful have been their effects on women and nature. In her novel *The Wanderground,* for instance, Sally Gearhart (1983) envisages a feminist utopia in which technological means of communication are eliminated and women communicate through psychic power (Schweickart, 1983).

There is, of course, nothing new to the argument that we should reject science and technology, that it wrongly interferes with the purposes of God or nature—a nature mistakenly taken to be distinct from society although it conditions and in turn is conditioned by society. Such appeals were commonplace in eighteenth- and nineteenth-century debates about science and religion, as in Blake's 1804 poetic evocation of Jerusalem counterposed to England's "dark satanic mills"—a hymn long used to introduce Women's Institute meetings in England. Similar arguments are voiced today by creationists and religious fundamentalists in the United States (Gould, quoted in Cherfas, 1984). But the rejection of science on these grounds ignores the fact that women's and men's nature is produced by their social being (Marx, 1970), by the stage of development of our means of production and reproduction (Engels, 1970). Moreover, back-to-nature arguments have been, and continue to be, more often used against rather than in the service of women's needs and interests, as in current British and American antiabortion campaigns (Hume, 1985). Feminists who challenge existing sexual divisions in society are regularly accused of wrongly seeking to interfere with nature, with a status quo ordained by biology. They are constantly criticized as unnatural, as deviating biologically from the norms of their sex, as guilty of "psycho-sexual aberrancy" (Weir, 1895: 819). Women have repeatedly been told to accept their traditional social lot—portrayed as given by nature if not by God—that their proper role is to temper the brutality of men rather than to be equal to them (Scruton, 1983).

It is therefore not surprising that many feminists take issue with those who argue that women should abandon science and return to their "true nature"— so antithetical are such appeals generally to the cause of women's liberation. Feminist writers stress that women's experience of themselves as closer to nature is not self-validating (Jaggar, 1983), that this experience is socially produced (Wittig, 1979) and itself stands in need of scientific, psychological (Keller, 1983), historical, and cross-cultural investigation (Tilly, 1978). Criticizing the hostility to science of some feminists, historian of science Elizabeth Fee (1983) asserts,

> The concept of creating knowledge through a constant process of practical interaction with nature, the willingness to consider all assumptions and methods as open to question and the expectation that ideas will be subjected to the most unfettered critical evaluation are all aspects of scientific objectivity that should be preserved and defended [1983: 16].

In this, Fee is at one with Wollstonecraft, who two centuries ago also urged women to engage with science and cultivate their reason rather than simply act on the experience of the moment.

At present, however, this experience risks being entirely overlooked by science. Scientists take little account of the experiences of women in transforming the world in the production and reproduction of their own and others' lives. In this sense science does indeed render women's experience silent or invisible. Feminists both opposed and sympathetic to science have rightly drawn attention to its failure in this respect. As biologist Ruth Hubbard (1983a) points out, science all too often ignores women's "knowledge and experience of how our bodies function within the context of our lives" (1983a: 7). Nor is this any wonder:

> Because of their sex and class, the large majority of scientists are less likely than the general population to be interested in such topics as the occupational exposures that present a risk to the nursing mother, alternative (non-hormonal) treatments for the discomforts of menopause, how a woman can give herself a safe (and, where necessary, secret) abortion, what work postures increase the likelihood of menstrual cramps, and how a low-income family can provide itself with nutritious meals [Messing, 1983: 78].

But this does not excuse many scientists' all too ready dismissal of women's practical day-to-day knowledge and experience as "old wives' tales," as mere folly and folklore compared to the theories of science. All too often feminist criticisms of science are labeled hysterical, subjective, and biased (Bleier, 1978; Fee, 1983). Popular magazines, for instance, have described feminists as putting scientists under "Lysenkoist pressure to hew to women's liberation orthodoxy" while these self-same magazines herald biological determinists as "pioneers" in the scientific quest for truth (Beckwith, 1984). Similarly, while academic journals that publish articles reiterating dominant beliefs about sexual difference are considered politically neutral, those critical of these beliefs—journals such as *Feminist Studies* and *Science for the People*—are treated as politically biased and therefore not worthy of being cited for academic promotion or tenure, at least in the United States.

THE FUTURE

The primary reason that mainstream scientific research appears to be neutral and untainted by emotional, subjective, or partisan bias and interest (despite the fact that its organization and funding are clearly determined by political, economic, and military factors) is that its biases are those of the dominant interests governing our society and its knowledge of the world (Rose, 1984). Those who currently benefit from the way science is organized have little reason, apart from the protest of those against whom their work is used, to recognize that their experience and interests are limited and not universally valid. Scientists, for instance, are by and large unaware of the biases—including the sex bias—that informs their work (a point noted by Stéhelin, 1976, for example). Nor do they have any reason to recognize that the society and science they enjoy are not constant and unchanging. As philosopher Alison Jaggar (1983) points out, "Because their class position insulates them from suffering of the oppressed," and because they "experience the current organization of society as basically satisfactory . . . they accept [as natural] the interpretation of reality that justifies that system of organization" (1983: 370).

Furthermore, to the extent that the interests and biases of the dominant class, race, and sex shape the current organization of science and society, this group's experience of the world as unchanging and constant, as given by nature, tends to be treated both by them and by those they rule as the whole truth. This is evident, for instance, in many women's experience of themselves, in conformity with currently dominant beliefs about sexual difference, as essentially and eternally closer to nature, as less aggressive and less individualist, and as more moral and attuned to personal relations than are men. So pervasive are these beliefs that feminist challenge to them is easily dismissed as subjective, hysterical, unrealistic, "distorted, crazy or perverse" (Jaggar, 1983: 382).

The feminist challenge arises from the fact that women experience themselves as not only different but as also similar to men, as not only merged with nature but also separate from it, as not only nurturant and caring but also aggressive and selfish (Sayers, 1986). It arises from women's understanding of their household labor not only as a labor of love but also as one of toil and drudgery (Hartsock, 1983). Experiencing the current social order not only as heaven but also as hell, women have more at stake than do those whose interests this order serves in recognizing that social change is possible and that existing sexual inequalities and differences are not eternally fixed by biology. It is the contradiction in women's social experience that galvanizes them and other oppressed groups in society "toward realizing that something is wrong with the prevailing social order," and toward "criticizing accepted interpretations of reality" (Jaggar, 1983: 373; see also Keller, 1983: 144). It is this realization that leads them to question received scientific wisdom that holds existing psychological sex differences to be static, unchanging, and natural. And just as such scientific claims have to be tested in practice —a test from which they hardly emerge unscathed—so the ideas of feminism likewise have to be tested in practice to determine whether they in fact accurately reflect and serve women's current needs and interests (Jaggar, 1983: 384). This is all part of the process of forging a science that pays due attention to women.

Achievement of this goal depends on women gaining equal status and power with men in science and society generally. Today, as in the past, it is only by women gaining greater social equality with men that their interests and needs have begun to shape the priorities, methods, and use made of research. I shall illustrate this point by again treating separately these overlapping facets of scientific practice.

First, the *priorities* of research: As women's labor force participation rates continue to rise, scientists have at last abandoned the attempt to demonstrate the supposed inevitably deleterious effect on children of their mothers going out to work (Hoffman, 1984). Instead, some increased research effort is now being put into investigating ways of improving the quality of care provided children while their mothers work (New and David, 1985). However, the priorities of research still do not reflect women's interests as well as they might. There remains a crying need for more information on the damage done to women's chances of bearing healthy children by inadequate nutrition, dangerous work conditions, and by the side effects of contraception (Berer, 1985). Instead, current research, at least in reproductive biology, is much more concerned with *in vitro* fertilization (IVF)—a concern that reflects the professional and financial interests of the scientists involved (Sattaur, 1984; Rothman, Chapter 5 in this volume), and the commercial interest of the drug companies, which stand to profit from this research (Hubbard, 1983b), rather than the interests of women and their children.

Second, as regards the *methodology* of research: Women's greater involvement in public life has finally led to Terman's M-F test being replaced by measures that tap the similarities as well as differences in women's and men's personalities (Bem, 1974)—similarities that have become more obvious as women and men increasingly work alongside each other in psychology, science, and society generally. On the other hand, there is still a long way to go before research methods take sufficient account of women's experience and interests. Research on contraception, for instance, is all too often conducted on those with least power and status in society, such as working-class, ethnic minority, and Third World women—women who have little means of redress when they fall ill or become pregnant from such research (Messing, 1983; Bunkle, 1984).

Third, the use made of the *results* of scientific research: It is clear that as women's social status has improved greater objectivity has been accorded feminist-inspired research. Thus some, if not all, feminist-oriented journals— *Signs* and *Sex Roles* for example—are now regarded as respectable, tenure-track journals. In addition, the findings of feminist research now receive coverage in both academic and popular journals and are increasingly being used in practice, for instance in therapy. Again, however, there is much room for improvement. Feminist research reporting differences between the sexes in line with evangelical notions about women as the more caring sex (e.g., Chodorow, 1978; Gilligan, 1982) is still given greater publicity than research reporting similarities between the sexes in these and other respects. Further, the use of science in developing alternative technology still does not pay sufficient attention to the practical needs of the women for whom this technology is designed, as when solar cookers now being developed for Third World women do not take into account their need for cookers large enough to support the pots used in preparing food for their extended families (Carr, 1981). Similarly, in the West, women's experience is not incorporated into the design of data processors which, by increasing the pace of work, step up the stress on women using them. Nor is sufficient attention paid to the potential health hazards of video display terminals (Rothschild, 1983). Women's needs and rights as mothers are also not sufficiently heeded in the use made of IVF techniques where the decision as to who should benefit from them is made by physicians rather than by their women patients. Finally, lawyers in the United States are now arguing that women should not have the right to refuse medical treatment of their fetuses, treatment made possible by IVF research (Hubbard, 1984; Rothman, Chapter 5 in this volume).

Women's needs and interests have, of course, been transformed by advances in reproductive technology and by scientific and social progress generally. But if these interests are to be adequately served women must gain greater social power and influence. They cannot count on men alone to represent their concerns, especially where they conflict with those of men (a point discussed by Virginia Woolf in her *Three Guineas* and by many others). This means that women must struggle on their own behalf. In the Third World, this entails resisting both patriarchy and the imperialism of the multinational companies that make women the mere servants of science (e.g., drug "guinea pigs" or assembly-line producers of computer components) in situations in which they have little means of influencing the use made of their reproductive or productive capacities.

In the West, scientific research has become increasingly stratified as it has expanded in response to the needs of industrial and particularly of military concerns. The latter now commands over half of U.S. and British research and development budgets (Birke, forthcoming). Despite such expansion, women still find themselves concentrated in the lower ranks of the scientific establishment (Rossiter, 1980). As a result, they have little means of influencing the direction of research (Couture-Cherki, 1976), serving rather as handmaidens to scientists—whether at home as mothers, wives, sisters, or daughters, or at work as cooks, cleaners, lab technicians, and factory operatives. In science, as elsewhere, women remain identified with manual, men with mental labor (Rose, 1983).

Such is women's general lack of power in society, that even when they have contributed to the development of scientific and technological knowledge, their contribution has regularly gone unnoticed. Few, for instance, know that the cotton gin was the brainchild of a woman, Eli Whitney's landlady, for it was he who had the wherewithal to realize her idea (Amram, 1984). Anonymity likewise veils the contribution of women to the development of botany (Kohlstedt, 1978)—an unanticipated consequence of middle-class women's increased involvement in gardening when they moved to the suburbs (Davidoff and Hall, 1983). The invisibility of women's contribution to science is not surprising as they have regularly been told to keep a low professional profile. For example Mary Treat, a popular nineteenth-century botanist, was congratulated for having a "modesty so shrinking as to make any public recognition of her services painful to her" (Kohlstedt, 1978: 90). More recently there was the shameful neglect of Rosalind Franklin's contribution to the discovery of the structure of DNA—a neglect that in her case, as in others, partly reflects women's lack of the old-school tie and support networks that help men to advance in science (Exum et al., 1984).

The image of science as men's natural preserve has intimidated many women from entering the field at all. Nineteenth-century women, educated to regard themselves in the light of evangelical morality, as pure beings uncontaminated by nature (Cott, 1978), often only became scientists as a last resort. Elizabeth Blackwell, for instance, initially responded with horror to the idea of becoming a doctor, saying that she 'hated everything connected with the body and could not bear the sight of a medical book' (Blackwell, 1914: 233). She nevertheless struggled against the odds to be a doctor because of the freedom it would give her from marriage. Similar considerations led Alice Hamilton to train as a physician despite the fact that she dreaded the bodily contact it involved, a dread that eventually caused her to abandon medical practice for research (Strouse, 1985). So much for the claim that women are closer to nature and to the fluidity of life (Hein, 1981), that they have a greater sense than men of connection with the nature they study (Keller, 1983) and perceive that "everything is connected with everything else" (Daly, 1978: 11)!

Over two hundred years ago Hannah More (1778) wrote that "the female mind, in general, does not appear capable of attaining so high a degree of perfection in science as the male" (1778: 6). This belief persists today. Parents, teachers, girls, and women believe females to have so little natural capacity for science that they must work much harder to achieve the same level of attainment as boys (Eccles et al., 1985). And, of course, this belief is reinforced by the widespread publicity given to scientifically spurious claims that boys are innately better suited to these subjects than are girls (Benbow and Stanley, 1980).

Such was the strength of the nineteenth-century women's movement that many women recognized that the undermining of their scientific ability could only be countered by women challenging it collectively. In the 1870s women like the astronomer Maria Mitchell became involved in the Association for the Advancement of Women (Rossiter, 1980), and in 1897 zoologist Ida Hyde set up a project to help fund women to do research in the Naples marine laboratory (Sloan, 1978).

With the winning of the vote and the decline of feminism in the early decades of this century, such women-only organizations also declined. Identifying more with science than with their sex, many women scientists urged their sisters "to lose themselves in their profession" (Morantz, 1982: 27). They opposed women's organizations in science, which they felt unduly emphasized women's difference from men.

But, whether they like it or not, women in science, as elsewhere, are perceived as different from men and are discriminated against on this account.

Renewed recognition of this fact has been responsible for the current resurgence of feminism and appreciation of the need for separate organizations to meet women's needs as producers and consumers of science. There are now women scientists' and women engineers' associations in the United States and England (Henifin and Amatniek, 1982; Amram, 1984). Both countries now have flourishing women's health movements dealing with general and specific issues affecting women such as reproductive rights (Gladwin, 1985) and cystitis (otherwise all too readily dismissed as hysterical and unreal; Fee, 1983).

In sum, the struggle of these organizations to achieve a science that meets the real needs of women as of men has been, and continues to be, one with the women's movement in general. It is "linked inseparably with a transformation of power relations between the sexes" (Jaggar, 1983: 387). This transformation depends on women struggling both alongside men and separately from them around the similarity and difference of their vision of a society in which they might equally benefit from scientific advance. Only thus can science some day fulfill its promise of being truly a force for good rather than ill in all our lives.

REFERENCES

ADDAMS, J. (1907) Newer Ideals of Peace, excerpted in A. Rossi (ed.) The Feminist Papers (1974). New York: Bantam Books.
ADDAMS, J. (1922) Peace and Bread in Time of War. New York: Macmillan.
ALAYA, F. (1977) "Victorian science and the 'genius' of woman." Journal of the History of Ideas 38:261-280.
ALEXANDER, S. (1976) "Women's work in nineteenth-century London: A study of the years 1820-50," in A. Oakley and J. Mitchell (eds.) The Rights and Wrongs of Women. Harmondsworth: Penguin.
ALLAN, J. M. (1869)"On the real differences in the minds of men and women." Anthropological Society of London Journal 7: 195-219.
AMRAM, F. (1984). "The innovative women." New Scientist (May 24): 10-12.
ANASTASI, A. (1981) "Sex differences: Historical perspectives and methodological implications." Developmental Review 1: 187-206.
ANDERSON, E. G. (1874) "Sex in mind and education: A reply." Fortnightly Review 15: 582-594.
ARDENER, S. (1978) "Introduction: The nature of women in society," in S. Ardener (ed.) Defining Females. London: Croom Helm.
ARNOLD, E. and W. FAULKNER (1985) "Introduction," in W. Faulkner and E. Arnold (eds.) Smothered by Invention: Technology in Women's Lives. London: Pluto.
BARRETT, M. and M. MCINTOSH (1980) "The 'family wage': Some problems for socialists and feminists." Capital and Class 11: 51-72.
BECKWITH, B. (1984) "How magazines cover sex differences." Science for the People 16, 4: 18-23.
BECKWITH, J. and J. DURKIN (1981) "Girls, boys and math." Science for the People 13, 5: 6-9, 32-35.

BEM, S. (1974) "The measurement of psychological androgyny." Journal of Consulting and Clinical Psychology 42: 155-162.

BENBOW, C. P. and J. C. STANLEY (1980) "Sex differences in mathematical ability: Fact or artifact?" Science 210: 1262-1264.

BERER, M. (1986) "Infertility—a suitable case for treatment?" Marxism Today (June): 29-31.

BIRKE, L. (forthcoming) Women, Feminism and Biology. Brighton: Harvester.

BLACKWELL, E. (1914) Pioneer Work for Women. New York: E. P. Dutton.

BLAKE, W. (1804) "Jerusalem," in Poetry and Prose of William Blake, London: Nonesuch Library.

BLEIER, R. (1978) "Bias in biological and human sciences: Some comments." Signs 5, 1: 159-162.

BLEIER, R. (1984) Science and Gender: A Critique of Biology and Its Theories on Women. Oxford: Pergamon.

BRANCA, P. (1974) "Image and reality: The myth of the idle Victorian women," in M. S. Hartman and L. Banner (eds.) Clio's Consciousness Raised: New Perspectives on the History of Women. New York: Harper & Row.

BRONTE, C. (1847/1966) Jane Eyre. Harmondsworth: Penguin.

BUNKLE, P. (1984) "Calling the shots? The international politics of depo provera," in R. Arditti et al. (eds.) Test-Tube Women: What Future for Motherhood? London: Pandora.

CAPLAN, P. J., G. M. MACPHERSON, and P. TOBIN (1985) "Do sex-related differences in spatial ability exist?" American Psychologist 40, 7: 786-799.

CARR, M. (1981) "Technologies appropriate for women," in R. Daubar and M. Cain (eds.) Women and Technological Change in Developing Countries. Boulder, CO: Westview.

CHERFAS, J. (1984) "The difficulties of Darwinism." New Scientist (May 17): 28-30.

CHODOROW, N. (1978) The Reproduction of Mothering. Berkeley: University of California Press.

COMSTOCK, G. (1985) Paper given at the American Association for the Advancement of Science, reported in The Listener (June 20): 16.

CONTRATTO, S. (1984) "Mother: Social sculptor and trustee of the faith," in M. Lewin (ed.) In the Shadow of the Past: Psychology Portrays the Sexes. New York: Columbia University Press.

COTT, N. (1978) "Passionlessness: An interpretation of Victorian sexual ideology, 1790-1850." Signs 4, 2: 218-236.

COUTURE-CHERKI, M. (1976) "Women in physics," in H. Rose and W. Rose (eds.) The Radicalisation of Science. London: Macmillan.

DALY, M. (1978) Gyn/Ecology. Boston: Beacon.

DAVIDOFF, L. and C. HALL (1983) "The architecture of public and private life: English middle class society in a provincial town, 1780-1850," in A. Sutcliffe (ed.) The Pursuit of Urban History. London: Edward Arnold.

DAVISON, G. (1978) The Rise and Fall of Marvelous Melbourne. Melbourne: Melbourne University Press.

DAWKINS, R. (1976) The Selfish Gene. New York: Oxford University Press.

DE BEAUVOIR, S. (1972) The Second Sex (H. M. Parshley, trans.) (1949). Harmondsworth: Penguin.

DICKENS, C. (1865) Our Mutual Friend. London: Collins.

DISTANT, W. L. (1984) "On the mental differences between the sexes." Journal of the Royal Anthropological Institute of Great Britain and Ireland 4: 78-87.

DONZELOT, J. (1980) The Policing of Families (R. Hurley, trans.) (1977). London: Hutchinson.

DWORKIN, A. (1980) "Why so-called radical men love and need pornography," in L. Lederer (ed.) Take Back the Night. New York: Morrow.

ECCLES, J., T. F. ADLER, R. FUTTERMAN, S. B. GOFF, C. M. KACZALA, J. L. MEECE, and C. MIDGLEY (1985) "Self-perceptions, task perceptions, socializing influences, and the decision to enroll in mathematics," in S. F. Chipmen et al. (eds.) Women and Mathematics: Balancing the Equation. Hillsdale, NJ: Lawrence Erlbaum.

EHRENREICH, B. and D. ENGLISH (1979) For Her Own Good. Garden City, NY: Doubleday/Anchor.

ENGELS, F. (1958) The Condition of the Working Class in England (W. O. Henderson and W. H. Chaloner, trans.) (1849). Oxford: Basil Blackwell.

ENGELS, F. (1970) The Origin of the Family, Private Property and the State, in Karl Marx and Frederick Engels: Selected Works (1884). London: Lawrence & Wishart.

EXUM, W. H., R. J. MENGES, B. WATKINS, and P. BERGLUND (1984) "Making it at the top: Women and minority faculty in the academic labor market." American Behavioral Scientist 27, 3: 301-324.

FAULKNER, W. (1985) "Medical technology and the right to heal," in W. Faulkner and E. Arnold (eds.) Smothered by Invention: Technology in Women's Lives. London: Pluto.

FEE, E. (1983) "Woman's nature and scientific objectivity," in M. Lowe and R. Hubbard (eds.) Woman's Nature: Rationalizations of Inequality. New York: Pergamon.

FEYERABEND, P. (1984) "On the limits of research." New Ideas in Psychology 2, 1: 3-7.

GARDINER, J. (1974) "Women's work in the industrial revolution," in S. Allen et al. (eds) Conditions of Illusion. Leeds: Feminist Books.

GEARHART, S. (1983) "An end to technology: A modest proposal," in J. Rothschild (ed.) Machina Ex Dea: Feminist Perspectives on Technology. New York: Pergamon.

GILLIGAN, C. (1982) In a Different Voice. Cambridge, MA: Harvard University Press.

GITTINS, D. (1983) "Inside and outside marriage." Feminist Review 14: 22-34.

GLADWIN, M. (1985) "The rape of the womb." M.A. thesis, University of Kent, Canterbury.

GOLDBERG, S. (1977) The Inevitability of Patriarchy. London: Temple Smith.

GRAY, M. A. and A.W.H. BUFFERY (1971) "Sex differences in emotional and cognitive behaviour in mammals including man: Adaptive and neural bases." Acta Psychologica 35: 89-111.

GRIFFIN, S. (1980) Woman and Nature: The Roaring Inside Her. New York: Harper & Row.

HARAWAY, D. (1979) "The biological enterprise: Sex, mind, and profit from human engineering to sociobiology." Radical History Review 20: 206-237.

HARRIS, B. J. (1984) "'Give me a dozen healthy infants . . .': John B. Watson's popular advice on childrearing, women and the family," in M. Lewin (ed.) In the Shadow of the Past: Psychology Portrays the Sexes. New York: Columbia University Press.

HARTMANN, H. (1979) "The unhappy marriage of Marxism and feminism: Towards a more progressive union." Capital and Class 8: 1-33.

HARTSTOCK, N. (1983) Money, Sex, and Power. London: Longman.

HEIN, H. (1981) "Women and science: Fitting men to think about nature." International Journal of Women's Studies 4: 369-377.

HENIFIN, M. S. and J. C. AMATNIEK (1982) "Bibliography: Women, science, and health," in R. Hubbard et al. (eds.) Biological Woman—The Convenient Myth. Cambridge, MA: Schenkman.

HOFFMAN, L. W. (1984) "The study of employed mothers over half a century," in M. Lewin (ed.) In the Shadow of the Past: Psychology Portrays the Sexes. New York: Columbia University Press.

HOLCOMBE, L. (1973) Victorian Ladies at Work. Newton Abbot, England: David & Charles.

HOLLIDAY, C. (1978) The Violent Sex. Guerneville, CA: Bluestocking Books.

HUBBARD, R. (1983a) "Social effects of some contemporary myths about women," in M. Lowe and R. Hubbard (eds.) Woman's Nature: Rationalizations of Inequality. New York: Pergamon.

HUBBARD, R. (1983b) "Human embryo and gene manipulation." Science for the People 15, 3: 24-27.

HUBBARD, R. (1984) "'Fetal rights' and the new eugenics." Science for the People 16, 2: 7-9, 27-29.

HUME, B. (1985) "Why Warnock is wrong." The Times (June 6): 12.

HUMPHRIES, J. (1981) "Protective legislation, the capitalist state, and working class men: The case of the 1842 Mines Regulation Act." Feminist Review 7: 1-33.

IRIGARAY, L. (1982) "Le sujet de la science est-il sexúe?" Temps Modernes 39, 434: 960-974.

JACOBI, M. P. (1877) The Question of Rest for Women During Menstruation. New York: Putnam's

JAGGAR, A. (1983) Feminist Politics and Human Nature. Brighton: Harvester.

JORDANOVA, L. (1980) "Natural facts: A historical perspective on science and sexuality," in C. MacCormack and M. Strathern (eds.) Nature, Culture and Gender. Cambridge: Cambridge University Press.

KELLER, E. F. (1983) "Women, science, and popular mythology," in J. Rothschild (ed.) Machina Ex Dea: Feminist Perspectives on Technology. New York: Pergamon.

KERR, M. (1985) "Sharing in a common plight?" Poverty 60: 22-26.

KIMBALL, M. (1981) "A critique of biological theories of sex differences." International Journal of Women's Studies 4: 318-333.

KING, Y. (1983) "Toward an ecological feminism and a feminist ecology," in J. Rothschild (ed.) Machina Ex Dea: Feminist Perspectives on Technology. New York: Pergamon.

KOHLSTEDT, S. G. (1978) "In from the periphery: American women in science, 1830-1880." Signs 4, 1: 81-96.

KUHN, T. S. (1970) The Structure of Scientific Revolutions. Chicago: University of Chicago Press.

LAKATOS, I. (1970) "Falsification and the methodology of scientific research programmes," in I. Lakatos and A. Musgrove (eds.) Criticism and the Growth of Knowledge. Cambridge: Cambridge University Press.

LAMBERT, H. H. (1978) "Biology and equality: A perspective on sex differences." Signs 4, 1: 97-117.

LEWIN, M. (1984) "'Rather worse than folly?' Psychology measures femininity and masculinity," in M. Lewin (ed.) In the Shadow of the Past: Psychology Portrays the Sexes. New York: Columbia University Press.

LLOYD, B. (1976) "Social responsibility and research on sex differences," in B. Lloyd and J. Archer (eds.) Exploring Sex Differences. London: Academic Press.

LONGINO, H. and R. DOELL (1983) "Body, bias, and behavior." Signs 9, 2: 206-227.

LOWE, M. (1983) "The dialectic of biology and culture," in M. Lowe and R. Hubbard (eds.) Woman's Nature: Rationalizations of Inequality. New York: Pergamon.

MACCOBY, E. E. and C. N. JACKLIN (1974) The Psychology of Sex Differences. Stanford: Stanford University Press.

MARX, K. (1970) "'Preface' to A contribution to the critique of political economy," in Karl Marx and Frederick Engels: Selected Works (1859). London: Lawrence & Wishart.

MAUDSLEY, H. (1874) "Sex in mind and in education." Fortnightly Review 15: 466-483.

MCKENNA, W. and S. J. KESSLER (1977) "Experimental design as a source of sex bias in social psychology." Sex Roles, 3, 2: 117-128.

MERCHANT, C. (1980) The Death of Nature. San Francisco: Harper & Row.

MESSING, K. (1983) "The scientific mystique: Can a white lab coat guarantee purity in the search for knowledge about the nature of women?" in M. Lowe and R. Hubbard (eds.) Woman's Nature: Rationalizations of Inequality. New York: Pergamon.

MORANTZ, R. M. (1982) "Introduction. From art to science: Women physicians in American medicine, 1600-1980," in R. M. Morantz et al. (eds) In Her Own Words: Oral Histories of Women Physicians. Westport, CT: Greenwood.

MORE, H. (1778) Essays on Various Subjects, Principally Designed for Young Ladies. London: J. Wilkie and T. Cadell.

MORE, H. (1799) Strictures on the Modern System of Female Education, Vol 2. London: T. Cadell and W. Davies.

NEW, C. and M. DAVID (1985) For the Children's Sake. Harmondsworth: Penguin.

NICHOLSON, J. (1984) Men and Women: How Different Are They? Oxford: Oxford University Press.

OAKLEY, A. (1976) "Wisewoman and medicine man: Changes in the management of childbirth," in A. Oakley and J. Mitchell (eds.) The Rights and Wrongs of Women. Harmondsworth: Penguin.

RICH, A. (1977) Of Woman Born. New York: Bantam.

ROSE, H. (1983) "Hand, brain, and heart: A feminist epistemology for the natural sciences." Signs 9, 1: 73-90.

ROSE, S. (1984) "The limits to science." Science for the People 16, 6: 16, 24-26.

ROSENBERG, C. S. (1982) Beyond Separate Spheres. New Haven, CT: Yale University Press.

ROSSI, A. (1977) "A biosocial perspective on parenting." Daedalus 106: 1-32.

ROSSITER, M. (1980) "'Women's work' in science, 1880-1910." ISIS 71 (Sept.): 381-398.

ROTHSCHILD, J. (1983) "Machina ex dea and future research," in J. Rothschild (ed.) Machina Ex Dea: Feminist Perspectives on Technology. New York: Pergamon.

SARAGA, E. and D. GRIFFITHS (1981) "Biological inevitabilities or political choices?" in A. Kelly (ed.) The Missing Half. Manchester: Manchester University Press.

SATTAUR, O. (1984) "New conception threatened by old morality." New Scientist (Sept. 27): 12-17.

SAYERS, J. (1982) Biological Politics. London: Tavistock.

SAYERS, J. (1986) Sexual Contradictions: Psychology, Psychoanalysis, and Feminism. London: Tavistock.

SCHWEICKART, P. (1983) "What if . . . science and technology in feminist utopias," in J. Rothschild (ed.) Machina Ex Dea: Feminist Perspectives on Technology. New York: Pergamon.

SCRUTON, R. (1983) "The case against feminism." The Observer (May 22): 27.

SÈVE, L. (1975) Marxism and the Theory of Human Personality (D. Pavett, trans.) (1968). London: Lawrence & Wishart.

SHERIF, C. (1979) "Bias in psychology," in J. A. Sherman and E. T. Beck (eds.) The Prism of Sex. Madison: University of Wisconsin Press.

SHERMAN, J. (1977) "Effects of biological factors on sex-related differences in mathematics achievement," in L. H. Fox et al., Women and Mathematics. Washington: National Institute of Education.

SHIELDS, S. A. (1975) "Functionalism, Darwinism, and the psychology of women: A study in social myth." American Psychologist 30: 739-754.

SHIELDS, S. A. (1982) "The variability hypothesis: The history of a biological model of sex differences in intelligence." Signs 7, 4: 769-797.

SHIELDS, S. A. (1984) "To pet, coddle, and 'do for': Caretaking and the concept of maternal instinct," in M. Lewin (ed.) In the Shadow of the Past: Psychology Portrays the Sexes. New York: Columbia University Press.

SLOAN, J. B. (1978) "The founding of the Naples Table Association for Promoting Scientific Research by Women, 1897." Signs 4, 1: 208-216.

SPENCER, H. (1873) "Psychology of the sexes." Popular Science Monthly 4: 30-38.

STARK-ADAMEC, C. and M. KIMBALL (1984) "Science free of sexism: A psychologist's guide to the conduct of nonsexist research." Canadian Psychology 25, 1: 23-24.

STÉHELIN, L. (1976) "Sciences, women and ideology," in H. Rose and S. Rose (eds.) The Radicalisation of Science. London: Macmillan.

STORER, H. R. (1868) Criminal Abortion. Boston: Little, Brown.

STRACHEY, R. (1979) The Cause (1928). London: Virago.

STROUSE, J. (1985) "Review of Alice Hamilton by Barbara Sicherman." New York Review of Books (May 9): 38-40.

TANNER, N. and Z. ZIHLMAN (1976) "Women in evolution." Signs 1, 3: 585-608.

TENNYSON, A. (1984) "The princess," in The Works of Alfred Tennyson (1847). London: Macmillan.

TERMAN, L. M. and MILES, C. C. (1936) Sex and Personality. New York: Russell and Russell.

TILLY, L. A. (1978) "The social sciences and the study of women." Comparative Studies in Society and History 20, 1: 163-173.

WATSON, J. (1925) Behaviorism. New York: Norton.

WAINWRIGHT, H. (1983) "The women who wire up the weapons," in Women Against the Bomb (eds.) Over Our Dead Bodies. London: Virago.

WEIR, J. (1895) "The effect of female suffrage on posterity." American Naturalist 29: 815-825.

WEISSTEIN, N. (1982) "Adventures of a woman in science," in R. Hubbard et al. (eds.) Biological Woman—The Convenient Myth. Cambridge, MA: Schenkman.

WITTIG, M. (1979) "One is not born a woman," in Proceedings of the Second Sex Conference. New York: New York Institute for the Humanities.

WOOLF, V. (1938) Three Guineas. London: Hogarth.

ZIPES, J. (1982) The Trials and Tribulations of Little Red Riding Hood. London: Heinemann.

3 Thinking About Gender

KAY DEAUX
New York University

MARY E. KITE
Purdue University

THE nature of women and men is a seemingly endless topic for debate. For decades, scientific studies have attempted to delineate the fundamental similarities and differences between the sexes (see Rosenberg, 1982; Shields, 1975, 1982, for accounts of some early psychological investigations). The frequent failure of these efforts to provide definitive answers has not deterred those who would offer less documented but fervently held opinions. Seventeenth-century observations, such as those of La Bruyere ("Women run to extremes; they are either better or worse than men") or George Herbert ("Words are women; deeds are men") are not unfamiliar in twentieth-century discourse. Nor are alternative conclusions absent. For example, consider Liv Ullman's seeming response to the question often attributed to Freud: "What does a woman want?" "To be a woman is to have the same needs and longings as a man" (Ullman, 1976).

Within psychology, the attempts to look at women and men have been most frequently associated with the term "sex differences," the term itself suggesting the conclusions that are often sought. Whether such differences are inherent to the species or the product of socialization practices and pressures has been an issue of continuing debate, but both nature and nurture proponents generally focus on the individual as the source of the differences.[1]

More recently, an alternative perspective on these questions has emerged. Without denying that there may be both biological and behavioral differences between the sexes, this perspective suggests that it is equally important to consider the perceiver and the beliefs that he or she brings to bear. How is gender, as a social category, construed in our society? What are the contents and scope of what we will call the gender belief system? And how do these beliefs about gender affect the course of social interaction, particularly when reality does not support the held beliefs? These are the kinds of questions that we will consider in this chapter. Although our own background is in social

AUTHORS' NOTE: Support for writing this chapter was provided in part by a grant from the National Science Foundation (BNS-8217313). The authors are grateful to the following people and to the very dedicated editors who provided helpful comments on an earlier draft: Nyla Branscombe, Alice Eagly, Eliot Smith, and Janet Spence.

psychology, the cognitive perspective that we adopt is not bound to any one discipline. Anthropologists as well as sociologists have been looking at gender as a belief system, using related terms such as "folk models" to describe the domain. Thus we see that beliefs about gender, although resident in individual heads, reflect a cultural system that demands an interdisciplinary interpretation.

Before considering these belief systems, however, we need to look at the history of the investigation of gender within psychology. An examination of these earlier attempts serves at least two purposes: First, it informs us as to what is really known about the similarities and differences between the sexes; and second, it provides an instructive lesson in the nature of scientific inquiry in an area where ideology is a constant companion.

MEN AND WOMEN, M AND F

As already noted, the search for sex differences has been a major activity of psychologists. Further, despite some ebb and flow, it has persisted for more than a century with variations only in the variables for which differences are sought. In the late nineteenth and early twentieth century, differences in intelligence were the major issue. Nineteenth-century craniometrists, led by Paul Broca, purported to show scientific proof of sex differences in intellectual capability. Although the smaller average stature of women was acknowledged to be a partial cause of brain size differences between women and men, stature was not believed to be the major determinant of brain differences. As Broca himself noted,

> We must not forget that women are, on the average, a little less intelligent than men, a difference which we should not exaggerate but which is, nonetheless, real. We are therefore permitted to suppose that the relatively small size of the female brain depends in part upon her physical inferiority and in part upon her intellectual inferiority [quoted in Gould, 1980: 154].

More savage in his comments was Gustave LeBon (often considered to be a founder of social psychology). "All psychologists who have studied the intelligence of women," he declared in 1879, "recognize today that they represent the most inferior forms of human evolution and that they are closer to children and savages than to an adult, civilized man" (quoted in Gould, 1980: 155).[2]

The biases underlying these investigations were not missed by all. Surveying the developing field of sex difference research in 1910, Helen Thompson Woolley concluded, "There is perhaps no field aspiring to be scientific where flagrant personal bias, logic martyred in the cause of supporting a prejudice, unfounded assertions, and even sentimental rot and drivel, have run riot to such an extent as here" (Woolley, 1910: 340). In her own research, Woolley conducted a careful comparison of males and females on a series of intellectual, sensory, and motor tasks, carefully matching subjects on a number of background variables. She looked at variability as well as averages and carefully presented graphed distributions on all the measures of the study. In general, Woolley found that differences between women and men were small and directionally inconsistent. Other investigators echoed her conclusions, finding differences more random than systematic, often more apparent than real. By 1918, Leta Hollingworth could state that a reviewer hoping to focus on sex differences in mental traits would "automatically tend to do himself out of his review. He would have very little to report" (Hollingworth, 1918: 428).[3]

The developing field of intelligence testing paid heed to this research by standardizing tests on an assumption of no sex differences. Nonetheless, the quest for sex differences in mental abilities persisted. Whereas general intelligence is most often conceded to be genderless, sex differences are often posited in terms of specific cognitive abilities—a more segmented approach to intelligence. Currently the questions are posed in terms of sex differences in verbal ability, mathematical ability, visual-spatial ability, and other concretely operational skills. Echoing their turn-of-the-century predecessors, current investigators debate not only the existence of such differences but their determinants as well.

Of the domains named above, visual-spatial ability is generally believed to show the largest sex difference (Hyde, 1981); consequently, consideration of those findings can prove instructive. First, the sex differences are not as large as the terminology might suggest, accounting for 5% or less of the variance (but sometimes representing a difference of as much as one standard deviation). Second, results vary sharply depending on the particular task that is used: Sex differences are evident on one particular type of spatial task (mental rotation) but are not reliably present on many others (Linn & Petersen, 1985). Third, attempts to implicate specific biological mechanisms to account for apparent differences often fail to acknowledge the considerable variation among tasks. These same qualifications can rather easily be applied to similar investigations of mathematical ability (see, for example, Benbow & Stanley, 1980, 1983). In each case, the differences between women and men, although real at one level, are often magnified and oversimplified in the telling.

The search for differences in personality characteristics and social behaviors of women and men is only slightly more recent and no less intense. One of the earliest attempts to document such behavioral differences was reported by H. T. Moore (1922). Disparaging the "inadequacy of the psychological test to get at the most important features of mental differentiation" (1922: 210), Moore sought to explore "emotional aptitudes" as reflected in the everyday conversations of women and men. The overheard tendency of men to talk more about business and sports and women to talk more about people provided no argument for innate sex differences, but did signal the future exploration of social and behavioral differences.[4]

The range of behaviors covered in those subsequent explorations has been extensive, as the reviews of Maccoby and Jacklin (1974), Eagly (1987), and others document. Further, the temptation to invoke biological causation has not been resisted, particularly in the case of aggression. It is a matter of some debate as to what this body of literature shows. Unquestionably, there are some reliable sex differences to be observed. These include such diverse behaviors as aggression, helping behavior, nonverbal communication, and social influence (see Eagly and Carli, 1981; Eagly and Crowley, 1986; Eagly and Steffen, 1986; Hall, 1978, 1984; Hyde, 1984).

How large and how meaningful these differences are is disputable. Many investigators have suggested that the limited explained variance of these sex comparisons cautions against conclusions that emphasize differences between women and men. In contrast, counter to the prevalent trend of deemphasizing sex differences, Eagly (1987) argues that male-female differences in social behavior are far from trivial and in fact are predicted by social-role analysis. That is, people are members of social groups and are subject to the pressures of these groups. Accordingly it is argued that the pressures of this group membership almost inevitably result in distinctive social behaviors resulting from the roles that men and women occupy in the social structure.

Endorsement of psychological sex differences is also evident in the field of personality, where some of the most publicized work on gender has dealt with hypothesized sex differences in personality dispositions: Witness Matina Horner's (1972) introduction of the concept "fear of success" and Carol Gilligan's (1982) emphasis on the morality of attachment and responsibility. In both instances, the investigators reacted to a perceived imbalance in the extant research literature and introduced an alternative motive or disposition that could account for differences in female performance. Although neither author would claim exclusive domain—some men can fear success, for example, as some men emphasize attachment or women separation— nonetheless both Horner and Gilligan stressed differences rather than similarities between the sexes. The empirical work is far less supportive of a sex difference on these measures. In the case of moral development, for example, recent critiques have suggested an absence of sex differences in both the traditional measures and in the newer Gilligan concept (Broughton, 1983; Smetana, 1984; Walker, 1984).

A variant on the sex difference approach has been the attempt to define psychological dimensions of masculinity and femininity (often abbreviated as M and F). This strategy also has a lengthy history: Masculinity and femininity scales were first developed by Lewis Terman and Catherine Cox Miles (1936) in order to provide an objective measure parallel to the measurement of intelligence, an area in which Terman had worked earlier. More specifically, Terman and Miles wanted to be able "to locate the subject, with a fair degree of approximation, in terms of deviation from the mean of either sex" (1936: 3). To do so, they developed a battery of items, the answers to which were believed to indicate either a masculine or a feminine orientation. The choice of these items, although carefully done, was made on empirical rather than logical or conceptual grounds, thus accounting for the seeming randomness of masculinity-defining topics such as dislike for foreigners, religious men, guessing games, and thin women, or the parallel femininity of antipathy to bashful or bald-headed men, sideshow freaks, and riding bicycles.[5]

For several decades, this M-F scale and others developed in its image both reflected and promoted a number of basic assumptions about the nature of "maleness" and "femaleness." From the onset, normative responses were considered a sign of psychological health. Thus deviation from the average scores was believed to be not simply a statistical issue but a valid psychological diagnosis as well. In particular, homosexuality and familial troubles were predicted to link with deviant M-F scores (Morawski, 1985). Other underlying assumptions of this approach to assessing an individual's presumed masculinity and femininity were most effectively exposed by Constantinople (1973). She questioned three central tenets of the M-F research: the unidimensionality of masculinity-femininity, the assumed bipolarity or opposition of the two concepts, and the purely empirical basis on which the original items had been selected.

In the wake of Constantinople's critique, a number of alternative assessment tools were developed. The best known of these is the Bem Sex Role Inventory (Bem, 1974), designed to measure masculinity and femininity as separate and independent dimensions. Out of this particular research program also emerged the concept of androgyny, a label used to identify non-sex-typed individuals—that is, those whose scores on the masculinity and femininity scales were approximately equivalent. People categorized as androgynous were purported to be at an advantage in a number of ways, including mental health. Other investigators, most notably Spence et al. (1974), also developed two-dimensional measures of gender-related traits. These latter investigators were more cautious in their formulations, however, describing the scales as measures of the more limited traits of expressiveness and instrumentality rather than a global assessment of masculinity and femininity, and limiting their claims of its predictability to the corresponding domains rather than to the more broadly defined realm of gender-related behaviors (see Spence & Helmreich, 1978).

Such caution has proved appropriate. The concept of androgyny is far more limited than initially envisioned, neither indexing psychological health nor predicting to the broad domain of gender-related behaviors one might identify. (See Deaux, 1984, 1985; Morawski, 1985; Spence, 1984; Taylor & Hall, 1982, for more extensive analyses.) Furthermore, as Spence (1984, 1985) has articulated most clearly, it is important to distinguish between the theoretical concepts of masculinity and femininity and the range of gender-differentiating behaviors that are multidetermined and often only weakly linked to the more global theoretical concepts.

The scientific record on questions of sex differences, based on either biological or psychological distinctions, is shaky at best. Examples of bias are numerous, suggesting that gender beliefs can influence the actions of scientists as well as those of laypersons. There are without question some behavioral differences between women and men. Yet the size of these differences is often smaller than purported and their appearance is often highly dependent on context. Indeed the variability of gender-related behaviors and their dependence on specific situational contexts are increasingly recognized by a broad range of psychological investigators (see Deaux & Major, 1987; Eagly, 1987; Sherif, 1982; Unger, 1983).

Yet despite evidence of considerable overlap and situational specificity of gender-related behaviors, beliefs in sex differences are held tenaciously. Precisely because these beliefs have such impressive staying power it is important to understand more clearly just what they are. In the succeeding pages we will describe the form and content of the gender belief system, such as it is now known, and consider the consequences of these beliefs for ongoing social interaction.

GENDER BELIEF SYSTEMS

The term "gender belief system" refers to a set of beliefs and opinions about males and females and about the purported qualities of masculinity and femininity. This system includes stereotypes of women and men, attitudes toward the appropriate roles and behaviors of women and men, and attitudes toward individuals who are believed to differ in some significant way from the modal pattern (e.g., homosexual). Gender belief systems, conceptualized in this broad manner, include both descriptive and prescriptive elements— beliefs about what is and opinions about what should be.

Many aspects of the gender belief system are shared by substantial numbers of individuals within a society, so one can speak of consensual categories and normative beliefs. At the same time, it is also possible to assess individual variation in the endorsement of various aspects of this belief system. Such an individualized approach allows the formulation of more precise predictions of the behavioral consequences of gender-related beliefs, thereby suggesting routes of individual change as well.

The concept of gender belief systems, coined by us in the realm of psychology, finds its expression in other disciplines as well. Cognitive anthropologists have considered the ways in which cultural knowledge is organized, using the term "folk models" to describe the set of characteristics that are associated with a concept. More specifically, Holland and Davidson (1983) have defined a folk model as "a cognitive gestalt that guides the individual's inference making, information-seeking about, and action toward a particular aspect of the world" (1983: 7). Elements of such folk models include not only the word-plus-attribute unit (analogous to the stereotype and its associated verbal trait descriptors) but also scripts, causal propositions, action sequences, and functional assemblages (Holland & Davidson, 1983). Holland and Davidson argue that the folk model approach is superior to the more limited stereotype approach because it encompasses a broader domain of cultural knowledge. The concept of a gender belief system incorporates a similarly broad perspective and understanding.

It would be wrong to assume that these gender beliefs are inherently false. Indeed, there is little question that some aspects of gender stereotypes and beliefs about what women and men do are based on reality, reflecting the distribution of women and men into different roles in our society (see Eagly, 1983, 1987). At the same time, it is indisputable that people's beliefs are not a totally accurate mirror of reality, but rather are subject to numerous perceptual biases and interpretational errors. Work in social cognition has provided firm evidence of these cognitive "shortcuts" (see Fiske & Taylor, 1984). The problem of precisely how accurate people are seems to us an intractable one. More productive, we believe, is the identification of the belief system and an analysis of how it affects social interaction, based on an underlying assumption of partial truth and partial falsehood.

To appreciate fully how extensive the gender belief system is, we need to consider some of its elements in more detail. In the following sections, we will consider the characteristics typically ascribed to men and women, the types of women and men that people think of, and the attitudes that people hold toward gender-related issues, particularly in the realm of prescriptive roles. For reasons of both historicity and simplicity, we begin with the traditional stereotype approach.

Stereotypic Characteristics of Women and Men

Although the term stereotype was used in the printing trade in the early part of the nineteenth century, the concept did not become part of mainstream social scientific thought until Walter Lippmann's treatise on public opinion in 1922. The initial efforts of social scientists to quantify the concept focused on ethnic stereotypes, the most notable of these projects being Katz and Braly's (1933) study in which subjects were asked to say whether each of 84 traits was or was not characteristic of each of 10 ethnic groups. Early stereotype work continued in this tradition and, within a couple of decades, attention was directed toward identifying the content of gender stereotypes as well (e.g. Fernberger, 1948; McKee & Sheriffs, 1957; Sheriffs and McKee, 1957).

Expressiveness and instrumentality. Since the late 1960s, the work of Paul Rosenkrantz, Inge Broverman, and their colleagues (Broverman et al., 1972;

Rosenkrantz et al., 1968) has served as a benchmark for gender stereotype research. The major aim of this work was to identify some of those traits that are consensually believed to describe the typical man and the typical woman in contemporary U.S. society. These investigators identified two clusters of traits: a warmth-expressiveness cluster believed to be more characteristic of women than men, and a competence cluster believed to be more characteristic of men than women. Both groups of traits were considered socially desirable, although Rosenkrantz and his colleagues observed that a larger number of masculine traits were evaluated positively than were feminine traits. In terms of mean ratings, however, there was no difference in the average "goodness" of the two stereotypic clusters.

More recent research has continued to show the prominence of these two general dimensions in the stereotypes of women and men. Spence et al. (1974) began with a larger set of traits but two similar dimensions emerged, both in individual self-description and in stereotypic assignments to others. Nor are these stereotypic beliefs limited to U.S. populations. In research covering 30 different nations, Williams and Best (1982) observed considerable consensus in the perceived attributes of women and men, providing evidence for "pancultural generality." Men were typically seen as stronger and more active, characterized by high needs for achievement, dominance, autonomy, and aggression. Women, in contrast, were viewed as weaker and less active, more concerned with affiliation, nurturance, and deference. At the same time, in a caution against assumptions of complete universality, Williams and Best also found some variations across countries. In Catholic countries, for example, women were viewed as stronger, perhaps reflecting the prominent role of females in the religious belief system.

In a recent study of the perceptions that U.S. college students hold of men and women in 28 nations, Eagly and Kite (1986) compared the general nationality stereotype to specific male and female stereotypes of that nationality—for example, Swiss people versus Swiss women versus Swiss men. They found that stereotypes of men were closer to the corresponding national stereotype than were those of women, a finding that corresponds to the Broverman et al. (1972) study of judgments of mental health (in which judgments of healthy men and healthy persons were quite similar, while healthy women were viewed as different from either group). However, the size of the perceived differences varied by country. People saw greater similarity between stereotypes of men and their nationalities than between women and their nationalities to the extent that the countries were not positively evaluated (e.g., were seen as unlikable and without an attractive natural environment), were seen as possessing negative political characteristics (e.g., militaristic, conservative), and were not viewed as a country that emphasized equality between the sexes. As with the Williams and Best (1982) results, patterns of gender belief show elements of both similarity and variability across cultures.

A general finding that pervades the work on stereotypic attributes of women and men is their perceived bipolarity. Thus whereas numerous investigations of self-described attributes show that expressive and instrumental traits are independent dimensions, perceivers continue to cling to the belief that these traits, as well as other male- and female-related attributes, are polar opposites. Thus a person described as lacking expressive characteristics will be assumed to have instrumental traits (Foushee et al., 1979); and homosexuals are assumed to possess the attributes of the other biological sex (Kite & Deaux, 1987). This oppositional pattern of thought not only underlies the association of particular characteristics with women and men but the categorical process itself. (This assumption was clearly evident in the scientific construction of masculinity-femininity measures.)

Multiple components. The reliance on personality trait terms to define gender stereotypes has been a persistent but not particularly defensible strategy among social scientists. It is quite clear that the terms "man" and "woman" conjure up a variety of associations, yet it is only recently that the multidimensionality of gender stereotypes has begun to be explored in a systematic way. Deaux and Lewis (1983, 1984) have shown that there are clear gender-linked associations in a number of realms. Certain role behaviors, such as being a financial provider and taking the initiative with the other sex, are strongly associated with men, while other behaviors such as cooking meals and taking care of children are associated with women. Occupations also differ in their gender-linked associations, typically reflecting the actual distribution of women and men in occupational categories within the society. Thus secretaries and telephone operators are assumed to be women, while truck drivers and chemists are thought more likely to be men. Perhaps most important, there are specifiable physical features that are reliably associated with men and women. Although these ideas are intuitively obvious, the implications that these multiple components and their interrelationships have on people's perceptions of men and women have only begun to be understood. Deaux and Lewis (1984) suggest that the various gender-related associations are linked under a common umbrella, allowing a broad range of inferences to be made from relatively limited amounts of information, and provide evidence to support their claim.

Information about physical appearance appears to be particularly influential in the gender belief system.[6] Deaux and Lewis (1984) found that people weigh such information much more heavily than other kinds of gender-related information, using physical appearance to predict a wide variety of traits and behaviors. For example, told that a male is short and has a soft voice, people were quite apt to predict that the male in question is expressive, engages in female role behaviors, and has a relatively high probability of being homosexual. Ashmore and Del Boca (1979) also stress the importance of physical features to the gender stereotype and they have begun to analyze the specific physical features that are associated with a particular stereotypic category. In a provocative review of this issue, McArthur (1982) explores the relationship between physical appearance and stereotyping, including the self-fulfilling nature of such information and implications for changing stereotypes that are closely tied to physical appearance. As McArthur (1982) points out, visual stimuli are primary—they are generally seen and categorized before any other information about a person is obtained. Such categorization on the basis of physical appearance may result in later information being selectively noticed, remembered, and organized by the assumptions made about persons in that group; this information, in turn, is likely to create expectancies about that person's behavior.

Sexuality. Beliefs about sexuality of males and females are another important but relatively ignored aspect of the gender stereotype.[7] As early as 1957, Sheriffs and McKee found sexuality to be one of the most frequently mentioned attributes of women and men. Only recently, however, have attempts been made to incorporate sexuality into models of gender stereotypes. Ashmore and Del Boca (1983) suggest that both sex and violence are integral parts of the gender belief system. Holland and Davidson (1983) found that sexuality was one of the three major themes in both females' listing of types of males and males' listing of types of females. People are quite willing to infer sexual orientation on the basis of trait, role, or physical appearance information (see Deaux & Lewis, 1984). The reverse is also true: Kite and Deaux (1987) provide evidence of the close association between known homosexual orientation and the inferred possession of the other-sex attributes. These results and others (e.g., Storms, 1978a, 1978b) suggest that observers rely on information about sexuality to predict a range of gender-related behaviors, just as they infer sexual preference from information in other domains. Further, these results provide added support for the bipolarity of people's gender belief system.

Types of Women and Men

The act of labeling members of the human species as either male or female appears to be universal. As Kessler and McKenna (1978) have argued in considerable detail, gender attributions are a nearly automatic process, often based on the identification of genitals. In the absence of such intimate information, observers will use secondary physical characteristics, such as body build and amount of hair, to make a dichotomous judgment. Because there is a biological basis (although an admittedly imperfect one) for dividing people into males and females, it has been common practice to think of stereotypes as a two-category system as well. Such a two-category system undoubtedly encourages the belief in bipolarity. Indeed, the temptation to treat two categories as opposites may be irresistable (Belle, 1985). In a recent dissertation, Barnes (described in Belle, 1985) found that parents with two children describe their children in terms of opposition (e.g., "Susie is a leader and Brad is a follower"), whereas parents with more than two children use separate and unique dimensions in describing each child. Both lay observers and scientific investigators may fall into this same oppositional trap.

Although a two-category system is the strategy of first choice, it is not the only basis for stereotyping women and men. It has become increasingly evident that the gender belief system is peopled with many different types of women and men. Thus while we associate certain characteristics with women and men in general, we also have more detailed conceptions of, for example, career women and businessmen, sexy women and macho men. Such subtypes do not invalidate the broader concepts but seem to coexist with them.

In one of the first efforts to look at gender beliefs in this more particularized way, Clifton et al. (1976) noted the existence of "housewife" and "bunny" as distinct female stereotypes. Noseworthy and Lott (1984) found that traits are reliably clustered around four clear types of women: sex object, career women, housewife, and athlete. Virtual identical female categories are reported by Deaux et al. (1985); these authors also introduce a set of male categories, including businessman, athletic man, blue-collar working man, and macho man. Multidimensional scaling, as used by Ashmore et al. (1984), has pointed to three dimensions of classification for gender. Briefly summarized, their results suggest three major types of women—the nurturant wife and mother, the sexual (and negatively evaluated) woman, and an independent career woman. The male solution for this scaling analysis was less clearly articulated and varied in some important ways between male and female respondents. Most notable were differences in the evaluation of sexuality, where men view sexual prowess as central to the definition of masculinity. Women, in contrast, distinguished between sexy lovers, who were also seen as gentle and respectable, and a more negative manifestation of sexuality in the Don Juan and stud types. Three-dimensional solutions were also reported by Holland and Davidson (1983).

Although there are some variations across experimental investigations, it seems quite clear that people can and do conceptualize women and men in terms of specific types, as well as the more generic male and female categories. Furthermore, people can quite easily list numerous characteristics that these various types of men and women possess (Deaux et al., 1985). The role of physical characteristics in identifying these types of women and men should not be ignored. When listing attributes of the various types, people are quite apt to mention identifying physical features. Physical characteristics may in fact be one of the major ways by which types of women and men are distinguished from one another, thus accounting for the importance of physical appearance information to other judgments, as noted earlier.

Of course, the exact types of women and men that are contained in the belief system may vary across cultural and subcultural groupings. For example, college students in the Holland and Davidson (1983) studies identified such idiosyncratic types as "fratty-bagger," a category probably not recognizable off the university campus. More broad-ranging cultural inquiries would undoubtedly produce more diverse types.

The consequences of such a typology may be ultimately more interesting than identification of the types specific to any one culture. Within cognitive psychology, investigators have suggested that categories are organized in a hierarchy, with some categories superordinate and others subordinate to the more basic level of categorization (see Rosch, 1978). In the example used most often, "tables" and "chairs" are viewed as basic-level categories, more detailed than "furniture" and less particular than "card table" or "Breuer chair." Such basic levels of categorization, it is argued, represent the richest level of conceptualization and thus of use.

The parallel argument for gender beliefs would be that specifiable subtypes of women and men are relied on more extensively than the subordinate categories of "women" and "men" (see Hamilton, 1981; Taylor, 1981, for statements of this position). However, available data do not support these predictions, suggesting instead that people have developed stereotypes of equivalent richness at more than one level of categorization. In contrast to the neatness of object categorization, social perception is far more muddied (see Lingle et al., 1984).

This diversity of stereotypic categories may be quite adaptive. Equipped with varying levels of specificity, people can have a belief appropriate to each occasion. With little distinguishing information, a general concept of "woman" and "man" may be serviceable. Additional information, either physical or verbal, may call for a more differentiated concept and more specific associations. Indeed, some beliefs about women and men may be linked to particular contexts, their utility limited to those situations in which a male or a female appears in the imagined setting. Thus "professional football player in a locker room" may trigger some very specific beliefs, only weakly related to general concepts of men.

Attitudes Toward the Roles of Women and Men

The social and cognitive psychological traditions have tended to emphasize the generality of gender beliefs, stressing the consensually shared beliefs about women and men and, more recently, the general structure of those beliefs. The attitudinal perspective, similarly steeped in tradition, also deals with the generality of shared beliefs, but its emphasis is on individual differences in the strength of those beliefs. Attitudinal measures differ from stereotype endorsement in at least two other respects. First, at least historically, attitudes have had a more studied link to behavioral outcomes. Second, attitudes have a more explicitly evaluative component, whereas stereotypic beliefs do not necessarily imply a good-bad dimension.

A number of specific measures have been developed to assess attitudes toward women and men (most often toward specific role behaviors of women and men), in addition to sets of questions used in survey research. The Attitudes toward Women Scale (AWS), developed by Spence and Helmreich (1972; Spence et al., 1973), solicits people's opinions on the rights, roles, and privileges that women ought to have. The FEM scale, developed by Smith et al. (1975), assesses acceptance of feminist ideology in a variety of social and occupational domains. The more specific domain of attitudes toward women as managers is assessed through a scale developed by Peters et al. (1974).

Such attitudinal measures can be approached in at least two ways. From a social-demographic perspective, comparisons of mean scores across groups and across time periods can indicate changes in the beliefs held by various samples of the population. Most studies directed at this question have indicated gradual changes in the direction of less traditional views over the past 10 to 20 years. Thus on average Americans are now more likely to endorse such concepts as paid employment among mothers with small children and male participation in household chores than they were 10 to 15 years ago.[8]

From an individual difference perspective, one can explore the degree to which individual attitudes predict subsequent behavior in related domains— for example, whether an individual who endorses feminist ideology would be more apt to belong to the National Organization for Women, to donate money to female political candidates, or to have an equitable division of labor in the household. To illustrate, Spence and Helmreich (1978) demonstrated that profeminist students are more positive toward competent women than are less feminist students; Robinson and Follingstad (1985) found that feminist women are more likely to report that they participate in feminist behaviors than women with more traditional attitudes toward women. In validating their FEM scale, Smith et al. (1975) reported associations between liberality and level of involvement in the feminist movement. People whose attitudes toward women in management positions are most negative are also most likely to attribute the success of an individual woman to luck or an easy task assignment (Garland & Price, 1977).

Yet undone is research that would help us understand more about the determinants of individual differences in these measures. Furthermore, although there is some evidence that attitudes toward gender roles are related to political and religious views, there is considerable variability among these domains. Nor is it the case, despite frequent assumptions, that prescriptive attitudes toward male and female roles are identical with descriptive beliefs about differences in male and female characteristics. One may value certain things without believing that they are so.

Cognition, Evaluation, and Judgment

The gender belief system, as we conceive it, is broadly defined, encompassing a range of beliefs, evaluations, and judgments. Although these diverse elements are related by virtue of their substantive focus, the links between them are yet to be forged. There has been an unfortunate tendency to assume one-to-one correspondence among these elements without empirical support. In fact, the available data raise serious questions about the isomorphism of these seemingly related elements.

Research efforts that assume too quickly the parallelism between various elements of the gender belief system have encountered considerable difficulty. In her initial formulation of androgyny, for example, Bem (1974) implied that self-descriptive masculinity (instrumentality) and femininity (expressiveness) should predict a wide range of gender-related behaviors, including attitudes toward feminist issues. These assumptions have generally not been supported. More recently, in introducing a model of the gender schema, Bem (1981, 1985) has used the same self-assessment tool to predict cognitive organization and reactions to male and female target persons. According to gender schema theory, the Bem Sex Role Inventory (BSRI) can be used as a basis for predicting who will process information on the basis of sex-linked associations (gender schematic individuals) and who does not possess this general readiness to view the world in gender-linked terms (gender aschematic individuals). Again, empirical findings make this assumed linkage doubtful (Deaux et al., 1985; Edwards & Spence, 1985; Mills & Tyrell, 1983). Theoretical criticisms provide further reason to doubt the utility of this approach (see Spence, 1984, for a summary of these issues).

The critical factors that differentiate among the elements of the gender belief system remain to be charted. Gender alone is not sufficient to link all of the elements, despite the ease with which such assumptions are made. Without attempting to be exhaustive, we can suggest a number of factors that need to be considered. First, the number of beliefs relevant to gender is substantial, and the specificity-generality issue is one that cannot wisely be ignored (see Ajzen and Fishbein, 1977, for a discussion of these issues in the general attitude realm). That is, because attitude scales—such as the FEM and the AWS—measure global tendencies to view women and men in traditional ways, it is unlikely that scores on such measures would reliably predict any single behavior. Rather, the scales should provide greatest utility for predicting individual differences in reactions toward women and men when the behavior itself is also measured at a global level. Nor should strategies for adequately assessing behavior be ignored, such as the value of aggregating across a variety of conceptually related behaviors and occasions (see Ajzen, 1982; Fishbein & Ajzen, 1974; Epstein, 1979, 1983). Second, affective weightings and motivational needs must be considered, echoing our earlier distinction between descriptive and prescriptive elements. Third, the context in which these elements are explored is important but too often ignored. Although some of these points are fairly technical, each of them raises questions about the presumed link between gender beliefs and actions directed toward women—a link that, while it surely exists, cannot be considered automatic.

WHEN COGNITION MEETS REALITY

Do people who hold different concepts of women and men act differently? The assumption, one that underlies most of the cognitive work on gender issues, is that such representations do affect behavior. But how?

There are a number of questions that can be raised here. First, when and how are the beliefs of an observer translated into action toward a target person who fits one of the categories of belief? Second, what effects do these beliefs and actions have on the behavior of the recipient? And third, are there any ways in which these beliefs may be altered? In other words, can stereotypes be disconfirmed by the actions of a target, and does this disconfirmation feed back to the original belief system?

To ground these questions in an example, consider the employer who believes that women are generally emotional, illogical, and ill-suited for the managerial role. If a female graduate of a prestigious M.B.A. program applies for a management training position, how will the beliefs of this employer be translated into action? An obvious but discriminatory possibility is refusal to hire the applicant. More subtle translations of beliefs into action might involve assignment of less challenging projects, overly harsh performance evaluation, and the like. A women in this position would have several avenues of response. Constrained by the structure and unable to alter the biased judgment process, the woman might in at least some respects confirm the beliefs, appearing less qualified than a male colleague. Alternatively, the woman might strive to refute the conveyed message, performing exceptionally in the face of doubts about her performance. Given the latter alternative, would the beliefs of the employer be altered? And if so, would this employer now have a different view of women in general, a more articulated set of beliefs about career women, or, more narrowly, only some specific beliefs and attitudes about this individual woman? Questions such as these bring life to the cognitive inquiry, directing our attention to the realm of social interaction in which men and women engage.[9]

From Beliefs to Actions

The expansive network of beliefs about the characteristics and behaviors of women and men that each person holds forms the basis of specifiable actions toward individuals and groups in the social context. Thus if one assumes that women are skilled in some domains and men in others, one may look to a member of one group and not the other when attempting to get a particular task accomplished. As a concrete example, imagine yourself in a room with a man, a woman, and a very young child. With the onset of tears and cries from the child, to which person would you look for help?

There are a number of ways in which beliefs can be manifested in actions. Direct expression of attitudes is one way in which the perceiver indicates a belief system. For example, one might compliment a woman on her dress and commend a man for his insightful analysis of a problem. Such choices reflect the associations that are linked to a particular category and that thus become activated when the category is salient (see also Rothbart & John, 1985). Expectancies may also be conveyed in more subtle ways. Using meta-analytic techniques to detect consistent patterns in a body of research, Harris and Rosenthal (1985) analyzed 31 different ways in which expectancies might be conveyed to a target. Several behaviors were found to lead reliably to positive interaction, including length of the interaction, frequency of interactions, and amount of smiling and eye contact between the participants.

The operation of such beliefs in the gender realm has been demonstrated quite convincingly in two laboratory studies by Mark Snyder and his colleagues. In the first study (Snyder et al., 1977), men were led to believe, by the provision of photographs, that they were interacting with either a highly attractive or a less attractive woman. Communicating only via intercoms, the men in the study showed substantially different behavior toward women in the two different conditions, behaving in a much more positive and friendly manner when they believed their partner was physically attractive. In a second study (Skrypnek & Snyder, 1982), male students assigned gender-related tasks to a partner in accordance with his or her alleged sex. (Lewis, 1985, replicated this for female subjects as well.) In yet another demonstration of the influence of gender beliefs, Kite and Deaux (1986) found that students who hold negative attitudes toward homosexuality will act differently toward a male identified as a homosexual than do students whose attitudes are less negative.

Beliefs can also inhibit action. Thus a person who holds negative beliefs about macho men, for example, may simply avoid encounters with males believed to typify that category. (In a similar manner, the racial bigot may avoid contact with blacks, allowing the belief system to remain unchallenged by potentially contradictory evidence.)

Given that a person holds particular beliefs about gender, is it necessarily true that such beliefs will be activated on all occasions? In an initial encounter, for example, when do beliefs about women and men come to the fore in priority over beliefs about, for example, whites and blacks, tall and short people, academicians and laypersons, or any of a wide variety of other categories that may be coded in memory and be applicable in the specific instance? In general, we would argue, categories that are readily cued by physical information should come to the fore more quickly than those that depend on less visible cues. Thus beliefs about women and men (and about blacks and whites) should be activated more readily than beliefs about occupational groups or political parties.[10]

More differentiated beliefs about women and men, or specific subtype stereotypes, may also be activated by physical cues. For example, the navy business-suited women may elicit the career woman stereotype, whereas a low-cut blouse may call for the "sexy woman" image. Ashmore and Del Boca (1983) have recently begun to explore the very specific physical features that particular gender stereotypes contain, attempting to describe the visual prototype for each of several common gender subtypes. The more closely an individual resembles an observer's prototypical category, the more likely it is that the stereotype will be activated.[11]

The salience of a target in the context of a particular environment will also influence the activation of gender beliefs. Taylor and her colleagues (Taylor et al., 1979; Taylor et al., 1978) and McArthur and her colleagues (McArthur & Post, 1977; McArthur & Solomon, 1978) have shown that salience can be manipulated in a variety of ways, including having a solo male in a group of females, having a moving person in a group of stationary others or having perceivers focus on a particular person in a group. Further, these studies have consistently shown that salient individuals are rated more extremely (either positively or negatively) and are generally thought to be more influential than other members of the group (see McArthur, 1981, and Taylor and Fiske, 1978, for detailed reviews of this literature). Thus if a female is interacting with a group of males, it is likely that her sex will be more salient and that the gender stereotypes of the perceivers will be more readily activated than if she were in a group of females. These are essentially the issues that Kanter noted in discussing the problems of the token woman in a predominantly male organization—or, less frequent but equally applicable, the problems of a token male in a predominantly female organization (Kanter, 1977).

Behavior of the Target

"If men define situations as real, they are real in their consequences." Although originally proposed by W.I. Thomas, the concept of the self-fulfilling prophecy owes much to the extended analysis of sociologist Robert K. Merton (1948). More recently its implications have been developed extensively in the psychological literature (see Darley & Fazio, 1980; Rosenthal & Jacobson, 1968). With regard to gender, we suggest that the behavior of women and men is often channeled in such a way as to confirm aspects of the gender belief system. Such a position in some respects brings us back to the "sex difference" position. Yet differences between women and men, in the present interpretation, are the outcome of certain processes, are contingent on context, and are variable in their appearance.

The Snyder et al. (1977) study provides a striking illustration of the behavioral confirmation process as it operates in the gender realm. Not only did the male subjects in this study act differently depending on their beliefs about their partner's attractiveness but the males elicited differential behavior from their female partner as well. Women believed to be highly attractive (who were in fact no different from the others) were rated by neutral observers as being more confident, more animated, and as enjoying the conversation more than were women believed to be less attractive.

Although much of the behavioral confirmation literature suggests a rather automatic adherence on the part of the target to the sent messages, the process is considerably more complicated and less unidirectional. Individuals choose, often with very conscious intent, how to present themselves in various situations. Such presentations may be affected both by general concerns with self-presentation as well as with specific masculine and feminine identities.[12] Recipients of stereotypical messages may be quite aware of the message and may consciously choose to confirm or disconfirm the belief that is conveyed.

An individual's willingness to confirm or deny the stereotypical expectancies is also influenced by the situational context and by characteristics of the person who conveys the expectancies. The power and resources of the message-sender, for example, may influence a target's choice, as has been shown by Zanna and his colleagues (Zanna & Pack, 1975; von Baeyer et al., 1981). College women were willing to modify their views and their appearance when a male was socially attractive or when he had economic power, but not when he was less appealing. So too may a person's goals for a particular interaction influence how readily he or she confirms the conveyed beliefs. When future contact is desired, the individual may be much more prone to "set the record straight" than if the encounter holds no promise for repetition.

The Consequences of Nonconfirmation

Although there are numerous occasions when behavioral confirmation may occur, there are also a host of occasions on which a specific target does not confirm the stereotypic beliefs of the perceiver. Such actions, it would seem, should cause an alteration in the stereotype, forcing the products of experience to be incorporated into the belief system. Ultimately a series of such experiences should result in isomorphism between reality and the mental representation of that reality. Yet as investigators have pursued the question of stereotypic change over the past several decades, it has become evident that the process of change is not so easily accomplished.

One factor that inhibits change is cognitive confirmation, whereby the observer finds evidence for his or her beliefs in the target's actions, independent, in a sense, of what the target actually does. Darley and Gross (1983), for example, found that observers led to believe that a child was either lower or upper class saw evidence of poor or good academic performance, respectively, when viewing identical videotapes. Similarly, the person who believes that men are nonemotional may either ignore outbursts that disconfirm the premise or, alternatively, reinterpret the behavior as nonemotional and thereby consistent with the stereotype. At the same time that observer might be particularly attuned to the raised voice of the presumably emotional woman.

Some investigators have suggested that category-based beliefs can be abandoned quite easily in the face of more individuating information (Locksley et al., 1980; Locksley et al., 1982). Under certain conditions this is indeed the case, such as when the individuating information is very closely linked to the subsequent judgment that needs to be made. In other words, if you think that women are warm and empathetic, but I describe a certain Stephanie as cold and unresponsive, it is quite likely that you would expect Stephanie to be cold when you meet her. There are definite limits to this effect, however, and part of the impact of stereotypes is the degree to which logically unrelated attributes are nevertheless linked in a common category, permitting generalizations and expectations that are not warranted by the evidence itself (see Deaux & Lewis, 1984; Grant & Holmes, 1981).

Rothbart and John (1985) have suggested that observers apply a "goodness of fit" test to specific individuals they meet. Thus if a woman seems to match the prototype of women that an individual carries in his or her head, then that particular woman will be coded as an instance of the more general category. Rothbart and John further suggest that one will incorporate disconfirming evidence into the general category to the extent that the majority of the features are similar. In contrast, an exemplar who differs on a wide variety of characteristics from the prototype would not be coded in that category, precluding change in the general categorical belief. Weber and Crocker (1983) report data consistent with this hypothesis. Concentration of stereotypic-inconsistent information in a few examples led people to create subtypes rather than to revise the stereotype. In contrast, the same amount of inconsistent information dispersed over a larger number of group members resulted in some modification of the overall stereotype.

Consider how this subtype formation might work. If one's beliefs about women include traits such as passivity, emotionality, and total dependence on a husband, the example of Margaret Thatcher would probably not alter that belief. Instead one might construct a separate category of women to handle Prime Minister Thatcher, perhaps labeling that category "political women." Gordon Allport graphically referred to this phenomenon as "re-fencing": "When a fact cannot fit into a mental field, the exception is acknowledged, but the field is hastily fenced in again and not allowed to remain dangerously open" (1954: 23).

Eventually, Rothbart and John (1985) suggest, continual subtyping may lead to the dissolution of the general category. Thus a stereotype of women built on the premise of passivity and domesticity may crumble in the face of a continuing parade of Margaret Thatchers, Indira Gandhis, and (equally stereotypical) career women. Such dissolution will only occur, however, to the extent that the general category loses its ability to predict outcomes successfully. If many of the women that our hypothetical perceiver encounters do in fact evidence passivity and domesticity, then the predictability of the belief system may not be challenged and the stereotypes can remain unchanged. Somewhat similar arguments have been made by Eagly (1983; Eagly & Steffen, 1984), who uses a social role analysis to interpret variations in the perceptions of male and female behavior. For example, to the extent that women occupy lower-status positions in the society, it is not unreasonable to assume that they will on the average be more easily influenced than will high-status occupants (such as males). Similarly, women defined as home-makers are perceived to be more easily influenced than employed women (Eagly & Steffen, 1984). As long as women and men continue to be found disproportionately in some roles and not in others, beliefs consistent with those distributional patterns can be maintained.

CONCLUDING THOUGHTS

Consideration of the gender belief system—that complex set of attitudes and thoughts about women and men—is a definite shift in focus from earlier work that considered men and women as subjects only. Rather than assume all differences to be real, only awaiting the calibration of the social scientist, we now look to the observer as more than a passive receptor. In treating men and women as the objects of perception, we are suggesting that these beliefs may have a reality and an influence of their own. It would be a mistake, however, to conclude that all cards are in the observer's deck. Although we have in this chapter emphasized the eye of the beholder as a corrective to earlier endeavors, we at the same time stress the importance of context and of the social interaction process. Such contextual approaches to gender are essential, we believe, and are being advocated by scholars in a variety of disciplines (see, e.g., Gerson & Peiss, 1985). Gender is not static but flexible, and its meaning becomes clear in the beliefs that people hold and in the context of social interaction, where those beliefs are manifested, rather than in any inherent qualities of the male or female.

NOTES

1. The distinction between the terms "sex" and "gender" used in this chapter is similar to that offered by Gailey in Chapter 1 of this volume. In line with an earlier discussion of this point (Deaux, 1985), sex refers to the biologically based categories of male and female. Gender refers to the psychological characteristics associated with men and women or, more broadly, to the social construction of these categories.

2. The racism in the statement is evident. Not surprisingly, investigations of possible intelligence deficits in blacks and in women show a number of parallels. In the case of blacks, however, assumptions of general intellectual inferiority have proved more durable than they have with regard to women.

3. Rosenberg (1982) presents a highly informative account of these pioneer investigators, their research, and the reception that their work received.

4. Morawski (1985) presents a more extensive analysis of this early work, showing how it laid the foundation for the conceptualization of masculinity and femininity.

5. See Lewin (1984) and Morawski (1985) for more extended discussion of the development of these measures.

6. Gordon Allport (1954) recognized the importance of physical appearance to racial prejudice. "Visibility and identifiability aid categorization" (1954: 127), he stated, arguing that categorization is often based on ethnicity specifically because members of ethnic groups tend to share identifiable physical characteristics, such as skin color or facial features.

7. It is interesting to note that sexual orientation was an integral part of early conceptions of M-F but was abandoned in the more recent work on androgyny and related scales of so-called masculinity and femininity (see Morawski, 1985).

8. See Spence et al. (1985) for a more thorough review of this literature.

9. Deaux and Major (1987) have developed a process-based model of gender that incorporates perceiver expectancies, self-presentation concerns, and situational influences. The processes discussed in this section are developed much more thoroughly in that paper.

10. See McArthur (1982) for an excellent discussion of the importance of physical characteristics in the social judgment process.

11. Individuals can obviously take advantage of this situation, altering their dress and appearance to make a particular set of beliefs salient to the perceiver. Recommendations to "dress for success," for example, emphasize the importance of a particular wardrobe for eliciting a particular set of beliefs. In such cases, however, the elicited category (e.g., businesswoman) may still contain beliefs detrimental to the success of the individual.

12. Deaux and Major (1987) present a more detailed analysis of these moderating conditions, which include the social desirability and the saliency of the conveyed expectancy, the strength of the individual's self-presentation concerns, and the strength of situational pressures.

REFERENCES

AJZEN, I. (1982) "On behaving in accordance with one's attitude," in M. P. Zanna et al. (eds.) Consistency in Social Behavior: The Ontario Symposium, Vol. 2. Hillsdale, NJ: Lawrence Erlbaum.

AJZEN, I. and M. FISHBEIN (1977) "Attitude-behavior relations: A theoretical analysis and review of empirical research." Psychological Bulletin 84: 888-918.

ALLPORT, G. W. (1954) The Nature of Prejudice. New York: Addison-Wesley.

ASHMORE, R. D. and F. K. DEL BOCA (1979) "Sex stereotypes and implicit personality theory: Toward a cognitive-social psychological conception." Sex Roles 5: 219-248.

ASHMORE, R. D. and F. K. DEL BOCA (1983) "Pictures of women and men: Where's the sex and violence?" Presented at the Society of Experimental Social Psychology, Pittsburgh, October.

ASHMORE, R. D., F. K. DEL BOCA, and D. TITUS (1984) "Types of women and men: Yours, mine, and ours." Presented at American Psychological Association meeting, Toronto.

BELLE, D. (1985) "Ironies in the contemporary study of gender." Journal of Personality 53: 400-405.

BEM, S. L. (1974) "The measurement of psychological androgyny." Journal of Consulting and Clinical Psychology 42: 155-162.

BEM, S. L. (1981) "Gender schema theory: A cognitive account of sex-typing." Psychological Review 88: 254-364.

BEM, S. L. (1985) "Androgyny and gender schema theory: A conceptual and empirical integration." In T. B. Sondregger (ed.), Nebraska Symposium on Motivation: Psychology and Gender, 1984. Lincoln: University of Nebraska Press.

BENBOW, C. P. and J. C. STANLEY (1983) "Sex differences in mathematical reasoning: More facts." Science 222: 1029-1031.

BROUGHTON, J. M. (1983). "Women's rationality and men's virtues: A critique of gender dualism in Gilligan's theory of moral development." Social Research 50: 597-642.

BROVERMAN, I. K., S. R. VOGEL, D. M. BROVERMAN, F. E. CLARKSON, and P. S. ROSENKRANTZ (1972) "Sex-role stereotypes: A current appraisal." Journal of Social Issues 28, 2: 59-78.

CLIFTON, A. K., D. MCGRATH, and WICK (1976) 'Stereotypes of women: A single category?" Sex Roles 2: 135-148.

CONSTANTINOPLE, A. (1973) "Masculinity-femininity: An exception to a famous dictum?" Psychological Bulletin 80: 389-407.

DARLEY, J. M. and R. H. FAZIO (1980) "Expectancy confirmation processes arising in the social interaction sequence." American Psychologist 35: 867-881.

DARLEY, J. M. and P. H. GROSS (1983) "A hypothesis-confirming bias in labeling effects." Journal of Personality and Social Psychology 44: 20-33.

DEAUX, K. (1984) "From individual differences to social categories: Analysis of a decade's research on gender." American Psychologist 39: 105-116.

DEAUX, K. (1985) "Sex and gender." Annual Review of Psychology 36: 49-81.

DEAUX, K., M. E. KITE, and L. L. LEWIS (1985) "Clustering and gender schemata: An uncertain link." Personality and Social Psychology Bulletin 11: 387-397.

DEAUX, K. and L. L. LEWIS (1983) "Components of gender stereotypes." Psychological Documents 13: 25 (Cat. #2583).

DEAUX, K. and L. L. LEWIS (1984) "The structure of gender stereotypes: Interrelationships among components and gender label." Journal of Personality and Social Psychology 46: 991-1004.

DEAUX, K. and B. MAJOR (1987) "Putting gender into context: An interactive model of gender-related behavior." Psychological Review 94: 369-389.

DEAUX, K., W. WINTON, M. CROWLEY, and L. L. LEWIS (1985) "Level of categorization and content of gender stereotypes." Social Cognition 3: 145-167.

EAGLY, A. H. (1983) "Gender and social influence: A social psychological analysis." American Psychologist 38: 971-981.

EAGLY, A. H. (1987) Sex Differences in Social Behavior: A Social-Role Analysis. Hillsdale, NJ: Lawrence Erlbaum.

EAGLY, A. H. and L. L. CARLI (1981) "Sex of researchers and sex-typed communications as determinants of sex differences in influenceability: A meta-analysis of social influence studies." Psychological Bulletin 90: 1-20.

EAGLY, A. H. and M. C. CROWLEY (1986) "Gender and helping behavior: a meta-analytic review of the social psychological literature." Psychological Bulletin, 100: 283-308.

EAGLY, A. H. and M. E. KITE (1987) "Are stereotypes of nationalities applied to both women and men?" Journal of Personality and Social Psychology, 53: 451-462.

EAGLY, A. H. and V. J. STEFFEN (1984) "Gender stereotypes stem from the distribution of women and men into social roles." Journal of Personality and Social Psychology 46: 735-754.

EAGLY, A. H. and V. J. STEFFEN (1986) "Gender and aggressive behavior: A meta-analytic review of the social psychological literature." Psychological Bulletin, 100: 309-330.

EDWARDS, V. and J. T. SPENCE (1985) "Gender-related traits, stereotypes, and schemas." Manuscript in preparation.

EPSTEIN, S. (1979) "The stability of behavior: II Implications for psychological research." American Psychologist 35: 790-806.

EPSTEIN, S. (1983) "Aggregation and beyond: Some basic issues on the prediction of behavior." Journal of Personality 51: 360-392.

FERNBERGER, S. W. (1948) "Persistence of stereotypes concerning sex differences." Journal of Abnormal and Social Psychology 43: 97-101.

FISHBEIN, M. and I. AJZEN (1974) "Attitudes towards objects as predictors of single and multiple behavioral criteria." Psychological Review 81: 59-74.

FISKE, S. T. and S. E. TAYLOR (1984) Social Cognition. Reading, MA: Addison-Wesley.

FOUSHEE, H. C., R. L. HELMREICH, and J. T. SPENCE (1979) "Implicit theories of masculinity and femininity: Dualistic or bipolar?" Psychology of Women Quarterly 3: 259-269.

GARLAND, H. and H. K. PRICE (1977) "Attitudes toward women in management and attributions for their success and failure in a managerial position." Journal of Applied Psychology 62: 29-33.

GERSON, J. M. and K. PEISS (1985) "Boundaries, negotiations, consciousness: Reconceptualizing gender relations." Social Problems 32: 317-331.

GILLIGAN, C. (1982) In a Different Voice. Cambridge, MA: Harvard University Press.

GOULD, S. J. (1980) The Panda's Thumb. New York: Norton.

GRANT, P. R. and J. G. HOLMES (1981) "The integration of implicit personality theory schemas and stereotype images." Social Psychology Quarterly 44: 107-115.

HALL, J. (1978) "Gender effects in decoding non-verbal cues." Psychological Bulletin 85: 845-875.

HALL, J. (1984) Nonverbal Sex Differences: Communication, Accuracy and Expressive Style. Baltimore, MD: Johns Hopkins Press.

HAMILTON, D. L. (1981) Stereotyping and intergroup behavior: Some thoughts on the cognitive approach, in D. L. Hamilton (ed.) Cognitive Processes in Stereotyping and Intergroup Behavior. Hillsdale, NJ: Lawrence Erlbaum.

HARRIS, M. J. and R. ROSENTHAL (1985) Mediation of interpersonal expectancy effects: 31 meta-analyses. Psychological Bulletin 97: 363-386.

HOLLAND, D. and D. DAVIDSON (1983) "Labeling the opposite sex: Metaphors and themes in American folk models of gender." Paper prepared for conference on folk models, Institute for Advanced Study, Princeton University, May.

HOLLINGWORTH, L. S. (1918) "Comparison of the sexes in mental traits." Psychological Bulletin 15: 427-432.

HORNER, M. S. (1972) "Toward an understanding of achievement-related conflicts in women." Journal of Social Issues 28, 2: 151-175.

HYDE, J. S. (1981) "How large are cognitive gender differences? A meta-analysis using ω^2 and d." American Psychologist 36: 892-901.

HYDE, J. S. (1984) "How large are gender differences in aggression? A developmental meta-analysis." Developmental Psychology 20: 722-736.

KANTER, R. M. (1977) Men and Women of the Corporation. New York: Basic Books.

KATZ, D. and K. W. BRALY (1933) "Racial stereotypes of one hundred college students." Journal of Abnormal and Social Psychology 28: 280-290.

KESSLER, S. J. and W. McKENNA (1978) Gender: An Ethnomethodological Approach. New York: John Wiley.

KITE, M. E. and K. DEAUX (1986) "Attitudes toward homosexuality: Assessment and behavioral consequences." Basic and Applied Social Psychology, 7: 137-162.

KITE, M. E. and K. DEAUX (1987) "Gender belief systems: Homosexuality and implicit inversion theory." Psychology of Women Quarterly 11: 83-96.

LEWIN, M. (1984) "'Rather worse that folly?' Psychology measures femininity and masculinity, 1: From Terman and Miles to the Guilfords," in M. Lewin (ed.) In the Shadow of the Past: Psychology Portrays the Sexes. New York: Columbia University Press.

LEWIS, L. L. (1985) "The influence of individual differences in gender stereotyping on the interpersonal expectancy process." Unpublished Ph.D. dissertation, Purdue University.

LINGLE, J. H., M. W. ALTOM, and D. L. MEDIN (1984) "Of cabbages and kings: Assessing the extendibility of natural object concept models to social things," in R. S. Wyer and T. K. Srull (eds.) Handbook of Social Cognition, Vol. 1. Hillsdale, NJ: Lawrence Erlbaum.

LINN, M. C. and A. C. PETERSON (1985) "Emergence and characterization of sex differences in spatial ability: A meta-analysis." Child Development 56: 1479-1498.

LIPPMANN, W. (1922) Public Opinion. New York: Harcourt, Brace.

LOCKSLEY, A., E. BORGIDA, N. BREKKE, and C. HEPBURN (1980) "Sex stereotypes and social judgment." Journal of Personality and Social Psychology 39: 821-831.

LOCKSLEY, A., C. HEPBURN, and V. ORTIZ (1982) "On the effect of social stereotypes on judgments of individuals: A comment on Grant and Holmes's 'The integration of implicit personality theory schemas and stereotypic images.'" Social Psychology Quarterly 45: 270-273.

MacCOBY, E. E. and C. N. JACKLIN (1974) The Psychology of Sex Differences. Stanford, CA: Stanford University Press.

McARTHUR, L. Z. (1981) "What grabs you? The role of attention in impression formation and causal attribution," in E. T. Higgens et al. (eds.) Social Cognition: The Ontario Symposium, Vol. 1. Hillsdale, NJ: Lawrence Erlbaum.

McARTHUR, L. Z. (1982) "Judging a book by its cover: A cognitive analysis of the relationship between physical appearance and stereotyping," in A. H. Hastorf and A. M. Isen (eds.) Cognitive Social Psychology. New York: Elsevier.

McARTHUR, L. Z. and D. L. POST (1977) "Figural emphasis and person perception." Journal of Personal and Social Psychology 13: 520-535.

McARTHUR, L. Z. and L. K. SOLOMON (1978) "Perceptions of an aggressive encounter as a function of the victim's salience and the perceiver's arousal." Journal of Personality and Social Psychology 36: 1278-1290.

McKEE, J. P. and A. C. SHERIFFS (1957) "The differential evaluation of males and females." Journal of Personality 25: 356-371.

MERTON, R. K. (1948) "The self-fulfilling prophecy." Antioch Review 8: 193-210.

MILLS, C. J. and D. J. TYRELL (1983) "Sex stereotypic encoding and release from proactive interference." Journal of Personality and Social Psychology 45: 772-781.

MOORE, H. T. (1922) "Further data concerning sex differences." Journal of Abnormal and Social Psychology 17: 210-214.

MORAWSKI, J. G. (1985) "The measurement of masculinity and femininity: Engendering categorical realities." Journal of Personality.

NOSEWORTHY, C. M. and A. J. LOTT (1984) "The cognitive organization of gender-stereotypic categories." Personality and Social Psychology Bulletin 10: 474-481.

PETERS, L. H., J. R. TERBORG, and J. TAYNOR (1974) "Women as managers scale: A measure of attitudes toward women in management positions." JSAS Catalog of Selected Documents in Psychology 4: 27.

ROBINSON, E. A. and D. R. FOLLINGSTAD (1985) "Development and validation of a behavioral sex-role inventory." Sex Roles 13: 691-713.

ROSCH, E. (1978) "Principles of categorization," in E. Rosch and B. B. Lloyd (eds.) Cognition and Categorization. Hillsdale, NJ: Lawrence Erlbaum.

ROSENBERG, R. (1982) Beyond Separate Spheres: Intellectual Roots of Modern Feminism. New Haven, CT: Yale University Press.

ROSENKRANTZ, P., S. VOGEL, H. BEE, I. BROVERMAN, and D. M. BROVERMAN (1968) "Sex-role stereotypes and self-concepts in college students." Journal of Consulting and Clinical Psychology 32: 286-295.

ROSENTHAL, R. and L. JACOBSON (1968) Pygmalion in the Classroom. New York: Holt, Rinehart & Winston.

ROTHBART, M. and O. P. JOHN (1985) "Social categorization and behavioral episodes: A cognitive analysis of the effects of intergroup contact." Journal of Social Issues 41: 81-104.

SKRYPNEK, B. J. and M. SNYDER (1982) "On the self-perpetuating nature of stereotypes about women and men." Journal of Experimental Social Psychology 18: 277-291.

SHERIF, C. W. (1982) "Needed concepts in the study of gender identity." Psychology of Women Quarterly 6: 375-398.

SHERIFFS, A. C. and J. P. MCKEE (1957) "Qualitative aspects of beliefs about men and women." Journal of Personality 25: 451-464.

SHIELDS, S. A. (1975) Functionalism, Darwinism, and the psychology of women: A study in social myth." American Psychologist 30: 739-754.

SHIELDS, S. A. (1982) "A variability hypothesis: The history of a biological model of sex differences in intelligence." Signs 7: 769-797.

SMETANA, J. G. (1984) "Morality and gender: A commentary on Pratt, Golding, and Hunter." Merrill-Palmer Quarterly 30: 341-348.

SMITH, E. R., M. M. FERREE, and F. D. MILLER (1975) "A short scale of attitudes toward feminism." Representative Research in Social Psychology 6: 51-58.

SNYDER, M., E. D. TANKE, and E. BERSCHEID (1977) "Social perception and interpersonal behavior: On the self-fulfilling nature of social stereotypes." Journal of Personality and Social Psychology 35: 656-666.

SPENCE, J. T. (1984) "Masculinity, femininity, and gender-related traits: A conceptual analysis and critique of current research." Progress in Experimental Personality Research 13: 1-97.

SPENCE, J. T. (1985) "Gender identity and its implications for concepts of masculinity and femininity," in T. Sondregger (ed.), Nebraska Symposium on Motivation: Psychology and Gender. Lincoln: University of Nebraska Press.

SPENCE, J. T., K. DEAUX, and R. L. HELMREICH (1985) "Sex roles in contemporary American society," in G. Lindzey and E. Aronson (eds.) Handbook of Social Psychology. New York: Random House.

SPENCE, J. T. and R. HELMREICH (1972) "The Attitudes toward Women Scale: An objective instrument to measure attitudes toward the rights and roles of women in contemporary society." JSAS Catalog of Selected Documents in Psychology 2: 66.

SPENCE, J. T. and R. L. HELMREICH (1978) Masculinity and Femininity: Their Psychological Dimensions, Correlates, and Antecedents. Austin: University of Texas Press.

SPENCE, J. T., R. HELMREICH, and J. STAPP (1973) "A short version of the Attitudes toward Women Scale (AWS)." Bulletin of the Psychonomic Society 2: 219-220.

SPENCE, J. T., R. L. HELMREICH, and J. STAPP (1974) "The personal attributes questionnaire: A measure of sex-role stereotypes and masculinity/femininity." JSAS Catalog of Selected Documents in Psychology 4: 43.

STORMS, M. D. (1978a) "Attitudes toward homosexuality and femininity in men." Journal of Homosexuality 3: 257-263.

STORMS, M. D. (1978b) "Sexual orientation and self-perception," in P. Pliner et al. (eds.) Advances in the Study of Communication and Affect, Vol. 5: Perception of Emotion in Self and Others. New York: Plenum.

TAYLOR, M. C. and J. A. HALL (1982) "Psychological androgyny: Theories, methods, and conclusions." Psychological Bulletin 92: 347-366.

TAYLOR, S. E. (1981) "A categorization approach to stereotyping," in D. L. Hamilton (ed.) Cognitive Processes in Stereotyping and Intergroup Behavior. Hillsdale, NJ: Lawrence Erlbaum.

TAYLOR, S. E., J. CROCKER, S. T. FISKE, M. SPRINZEN, and J. D. WINKLER (1979) "The generalizability of salience effects." Journal of Personality and Social Psychology 37: 357-368.

TAYLOR, S. E. and S. T. FISKE (1978) "Salience, attention and attribution: Top of the head phenomena." Advances in Experimental Social Psychology 11: 249-288.

TAYLOR, S. E., S. T. FISKE, N. L. ETCOFF, and A. J. RIDERMAN (1978) "The categorical and contextual bases of person memory and stereotyping." Journal of Personality and Social Psychology 36: 778-793.

TERMAN, L. M. and C. C. MILES (1936) Sex and Personality: Studies in Masculinity and Femininity. New York: McGraw-Hill.

ULLMAN, L. (1976) Changing. New York: Knopf.

UNGER, R. K. (1983) "Through the looking glass: No wonderland yet! The reciprocal relationship between methodology and models of reality." Psychology of Women Quarterly 8: 9-32.

VON BAEYER, C. L., D. L. SHERK, and M. P. ZANNA (1981) "Impression management in the job interview: When the female applicant meets the male (chauvinist) interviewer." Personality and Social Psychology Bulletin 7: 45-51.

WALKER, L. J. (1984) "Sex differences in the development of moral reasoning: A critical review." Child Development 55: 677-691.

WEBER, R. and J. CROCKER (1983) "Cognitive processes in the revision of stereotypic beliefs." Journal of Personality and Social Psychology 45: 961-977.

WILLIAMS, J. E. and D. L. BEST (1982) Measuring Sex Stereotypes: A Thirty-Nation Study. Newbury Park, CA: Sage.

WOOLLEY, H. T. (1910) "A review of the recent literature on the psychology of sex." Psychological Bulletin 7: 335-342.

ZANNA, M. P. and S. J. PACK (1975) "On the self-fulfilling nature of apparent sex differences in behavior." Journal of Experimental Social Psychology 11: 583-591.

II

SOCIAL CONTROL
OF FEMALE SEXUALITY

4 Female Sexuality: Looking Back Into the Future

BETH E. SCHNEIDER
University of California, Santa Barbara

MEREDITH GOULD
Rutgers University-Camden College

T HE study of sexuality[1] is one area of sociological inquiry that is only now being recast in feminist terms. While feminist activists and theorists have recognized and written about the role of sexuality in constructing, organizing, maintaining, and occasionally challenging the social arrangements of women's lives (e.g., Vance, 1984; Snitow et al., 1983; MacKinnon, 1979; Rich, 1980), many of these insights are just beginning to affect the directions of research and theoretical development in the sociology of sexuality.

The sociology of sexuality is today where the sociology of gender was in the mid-1970s. For example, 10 years ago, one influential anthology whose purpose was the documentation of the exclusion of women from sociology and its subsequent distortion of knowledge (Millman and Kanter, 1975), contained no sustained and coherent analysis of this subfield; rarely were sexuality and sexual relationships even mentioned. This startling omission speaks eloquently to the devaluation of the substantive content of the field itself.

Problems of Studying Sexuality

The topic of sexuality is professionally taboo. Sociological researchers studying sexuality face several formidable obstacles. First, despite the profusion of talk about sexuality, its heightened cultural importance, and a popular literature whose emphasis is the encouragement of more and "better" sexual relations, sexuality itself still carries a heavy burden of moralistic, naturalistic, and mythical components that limits its study and stigmatizes its students. British sociologist Kenneth Plummer (1975) has observed that "while in other areas of life, the search for understanding through research is seen as a *sine qua non* of progress, in sexual matters it is decried as irrelevant, dehumanizing and pernicious" (1975: 5). Hence, relative to other fields there are startlingly few sociologists of sexuality, even fewer female sociologists of sexuality. And the research enterprise is hindered by monumental impediments, not the least of which is others' tendency to devalue, ignore, or deny the importance of the research.

Second, firmly entrenched cultural and sociological understandings presuppose that legitimate sexuality occurs only in the private world and not in the public. This tendency to equate sexuality with the intimate world results in the imposition of psychological and social-psychological rather than sociological models on individual behavior and the automatic but untested assumption that all sexual relations enacted in public settings are deviant. The result has been a tendency to cede the study of sexuality to social-psychologists and the entrapment of this area between two competing frameworks: the sociology of deviance, and the sociology of marriage and the family. Consequently, distinct types of sexual expression are consigned to different (and noncommunicating) substantive fields so that a theoretical and methodological wedge is driven between those sexualities understood as culturally normative and those that are not.

Third, funding sources set the context within which research on sexuality proceeds. What is problematic to funders draws wide, but not unlimited, parameters around what will be problematic to the funded researcher. This affects the direction of the field for the nonfunded as well, through the influence of what *is* funded. Since Alfred Kinsey in the 1940s, there has been virtually no significant foundation or grant support for research directly on sexual expression or relations. Some exceptions to the general rule, such as funding in the area of adolescent heterosexual activity by the Department of Health and Human Services and in the area of sexual violence by the Department of Justice and the National Institutes of Mental Health, speak to a social problems orientation rather than one that focuses on the vast array of sexual expression in everyday life. Since the 1960s, several large-scale studies of sexual behavior and sexual attitudes have been financed by commercial magazines such as *Playboy, Cosmopolitan,* and *Redbook,* whose motivation surely is profit and reader service rather than an increase in knowledge. Our desire is not to discredit this work. Much of it has extended our understanding of the frequency and types of sexual behaviors engaged in by certain selected populations. Nevertheless, funding priorities limit the range of researchable topics and constitute formidable professional roadblocks to the entry of new scholars.

In addition we believe that feminist thinking about sexuality has itself *unintentionally* posed intellectual dilemmas for sociologists who might have been interested in pursuing its crucial insights. Feminist concerns with sexuality have taken several contradictory twists and turns in the last 15 years. The early analyses of sexuality, fueled by the excitement and necessary struggle of asserting first feminist truths, were themselves contradictory. There was an urgent rhetorical insistence that women control their own bodies and be equal to men in their heterosexual sexual activity. At the same time, the talk of women in consciousness-raising groups emphasized the problems but not the pleasures of satisfactory heterosexual sex (see Shulman, 1980; Snitow et al., 1983, for lengthy descriptions of the content of these initial conversations about sexuality). In the face of these critiques it was not long before lesbianism was reclaimed as a significant social category. Lesbian relationships and lesbian sexuality were proferred as positive alternatives for women who would thereby free themselves from oppressive heterosexual relationships. This path, fueled as it was by the growing influence of both the women's and gay liberation movement, did result in research on lesbians' behavior, identity, and community. A significant portion of this research was, for the first time, undertaken by female scholars. Only a few, however, were sociologists.

Increasingly this feminist dialogue about the dangers of heterosexual relations called attention to the multitude of ways in which violence is perpetrated against women (Brownmiller, 1975; Griffin, 1979; Sheffield, Chapter 6 in this volume) and to the institutional nature of heterosexuality and the social practices that make it compulsory (Rich, 1980; Bunch, 1975). Coupled with the valorization of lesbians, this focus on violence cast male and female sexuality as opposites: aggressive, hostile, violent, and domineering versus nurturant, tender, caring, and mutual. The result, in terms of research, was a wide-ranging and crucially important proliferation of studies about rape (including that within marriage), sexual harassment, child sexual assault, and wife battering (Russell, 1984; MacKinnon, 1979; Herman, 1981). Again this research was accomplished for the most part by researchers who do not identify themselves as sociologists of sexuality.

A predictable kind of disjuncture occurred from this emphasis on the dangers of heterosexuality. Feminists were less than willing to openly concede enjoyment in heterosexual relations since doing so would admit to pleasure where only violence and domination were understood to reside. Second, significant insights about the social construction of gender and gender domination became conflated with the social construction of sexuality and sexual domination, leaving the stark impression that sexuality and violence were necessarily related and that sexual pleasure in heterosexual relations was not possible. Though it is difficult to demonstrate conclusively that this perspective directly affected research within the sociology of sexuality, it did make feminist scholars unusually reticent about challenging this equation.

In the last few years sexuality has reemerged as a topic of intense debate in feminist circles. Pornography, sadomasochism, and the meaning of sexual liberation for women are the focus of heated discussion and passionate polemics. With an emphasis on efforts to define and explore their own sexualities, women are cast as subjects of their own desires, not simply as objects of male desire.

In sum, the development of a sociology of sexuality has been impeded by its status as a taboo object of inquiry, poor funding prospects, the language of psychology and deviance, and a proliferation of feminist thought tending to emphasize domination and victimization rather than empowerment and pleasure. Theorizing about sexuality within sociology lags behind empirical research, which is itself scanty.

A Feminist Perspective on Sexuality

Nevertheless, the field has changed in the last decade as increasing numbers of new sociologists embark on studies of adolescent sexuality, extramarital relations, and homosexuality. In addition, provocative insights about sexuality have emerged from sociological researchers whose primary focus is not exclusively sexuality (Luker, 1984; Rubin, 1976), and the field has been affected by significant contributions from scholars outside sociology, particularly anthropologists and historians. Because feminist scholarship in history has been more readily and decisively incorporated into the historical tradition than is the case of sociology (Stacey and Thorne, 1985), research on the *history* of sexuality offers more feminist insights than the sociology of sexuality despite the fact that historical materials are often uneven, more prescriptive than behavioral, and markedly limited by racial and class constraints in their substantive content.

The sociology of sexuality is concerned with the study of sexual attitudes and behavior, the contexts in which these occur, and the social organization of sexual relations at the individual, community, and societal level. By the very nature of the subject matter and the necessary reliance on research by scholars from other disciplines, this field is strongly interdisciplinary. Still, there are areas of consensus among sociologists researching and writing about human sexuality. Although their conceptual language varies, these scholars agree that sexuality is a social phenomenon, an activity charged with social meaning. Social actors possess genitals rather than the other way around. Sexual arrangements are constructed. Sexual behaviors are enacted. Blueprints for construction and scripts for enactment are culturally and historically contingent rather than constant. Biological factors are, more often than not, considered secondary to culture and history, although the body, through which sexual sensation is experienced, *is* acknowledged more than in other sociological fields. Human sexuality cannot be derived from the sexual experiences of animals, though each of us is "born into a state of sexual multipotentiality," that is, a capacity for sexual arousal in response to a varied range of stimuli. Our anatomical structure and hormonal inheritance enhance and constrain what we can and cannot do sexually (Goode and Troiden, 1974). Nevertheless, even evolutionary theory can be used to argue that "the culturization of sex, the social production and reproduction of our sexual beings, is precisely that which is 'natural' about human sexuality" (Caulfield, 1985: 356).

At this historical juncture more can be said about the *potential* impact of feminism on the field than about its actual influence, but its effect is beginning to be evidenced in four related theoretical concerns. First is the recognition among feminist scholars that social reality is a gendered construction. Virtually all data are transformed by attending to the social construction of gender because the imputation of particular meanings to the biological status of maleness and femaleness shapes all other social arrangements, including sexual ones. Until recently, the relationship between gender and sexuality had not been systematically explored either by sociologists studying gender or those studying sexuality, leaving it surprisingly unexamined despite its importance (Allegier and McCormick, 1983; Gould, 1983; Miller and Fowlkes, 1980; Vance, 1984). Unraveling and exposing the ways in which gender has been enlisted to construct female sexuality is becoming an important project for sociologists who have already demonstrated the social as opposed to "natural" character of other institutions. One such effort is evident in Millman's (1980) gendered analysis of the association of female obesity with asexuality.

Second, sexuality and gender are deeply intertwined but not identical. Some feminists conflate sexuality and gender to assert that "sexuality is that social process which creates, organizes, expresses and directs desire" (MacKinnon, 1982: 517). Sexuality, like gender, is socially constructed and historically contingent. Shifts in gender organization are bound up with shifts in sexual meanings and taboos. However, while changing definitions of female sexuality may well reflect these shifts, legitimate questions need to be addressed to the ways in which sexuality and gender are *not* intertwined. Rubin (1984: 307) argues, "Feminism is the theory of gender oppression. To automatically assume that this makes it the theory of sexual oppression is to fail to distinguish between gender, on the one hand, and erotic desire, on the other."

Careful attention to the ways in which the suppression of female sexuality has occurred, as well as to those ways in which women resist and rebel against that oppression in their everyday lives, is required to explicate the connections and disjunctures between the experience of sexual victimization and sexual empowerment. So too, careful reflection is needed about the ways in which women, especially lesbians and other sexual minorities, are specifically oppressed sexually, rather than simply asserting that their oppression is directly derived from gender domination.

Flowing from these points comes a third: Feminist work on female sexuality attends to the political dimensions of sexual intimacy. For sociologists, the study of female sexuality offers an opportunity to examine a special type of power. Studying the distribution of power in erotic activity is another way of studying gender inequality, one that requires asking different questions about the construction of sexual meaning. Where does meaning come from? Do women have the power to define sexual vocabularies and to create their own meaning? At another level of analysis, questions abound about the politics of sexual expression: When is sexual activity repressed, by whom, and for what ends?

Finally, much of the current material on female sexuality can be located within the growing tradition of feminist scholarship that reflects a disenchantment with positivism and argues that distinctions between theory and method are suspect (see Bowles and Duelli-Klein, 1983, and Stanley and Wise, 1983, for examples of this feminist critique). Theory and method do more than inform one another; they construct one another. Data collection as well as the analytic apparatus for explaining data depend on understanding the sex/gender system. Knowing the meaning of gender as it is constituted in social arrangements—or, more fundamentally, knowing that gender *is* constituted in social arrangements—has an impact on the way such arrangements are perceived (Smith, 1979a; Roberts, 1981). Increasingly, methodological strategies for studying female sexuality are being developed from what women actually say (Krieger, 1983) and subsequent theorizing reflects this.

We bring these four basic feminist insights to a review of the traditional field of the sociology of sexuality, highlighting problems ignored in that work or the puzzles it poses for subsequent research on female sexuality. We focus on current scholarship by sociologists and nonsociologists alike to address three important questions: How is sexual identity constructed? Do women have vocabularies of desire sufficient to explicate their own experiences? How, if at all, has female sexual behavior been changing? For each question we have chosen to highlight articles and monographs that have either created current issues for debate about female sexuality or that portend future developments in this area.

THE TRADITIONAL FIELD:
OMISSIONS AND DISTORTIONS

The sociology of sexuality has several distinct literatures: "sexual bookkeeping" (Gagnon, 1984: 12), survey research, theoretical, and ethnographic. Female sexuality has been either ignored, or, more often, distorted in each of these published literatures. Once noted, it is perhaps patently obvious that because so much of what we culturally assume is the heterosexuality of erotic expression, which necessarily includes women, women's presence cannot be ignored in the research on sexuality. Instead, we argue, female sexuality has been distorted. These distortions rather than the omissions of female experience are emphasized in our review.

Sexual Bookkeeping

The sociology of sexuality as it is currently constituted has been shaped primarily by a longstanding tradition of empirical research in the United States conducted, for the most part, by nonsociologists. Although there were a few researchers before him, Alfred Kinsey is considered the father of this empirical tradition. Almost 40 years ago, Kinsey and his associates emphasized the salience of social indicators for explaining sexual behavior (Kinsey et al., 1948: Kinsey et al., 1953).

Kinsey's focus was on what people do, not what they think, believe, or feel. He found that females' sexual behavior was more uniform than that of males. Women were consistently less sexually responsive and showed lower frequencies of orgasm than men, a fact attributed to the latter's greater "psychologic conditionability" (1953: 684). Kinsey's focus on orgasmic outcomes from whatever erotic source betrayed an insidious double standard, despite his generally tolerant views regarding whatever people do sexually, including homosexuality. Female sexuality, including female orgasm, was understood as being in the service of greater male satisfaction, both psychological and sexual (see Miller and Fowlkes, 1980). Despite his failure to explore the social and gendered context in which sexual relations are enacted, Kinsey's impact on the field cannot be overstated. All too frequently his 1940s interviews are still cited as evidence today.

Much of Kinsey's analysis of women's unresponsiveness and derivative sexuality was rendered obsolete during the 1960s by Masters and Johnson's research on the physiologic dimensions of sexual response (Masters and Johnson, 1966). Their work had a formidable impact on the study of female sexuality. First, their laboratory results demonstrated conclusively that women have the same or greater orgasmic capacity as men and that the site of physiological sexual response is the clitoris. Second, they argued that the kind of sexual attention women receive is important to the accomplishment of female pleasure. Yet while completely overturning mythologies about women's "diminished sexual capacities" and also implying that women had a right to sexual pleasure, Masters and Johnson staunchly defend conventional heterosexual relations and sexual intercourse, raising the achievement of coital orgasm to the highest and most meaningful level of sexual activity.

In the decades since Kinsey's research, several large-scale studies of sexual behavior were published, accessible to a lay as well as scholarly audience (Bell and Weinberg, 1978; Hite, 1976, 1981; Hunt, 1974; Sarrel and Sarrel, 1980; Tavris and Sadd, 1977). There were also several important studies aimed exclusively at professionals (Kantner and Zelnick, 1972, 1977). Much of this work has been criticized on methodological grounds since these studies utilize large samples of volunteers, usually readers of magazines such as *Playboy*,

Redbook, and *Cosmopolitan.* The self-selected nature of these samples and the bias of "convenience" samples such as undergraduate students necessitates considerable caution in generalizing from their findings (Delamater, 1981).

Nevertheless, most sociologists have relied on this research tradition. In its own terms, the "sexual bookkeeping" approach clarifies the base line behavioral experience of women and men. From it, we are cautiously able to demonstrate changes in sexual practices among adolescents and adults, both within and outside the marital context.

Survey Research

The survey research tradition is often empirical at the expense of theory. These studies are "profuse in nuance" (Keller, 1985) but limited in theoretically sound explanations of the behaviors being so carefully counted. For example, both Hunt (1974) and Petersen et al. (1983) found higher reported frequencies of oral sex among heterosexuals than had Kinsey. Each attributes this change to the impact of sexual reform in the last two decades; yet little is known from these accounts about the actual experience of persons engaging in these activities. What they think about what they are doing and why, and how these practices have been incorporated into their sexual repertoires? From these accounts alone we know little about whether women and men experience oral sex similarly, though Rubin's (1976) examination of the lives of working-class marital partners beautifully illustrates how markedly different are the motivations for participation of females and their partners.

A strong androcentric bias in empirical research design has limited our knowledge of female sexuality even in studies that include women. For example, Bell and Weinberg (1978) recruited their samples of lesbians and male homosexuals primarily from sources in which men are more likely to be found (bars, baths, public places) and their resulting male sample is more than twice as large as their female one, thus perpetuating the view of lesbians as a homogeneous group. While their recruitment of greater numbers of male respondents is partially explained by the interests of their funding source, Bell and Weinberg also assume the problems of adaptation of male homosexuals are greater than those of lesbians because of their greater numbers, visibility, and more open engagement in the gay (male-defined) world (1978: 29-34). This assumption is subject to direct empirical investigation, since it may well be that lesbian invisibility is itself a source of significant difficulty.

This research tradition can be improved in several distinct ways. In his review of the literature on the social control of heterosexual activity, Delamater calls for a "general conceptualization of the sociological determinants of sexual expression" (1981: 287) to remedy the lack of integration among studies about various forms of sexual expression. Premarital, marital, and extramarital aspects of heterosexual sexuality are studied by different researchers, often without recognition of developmental links between stages of the life cycle and often without recognition of the differing paradigms that inform their work.

Second, the need for more research is obvious, especially with respect to populations traditionally disqualified from having any sexuality at all, such as women, children, the disabled, and the aging.[2] Research about sexual minorities should focus on normative patterns rather than subcultural exotica in order to correct distorted notions about the alleged promiscuity or sexual superiority of certain racial/ethnic groups, especially blacks (Staples, 1978). Most race comparisons concern the premarital sexual activity of black and white populations (Zelnick and Kantner, 1980). With rare exceptions (Bell and Weinberg, 1978) these works reinforce the impression of intracultural homogeneity, so that little is actually known to challenge widely held racial stereotypes. The difficult work of attempting to integrate sociological insights about racial minorities into the study of sexuality would force a rethinking of the means by which racial oppression intersects with not only gender oppression but sexual oppression as well. For example, Espin (1984: 160) alerts us to the interplay of the personal and political among Latin women when she notes that "rebellion against the culture of origin or loyalty to it can, in many instances, be expressed through sexual behavior." And surely more research is needed about the multiple stigma of being a member of both a sexual and a racial/ethnic minority. A small body of literature has recently emerged on the life-styles of racial/ethnic lesbians. Though not specifically about sexual practice, it nevertheless provides important information about the context in which minority women enact their sexual identities (Allen, 1984; Hidalgo, 1984).

Theories of Sexuality

The theoretical literature is only nominally grounded in empirical work, whether quantitative or ethnographic. It draws selectively on previous research findings, notably Kinsey's, to make larger statements about the development of sexual identity (Gagnon and Simon, 1973) or the meaning of that identity once acquired (Plummer, 1975).

The work of Gagnon and Simon (1973) has significantly shaped theoretical understanding of sexuality. Feminist sociologists have used the concept of "sexual scripts" to articulate the particular dimensions of female sexuality (Laws and Schwartz, 1977; Atwater, 1982). "Scripts are the plans that people may have in their heads for what they are doing and what they are going to do, as well as being the devices for remembering what they have done in the past" (Gagnon, 1977). All social behavior, including all sexual behavior, is scripted. The sexual script, again like all scripts, has five components: (1) *Who* does a woman have sex with, that is, what are the limits and constraints of appropriate partners; (2) *what* acts does a woman engage in sexually from the whole range of possible sexual acts; (3) *when* is sex done, that is, at what times of the day, month, or year and in one's life cycle; (4) *where*, in setting or circumstance, does sex occur; and (5) *why* do people have sex, that is, what are the culturally approved accounts for doing sexual things that people provide for themselves and others (Gagnon, 1977: 6-9). Scripts vary by gender, from culture to culture, and by subgroup within the culture. So too, individual behavior may vary from the given cultural prescriptions and, indeed, may vary across concrete situations.

Sexual scripts are an important corrective to a biological or psychological perspective since the notion calls attention to a critical component of sexuality: meaning and identity and how they emerge out of social control and definition. Socially constructed scripts alert us to the cultural meanings attached to particular acts and their consequent regulation. Interactionists seek to understand the social construction of sexual meanings despite a dearth of empirical research about the content, source, and transmission of such beliefs (Plummer, 1975: 30). The interactionist approach to sexuality is perhaps most clearly and coherently explained by Plummer, who captures its essence in one neat sentence: "Nothing is sexual but naming makes it so" (1975: 30). Yet this naming process is neither simple nor easy; "sexual meanings are not universal absolutes, but ambiguous and problematic categories" (Plummer, 1975: 31). Meanings emerge in a cultural context. They have social and historical sources. Sexual meanings are not universal or unambiguous, although there is a range shaped and constrained by biology, culture, and human interaction (Plummer, 1975: 32-41; Gagnon, 1984). Scripts conceptually provide an important corrective to the direction and implications of much of the empirical research; with a focus less on behavior and outcomes, and more on the meanings applied by sexual actors to their behavior and situations, the approach brings us closer to the grounded experience of sexual actors. Theoretical work is needed about the sexual meanings developed, learned, and imparted to social actors (Plummer, 1975: 30-41).

In this focus on meaning, however, it is possible to lose sight of sexual practice itself, as if erotic acts had a universal quality that requires no explanation. This view raises questions about the inherent "naturalness" of sexual acts and desires. How are sexual fantasies created as a reaction to particular social and historical forms and structures? Does sexual expression and behavior change historically? It is possible that not only meaning or identity are historically transformed but that actual behavior changes over time and affects the identity of the actors and the meanings assigned to behavior and fail to incorporate the real diversity of response (Miller and and the analyses that utilize these concepts can mute the richness and complexity of the interactional process. Theories often rely on stereotypical descriptions of the influence of social norms on women's identity and behavior and fail to incorporate the real diversity of response (Miller and

Fowlkes, 1980). Third, the focus on meanings, if not studiously avoided, can obscure inequalities of interpersonal and institutional power. The existence of gender domination suggests that women's sexual meanings and sexual language flow from male experience and male definitions of desire.

Theoretical observations about women's lives as sexual actors and intimate partners are also limited by biases in existing data bases (Gagnon and Simon, 1973; Simon and Gagnon, 1967a, 1967b). For example, Gagnon and Simon (1973) were among the first scholars to recognize that there might be differences between female and male homosexuality and that previous research had treated the sexual object choice of lesbians, the choice that lesbians make as to what is erotic, as *the* only matter of interest, failing to explore lesbian existence as a uniquely female experience. Hence in their 1973 analysis of lesbian identity, Gagnon and Simon wrote that the "female homosexual follows conventional feminine patterns in developing her commitment to sexuality and in conducting not only her sexual career but her nonsexual career as well" (1973: 178). This analysis was informed by little prior substantive literature and was steeped in a model of the conventional women that accepted untested normative assertions about women's limited sources of sexual knowledge and need for emotional involvement for sexual gratification. Gagnon and Simon thus preclude the possibility that lesbian erotic interest and activity might be diffeent from their heterosexual counterparts and might vary also among lesbians. This conceptual limitation has been reproduced in others' work until quite recently when Peplau et al. (1978) began to discuss some of the diversity within lesbian relationships.

Ethnography

The ethnographic tradition often sacrifices explanation to description (Humphreys, 1970; Warren, 1974; Weinberg and Williams, 1974). Work in this category tends to rely on phenomenological theories to validate the methodology. Most of this research explores sex as it is enacted by heterosexual and homosexual men in public places (bars, public toilets, bath houses). Such studies are crucially important in demonstrating the ways in which the desire for sex is communicated and met, and examining the kinds of community settings available to males for sexual expression. They provide a contextual rendering of physical spaces in which sexual outcomes are possible, and hence, offer much more situated knowledge on sexual frequency than do surveys. But ethnographic depictions of women's lives in all-female communities did not even reach publication until recently (Ettorre, 1980; Krieger, 1983; Ponse, 1978; Wolf, 1979). This is not surprising. Women, with the exception of prostitutes, have not been accorded nor have they created such public avenues to sexual activity. Moreover, only in the last 15 years have fully developed, separate lesbian communities existed.

Toward Conceptual Clarity

The theoretical development of a more accurate and complete sociology of sexuality cannot take place without a critical rethinking of categories that have heretofore organized the study of sexuality and society. Four major assumptions construct current understanding and constrict the development of this field in general and of new perspectives on women in particular.

First, as this selective review indicates, maleness and masculinity provide the normative base line for understanding all human sexuality. The consequences of relying on masculine sexual stereotypes have emerged most flagrantly in the vaginal/clitoral controversy and in the struggle over meaning. This is an issue we will explore later in greater depth. An androcentric approach to knowledge does little to inform what we know about women and, indeed, offers little by way of grounded knowledge about males, for their sexuality is also constrained by gender.[3]

Second, heterosexuality is viewed as the only normal expression of sexual intimacy. This is an observation about value and meaning, not an empirical fact. Sociologists have yet to examine systematically the way heterosexuality has acquired such social meaning that all other sexual conduct is evaluated with reference to it. Measuring sexual expression, not to mention social identity, in heterosexual terms constrains the range of meaning that might be ascribed to relationships between women, between men, and even between women and men. In addition, it is important to trace the way in which *homophobia*, fear of homosexuals and homosexuality, has limited the sociology of sexuality (Kayal, 1977; Kayal and Giovanni, 1980).

Third, confusing sexuality with reproduction blurs the intricate meanings of both phenomena, especially for women. While sex in the service of procreation is one of the hallmarks of Judeo-Christian thought on heterosexual sexuality, more modern perspectives emphasize the personal pleasure of sexual experience. Feminists have long dismissed biological accounts for women's behavior, but the fact that women reproduce and men do not may well constitute grounds for rethinking female sexuality. Miller and Fowlkes (1980) have rightfully criticized others in the field for seeing female reproduction as "incidental to or contingent upon sexuality rather than as interactive with a woman's sexual self-concept and responsiveness" (1980: 264). Indeed the increase in self-insemination by lesbians (Wolf, 1984: Duelli-Klein, 1984) suggests that reproductive processes are not the exclusive domain of heterosexual women. Research on women who have sought abortions (Luker, 1975) and evidence that women are more orgasmic after the birth of their first child provide evidence that the uniquely female experiences of pregnancy and the whole range of reproductive processes have meanings that are sexual, with implications for female sexual behavior that have not yet been explored.

And finally, it is empirically unsound and conceptually unwise to detach sexuality from economic and political relations. Sex is not merely a private matter. Assumptions about sex and sexual behavior underlie a great deal of state activity and regulation (see Baron, Chapter 17 in this volume). Sexuality as a group of social relations may occur anywhere, and equating the sexual with the personal and private world is a serious mistake. Research on the sexualization of the work place in the last decade has forced us to confront the homophobic and androcentric assumptions embedded in sociological notions of the public world of work. Because no women were assumed to be present, no sexual expressions, activities, or problems were thought to exist (Schneider, 1985). In terms of the sociology of sexuality, the research on sexual harassment and "office affairs" demands a recognition and reconceptualization of the context in which sexuality may be enacted, the variable meanings women bring to these experiences, the consequences of such sexual interactions for women, and the ways in which sexual interests and relationships are often constructed in the face of the alienating, fragmented, and competitive conditions of work (Schneider, 1984). A significant number of women engage in risky, secret relationships with persons from work, and the experience of risk may itself be a source of pleasure.

Indeed, the whole notion of public sex needs to be reexamined. We concur with Altman (1982: 79) about the confusion inherent in the notion itself:

> Public sex is used to describe a whole range of behavior associated with two interrelated but separate acts: sex outside the framework of an ongoing relationship and sex that takes place in other than a private home or hotel. Thus the term itself raises all those images of "promiscuous," "impersonal," "anonymous" sex that have long been used to condemn gay men. . . . When heterosexuals indulge in similar behavior the term used is "recreational sex."

Among other considerations, public sex raises perplexing issues about the links between biology and culture in the organization of sexuality, because women, whether self-identified as heterosexual or lesbian, have minimal access to the zones of public sex.

In what follows we explore three issues that bridge the gap between the older tradition and emergent research in the sociology of sexuality. The first explores the historically specific and complex ways in which sexual identity, behavior, and community are organized. The second demonstrates that the terms for speaking about sexuality have been systematically unavailable to women and suggests how changing these terms enhances understanding of female sexuality. The third utilizes the theoretical perspective of sexual scripts to discuss possible changes in women's actual experience of sexuality in the last decade. The new tradition of feminist scholarship, as we hope to show, recognizes the validity of interdisciplinary contributions. Female sexuality is being studied in a way that anchors theory to the subjective realities of women's lives, lives that are recognized as having cross-cultural and historically specific meanings.

THE SOCIAL CONSTRUCTION
OF SEXUAL IDENTITY

For decades, sociologists of sexuality have worked from an often implicit assumption that the sexual acts in which a person engages do not necessarily relate to sexual identity consistently. Kinsey et al. (1953; 1948) alerted researchers to the vast frequency of homosexual acts among persons who as adults considered themselves heterosexual, and to the heterosexual activity of many who as adults defined themselves as homosexual. Historians in this decade have turned their attention to the historically specific ways in which certain behaviors and relationships are culturally defined as sexual or not, normal or deviant, and the ideological and economic conditions through which homosexual acts are distinguished from homosexual identity.

The publication of Carroll Smith-Rosenberg's (1975) powerful analysis of friendship networks among women during the nineteenth century marked the beginning of an academic debate about the conditions under which certain activities come to be defined as sexual and deviant. Using letters and diaries, she traced what were often lifelong passionate and loving commitments between friends, sisters, and mothers and daughters during the last century. She concentrated on ideology and consciousness rather than sexual behavior, which she presumed was shaped by systems of sexual meaning.

Her observations and interpretations radically reorganized subsequent discussions of female sexuality. First, Smith-Rosenberg questioned the validity of explaining these intimate networks by applying Freud's libidinal theory, which tends to separate abnormal and normal, and sexual from platonic. She proposed an alternative analysis, essentially sociological in its recognition of the societal and familial structures of the nineteenth century. Citing an abundance of structural conditions that made the family an important sphere for women, Smith-Rosenberg argued that a female world developed within which women shared and celebrated important life events with one another. The homosociality of this world was reinforced by a strict division of the sexes in virtually all aspects of life. Within "such a world of emotional richness and complexity, devotion to and love of other women became a plausible and socially accepted form of human interaction" (1975: 9). Indeed, the intense and physically demonstrative intimacies of these women surpassed those they seemed to experience with men at that time. Smith-Rosenberg did not distinguish between genital and nongenital physicality. Although she characterizes at least one loving friendship as both "sensual and platonic" (1975: 4), she maintains that the question of genital contact is irrelevant. Instead Smith-Rosenberg notes that these expressions of love between women were accepted, not taboo, and not necessarily presumed to lead to genital sex.

Several interrelated questions emerged from the Smith-Rosenberg piece. First, what is the centrality of genital acts to sexual identity? Second, how are sexual acts, sexual identity, and sexual community related for any person or group? Third, has women's sexual identity been suppressed? Fourth, how modern is the idea of sexual identity as distinct from sexual acts?

Sexual Identity and Genital Acts

One hallmark of feminist historians who elaborated on the Smith-Rosenberg analysis is their insistence on the recognition of the political dimensions in the organization of human intimacy. For example, Blanche Wiesen Cook (1977) discovered the pervasiveness of "networks of love and support" while studying the contributions to the early twentieth-century peace movement made by Lillian Wald, Jane Addams, Crystal Eastman, and Emma Goldman. Cook argues that such networks played a crucial role during the eighteenth and nineteenth centuries in enabling politically active women to accomplish their work unencumbered by patriarchal constraints. Historian Nancy Sahli (1979) goes further to argue that loving friendships between politically active and independent women "posed a basic threat to a system where the fundamental expression of power was that of one sex over another" (1979: 27).

Following Smith-Rosenberg, Faderman (1981) suggests that these love relationships were probably not genital because "women in centuries other than ours often internalized the view of females as having little sexual passion" (1981: 16). Sahli takes an essentially similar position, noting that women in the nineteenth century imbued their love for other women with spiritual meaning (1979: 26).[4]

In contrast, Cook, whose work attempts to demonstrate the historical denial of lesbianism (1979a, 1979b), scoffs at a biographer of two adult women of the early twentieth century who "seriously expects us to believe that two women who lived together for almost fifty years never hugged, never kissed, never warmed each others' bodies on a cold South Hadley night" (1979b: 64). According to Cook, "Women who love women, who choose women to nurture and support and to create a living environment in which to work creatively and independently, are lesbians" (1977: 48). She also argues that "genital proof" is irrelevant as it "derives from a male model that has very little to do with the love, support and sensuality that exist between women" (1977: 53). In another article, Cook criticizes the double standard used in "genital proofs," which are "never required to confirm the heterosexuality of men and women who live together for 20 to 50 years. Such proofs are not demanded even when discussing ephemeral love relations between women and men" (1979b: 64).

Sexual Identity and Sexual Community

This scholarly debate did not emerge from the chance publication of an academic study. The historical study was made significant by the political context of the 1970s, where the social and sexual meaning of women's ties to one another was a burning intellectual question, particularly in the emerging literature about contemporary lesbians. While it might seem ironic that there should be some tension in this literature about lesbianism, there was and still is continuing debate over the meaning of these relationships as well as conjecture about the genital sexuality of these loving friends. This highlights the importance of understanding lesbianism as a social as well as sexual category. The issue exemplified a basic conflict for feminist scholars who wish to acknowledge the existence of female sexuality without reducing women to their genitals. It also reflects a basic schism among contemporary lesbians about the importance of same-sex sexual behavior to a self-conscious commitment to a lesbian identity and to the emergent lesbian political community (Rich, 1980; Ferguson, 1981; Zita, 1981; Addelson, 1981).

In addition, this debate directs attention to the complex ways in which sexual acts, sexual identities, and sexual communities are organized, not just for those who identify as lesbians but for all women. That heterosexuality is socially constructed requires explication. Rich, in her essay on "compulsory heterosexuality" asks how it can be assumed that women in Smith-Rosenberg's study "chose" heterosexual marriage. She argues,

> Women have married because it was necessary, in order to survive economically, in order to have children who would not suffer economic deprivation or social ostracism, in order to remain respectable, in order to do what was expected of women because coming out of "abnormal" childhoods they wanted to feel "normal," and because heterosexual romance has been represented as the great female adventure, duty, and fulfillment [1980: 654].

While Rich's claims are true, they do not necessarily invalidate Smith-Rosenberg's analysis. If anything, Smith-Rosenberg's thesis forces attention precisely to the interplay of oppression and resistance. The women she studies can be cast as those who chose one complex route to meeting their needs within the cultural prescriptions of that time. Evidence of women who "passed" as men in the nineteenth century, doing men's work, voting, and even marrying women, attests to an alternate and less condoned avenue of resistance (Katz, 1976).

Recently several other historians have attempted to chart the changes in notions of sexuality that parallel the development of capitalism, tracing the emergence of sexual communities where none existed, on the one hand, and sexual persons rather than sexual acts, on the other (Adam, 1985; Weeks, 1981; D'Emilio, 1983). These efforts tell us a great deal about the shifts in the social control of sexuality through their focus on changing laws and other sources of ideology, particularly science (Weeks, 1981; Foucault, 1980), though they are less clear about the interactions between social regulation and actual sexual practices.

However, this historical work does indicate that the separation of people into heterosexual and homosexual is a relatively recent practice whose origins lie in the nineteenth century. Only the modern idea of homosexuality involves a sense of difference in terms of personhood, and this sense coincides with the development of a distinctly homosexual identity, community, and politics. Lesbian sexual identity seems to emerge most strongly in the early twentieth century when the new ideology of companionate marriage took hold and when greater numbers of women had, for the first time, the potential for economic independence—that is, when major transformations occurred in the sex/gender system (Weeks, 1977; Simons, 1979; Ferguson, 1981).

The significance of these studies cannot be overemphasized. First, they make it virtually impossible to think or write about women's communities and female sexuality without acknowledging the history of women's relationships. Second, they raise important issues about the extent to which a "male model" of sexuality, narrowly genital and mechanical, has been the framework from which all sexual relationships are judged rather than being defined by passion, love, and commitment. Third, questions emerge about the relationship of identity to behavior and which behaviors define specific identities. Four, this work directs attention to questions about why and under what conditions certain behaviors become stigmatized and devalued (e.g., Schur, 1984: 118-132). And finally, it reveals change, continuity, and diversity of women's sexual scripts in the past, forcing recognition of such difference in the present.

VOCABULARIES OF DESIRE

Being interested in sex and, indeed, talking about sex are primary taboos for contemporary American women (Vance, 1984; Webster, 1984; Laws and Schwartz, 1977). Many women cannot easily talk about sex. Our language does not have a selection of good words to describe what we do. For example, we have scientific language ("sexual intercourse"), slang ("fuck"), and euphemisms ("make love"). Most talk about sex, especially slang, is accomplished by men, using language created by men. Whether cold, "dirty," or coy, the absence of words coupled with the lack of admissible sexual feelings inhibits communication at the interpersonal level. We know our partners well enough to be sexual but not to talk about it.

While sexual acts and genital arrangements seem to possess an aura of constancy, their meanings clearly do not. In the sociology of sexuality, much of the feminist critique, as in other substantive areas, focuses on the socially constructed nature of meaning—that is, on "naming" as a problematic (Daly,

1973; Spender, 1980; Smith, 1979b). Those who name an experience control its meaning, and women have traditionally been excluded from this source of power. Thus constructing a vocabulary of desire that captures female sexual experience has emerged as a central task for feminists. This task, while compatible with the social constructionist perspective, clearly evolves out of the feminist analysis of the social organization of gender and the ubiquity of power inequalities, including the power to define.

The range of sexual meanings available to women has been so constrained that sexual vocabularies must be developed to accomplish at least two goals. First, a vocabulary is required by researchers to describe adequately the physiological and emotional experiences of a distinctively female sexuality. Second, a "more precise sexual vocabulary" (Newton and Walton, 1984) is needed to communicate women's sexual wishes, desires, and identities to others and to oneself. In both situations, women's subjective understandings are the grounds for the emergence of such a vocabulary. Shifts in the meaning of female orgasm illustrate the first point. The feminist critique of "foreplay" illustrates the second. While it is not clear that one adequate vocabulary can be devised to fit both these goals, explicit use of feminist methodological insights should eventually bring them closer together.

The Orgasm Discourse

By far the most intense debate in the history of female sexual response is the vaginal/clitoral controversy, which clearly illustrates what happens when women's subjective experience is finally taken into account. As Laws and Schwartz (1977) have pointed out, this argument is about competing constructions of female sexuality: passive and in the service of men, or active, autonomous, and in the service of female desire. Although empirical studies (Masters and Johnson, 1966) challenged the Freudian insistence on the superiority and "maturity" of vaginal orgasm, it was radical feminists outside the mainstream of scientific and intellectual production who brought the importance of clitoral stimulation to public consciousness (Koedt, 1970; Laws and Schwartz, 1977; Shulman, 1980). These writers challenged the dominant paradigm, arguing that women must repudiate constructions that measure female sexuality in terms of male sexual gratification. The clitoris, they claimed, was the *only* site for female orgasm. Women who thought otherwise were confused because of anatomical ignorance and a desire to fit their sexual experience to male definitions. Five years later, the radical feminist insistence that vaginal orgasm did not exist was challenged by *The Hite Report* (Hite, 1976).

Shere Hite set out to present "what the women who answered said—in their own words and in their own way . . . to get acquainted, to share how we have experienced our sexuality, how we feel about it—and to see our personal lives more clearly, thus redefining our sexuality and strengthening our identities as women" (1976: xi). Criticisms about methodology notwithstanding (Melosh, 1978), this is what she accomplished, making a set of subjective interpretations about female sexuality available and accessible to a wide public. Her respondents, both heterosexual and lesbian, identified two interconnected orgasmic responses. Other recent empirical work confirms her findings (Newcomb and Bentler, 1983; Butler, 1976). By 1976, it seems, women were more articulate about their sexual response, in contrast to previous decades when, as de Beauvoir pointed out, "statements by women on the matter [of orgasm] are rare, and they remain extremely vague even when precision is attempted" (1953: 371).

What seems clear is that the radical feminists were not wrong in the specification of the physiological site of orgasm or in their insistence on the need to confront directly the cultural myth of the "immature" clitoral response. Those analyses failed, however, to make the crucial distinction between the physiological site at which arousal occurs and the subjective meanings different kinds of sexual experiences hold for women. That women seem to be able to distinguish sensory differences in experiences says little about the value they impart to each of these sites or the extent to which women might still believe that one site or another is superior or inferior. Many heterosexual females still seem to prefer vaginally induced orgasms, not because the physical pleasure is greater, either in intensity or in frequency of orgasmic response, but because of the greater emotional meaning in partner-related sex activity (Butler, 1976; Hite, 1976; Tavris and Sadd, 1975). The social context within which a woman achieves orgasm and the psychological influence of the environment have a substantial impact on how the physiological aspects of orgasms are subjectively perceived (Newcomb and Bentler, 1983). In this regard women have not constructed a new way of describing these sexual experiences, and this will not be an easy task since they are bombarded with new, purportedly scientific studies in popular books that illustrate the persistence of a male-dominated vocabulary for female sexuality (Ladas et al., 1982).

Relabeling Female Experience

As yet, the conceptual vocabulary to describe female sexuality in any terms other than those already in use is unavailable. A conceptual vocabulary cannot be developed as long as male sexuality is considered the normative base line for all sexual experience. As Spender (1980) points out, "males began by naming themselves as sexual beings and in accordance with their male subjective logic name females as minus males and minus sexuality" (1980: 172).[5]

Spender, in fact, offers one creative solution to the problem of naming female sexuality in an androcentric social world: Simply transform existing terms (1980: 171-190). Exactly how this is to be accomplished is unclear, although lesbian feminists have been relatively successful (in some circles) in transforming the term "dyke" from a pejorative to an emblem. Spender writes about the term "frigidity," suggesting that it could be

> renamed as an autonomous and independent state, an outcome of conscious debate and decision, freely arrived at in the face of possible alternatives. It could be a form of power against an oppressor, a form of passive resistance or unavailability. In such circumstances it is very different from impotence which would seem not at all to be freely arrived at as a deliberate choice [1980: 177].

She also argues for inventing new terms to encode female experience, suggesting that "vagina gratitude is quite a good corrective in a society which has only, and falsely, named penis envy" (1980: 182).

Other feminists have also argued for transforming existing terms and creating new ones. Brownmiller (1977: 334) cites Mehrhof as suggesting that the term "penetration" might from a female perspective be more properly termed "enclosure." Along with others, Gould has suggested promoting what has been ignominiously labeled "foreplay" to the status of sexual activity, and demoting intercourse to just one feature of "heterosexual afterplay" (Gould, 1983; Laws and Schwartz, 1977: 55-57; Spender, 1980: 178).

The feminist critique of foreplay invokes an additional facet of the problem of naming, that of communicating sexual desire. Gagnon and Simon (1973) have written both about the importance of sex talk and silence:

> While talk is significant in shaping behavior, it often does so through its imprecisions and its absences. In a very immediate and concrete way, most people remain untrained in the ability to talk about their own sexual activity or scripts, particularly with persons with whom they are having sex [1973: 105].

Women, who have been socialized into silence about much of their inner lives, feel this most acutely, especially when their subjective reality is discontinuous with the dominant, expected sexual script. Constructing the meaning of female sexuality differently may mean taking seriously all those subjective accounts, collected by every sex researcher to date, in which women say that kissing, holding, and touching often mean more and feel better than intercourse (Denny et al., 1984). For women this *is* sex, not foreplay. As Laws and Schwartz put it, "women like foreplay before, during, and after. As a social construction, foreplay clearly embodies male priorities and practices in the sexual encounter" (1977: 56). Articulating this and other sexual preferences is problematic because the current vocabulary of desire does not and clearly cannot capture the subjective experience of female sexuality. Sexual discourse is one that is thick with meaning. It can only be decoded and refined by an analysis that recognizes the impact of gender on human sexual identity and the distribution of power in intimate, personal life. What feminists have begun is more than lexicography; it is, in fact, a struggle for power.

Atwater's (1982) research on extramarital relationships illustrates an additional problem of naming, one that focuses on defining the context of sexuality. This is not, of course, a problem unique to women. Nevertheless, our cultural tradition of assigning a voracious sexuality to men and minimal level of erotic desire to women is supported by constraints on female sexual expression. These constraints include the institution of "compulsory heterosexuality" (Rich, 1980) and the institution of marriage. Atwater's study highlights problems with the latter, specifically that of always defining sexuality in relation to marriage: "Our language still reflects that traditional value, for even when sexuality does take place outside of marriage, it is still defined by marriage" (1982: 188). This is especially self-evident in the terms "*pre*marital" and "*extra*marital" sex. It is also implied by the absence of terms for sexual activity after the divorce or death of a spouse, or to describe sexual activity between voluntarily single adults (Atwater, 1982: 189). Growing use of the term "*post*marital" sex only underscores the fact that sexuality is persistently defined by marital norms. For women, the absence of more neutral terms to describe nonmarital sexual relationships serves to reinforce linkages between women and marriage, an institution which, despite its romantic gloss, enforces women's social, legal, and economic inequality.

Finally, to name adequately and speak of all of the experiences women can have that might be considered sexual requires a departure from a male-centered approach to bodily sensation and a positive reappropriation of those features of female experience that men do not have. In doing so, we must take seriously those rarely expressed but uniquely female bodily functions associated with fertility. Laws and Schwartz (1977) provide a useful listing of those occurrences for which women do not have a vocabulary: the pleasurable features of menstruation; monthly vaginal secretions; sensations and transformations of body image connected with pregnancy, birth, and nursing; sexual intercourse during and after pregnancy. A few writers have explicitly commented on the sexual meanings women impart to pregnancy (Luker, 1975) and on the sexual feelings evoked by nursing and giving birth (Rossi, 1973; Weisskopf, 1980; Masters and Johnson, 1966), but the powerful prescriptive image of asexual motherhood remains unchanged. The omission of these experiences in the vocabulary of desire graphically illustrates how markedly our model of sexuality relies on male experience, how little men are interested in those aspects of life that they do not share, and how great has been the suppression of female experience in the language of sexuality.

CHANGING SEXUAL SCRIPTS

Although the language to describe female sexuality remains largely inflexible for now, there is evidence of some change in women's sexual scripts.

Traditional scripts, mentioned in virtually every text about sexuality, are heterosexual ones, resting squarely on dichotomously gendered notions of male and female sexuality. According to this script, men always want and are ready for sex; sex is centered in male orgasm and no physical pleasure is possible without sexual intercourse; men initiate sex and sexual expertise is a man's responsibility; men separate sex from emotions (Zilbergeld, 1978; Gross, 1978). Conversely, women deny their sexuality; women learn *not* to be sexual and do not talk about sex; women do not initiate sex but rather manipulate men to get their own needs met; women conflate sexual relations and intimacy (Strong and Reynolds, 1982). Finally, women's sexuality is for something (reproduction) or someone else: "For the female sexual activity does not occur for its own sake, but for the sake of children, family and love. . . . This vision of sexuality as a form of service to others is continuous with the rest of female socialization" (Gagnon and Simon, 1973).

Despite these highly abstract normative strictures, changes are visible in the area of female sexuality for several reasons. First, the development of more sophisticated contraceptive technology during the 1950s has effectively separated reproduction from sexual activity, enabling women, if they so desire, to alter the traditional procreative script. While procreating may have been "statistically the least important and most defunct meaning to actors"(Plummer, 1975: 33), this new technology has moved sexual activity irrevocably away from its Judeo-Christian moorings as reproductive behavior occurring within the context of marriage. Since women are the ones who get pregnant, the effect of new contraceptives on the female sexual script should not be minimized.

However, not all women have an interest in separating sexual relations and procreation through this improved technology. Analysis of the beliefs of antiabortion activists provides a finely etched portrait of the links these women make between their ability to control male sexuality when contraceptives are renounced, their childbearing choices, and the limited power they perceive they have in the rest of their lives (Luker, 1984).

Second, feminist activity during the 1970s injected a rhetoric of sexual equality as part of the call for gender equality, at least in part as a response to the shallow and sexist claims of the "sexual revolution" of the preceding few years. The sexual double standard by which men are entitled to be sexual and women are not, outside as well as within marriage, was challenged. Sexual equality sometimes meant that women might behave as men have, sometimes that women are entitled to sexual pleasure and sexual satisfaction just as surely as men have been.

Finally, the spread of modern sex education means that important information is no longer withheld from girls or women, or learned abruptly at marriage (Gagnon and Simon, 1973: 110-128). Women's traditional ignorance about their own bodies and desires no longer poses such a formidable obstacle to their search for pleasure; women no longer need to rely on men for information. In sum, the possibility of a separation of reproduction from sexuality, new values placed on female pleasure, and women's access to sexual information suggest that female sexuality in all contexts, including marriage, should be changing.

However, while there are hundreds of studies on premarital and extramarital relations, there is virtually nothing on marital sex (Williams, 1980). And unfortunately, most studies of adolescent sexuality, while showing increased practice, expectation, and acceptance of premarital sex and sexual intercourse, focus primarily on the frequency of coitus and pregnancy as its outcome (Zelnick and Kantner, 1980). This research fails to illuminate the female sexual experience because it ignores the links young women make between pregnancy, romance, and relationships (see Thompson, 1984, for a very recent effort to rectify this omission). Hence we know very little about how young women's sexuality has altered due to the purported changes in the last two decades. Normatively, it is obvious that the cultural link between sexuality and youth remains. The entire substantive terrain of women's sexual responsiveness and interest over the life course is made problematic by the privileging of young women and the persistence of an androcentric model of sexuality, which presupposes declines in sexual responsiveness with age.

While marriage has lost some of its power as the only legitimate setting for sexual intercourse (Furstenberg, 1980), marriage still dominates the lives of most women. Yet in the available research on marriage, females seem to be missing. The unit of analysis is the couple, with sexuality assumed to be private, restricted to certain times, interrupted by children, and frozen in an unchanging pattern over the life course. The feminist literature through 1984 also provided virtually no new insights into women's sexual experiences within marriage. Indeed, positive descriptions of heterosexual genital sexuality and heterosexual intimacy and orgasm are all but lost in the wealth of more controversial debates (Gardetto, 1984).

Miller and Fowlkes (1980) take other sociologists to task for failing to elaborate the range of normative social arrangements that can provide the context for female sexuality. Marriage is one such arrangement, but gendered notions preclude adequate explication of female sexuality even in this setting. As they point out,

> Our culturally cherished notion of the sexually settled, mature, and nurturing adult woman may account for the persistent sociological bias that, once a woman is anchored in the socially approved heterosexual world of marriage, her sexuality speaks for itself and is not a subject for investigation. Yet there is every reason to believe that a women's sexuality is emergent and takes on new meanings and qualities in the context of the emergent marriage relationship [1980: 265].

Two themes emerge from this analysis: Women's sexuality in marriage is not static, and marriage is not the only context for female sexuality. The first of these points is given some credence by the research on heterosexual women's experiments with sexual play. The second is well illustrated in Atwater's (1982) research on women's extramarital relationships.

Baumann's work on sex parties (1985) suggests that married women may indeed be living out some shift in sexual scripts as they partake of Tupperware-type parties in homes of their friends that introduce them to sex toys, sexy clothing, and sex talk that seem premised on a more active, playful, and initiating role for women in their heterosexual activities. The parties encourage sex talk and the learning about sex in an open, supportive way that permits admission of ignorance and embarrassment. In this context, women seem to experience a decrease in self-consciousness about their bodies and an enhanced reassurance about their physical selves. Galler (1984) argues that pressure to measure up to a physical ideal and the fear of being different create anxiety about being sexual: Not being physically perfect is "equated with the lack of entitlement to a sexual life" (1984: 68). Baumann's study indicates that heterosexual women, once married, do not abandon sexual display and experimentation and are not prepared to grant to young women the sole right to a sexual life.

In contrast, Blumstein and Schwartz (1983) found continuation of the traditional script in a least one aspect of marital sexual activity: Married women are hesitant to initiate sex with their husbands even when encouraged to be more assertive, deferring to the men especially when their husbands are feeling insecure. Hence despite some change in scripts, male power in sexual terms is still perpetuated.

Similar patterns of change in scripts, though not without some contradictions, appear in the literature on extramarital relations. *The Extramarital Connection* (Atwater, 1982) is an important piece of feminist research indicating that women rewrite their sexual scripts when there is a conflict between their personal reality and traditional social constructions. Of special interest is Atwater's discussion of the meaning that extramarital relationships have for her respondents. Writing in the new tradition of feminist research, Atwater lets her respondents speak. What emerges from these women, all white and readers of a feminist publication but otherwise diverse in education, employment, and mothering experiences, is a "remarkable uniformity of the meanings of their experiences" (1982: x).

Atwater finds "virtually no evidence of the traditional model of female sexuality in the descriptions women gave of their extramarital sexual activity" (1982: 140). Extramarital sex itself seems to alter at least one aspect of the female sexual script, that which concerns women's services to others. Her respondents became more acutely aware of their sexual power during extramarital liaisons with other men and women. They developed a sense of entitlement during their affairs that they then brought back into their marriages or extended to other areas of their lives. While a shift in the female sexual script toward female pleasure and self-satisfaction was indicated in Hite's research (1976), Atwater's data demonstrate how this shift has been effected by women in fairly conventional marital settings. Atwater suggests that rather than being an extension of routine sexual feelings and practice,

> extramarital behavior may be an area in which women are now unusually free to establish the kind of sexual patterns they prefer . . . because the extramarital area is not governed by the social rules and inherited patterns that have long dominated marital and premarital interaction [1982: 190].

Others are less optimistic about this change and suggest that "much, if not most, of the increase in female participation in extramarital sex may not be an expression of a feminist revolution so much as it is a more comfortable alternative to a revolution" (Gagnon, 1984: 59). Either way, we might ask, How does behavior that is generally disapproved, such as extramarital relationships (Glenn and Weaver, 1979), become desirable? What happens to the differences in the rates of extramarital relationships when the focus is not exclusively on sex but also on emotions? Thompson (1984) finds that the rates become similar, suggesting the need for serious refinements in the measurement of extramarital affairs so that it elicits more accurately the experience of women and is based less on an implicit male model.

The research on extramarital sex and, for that matter, bisexuality in women (Blumstein and Schwartz, 1976) illustrates ways in which women have authored new scripts. However, the power of gender socialization requires adopting a stance of cautious optimism about the ease with which women are willing or able to reorganize traditional scripts, no matter how dissonant with the subjective reality of their own sexuality. What happens, for example, when women choose to exclude men from their social, emotional, and sexual worlds? What, if anything, happens to female sexual identity when women must simultaneously manage other minority statuses? Because erotic activity is tied to social context, variation in that context is of particular interest to sociologists. Just how much room is there for change in a society that constructs the "female world" (Bernard, 1981) in a particular way?

For example, the historical transformation of lesbian identity and community indicates shifting patterns of freedom and constraint. In the last 15 years, lesbian visibility has increased dramatically for individuals and in the emergence of public communities and activities. Perhaps more than with any sort of heterosexuality, the meaning of lesbianism has been transformed by feminism. Yet recent work by Susan Krieger (1983) suggests there is not much leeway for change at all. Her study, appropriately characterized as "both document and analysis," of one lesbian community illustrates a tyranny of lesbian norms. In her introduction, Krieger writes about the tension community members feel about being validated in their lesbian identities while being invalidated as individual selves:

> This, I came to feel, was true in large part because the community was a community of likeness, one in which individuals were encouraged to value a

common identity as women. It was also a community of intimacy in which members were given support for experiences of closeness and union, including those which might reach their peak in shared sexuality [1983: xiii].

Krieger's work is a synthesis of a particular literature on lesbianism. Others have written about the tension between identity and community (Ettorre, 1980: Ponse, 1978) and specifically the relationship between gender and lesbian identity (Simon and Gagnon, 1967a, 1967b; Peplau et al., 1978; Peplau and Gordon, 1982). While this work is not specifically about sexual practices, it demonstrates a certain tenacity of gender socialization. Such research helps us understand Blumstein and Schwartz's (1983) empirical findings about the sparse and generally monogamous sex lives of lesbian couples, which they explain by noting that lesbians "have been taught the same standards of appropriate female conduct as heterosexual women" (1983: 197). It reminds us of the extent to which women's sexuality is contingent and embedded in a social world not of women's own making. By extension, this research suggests the enormous power that must be brought to bear to effect change in society as well as in intimate relationships.

On the other hand, Krieger fails to note the political importance of creating bonds of intense communality in the development of these lesbian communities, a pattern similar to most community-building done in opposition to the dominant culture. She and others also overlook the diversity of lesbians by class, race, and cultural heritage, which makes any notion of a single pattern of female socialization inaccurate and limiting. Lorde (1984) succinctly summarizes these paradoxical features of sexual communities:

> Without community, there is no liberation, only the most vulnerable and temporary armistice between an individual and her oppression. But community must not mean a shedding of our differences, not the pathetic pretense that these differences do not exist [1984:112].

DEBATE AND NEW DIRECTIONS

Throughout this chapter we have pointed to gaps and distortions in knowledge about female sexuality. In conclusion, we want to comment on the meaning and implications of recent feminist debates for the work of sociologists of sexuality and call attention to several other specific directions for research in the next decade.

Sexuality can be a terrain of both oppressive inequality and creative struggles toward women's eventual freedom. This duality of meaning causes confusion for feminists, as does the important insight that sexuality, gender, and reproduction can be separated into relatively distinct spheres of power. Feminist discussion of sex emerged in the late 1960s and continues today in the context of a society that discourages critical analysis of sexuality and in which many women are still unable to talk about sex.

The most recent feminist sexuality debate initially centered on the issue of pornography. This concern emerged from activism around rape, battering, and other violence against women. Pornography, as symbol and fact, was seen by some feminists primarily as another manifestation of violence against women and as a critically important way in which female sexuality is repressed, objectified, and distorted. Some feminists have argued against these antipornography activists on several grounds. First, it is said that these activists are conflating sexuality and violence, leaving no room for sexual pleasure. Second, they are promulgating antisexual attitudes. Third, some argue that control over pornography through legal channels would result in the suppression of all sexually explicit materials, including feminist and gay publications and art. (The literature on this issue is voluminous; for those interested readers we suggest the articles and the materials cited within them in "Forum: The Feminist Sexuality Debates," in *Signs* 1984, and the May 1986 issue of the *Women's Review of Books*.)

At the same time, the politics of sexuality emerged on the national political agenda (Eisenstein, 1981; Altman, 1982). The political right, whose analyses rest squarely on fear and loathing of sex itself, continues to redefine everyone's sexual lives by reasserting the equation of sexuality with procreation and attacking abortion, contraception, teenage sex, and homosexuality (Petchesky, 1981; Hollibaugh, 1979; Gordon and Hunter, 1977). This antifeminist countermovement has taken as its terrain many of the implicit and explicit issues raised by feminists who view sexual freedom, openness, and equality as one goal among many in the struggle for women's self-determination. This challenge to feminist thought and to the women's movement forced greater recognition and understanding of the relationships of sexuality and politics.

Recently the discussion has moved beyond pornography to encourage political talk about female sexuality and to examine the nature of female sexual expression itself; for example, to ask whether women's sexuality has been muted by repression or is entirely different than men's. Based on social constructionist views of sexuality, the debate now encompasses new questions about the experience of sexual minorities, how objects and acts become eroticized, the impact of the sexual revolution on women, and the ways in which race and class shape sexual experience. If there is any one question that fuels all the others, it is precisely how much freedom women have to be sexual and to set the terms of their own sexuality within the constraints of a heterosexist, racist, sexist, and erotophobic system of domination. (Vance, 1984, and Snitow et al., 1983, are two of the important collections of historical and sociologically grounded work concerning these topics.)

For sociologists of sexuality, two important questions remain to be addressed. First, what is the relationship between sexuality, violence, and pleasure in feminist theory and individual practice, and how are these dimensions related to each other in the experience of sexual relations? Second, if sexuality is, at least in part about fantasy, how does fantasy relate to actual behavior, which is tied to political and social structural systems of domination? How can we account for the prevalence in the dominant discourse of links between sexuality, violence, and death? Answers to these difficult questions could change the terms of the debate over the role of pornography in the sexual apparatus of the culture.

There is also a serious problem of dichotomous thinking apparent in feminist discussions of sexuality. Either there is sexual liberation or there is sexual regulation and control. These are seen as separate and antagonistic extremes against which behavior, ideology, and social trends can be judged. But such dualism does not help make sense of the complexity of women's everyday social reality. A sociology of sexuality that concurrently uses the concept of sexual scripting and the insights of feminism should be able to explain how individuals and selected groups manage elements of the contemporary culture that simultaneously repress sexual experience while offering freedom of expression.

In addition to the questions about liberation raised by the sexuality debate, the general issue of social change requires serious attention by sociologists of sexuality. For example, given what we know about the current trends in marriage, divorce, and remarriage rates, as well as in sexual practice, it appears likely that women in the future will have a series of sexual partners, that female sexuality will not be limited to experience only with partners, that women will take more responsibility for their own sexuality, and that women will be more continuously sexual over the course of their lives. These expectations should change the sexual landscape appreciably but in ways as yet uncharted.

Other empirical gaps must be filled. Sexuality in the middle years is already getting some attention, but the sexuality of the aged is invisible. Older women face unfavorable sex ratios, the likelihood of widowhood, normative constraints against sex and/or marriage with younger men, lower probability of remarriage, and doubts about their sexual appeal. What are women doing about these circumstances? Have older women initiated new sexual scripts to deal with these contingencies?

Despite the research on premarital pregnancy, we know less than we should about female adolescence and its nature, values, and accompanying sexual behaviors. While it seems clear that the sexual script is primarily heterosexual and oriented toward marriage, we know virtually nothing about girls' sexual experiences that deviate from cultural expectations, such as in homosexual or autoerotic activity. One other aspect requires significant attention from sociologists of sexuality. Ever since the work of Kinsey et al. (1953; 1948) evidence abounds that the male peer group assumes a major role in validating sexuality for adolescent males, but we lack research on whether similar social supports exist for women.

Sociologists of sexuality also must attempt to clarify theoretically the confusion about sexuality, sexual standards, and values that currently permeates feminist and everyday thought. To understand the relationship among sex, politics, and society we need to see how all forms of sexuality—perhaps most important, conventional heterosexuality—are socially and historically constituted. Heterosexual women enjoy sex. How did they come to enjoy it? In what sorts of relationships is enjoyment possible? How important is the quality of the relationship to the quality of the sex? How has the ideology of feminism and the focus on technique in the last two decades affected most heterosexual women? Are sexual relations a sphere in which women feel power over men, as several of our students so naively report ("I feel a special power over men in sex because I can bring them to their knees")?

Feminist theory has successfully introduced the issue of power as a component of sexuality into public discourse and into the sociology of sexuality. However, consent is rarely raised as an issue except when scholars are examining various types of violence against women: marital rape, child sexual assault, rape, and sexual harassment. Even with regard to consensual relations, a critical examination of the existing material basis of consent, the power relations involved in sex, and the complex relationships between desire and reality still await intensive investigation.

The seeming monogamous nature of lesbian relationships also needs further examination since failure to do so may sustain the myth, albeit a politically motivated one, that lesbians are completely similar to heterosexual women and utterly different from homosexual males in sexual practice and interest. This assertion is now so well substantiated and reproduced in sociological literature that proposing to research the issue seems heretical. True, the development of lesbian cultures and life-styles has not generated the sort of visible assertion of sexuality common among gay men (at least before public awareness of AIDS). But the reason for this difference is not apparent. Lesbians are themselves divided about its source: Is it evidence of deep repression of female sexuality, or of the basic difference between women and men?

Yet another interesting arena for further work lies in explicating how people who experience the disjuncture between sexual identity and behavior manage and interpret what and who they are. While we know a great deal about the coming-out process for adults self-identified as homosexuals, we know virtually nothing about how people who come from a history of homosexual acts foreclose homosexuality as adults or manage ambisexual identities. Women do this often, and it would further our understanding of the nature of "compulsory heterosexuality" if the processes of sexual identity formation for heterosexual women were not taken for granted but rather were explored in greater detail and complexity.

Finally, if we are ever going to attain the transformation of knowledge promised by the feminist critique of social science (Duelli-Klein, 1984; Stanley and Wise, 1983; Roberts, 1981: Smith, 1979a), the dominant androcentric model of sexuality must be thoroughly dissected. To date, the "truth" about female sexuality has been defined in contrast to what might even be a false reality for men. Nothing less than a monumental overhaul begun by feminists of the entire apparatus of thought about sexuality is needed. Without a more complete sociological understanding of the role sexuality plays in the lives of all gendered actors, female sexuality will remain distorted and unarticulated.

NOTES

1. In this chapter, the terms "sexual," "sexuality," "sexual identity," and "sexual relations" are used to describe those elements of thought, feeling, and behavior that persons themselves or researchers consider sexual or erotic. These are distinguished throughout from the terms "gender," "gender identity," and "gender relations." Our discussion will demonstrate the manifold ways in which these concepts are linked as well as those occasions when they may not be, and our language is intended to highlight and give focus to the sexual realm.

2. The question as to what research is needed gets addressed annually at meetings of the Sexual Behavior Division of the Society for Study of Social Problems and at in-house sessions of the Sociologists Gay Caucus. Sessions of the Sexual Behavior Division between 1983 and 1985 include yearly discussions of the problems, both practical and ethical, of teaching and doing research on sexuality; violence and sexuality; controversial topics in sexuality; support for sociosexual research; cross-cultural analyses of sexual variations in ethnic communities; female sexuality; and since 1984, a session each year on AIDS.

3. With the exception of male homosexuals, it is unusual to find papers on male sexuality at professional meetings, a paucity that seems to reflect a continued male bias in the research on heterosexuality in which the sexuality of males is considered normative, and that of females is thought of as deviant or at least in need of explanation. While there is an ongoing effort to close the gap in the sheer quantity of what is known about women and men, all of the movement improves and enhances the female side, leaving utterly unexplored the real rather than the ideological nature of male sexuality.

4. According to Faderman (1981), networks of loving women friends were not unique to the eighteenth and nineteenth centuries. She notes in the introduction to her book that even knowing Smith-Rosenberg's work did not prepare her to "discover that it was virtually impossible to study the correspondence of any 19th century women, not only in America but also of England, France, and Germany, and not uncover a passionate commitment to another woman at some time in her life" (1981: 15-16). She also found "romantic friendships in the 17th century as well," and "came upon the genesis of that institution in European and American romantic friendship in the Renaissance" (1981: 16).

5. One staggering popular example of this is David Rubin's comments about lesbians: "One vagina plus another vagina still equals zero" (1969: 269).

REFERENCES

ADAM, B. (1985) "Structural foundations of the gay world." Comparative Studies in Sociology and History 27 (October): 658-671.

ADDELSON, K. P. (1981) "Words and lives." Signs 7 (Autumn): 187-199.

ALLEN, P. G. (1984) "Beloved women: The lesbian in American Indian culture," in T. Darty and S. Potter (eds.) Women-Identified Women. Palo Alto, CA: Mayfield.

ALLGEIER, E. R. and N. McCORMICK [eds.] (1983) Changing Boundaries: Gender Roles and Sexual Behavior. Palo Alto, CA: Mayfield.

ALTMAN, D. (1982) "Sex: The new front line for gay politics." Socialist Review 12 (September-October): 75-84.

ATWATER, L. (1982) The Extramarital Connection. New York: Irvington.

BAUMANN, E. (1985) "The underwear comes in flavors: Eroticism, humor, and expressivity at 'naughty lady' parties." Presented at the Society for the Study of Social Problems Annual Meetings.

BELL, A. P. and M. WEINBERG (1978) Homosexualities: A Study of Diversity Among Men and Women. New York: Simon & Schuster.

BERNARD, J. (1973) "My four revolutions: An autobiographical history of the ASA," in J. Huber (ed.), Changing Women in a Changing Society. Chicago: University of Chicago Press.

BERNARD, J. (1981) The Female World. New York: Free Press.

BLUMSTEIN, P. and P. SCHWARTZ (1983) American Couples: Money, Work, Sex. New York: Morrow.

BLUMSTEIN, P. and P. SCHWARTZ (1976) "Bisexuality in women." Archives of Sexual Behavior 5, 2: 171-181.

BOWLES, G. and R. DUELLI-KLEIN [eds.] (1983) Theories of Women's Studies. London: Routledge & Kegan Paul.

BROWNMILLER, S. (1975) Against Our Will: Men, Women and Rape. New York: Simon & Schuster.

BUNCH, C. (1975) "Not for lesbians only." Quest: A Feminist Quarterly 2 (Fall): 50-56.

BUTLER, C. A. (1976) "New data on female sexual response." Journal of Sex and Marital Therapy 2: 40-46.

CAULFIELD, M. D. (1985) "Sexuality in human evolution." Feminist Studies 11 (Summer): 343-363.

COOK, B. (1979a) "Women alone stir my imagination." Signs 4 (Summer): 718-739.

COOK, B. (1979b) "The historical denial of lesbianism." Radical History Review 20 (Spring/Summer): 60-65.

COOK, B. (1977) "Female support networks and political activism." Chyrsalis 3: 43-61.

DALY, M. (1973) Beyond God the Father. Boston: Beacon.

DE BEAUVOIR, S. (1953) The Second Sex. New York: Alfred Knopf.

DELAMATER, J. (1981) "The social control of sexuality." Annual Review of Sociology 7: 263-290.

DELAMATER, J. and P. MACCORQUODALE (1979) Premarital Sexuality: Attitudes, Relationships, Behavior. Madison: University of Wisconsin Press.

D'EMILIO, J. (1983) Sexual Politics, Sexual Communities. Chicago: University of Chicago Press.

DENNY, N. W., J. K. FIELD, and D. QUADAGNO (1984) "Sex differences in sexual needs and desires." Archives of Sexual Behavior 13: 233-245.

DUELLI-KLEIN, R. (1984) "Doing it ourselves: Self insemination," in R. Arditti et al. (eds.) Test-Tube Women. London: Pandora.

EISENSTEIN, Z. (1981) "Antifeminism in the politics and election of 1980." Feminist Studies 7 (Summer): 187-205.

ESPIN, O. (1984) "Cultural and historical influences on sexuality in Hispanic/Latin women," in C. S. Vance (ed.) Pleasure and Danger. Boston: Routledge & Kegan Paul.

ETTORREE, E. M. (1980) Lesbians, Women and Society. London: Routledge & Kegan Paul.

FADERMAN, L. (1981) Surpassing the Love of Men. New York: Morrow.

FERGUSON, A. (1981) "Patriarchy, sexual identity, and the sexual revolution." Signs 7 (Autumn): 158-172.

Forum: Feminist Sexuality Debates (1984) Signs 10 (Autumn).

FOUCAULT, M. (1980) Herculine Barbin. New York: Pantheon Books.

FURSTENBERG, F. (1980) "Reflections on marriage." Journal of Family Issues 1 (4): 443-453.

GAGNON, J. (1984) "Notes toward an understanding of the transformation of sexual conduct." Concilium-Sociology of Religion 193: 11-19.

GAGNON, J. and W. SIMON (1973) Sexual Conduct. Chicago: Aldine.

GALLER, R. (1984) "The myth of the perfect body," pp. 165-172 in C. Vance (ed.) Pleasure and Danger. Boston: Routledge & Kegan Paul.

GARDETTO, D. (1984) "Heterosexuality and silence." Sojourner (October): 13-14.

GOODE, E. and R. TROIDEN [eds.] (1974) Sexual Deviance and Sexual Deviants. New York: Morrow.

GLENN, N. D. and N. WEAVER. (1979) "Attitudes toward premarital, extramarital, and homosexual relations in the United States in the 1970's." Journal of Sex Research (May): 108-119.

GORDON, L. and A. HUNTER (1977) "Sex, family and the new right." Radical America ll (November/February).

GRIFFIN, S. (1979) Rape: The Power of Consciousness. San Francisco: Harper & Row.

GROSS, A. (1978) "The male role and heterosexual behavior." Journal of Social Issues 34: 87-107.

GOULD, M. (1983) "Constructing the meaning of female sexuality." Presented at the American Sociological Association Annual Meetings.

GOULD, M. (1980) "The new sociology." Signs 5, 3: 459-467.

HERMAN, J. (1981) Father-Daughter Incest. Cambridge, MA: Harvard University Press.

HIDALGO, H. (1984) "The Puerto Rican lesbian in the United States," in T. Darty and S. Potter (eds.) Women-Identified Women. Palo Alto, CA: Mayfield.

HITE, S. (1976) The Hite Report on Female Sexuality. New York: Macmillan.

HOLLIBAUGH, A. (1979) "Sexuality and the state: The defeat of the Briggs initiative." Socialist Review 45 (May-June): 55-72.

HUMPHREYS, L. (1970) The Tea Room Trade: Impersonal Sex in Public Places. Chicago: Aldine.

HUNT, M. (1974) Sexual Behavior in the 1970's. Chicago: Playboy Press.

KANTNER, J. and M. ZELNIK (1972) "Sexual experience of young unmarried women in the United States." Family Planning Perspectives, 4(4): 9-18.

KANTNER, J. and M. ZELNIK (1977) "Sexual and contraceptive experience of young unmarried women in the United States, 1971-1976." Family Planning Perspectives, 9(2): 55-71.

KATZ, J. (1976) "Passing women," in Gay American History. New York: Crowell.

KAYAL, P. (1977) "Homophobia in sociology." Gai Saber 1 (Summer).

KAYAL, P. and L. GIOVANNI (1980) "Sociological biases in the study of sexuality." Presented at the Society for the Study of Social Problems Annual Meetings.

KELLER, S. (1985) Personal communication, June 7.

KINSEY, A., W. B. POMEROY, C. E. MARTIN, and P. GEBHARD (1953) Sexual Behavior in the Human Female. Philadelphia: W. B. Saunders.

KINSEY, A., W. B. POMEROY, and C. E. MARTIN. (1948) Sexual Behavior in the Human Male. Philadelphia: W. B. Saunders.

KOEDT, A. (1970) "The myth of the vaginal orgasm," in L. Tanner (ed.) Voices from Women's Liberation. New York: New American Library.

KRIEGER, S. (1983) The Mirror Dance. Philadelphia: Temple University Press.

KRIEGER, S. (1982) "Lesbian identity and community: Recent social science literature." Signs 8, 1: 91-108.

LADAS, A., B. WHIPPLE, and J. PERRY (1982) The G-Spot and Other Recent Discoveries about Human Sexuality. New York: Holt.

LAWS, J. and P. SCHWARTZ, (1977) Sexual Scripts: The Social Construction of Female Sexuality. Hinsdale, IL: Dryden Press.

LORDE, A. (1984) "The master's tools will never dismantle the master's house," in A. Lorde, Sister Outsider. Trumansberg, NY: Crossing Press.

LUKER, K. (1984) Abortion and the Politics of Motherhood. Berkeley: University of California Press.

LUKER, K. (1975) Taking Chances: Abortion and the Decision Not to Contracept. Berkeley: University of California Press.

MACKINNON, C. (1982) "Feminism, Marxism, method and the state: An agenda for theory." Signs 7, 3: 515-544.

MASTERS, W. H. and V. JOHNSON (1966) Human Sexual Response. Boston: Little, Brown.

MILLER, P. Y. and M. R. FOWLKES (1980) "Social and behavioral constructions of female sexuality." Signs 5 (Summer): 783-800.

MILLMAN, M. (1980) Such a Pretty Face: Being Fat in America. New York: Norton.

MILLMAN, M. and R. KANTER [eds.] (1975) Another Voice: Feminist Perspectives on Social Life and Social Science. Garden City, NY: Doubleday/Anchor.

NEWCOMB, M. D. and P. M. BENTLER (1983) "Dimensions of subjective female orgasmic responsiveness." Journal of Personality and Social Psychology 44: 862-873.

NEWTON, E. and S. WALTON (1984) "The misunderstanding: Toward a more precise sexual vocabulary," in C. Vance (ed.) Pleasure and Danger. Boston: Routledge & Kegan Paul.

PEPLAU, L. and S. GORDON (1983) "The intimate relationships of lesbians and gay men," in E. Allgeier and N. McCormick (eds.) Gender Roles and Sexual Behavior. Palo Alto, CA: Mayfield.

PEPLAU, L. A., et al. (1978) "Loving women: Attachment and autonomy in lesbian relationships." Journal of Social Issues 34 (Summer): 7-27.

PETCHESKY, R. P. (1981) "Antiabortion, antifeminism and the rise of the new right." Feminist Studies 7 (Summer): 206-246.

PETERSON, J. R., et al. (1983) "The Playboy readers sex survey." Playboy (March).

PLUMMER, K. (1975) Sexual Stigma: An Interactionist Approach. London: Routledge & Kegan Paul.

PONSE, B. (1978) Identities in the Lesbian World. CT: Greenwood Press.

RICH, A. (1980) "Compulsory heterosexuality and lesbian existence." Signs 5 (Summer): 631-660.

ROBERTS, H. [ed.] (1981) Doing Feminist Research. London: Routledge & Kegan Paul.

ROSSI, A. (1973) "Maternalism, sexuality and the new feminism," in J. Zubin and J. Money (eds.) Contemporary Sexual Behavior. Baltimore, MD: Johns Hopkins University Press.

RUBIN, D. (1969) Everything You Always Wanted to Know About Sex. New York: Bantam.

RUBIN, G. (1984) "Thinking sex: Notes for a radical theory of the politics of sexuality," in C. Vance (ed.) Pleasure and Danger. Boston: Routledge & Kegan Paul.

RUBIN, L. (1976) Worlds of Pain. New York: Stein & Day.

RUSSELL, D. (1975) The Politics of Rape. New York: Stein & Day.

RUSSELL, D. (1984) Sexual Exploitation: Rape, Child Sexual Abuse, and Workplace Harassment. Newbury Park, CA: Sage.

SAHLI, N. (1979) "Smashing: Women's relationships before the fall." Chrysalis 8 (Summer): 17-28.

SARREL, P. and L. SARREL (1980) "The Redbook report on sexual relationships: Part I." Redbook, October: 73-80.

SCHNEIDER, B. (1985) "The sexualization of the workplace: A challenge to sociological theory." Presented at the American Sociological Association Annual meetings.

SCHNEIDER, B. (1984) "The office affair: Myth and reality for heterosexual and lesbian women workers." Sociological Perspectives (October): 443-464.

SCHUR, E. (1984) Labeling Women Deviant. New York: Random House.

SHULMAN, A. K. (1980) "Sex and power: Sexual bases of radical feminism." Signs 5 (Summer): 590-604

SIMON, W. and J. GAGNON (1967a) "The lesbians: A preliminary overview," in J. Gagnon and W. Simon (eds.) Sexual Deviance. New York: Harper & Row.

SIMON, W. and J. GAGNON (1967b) "Femininity in the lesbian community." Social Problems 15: 212-221.

SIMONS, C. (1979) "Companionate marriage and the lesbian threat." Frontiers 4 (Fall): 54-59.

SMITH, D. (1979a) "A sociology for women," in J. A. Sherman and E. T. Beck (eds.) The Prism of Sex. Madison: University of Wisconsin Press.

SMITH, D. (1979b) "Using the oppressor's language." Canadian Newsletter of Research on Women (Spring).

SMITH-ROSENBERG, C. (1975) "The female world of love and ritual: Relations between women in nineteenth century America." Signs 1 (Autumn): 1-29.

SNITOW, A., C. STANSELL, and S. THOMPSON [eds.] (1983) Powers of Desire: The Politics of Sexuality. New York: Monthly Review Press.

SPENDER, D. (1980) Man Made Language. London: Routledge & Kegan Paul.

STACEY, J. and B. THORNE (1985) "The missing feminist revolution in sociology." Social Problems, 32(4): 301-316.

STANLEY, L. and S. WISE (1983) Breaking Out: Feminist Consciousness and Feminist Research. London: Routledge & Kegan Paul.

STAPLES, R. (1978) "The myth of black sexual superiority: A reexamination." Black Scholar 9 (April): 16-23.

STRONG, B. and R. REYNOLDS (1982) Understanding Our Sexuality. St. Paul, MN: West Publishing.

TAVRIS, C. and S. SADD (1975) The Redbook Report on Female Sexuality. New York: Delacorte Press.

THOMPSON, A. (1984) "Emotional and sexual components of extramarital relationships." Journal of Marriage and the Family (February): 35-42.

THOMPSON, S. (1984) "Search for tomorrow: On feminism and the reconstruction of teen romance," in C. Vance (ed.) Pleasure and Danger. Boston: Routledge & Kegan Paul.

VANCE, C. [ed.] (1984) Pleasure and Danger: Exploring Female Sexuality. Boston: Routledge & Kegan Paul.

WARREN, C. (1974) Identity and Community in the Gay World. New York: Wiley.

WEBSTER, P. (1984) "The forbidden: Eroticism and taboo," in C. Vance (ed.) Pleasure and Danger. Boston: Routledge & Kegan Paul.

WEEKS, J. (1977) Coming Out: Homosexual Politics in Britain from the Nineteenth Century to the Present. London: Quartet Books.

WEEKS, J. (1981) Sex, Politics, and Society: The Regulation of Sexuality Since 1800. London: Longman.

WEINBERG, M. and C. WILLIAMS (1974) Male Homosexuals: Their Problems and Adaptations. New York: Oxford University Press.

WEISSKOPF, S. C. (1980) "Maternal sexuality and asexual motherhood." Signs 5 (Summer): 766-782.

WILLIAMS, J. (1980) "Sexuality in marriage," in B. Wolman and J. Money (eds.) Handbook of Human Sexuality. Englewood Cliffs, NJ: Prentice-Hall.

WOLF, D. C. (1984) "Lesbian childbirth and woman-controlled conception," in T. Darty and S. Potter (eds.) Women-Identified Women. Palo Alto, CA: Mayfield.

WOLF, D. C. (1979) The Lesbian Community. Berkeley: University of California Press.

Women's Review of Books (1986) Reviews by Tong; Gardner; Cantarow; Ferguson (May).

ZELNIK, M. and J. KANTNER (1980) "Sexual activity, contraceptive use and pregnancy among metropolitan-area teenagers: 1971-1979." Family Planning Perspectives 12 (September/October): 230-236.

ZILBERGELD, B. (1978) Understanding Male Sexuality. New York: Bantam.

ZITA, J. (1981) "Historical amnesia and the lesbian continuum." Signs 7 (Autumn): 172-187.

5 Reproduction

BARBARA KATZ ROTHMAN
Baruch College, CUNY

T HIS is not an easy time to be writing a review of feminist work in reproduction. Just a decade ago, the issues for feminists concerned with reproduction were comparatively simple. They had to do with motherhood and with choice. Because women's rights to become mothers needed to be ensured, feminists were opposed to forced sterilization. Because women's rights *not* to become mothers also needed to be ensured, feminists were in favor of access to contraception and, as necessary, abortion. That was pretty much it. Just bearing those two issues in mind, one could develop a cohesive feminist reproductive policy. Women needed choices, and to make choices they needed information. From this flowed most of the work in the reproductive rights movement.

Today's issues are more complex. Contemporary feminist thinking about reproduction must grapple with such situations as surrogate motherhood, embryo transfers, fetal diagnosis and selective abortion, fetal surgery and fetal patienthood, forced cesarean sections, neonatal intensive care units, and much, much more. Where once the answers seemed to lie in personal choice— to have or not to have babies; where, when, and with whom to have babies— the issues today confront the limits of individual autonomy. Questions about prenatal diagnosis and selective abortion to achieve the "perfect" child, for example, have no simple answers in "greater choice." Abortions for potential disability threaten to divide the women's health movement as women active in the disability rights movement, courted by the New Right, find themselves isolated from women who are abortion rights activists. Abortion for preferred sex similarly shakes the reproductive rights movement. Class issues inherent in the institutionalization of purchasing reproductive services or products ("surrogate" mothers, the sale of semen or ovum or even of fetuses and embryos) open up new schisms in the women's health movement.

Some causes of the new complexities are recent reproductive technologies: in vitro fertilization, embryo transplants, embryo freezing, and more sophisticated prenatal diagnostic techniques. But there are also nontechnological, social changes: the commercialization of "surrogate motherhood"; court-

AUTHOR'S NOTE: I wish to express my appreciation for the thoughtful comments of Eileen Moran and Maren Lockwood Carden.

ordered cesarean sections; "Baby Doe" squads, hot lines, and ethics com-
mittees; and abortion clinic bombings. These are just some of the social
changes of the last decade. Interesting times, these.

The social and technological changes are all entangled, of course. A certain
kind of social environment opens the door for particular technological
development, while new technologies can call social expectations into
question and encourage social change. I have attended countless meetings in
the past few years where people have gathered, often as feminists, to discuss
the new reproductive technology. But what was ultimately discussed was not
the technology but the new reproductive ideology: how our ideas about
reproduction are changing. Much of the confusion at such meetings, as in
both the popular and the scholarly press, centers on finding suitable
theoretical and ethical frameworks in which to place the technology and our
concerns about it. What, after all, is or should be the feminist response to in
vitro fertilization? surrogate motherhood? charges of "fetal abuse" against
pregnant women? Baby Doe cases? sex selection? frozen embryos? If you find
yourself shaking your head, shrugging your shoulders, feeling a bit overwhelmed by it all, you're not alone.

Before considering these new issues and concerns, this chapter will first
explore such familiar topics as "maternal instincts," pregnancy discrimination,
the management of childbirth, and abortion rights. By grounding ourselves in
these familiar and comparatively well thought out areas, perhaps we can
approach the new questions with greater clarity.

TRADITIONAL CONCERNS:
THE MAXIMALISTS AND THE MINIMALISTS

Even without the new reproductive technology, reproduction has long been
one of the most challenging issues for feminists. The implications of male-
female reproductive differences present difficulties because reproduction is
one area in which such basic liberal feminist tenets as equality and
comparability do not apply. What, after all, is "equal" to pregnancy? What
would be "comparable"? The challenge has been to find a way of thinking
about that which is unique to women that will not be used against women in a
patriarchal society.

One way to handle the problem is to point out that, in most modern
industrial societies, it hardly matters: typically, a woman today spends
perhaps a year and a half of her life pregnant, and just a couple of days giving
birth. Reproduction is such a small part of our lives, such a tiny slice of our
time on earth, that there is no reason to let ourselves be defined by capacities
we so very rarely use. Although our biological roles in reproduction are
different, socially, as parents, we can be interchangeable: Our abilities to hold,
comfort, teach, discipline, love, and guide are the same. Men and women are
much more alike than different.

This perspective is what Catherine Stimpson (1980) calls "minimalist" feminism. The differences, particularly in reproductive capacities, between women and men can be socially insignificant—*if we choose to make them so*. "Parent" then is a better word than "mother" or "father" to describe the nurturant adult-to-child relationship: "Parenting" implies gender-free care, a social role that women and men are presumably equally competent to assume.

There is another, contrasting perspective, aptly dubbed by Stimpson (1980) "maximalist" feminism. The work of Alice Rossi (1977) is a good example. At first glance, it may sound much like the old nonfeminist biological determinism. In fact, minimalist feminists tend to see maximalist work as nonfeminist, perhaps even part of an antifeminist backlash. The maximalists emphasize that there are sex differences, genuine differences between men and women in biological parenthood and potentially in social parenthood as well. To be a mother, a biological mother, is not the same thing, they point out, as to be a biological father, and a very different social as well as biological relationship will exist at birth between parent and child.

These issues were brought to the forefront in Rossi's "Biosocial Aspects of Parenting" (1977), in which she argued that biological differences not only exist in pregnancy but continue to affect parental behavior after birth. Rossi evoked the concept of maternal instincts to explain these differences, basing her argument on some of the studies of maternal-infant bonding that began to appear in the 1970s (e.g., Klaus and Kennel, 1976). Unfortunately, she did not recognize the severe methodological limitations of these studies as did the authors in a recent recantation of their earlier thesis (Klaus and Kennel, 1983). Pulling from a variety of sources to conclude that mothering is in part "instinctual" behavior, Rossi wrote,

> Mother-infant interaction carries a cluster of characteristics that suggest the presence of unlearned responses. On a strictly physiological level, infant crying stimulates the secretion of oxytocin in the mother, which triggers uterine contractions and nipple erection preparatory to nursing. Without even being aware of it, the majority of women cradle their infants in their left arm, regardless of their particular handedness, where the infant can hear and be soothed by the maternal heartbeat familiar from uterine life. Close-up films of women after childbirth show a common sequence of approaches when their nude babies are placed at their side. They touch its fingers and toes with their own fingertips, put the palm of their hand on the baby's trunk, then enclose the infant with their arms, all the while rotating their heads to an *en face* position to achieve full, parallel eye contact, with increasing tension in the mother until her baby's eyes are open and eye contact is made. Even mothers of premature infants peering into incubators at their babies engage in head rotation to achieve *en face* contact [Rossi, 1977].

Rossi's work was like a lightning rod, drawing energy, heat and some light from its critics. The basic minimalist argument was summed up by Judith Lorber: "The crucial issue, it seems to me, is not whether mother-child bonding is in our genes, our evolutionary heredity or our physiology, but what are the social consequences of mother-child bonding?"(Lorber, 1977). There may or may not be some biological differences in parenting beyond the period of gestation, and even beyond lactation: The real question for the minimalists is, so what? Why should these differences, assuming they do exist, influence the gender distribution of family control, work relations, patterns of ownership, and the general social structure?

Before considering the implications of the maximalist/minimalist controversy, let us deal directly with the "maternal instincts" argument. Can the data presented by Rossi really demonstrate the existence of instincts that affect mothering behavior? Rossi says that infant crying stimulates oxytocin secretion, which triggers breast and uterine responses "on a strictly physiological level"—that is, the oxytocin secretion is perceived by the mother as a milk "let down," milk rushing into the main sinuses under the nipple, or even dripping or spraying from the duct opening. But leaking of milk is experienced by the majority of new mothers in response not only to the infant crying but also to sexual arousal, emotional arousal, leaning over, and just running up or down stairs. Gradually the let down becomes less of an immediate response, often taking a minute or two of actual sucking to activate. The leaking also becomes increasingly specific, which is a good indication of a learned response. Mothers, it seems, are not really responding so much to the physical sensation of infant crying but to the *social meaning* of the sound. "Let down," therefore, is a social as well as a physiological response, just as a person may respond with a pounding heart and clammy hands to a threateningly aimed gun. Adrenaline is secreted in response to the socially learned danger signal, and the physiological effects follow. Oxytocin too is stimulated by a socially learned stimulus, the crying of the baby, and it too has physiological effects.

Similarly, mothers holding infants on the left, over their hearts, may not be instinctual behavior but may be learned: Infants do calm down when they are held over a human heartbeat. And it is not a response geared to the familiar maternal heartbeat; tapes of strange heartbeats also soothe babies. When people do something that achieves a consciously desired end, it may be that they have learned, with or without complete awareness, that it works. Because it works that is the way people tend to hold babies. It not only feels right because the baby settles down, it also looks right because that is how we have seen it done.

The second major limitation of the studies Rossi (1977) cites is that they are all based on research on mothers, which tells us something about maternal responsiveness but nothing about the responsiveness of others. If these are instincts, how do we know they are uniquely maternal instincts? Do women without children, do men, do children, hold babies differently than do mothers? Or do they too put the baby on the left, and rotate their face to the parallel, en face position? Is what we are looking at maternal behavior, female behavior, or human behavior?

The "first touch" study referred to earlier is a particularly good case in point. The observed behaviors were indeed startlingly similar from one mother to the next, beginning with "fingertip touching of the infant's extremities and proceed[ing] in four to eight minutes to massaging and encompassing palm contact with the trunk"(Rossi, 1977). Taken at face value, it appears to be an example of an instinctual maternal response. But there are two problems with this study. One is that it still does not tell us what nonmothers do when presented with newborn infants under the same circumstances; the second is the interpretation of such behavior as natural and universal. These mothers were observed in the unique social environment of an American hospital. Frequently, more than an hour elapsed between the birth and the "greeting." The babies were born in standard delivery room settings, and presented to their mothers by hospital staff in a different room and at a later time. In human birth generally, without the constraints of the modern Western hospital, mothers and infants are *not* separated at the time of birth. Mothers either take the babies immediately from their bodies themselves, or are handed infants immediately upon emergence. The hesitant approach from the extremities is simply not possible with a newly born, slick, and squirming infant. In addition, in order to separate the effects of the nursing relationship from other maternal behavior, bonding studies intentionally chose *non-nursing* mothers—a rather strange notion in itself. Can there be an instinctual greeting sequence that never gets the baby to the breast?

The very idea that we can identify pure, instinctual maternal behavior by observing interaction between mothers and babies is naive. The mothers, whatever their instincts or lack of instincts, are fully socialized members of our society. Their behavior will always reflect social expectations. If there are maternal instincts, how could we ever know?

MAXIMALISTS AND MINIMALISTS AT WORK

While Rossi (1977) may have been naive in her use of research, she nevertheless struck a responsive chord. Whether responses are instinctual or learned, biological or social, who could deny the significance of the pregnancy and birth experience *to the mother*? Women feel these responses, feel this tug toward the baby, feel the significance of the pregnancy relationship for motherhood. The minimalist attempt to deny the unique nature of the pregnancy and birth experience, to consider these events as comparable to other experiences that men can and do have, may not meet the needs of women. Most profoundly, what has actually happened is that pregnancy and childbirth have been "medicalized," that is, rendered comparable to other medical or illness conditions. What is minimized turns out to be the emotional, social, and psychological components of motherhood. What is left as irreducible reality are the physical phenomena, which are then treated as medical problems from which one can "recover" with "treatment."

The medicalization of childbirth occurred in two areas. One, to be discussed later in this chapter, is in the direct management of maternity care. The second is in the occupational arena. To achieve comparability, minimalists must view pregnancy as a disability condition, similar to other disabilities, so that childbirth falls under sick-leave provisions. Thus women workers are made to seem comparable to men workers: They can become disabled, they can be sick, but when they recover, they regain their prior status. Jobs are to be held open until the worker recovers, whether the recovery is from a pregnancy or, say, a broken leg.

This way of minimalizing the uniqueness of pregnancy and the birth experience has not always served women well. Actual "recovery" from birth is a matter of days. A woman can certainly return to a typing job within a few days of a normal, healthy vaginal birth. The fact of the matter is that she is not sick. But biological motherhood comes in a social context. A day or so after the birth a new mother is usually in no mood to be sitting at a typewriter in an office. She is busy, tired, exhilarated, entranced with her baby, with more important things than her paid job on her mind. At a month, or six weeks, when the sick-leave or disability coverage begins to run out, the baby is not sleeping through the night—and so usually neither is the mother. The baby is beginning to smile at her. Women may not *want* to leave the baby to spend the day typing, filing, doing factory work. Even women in personally fulfilling jobs have been known to prefer spending their time with the new baby. And this is not a matter of physical health or disability.

For many women, fully paid but brief pregnancy disability leave and then child care—even free, high-quality child care—would not necessarily be the preferred solution. Women who do not want a maternity experience essentially comparable to men's experiences may find that the dominant, minimalist thinking in the feminist movement does not represent their concerns.

These work issues have been addressed by feminist attorneys. At a recent conference on women and the law (Women and the Law Conference, 1983), for example, participants debated "Pregnancy: Equal Treatment Versus Special Treatment." They "struggle[d] with the question whether, and if so, how, pregnancy, a unique physical condition of women, can be incorporated into a theory of women's equality under the law"(1983: 176). Those at the workshop discussed whether pregnancy "can be or should be compared, as a legal matter, to other physical conditions that similarly affect how a person functions, as required by the Pregnancy Discrimination Act, or whether a doctrine of special accommodation to pregnancy should be developed" (p. 176). Dominating the discussion was the awareness of all concerned that, given a fundamentally patriarchal society in which women are placed at a disadvantage, either way of treating pregnancy can be used against women.

The dangers in the maximalist approach—pregnancy and birth as unique female events—is that women will be trapped by biological roles into traditional social roles. The dangers in the minimalist approach—that pregnancy is like, say, a twisted ankle, and birth comparable to gall bladder surgery—is that women's lives will be limited, not expanded, by nontraditional roles.

Recent political gains by women have been made mostly by emphasizing the minimalist approach. In a society such as ours, where the rights of individuals (rights to try rather than to succeed) dominate, collective solutions are rarely available. There is no free and wonderful child care so that, whatever changes have been made in occupational opportunities, women still remain largely responsible for the care of children and families. Women at the top of the economic structure are able to "buy out" of some of those responsibilities by hiring other women as housekeepers. Women at the bottom of the economic structure have no such alternative. The unanticipated consequences of the class limitations of contemporary feminism and of the minimalist approach were the denial of how much time and energy these responsibilities take and the denial of the possible satisfaction and joys available to women in the family.

CHILDBIRTH

While the implications of a disability model for pregnancy are still hotly debated, the issue of direct management of pregnancy and childbirth brings a surprising consensus. The consensus comes not only from those taking the maximalist and minimalist feminist stances but also from the most traditional of women. Rossi and others who speak of maternal instincts speak strongly to placing birth back in women's hands, under women's control, redesigned to meet the needs of women rather than those of physicians. Feminist women are more comfortable when the issue is phrased in terms of individual rights of bodily autonomy, and more traditional women when it is phrased as a concern with the autonomy and integrity of families, but all agree that power must be removed from the institutions of medicine.

The medicalization of childbirth, the treatment of pregnancy and of birth as medical events, has not served the interests of women. That is not to say that individual women have not benefited from specific medical services such as the necessary cesarean section and the appropriately used antibiotic. These and other procedures have certainly saved lives and health, but the institutionalization of childbirth as a medical event goes far beyond individual treatments. It has meant placing doctors in the active role, and women in the passive position of patient, a recipient of services rather than controller of birth.

When childbirth became a medical event, women lost control over their own birth experiences. The medicalization began with the eradication of midwifery as a profession and continued largely unabated until the home midwifery movement of the 1970s. Observing childbirth in Boston hospitals at the end of this period, in the early 1970s, Nancy Stoller Shaw (1974) described the typical American birth. The women were placed on a delivery table similar to an operating table. The majority were numbed from the waist down, while they lay in the lithotomy position (legs spread apart and up in stirrups), with their hands at their sides, often strapped there, to prevent their contaminating the "sterile field." The women were unable to move their bodies below the chest. Mothers were clearly not the active participants in the birth. That role was reserved for the doctor.

> This does not mean that the woman becomes unimportant, only that her body, or more specifically, the birth canal and its contents, and the almost born baby are the only things the doctor is really interested in. This part of her and, in particular, the whole exposed pubic area, visible to those at the foot of the table, is the stage on which the drama is played out. Before it, the doctor sits on a small metal stool to do his work. Unless he stands up, he cannot clearly see the mother's face, nor she his. She is separated, as a person, as effectively as she can be from the part of her that is giving birth [Shaw, 1974: 84].

And in Boston hospitals over a decade later, Michelle Harrison (1982), an obstetrical resident, made virtually the same observations. Although the situation may be very different in home births and in some midwife-run birth centers, the pattern in hospitals remains the same: Doctors deliver babies from the bodies of women. The women may be more or less awake, more or less aware, more or less "prepared," and more or less humanely and kindly treated, but within the medical model the baby is the product of the doctor's services.

This alienation of the woman from the birth, and more fundamentally, from the *baby*, is, I believe, the most important and consistent theme in modern obstetrics. The perception of the fetus as a person separate from the mother has its roots in patriarchal ideology. In patriarchal societies, and in modern obstetrics as developed in such societies, the woman is pregnant with the man's child: Daddy plants a seed in Mommy; fetuses are "parasites" in maternal "hosts." This has been the underlying ideology in Western society and can be documented at least as far back as the early use of the microscope to see the "homunculus," the little man curled up in the sperm. But until recently the effects of this ideology on the management of pregnancy could only be indirect. For all practical purposes, the mother and fetus had to be treated as one unit while the fetus lay hidden inside the mother.

Radical change began with the development of techniques for fetal monitoring. Only a decade ago the way that medicine "monitored" or, to put it simply, "watched" a labor was to observe the laboring woman. *Her* heart rate, *her* blood pressure, the frequency and intensity of *her* contractions, and the rate at which *her* cervix, the neck of the uterus, was opening up provided the information on how the labor was going. An additional technique, more directly a measure of the fetus, allowed the heartbeat of the fetus to be heard by placing a stethoscope to the mother's abdomen.

Electronic fetal monitoring was first introduced for high-risk pregnancies but, as is so often the case, its use rapidly became widespread. Electronic monitoring provides direct information about the status of the fetus in three ways: externally, by ultrasound monitoring of the fetal heart rate and uterine contractions; internally, by fetal electrocardiogram obtained with electrodes passed into the uterus through the cervix; and by sampling of fetal scalp blood, obtained from an electrode screwed into the fetal head. As it turns out, electronic fetal monitoring may not really provide all that much more information than does good nursing care, but it certainly looks like more information, producing endless strips of printout for the duration of the labor.

But more important than the sheer quantity of the data, impressive though it is, is that the information comes in a new context. Instead of having to approach the woman, to rest your head near her belly, to smell her skin, you could now read the information on the fetus from across the room, from down the hall. While woman and fetus were still one being on the bed, medical personnel came to see them as two separate and different patients. This problem was exacerbated by continued development of a technology that renders the fetus visible, giving obstetricians more and more direct access to the fetus itself, its tissue and blood, and the direct observation of its movements provided by sonography. Within patriarchy, the separation between mother and fetus was already there conceptually; the new technology allows the separation to be reified. More and more, doctors developed a relationship with the fetus, which they saw as the separate patient within.

This technology was introduced at just the moment that increasing numbers of women were rejecting the patient role in pregnancy, often to the irritation and distress of their doctors. Wherever midwifery services were offered, women flocked to them. Home birth, virtually unheard of in the United States outside of rural poverty areas, reemerged as a respectable alternative. Out-of-hospital birthing centers were opened in cities and towns all over the country. As pregnant women increasingly declared themselves healthy and rejected the labeling of pregnancy as an illness, as a fundamentally medical process needing medical control, the doctors began looking more and more closely at the fetus within, the tiny, helpless, dependent fetus.

FETAL ABUSE?

As Ruth Hubbard (1984) has pointed out, pregnancy is increasingly seen as a conflict of rights between a woman and her fetus. In part, this is a response to the new technology that enables the obstetrician to see and perhaps to diagnose and even to treat the fetus; but it is also in part a response to the growing consumer movement in medicine and in part a continued growth of men's domination of reproduction. When the obstetrician perceives the fetus as a separate patient, the mother becomes a potential adversary, a barrier to the optimum medical care of the fetus.

The conflict in this situation has recently been dramatized in court-ordered cesarean sections. When women in labor or in late pregnancy have disagreed with their physicians (or who they thought were their physicians) over how to manage the pregnancy or labor, the doctors have turned to the courts (Hubbard, 1982). In several bedside juvenile court hearings, with one lawyer appointed to represent the unborn fetus, another to represent the pregnant women, and yet others representing the hospital, women have been ordered to submit to cesarean sections, the fetus within them claimed by the state as a "dependent and neglected child" (Gallagher, 1984). In 1981, the professional journal *Obstetrics and Gynecology* (cited in Gallagher, 1984) reported one such case in which the woman, although found to be psychologically competent, was forced to undergo a cesarean section very much against her will. The article quoted the current edition of one of the classic obstetrics textbooks, which states that the fetus has "rightfully achieved the status of the second patient, a patient who usually faces much greater risk of serious morbidity and mortality than does the mother"(cited in Gallagher, 1984).

Not all of these forced cesarean sections turn out to have been medically correct decisions. The condition of the baby in the case just described was actually far less serious than the doctors had anticipated. In another case, of a woman in Georgia with a *placenta previa* (placenta blocking the cervical opening), doctors testified that there was a 99% certainty that the fetus could not survive vaginal delivery and at least a 50% chance that the woman herself would die. Two weeks later the placenta had shifted and the woman had a normal vaginal birth of a healthy baby. The Georgia Medical Society headlined the story: "Georgia Supreme Court Orders Cesarean Section—Mother Nature Reverses on Appeal." But as attorney Janet Gallagher points out, a legal and political precedent had been set (Gallagher, 1985).

This has been made very clear to me in recent panels I have shared with obstetricians, where similar stories have been told of doctors who felt a cesarean section was necessary and got a court order, but in the interim the woman gave birth vaginally. As one obstetrician explained, "Mother Nature intervened." When I suggested that perhaps the moral of the story was that the woman was right and the doctor was wrong, he was offended. The mother was not right, he insisted—she was lucky.

Cesarean section is one of the most common operations performed on women, but is rarely done to save the life or health of the mother. Much more commonly, they are done in response to fetal indications because obstetricians, rightly or wrongly, believe that the laboring uterus is potentially dangerous to the fetus. Major abdominal surgery is conducted on the body of the women to help her fetus. In the crisis-like situation of a labor going poorly or which doctors believe is going poorly, the conflict of rights between the mother and the fetus are readily blurred.

The situation becomes even more problematic when surgery is performed on the fetus itself, with the mother opened up only to gain access to the fetus. Several operations of this sort have been done, including placing a shunt in a hydrocephalic fetus, to prevent fluid from building up in the brain. The procedures are experimental and have had little real success—the only babies to have survived appear to be those that probably would have survived without the surgery. But hopes are high that such procedures will eventually work. Anticipating women's possible objections, doctors, lawyers, and philosophers are already talking about "fetal advocates," people who can make decisions on behalf of the fetus and represent the fetus's interests, presumably particularly in those cases where the mothers resist experimental or personally dangerous surgery.

Fetal advocacy and fetal rights are also being urged in cases where a woman's behavior during pregnancy does not meet the standards established by her physicians. Women who behave in ways doctors believe are harmful to the fetus, such as smoking or using drugs or alcohol, may find themselves charged with "fetal abuse." One drug-using woman has already been incarcerated for the duration of her pregnancy, against her will, to protect her fetus. While no one likes to see pregnant women engaged in behavior that could be harmful to the fetus, the loss of basic civil rights of pregnant women, and perhaps all women of reproductive age, has frightening implications. The social and legal status of pregnant women is in danger of being reduced to that of vessels or containers for the products of conception within them (for further discussion, see Rothman, 1986a).

ABORTION

The fetus has replaced the woman as prime patient not only in childbirth but increasingly earlier in the pregnancy as prenatal screening and diagnosis have become more sophisticated. The technology that renders the fetus visible, and the woman by implication transparent, encourages obstetricians to identify increasingly with the fetal patient.

It is ironic to note that this focus on fetal diagnosis and screening has been used—with great passion and power—on both sides of the abortion debate in the United States. Right-to-life advocates have used the techniques of prenatal diagnosis, notably ultrasound, to make the fetus increasingly visible and *real*. The most dramatic example is, of course, the film "The Silent Scream," in which a sonogram (ultrasound picture) of a 12-week fetus is shown during an abortion. With the use of special effects (dramatic slowing and speeding up of the film to make fetal movement appear to change in intensity) and powerfully suggestive language (the "child" in its "sanctuary") the audience is asked to share the identification with the fetus within, and to ignore entirely the woman—never shown—in whom it resides. Sonography shows us the fetus as if in empty space, abandoned rather than protected in the womb.

On the other hand, these same techniques of prenatal diagnosis are being marshalled in support of the right to abort. Abortions where the fetus would be "defective" are among the most socially acceptable in America. Called "selective" abortion, this relatively new type occurs not because the woman wishes to avoid pregnancy but because she does not want to be pregnant with the particular fetus she carries—a fetus that may have a terminal disease, a profoundly disabling condition, or, as some fear, be of the "wrong" sex.

One of the most important tasks facing feminists today is coming to grips with the various uses of abortion and its many consequent meanings. A simple pro-choice or right to abortion position is not enough when faced with the complex issues brought by today's technology.

Kristen Luker (1984) has contributed to our understanding of abortion as a social issue by exploring the ideology of the activists in both the right-to-life and the pro-choice movements, and placing them in their historical context. Abortion has probably always been a personal problem for women, but as a political issue in America it dates back only to the mid-nineteenth century, when physicians used abortion as one more wedge toward gaining their professional status. Abortions were apparently widely available in America at that time, advertised in newspapers and performed by people with a variety of backgrounds. In driving out the "quacks," physicians in one sense were doing what they were doing in other areas of practice. They replaced midwives at childbirth in the same way: by attempting to redefine the services provided as "medical" in nature. But with abortion, another dimension was added. Physicians argued that their knowledge of embryonic and fetal development, minimal as it truly was at the time, enabled them to know what the women having abortions presumably did not know: that the embryo was a baby. Having made this claim, doctors were able to say that abortionists were not only incompetent, dirty, backward—all the charges they leveled at the midwives—but also that what they were doing was fundamentally wrong, immoral.

Physicians did not, however, want an absolute ban on abortions. What the doctors claimed, a contradiction highlighted by Luker, was that abortion was wrong, but physicians alone could determine when it was necessary. For example, abortion was necessary when the pregnancy threatened the life of the mother, a determination over which the doctors claimed technical expertise. Thus there were two kinds of abortions: the ones the doctors did not do, which were "immoral," and the ones the doctors did do, which were both moral and, almost by definition, "therapeutic."

As the overall health of the population improved, and as medical technology improved also, abortion to save the life of the mother became increasingly rare. While some physicians and hospitals continued to use abortion only to save the life of the mother in the strictest interpretation of that phrase, others began to take into consideration the woman's general physical health and eventually her emotional health. A gap opened between what Luker (1984) calls the "strict constructionists" and the "broad constructionists" in the way that they defined the preservation of the mother's life. The broad constructionists eventually sought to legitimate their interpretation of the law, through legalization of abortions for women's health, including emotional health. Once a "broad" definition or "liberal" abortion law was allowed, the inherent and often arbitrary power of physicians to do the interpreting was laid bare.

It is in this context that Luker places what she sees as a new force entering the abortion discussion: women, as women, claiming abortion as a right not dependent on the approval of their physicians but as a basic human right to control their own bodies, essential to their civil liberties and to genuine equality.

To oversimplify somewhat, there are the two ideologies concerning abortion today: On the one hand, there is the view that the fetus is a baby, with all the rights of a person—including the right not to be deprived of life except in self-defense. And on the other hand, there is the view that women have the right to control their own bodies, including the right to end an unwanted pregnancy. As important as these two ideologies are in shaping the abortion debate in America today, however, there is another equally important but less clearly verbalized ideology centered on population control and eugenics. Most Americans—in fact, the overwhelming majority of Americans—support legal abortion. And yet, it seems to me, most Americans are not feminists at heart. There is more to the abortion debate than the two ideologies proffered by abortion activists.

Consider again the very strong support, by over 80% of Americans according to a *New York Times* survey, for abortion when the fetus would be "defective." For those who are neither in the right-to-life movement nor particularly concerned with abortion as a specifically feminist issue, other considerations come into play. Fears of disability, extreme repugnance toward the mentally retarded, and firmly embedded cultural ideas about health combine to shape our attitudes toward abortion for "fetal defect." Thus a deeply felt and painful schism has opened up within the women's health and reproductive rights movement. Women in the disability rights movement are being actively and sometimes successfully courted by the New Right and the right-to-life movement. And other feminists, while rejecting "anatomy is destiny," somehow find themselves evoking anatomy as destiny and disability as doom to justify abortions. Addressing this issue, Adrienne Asch and Michelle Fine (1985) urge that

> the reproductive rights movement and other feminists not presume nor prescribe any reason, e.g., "the tragedy of the 'defective fetus'" for an abortion . . . activists cannot continue to exploit the disabled fetus as the good or compelling reason to keep abortion safe, legal, and funded. On the basis of women's rights alone,

abortion must be safe, legal and funded—not to rid our society of some of its "defective" members [1985: 52].

In my own work, I have explored the very painful dilemma of women pregnant with fetuses the world very clearly does not want and will not support: fetuses who would be mentally or physically disabled (Rothman, 1986b). Even when the woman does not herself share the cultural repugnance toward physically disabled or mentally retarded people, she must be cognizant of the world in which her child will live, and especially what that will mean after her own death. As Rosalyn Petchesky (1980) has stated about abortion and all reproductive decision making,

The "right to choose" means very little when women are powerless. . . . Women make their own reproductive choices, but they do not make them just as they please; they do not make them under conditions which they themselves create, but under social conditions and constraints which they, as mere individuals, are powerless to change [1980].

The women's health and reproductive rights movement emerged at a time when medical control was at its peak, when doctors exercised autocratic control over the reproductive lives of women. The profession of medicine determined what kind of contraception was available and made that contraception available, or not, to individual women. Abortion was available only with the approval of physicians. Women gave birth where doctors were willing to attend them, under circumstances arranged for the convenience of doctors.

Understandably, the first battle was to wrest control away from medicine. That battle is far from won, but already we can see beyond it. We can see that taking power away from doctors does not necessarily give power to women. There are other forces—economic, cultural, social—more subtle and ultimately more constraining than people in white coats.

LOOKING BEYOND

The new reproductive technology arrives, as everything always does, in a social context. It comes to us in a society that is still deeply patriarchal in its attitude toward reproduction. It comes in a society that individualizes social problems, and it comes in a society that takes little collective responsibility for its children.

Earlier I said that the most profound and consistent theme in modern obstetrics is the separation or alienation of the woman from her labor and from her baby. This trend accelerates with the new reproductive technology because it reifies the fetus as separate from the mother. The new technology goes even further, dividing formerly entwined aspects of motherhood, separating the genetic relationship from the pregnancy relationship. To become a biological mother used to mean to have a baby, half of whose genetic make-up came from your egg, grow in your body. No more. Women's eggs can now be removed from their bodies and fertilized elsewhere: If fertilization takes place in a petrie dish, we call it "in vitro" fertilization, fertilization "in glass." The fertilized egg can be returned to the same woman's body, but it can just as well be placed—and has been—in a different woman's body. Thus women, like men, can have their seed planted in another body, have a baby that is genetically "theirs," as we speak of men's babies as "theirs," but, like men, without pregnancy. Women, like men, can become genetic parents without gestation. Women, like men, can now become fathers.

But women can also do what men cannot (yet) do. Women can grow babies within their bodies. The change is that these babies need no longer be "of their seed." The baby can now be genetically unrelated to the woman in whose body it grows.

Why are we developing such technology? Ostensibly, it is to solve problems. This technology is most often presented in the popular media as a solution to the distressing problem of infertility: "New Hope for the Childless" is a typical headline heralding the latest breakthrough. In vitro fertilization can be used, as it was introduced, to bypass blocked fallopian tubes. Embryo transplants can be used to allow women with functioning uteri but non-functioning ovaries to become pregnant. Noble goals: While no woman should feel she *must* become a mother, surely it is a pity when a woman who *wants* to become a mother cannot.

The medical treatment of infertility, much like the medical treatment of childbirth itself, is decidedly a mixed blessing. True, some women have been helped to achieve pregnancies they would not otherwise have had. But the success rate for in vitro fertilization is only around 10%. Nine of ten women experience failure, a failure to achieve and maintain a pregnancy, after being treated with dangerous hormornes, after enduring several surgical procedures, and after spending much money.

Beyond the few women who do get pregnant, and the many who do not, this technology changes our ideas about what it means to "get pregnant," what it means to become a mother. Gena Corea (1985), in her research on the new reproductive technology, *The Mother Machine*, sees the technology as transforming the experience of motherhood and placing it under the control of men. "Women's claim to maternity is loosened," she argues, while men— and most of the "pioneering" doctors in this field are men—gain more control. The claim to maternity is loosened as motherhood is divided up between women, between genetic mothers (the source of the egg), gestational mothers (the women who carry the pregnancy), and social mothers (the women who rear the children). Under what Corea calls "this system of dismembered motherhood, none of these three women will have a compelling claim to the child"(1985: 290).

And so we confront the total alienation of the woman from the baby. The technology being developed is geared to making the separation ever more possible. At the beginning of pregnancy—with in vitro fertilization and embryo freezing and transplants—a woman's fertilized egg can be sustained outside her body. And at the end of pregnancy, with more sophisticated neonatal intensive care units, a woman's fetus can again be sustained outside of her body. The technology makes possible new questions about the relationship between the woman and the products of conception. Is the embryo hers? Does she own it, have rights over it, control its disposal, when it is not in her body? When in vitro fertilization produces "extra" embryos, who owns them? Who owns an embryo that can be frozen long after the death of the woman from whom it came? And at the end of pregnancy, again we must ask: Is the fetus hers, to do with as she will, after it leaves her body? When the rare late-term abortion results in a fetus no smaller or less viable than the premature infants in neonatal intensive care units, who owns that fetus (Rhoden, 1984)? Is it a fetus? Is it an "abortus"? Or is it a baby? And whose baby is it if it is the product of an abortion?

CONCLUDING THOUGHTS

These are some of the questions that complicate contemporary thinking about reproduction, making simplistic notions on "choice" and "information" insufficient to inform a feminist policy. New technology is changing women's relationship to reproduction and to motherhood, and the technology is being developed in and by a society that values neither mothers nor children. The most important work facing feminists in the area of reproduction is the articulation of a feminist ideology that can embrace the feelings of women as mothers, the technology of reproduction, and the social context in which both belong.

POSTSCRIPT

The editors of this volume have been asking, reasonably but insistently, that I add a final page or two on "where we are headed" or "theoretical directions for the future" or some such. And with equal insistence, and I hope with equal reason, I have refused.

It is tempting to wrap up troubling issues with some vague guidelines for future work, research, or theory. But I genuinely believe what I have said in concluding this paper: Coming to grips with these issues brought by the new reproductive technology and ideology is *the most important work facing feminists today*. If I could *do* that work, if I could point us clearly off into the future, I would. But I feel these issues are too complex, too divisive, and far too important for a simple summary and conclusions.

In my work on women's experiences with amniocentesis (Rothman, 1986b) I have tried to develop some of the vision I think we need—but even there, without limitations of space, it is only a beginning. There are no easy answers, and any attempt to formulate suggestions for future developments and theory at this time would be at best premature, and at worst misleading.

REFERENCES

ASCH, A. and M. FINE (1985) "Shared dreams: A left perspective on disability rights and reproductive rights." Radical America (May): 52.

COREA, G. (1985) The Mother Machine. New York: Harper & Row.

GALLAGHER, J. (1984) "The fetus and the law: Whose life is it anyway?" Ms. (September).

GALLAGHER, J. (1985) "Fetal personhood and women's policy," in Sapiro (ed.) Biology and Women's Policy. Newbury Park, CA: Sage.

HARRISON, M. (1982) A Woman in Residence. New York: Penguin.

HUBBARD, R. (1982) "Legal and policy implications of recent advances in prenatal diagnosis and fetal therapy." Women Rights Law Reporter 7: 201-208.

HUBBARD, R. (1984) "Personal courage is not enough: Some hazards of childbearing in the 1980s," in Arditti et al., Test Tube Women. Boston: Pandora Press.

LORBER, J. (1977) "Power politics and motherhood." Prepared for the Biosocial Perspective on Parenting: A Review Panel. Sociologists for Women in Society annual conference, Chicago, September.

LUKER, K. (1984) Abortion and the Politics of Motherhood. Berkeley: University of California Press.

PETCHESKY, R. (1980) "Reproductive freedom: Beyond a woman's right to choose." Signs 5: 661-685.

RHODEN, N. K. (1984) "The new neonatal dilemma: Live births from late abortions." Georgetown Law Journal 75, 5: 1451-1509.

ROSSI, A. (1977) "Biosocial aspects of parenting." Daedalus 106 (Spring): 1-32.

ROTHMAN, B. K. (1986a) "Case commentary: When a woman abuses her fetus." Hastings Center Report, February: 24-25.

ROTHMAN, B. K. (1986b) The Tentative Pregnancy: Prenatal Diagnosis and the Future of Motherhood. New York: Viking.

ROTHMAN, B. K. (1982) In Labor: Women and Power in the Birthplace. New York: Norton.

SHAW, N. S. (1974) Forced Labor: Maternity Care in the United States. New York: Pergamon.

STIMSON, C. (1980) "The new scholarship about woman: The state of the art." Presented at the CUNY Graduate Center, New York, October 8.

Women and the Law Conference (1983) "Sourcebook." Women and the Law 14th National Conference, Washington, DC, April 7-10.

6 Sexual Terrorism: The Social Control of Women

CAROLE J. SHEFFIELD
William Paterson College

A T a time when the media, the political right, and many of my students, male and female, have proclaimed the end of the women's movement, we must ask some hard, direct questions about the status of women in American society. In an era when women are indeed exercising hard-won options in areas such as employment, childbearing, and politics, they often seem to be limited in simpler choices—whether to go to the movies alone, where to walk or jog, whether to answer the door or telephone. Can we measure the success of a social movement for equality if we do not include an assessment of the quality of life of the affected groups? No aspect of well-being is more fundamental than freedom from personal harm motivated by hatred or fear of one's ascribed characteristics, that is, freedom from ideologically justified violence against one's person. Without such freedom it is impossible to implement other choices. To the extent that women's personal freedom is still restricted and denied, we can continue to speak of oppression.

All systems of oppression employ violence or the threat of violence as an institutionalized mechanism for ensuring compliance. "Inferior" peoples— whether they be blacks in South Africa, peasants in South America, or females in the United States—are kept in their place by fear, which is generated by periodic displays of force. Subordination, as described by Dworkin (1985), is a social/political dynamic consisting of hierarchy, objectification, submission, and violence. This chapter is largely concerned with the last element—violence—as a crucial element in the ongoing process of female subordination.

Sexual terrorism is the system by which males frighten, and by frightening, dominate and control females. It is manifested through actual and implied violence. All females are potential victims—at any age, any time, or any place, and through a variety of means: rape, battery, incest, sexual abuse of children, sexual harassment, prostitution, and sexual slavery. The subordination of women in all other spheres of the society rests on the power of men to intimidate and to punish women sexually.

In this chapter we will analyze the ways in which male dominance is established and maintained through sexual terrorism, primarily as manifested in our society today. That is, we shall consider terrorism as a crucial strategy in sustaining the power relationships of *patriarchy*, whereby maleness is glorified and femaleness denigrated. As the institutionalized mechanism for the social control of women, sexual terrorism operates at several levels: through (1) the normative dichotomy of good woman/bad woman; (2) the production of fear through expressions of the popular culture—rituals of degradation, music, literature, films, television, advertising, pornography; and (3) providing legitimation and social support for those who act out their contempt for women (e.g., rapists, men who beat "nagging" wives, and so forth).

Thus, while sexual terrorism is the objective condition of female existence—that is, living in fear of bodily harm—it also provides a theoretical framework for examining how patriarchal social orders are created and maintained. The three levels at which sexual terrorism operates—normative, cultural, and social—can be integrated into a broader conceptual model of terrorism in general, in which five basic components have been identified: ideology, propaganda, indiscriminate violence, "voluntary compliance," and perceptions of victim and oppressor characteristics.

IDEOLOGY

Terrorism must be "explicitly rationalized and justified by some philosophy, theory, or ideology—however crude" (Johnson, 1978: 273), and indeed no bomb thrower or world power is without a claim to a "higher principle" or "greater good." In the case of sexual terrorism, the ideological underpinnings of patriarchal power relationships serve as ample justification for violence against women. If maleness is superior to femaleness, then females must be described in terms of some basic flaw, some trait that makes their subordination both necessary and legitimate. Many feminist thinkers (e.g., Tavris and Wade, 1984) have identified this presumed "basic flaw" as female sexuality itself—tempting and seductive, and therefore disruptive; capable of reproducing life itself, and therefore powerful. Out of their own fear, men have sought to bring this threatening force under control by both physical and psychological means.

Although there is still much debate over the original basis for male dominance and the role of sheer physical force in that equation, by the time of full-fledged archaic states the ideological components were well in place. The story of Adam and Eve, along with its counterparts throughout the world, can stand as the basic cautionary tale of the dire consequences of unfettered female sexuality.

Moreover, if maleness becomes the standard of normality, femaleness (whether manifest by females or males) is necessarily abnormal. The definition of female behavior as somehow non-normative, a neat example of the social construction of deviance (Schur, 1984), sets in motion the process of stigmatization, which in turn becomes the rationalization for both gender stratification (patriarchy) and sexual terrorism.

The concept of female "deviance" reflects—indeed, some structuralists would claim that it is the original instance of—a basic division of the world into dichotomous types: female/male, nature/culture, emotion/reason, body/brains, and so forth. Not only is masculinity defined in opposition to femininity, but males are seen as self-reliant, courageous, competent, and rational. In contrast, females must therefore be dependent, sensual, emotional, and evil. If man is the maker of history, the one who does things, woman is "the mediating force between man and nature, a reminder of his childhood, a reminder of the body, and a reminder of sexuality, passion, and human connectedness . . . the repository of emotional life and of all the nonrational elements of human experience" (Lowe and Hubbard, 1983: 12; see also Sayers, Chapter 2 in this volume). To the extent that men must not harbor such traits and must distance themselves from femininity, contempt and fear of femaleness are logical concomitants of this dualistic conception of gender.

Yet another dichotomy lies *within* the construct of femininity itself: between the "good" woman and the "bad" woman. Somehow, some women are going to have to become "good" enough to serve as marriage partners. Apparently, this is achieved by accepting their limitations, controlling their basically evil nature, and placing themselves under the protection of a man. The "good" woman becomes the wife; or more likely, the wife is compelled to have these attributes, as one outcome of the complex historical process whereby women are transformed into private property (Firestone, 1972).

The pressure to achieve "goodness" is a powerful mechanism of social control; one must work constantly to earn the label of "lady," an accolade that can only be bestowed by men (Fox, 1977). Although some women may achieve instant respectability through wealth or lineage, most must strive to acquire and maintain that status. Further, becoming a good woman in order to secure protection from male violence is a rather dubious bargain; the home is hardly a haven from sexual assaults, nor does marriage shield women from nonfamily attacks.

The good woman/bad woman dichotomy has particularly troublesome consequences for black women in our society. In general, racism and sexual violence, particularly rape, are part of the same oppressive structure. Historically, U.S. rape laws were enacted to maintain the property rights of white men and to control black men and women. Although it was a capital offense for a black man to rape a white woman, the rape of a black woman (by either a black or a white man) was not considered a crime. According to the racist ideology, the black woman was inherently inferior and could therefore never achieve goodness. Thus, "to assault her and exploit her sexually . . . carried with it none of the normal sanctions against such behavior" (Lerner, 1973: 163).

Hooks (1981: 108) carries the argument one step further, to suggest that black women have had great difficulty forming alliances with men from either group in order to gain protection from the other. Neither the abolition of slavery nor the 120 years of American history since the Civil War have had much effect on the way in which black women are regarded, especially by white men. Their "blackness" continues to define their sexuality. Given the continued pervasiveness of racism in our society, it is reasonable to assume that women of color experience additional humiliation when they encounter the predominantly male judicial system.

In sum, all aspects of male supremacist ideology provide a justification for sexual terrorism as a means of keeping women in their place and thus reinforcing the gender stratification system of patriarchy across time and place. But the effectiveness of ideologies depends on how broadly and thoroughly they are disseminated and on how they are given concreteness.

PROPAGANDA

The second component of terrorism is propaganda—the methodical dissemination of information promoting this ideology. By definition, the information is biased, even false, designed to present one point of view and to discredit all contrary opinion (LaBelle, 1980). "Terrorism must not be defined only in terms of violence, but also in terms of propaganda. . . . Violence of terrorism is a coercive means for attempting to influence the thinking and actions of people. Propaganda is a persuasive means for doing the same thing" (Watson, 1976: 15).

Other chapters in this volume suggest the degree to which patriarchal ideology has shaped what passes for "knowledge" in such diverse realms as anthropology, sociology, psychology, economics, political science, medicine, and the law. These are all areas in which the new feminist scholarship has questioned and corrected many misconceptions (although the public remains largely unaware of this reshaping and reconstruction of knowledge).

The avenues of propaganda central to the theme of this chapter, however, are those of the modern mass media: television, radio, films, music, and advertising. It is not difficult to find telling examples in which the theme of violence toward women dominates. Battered women appear nightly on television (and even the programs presumably devoted to "educating the public" have a high titillation factor). Moviemakers such as Brian DePalma outdo one another in finding ever more gory ways to mutilate female bodies (a recent one being with a power saw). Lyrics for rock music have become offensive enough to elicit an agreement from record companies to provide warning labels. Pictures of women in bondage appear on album covers, in the pages of *Vogue* magazine, and in the windows of Bloomingdale's department store.

But the propaganda of sexual terrorism is most fully embodied in the books and films and paraphernalia exclusively devoted to the sexual degradation of women—pornography. The word itself is derived from the Greek *porne,* referring to the lowest class of sexual slave. Here the line between good and bad women may be erased, as all female bodies and all parts of the body exist for the pleasure of men. To its most severe critics, then, pornography teaches men not only what they can do with/to whores but also what can be done with/to one's wife, lover, or daughter (Barry, 1979; Russell, 1982). This view has received support from recent research on the link between exposure to pornography and subsequent tolerance of violence against women (Donnerstein, 1980; Malamuth, 1981).

There is no question that most pornography today articulates a male fantasy world in which women are typically depicted as depraved and insatiable, and therefore appropriate objects for rape, bondage, mutilation, and even murder. But there is a very heated controversy among feminists about the effects of pornography, the distinction between eroticism and pornography, the threat to civil liberties of antiobscenity campaigns, and the dangers of alliances with antifeminists.[1]

Pornography, however, is more than a sexual—or even legal—issue; it is also about power. Its economic power is immense; it's a multi-billion-dollar industry, involving a network of producers, distributors, retailers, and consumers. Even more important, pornography is about the power of naming, of naming women as body parts and their sexuality as depraved, thus literally "doing the dirty work" in the spread of the ideology of patriarchy.

The ultimate power of pornography is terrorization. Pornography embodies acts of sexual terrorism (rape, battery, incestuous assault, bondage, torture), symbols of sexual terrorism (gun, knife, fist, whip, etc.), and the legend of sexual terrorism (the male as dangerous; Dworkin, 1979). The extreme manifestations of physical violence found in much of contemporary pornography are considered by many people, feminist and antifeminist alike, to pose a threat to the safety of women and girls insofar as these images normalize sexual abuse and raise the level of tolerance for such behavior.

INDISCRIMINATE AND AMORAL VIOLENCE

According to classic theories of political terrorism, an ideology and its spread through propaganda are both necessary *and* sufficient causes of overt violence directed at people who possess a particular ascribed characteristic that legitimates their victimization. As described by Wilkinson (1974: 17), all terrorism involves "indiscriminateness, unpredictability, arbitrariness, ruth-less destructiveness and amorality." Sexual terrorism, then, is violence perpetrated on girls and women *simply because they are female*, as when the threat of sexual assault keeps many girls and women in a state of fear, regardless of their actual risks (Warr, 1985).

The element of amorality can be seen in the fact that only rarely do those who commit acts of sexual violence perceive themselves as having done "wrong"—even child molesters and incestuous fathers. Rather, like the rapists studied by Scully and Marolla (1985), they construct a vocabulary of motives and rationales from the surrounding culture that they feel will be acceptable to others. That this vocabulary is often shared by police officers, lawyers, and judges can be seen in the low rate of prosecution of crimes of sexual violence in our society (Polk, 1985). Indeed, the rationalizations may also be shared by an entire community. In the case of the New Bedford, Massachusetts, gang rape, for example, the largely Portuguese community interpreted the prosecution of the rapists as an incident of ethnic discrimination rather than a response to sexual violence.

Although from the viewpoint of women sexual terrorism could be defined inclusively, public perception will often be based on those acts that fall within the criminal law (keeping in mind that each state defines its own standards of appropriate sexual behavior, and that the federal law may hold to yet another standard). Despite such diversity, there is at least one unifying strand: The laws have been promulgated by male-dominated legislatures and interpreted by a male-dominated judiciary (MacKinnon, 1983; Bart and Scheppele, 1980). Changing these laws to take into account women's own definitions of their experience is perhaps the most difficult yet most crucial task for feminist activists in the coming decades (see Schneider and Gould, Chapter 4, and Baron, Chapter 17 in this volume).

At the moment, however, the generally recognized acts of sexual violence that have been prohibited by law include the following: rape, wife assault, sexual abuse of children, sexual harassment, and sexual slavery. And each has been defined from a male point of view.

Rape. The definition of rape, for example, was originally drawn to exclude the possibility of marital sexual assaults on the assumption that a wife's sexual services were part and parcel of the marriage contract (Russell, 1982). That is, the laws were designed precisely to protect a husband's sexual property.

In addition, the description of the forbidden act was based on the traditional model of sexual intercourse (i.e., vaginal-penile penetration), thus obscuring the whole context of violence in which the act takes place. This exclusive focus on the sexual component, then, requires some evidence that the victim was not "willing," in other words, that she resisted. For no other crime is a victim required to prove nonconsent; rape, however, is still viewed largely in terms of women's sexuality rather than men's coercion (Stanko,

1985). Women must prove that they resisted, or consent is presumed. Yet at the same time they are warned of the potential bodily harm that their resistance might encourage—a veritable "catch-22": If you fight back you'll get hurt, but if you don't we'll think you welcomed the attack. Yet recent research strongly suggests that women who physically resist are more likely than nonresisters to *avoid* being raped, without necessarily increasing the rapist's level of violence (Bart and O'Brien, 1984).

Redefining rape to include forms of sexual violation other than intercourse would be a first step in directing attention to the inherent violence and degradation of the phenomenon but would not necessarily advance a deeper understanding of the victimization of women. The value of Brownmiller's (1975: 5) claim that rape is a "more or less conscious process of intimidation by which *all* men keep *all* women in a state of fear" is that it draws attention to the power dimension of the act. But power relationships are themselves a function of complex historical/economic processes.

Other social scientists have argued that not all men are potential rapists and not all cultures provide a vocabulary of motives; rather, we should look to the links among socioeconomic inequality, general levels of violence in a society, and variations in gender stratification systems (e.g., Leacock, 1981; Sanday, 1981; Schwendinger and Schwendinger, 1983). The general finding from these reviews of the anthropological and sociological literature is that rape is part of an entire sociocultural complex in which men lose control over their own destinies and in which violence toward women is a response to powerlessness in other spheres of activity.

Yet when looking at contemporary America, Brownmiller's thesis receives qualified support from rape researchers Holmstrom and Burgess (1983: 36), who conclude that while it would have been more accurate to say that "rape is one way in many (but not all) societies that men *as a class* oppress and control women *as a class*," it is a fact that "macho" values are institutionalized in the United States today and that "male-dominated patterns of aggressive behavior and male-dominated institutions oppress and control women" (1983: 36).

Wife-assault. Here again in dealing with behavior that takes place within the privacy of the marriage, the law—and public opinion—often reflect the traditional assumptions of appropriate gender roles and power relationships. Yet much has changed over the past two decades as certain types of family violence have been redefined as "social problems," with the result that both public opinion and the law are changing.

As analyzed by Breines and Gordon (1983), these changes in the perception and definition of family violence are the result of a number of societal trends, including the feeling that intrafamily violence is a symptom of a deeper "crisis" in the American family; the notion of child-centered parenthood, which makes violence toward children less acceptable than in the past; the feminist emphasis on the family as source of oppression and on the translation of the personal into the public; and the growing acceptance of a "confessional mode" in which people are encouraged to "tell all." It would be a mistake, however, to lump all family violence together, as there are very different historical developments in both the incidence and the recognition of each type as a social problem. Note, however, that as these acts receive public attention they are also being privatized through the use of terms such as "family" or "domestic" violence (i.e., that these are really personal problems of unhappy individuals, and most likely due to a failure on the part of the wife/mother whose task it is precisely to maintain harmony in the home). This language also obscures the primary victims (Bush, 1985). Russell (1982) makes a similar point by suggesting that the term "wife-rape" is preferrable to either "marital rape" or "spousal rape" specifically because wife-rape is not gender neutral.

The recognition of wife assault as a social problem, for example, is primarily a product of the women's movement (Tierney, 1982) and has been the subject of an outpouring of feminist research and analysis over the past 15 years (reviewed in Breines and Gordon, 1983; Pagelow, 1985). The theme has also been taken up by the mass media, although not without an element of voyeurism and typically in a way that emphasizes the psychological problems of the abuser or of the marital pair. So while the personal has become public, it has not yet been transformed into the political. A feminist analysis of gender-power relationships in the wider society is still missing. Instead, violence against women has typically been treated by clinicians, law enforcement personnel, and the judiciary as a consequence of victim characteristics that either arouse or anger the batterers (i.e., the "victim provocation" thesis). It follows from this view that the solution lies in training women to watch themselves—to become, as it were, the monitors of their own actions. This is victimization internalized. Also, the simplistic solution to wife-abuse—that women should leave batterers—suggests that women are to blame if they do not leave. Blame, then, comes back on the victim for "accepting" this behavior. Only rarely, and only in the feminist literature, are the roots of such violence located in culture and social structure—the gender stratification system, the socioeconomic system, or the structure of the family (for this type of analysis see Schechter, 1982; Schwendinger and Schwendinger, 1983).

Yet as women begin to speak out and as others realize the extent of the phenomenon, pressures are generated on lawmakers and judges, who, despite their patriarchal interests, are slowly changing the legal definitions of appropriate marital behavior. Only a few states define wife-abuse as a felony per se, and in most other states the general assault statutes apply to violence directed against a wife. But lawmakers are loath to tackle the subject of wife-rape, particularly if the couple is living together, and in a few states a husband cannot be charged even if the couple is legally separated (Russell, 1982).

Although it is difficult to estimate the incidence or prevalence of wife-rape—in part because the wife may not interpret the situation in those terms—it is interesting to note that when researcher Irene Frieze (1983) sought a matched sample to compare with a group of 137 women who had reported being physically assaulted by their husbands, she discovered that close to 30% of the presumably violence-free comparison group had also experienced marital attacks. The findings from this study of wives indicate that wife-rape is strongly associated with other acts of personal violence; that wives do *not* precipitate such incidents by refusing sex or being unfaithful; and that husbands who rape appear to like violent sex and lots of it, and feel they have the right to demand it.

Sexual abuse of children. This category includes a number of different types of behavior, from incest to indecent exposure. Again, the statutes vary from state to state with regard to what acts are included, how they are defined, and how the offense will be treated (as a felony, misdemeanor, or a form of assault). In general, the phrases most often used to describe the sexual abuse of children are the following: (by definition) statutory rape, incest, molestation, carnal knowledge, indecent liberties, and impairing the morals of a minor. It is assumed that a child cannot give informed consent, even though it is possible that some adolescents are willing partners. In the case of incest, Butler (1978) argues that the term "incestuous assault" is more useful because it implies nonconsensual, essentially coercive behavior. Increasingly the use of children as models in pornography is specifically included in the statutes, although this behavior also falls well within several of the existing definitions.

It is impossible to know the true extent of sexual abuse of children; estimates vary from 1% to 10% for man/girl incest to 25% of all females being victims of some form of "sexual molestation" by the time they reach 18 years of age (data reviewed in Breines and Gordon, 1983: 521-522). The sexual abuse of children, unlike child abuse in general, is overwhelmingly committed by men against girls, a fact that the clinical literature succeeded in ignoring until the recent wave of feminist scholarship. By denying the male-dominant nature of incest, for example, the clinical establishment could continue to consider it a problem of individual psychopathology—on the part of the victim who may have acted "seductively," or on the part of the mother who "failed" to protect her daughter or who "collaborated" with her partner in "allowing" the assault—and not on the part of the assailant, who was only following his sexual nature.

Despite the existence of statutory prohibitions (and certain types of incest have always been criminalized), the sexual abuse of children is notoriously difficult to prosecute. The victims, if they recognize themselves as such, are relatively powerless; adults employ denial mechanisms; the perpetrator has the power to punish; and few outsiders can pierce the veil of privacy that protects the modern family. As in the case of wife assault, the women's movement has given many women the courage to speak out about their own childhood experiences, making it quite clear that they were not willing participants, that it was not pleasurable (a common male fantasy), and that they still bear deep psychological scars. Feminism has also spurred an analysis based on cultural and societal variables, to which gendered power relationships are central. Childhood victimization is a powerful socialization to that fear so essential to the entire system of sexual terrorism.

Sexual harassment. Although coined only recently, "sexual harassment" (Farley, 1978) is a phenomenon with which women were well acquainted before it was named. Sexual harassment refers to a wide range of coercive and intimidating behaviors that reinforce the basic fears of women by implying the ultimate use of force.

Although sexual assaults, in the work place or anywhere else, were already covered by the criminal law, other less physical but nonetheless threatening behaviors are now also forbidden. The most common legal definition includes any deliberate, repeated, or unwelcome verbal comments, gestures, or physical contacts of a sexual nature. A specific definition covering academic sexual harassment is that of the National Advisory Council on Women's Educational Programs: "The use of authority to emphasize the sexuality or sexual identity of a student in a manner which prevents or impairs that student's full enjoyment of educational benefits, climate, or opportunities" (Till, 1980: 7).

Under 1980 federal guidelines, sexual harassment has been subsumed under the rubric of discrimination as an unfair impediment to an individual's ability to get the job done or to advance on one's own merits. Many organizations now have written rules spelling out the proscribed conduct and providing channels for handling complaints, which may provide women with some protection or redress. However, the fact that sexual harassment is analogous to rape in that it is less an expression of sexuality than of power and represents a process of intimidation must not be overlooked. Only in the feminist literature and scholarship do we find the link to the larger system of gender stratification.

There is, therefore, some question about the effectiveness of anti-harassment laws given the "combined effects of occupational segregation, employment discrimination, and economic dependency [that] force women to remain in workplace situations that are decidedly threatening and coercive" (Schneider, 1985: 26). As Schneider also points out, because workplace harassment occurs almost by definition among people who know one another, the victim has the same problem as the victim of "acquaintance rape" in interpreting the event as totally unprovoked and in being believed by others.

With respect to antiharassment regulations drawn up by universities, Crocker (1983) notes that they cover a wide spectrum of actions, acknowledge the potentially damaging consequences for victims, provide ample warning to possible violators, and also raise community consciousness—all generally constructive outcomes. Yet Crocker also suggests that using the words "inappropriate" or "unwelcome" implies that there are appropriate or welcome leers and pinches that will not be considered harassment. Similarly, the use of words such as "coercion" and "force" implies that unforced sexual favors are acceptable. But is it really possible, given the power of professors over students, that even uncoerced sexual favors are truly willingly bestowed? Then, too, the ranking of offenses—the general assumption that threat of punishment ("fuck or flunk") is a more serious offense than promise of reward ("A for a lay")—makes little difference to the student, who may not even need to have the alternatives articulated in order to protect herself (Crocker, 1983).

In other words, in both the work place and academe, sexual harassment regulations may alert women to their rights, may restrain some men, and may raise the general level of consciousness of all members of the community, but as long as the gender stratification system remains intact, sexual threats will continue to characterize the lives of women outside the family as well as within.

Sexual slavery. Sexual terrorism may well reach its ultimate form in the practice of what Barry (1979) calls "female sexual slavery"—the international traffic in women and forced street prostitution. Although prostitution is illegal in most jurisdictions, our legal conception is actually very limited and misleading. Prostitution was defined as illegal in order to protect men (primarily from disease) and is viewed as a crime that women commit willingly. Barry argues that "female sexual slavery is present in all situations where women or girls cannot change the immediate conditions of their existence; where regardless of how they got into those conditions, they cannot get out; and where they are subject to sexual violence and exploitation" (1979: 33).

Another form of sexual slavery, practiced by individual pimps who employ intimidation or overt violence to force women and girls to sell their bodies for his profit, is more well known. The situation of runaway girls has recently been exploited by the mass media, along with general concern over the potential sexual abuse of "missing children"—both boys and girls (although we suspect that cases of male prostitutes receive disproportionate attention).

Procurers employ a variety of subtle as well as openly coercive techniques to attach their women to them, including both emotional and drug dependencies. Among urban blacks, where so many other forms of achievement are systematically blocked, Bell Hooks (1981: 108) notes that "the male who overtly reveals his hatred and contempt of women is admired," so that the pimp becomes a hero.

The newest pimp may be the broker who arranges marriages between American men and Asian women. These brokers, who sell women for a lifetime rather than for an hour or an evening, or who arrange for increasingly popular sex tours of Southeast Asia, combine racism—that is, the stereotypical view of submissive and exotic Asian women—with the traditional view of women as chattel.

Barry (1979) also extends the definition of sexual slavery to include situations where fathers and husbands use force to keep wives and daughters submissive and powerless. As we have noted for other types of family violence, it is often difficult to prove that victims were not volunteers, and the authorities are far more prone to see complicity rather than coercion. Few have asked the crucial question posed by Barry (1979: 70): "Are these women able to change the conditions of their existence?" If not, their complicity cannot be assumed.

VOLUNTARY COMPLIANCE

An institutionalized system of terror requires mechanisms other than sustained violence to achieve its goals. Sexual terrorism is maintained by a system of sex-role socialization that encourages men to be terrorists in the name of masculinity and women to be victims in the name of femininity. Therefore, the fourth element in the model of terrorism, "voluntary compliance," is almost an automatic assumption in cases of sexual terrorism. Not only do women "ask for" this type of treatment, but deep down they really "want it"—a belief bolstered by the pseudo-scientific authority of psychoanalysis. To the extent that the essence of femininity is defined as an innate masochism, coerciveness is rationalized away. This image is perhaps the quintessential aspect of the ideology, the basic theme of so much propaganda, a key to the vocabulary of motives, and an effective means of interjecting fear.

As long as each women clutches her self-doubts to herself, the line between compliance and coercion can be blurred. In one recent study of the responses of victims of sexual violence, Stanko (1985) found three common reactions among women, whether they were raped, battered, harassed, or incestuously assaulted: self-blame, shame, and guilt (responsibility). Such feelings complete the circle of the self-fulfilling prophecy as women internalize the identity of "bad women," the one who must deserve her fate (see also Burgess, 1985). This is also one way to resolve the cognitive dissonance of maintaining the image of a good woman while recognizing that awful things have been done to you: Either you're not all that good or what's happened to you isn't all that bad.

A third possibility is to realize that you are good and that you don't deserve to be attacked—neither perception being nurtured in the patriarchy. And here is precisely where the feminist reconstruction of reality can begin to erode the forces of fear. As Bart and O'Brien (1984) found, the women who resisted rapists also defied the traditional vocabulary of motives, and whether their resistance was successful or not, were less likely than other victims to feel depressed or to blame themselves. It is not quite clear what led to the original decision to resist, but there is no question that the experience of having resisted brought a psychic liberation. If rape is the purest expression of male dominance, than resisting (not just avoiding) rape is a powerful statement of self-worth.

PERCEPTIONS OF VICTIMS
AND TERRORISTS

Among the major goals of any system of terror are the erosion of public support for victims and acquisition of respectability for one's own cause. The effectiveness of all the other elements of terrorism can be judged by an examination of societal responses. With regard to sexual terrorism, the evidence is that such acts are the least reported of crimes and that when reported are least likely to be brought to trial or to result in conviction.

In addition, the exclusive focus of the law and the media is on the sexual nature of the crime; and because the victim and terrorist are usually known to one another, sexual assaults are treated as "acquaintance crimes" (i.e., the result of some personal problem between the individuals involved).

Yet sexual violence is pervasive (Stanko, 1985; Finklehor, 1984; Straus et al., 1980) and cuts across lines of age, religion, ethnicity, and social class. Although some research suggests no relationship to social class (e.g., Adler, 1985), other scholars disagree (e.g., the studies reviewed by Schwendinger and Schwendinger, 1983). These mixed findings reflect, in part, a political agenda. That is, if you see sexual violence as a response to socioeconomic conditions— at the macro and micro levels—you have a vested interest in finding that lower status subgroups are most likely to engage in sexual terrorism. If, conversely, you believe that sexually aggressive behavior is a generalized male trait or that all men in a society benefit from the patriarchal system, you will look for support in the finding of no social class effect.

It is always comforting to believe that crimes and other antisocial behaviors are restricted to people unlike those who make and enforce the laws—poor, uneducated, or nonwhite people. And it is easy to deny disconfirming evidence. Thus it seems likely that sexual terrorism is more widely distributed across the social class structure than is commonly assumed. But it is also possible that the proximate causes of sexual violence are disproportionately experienced by the less affluent.

In any event, whoever commits the crime stands very little chance of having a complaint filed or of being prosecuted. For example, in 1984, over 84,000 rapes were reported to the police (FBI, 1985), a 7% increase over 1983 and 50% increase since 1975. It is doubtful that, in such a short time span, this increase reflects only a greater willingness to report a rape or more effective law enforcement. The FBI calculates that, correcting for under-reporting, a rape occurs every two minutes. Yet rape has the lowest conviction rate of all violent crime.

As with rape, the true prevalence of wife-assault is unknown because the crime is so seldom reported. Although wife-assault is not yet an FBI crime category, federal analysts recognize that it is widespread and estimate that it is three times as common as rape. Russell's (1982) random sample of 644 women revealed that 21% had been subjected to physical violence by a husband. In their national study of violence in American homes, Straus et al. (1980) found husbands violent in 27% of the marriages analyzed. They suggest, however, that the true rate is much higher.

Similarly, the incidence of the sexual abuse of children is unknown. Finklehor (1984) estimates that 75% to 90% of the incidents are never reported. In spite of this, studies clearly suggest that child sexual abuse is of great magnitude. Reviewing the evidence from five surveys on incest between 1940 and the present, Herman (1981) found that one-fifth to one-third of all the respondents reported that they had had some kind of childhood sexual encounter with an adult male; between 4% and 12% reported a sexual experience with a relative, and 1 female in 100 reported having had a sexual experience with her father or step-father. In spite of the acknowledged prevalence of wife-assault and child sexual abuse, arrest and prosecution is arduous and discouraging and convictions are rare.

An identical pattern emerges when examining the data on sexual harassment. While accurate data are impossible to obtain, studies suggest that sexual harassment is pervasive. Farley (1978) found that within the federal government, accounts of sexual harassment are extensive, and that surveys of working women in the private sector suggest a "dangerously high rate of incidence of this abuse." The U.S. Merit System's Protection Board surveyed 23,000 federal employees in 1981 and found that within the two years prior to the survey 42% of the respondents experienced sexual harassment (Stanko, 1985). Moreover, younger, single women reported a higher incidence of harassment. According to Dziech and Weiner's (1984) study of academic sexual harassment, 20% to 30% of female students are victims of sexual harassment during their college years. While victims of sexual harassment are increasingly breaking silence and some are even successful in bringing cases to court, adjudication and conviction in these cases are rare.

CONCLUSIONS

As the task of confronting men's power to intimidate and violate females is manifold, the agenda for feminist research and activism must be diverse and bold. Therefore, in an effort to deepen and broaden our understanding of sexual terrorism, I would like to offer several suggestions for further research.

First, we must expand our understanding of the definitions and scope of sexual violence. Since 1971 when the first speak-out on rape was held, both feminist scholars and courageous survivors of sexual terrorism have broken silence on the darkest aspects of patriarchy. In the past 15 years we have pierced the curtain of ignorance of what W. W. Visser't Hofft (1982) calls "the twilight between knowing and not knowing." The breaking of the tradition of silence surrounding rape, wife-assault, wife-rape, sexual harassment, sexual slavery, incestuous assault, and pornography is truly revolutionary. Because women have been constructed within a male-dominated society, women's experiences of sexual violence have been viewed through a patriarchal lens, resulting in an illusion of at best insignificance, and at worst complicity. What was lost—or rather, what was denied—was a woman-defined understanding of sexual terrorism. As feminist theory comes largely from the experience of women, the breaking of silence has informed and transformed the study of violence against women. While the gap between women's experiences of male violence and men's definition of sexual violence still must be bridged, the recognition that violence must be defined, in large measure, by those who experience it provides a meaningful foundation for future research.

We still need, however, to know more about the actual extent of violence against women. Hence a national random incidence survey is imperative. Such a study should not be limited to the conventional criminal categories, but should include the opportunity for women and girls to provide subjective understanding and definitions.

Second, we need to bring together the various forms of violence against females in order to see the patterns. In furthering our understanding of the commonalities of forms of sexual violence, we can then examine areas of women's oppression that have been previously neglected in the literature on violence. For example, the link between medicine and sexual violence has yet to be fully explored. Corea's (1985) analysis of medicine as a form of social control, and the work of Stark et al. (1979) on the treatment of battered women in a hospital emergency room, represent an important introduction to this uncharted terrain. Additionally, the diagnosis and treatment of women in psychiatric care should be analyzed from the perspective of societal attitudes toward sexual violence and the role of violence in keeping women subordinate in institutions of care.

We need to know more about multiple personality syndrome and its connection to sexual violence. Similarly, an investigation of female self-abusers and studies of suicide and attempted suicide relative to sexual violence are necessary. Research into these areas would not only enlarge the scope of our understanding of sexual violence but would provide insight into the coping/survival strategies of victims and the ways sexual violence is processed by agencies of the culture.

Third, the role of violence in structuring and maintaining male-female relationships remains inadequately considered. This needs to be addressed at the macro level, where force and the threat of violence are functional to male supremacy and provide the foundation for other forms of domination and control. At the micro level we need to study the psycho-sexual processes that underscore the heterosexual social system. From this perspective, Hanmer and Saunders (1984) suggest that we look at the concepts of authority and obedience in personal relationships. Also, we should continue exploring the interconnections between the socially constructed dependencies of women and the further powerlessness engendered by physical intimidation and violence.

Moreover, the study of women should illuminate the study of men. This is generally, and notably, not the case in the study of sexual violence. For example, the majority of offenders are known to the victims, yet the significance of this has yet to be explored. To date, most of the studies involving offenders (Groth, 1979; Scully and Marolla, 1985) have been done with *convicted* sex offenders. Given that victims are least likely to report when the offender is known to them, and acquaintance rapes rarely result in conviction, studies on convicted offenders are limited in their ability to inform us about the complexities inherent in the phenomenon of men committing violence against women and girls whom they profess to love.

Fourth, there is a need for much more research into the legal system and its response to offenders and victims. While there has been both evidentiary and statutory reform in the legal codes, the greater problem in the litigation of sexual violence seems to be discriminatory enforcement. The chasm between legislative reform and women's experiences of the legal process as "the second assailant" (Stanko, 1985) remains wide.

Finally, I believe that the continuing study of the relationships between sexual terrorism and popular culture is crucial. The expressions of popular culture—literature, films, television, music, advertising, and so on—are vehicles for the transmission of patriarchal myths and attitudes.

Furthermore, the level of violence against females is not only at an all-time high, but indications are that it is increasing. To say that it is pervasive is not enough; acts of sexual violence are more severe and brutal than ever before. There is an apparent increase in gang rapes, serial rapes, and murders (which often involve dismemberment of women's bodies). This alarming phenomenon should be analyzed in relation to the propaganda of sexual terrorism and the production of fear.

Strategies to free women must be based on a thorough understanding of the roots and range of the system of sexual terrorism. The task of feminist scholarship is to forward the search for truth and, in so doing, develop a body of knowledge and a new curriculum about women, and to inform public policy. As Kathleen Barry (1979: 11) put it, "knowing the worst frees us to hope and strive for the best."

NOTE

1. This debate, or "sex war," as explicated by Ferguson et al. (1984), hinges on two radically different visions of feminist sexual morality. One group—the "radical feminists"—perceives not

only pornography but all forms of sexuality based on dominance and power inequality as supportive of the patriatrchal sex/gender system. The other group—"libertarian feminists"—argues that feminism must stand for liberation from the narrow confines of male-defined traditional sexuality, that women must be allowed to find sexual pleasure in a variety of hitherto forbidden ways, provided only that the relationships are consensual.

Libertarians claim that the antipornography activists would turn the clock back to a repressive morality in which female sexuality would be once more stifled. The radicals perceive libertarians as reinforcers of brutality in the larger society and among women. The debate among feminists, however, may make it possible to find some third path to defining a female sexuality that is both liberating and noncoercive.

In addition, many feminists doubt the effectiveness of using the law to control pornography when both are defined by male perspectives (Baron, Chapter 17 in this volume). Nonetheless, other feminists have written and promoted local ordinances that would define pornography as a threat to women's rights to move freely in the community and to enjoy equal protection of the laws (Blakely, 1985).

The antifeminists have, of course, an entirely different agenda in their crusade against "obscenity," one that has more to do with a fear of rampant sexuality (echoing the basic patriarchal position) than with the issue of gender power (Diamond, 1980). There is, then, a way in which the suppression of pornography, along with the suppression of contraception and access to abortion, could herald a new wave of puritanism that would once more deny to women the ability to define and control their own sexuality.

REFERENCES

ADLER, C. (1985) "An exploration of self-reported sexually aggressive behavior." Crime and Delinquency 31, 2: 306-331.

BARRY, K. (1979) Female Sexual Slavery. Englewood Cliffs, NJ: Prentice-Hall.

BART, P. B. and P. H. O'BRIEN (1984) "Stopping rape: Effective avoidance strategies." Signs 10, 1: 82-101.

BART, P. B. and K. L. SCHEPPELE (1980) "There ought to be a law: Women's definitions and legal definitions of sexual assault." Presented at the American Sociological Association meeting.

BLAKELY, M. K. (1985) "Is one woman's sexuality another woman's pornography?" Ms. (April).

BREINES, W. and L. GORDON (1983) "The new scholarship on family violence." Signs 8, 3: 490-531.

BROWNMILLER, S. (1975) Against Our Will: Men, Women and Rape. New York: Simon & Schuster.

BURGESS, A. W. (1985) Rape and Sexual Assault. New York and London: Garland Publishing.

BUSH, D M. (1985) "Doublethink and newspeak in the real 1984: Rationalizations for violence against women." Humanity and Society, 9(3): 308-327.

COREA, G. (1985) The Hidden Malpractice: How American Medicine Mistreats Women. New York: Harper & Row.

CROCKER, P. L. (1983) "An analysis of university definitions of sexual harassment." Signs 8, 4: 696-707.

DIAMOND, I. (1980) "Pornography and repression: A reconsideration of who and what," in Laura Lederer (ed.) Take Back the Night: Women on Pornography. New York: William Morrow.

DONNERSTEIN, E. (1980) "Aggressive erotica and violence against women." Journal of Personality and Social Psychology 39, 2: 269-277.

DWORKIN, A. (1979) Pornography: Men Possessing Women. New York: Perigree Books.

DWORKIN, A. (1985) "A word people don't understand." Ms. (April).

DZIECH, B. W. and L. WEINER (1984) The Lecherous Professor. Boston: Beacon.

FARLEY, L. (1978) Sexual Shakedown: The Sexual Harassment of Women on the Job. New York: McGraw-Hill.

FERGUSON, A., I. PHILIPSON, I. DIAMOND, L. QUINBY, C. S. VANCE, and A. B. SNITOW (1984) "The feminist sexuality debates." Signs 10, 1: 102-153.

FINKELHOR, D. (1984) Child Sexual Abuse: New Theory and Research. New York: Free Press.

FIRESTONE, S. (1972) The Dialectic of Sex. New York: Bantam.

FOX, G. L. (1977) "Nice girl: Social control of women through a value construct." Signs 2, 4: 805-817.

FRIEZE, I. H. (1983) "Investigating the causes and consequences of marital rape." Signs 8, 3: 532-553.

GROTH, N. (1979) Men Who Rape: The Psychology of the Offender. New York: Plenum.

HANMER, J. and S. SAUNDERS (1984) Well-Founded Fear: A Community Study of Violence to Women. London: Hutchinson.

HERMAN, J. L. with L. HIRSCHMAN (1981) Father-Daughter Incest. Cambridge, MA: Harvard University Press.

HOLMSTROM, L. and A. W. BURGESS (1983) "Rape and everyday life." Society (July/August): 33-40.

LABELLE, B. (1980) "The propaganda of misogyny," in Laura Lederer (ed.) Take Back the Night: Women on Pornography. New York: William Morrow.

HOOKS, B. (1981) Ain't I A Woman: Black Women and Feminism. Boston: South End Press.

JOHNSON, C. (1978) "Perspectives on terrorism," in Walter Laqueur (ed.) The Terrorism Reader. Philadelphia: Temple University Press.

LEACOCK, E. B. [ed.] (1981) Myths of Male Dominance: Collected Articles on Women Cross-Culturally. New York: Monthly Review Press.

LERNER, G. [ed.] (1973) Black Women in White America: A Documentary History. New York: Vintage Books.

LOWE, M. and R. HUBBARD (1983) Women's Nature: Rationalizations of Integrity. New York: Pergamon.

MACKINNON, C. A. (1983) "Feminism, Marxism, method and the state: Toward feminist jurisprudence." Signs 8, 4: 635-658.

MALAMUTH, N. M. (1981) "Rape proclivity among males." Journal of Social Issues 37: 138-157.

PAGELOW, M. D. with L. W. PAGELOW (1985) Family Violence. New York: Praeger.

POLK, K. (1985) "Rape reform and criminal justice processing." Crime and Delinquency 31, 2: 191-205.

RUSSELL, D.E.H. (1982) Rape in Marriage. New York: Macmillan.

SANDAY, P. R. (1981) "The socioculture context of rape." Journal of Social Issues 37, 1.

SCHECHTER, S. (1982) Woman and Male Violence: The Visions and Struggles of the Battered Women Movement. Boston: South End Press.

SCHNEIDER, B. E. (1984) "Put up and shut up: Workplace sexual assaults." Presented at the American Sociological Association Meeting.

SCHUR, E. M. (1984) Labelling Women Deviant: Gender, Stigma, and Social Control. New York: Random House.

SCHWENDINGER, J. R. and H. SCHWENDINGER (1983) Rape and Inequality. Newbury Park, CA: Sage.

SCULLY, D. and J. MAROLLA (1985) "Riding the bull at Gilley's: Convicted rapists describe the rewards of rape." Social Problems 32, 3: 251-263.

STANKO, E. A. (1985) Intimate Intrusions: Woman's Experience of Male Violence. London: Routledge & Kegan Paul.

STARK, E., A. FLITCRAFT, and W. FRAZIEW (1979) "Medicine and patriarchal violence: The social construction of a 'private' event." International Journal of Health Services 9, 3: 461-492.

STRAUSS, M., R. GILES, and S. STEINMETZ (1980) Behind Closed Doors. Garden City, NY: Anchor/Doubleday.

TAVRIS, C. and C. WADE (1984) The Longest War: Sex Differences in Perspectives. New York: Harcourt Brace Jovanovich.

TIERNEY, K. J. (1982) "The battered women's movement and the creation of the wife beating problem." Social Problems 26, 2: 207-220.

TILL, F. J. (1980) Sexual Harassment: A Report on the Sexual Harassment of Students. Washington, DC: National Advisory Council on Women's Educational Programs.

U.S. Department of Justice, Federal Bureau of Investigation (1985) Uniform Crime Report. Washington, DC: U.S. Government Printing Office.

VISSER'T HOFFT, W. W. (1982) The Terrible Secret: The Suppression of the Truth About Hitler's Final Solution. New York: Penguin.

WARR, M. (1985) "Fear of rape among urban women." Social Problems 32, 3: 238-250.

WATSON, F. M. (1976) Political Terrorism: The Threat and the Response. Washington, DC: R.B. Luce.

WILKINSON, P. (1974) Political Terrorism. New York: John Wiley.

7 Popular Culture and the Portrayal of Women: Content and Control

MURIEL G. CANTOR
The American University

T HIS chapter is about the messages women receive from the mass media and how these messages are created and distributed. Of special interest are the messages about women's place in society and their relationships with men. This essay will examine the presentation of sexual relationships in the most popular women's media: popular fiction such as confession short stories, other magazine fiction, Harlequin-type romance novels, and soap operas. Women are usually depicted as subordinate to men and passive-dependent, but even when presented as relatively independent the basic message is that sexual relationships are central and all-important in women's lives—more important than family, children, and career at the individual level, and, of course, more important than politics, the economy, or war and peace at the societal level. In other words, women's popular fiction presents a unidimensional world where neither women nor men are actively involved in the main events of the larger society. Romance, sexual activity, and sometimes even love are primary, with other traditional feminine concerns secondary.

Women's fiction has been scrutinized through a variety of methods, ranging from systematic content analyses to critical humanistic and feminist study. Numerous books and articles on the subject are now available and, with

AUTHOR'S NOTE: This article is dedicated to Phyllis Diness who died on September 24, 1985. She gave generously of her time and skills so that the content analysis reported here could be completed during a no-cost extension of an NIMH grant (No. 5R01MH32970-02). Without Phyllis, Eileen Zeitz, and Elizabeth Jones, this chapter could not have been written. Eileen and Liz helped draft the final report (Cantor et al., 1983) for NIMH, sections of which have been incorporated here. Also, I am especially grateful for the editorial assistance I received from Beth Hess and Myra Marx Ferree, to Kay Mussell for her critical reading, to NIMH for its support, and to the local chapter of Sociologists for Women in Society (SWS) for giving me the opportunity to present some of this material at a chapter meeting.

the surge of interest in popular culture and women's studies in the 1970s, courses on women's fiction are often included in college curricula. Yet most of the scholarship is in the literary criticism tradition (e.g., Radway, 1984; Modleski, 1982; Mussell, 1981, 1984; Honey, 1983). As an area of research, women's popular fiction has generated little interest from social scientists and even less from students of the mass media.

The few works that do exist in the sociological and mass media literature are either content analyses, showing that women are presented differently from men in all public media (see Tuchman et al., 1978, Gallagher, 1980; and Butler and Paisley, 1980, for reviews) or audience studies showing that women's tastes differ from men's. Although these studies are useful and informative, scholars (Gans, 1974; Ferguson, 1983; Cantor, 1980; Swidler et al., 1986) contend that it is not possible to understand culture, especially popular culture, without also examining the commercial system within which it is created. To understand any popular genre and the medium through which it is distributed, it is necessary to consider not only the content but also the organization of artistic production, including the economic context in which it is produced, its creators (writers, editors, producers), distributors (networks and publishers), and target audiences.

The items of popular culture considered in this chapter are manufactured and usually distributed through the mass media (magazines, books, radio, and television). Their primary function is to make a profit for those who own and run the companies that produce and distribute the fiction. However, fiction as a product differs from those items that are usually associated with the manufacturing and the industrial sector of the economy. Whether consciously determined or not, popular fiction as a symbol system has an *ideological* function as well as economic utility.

Women's fiction is defined as fiction written *for* women, usually with women as central characters. Because it is an economic commodity, the target audience is very important in determining the nature of the messages and ideology that are communicated. Not only is women's fiction written primarily for women, much of it is written *by* women. However, to qualify as women's fiction the writer does not have to be a woman, nor does the audience have to be all female. It is the audience *targeted* by the creator or distributor that must be female. The industrial system through which fiction is created and distributed is based on a consumer model of target audiences with different tastes and interests, audiences segmented by intellectual, economic, and social (age, gender, and community) characteristics. In the entertainment and publishing industries, most writers aim at particular taste segments or markets, and editors and publishers buy for those markets. Thus, although the fiction being discussed here is written and published primarily for women, each fiction type varies according to the medium, how it is supported, and how the target audience is defined.

This chapter will examine three fundamental questions:

(1) What messages (issues, themes) are brought up in this fiction and how have they changed over time?
(2) Who creates the fiction and under what circumstances?
(3) In what ways do the readers and viewers affect what is created for them?

We will not deal with the way women and women's issues have been portrayed in the news or in the movies. Gaye Tuchman (1978) has demonstrated that women are not considered newsmakers or even major news consumers and that political and policy issues relating to women have been relegated to the women's pages. Nor will we analyze the nonfictional material in women's magazines, although the few studies of women's magazines suggest that their nonfictional content leads the fictional in presenting a more "liberated" and independent women. But as Nona Glazer (1980) showed in her study of new magazines directed to women who work outside the home, while women may be in the labor force and released from the prison of enforced pregnancy if sexually active, they remain irrevocably tied to the female world of love, duty, and family.

Both gender and class are considered important audience characteristics. As is well documented, women and men, as separate target audiences, are presented with different world views (ideologies) in different media (Ehren-reich, 1984; Smith and Matre, 1975; Gerbner and Signorielli 1979). To understand the relationship between ideology and economic context in fiction targeted to middle-class and working-class women, this analysis will focus primarily on how messages about sexual relationships and activities changed from before World War II to the present, and secondarily on how these messages are manufactured and distributed.[1] Before presenting the major issues relating to the content and manufacture of popular fiction, some background material is presented.

BACKGROUND

The study of mass media and mass communications has a long and rich history in the United States. Except for a few classic studies done during the heyday of media research (1940s and early 1950s), the study of mass communications was at best gender neutral and at worst sexist. The classic research that considered women as not just another variable but as central includes *Personal Influence* (Katz and Lazarsfeld, 1955), the radio soap opera studies in *Radio Research 1942-43* (Lazarsfeld and Stanton, 1944), and *Workingman's Wife* (Rainwater et al., 1959) a study of *True Story* readers. Except for several content analyses of confession magazines and soap operas (Arnheim, 1944; Johns-Heine and Gerth, 1949), these studies focused on the audience. Because the research was funded by the advertising and publishing industries, women were primarily seen as consumers or opinion leaders in areas relating to fashion, the movies, and other frequently advertised consumer products. These early researchers were rarely concerned with the issue of women's status in society and how women and women's concerns were being portrayed in the media. (An early exception is Gerbner, 1958.)

This lack of concern is perplexing because specialized periodicals and novels have been published for women in Great Britain for almost 300 years and in the United States from the early nineteenth century (White, 1970). The rise of both magazine fiction and the novel was an outcome of the Age of Enlightenment (Ferguson, 1983; Fielder, 1960; Watt, 1963) and their history parallels the growth of the popular press (White, 1970). Although one might argue that newspapers were produced for a heterogeneous readership, it is clear that women were meant to be the readers of the new fiction produced in the late eighteenth century. Nor is there any doubt that this fiction was created not for art's sake but for profit, thus starting an industry that still flourishes. The bookseller was also the publisher who decided what would be printed, and decisions to support a particular genre often were made on the basis of previous sales.

Most of the nineteenth-century women's fiction was written for the middle-class "lady of leisure," herself a product of the industrial revolution. As literacy increased by the middle of the nineteenth century, a new group of female readers emerged—factory workers and shop clerks, who were avid readers of women's magazines such as *Godey's Lady's Book*, first published in 1837 (Beasley and Gibbons, 1977), domestic novels, and "papernovels." Most of this fiction can be classified as about romance or manners or both. From the early nineteenth century to the present, both the themes and the issues brought up in the story lines varied with the class membership of the target audience, but the underlying or deep message was the same: From Samuel Richardson's *Pamela* (1740-1741) to the latest supermarket Harlequin novel, women have been told that their most important task is to "find a man," usually for marriage. The techniques for finding this man (and keeping him) have changed over the past 200 years. The basic theme remains essentially intact but not static. For example, messages about sex per se have changed dramatically. In early fiction, marriage (the ideal state for a woman) was possible for those who remained virginal during courtship; today sex before marriage is not only considered appropriate but desirable. Yet despite this new sexual morality, the primacy of marriage and interpersonal relationships in women's lives has changed little. Similarly, although women are portrayed as more or less independent and autonomous in different periods, the underlying focus is love and romance, ideally leading to marriage.

Ever since Richardson's *Pamela* (1740-1741), the first "modern" novel, fiction has been subject to critical analysis. Although interpretive canons vary widely, there seems to be general agreement that domestic and sentimental fiction has from the outset contained didactic lessons concerning appropriate behavior in sexual relationships. The stories and themes found in the modern short story, the Harlequin-type romantic fiction, and the soap opera all have their roots in *Pamela,* the tale of a female servant whose employer tried every way he could imagine to seduce her. Failing in these efforts, he finally marries her. Conversely, in Richardson's next novel, *Clarissa Harlowe* (1747-1748), the protagonist succumbs to her seducer and dies. The legend of these two novels has remained salient for the next 200 years: "Bad women" had sexual relations before marriage or committed adultery and paid for their sins; "virtuous women" resisted temptation and ultimately triumphed. In the movies, television entertainment, soap operas, romances, and confession fiction, including the dime novels that were popular with men at the end of the nineteenth century, the dichotomy of "bad girls" and "good girls" also supports a double standard as men enjoy the bad girls before marrying the good ones. One might argue that although the tone and direction of men's fiction is more action oriented and adventurous than women's fiction, the portrayal of women is similar.

Most analysts consider the images of women in romance and domestic fiction in the nineteenth century, whether through books or magazines, as overly sentimental and passive (Douglas, 1978; Cohn, 1943). Although there have been revisionist analyses of women's fiction, showing that many women characters are independent, capable, and strong (Baym, 1978), critics of domestic and romance fiction are generally unsympathetic to the way women are portrayed and often unsympathetic to women in general. For example, Helen Papshasvily (1956) in her analysis of both nineteenth-century novels and magazine short stories considers the portrayal of sexual relationships in romance fiction as a reflection of the "real" world in which women ruthlessly use feminine wiles in their efforts to gain superiority and control over men.

This interpretation of women characters as strong and dominant and men as ineffectual, helpless, and often hapless clowns was widely shared by men and women in the publishing business in the period immediately following World War II. Although there was tacit recognition that the women's sphere was limited to sexual and domestic concerns, many critics believed that within the home women had usurped male authority. For example, one analysis of women's magazines (Woodward, 1960) argues that women have gone too far in their desire for power, blaming women's magazines for the reduction in high school math courses and for the prevalence of emasculated men in the United States. The themes of female dominance and the breakdown of male authority appear in many media of this period—from the comic strips, *Maggie and Jiggs* and *Blondie and Dagwood*, and early television shows such as *Life With Riley* and the *Honeymooners* to the vilification of mothers in Philip Wylie's *The Generation of Vipers* (1942).

Yet women's fiction and nonfiction can be read with different definitions of power, leading to entirely different conclusions. Even before the resurgence of the women's movement in the 1960s, some analysts recognized that the exclusive focus on the sentimental and domestic aspects of life found in all women's fiction presented women with a limited view of social reality. Women were certainly not portrayed as powerful in the marketplace (except as consumers in the twentieth century) or in the political arena. Although the overly sentimental story found in women's magazines disappeared around 1888, the basic message in 1940 was similar to that found in 1878: A woman's place is in the home, preferably a home where she can have lots of babies (Cohn, 1943). In the 1940s middle-class women's magazines were little different in essentials from their inception earlier in the nineteenth century, though more modern in their details.

MESSAGES AND ISSUES

This section will examine the changes in messages and issues found in women's fiction since 1940. Through reviews of both published and unpublished research, changes in four genres will be examined: fiction in a traditional women's magazine, a confession-romance magazine, soap opera, and romance novels. Women's fiction, both in print and in the electronic media, provides important clues as to the content, myths, and reality that constructed (and constrict) the world in which women live (Bernard, 1983).

Magazine Fiction

To document how women's position changed from the pre-World War II period to the post-World War II period, Betty Friedan (1963) looked at women's fiction in four popular magazines and found that before the war the stories showed "career women—happily, proudly, adventurously attractive career women—who loved and were loved by men" (1963: 38). By the end of 1949, however, only one out of three heroines in these magazines was a career woman—and she was shown in the act of renouncing her career and discovering that what she really wanted to be was a housewife (p. 44). From this analysis, Friedan contends that a new feminine mystique made the housewife-mother the model for all women (p. 37). To be fulfilled women must accept male domination and be sexually passive.

Other content analysis of women's magazine fiction also reveal the extent to which women are portrayed as defined by the men in their lives. A random sample of issues of *Ladies Home Journal, McCalls', and Good Housekeeping* between the years 1940 and 1979, for example, found four roles for women: "single and looking for a husband, housewife-mother, spinster, and widowed or divorced—soon to remarry"; all are categorized in relation to men and marriage (Franzwa, 1974). These findings are confirmed by Flora's (1971) study of *Redbook* and *Cosmopolitan*, targeted to middle-class women, and *True Story* and *Modern Romance,* targeted to working-class women. She found that female dependence and passivity are highly valued; on the rare occasions that male dependence is portrayed, it is seen as undesirable. Getting and keeping a man was also the central theme in English magazines between 1949 and 1974 (Ferguson, 1983). In this fiction, romantic love was both a necessary and sufficient condition for marriage, a state of existence to be sought and welcomed, just as its absence was to be avoided and feared. In the 20 years covered by her sample, there were only four instances of women who were not married or on their way to that happy state: two spinsters (in the sense that they had neither hope nor scheme), one widow, and one divorcee (1983: 47-48).

Data from our unpublished study of a middle-class (*Redbook*) and a working-class (*True Story*) magazine show that although there are consistent differences between the two in theme, literary style, and emphasis, marriage for all women was paramount (Cantor et al., 1983). This study had two specific objectives: (1) to find out if the messages about sex per se and rape differ in middle-class magazines as compared to working-class magazines, and (2) to see if the messages varied over the period between 1930 and 1979. We were especially interested in seeing whether the messages about love, marriage, and sex directed to women through popular magazine fiction changed during the postwar period. We found that although women's relationships with men remain central in this fiction and most women were portrayed as passive in political and social roles throughout five decades, not all women were presented similarly. For example, middle-class women are presented with a different world view through fiction than are their working-class counterparts. In particular, the message about sex and sexual violence varied significantly.

The content analysis focused on sexual interactions with emphasis on stories about rape. Whether a woman has been raped or not, the threat of rape is ever present, a fact of life reflected in literature and myth (Brownmiller, 1975). "Little Red Riding Hood," for example can be interpreted as the prototype of the most common rape theme—the woman (or girl) in the wrong place, without protection of family or friends, accosted by an evil man with uncontrollable sexual appetites, and saved by the "good" father or suitor.

True Story: Confession-Romance Fiction

Of all women's fiction, the most maligned by critics are the stories in confession magazines (Cantor and Jones, 1983).[2] Yet this genre has existed in its present form since 1919 when Bernarr McFadden decided to publish a magazine for women in which accounts of personal problems could be told in the first person in language that the average working class woman could read, relate to, and understand. Most of these "true" stories, however, are authored by people (mostly women) who are or aspire to be fiction writers (Cantor and Jones, 1983).

With the exception of the 1940s, the most common topic of *True Story* fiction was sex. In the 1940s, the dominant theme was not war but marriage, with all its accompanying difficulties such as discontent, boredom, quarrels and reconciliation, and mother-in-law troubles. Out of the 55 issues sampled from the 1940s, half the stories are about marriage. In every other decade samples, more than 35% of *True Story* fiction is about sex. Although there are some continuities, the way in which the topic is presented and the types of sexual interactions in which the characters engage vary from one decade to another. Overall, women rarely initiate sexual interactions. In the 1930s and the 1940s there are frequent references to "giving in" or "succumbing to his passion." In the 1950s through the 1970s that same type of act is referred to "as being seduced by his charms" or "giving in to his needs." The sexual drive is male, not female. Despite the reader's awareness that sexual interaction is taking place, sex is never graphically described in any of the sampled stories. Instead, various euphemisms and implications are used to tell the reader what is transpiring.

Confession fiction always has a moral expressed in terms of appropriate behavior, but appropriate behavior changes over the decades. For example, certain behaviors that were inappropriate during the 1930s through the 1950s, such as premarital sex, are now generally accepted. Up until 1964 virginity and chastity before marriage were among the most popular story topics; since 1970, these themes have virtually disappeared.

In stories involving the issue of premarital sex, all female characters who engaged in such behavior were punished. Nice girls said no, but it was recognized that even a "good" girl could transgress. In the 1930s there was almost no forgiveness for those engaging in premarital sex, regardless of the circumstances. In the 1940s and especially after World War II the scenario changed somewhat depending on the character of the "girl." A standard story across time is that a young woman is pressured into sex by a boyfriend, as conveyed in titles such as "Prove That You Love Me Now" and "If You Loved Me You Would." These stories can have different endings and punishments. For example in one story, a young woman who becomes pregnant is forced into a "shotgun" wedding, and the marriage ends in conflict and disaster. Another story also involves a woman who "gives in" but then "comes to her senses" and ends the relationship, or is jilted and so "brought to her senses" before she gets pregnant. Both women are punished for violating sexual mores; one by shame and having to live with a bad marriage, the other by guilt, remorse, and the dilemma of whether or not to tell future partners. Women in these stories have learned appropriate behavior from religious or family teachings; the "good" women who "fall" temporarily are frequently portrayed as shy, demure, and modest, and vulnerable to excessive pressure coupled with the desire for affection. The "bad" women who become pregnant and live with the consequences are frequently described as rebellious toward their families, often coming from broken homes, doing poorly in school, running with a wild crowd, and seeking love from more than one man.

If virginity is no longer valued, promiscuity and sex without love are still punished, often severely by rape or attempted rape. The rape stories follow a pattern regardless of the decade in which they appear. Women who are raped or involved in an attempted rape were typically engaged in some sort of inappropriate behavior prior to the event—out alone at night, in a bar unescorted, or otherwise acting independently. These stories repeat the double-edged message of most confession-romance magazine stories: Because women are unable to care for themselves, they had better not break any fundamental rules of behavior. There is, however, at least one contradiction in these stories. Although women need to be careful of men's darker nature, they also need men to take care of them. For example, in the 1960s several stories depicted women who were raped (or suffered an attempted rape) and were offered marriage (permanent safety) by their boyfriends. As the hero says, "No woman is safe out alone at night and I hope you know it now! Just let me look after you from now on, will you?" In another story, the boyfriend wanted marriage all along, but the woman, a new feminist, wanted her independence. Her subsequent rape brought her to her senses, and she accepted the offer of marriage.

There are rape stories to fit every cultural myth: rapes occur to women who hitchhike, swim in the nude on a deserted beach, go out to buy a newspaper alone after dark, refuse the advice of parents, and select unsuitable men for romance. In all cases, the woman is in the wrong place, she has chosen not to accept advice, or she acts too independently.

Redbook: A Middle-Class Magazine

When one tries to compare *True Story* to *Redbook* or similar magazines, the notion that all women's fiction is alike quickly dissipates. For example, sex is almost nonexistent in *Redbook*. Out of a total of 330 stories analyzed over a 50-year period, just 41 concerned sexual behavior of any kind. There were no stories about premarital sex, adultery, or any kind of deviant behavior. Also, none of the 41 sex stories describes explicit sexual behavior. Even in the 1970s, when sex became more prevalent as a topic, it is presented with "taste" and "decorum"; all is subtly implied. In the 1970s there are stories about women having affairs with married men, married women having extramarital affairs, and women living with men to whom they are not married, but most of these women ultimately come to see that such behavior is self-defeating though not necessarily wrong in moral terms. Affairs are ended because they are not satisfactory or because they offer no future benefits. The heroine usually comes to the conclusion that some other course of action is more appropriate, such as learning a new skill, getting a new job, or returning to school. As Marjorie Ferguson (1983) in her content analysis of British magazines points out, there are increasing numbers of stories in the 1970s in which the women characters seek self-improvement. Apart from the few stories about infidelity, there is almost no "deviant" sexual behavior. Only one rape story appeared in the entire sample of *Redbook* fiction, and it was similar to those found in *True Story*—the heroine was engaging in inappropriate behavior: She answered the door wearing only a slip.

Redbook's editorial policy for fiction differs from that for nonfiction. The problems of the "new" independent woman are more commonly discussed in nonfiction articles than in short stories. Most stories throughout the entire 50 years depict women as centrally identified with home, family, and romance. The emphasis is, and has been, on domestic conflicts. Specific details have changed over time (for example, more women work outside the home in the 1970s) but the themes have generally remained focused on love (getting and keeping a man), home (children's problems, husbands who stray, whether to work outside the home or not), and community (meeting neighbors, being included in neighborhood activities). Over the five decades stories remained similar in one respect that is difficult to document quantitatively: The *Redbook* story, both before and after a major editorial policy change in the 1960s, centers on problems faced by middle-class women who live in a world where they are essentially alone, whether married or single. Although many stories end with the woman accepting or seeking advice or help from her mate if married, or "catching her man" if single, the plot revolves around the inner thoughts of a heroine in conflict. In the 1930s and 1940s this conflict was often over career or marriage; in the 1970s there was at least one story in our sample in which the heroine had a conflict over whether to work outside the home as did her next-door neighbor or inside the home at a craft for less money so that she could be available to her school-aged children and her own aging mother. In the 1940s and especially in the 1950s, the conflict was over the guilt, loneliness, and frustration experienced through marriage. Although we do not claim expertise in psychological analysis, these soul-searching, guilt-generating introspections could be interpreted as reflecting a lack of intellectual excitement in daily life. Most *Redbook* readers are college educated, and after 1964 the magazine itself became an advocate of women's rights, especially the Equal Rights Amendment (ERA). There were nonfiction articles as early as 1960 discussing how women could combine marriage, child rearing, and career. Yet the fiction had quite a different message, far more traditional, stressing the mundane conflicts of domestic life. Most of the fiction revolved around an individual woman and her adjustment to her fate, especially if her fate was to be a wife and mother.

Modern Romance Novels

Throughout the 300 years that women's magazines have been published, their function has been to reach target audiences in need of guidance, either in the sexual or domestic sphere. Although the romance novel also had its origins in the industrial and communication revolution, its contents are different from both that found in *True Story* and *Redbook*. Rather than disseminating overt and concrete advice, the romance novel deals in fantasy and escape. Readers are rarely confronted with a mean world as they are in *True Story*, nor are they confronted with the problems of the domestic life as they are in both magazines. Rape and violence are present in some of the romances to add excitement, but the ideal romance always has a "happy ending" and there is only one moral: Romance is everything for women. The striking characteristic of this genre is its exclusive focus on the love relationship between the hero and heroine. Regardless of how realistic romance fiction has become, these books, targeted mostly to women of limited education and distributed in supermarkets and drugstores as well as bookstores, are fantasies and are usually remote from the reader's experience. (Both *Redbook* and *True Story* stories are "realistic" in the sense that they tap everyday problems.)

Although romance novels have recently attracted scholarly attention, there is no systematic analysis of their contents, largely because they are written by formula. Thus it is possible to speak of the "ideal romance," as Kay Mussell (1984), Janice Radway (1984), and Margaret Jensen (1984) have done, without necessarily examining the minute details of the stories. All three researchers acknowledge the existence of various types of romance—the gothic, the historical, the romance for the "aging" reader (in her thirties), and now even stories specifically written for teenagers (always a strong market for all women's popular fiction). Mussell, Radway, and Jensen agree that the triumvirate of love, sex, and marriage constitutes the essence of the romances, so that all other interests and activities fade in significance. For example, Radway's in-depth study of 20 romance readers convincingly demonstrates that after reading the novel, the reader is reassured that men and marriage really do mean good things for women. Regardless of the heroine's adventures, her occupational or community role, or her innate ability and intelligence, the married state remains the ideal in 1987 as it did in 1740.

However, there is another message in these novels and in this they differ from magazine stories and from the modern television soap opera: There is often a tenderness and love between the hero and heroine that is missing in the other fiction. Although violence is depicted, it rarely happens between the hero and the heroine. One overriding theme is the commitment of two people to each other. In this sense, the romance represents the essence of feminine values. According to Radway (1984), the fundamental message is that women want an exclusive and intense emotional relationship with a tender, life-giving individual. This longing is implicit and sometimes explicit in all romance fiction and may be the feature that distinguishes it from other kinds of women's fiction or romances of a different period.

For all its standardization and formula plots, this genre may be most representative of the new era that has emerged in the last two decades in the

United States, reflecting the contradictions in women's lives. While women have been liberated sexually, and a select few have rewarding careers, the new opportunities bring fears of failure in both arenas. On the one hand, the romance novels offer escape from the mundane realities of everyday life, and on the other, the contradictions, dilemmas, and paradoxes of women's position in the social order are played out, again and again. In these novels, women recognize that independence through waged work is a necessity, but still the ideal situation for women is to marry for both love and money. Women's work is always less important and secondary to men's. Although premarital sex with the "right" man is included in almost every modern romance as part of the formula, the heroine does not succumb early or without guilt. In the romances, sex is likely to be far more explicit than in the soap operas or confession magazines, but also less casual.

Both Jensen (1984) and Radway (1984) believe that the new romances reflect more sexual equality and represent women as stronger and more independent than they were portrayed previously. But as Radway (1984: 221) points out, most romances are ideologically conservative in that they support, at least temporarily, existing institutions and practices (especially love and marriage) and, in the end, the heroine's personal goals are always put aside for a deep relationship with a man.

Heroines are much more likely today than formerly to be well-educated professionals themselves; and many of the current heroines do not give up everything to marry, but rather there is an affirmation of the superwoman syndrome in some of the new fiction. As Mussell (1986) points out, heroines can now combine career and family. Because all romances end with marriage, the difficulties and problems of trying to "have it all" are never described (Rose, 1985).

A common claim in some of the newer romances is that economic security and even wealth are assured for women with strength and drive. More relevant here is the message that even if most people reject independent, strong women, there is always a man (sometimes equally strong, but often weak) for this woman to marry, and economic success, although an important part of the fantasy, is secondary. In the romance novel, whether the heroine is traditional and domestic or modern and active economically, romance leading to marriage remains primary.

Television

This section looks at television, the dominant medium in American life. The emphasis is on the soap opera but some aspects of prime-time television are also discussed. The first soap opera was broadcast on national network radio in the early 1930s, and since that time soap operas have continued to engage primarily female audiences. Yet, until recently, researchers failed to consider the soap opera as an integral part of television. As a genre (or program type) it has rarely been considered an important research topic. Thus most of what is known about television comes from studies of prime time.

Prime-Time Television

From the first content analyses of entertainment programs to the present, researchers have found that women are greatly underrepresented as leading characters or, in Gaye Tuchman's (1978) phrase, "symbolically annihilated." George Gerbner (1978) and Butler and Paisley (1980) reach similar conclusions after reviewing the content analyses available at the end of the 1970s. In addition, Butler and Paisley found the same pattern in children's programs, where males not only outnumber females but women are almost exclusively shown in family roles.

Despite an increase in participation of active women in prime-time entertainment during the past 20 years, almost all television continues to feature male authority in advertising, in children's programs, on the national news, and in prime-time shows. Reviewing 11 content analyses of television commercials carried out between 1972 and 1978, Butler and Paisley (1980) found that 90% of the voice-overs in advertisements are male. The assumption behind this practice is that women depend on men for advice and assistance in the purchase and use of products, even those associated with tasks considered traditionally female. From the earliest days of television to the present, oversized men have come out of the walls and down from the skies to tell women how to clean their kitchens and bathrooms. Women passively accept their advice, but actively engage in the actual cleaning and in serving meals to husbands, lovers, and children. The major difference between 1972, when researchers first looked at advertisements systematically, and 1986 seems to be that women are increasingly portrayed as those who earn money to buy the bread as well as serve it to their families.

Although there has been an increase in the number of women in starring roles in prime-time television, there has been little change in the actual overall proportion of women to men since 1969, when the Cultural Indicators at the Annenberg School of Communications in Philadelphia was established. Since then all types of evening and Saturday morning children's programs have been analyzed (Gerbner and Signorielli, 1979; Signorielli, 1986). The results show that the world of prime-time also is dominated by males and masculine values; of all characters portrayed on prime-time during the years 1969 through 1983, 75% were male, over 90% of whom were white. According to a report by Gerbner and Signorielli (1979), much of the world of prime-time revolves around questions of power and violence, which they equate with masculine values. Fifty-six percent of all prime-time characters and 80% of all weekend daytime characters (children's programming, primarily) are involved in violence. However not all groups are equally involved. For example, for every 10 characters who commit violence, the average number of victims is 12 for white males, 13 for nonwhite males, 17 for lower-class women, 18 for young women and nonwhite women, and 33 for old women. Although the report shows that more women are playing leading roles in recent years than they were in 1969, it also finds that young women predominate over older women and that most women are relegated to romantic and domestic roles.

Soap Operas

Some prime-time programs, particularly domestic and situation comedies, are targeted to female audiences, but only the daytime soap operas, as women's fiction, have a coherent and uninterrupted history. They were consciously designed and originated in the early 1930s for women in general and housewives in particular, and historically women have been portrayed differently during the day than they have in the prime-time hours in terms of both numbers and types of roles. In some respects the world of the soap operas is more realistic than nighttime drama. The social demography of the soaps, their locales, and the way social status, love and romance, sickness and health, crime and violence are presented appear as stylized representations of the real world. Like their prime-time counterparts, the soap operas also reflect the continuing inequalities and disparities among races, classes, and sexes in American society, but the inequalities between the sexes are not as obvious or as wide as they are in the evening programs. For example, the number of women characters in a soap opera usually is equal to the number of men (Weibel, 1977; Cantor and Pingree, 1983).

In the following discussion, soap opera content will be discussed to show how sex and moral issues have changed over time, with emphasis on the present.

Sex on the Soaps

The portrayal of sex on the soaps has been a controversial subject, receiving a great deal of popular media attention (e.g., People, 1982). Although the soaps seem to get increasingly steamy, actual sex acts are never shown on over-the-air television and could only be imagined on radio. In recent years, couples not necessarily married to each other are shown in bed, usually talking, but a scene can now end with an embrace. However, most of what has been called "sex" on television involves only intimations of sexual acts such as crimes of passion, rape, adultery, and premarital intercourse, or outcomes of such acts, such as pregnancy and abortion. As in the other media, the greatest change over time in the United States has been in the way sex and morality are presented.

In radio soap operas, for example, puritanism was the fundamental ideology; though people did divorce, virginity before marriage was highly valued; and sex outside of marriage was definitely taboo. As playwright and humorist James Thurber (1948) put it, my persistent eavesdropping has detected nothing but coy and impregnable chastity in the good women, nobly abetted by a kind of Freudian censor who knocks on doors or rings phones at crucial moments. Young Widder Brown has kept a doctor dangling for years without benefit of her embraces, on the ground that its would upset her children if she married again. Helen Trent, who found that she could recapture romance after the age of thirty-five, has been tantalizing a series of suitors since 1933. (She would be going on fifty if she were a mortal but, owing to the molasses flow of soap-opera time, she is not yet forty.) Helen is soap opera's No. 1 tormentor of men, all in the virtuous name of indecision, provoked and prolonged by plot device. One suitor said to her, "After all, you have never been in my arms" . . . Helen, thereupon went into a frosty routine about marriage being a working partnership, mental stimulation, and, least of least, "emotional understanding." "Emotional understanding, " a term I have heard on serials several times, seems to be the official circumlocution for the awful word "sex" [1948: 169].

Robert Stedman (1977) claims that sex on early television was far more "realistic" than on radio and that there was more of it. An extreme example of frankness was reached on *Love of Life* in 1958 when one of the heroines announced that she would not complete an unwanted pregnancy and had found a doctor to help her with her "problem." Although the word "abortion" was not used, the implication was clear. Such an event was not possible on radio soap operas because good women (and the character was a good woman) did not break the law knowingly (and abortions were illegal before 1973).

Unfortunately, there are no systematic qualitative or quantitative content analyses of television soaps from the early 1950s, when they were first televised, until Nathan Katzman's 1972 study. There is, however, much evidence from the 1970s and 1980s to show that sex is presented differently on the television soaps than it was on radio. For example, Katzman reported eight cases of marital infidelity, one bigamous marriage, four children born from parents not married to each other, and various other romantic problems involving infidelity and premarital sex. Rose Goldsen (1977), in a study of soap operas in the first half of 1975, found eight divorces, two bigamous marriages, four married couples who had separated, six divorces being planned, and 21 unmarried couples either living or sleeping together. Two women had more than one bed partner, and several children has been born or conceived with their paternity in doubt.

Although it is impossible to date precisely when the presentation of sex changed on television, there is no doubt that the message has been radically altered in both daytime and prime-time television. The pure and virginal heroine is gone: Premarital sex and adultery are now commonplace for all characters, whether portrayed as good or bad. Change is evident also from the kinds of stories that have become commonplace but were taboo a few years ago. Characters commit rape, homosexuals (both male and female) have come out of the closet, and prostitutes are often rehabilitated. Not only are such story topics and characters acceptable in this postpuritan age, but the clear-cut distinction between good and bad that marked the radio soap is long gone.

Characters may still describe transgressors as committing sinful acts, but these messages are not supported by the outcomes of the stories. Punishment is no longer handed out to the "bad" character as it was inevitably in the past. As an example, in *General Hospital* several years ago, Laura was raped by Luke and finally married him even though she was married to someone else when the rape occurred.

Different from the romance novel or the short story (or even most prime-time television), the soap opera goes on forever, presenting a world where no marriage is sacred and no love affair lasting. Most stories revolve around "love" triangles with participants trying to break up relationships so that new ones can form. Soap operas can be compared to mating dances with no end. When last counted in 1985, a favorite soap opera character in *All My Children*, Erica Kane, had been married numerous times in the 15 years the show had been on the air.

Although Cantor and Pingree (1983) found more women characters in the work force in the late 1970s and early 1980s than in previous decades, the soap opera, like all women's fiction, is never about work, politics, war, or peace but primarily about social relationships with dramatic elements provided by the characters' involvement with social and personal problems. For example, although characters have occupations, few are ever shown as working, while love and talk of love dominates (Downing, 1980). In the soap opera women (and men, too) are still prisoners of their sexuality. Nothing else, not even family (although these stories are essentially family sagas) is more important than bedding down with a current lover or, if without a lover for the moment, finding one. Women, both good and bad, can use any means they wish to accomplish their goals with little fear of punishment. The soap opera world of today is one in which everything and anything is fair in the quest for love and romance.

CREATIVE CONTROL

There has been increased interest among social scientists in the production of culture and the social organization of artistic production (Peterson, 1979). However, most analysts rarely consider how women's culture is created or how the industrial system in which popular culture is created relates to the kind of content received by audiences. Jessie Bernard (1983: 414) makes a distinction between "female culture" and the "culture of the female world." According to Bernard, a large part of the "culture of the female world" includes products created by men, so that much of the cultural diet consumed by women portrays them as they look to men, in a male context, and in situations of interest to men. "Female culture," in contrast, refers to that which is created by and for women themselves. Yet is is not always easy to make such a distinction when analyzing women's fiction, which often is written by women for women but is financed, produced, and distributed by industries predominantly under the control of men.

Women have been writing fiction since the modern novel and short story emerged, but just a few have been highly successful. Most writers of this fiction remain unknown even after they are published (Cantor and Jones, 1983; Cantor, forthcoming). Few make a living from writing, and most find it difficult to get their work published at all. Even those writers who do get published cannot be confident that future stories will be printed. However, as Fiedler (1960) also notes, the manufacture of novels was the first "business" (in the modern sense) that women could enter in large numbers. From the eighteenth century on, women fiction writers competed directly with males, and often their fiction achieved greater financial success although it was usually critically maligned.

Almost from the beginning women's fiction was a consumer product, created within an "industrial" setting. Writers, both men and women, who write formula fiction serve those in commercial enterprises that publish, produce, or distribute their products. As far back as 1725, Daniel Defoe argued,

> Writing is becoming a very considerable Branch of the English Commerce. The Booksellers are the Master Manufacturers or Employers. The several Writers, Authors, Copyers, Sub-writers, and all other Operators with Pen and Ink are the workmen employed by the said Master Manufacturers [quoted in Watt, 1974: 53].

That relationship has not changed. Rather, as publishing became even more businesslike and institutionalized, writers continued to lose control over their own work. Today publishing is still commerce, and although writing is a craft, writers are constrained by the realities of the marketplace. While writers still work in a cottage-industrial setting, their works are treated as products in a major world of conglomerates and corporate profits, as publishing has become increasingly interconnected with other means of communication such as the movies and television. One result has been greater selectivity in what and how much is published.

Although more people than ever are writing fiction, the number of books and short stories actually published has declined. While the population of the United States rose 83% between 1929 and 1980, the number of novels published increased by only 32% during the same period. The market for short stories has also declined. Over the years, women's magazines have chosen informative articles and advice over fiction, and of all women's magazines only *Redbook* will publish more than one or two stories a month. This policy remains intact even though the number of story submissions seems to increase monthly. According to *Writer's Yearbook* (1982), *Redbook* received 40,000 submissions; and the total number of submissions to all short story publishers reached 250,000 while only 500 were published.

The only fiction market that has grown substantially in the last decade is that for paperback romances (Radway, 1984; Jensen, 1984; Business Week, 1983). The number of romances published since 1979 is high in comparison to the pre-1979 years, and the increased market for this type of formula fiction has resulted in a tremendous increase in the number of women writing (or trying to write) romances of all types. In 1983, there were eight major publishers of 30 different lines or series of romance fiction, with 140 titles added a month. (This compares with about 20 books a month in 1979.) However, the field has been very competitive and, as in all fiction writing, supply now far exceeds demand (Cantor and Jones, 1983; Cantor, forthcoming).

Although it could be argued that writers are responsible for the images, themes, and myths found in modern literature, all but a few writers (men and women) are powerless to control the outcome of their work or to establish unique identities in the commercial publishing world. The most successful short story and novel writers, regardless of genre, are represented by agents. Thus for a writer to have a manuscript accepted, she or he must first be accepted by an agent and then by an editor. Acting as gatekeepers, agents and editors select from the huge number of submissions those stories that they believe the readers want.

Regardless of the difficulties in getting published, the myth persists that writing provides an avenue to easy success. True, the system does occasionally provide exceptional rewards for unknown writers, but for the majority, the problem of earning a living is not solved even if the writer is published (Cantor and Jones, 1983). Because agents, editors, and publishers have the power to accept or reject manuscripts, it is not surprising that most potential writers seek to please the gatekeepers first and the audience or themselves second. Yet despite their dependence on editors and agents, fiction writers with tenacity, perseverance, or great talent are likely to get their books or stories published somewhere.

Creating for Television

Creating for television, however, is very different from publishing written texts. Because there are so few opportunities in the film and television industries, most who seek work there never get hired. Once hired, most creative workers merely carry out the ideas of others. Soap operas, like all broadcasting and film products, are manufactured collectively by directors, producers, writers, and actors with the final authority resting with those who control the means of production and distribution. For example, both Harding

LeMay (1981), who was head writer on *Another World* for eight years, and Michael Intintoli (1984), who did the only ethnographic study of soap opera production, give examples of direct advertiser censorship. I (Cantor and Pingree, 1983) interviewed several writers and producers who reported how network officials and producers stopped them from freely expressing ideas that they thought would appeal to the audience. Because there are "minority" outlets, such as feminist or black publishers for both magazine fiction and novels, fiction writers are more likely than television writers to be able to express their own ideas. Few people are offered the opportunity to create television drama, and those that are must satisfy the advertisers and the production companies, who in turn must satisfy the audience.

In any commercial medium, creative workers who have values different from those held by the publishers, editors, and advertisers will have trouble being hired in the first place, and if hired will often be stopped from introducing "disturbing" ideas. Because so many women are trying to write women's fiction, editors and publishers have no problem in finding stories to fit their conceptions of the target audience. Thus artists, whether male or female, are limited both by the genre and the organizational and economic constraints in the manufacture of popular art forms.

AUDIENCE CONTROL

Although it is important to study the creators of culture, their images of society, their values, and objective social, political, and economic positions, it is equally important to understand how audiences influence the kinds of culture they receive. (The term "audience" will be used to denote readers and viewers as well as listeners.) Most who study popular culture, both its production and content, either ignore the audience or else consider the audience passive recipients of whatever publishers and broadcasters decide to produce and distribute. Although the fiction being discussed here has been dissected and analyzed from various perspectives for over 200 years, few critics have asked how audiences contribute to the messages found in these genres.

Under the capitalist system, the important influence on content is the intended or *target* audience, not necessarily the actual audience or audiences who may be attracted to the fiction. However, both audiences must be included when considering how content is created, evolves, and changes. I am not postulating that there is a direct, immediate, linear causal relationship between the target audience and the content but rather a dynamic interaction based on several different kinds of feedback from the audience to the creators. It is well recognized that different categories (genres) of fiction in the United States and other parts of the Western world are specifically written and marketed for readers who vary in demographic, intellectual, and other social characteristics (see Writer's Market, 1984). Also, although not as commonly recognized by critics, there is diversity in television programs; some are targeted to younger audiences, some to adult women, and some (particularly sports) only to men (Cantor and Cantor, 1986).

Changes in market structure can influence change in cultural symbols (Peterson, 1979: 158). For magazines and romance novels, the obvious corollary is that changes in editorial policy produce changes in symbolic content. Policy about what to print or broadcast usually changes when readership or audience declines. Thus when the target audience no longer finds the symbolic message congruent with its values and norms, editorial policy must adapt or lose readers and viewers. Intintoli (1984) reports that writers are given increased freedom to innovate when ratings drop. Others (Cantor and Cantor, 1986) also argue that both the committed traditional viewer and the overall audience ratings are powerful influences on soap opera content. When ratings are high enough to keep the advertisers happy, the soap opera creators write with the traditional viewer in mind. When the ratings fall, new and innovative stories are tried in order to attract new audiences. Historically, the soap opera creators have preferred to target the 18- to 49-year-old housewife; but as more women in that age category entered the labor force, the proportion of younger women and older women in the audience grew. Over time, that reality did not go unnoticed by the advertisers, their agencies, and the producers who changed the content of their soaps selectively to keep pace with survey data and the changing composition of the daytime audience. Younger women not in the labor force, still at home attending high school, became a target for certain soap operas and the older audience the target for others. Although all soap operas have changed, those aimed at the younger audience have experienced a more radical change. (See Cantor and Pingree, 1983, for a fuller discussion.)

There is no controversy that women, whether they are conceptualized simply as passive readers and viewers or whether they are considered as members of an actively involved group (market) who accept or reject what is offered, enjoy reading or watching romance fiction. Also there is little controversy that this fiction embodies traditional, patriarchal values. The emphasis on sex and sexual relationships through the years shows that the patriarchal culture dominates popular women's literature. However, there is controversy concerning how audiences interpret and incorporate those values. Most feminist critics (Millet, 1969; Friedan, 1963; Flora-Butler, 1971, 1980; Snitow, 1983) believe that those who read this fiction adopt a world view that contributes to their own subordination. Both Radway (1984) and Jensen (1984) take a different position. According to Radway, readers of romances both affirm traditional values and at the same time engage in behavior that is subversive of those values. While her study does not challenge absolutely the notion that romance fiction (and other popular art forms) are ideologically conservative, she contends that real people use the romance to address unmet needs experienced precisely because the ideal relationship is made highly improbable by the institutional structures of contemporary society. That is, because the romances are fantasy, they point out the weaknesses of patriarchy and traditional marriages. Jensen, in contrast to other critics, believes that most women are casual readers who view romances as momentary escape into an imaginative world separate from their own, not as a way of life to be desired and emulated.

CONCLUSION

In this chapter, both working-class and middle-class women's fiction were examined to show that messages about women's position in the social structure and their relationships to the opposite sex remain that of subordination. Although some analysts suggest that a "new" woman has emerged in recent woman's fiction, she is essentially similar to the traditional woman in her desire for romance and marriage. The analysis also shows that although fictional women are increasingly depicted in the work force, they are usually located in traditional women's occupations, doing work of lesser importance than the men in their lives. Further, while heroines in romances are almost invariably successful outside the romance itself, they are rarely more successful than the hero. The fundamental change in all genres concerns sexual behavior. More women characters have sex before and after marriage, and "good" girls have to be distinguished from the "bad" by behaviors besides participation in sex. Rape is used as punishment in the more traditional fiction, such as the confession stories, and in the newer soap operas and series romances as a means to excite audiences. With all the changes, the basic message still given is that men are powerful and women depend on romance for happiness. Such deeply implanted ideology produces stories and articles that carry a basically conservative message: Happiness depends on having a heterosexual relationship. The message that women are able to domesticate men prevails in soap operas and romance novels, but not in magazine fiction. In all fiction, the ideal is to get the "protection" of men as sexual partners (preferably through marriage). How to get the man of your choice varies from genre to genre. In the soap opera women must be seductive, and sometimes deceitful and dishonest. In the Harlequin novels studied by Jensen (1984: 193), the heroine should be a wholesome, giving woman who works for a living, but her work cannot be as important or involving as the hero's. If women are reading or viewing this fiction to receive advice for living, as some suggest (e.g., Herzog, 1944; Gerbner 1958), they are receiving a mixed message on specifics, but a clear message about which sex is dominant.

Antonio Gramsci in his *Selections from the Prison Notebooks* (1971) argued that a subordinate group, working through direct personal experience and common sense, cannot construct a coherent oppositional world view.

What is experienced may be in contradiction to available explanations, but it is very difficult to understand why or how. Thus, despite the experience of contradictions, women (both readers and writers) accept the way things are as "natural." Greater emphases on the role played by ideology, patriarchy in particular, in influencing both change and consistency in themes is fundamental to understanding not only the continuing popularity of this fiction but also how this fiction influences readers, writers, and the publishing industry.

Here and elsewhere I have proposed that all popular cultural products will change as the social and material conditions of their audiences change. To understand change, the audience must be conceptualized in terms of demographic variables, such as age, social class, and gender, as well as "world view." However, such an approach cannot be used by itself; and even if larger economic and social structures are included, the analysis is essentially a consumer model because it specifies which taste cultures are satisfied and which are ignored by publishers and broadcasters. Such a model tells us more about the groups who have power to influence the fiction marketplace than why these groups want such fiction or what needs the fiction serves.

This examination of women's popular fiction shows that through five decades of material and social change in women's position in the home and the labor force, certain basic beliefs about women and their relationship to men have remained constant *regardless* of the apparent changing position of women in the social order. Moreover, although women of different social classes receive different messages about their roles and appropriate behavior, all women receive the same basic message: that men's work and life choices are more important than women's, and that in order to be happy and fulfilled, women must have a love-dependent relationship with some man.

Cultural products marketed through the mass media are designed to reflect changing ideologies in order to retain audiences. However, they also continue and maintain social order by reflecting and transmitting traditional beliefs deeply implanted in Western culture. In this analysis, I have shown that even though recent women's fiction is "modern" in that is presents new designs for living, especially about appropriate sexual behavior (Mattelart, 1978), it also perpetuates old myths about fundamental social inequalities.

NOTES

1. This analysis omits the debate about the role of fiction (culture) in society. Peterson (1979), Andrews (1978), and more briefly Swidler et al. (1986) review the debate. Most who study the content of fiction use one of two different models to account for that content. Reflection theorists contend that content reflects the fundamental preoccupations of the society in which it is produced. In other words, content mirrors society. Others use a variation, "manipulation theory," claiming that content is decided by those who control the culture industries and therefore represent the ideology of the dominant class. These two positions are not necessarily mutually exclusive.

2. In 1979, we received a grant from the National Institute of Mental Health to study sex and

sexual violence in fiction directed at women readers of magazine fiction. The objectives of the study were to describe and examine messages about sex acts, sexual behavior, and especially sexual violence being communicated to women in the United States through the medium of magazine fiction. The purpose was to show how cultural and societal "myths" concerning these topics changed over time and to see if these myths varied in fiction directed at women of different social classes. In all 435 stories from *True Story* and 330 from *Redbook* covering the 50-year period 1930-1979. Details about the methodology are available in Cantor et al. (1983) or directly from Muriel Cantor.

REFERENCES

ANDREWS, B. W. (1978) Fiction in the United States: An Ideological Medium Supporting Capitalism? Master's thesis submitted to the Department of Sociology, American University, Washington, DC.

ARNHEIM, R. (1944) "The world of the daytime serial," pp. 34-105 in P. F. Lazarsfeld and F. N. Stanton (eds.) Radio Research 1942-43. New York: Duell, Sloan and Pearce.

BALL-ROKEACH, S. J. and M. G. CANTOR (1986) Media, Audience, and Social Structure. Newbury Park, CA: Sage.

BAYM, N. (1978) Women's Fiction: A Guide to Novels by and About Women in America, 1820-1870. Ithaca, NY: Cornell University Press.

BEASLEY, M. and S. GIBBONS (1977) Women in Media: A Documentary Source Book. Washington, DC: Women's Institute for Freedom of the Press.

BERNARD, J. (1983) The Female World. New York: Free Press.

BROWNMILLER, S. (1975) Against Our Will: Men, Women, and Rape. New York: Simon & Schuster.

Business Week (1983) "Why book publishers are no longer in love with romance novels." December 5: 157, 160.

BUTLER, M. and W. PAISELY (1980) Women and the Mass Media. New York: Human Sciences Press.

CANTOR, M. G. (1980) Prime-Time Television: Content and Control. Newbury Park, CA: Sage.

CANTOR, M. G. (forthcoming) "Women who write popular fiction: a re-examination," in R. Rush and D. Allen (eds.) Communications at the Crossroads: The Gender Gap Connection. Norwood, NJ: Ablex.

CANTOR, M. G. and J. M. CANTOR (1986) "Audience composition and television content," pp. 214-226 in S. J. Ball-Rokeach and M. G. Cantor (eds.) Media, Audience, and Social Structure. Newbury Park, CA: Sage.

CANTOR, M. G. and E. JONES (1983) "Creating fiction for women." Communication Research: An International Quarterly 10, 1: 111-138.

CANTOR, M. G. and S. PINGREE (1983) The Soap Opera. Newbury Park, CA: Sage.

CANTOR, M. G., E. ZEITZ, and E. JONES (1983) "Sex and sexual violence in fiction directed to women." Report to the National Institutes of Mental Health (Grant No. 5R01MH32970-02).

CASSATA, M. and T. SKILL (1983) Life on Daytime Television: Tuning in American Serial Drama. Norwood, NJ: Ablex.

COHN, D. L. (1943) Love in America. New York: Simon & Schuster.

DOUGLAS, A. (1978) The feminization of American culture. New York: Alfred Knopf.

DOWNING, M. H. (1980) "American television drama—Men, women, sex, and love," pp. 299-341 in B. Dervin and M. J. Voight (eds.) Progress in Communication Sciences. Norwood, NJ: Ablex.

EHRENREICH, B. (1984) Hearts of Men: American Dreams and the Flight from Commitment. Garden City, NY: Anchor/Doubleday.

FERGUSON, M. (1983) Forever Feminine: Women's Magazines and the Cult of Femininity. London: Heinemann.

FIEDLER, L. (1960) Love and Death in the American Novel. New York: Meridan.

FLORA, C. B. (1971) "The passive female: Her comparative image by class and culture in women's magazine fiction." Journal of Marriage and the Family 33 (August): 435-444.

FLORA, C. B. (1980) "Women in Latin American fotonovelas: From Cinderella to Mata Hari." Women's Studies International Quarterly 3, 1: 95-104.

FRANZWA, H. (1975) "Female roles in women's magazine fiction, 1940-1970," pp. 42-53 in R. K. Unger and F. L. Denmark (eds.) Woman: Dependent or Independent Variable. New York: Psychological Dimensions.

FRIEDAN, B. (1963) The Feminine Mystique. New York: Dell.

FRIEDMAN, L. J. (1977) Sex Role Stereotyping in Mass Media. New York: Garland.

GALLAGHER, M. (1980) Unequal Opportunities: The Case of Women and the Media. Paris: UNESCO.

GANS, H. (1974) Popular Culture and High Culture: An Analysis and Evaluation of Tastes. New York: Basic Book.

GERBNER, G. (1958) "The social role of confession magazines." Social Problems 5: 29-40.

GERBNER, G. (1978) "The dynamics of cultural resistance," pp. 46-50 in G. Tuchman et al. (eds.) Hearth and Home: Images of Women in the Mass Media. New York: Oxford University Press.

GERBNER, G. and N. SIGNORIELLI (1979) "Women and minorities in television drama 1969-1979." A research report in collaboration with the Screen Actors Guild. Annenberg School of Communications, University of Pennsylvania, Philadelphia.

GLAZER, N. (1980) "Overworking the working woman: The double day in a mass magazine." Women's Studies International Quarterly 3, 1: 79-95.

GOLDSEN, R. (1977) The Show and Tell Machine: How Television Works and Works You Over. New York: Dial.

GRAMSCI, A. (1971) Selections from the Prison Notebooks (Q. Hoare and G.N. Smith, ed. and trans.). New York: International Publishers.

HERZOG, H. (1944) "What do we really know about daytime serial listeners?" pp. 3-34 in P. F. Lazarsfeld and F. N. Stanton (eds.) Radio Research 1942-43. New York: Duell, Sloan and Pearce.

HONEY, M. (1983) "The confession formula and fantasies of empowerment." Women Studies 10, 3: 352-358.

HONEY, M. (1984) Creating Rosie the Riveter: Class, Gender, and Propaganda During World War II. Amherst: University of Massachusetts Press.

INTINTOLI, M. J. (1984) Taking Soaps Seriously: The World of Guiding Light. New York: Praeger.

JENSEN, M. A. (1984) Love's Sweet Return: The Harlequin Story. Toronto, Canada: Women's Press.

JOHNS-HEINE, P. and H. GERTH (1949) "Values in mass periodical fiction, 1921-1940." Public Opinion Quarterly 13 (Spring): 105-113.

KATZ, E. and P. F. LAZARSFELD (1955) Personal Influence. New York: Free Press.

KATZMAN, N. (1972) "Television soap operas: What's going on, anyway?" Public Opinion Quarterly 36: 200-212.

LAZARSFELD, P. F. and F. N. STANTON [eds.] (1944) Radio Research 1942-43. New York: Duell, Sloan and Pearce.

LEMAY, H. (1981) Eight Years in Another World. New York: Atheneum.

MATTELHART, M. (1978) "Reflections on modernity: A way of reading women's magazines." Two Worlds 1, 3: 5-13.

MILLET, K. (1969) Sexual Politics. Garden City, NY: Doubleday.

MODLESKI, T. (1982) Loving With a Vengeance: Mass Produced Fantasies for Women. Hamden, CT: Archon Books.

MUSSELL, K. (1981) Women's Gothic and Romantic Fiction: A Reference Guide. Westport, CT: Greenwood Press.
MUSSELL, K. (1984) Fantasy and Reconciliation, Westport, CT: Greenwood Press.
MUSSELL, K. (1986) Personal communication, February 15.
PAPSHASVILY, H. (1956) All the Happy Endings: A Study of the Domestic Novel in America, the Women Who Wrote It, the Women Who Read It, in the Nineteenth Century. New York: Harper & Row.
People (1982) "Are soaps too sexy?" June 14.
PETERSON, R. A. (1979) "Revitalizing the culture concept," pp. 137-166 in A. Inkeles et al. (eds.) Annual Review of Sociology. Palo Alto, CA: Annual Reviews.
RADWAY, J. A. (1984) Reading the Romance: Women, Patriarchy, and Popular Literature. Chapel Hill: University of North Carolina Press.
RAINWATER, L., R. P. COLEMAN, and G. HANDEL (1962) Workingman's Wife: Her Personality, World and Life Style (1959). New York: McFadden Books.
ROSE, S. (1985) "Is romance dysfunctional?" International Journal of Women's Studies 8, 3: 250-265.
SIGNORIELLI, N. (1986) Personal communication, April 12.
SMITH, M. D. and M. MATRE (1975) "Social norms and sex roles in romance and adventure magazines." Journalism Quarterly 52, 3: 309-315.
SNITOW, A. B. (1983) "Mass market romance: Pornography for women is different," pp. 245-264 in A. Snitow et al. (eds.) Powers of Desire. New York: Monthly Review.
SONNENSCHEIN, D. (1972) "Love and sex in the romance magazines," pp. 66-74 in G.H. Lewis (ed.) Side-Saddle on the Golden Calf: Social Structure and Popular Culture in America. Santa Monica, CA: Goodyear.
STEDMAN, R. W. (1977) The Serials: Suspense and Drama by Installments. Norman: University of Oklahoma Press.
SWIDLER, A., M. RAPP, and Y. SOYSAL (1986) "Format and formula in prime-time TV," pp. 324-337 in S. J. Ball-Rokeach and M. G. Cantor (eds.) Media, Audience, and Social Structure. Newbury Park, CA: Sage.
THURBER, J. (1948) The Beast and Me. New York: Hearst Corporation.
TUCHMAN, G. (1978) Making News: A Study in the Construction of Reality. New York: Free Press.
TUCHMAN, G. (1979) "Women's depiction in the mass media." Signs 4: 528-542.
TUCHMAN, G., A. K. DANIELS, and J. BENET [eds.] (1978) Hearth and Home: Images of Women in the Mass Media. New York: Oxford University Press.
WATT, I. (1974) The Rise of the Novel: Studies in Defoe, Richardson and Fielding (1957). Berkeley: University of California.
WEIBEL, K. (1977) Mirror, Mirror: Images of Women Reflected in Popular Culture. Garden City, NY: Anchor/Doubleday.
WHITE, C. L. (1970) Women's Magazines 1693-1968. London: Michael Joseph.
WOODWARD, H. (1960) The Lady Persuaders. New York: Ivan Obolensky.
Writer's Market 1984 (1984) Cincinnati, OH: Writer's Digest.
Writer's Yearbook 1982 (1982) Cincinnati, OH: Writer's Digest.
WYLIE, P. (1942) The Generation of Vipers. New York: Farrar-Rinehart.

III

GENDER STRATIFICATION

8 Gender, Work, and World Capitalism: Third World Women's Role in Development

SUSAN TIANO
University of New Mexico

O
VERWORKED and underpaid is an apt description of women throughout the world. Women's labor accounts for two-thirds of the world's work hours, yet they receive only 10% of the income and own less than 1% of the property (United Nations, 1980: 7). Recognition of women's disadvantaged status led the United Nations to declare 1975-1985 the Decade for Women, convening international conferences, passing resolutions, and formulating plans for enhancing women's well-being. Yet the goals of the Decade for Women remain largely unfulfilled: Much of the earth's female population, particularly in the underdeveloped regions of Africa, Asia, and Latin America, remains poor and powerless. Why is this so? Have women always and everywhere been disadvantaged, or is gender inequality a product of the contemporary world? Is socioeconomic development the solution to women's problems, or does it merely subject them to more "modern" forms of oppression?

Exploring these questions requires information about women's role in international development. During the past decade, "women in development" has emerged as an important scholarly focus, catalyzing a wealth of ethnographic and cross-cultural studies on Third World women. The insight that gender is as important as class or race in structuring opportunities and life-styles has guided this rapidly accumulating body of research. While some researchers have begun to conceptualize and measure the slippery notion of women's status, others have documented changes in women's roles within their society's gender-based division of labor. This chapter will paint in broad strokes the image currently emerging within this multidisciplinary enterprise.

WOMEN AND DEVELOPMENT: COMPETING PERSPECTIVES

The effect of socioeconomic development on women is a hotly debated issue. Current viewpoints can be subsumed within three competing perspectives. The *integration* thesis holds that development leads to female liberation and sexual equality by involving women more centrally in economic and political life. The *marginalization* thesis maintains that capitalist development makes women peripheral to productive roles and resources. Finally, the *exploitation* thesis claims that modernization creates a female proletariat supplying low-wage labor for accumulating capital. A brief description of these perspectives will provide a framework for the following discussion.

The integration thesis shares many assumptions with modernization theory and the human capital school of neoclassical economics (Sokoloff, 1978; Tiano, 1984b). According to this view, economic development involves women more centrally in public life as the expansion of jobs for women in industry and related services integrates them into the modern labor market (Rosen, 1982). Wage work increases financial independence while developing productive skills and modern attitudes that enhance opportunities and motivation for advancement (Goode, 1970: 239; Moore, 1965: 89). Women who choose not to enter the labor force also benefit from economic development and the liberal values that buttress it. The spread of egalitarian, achievement-oriented norms increases women's power by undermining patriarchal control (Lerner, 1958: 99; Inkeles and Smith, 1974: 26, 313; Rosen, 1982). In sum, this thesis argues, modernization enriches women's opportunities while helping them acquire skills and aspirations to take full advantage of their options (Eisenstadt, 1966: 38; Hoselitz, 1970: 17-20). In this way, women who traditionally have been victims of repressive patriarchal structures become autonomous contributors to society and its development efforts.

The marginalization thesis is a key tenet of developmentalist theory, the most influential early theory of women in development (Elliott, 1977: 4-5; Jaquette, 1982: 268). This thesis holds that capitalist development isolates women from production and political control. Women in precapitalist societies, according to this view, are integral to household production; however, with capitalist modernization, socially valued production is transferred from the household to the modern firm and factory (Leacock, 1975: 33; McDonough and Harrison, 1978: 34). Men are drawn into the labor force to produce commodities in exchange for wages, while women are relegated to domestic and subsistence activities within the household (Kuhn, 1978: 48). Their isolation from production and resulting economic dependence on men limit their autonomy and access to cash, property, and other resources (Smith, 1975: 63; Rapp, 1982: 172). Women forced to generate an income are often channeled into poorly remunerated informal activities, such as washing and ironing clothes, housecleaning, cooking and selling food, and other extensions of women's domestic roles, which are peripheral to the modern capitalist economy (Arizpe, 1977; Bossen, 1984: 243). Thus despite the ideology of egalitarianism, development has generally increased women's economic and social marginality (Boserup, 1970; Tinker, 1976).

The exploitation thesis is consistent with Marxist feminist analyses of women's role in capitalist societies. This thesis assumes that development often makes Third World women more central to industrial production but that their involvement is more harmful than beneficial (Fernandez-Kelly, 1983a: 192). According to this view, women provide cheap and easily expendable labor because discriminatory hiring practices, sex-segregated labor markets, and inadequate preparation weaken their position within the labor market (Beechey, 1978; McIntosh, 1978: 278). Also, the typically intense competition for the jobs available to women keeps wages low and workers docile (Lim, 1981: 187). Because women rarely organize effective workers' unions, they are often powerless to change their circumstances (Grossman, 1979: 3; Enloe, 1983: 421). This thesis asserts that the exploitation of women is particularly pronounced in the Third World, where racism and dependency exacerbate gender inequalities (Saffioti, 1975; Bronstein, 1982). In sum, while capitalist development may provide jobs for women, because its *modus operandi* is the extraction of surplus value to accumulate capital, it jeopardizes women's well-being (Fuentes and Ehrenreich, 1983).

The debate centers on this basic question: Has development, a process intimately related to the rise of the world capitalist system, improved women's lives, both absolutely and relative to those of men in their society? A brief discussion of the world capitalist system will provide a context for probing this question.

DEVELOPMENT AND THE
WORLD CAPITALIST SYSTEM

The period between 1450 and 1900 witnessed the transformation of the United States and Western European nations into advanced industrial powers, establishing a global system of economic exchanges and interdependencies. Unlike previous empires that extracted tributes from subjects conquered militarily to increase imperial power, the capitalist world system was oriented toward constant economic growth through increasing the velocity and quantity of worldwide trade (Chirot, 1977: 20). Based on a highly rational method of bookkeeping and banking, and propelled by an economic elite of merchants, financiers, and manufacturers, the capitalist system aimed at extending and maintaining markets in order to increase profits (Chirot, 1977: 20).

Using sophisticated shipping and military technology to keep trade routes open, Westerners exchanged products manufactured in European factories for raw materials and agricultural goods from Africa, Asia, the Americas, and elsewhere. In many instances they enlisted the cooperation of local elites in the "peripheral" regions, who coerced their often reluctant populations to extract the raw materials and produce the agricultural goods for commerce with the West. To relatively underpopulated regions such as Brazil and the Caribbean, Western traders brought African slaves to labor on plantations. In Southern Africa and much of South America, indigenous populations were enslaved to work the mines. In many parts of Africa whole tribes were captured and sold into slavery by other Africans for cash to purchase Western-made products. India, China, Indonesia, and other Asian civilizations eventually came to be controlled by the Dutch and British merchant companies. Throughout the world, the Westerners combined the "carrot" of European-made commodities with the "stick" of superior military force to overcome indigenous resistance. By 1900, only the most remote and isolated regions of the world had been unaffected by the world capitalist system (Chirot, 1977: 21-23).

While the capitalist system brought progress and wealth to Western Europe and the United States, it led to massive dislocations, class polarization, and economic instability in peripheral nations. The commercialization of agriculture transformed village-based landholding arrangements into profit-oriented, private-property systems. A small landowning class grew wealthy at the expense of most of the rural population. Some displaced peasants crowded into increasingly fragmented farms in the most marginal areas; others became tenants on land leased from wealthy landlords; the most unfortunate became landless laborers competing for a dwindling number of poorly paid agricultural jobs. Many owners of large-scale enterprises increased profits by replacing their human labor force with heavy machinery, thereby fueling rural unemployment (Chirot, 1977: 122-126).

The dramatic expansion of the labor force due to rapid population growth exacerbated the rural proletariat's plight. Throughout most of human history, populations had grown slowly, maintaining an equilibrium with environmental resources. Infectious diseases, famine, and other natural population "checks" elevated death rates, requiring high birth rates to maintain population levels. Although contact with the Western world originally depopulated many Third World nations through massive epidemics and forced population transfers, by the late nineteenth century it began to have the opposite effect. The introduction of Western methods of disease control quickly reduced mortality, particularly among infants. Yet birth rates remained high in rural areas. Cultural norms favoring large families, which were demographically adaptive when many infants succumbed to infectious diseases, continued despite dramatic declines in infant mortality. Moreover, children were a needed source of income or labor power for families in precarious economic circumstances. Children were also the only form of insurance against destitution for elderly parents unable to support themselves. Raising many children was thus a rational survival strategy for poor rural households. At the national level, however, the combination of high birth rates and plummeting death rates was extremely problematic. Within a few generations, rapid population growth combined with concentrated land ownership, technological displacement of labor, declining global demand for many agricultural exports, and other economic and political factors to cause widespread rural poverty (Harrison, 1981: 217-224; Chirot, 1977: 126-128).

Many people have fled the countryside to seek economic survival in towns and cities. However, the slow-growing industrial and modern service sectors have provided limited employment options, forcing many to carve out a niche in the informal sector. Studies done in Bombay, Nairobi, São Paulo, Abidjan, Jakarta, and Lima estimate the informal sector to contain between 40% and 60% of the working population (Harrison, 1981: 200). Moreover, the lack of adequate housing for low-income people has jammed many migrants and urban natives into burgeoning squatter settlements that often lack schools, sewage, pure water, and other urban services. Shanty towns now encompass more than two-fifths of the population of large Third World cities. In Mexico City 46% of the residents live in squatter settlements; in Casablanca, proportions soar to 70%, and in Addis Ababa to 90% (Harrison, 1981: 161).

The urban shanty towns are a poignant illustration that development under capitalist auspices has not brought prosperity to most Third World people. While class stratification existed in all but the most simple subsistence societies prior to their integration into the capitalist system, capitalism tended to increase class inequality (Blumberg, 1981: 33). In each peripheral nation, capital accumulated in those sectors and regions producing exports for the international market. For those who owned or managed valuable resources, these "export enclaves" generated considerable wealth, some of which diffused to professionals, bureaucrats, and other white-collar workers. Industrialization added a new layer to the class system, creating what some have called a "labor aristocracy" of skilled workers enjoying state-mandated benefits and minimum wage incomes (Amin, 1973). At the bottom of the hierarchy is the informal sector, with its teeming mass of underemployed, frequently impoverished workers. Once considered a temporary aberration of overly rapid urbanization, the informal sector was expected to disappear as development caused the formal sector to expand. It is now clear, however, that the informal sector is a stable component of the urban economy that supports, rather than drains, the formal sector and the Third World state. Informal activities provide low-cost goods and services that reduce the cost of maintaining the formal labor force and increase the amount of capital accumulated in Third World cities. The class inequality that relegates many to the informal sector not only subsidizes the wealthy, but contributes to investment and growth in the Third World (Portes and Walton, 1981: 86).

Development under capitalist auspices has entailed a complex mix of costs and benefits for Third World people. Although this discussion has emphasized its negative effects, a number of beneficial consequences can be noted. As previously mentioned, improved public health practices have increased life expectancies and reduced infant mortality. Advanced technologies of birth control are also available in most regions. Formal educational facilities have made universal literacy a possibility for all but the poorest Third World nations. Third World governments have acquired the organizational capacity to respond to citizens who are more aware of and able to express politically their needs and aspirations. The GNP of some nations has risen considerably, enhancing the quality of life for many through higher incomes and expanded public services. Access to these advantages has depended, however, on one's social class. Moreover, gender inequalities have compounded class disparities to produce a doubly disadvantaged group.

WOMEN, DEVELOPMENT, AND
THE WORLD CAPITALIST SYSTEM

As Gailey (Chapter 1 in this volume) has demonstrated, the status of women in precapitalist societies is the subject of considerable controversy. Anthropologists generally agree, however, that gender inequality was less pronounced in hunting-and-gathering and simple horticultural societies than in peasant-based, agrarian societies. The relative benefits and losses attendant on development in part reflect women's circumstances before their societies embarked on the process.

Modernization's impacts on the status and roles of women also depend on their social class, their racial or ethnic status, and how their nations and households are linked to the international economy. Moreover, women respond to changing circumstances in diverse and often creative ways, some parlaying to their own advantage what for others would be insurmountable obstacles. Despite the tremendous range of individual (as well as regional and national) variation in both conditions and responses, overall trends are discernible.

In general, development through integration into the world capitalist system has eroded women's status relative to men of their social class. Whether modernization occurred through gradual incorporation into the world capitalist system or through development assistance projects implemented during the past three decades, the initial impact on women has been depressingly uniform. Women's originally vital role in production has deteriorated, jeopardizing their autonomy and material well-being.

RURAL WOMEN:
THE POOREST OF THE POOR

Although women have been involved in agriculture in most non-Western societies, their participation has varied among different types of farming systems (Boserup, 1970). In much of Africa and some parts of Southeast Asia and Central America, the relative abundance of land permitted a slash-and-burn technique in which men cleared the land and women did most of the cultivation. Women's integral role in subsistence production afforded them stable resource access and at least some decision-making influence in the household and the community (Blumberg, 1981: 52). In these "female farming systems," custom ensured women secure access to communally held land. In other parts of Asia and much of South America, by contrast, men worked the land with ploughs hauled by draft animals. Women's agricultural contribution in these "male farming systems" was limited to collecting feed for and tending the animals or, among the poorer classes, to laboring on land owned by other households. The male-centered plough-based system was the predominant form in European societies, contributing to the Western notion that farming is men's work (Boserup, 1970: 15-36).

When colonial administrations imposed the Western pattern on female-centered subsistence systems, rural women's workloads increased while their resource base diminished (Blumberg, 1981: 41). As communally held subsistence plots became privately owned farms producing cash crops for market exchange, women lost their customary access to productive resources. Colonial governments drew laborers into the market economy by imposing taxes requiring monetary payments; yet the cash crops and wage jobs necessary for monetary incomes were often available only to men. Women, whose child-rearing responsibilities made them less mobile, remained in the rural subsistence sector (Tinker, 1976: 25). The once reciprocal division of labor through which both sexes cooperated to produce subsistence crops gave way to a new system in which men were the primary growers of market crops while women assumed responsibility for raising food for family consumption. New varieties of seed, fertilizer, and other production-enhancing technologies were reserved for cash cropping, while less-productive traditional methods continued to be used for subsistence farming (Tinker, 1976: 27; Blumberg, 1981: 42).

In subsistence societies, women traditionally supplemented their agricultural production with spinning, weaving, basket and pottery making, and other types of traditional manufacturing. Proceeds from the sale or barter of these items were generally at women's disposal. As the incorporation of their societies into the global economy pitted traditional crafts against cheaply made, mass-produced commodities, women's income from these cottage industries diminished (Tinker, 1976: 25).

These changes adversely affected women, their families, and their societies. Women could only obtain cash necessary for essential commodities indirectly, through a male's wage or income. Furthermore, legal barriers to female land ownership gave men official title to land worked by their female partners. Women's resulting dependence on men limited their autonomy and material security. Many women became de facto household heads as their menfolk migrated to wage-paying jobs on plantations, in mines, or in urban centers. Constant farming of privately owned plots quickly depleted soils requiring the long fallow periods of the slash-and-burn system, yet fertilizers were generally unavailable to female subsistence farmers. Consequently, women labored on increasingly marginal soils, without male assistance, using primitive technologies. The resulting decline in food production led to inadequate caloric consumption and poor nutrition among many rural households. The famines currently plaguing many African regions in part reflect the dislocations stemming from this sexually unequal redivision of labor (Mead, 1976: 9; Blumberg, 1981: 40).

The economic changes sweeping the Third World countryside brought hardship to rural households. Fluctuating price and demand levels in the international market, rising costs of agricultural inputs, and declining yields due to land depletion led many cultivators into debt and bankruptcy; others sold their land before commercial enterprises drove them out of business. Customary patterns of partitioning land among sons, more of whom now survived to adulthood, so shrunk landholdings that they no longer supported households (Harrison, 1981: 74-89).

These trends have forced many rural women, even those from landowning households, into wage labor. In Guatemala, for example, women from highland villages migrate to harvest coffee on coastal plantations (Bossen, 1984: 68). Despite Pakistan's legacy of female seclusion, women constitute about a third of the labor force on commercial farms; in Ceylon and Vietnam they account for over 50% (Boserup, 1970: 76). Throughout much of Asia and Latin America, women also work in mining, construction, and transportation (Boserup, 1970: 79).

When economic circumstances force women into the labor force to help support their households, men rarely shoulder a larger share of domestic and child-rearing tasks. Rather, women must extend their work day to encompass their "double burden" (Palmer, 1979: 91; Huston, 1979: 64). One study concluded that men in Zaire did only 30% as much work as women did (Harrison, 1981: 441). In Upper Volta, women's average work days were 27% longer than men's (International Center for Research on Women, 1980a: 15). Boserup (1970: 78) describes the typical day of a North Indian tea plantation worker as follows:

> A woman's day begins at 4 or 5 a.m. with cooking for the family. Then, after seven or eight hours of plantation work, she must fetch water and firewood and cook another meal. Children are often brought to the fields, the smallest one strapped to the back of the mother.

The expansion of rural women's workload often jeopardizes their emotional and physical well-being, forcing them to impose their domestic and child-care duties on their daughters. An Upper Volta survey showed that 7-year-old girls worked over 5 hours a day, while boys of the same age worked only 40 minutes (Harrison, 1981: 443). Similarly, within peasant households in San Cosme, Mexico, daughters performed 34%, and sons only 12%, of domestic tasks (Rothstein, 1982: 73). Elder daughters often must abandon their studies in order to help shoulder their mothers' double burden. In 1975, 53% of Third World girls aged from 6 to 11 years old, compared with 70% of the boys in that age group, attended school. In the 12 to 17 year old age group, 42% of boys but only 28% of girls were pursuing formal education (Harrison, 1982: 443).

Young girls' domestic load is but one reason for the gender discrepancy in school enrollments; yet it illustrates how these inequalities are transmitted between generations, as education is one of the few ways in which women can enter the modern capitalist economy when other roles are eroded. Illiteracy impairs women's performance not only of modern tasks but also of traditional roles such as marketing. Although concerted efforts during the 1960s and 1970s decreased Third World illiteracy from 59% in 1960 to 41% in 1980, the number of illiterates increased from 701 million to 795 million (Harrison, 1981: 305). The level of female illiteracy rose over twice as fast as that of males, by 5 million a year compared with 2 million (Harrison, 1982: 443). In 1980, 73% of African women and 48% of men were illiterate; in Asia, 47% of women and 30% of men were unable to read and write; in Latin America, the percentages were 23% of women and 18% of men (Harrison, 1982: 443).

Most Third World illiteracy is confined to the countryside, reinforcing the disadvantages that rural women already face. Not only must they cope with the diminishing availability of land and jobs and gender-based inequities in their distribution, but they are often unable to pursue alternative opportunities. Despite decades of Western-oriented modernization, Third World rural women remain the poorest of the poor.

MIGRATION, URBANIZATION, AND HOUSEHOLD SURVIVAL STRATEGIES

A rural household adapts to its economic circumstance through "survival strategies" that depend on its size and composition, its share of land and other resources, and the job options in local and more-distant labor markets (see Schmink, 1984: 89-93). Most households, finding their landholdings inadequate for growing sufficient food and cash crops, must send one or more members into wage work. Because agrarian jobs are scarce and poorly paid, many rural dwellers seek employment in towns and cities. Some households opt to resettle together; others send members to support themselves, and, with luck, to remit money to those remaining in the countryside. Males more often migrate to Asian and African cities, whereas female migrants predominate in Latin America and some parts of Southeast Asia. These migration trends reflect the urban and rural economies' demand for male and female labor (Boserup, 1970: 183-193). In many parts of Africa, the tradition of female farming and the preferential hiring of men leads male members to take urban jobs while women and children remain in subsistence production. In Latin America, where male farming systems limit agricultural openings for women, older daughters are often sent to nearby towns to work as domestic servants, unskilled factory workers, or petty traders, while sons stay to work the land. Thailand, the Philippines, and other Southeast Asian regions have begun to deviate from the Asian pattern of predominantly male migration. The preference for female labor in electronics industries is pulling young women, who at one time would have remained in the countryside doing agricultural labor, toward the city (Fuentes and Ehrenreich, 1983: 16).

Whether women move alone or with other family members, their migrations typically follow previously established networks. Migrants usually join family, friends, or acquaintances from their home community who have already settled in the city and can help with the arduous task of finding employment. Although female (and male) migrants tend to be better educated than those who stay in the countryside, few have the educational attainment of urban natives (Sudarkasa, 1977: 185). Further, migrants are often members of indigenous groups who must overcome prejudice, language barriers, and cultural differences, which for women are overlaid with gender-based discrimination. Monetary incomes are especially essential in the city, for many goods and services previously provided through rural subsistence activities must now be purchased with cash (Boserup, 1970: 160). Economic insecurity leads some women to return to the countryside; most remain, however, or move on to another urban destination. Although city life may not bring financial security, it generally improves women's economic circumstances and offers them autonomy from traditional rural customs and family supervision.

WOMEN IN THE URBAN LABOR MARKET

In the countryside, where the subsistence mode of production coexists with commercial capitalism, the household is the locus of many productive activities. In the cities, which are more completely integrated into the capitalist system, socially valued production occurs at work places physically and symbolically separate from the household. Capitalist development entails a progressive division between the private sphere of home and the public sphere of work, with a corresponding distinction between reproductive or domestic labor, seen as women's work, and productive labor, seen as men's work. Supporting these social relations is an ideology that glorifies the monogamous nuclear family, viewing all women as wives and mothers with wage-earning husbands to support them and their children (see Tiano, 1984: 20).

As these notions and arrangements have taken root in developing nations, they have negatively affected women and their families. In some contexts, they have led to the widespread confinement of women to the household and their virtual exclusion from the formal labor force (Rothstein, 1982: 67-80). In others, women's domestic confinement has been symbolic; they have been able to enter the work force, but as subsidiary wage-earners limited to a narrow range of low-paying jobs seen as extensions of their primary reproductive roles (Lim, 1983: 77). Whether actual or symbolic, the exclusion of women from the public sphere not only limits their independence and resource access, but may jeopardize their family's financial well-being. In most Third World nations only relatively well-off urban households can support themselves with a single male breadwinner's income; most require the economic contributions of several members (Schmink, 1984: 91).

Moreover, between 20% and 30% of households in the developing world are headed by women (Buvinic et al., 1978: i) who bear sole responsibility for their families' support. Even stably partnered women often cannot rely on their men's incomes, for the amounts received may be inadequate, and many men spend their wages in other ways. Interviewing women from five Latin American countries, Bronstein (1982) heard the frequent complaint that their partners spent most of their own wages on alcohol, prostitutes, or supporting a second family. For women in such circumstances, exclusion from the labor force spells financial hardship. For women from wealthier households, it entails economic dependence and insecurity. Whether for economic or personal reasons, many urban women enter the formal or informal labor force at some point in their lives.

The form a woman's labor force participation takes depends on economic factors such as the demand for female labor and the woman's qualifications for formal jobs; psychological factors such as her interests, aspirations, and tolerance for various tasks; cultural factors defining appropriate work roles for women; and social factors, such as the size, composition, and economic needs of her household. Moreover, a woman's extra-domestic work is regulated by her reproductive roles as wife and mother, the demands of which vary at different stages of the life course.

Labor force participation is more variable among wealthy women, who can afford to devote themselves to full-time child care, than among poorer women who must generate household income regardless of child-rearing responsibilities. The proportion of upper-class and middle-class women in the formal labor market varies across developing nations. Women in Latin America and Central Asia face stronger cultural restrictions than do women in many parts of Africa, Southeast Asia, and the Caribbean, where women traditionally have participated in agriculture and marketing (Boserup, 1970: 122-138). Regardless of cultural context, many wealthier women never work outside the home, while others only work prior to their marriages. Although some may regret their economic dependence, they often cannot surmount their husbands' or families' objections to their paid employment. Others opt for full-time domesticity as a sign of their household's social status, or because they prefer domestic and child-care tasks to wage work. Some avoid the stigma of extra-domestic work by engaging in informal activities.

Informal and formal labor markets offer women different advantages. Jobs in the formal sector, whose conditions and pay scales are often legally regulated, are more stable, pay minimum wage or higher incomes, and offer benefits such as health insurance for workers and their children. These jobs' relative scarcity and more-demanding educational requirements, however, limit their availability to many urban women. Also, their physical separation from the household and their rigid schedules may make them incongruent with child care and domestic duties. The informal sector, by contrast, is more accessible to women whose formal participation is limited by language barriers, educational deficits, or newness to the city. Many informal tasks allow considerable independence from employer supervision, while their temporal and spatial flexibility make them more compatible with child care than are most formal jobs (Arizpe, 1977: 36). Also, men are less likely to object to their wives' and daughters' informal activities because they do not challenge accepted definitions of proper feminine roles (Fernandez-Kelly, 1983a: 176).

The distinction between formal and informal services is often fuzzy, depending less on the activity than the context in which it is performed (Arizpe, 1977: 36). Formal activities typically take place outside the household, in enterprises employing a certain number of workers whose wages are regulated by official pay scales. Informal enterprises employ no more than a few workers, who use rudimentary equipment, are not covered by state laws and regulations, and earn less than the minimum wage (Harrison, 1981: 199). These criteria are difficult to apply in many cases, particularly if the worker is self-employed and her income varies considerably in response to changing levels of demand for her services.

The educational and skill requirements of formal sector jobs are significantly different across societies and among activities. In general, the better educated the urban population, the more rigid are the entrance requirements for industrial and formal service jobs. Widespread illiteracy in Africa makes women with only a primary school education employable in formal labor markets (Boserup, 1970: 153). In much of Latin America and Southeast Asia, women often need secondary educations even for unskilled factory work, although sewing skills acquired in the home may enable less educated women to enter jobs in garment factories (Saffioti, 1986: 114; Fernandez-Kelly, 1983a: 52).

Ethnicity, race, language skills, and place of origin also structure formal job opportunities. Minority women often face discrimination, particularly if they were raised in rural areas speaking an indigenous language. The limited education of most rural-born minority women further diminishes their options for formal jobs (Bunster and Chaney, 1985: 17).

Formal employment also varies with life course stage and reproductive responsibilities. Young, childless women are more readily hired than mature women with children, whose employment chances decline further with each additional offspring (Fernandez-Kelly, 1983b: 220; Schmink, 1985: 139). Because all married women are seen as potential mothers, even those without children are usually less readily employable than single women. Women who found jobs when they were single may be eased out of the labor force as their marital and motherhood statuses change (Saffioti, 1986: 11). Even if women do not face discrimination because of their actual or imputed domestic roles, many will voluntarily exit from the labor force during their childbearing years (Arizpe, 1977: 37).

Formal labor force participation is rarely a lifelong activity for Third World women. Instead, they move between the informal and formal sectors according to the dictates of their reproductive roles. Some women engage in informal activities prior to formal employment. Girls who must contribute to household income but cannot meet minimum age requirements for formal jobs are often forced to take up informal activities (Fernandez-Kelly, 1983a: 53). Many learn informal tasks by helping their mothers or other female relatives. In Latin America, market traders and street vendors are frequently accompanied by young daughters who assist them in their work while minding younger children (Bunster and Chaney, 1985: 91). Similarly, Latin American girls often enter domestic service at early ages (Bunster and Chaney, 1986: 41; Fernandez-Kelly, 1983a: 53). Third World daughters also help family-based enterprises produce crafts or food items (Boserup, 1970: 107). Although informal tasks often interfere with girls' education, some manage to perform them while pursuing their studies. Most of these young workers remain in the informal sector throughout their lives, particularly if their work interrupted or prevented formal schooling. Some, however, find their way into formal jobs once they are old enough to be employable or after they complete their educations.

Women who enter the formal sector typically do so during their late teens or early twenties, usually to help support their parents' household (Fernandez-Kelly, 1983a: 51-56). Single mothers have limited chances of finding formal employment, although some succeed if they can arrange for child care through a household member or other agency. Once a woman marries and begins raising children, she may be able to continue working; it is probable, however, that she will choose or be compelled by her husband or employer to quit her job. At this point, she is likely to find an informal way to generate household income (Arizpe, 1977: 37). Unless she is highly skilled, she is apt to have difficulty reentering formal employment as her children mature. While some women rejoin the formal labor force, most continue in the informal sector throughout their remaining working years (Arizpe, 1977: 37). Aggregate statistics on Third World women's labor force participation, which exclude most informal activities, reflect this pattern. In most nations, employment rates peak among women aged 15 to 25 years, drop among women in the 25 to 35 age group, and remain stable among older age groups (Boserup, 1970: 145; Salaff, 1981: 60; Tiano, 1984: 7).

Although motherhood need not preclude a woman's formal employment, her ability to accommodate to the rigid schedules of formal jobs depends on her access to child care. Urban women are less able than rural women to rely on older daughters, for those not in school are often in the informal labor force. Moreover, urban households are more apt than rural families to be nuclear in structure, forcing many women to do without the assistance of extended family members. Women without resident babysitters must therefore find alternatives if they are to enter the labor force. Throughout Latin America, child care is often provided by resident domestic servants who work for such meager incomes that even some working-class households can afford to employ them. In many regions of Africa, women from polygamous households can share domestic duties, thereby freeing up one or more wives for full-time employment (Boserup, 1970: 43).

No matter how qualified or free from all-encompassing domestic responsibilities, women cannot enter formal employment unless jobs are available in the industrial or service sectors. Throughout the developing world, the industrial sector has not expanded rapidly enough to provide jobs for those displaced from agriculture and other traditional activities. Although women in some nations have joined the industrial work force in some types of manufacturing, the overall effect of industrialization prior to the 1960s was to displace women from manufacturing.

In precapitalist societies, manufacturing generally occurred in small, home-based industries producing for local consumption. Women actively participated in these cottage industries, whose domestic setting made them congruent with reproductive responsibilities. However, as competition with Western-made imports eliminated many cottage industries, women were displaced from traditional manufacturing (Boserup, 1970: 110-112).

During the initial stages of Third World industrialization, textile, leather goods, and food and beverage processing industries emerged to supply basic needs of urban consumers. In Latin America and some parts of Asia, women were drawn into these industries just as they had been in Europe and the United States (Schmink, 1985: 137). The demand for female labor reflected women's mastery of sewing and other domestically acquired skills and their lack of alternatives to tedious, low-waged labor (Towner, 1979: 49-50). By contrast, in northern Africa and Asian nations, where Islamic culture mandated female seclusion, women were rarely absorbed into modern industries (Boserup, 1970: 109).

Yet even in Latin America women's early involvement in manufacturing declined with subsequent industrialization. As the manufacturing sector became more capital-intensive, men came to predominate in the newer durable goods industries and increased their share of jobs in textiles and other light industries (Saffioti, 1985: 110). In turn-of-the century Mexico, for example, when textile and tobacco production dominated manufacturing, about 76,000 women held factory jobs; after 40 years of industrial diversification the female labor force was reduced by half (Vaughan, 1979: 78). The evolution of Brazilian industry reveals a similar pattern. In 1900, when textile production was the primary form of manufacturing, over 90% of the industrial labor force was female. The tremendous industrial growth during subsequent decades absorbed men rather than women, so that by 1940 women constituted only 25% of the industrial work force (Schmink, 1985: 137), and by 1970 only 12% (Saffioti, 1975: 87). Today women constitute between 9% and 14% of the manufacturing labor force in other Latin American nations; in Africa and most of Asia, they represent between 2% and 18% (Boserup, 1970: 109). Throughout the Third World, female industrial workers are confined to unskilled tasks in labor-intensive industries (Boserup, 1970: 141).

Women's relative wage levels reflect the segregation of the industrial work force. Throughout much of the developing world, skilled male workers typically earn three to four times more than their unskilled female counterparts (Boserup, 1970: 140). Further, the wage disparity appears to increase with industrialization. In 1920, for example, female textile workers in Brazil earned 70% as much as male workers; in 1970, their wages were only 60% as high as men's (Saffioti, 1985: 112).

Beginning in the 1960s, a new form of industrialization through foreign investment has taken root in some Third World nations. Rather than replacing women with machines and skilled male labor, "export processing industrialization" draws women into modern manufacturing. Multinational corporations based in the United States, Japan, and Western Europe have transferred labor-intensive production phases to Third World nations, which possess an abundance of low-wage labor. Using scientific management principles they have decomposed certain production stages into a series of steps that can easily be taught to unskilled workers. This "deskilling" essentially eliminates aptitude differences between labor in developed and developing nations, enabling corporations to select their work force chiefly on the basis of wage levels (Peña, 1982: 9). Wage rates are considerably lower in the Third World than in advanced nations: The average hourly wage in the United States in 1977 was $4.81; in Korea, it was $.70; in Indonesia, it was $.25 (Nash, 1983: 18; Fuentes and Ehrenreich, 1983: 9). Many Third World governments have offered incentives to foreign corporations, stimulating the proliferation of factories in northern Mexico, the Caribbean, Central America, and Southeast Asia. Their work force assembles components made elsewhere and packages the finished products for export to the world market (Ong, 1983: 426-428; Lim, 1981: 181-190; 1983: 79-82).

Women, most between ages 15 to 25 years, constitute over 85% of this assembly processing labor force (Grossman, 1979: 3; Fernandez-Kelly, 1983b: 209). The preference for female labor is rationalized by beliefs that women have a high tolerance for monotonous work, an inherent dexterity that suits them for minute tasks, and docile natures that enable them to withstand the pressure of rapidly paced, closely supervised production (Enloe, 1983: 412). Moreover, women work for lower wages than men and rarely organize unions or engage in collective protest (Lim, 1983: 77-78). Employers generally prefer young, inexperienced, single women on the assumption that their youth makes them submissive to authority, their inexperience minimizes previous contact with labor organizers, and their unmarried status reduces the likelihood of pregnancy (Tiano, 1985: 13; Fuentes and Ehrenreich, 1983: 12-13). Depending on the average educational attainment of the female population, workers are expected to have a primary- or secondary-level education. In short, export processing absorbs women from the least deprived sector of the female working class (Fernandez-Kelly, 1983a: 106).

Women assembly workers are often the primary wage-earners for large urban or rural households. A study of women workers in Juarez, Mexico, found that most came from households whose male head was absent, underemployed, or unemployed (Fernandez-Kelly, 1983b: 217). Similarly, assembly workers in Thailand, the Philippines, Malaysia, and Singapore are often the sole supporters of rural households that otherwise would face economic destitution (Ehrenreich and Fuentes, 1983: 18; Ong, 1983: 430). Families often dissuade their daughters from marrying until younger siblings complete their education or become old enough to take their sisters' places as primary breadwinners (Fuentes and Ehrenreich, 1983: 18).

Assembly work is tedious and monotonous, often exposing women to dangerous chemicals and other hazards that impair their eyesight and cause other physical ailments (Fuentes and Ehrenreich, 1983: 19). Operators also suffer from frequent layoffs and are frequently kept on temporary contracts affording little job stability (Fuentes and Ehrenreich, 1983: 22; Fernandez-Kelly, 1983a: 67). Moreover, multinationals rarely pay even experienced workers more than the state-mandated minimum wage (Tiano, 1985: 25). In countries such as Mexico, however, where 72% of working women earn less than a minimum wage (Arizpe, 1977: 32), such a salary is highly desirable, particularly when supplemented with paid vacations, health insurance, and medical benefits legally mandated for formal sector employees (Lim, 1983: 81). Further, many assembly workers enjoy the prestige attached to employment with large foreign corporations (Lim, 1981). These factors help explain the intense competition for export processing jobs. In northern Mexico only 1 applicant in 20 is hired by export processing firms (North American Congress on Latin America, 1979: 134).

To summarize, unlike the capital-intensive trend of most twentieth-century industrialization, export processing absorbs women into the manufacturing labor force. Assembly plants now employ half a million East Asian women (Fuentes and Ehrenreich, 1983: 16) and 150,000 northern Mexican women (Fernandez-Kelly, 1983a: 191). Women make up almost half of the industrial work force in Puerto Rico (Safa, 1985: 86) and one-third of that in South Korea (Fuentes and Ehrenreich, 1983: 16). Nevertheless, this phenomenon is both too recent and too geographically localized to have reversed the exclusionary global trend of capitalist industrialization or to have opened manufacturing to most Third World women. The vast majority continue to enter formal employment through the service sector, if at all.

Women from the higher classes, most of whom are more educated and have better contacts than lower-class women, have the widest options in the formal service sector. Nevertheless, they tend to cluster in a limited range of occupations. Among professional women in most countries, two-thirds are teachers and most of the remainder are nurses or other medical practitioners (Boserup, 1970: 125). Women in secluded societies, where custom mandates that only women can serve female clients, have better opportunities in the medical, education, and welfare professions than women in less sexually segregated societies (Tinker, 1976: 29). Clerical occupations also absorb middle-class women, although men outnumber them by 3 to 1 in Latin America and 10 to 1 in Africa and Asia (Boserup, 1970: 130-131). The proportion of women in administration is very low, averaging 10% in Latin America and the Philippines, and 3% everywhere else (Boserup, 1970: 123). Throughout much of the developing world, even highly educated women rarely occupy governmental or political posts (Chaney, 1979).

Whether in professions or other white-collar occupations, women's salaries seldom match those of men. The gap is smaller in Africa, where the general lack of education creates a demand for trained people of either sex, than in Latin America where education and skills are more widespread (Boserup, 1970: 153). Contrary to the integration thesis, income inequality between the sexes appears to increase with development. Although gender discrimination may be submerged when few people have modern skills, it appears to reassert itself once skill levels rise to meet the economy's demand for trained labor (Boserup, 1970: 153).

For relatively uneducated women, opportunities in the formal service sector are better in Latin America than in Asia and Africa, for the modern service sector is larger and its composition more heavily female (Boserup, 1970: 97). In African and Asian cities, where men outnumber women by as much as three to one (Boserup, 1970: 85), lower-class women's formal participation is confined to providing services for the male population. Women typically operate or work in restaurants, hotels, and entertainment establishments, where they compete with men for many of these jobs. Even though women may be heavily involved in informal marketing, sales jobs in small shops are reserved for men (Boserup, 1970: 95, 99). In Latin America, by contrast, women are as likely as men to be shopkeepers, and they predominate in restaurants, laundries, bakeries, beauty shops, and other commercial service establishments (Boserup, 1970: 91, 103; Arizpe, 1977: 33). While these regional differences may reflect cultural and historical factors, they also correlate with economic development level. It appears that jobs in modern services initially involve men, but as the formal sector expands the sex ratio becomes more equal (Boserup, 1970: 104).

It is the informal service sector, however, that supports most urban women. Women from the higher classes often choose informal jobs over white-collar employment as being more compatible with their reproductive roles. While lower-class women may also prefer informal tasks for this reason, they are most likely to perform them because they cannot secure formal industrial or service employment (Arizpe, 1977: 37). Informal occupations predominate among squatters and slum-dwellers, who often outnumber other residents of large Third World cities. Rural migrants generally enter the informal sector when they come to the city and most remain throughout their working years; many urban-born women also spend all or most of their lives performing informal tasks. In Lima, over half of all economically active women work in two informal service occupations: marketing and domestic service (Bunster and Chaney, 1985: 5). In Mexico City, 72% of working women, compared with 54% of men, are in the informal sector; three-quarters of them perform services (Arizpe, 1977: 32). Throughout the Third World, between one-half and three-fourths of informal service workers are women. Female informal workers earn 40% to 50% as much as their male counterparts and are considerably less likely than men to advance to higher-level service jobs (International Center for Research on Women, 1980: 68).

Marketing is the most prevalent informal service activity for lower-class women in sub-Saharan Africa and Southeast Asia. Of the women in Accra, Ghana, for example, 90% earn their living through informal trade (Little, 1976: 80). By contrast, in North Africa and Central Asia, where Hindu and Islamic cultures prohibit women from marketing, informal trade is primarily a male activity. Women predominate in marketing in those regions where they do the bulk of subsistence agriculture. Moreover, the products sold—women market eggs, poultry, milk, fruits, and vegetables, while meat is generally sold by men—are the same goods women and men produce (Boserup, 1970: 91). This suggests that the informal trade and the rural subsistence sectors are linked through female networks that direct the flow of agricultural surplus toward urban markets. For many women, marketing is an adjunct to agricultural and crafts production. In the Yoruba region of Nigeria, for example, two-thirds of women engage in selling; half of them do so as their sole activity while the rest market products they grow or manufacture (Boserup, 1970: 93).

Informal selling also occupies many Caribbean and Latin American women. Their participation is higher in Central America, Mexico, Ecuador, and Peru, where indigenous groups outnumber the mestizo or Hispanic populations, than in the Atlantic coast countries. Women constitute over a third of the informal trade sector in El Salvador, for example, but only 5% in Venezuela (Boserup, 1970: 89). While this contrast may stem from cultural differences in acceptable roles for women (Boserup, 1970: 91), it also reflects the discrimination against Indian women in the formal labor market as well as the widespread participation of lower-class women in domestic service. In Mexico City, Lima, and other cities to which large numbers of rural-born Indian women migrate, an informal division of labor exists between urban natives and rural migrants. The former tend to occupy stalls in established markets, while the latter, who lack capital and are unfamiliar with licensing, inspection, and formal business contracts, tend to be street vendors (Arizpe, 1977: 35; Bunster and Chaney, 1986: 5).

After marketing, domestic service is probably the most common informal service activity, particularly in Latin America, where it occupies a third of the female work force (Fernandez-Kelly, 1983b; 215). In Lima, 47% of all service workers are domestics, 93% of them women (Bunster and Chaney, 1985: 21). This occupation is especially common among female migrants to large cities. In Santiago, two-thirds of recent female migrants, compared to one-ninth of native-born women, work as domestics. Buenos Aires reveals a similar pattern: Domestic service occupies 52% of migrants from Argentina, 63% of movers from nearby countries, but only 5% of women born in the city (Jelin, 1977: 133). Female migration and domestic service are mutually reinforcing. Rural parents more readily allow their young daughters to move if they are immediately absorbed in urban households (Jelin, 1977: 136). Young girls are often recruited from their villages by urban women seeking servants for themselves and their friends. A study of domestic servants in Lima found that half of the migrants had been placed in urban households before they moved; two-thirds of those so sponsored were 11 years old or younger when they began working (Bunster and Chaney, 1985: 41). Conversely, the steady flow of rural migrants creates a pool of labor that urban households can employ at minimal cost, thereby stimulating demand for domestic servants (Jelin, 1977: 139). The poverty of many rural households and the shortage of employment options for women in the countryside propel young women toward the city. Some enter domestic service because it is the only alternative to street vending for relatively uneducated Indian women (Bunster and Chaney, 1985: 17). Many domestic servants, whether rural migrants or urban natives, were abandoned by their husbands or are *madres solteras* (single mothers). One study estimated that 40% of single mothers in Peru work in this occupation (Bunster and Chaney, 1986: 17).

Young girls in their first few years of work earn little or no salary; food, clothing, and shelter are their only remuneration for workdays that may stretch to 19 hours (Bunster and Chaney, 1985: 53). Older, experienced servants draw salaries that rarely approach the minimum wage levels officially determined for the occupation. Only 14% of the Peruvian domestic servants studied by Bunster and Chaney (1986: 49) earned a minimum wage salary.

Social scientists once considered domestic service to be a springboard to more lucrative occupations (Smith, 1973: 193). Recent studies suggest, to the contrary, that women forced to quit domestic service due to marriage or motherhood either become maids, cooks, or laundresses, or they take up street vending (Bunster and Chaney, 1985: 47). The move into informal marketing rarely brings economic improvement. In Lima, incomes for both occupations average $30 a month (Bunster and Chaney, 1986: 22). Thus women enter informal marketing not so much to better their economic circumstances but because changes in their reproductive status preclude continuation as resident servants.

Latin America is exceptional among Third World regions in the prevalence of domestic service openings for women. Such jobs are scarcer in Africa and Asia, and, with the exception of southern Africa, mostly held by men. Boserup (1970: 104) speculates that economic development tends to expand and to "feminize" the domestic service sector.

Urban women perform a variety of informal service activities in addition to selling and service. Middle-class women tutor in music, languages, and school subjects (Arizpe, 1977: 33). Lower-class women may work as day laborers at construction sites or haul materials or passengers across the city. Some are midwives or quasi-religious healers or fortune tellers. Some poorer women operate outside the law, distributing drugs or contraband items, performing abortions, operating gambling organizations, or engaging in prostitution. Such activities are probably the last resort for women pushed by economic need to generate an income for themselves and their families.

CONCLUSION: INTEGRATION, MARGINALIZATION, OR EXPLOITATION?

Has involvement in the world capitalist system integrated Third World women into the modern economy, or has it made them marginal members of their societies? Has it offered them meaningful, autonomous roles, or has it merely exploited their labor? Although a thoroughgoing analysis of integration, marginalization, and exploitation is beyond the scope of this discussion, considering these terms in light of the trends reviewed here raises issues that may help resolve the controversy.

First, marginalization is always relative to particular institutions and takes various forms. Marginality involves both the inability to contribute to socially valued production and the exclusion from rewards such as wealth, power, or prestige through which productive contributions are remunerated. The dominant mode of production in a society determines which contributions are socially esteemed and remunerated. Precapitalist, subsistence-based societies value and reward activities yielding products for household consumption; capitalist societies value activities producing commodities for market exchange.

In Third World nations only partially integrated into the world capitalist system, the subsistence and capitalist modes of production coexist. Peasant households often straddle the two sectors, allocating some members to subsistence production and others to market production. Through the household nexus, the subsistence sector supports the capitalist sector. By growing food for family consumption, subsistence producers bear part of the cost of supporting the household. This supplements the income of the wage earners, enabling their employers to pay wages less than the value of their labor power—the cost of reproducing the wageworkers and their families. The resulting savings increase the rate at which capital accumulates in the market sector, thereby stimulating the capitalist economy (Deere, 1976: 9-17; Blumberg, 1981: 45). However, subsistence activities have no market value; though useful to the household, they do not directly contribute to commodity production or exchange and therefore are not considered productive from the standpoint of the capitalist economy. In a sense, the transition to capitalism marginalizes the subsistence sector and its work force from socially valued production.

The domestic sphere also indirectly supports the capitalist economy. Like subsistence producers, domestic workers provide goods and services to wage-workers at a cost below their market value, thereby enabling the laborer and his or her family to survive on a lower wage than otherwise would be required. Moreover, domestic laborers bear and socialize new generations of workers for the capitalist labor force (Eisenstein, 1978; McIntosh, 1978). However, while these activities indirectly increase the rate of capital accumulation, they are not highly regarded by the capitalist system because they do not produce commodities with exchange value. By isolating the domestic arena from the market sector, capitalist development marginalizes domestic workers from socially esteemed production and its attendant rewards.

The informal economy is similar to the domestic sphere in that both are intimately related yet peripheral to the market economy; moreover, many informal tasks are extensions of women's domestic roles. Informal activities provide goods and services to formal workers at minimal cost, enabling them to survive on lower wages than they would need in order to purchase them on the formal marketplace. These activities thus stimulate the rate of capital accumulation in Third World cities (Portes and Walton, 1981: 86; Fernandez-Kelly, 1983a: 176). While informal goods and services may be purchased and sold for cash, thus appearing to be part of the market economy, most econo-mists consider them peripheral to the modern sector because they are not central to capitalist production and they replicate services provided more efficiently by formal or domestic workers (Bossen, 1984: 243). Moreover, many informal workers are severely underemployed, spending many hours to make or market products that in the formal economy would be dispatched within moments, and earning incomes so meager that they can barely survive (Bossen, 1984: 138). Informal activities are also marginal in that they are beyond the sphere of legal regulations that mandate minimum wage incomes, worker benefits, and protection against abuse and exploitation. In sum, informal activities are marginal in that they are considered superfluous from the standpoint of the modern capitalist economy and are neither highly valued nor well rewarded.

Domestic, subsistence, and informal workers are not idle; they work long hours at backbreaking tasks. Further, each type of activity contributes to the local and international economy by increasing capital accumulation in the Third World. Relative to the capitalist mode of production, however, they are all marginal. Women engaged in them are not considered "economically active" in occupational censuses or similar tallies of demographic data (International Center for Research on Women, 1980b). Their invisibility reinforces the ideology defining women solely in terms of their reproductive roles, as nonworking members of their society. To the extent that modernization draws men into the wage economy and women into the domestic economy, this process marginalizes women both in terms of their contribution to socially valued production and their access to material resources, power, and prestige. Similarly, if capitalist development draws men into the formal sector while affording women little or no alternative to informal jobs, it increases women's peripheral status.

At the same time, capitalist development also marginalizes women's roles and resources by relegating women to subsistence agriculture while their menfolk enter the wage economy. Yet modernization has also shrunk the subsistence sector, thereby expelling many women from subsistence production. On the one hand, by eroding women's once vital subsistence roles, modernization removes them from production and its rewards. On the other hand, because full-time subsistence workers are peripheral to the capitalist sector, undermining their traditional roles could lesson, rather then increase, their marginality.

Resolving this issue requires specifying the mode of production in the context of which marginality is considered. The integration thesis, which evaluates marginality relative to the modern, cash-based economy, assumes that development makes women less peripheral by drawing them out of the subsistence sector. The marginalization thesis emphasizes instead women's productive contributions to household and community regardless of mode of production. From this vantage point, development frequently marginalizes women relative to their previously essential roles in subsistence production. Once this conceptual distinction is clear, the debate hinges on whether women displaced from subsistence production are being drawn into formal employment.

The evidence presented here suggests, contrary to the integration thesis, that capitalist development is *not* absorbing most Third World women into the formal sector. Instead, it is confining many to the domestic sphere or the informal sector, thereby reducing their access to productive roles and resources. While middle-class status and education are enabling some women to enter white-collar jobs, they still suffer from a limited demand for their labor and from segregation into low-paying, powerless "female jobs."

Women's role in export-processing industrialization may appear to deviate from this pattern; yet it is likely a result of their tendency toward marginalization under capitalist industrialization. Multinational corporations locate their assembly operations in the Third World in order to use young women's inexpensive labor. Economic need forces many women to earn an income, yet the shortage of formal jobs limits their employment alternatives and forces many into the informal sector. It is precisely this socioeconomic marginality that makes young women a surplus labor pool that draws corporations to export-processing sites. Young women's economic vulnerability propels them into assembly plants, where they work under conditions that could be considered exploitative—for low wages under temporary contracts at jobs entailing neither employment security nor career advancement. A further set of links is apparent between marginality and women's role in export processing. Many women enter assembly plants because male wage earners could not support their households. Thus the economic marginality of lower-class men underlies women's exploitation by multinational corporations (Fernandez-Kelly, 1983a: 193).

This example suggests that exploitation and marginality are closely related, and the two theses linking them to capitalist development share the following basic assumptions: (1) Women play a major role in subsistence production; (2) this activity offers them autonomy and access to resources; (3) women's status erodes with capitalist development; and (4) the "modern" division of labor assigns women primarily to the wife-mother role. These propositions suggest that marginality and exploitation are the twin faces of women's subordinate status and that both reflect this dichotomous division of labor by gender. The notion that women's primary place is the home either isolates them completely from productive relations, or colors the terms of their participation in the labor force. Considered by others and raised to view themselves mainly as wives and mothers, women often do not acquire the education necessary for better jobs in the formal sector. They typically join and leave the formal labor force as reproductive responsibilities dictate, forfeiting not only their seniority but often their access to formal employment. The image that women are subsidiary wage earners who have men to support them becomes a justification for low wages and limited employment benefits. Moreover, sex-segregated labor markets confine most women to menial, poorly remunerated jobs viewed as extensions of their domestic tasks. In sum, the dynamics that marginalize women by confining them, actually or symbolically, to the domestic sphere make them vulnerable to exploitation. Their assignment to the wife-mother role limits many women's occupational options to peripheral positions in the informal sector or to insecure, low-paying jobs in the formal sector.

Theoretical explanations for these dynamics have taken several forms. Boserup (1970) attributed women's marginalization to cultural factors. In her view, as population growth led to increased pressure on land and other finite resources, less-productive technologies such as the handheld hoe were replaced by ox-drawn ploughs, which produced higher yields per acre. The change from female to male farming systems and the displacement of women from agriculture thus resulted, in her opinion, from demographic and technological factors (see Huntington, 1975: 1002; Beneria and Sen, 1981: 285). Women's subsequent marginalization during and after the colonial period, according to Boserup, reflected Western ideologies about proper feminine roles, which in some contexts were reinforced by traditional patriarchal values (Boserup, 1970: 54). Implicit in the work of Boserup and other developmentalists (Tinker, 1976; Palmer, 1979) is the notion that capitalist development is inevitable and basically beneficial, but that the culturally based prejudices of both Western and Third World peoples distort the process to women's disadvantage (Jaquette, 1982: 272; Huntington, 1975: 1007). For example, Boserup (1970: 113-220) attributes women's underrepresentation in modern industrial jobs to employers' preference for male workers, male worker's preference for male colleagues, and women's dislike of factory work (cited in Beneria and Sen, 1981: 282).

Boserup's critics have applauded her path-breaking work for documenting Third World women's productive contributions, for emphasizing the importance of gender in the division of labor and the allocation of resources, and for revealing development's negative impact on women (Beneria and Sen, 1981: 279-281). Nevertheless, they fault Boserup for neglecting women's reproductive roles and their subordination within the household (Huntington, 1975: 1007; Beneria and Sen, 1981: 291), and challenge the neoclassical economic underpinnings of her analysis (Beneria and Sen, 1981: 282). Siding with a host of critics of Western-oriented modernization, they argue that colonialism and capitalism have worked to the detriment of Third World nations. The critics further claim that the technological changes, population growth, and labor market discrimination to which Boserup attributes women's marginalization are themselves manifestations of capitalist development (Beneria and Sen, 1981: 286). In their view, the problem is not, as Boserup implies, that women are not sufficiently involved in an essentially beneficial modernization process. Instead, they claim, modernization under capitalist auspices has itself deepened women's oppression (Beneria and Sen, 1981: 290).

Socialist feminists advance an alternative explanation of Third World women's marginalization and exploitation. Their analysis centers on the way capitalism employs preexisting patriarchal relations (systems of male domination) to accelerate capital accumulation. According to this perspective, women's oppression originates in the household, the primary locus of patriarchal relations that assign women largely to reproductive roles. This patriarchal division of labor benefits capitalism, for women's unpaid domestic labor and child-rearing activities reproduce the labor force at minimal cost. Moreover, the argument continues, women's reproductive roles condition the terms of their participation in paid production. Considered subsidiary wage earners whose primary responsibility is to husband and home, they are relegated to insecure, poorly paid positions seen as extensions of their reproductive roles. Too, their child-rearing duties and frequent ambivalence about their roles as wage workers cause them to function as a surplus labor reserve, to be drawn into or expelled from the work force according to the system's labor needs. Contrary to classical economic models, which analyze women's productive roles in terms of labor demand, human capital, and other characteristics of the labor market, this view attributes women's occupational vulnerability to their reproductive roles and the patriarchal dynamics that emanate from the domestic sphere (Beneria and Sen, 1981: 290-297; Kuhn, 1978: Beechey, 1978).

Strategies for enhancing Third World women's situations reflect these theoretical assumptions about the nature of women's oppression and its links to capitalist modernization. Proponents of modernization theory and the integration thesis hold that socioeconomic development is the key to women's well-being, and that policies designed to foster modernization will raise living standards and expand formal sector openings for women workers. Developmentalists and other advocates of the marginalization thesis are less sanguine, however, for past experience has demonstrated that the benefits of growth do not automatically diffuse to all Third World people. Concerted efforts must be made to involve women in development planning, as participants and as beneficiaries, so that women's unique needs can be better addressed. Women must be given the means for self improvement—health care, schooling, credit access, child care, and so forth—so that they can compete on an equal footing with men in modern labor markets. Legal reforms are also needed to provide a constitutional basis for women's equality by removing male bias in existing legislation and by outlawing gender-based discrimination.

These reforms are insufficient for socialist feminists and other exponents of the exploitation thesis. They hold that Third World women's liberation and equality require radical transformation of three interlocking systems: imperialism, which subjugates all Third World people; capitalism, which exploits all workers; and patriarchy, which oppresses all women. A necessary condition is a socialist revolution that both eliminates capitalism and removes the nation from its dependent position in the world capitalist system. A sufficient condition is the destruction of patriarchy by eliminating the gender-based division of labor in the household, at the work place, and in the political arena, and by socializing reproductive tasks so men and society generally will assume their share of this responsibility.

As social scientists, we need not take a stand, either analytically or strategically, on the issues underlying this debate. As yet too little is known about the multifaceted dynamics involved in capitalist development and the varying ways it affects Third World women to be confident about our understanding of the past or our predictions for the future. Researchers must continue to explore the links between women's productive and reproductive roles and the factors that lead women into the work force. We must consider conditions affecting the economy's labor requirements to determine why in some contexts women's (typically low-wage) labor is in demand while in others women have few employment opportunities. We need to understand better the connection between household economic strategies and women's occupational aspirations and qualifications because these linkages determine the supply of female workers. We must also examine whether employment transforms women's lives and, if so, in what ways. Answers to these questions will help ameliorate development's exploitative and marginalizing effects and strengthen its liberating potential.

REFERENCES

AMIN, S. (1973) Unequal Development. New York: Monthly Review Press.

ARIZPE, L. (1977) "Women in the informal labor sector: The case of Mexico City," pp. 25-37 in Wellesley Editorial Committee (eds.) Women and National Development. Chicago: University of Chicago Press.

BEECHEY, V. (1978) "Women and production: A critical analysis of some sociological theories of women's work," pp. 155-197 in A. Kuhn and A. Wolpe (eds.) Feminism and Materialism. London: Routledge & Kegan Paul.

BENERIA, L. and G. SEN (1981) "Accumulation, reproduction, and women's role in economic development: Boserup revisited." Signs, 7(2): 279-298.

BLUMBERG, R. L. (1981) "Rural women in development," pp. 32-56 in N. Black and A. B. Cottrell (eds.) Women and World Change. Newbury Park, CA: Sage.

BOSERUP, E. (1970) Women's Role in Economic Development. New York: St. Martin's.

BOSSEN, L. (1984) The Redivision of Labor: Women and Economic Choice in Four Guatemalan Communities. Albany: SUNY Press.

BRONSTEIN, A. (1982). The Triple Struggle: Latin American Peasant Women. Boston: South End.

BUNSTER, X. and E. CHANEY (1985) Sellers and Servants: Working Women in Lima, Peru. New York: Praeger.

BUVINIC, M., N. YOUSSEF, and B. VON ELM (1978). Women-Headed Households: The Ignored Factor in Development Planning. Prepared for the Office of Women in Development, Agency for International Development, Washington, DC.

CHANEY, E. (1979) Supermadre: Women and Politics in Latin America. Austin: University of Texas Press.

CHIROT, D. (1977) Social Change in the Twentieth Century. New York: Harcourt Brace Jovanovich.

DEERE, C. D. (1976). "Rural women's subsistence production in the capitalist periphery." Review of Radical Political Economics 8, 1: 9-17.

EISENSTADT, S. N. (1966) Modernization: Protest and Change. Englewood Cliffs, NJ: Prentice-Hall.

EISENSTEIN, Z. (1978) "Developing a theory of capitalist patriarchy and socialist feminism," pp. 5-40 in Eisenstein, Capitalist Patriarchy and the Case for Socialist Feminism. New York: Monthly Review Press.

ELLIOT, C. (1977) "Theories of development: an assessment," pp. 1-8 in Wellesley Editorial Committee (Ed.), Women and National Development. Chicago: University of Chicago Press.

ENLOE, C. (1983) "Women textile workers in the militarization of Southeast Asia," pp. 407-425 in J. Nash and M. P. Fernandez-Kelly (eds.) Women, Men, and the International Division of Labor. Albany: SUNY Press.

FERNANDEZ-KELLY, M. P. (1983a) For We Are Sold, I and My People: Women and Industry in Mexico's Frontier. Albany: SUNY Press.

FERNANDEZ-KELLY, M. P. (1983b) "Mexican border industrialization, female labor force participation, and migration," pp. 205-223 in J. Nash and M. P. Fernandez-Kelly (Eds.), Women, Men, and the International Division of Labor. Albany: SUNY Press.

FUENTES, A. and B. EHRENREICH (1983) Women in the Global Factory. Boston: South End.

GOODE, W. (1970) "Industrialization and family change," pp. 237-259 in B. Hoselitz and W. Moore (eds.) Industrialization and Society. The Hague: Mouton.

GROSSMAN, R. (1979) "Women's place in the integrated circuit." Southeast Asia Chronicle 66: 2-17.

HARRISON, P. (1981) Inside the Third World: The Anatomy of Poverty. New York: Penguin.

HOSELITZ, B. (1970) "Main concepts in the analysis of the social implications of technical change," pp. 11-31 in B. Hoselitz and W. Moore (eds.) Industrialization and Society. The Hague: Mouton.

HUNTINGTON, S. (1975) "Issues in women's role in economic development: Critique and alternatives." Journal of Marriage and the Family, 37(4): 1001-1012.

HUSTON, P. (1979) "Learning, work, and aspirations." Development Digest 17, 1: 59-68.

INKELES, A. and D. H. SMITH (1974) Becoming Modern. Cambridge, MA: Harvard University Press.

International Center for Research on Women [ICRW] (1980a) Keeping Women Out: A Structural Analysis of Women's Employment in Developing Countries. Prepared for the Office of Women in Development, Agency for International Development, Washington, DC.

International Center for Research on Women [ICRW] (1980b) The Productivity of Women in Developing Countries: Measurement Issues and Recommendations. Prepared for the Office of Women in Development, Agency for International Development, Washington, DC.

JAQUETTE, J. (1982) "Women and modernization theory: A decade of feminist criticism." World Politics: 265-284.

JELIN, E. (1977) "Migration and labor force participation of Latin American women: The domestic servants in the cities," pp. 129-141 in Wellesley Editorial Committee (eds.) Women and National Development. Chicago: University of Chicago Press.

KUHN, A. (1978) "Structures of patriarchy and capital in the family," pp. 42-67 in A. Kuhn and A. Wolpe (eds.) Feminism and Materialism. London: Routledge & Kegan Paul.

LEACOCK, E. (1975) "Introduction," pp. 7-67 in F. Engels, The Origin of the Family, Private Property, and the State. New York: International Publishers.

LERNER, D. (1958) The Passing of Traditional Society. New York: Free Press.

LIM, L. (1981) "Women's work in multinational electronics factories," pp. 181-190 in R. Dauber and M. Cain (eds.) Women and Technological Change in Developing Countries. Boulder, CO: Westview.

LIM, L. (1983) "Capitalism, imperialism, and patriarchy: The dilemma of third-world women workers in multinational factories," pp. 70-92 in J. Nash and M. P. Fernandez-Kelly (eds.) Women, Men, and the International Division of Labor. Albany: SUNY Press.

LITTLE, K. (1976) "Women in African towns south of the Sahara: The urbanization dilemma," pp. 78-87 in I. Tinker and M. B. Bramsen (eds.) Women and World Development. Washington, DC: Overseas Development Council.

MCDONOUGH, R. and R. HARRISON (1978) "Patriarchy and relations of production," pp. 11-42 in A. Kuhn and A. Wolpe (eds.) Feminism and Materialism. London: Routledge & Kegan Paul.

MCINTOSH, M. (1978) "The state and the oppression of women," pp. 254-289 in A. Kuhn and A. Wolpe (eds.) Feminism and Materialism. London: Routledge & Kegan Paul.

MEAD, M. (1976) "A comment on the role of women in agriculture," pp. 9-11 in I. Tinker and M. B. Bramsen (eds.) Women and World Development. Washington, DC: Overseas Development Council.

MOORE, W. (1965) The Impact of Industry. Englewood Cliffs, NJ: Prentice-Hall.

NASH, J. (1983) "The impact of the changing international division of labor on different sectors of the labor force," in J. Nash and M. Fernandez-Kelly (eds.) Women, Men, and the International Division of Labor. Albany: SUNY Press.

North American Congress on Latin America [NACLA] (1979) Beyond the Border: Mexico and the United States Today. New York: Author.

ONG, A. (1983) "Global industries and Malay peasants in peninsular Malaysia," pp. 426-439 in J. Nash and M. P. Fernandez-Kelly (eds.) Women, Men, and the International Division of Labor. Albany: SUNY Press.

PALMER, I. (1979) "Rural women and the basic needs approach to development." Development Digest 17, 1: 89-98.

PĔNA, D. (1982) "Emerging organizational strategies of maquila workers on the Mexico-U.S. border." Prepared for the Tenth Annual Meeting of the National Association for Chicano Studies, Tempe, Arizona.

PORTES, A. and J. WALTON (1981) Labor, Class, and the International System. New York: Academic Press.

RAPP, R. (1982) "Family and class in contemporary America: Notes toward an understanding of ideology," pp. 168-187 in B. Thorne and M. Yalom (eds.) Rethinking the Family. New York: Longman.

ROSEN, B. (1982) The Industrial Connection: Achievement and the Family in Developing Societies. Chicago: Aldine.

ROTHSTEIN, F. (1982) Three Different Worlds: Women, Men and Children in an Industrializing Community. Westport, CT: Greenwood.

SAFA, H. (1985) "Female employment in the Puerto Rican working class," pp. 84-106 in J. Nash and H. Safa (eds.) Women and Change in Latin America. South Hadley, MA: Bergin & Garvey.

SAFFIOTI, H. (1975) "Female labor and capitalism in the United States and Brazil," in R. Rohrlich-Leavitt (ed.) Women Cross-Culturally: Change and Challenge. The Hague: Mouton.

SAFFIOTI, H. (1985). "Technological change in Brazil," pp. 109-135 in J. Nash and H. Safa (eds.) Women and Change in Latin America. South Hadley, MA: Bergin & Garvey.

SALAFF, J. (1981) "Singapore women: Work and the family," pp. 57-82 in N. Black and A. B. Cottrell (eds.) Women and World Change. Newbury Park, CA: Sage.

SCHMINK, M. (1984) "Household economic strategies: Review and research agenda." Latin American Research Review 19, 3: 87-101.

SCHMINK, M. (1985) "Women and urban industrial development in Brazil," pp. 136-165 in J. Nash and H. Safa (eds.) Women and Change in Latin America. South Hadley, MA: Bergin & Garvey.

SMITH, D. (1975) "Women, the family, and corporate capitalism." Berkeley Journal of Sociology 20: 55-90.

SMITH, M. (1973) "Domestic service as a channel of upward mobility for the lower-class woman: The Lima case," pp. 191-207 in A. Pescatello (ed.) Female and Male in Latin America. Pittsburgh: University of Pittsburgh Press.

SOKOLOFF, N. (1980) Between Money and Love. New York: Praeger.

SUDARKASA, N. (1977) "Women and migration in contemporary West Africa," pp. 178-189 in Wellesley Editorial Committee (eds.) Women and National Development. Chicago: University of Chicago Press.

TIANO, S. (1984a) "Maquiladoras, women's work, and unemployment in northern Mexico." Women in International Development Working Papers, No. 43, Michigan State University.

TIANO, S. (1984b) "The public-private dichotomy: Theoretical perspectives on 'Women and Development.'" Social Science Journal 21, 4: 11-28.

TIANO, S. (1985) "Women workers in a northern Mexican City: Constraints and opportunities." Prepared for the annual meetings of the Latin American Studies Association, Albuquerque, New Mexico.

TINKER, I. (1976) "The adverse impact of development on women," pp. 22-34 in I. Tinker and M. B. Bramsen (eds.) Women and World Development. Washington, DC: Overseas Development Council.

TOWNER, M. (1979) "Monopoly capitalism and women's work during the porfiriato," pp. 47-62 in W. Bollinger et al. (eds.) Women in Latin America: An Anthology from Latin American Perspectives. Riverside, CA: Latin American Perspectives.

United Nations (1980) Program of Action for the Second Half of the United Nations Decade for Women: Equality, Development, and Peace. New York: Author.

VAUGHAN, M. (1979) "Women, class, and education in Mexico, 1880-1928," pp. 63-80 in W. Bollinger et al. (eds.) Women in Latin America: An Anthology from Latin American Perspectives. Riverside, CA: Latin American Perspectives.

9   Gender and the GNP

PENELOPE CIANCANELLI
BETTINA BERCH
Barnard College

I F you were to ask the average neoclassical economist to explain the
economic basis of gender stratification, you would be directed, in
all likelihood, to the sociology department. The concepts of gender
and stratification are not part of economic discourse and no sensible answer
can be expected as long as the issue is framed in such terms.[1] To get the
economists talking, the question has to be recast in terms they can understand,
which is no easy feat.

Economics has been termed the dismal science in large part because it is
remorselessly narrow in its approach and relentlessly confident of its
explanatory power. Undeterred by epistemological self-doubt, orthodox
economics is mired in a crude nineteenth-century materialistic philosophy. All
behavior is reduced to individual utility maximization—a conjectural calculus
of pain and pleasure married to a crude social Darwinism, which in its latest
variant—sociobiology—turns out to ensure genetic optima for the species via
allocational efficiencies in household formation (Becker, 1981).

If one went instead to the average nonorthodox economist (an eclectic set
of institutionalists, radicals, etc.) hoping for a more weighty response to the
same question, one would in all likelihood be directed to their women's
caucus. Being relatively more broad-minded, nonorthodox economists have
settled on a division of labor in the production of knowledge on the subjects of
sex and class (proxies for gender and stratification). Behavior is thought to
have a more diffuse basis than maximizing utility, and some effort is made to
introduce structural variables (class, power, discrimination) that go beyond
individual choice. Doing so introduces more complexity but leaves these
models less mathematically tractable.

Since neither gender nor stratification are concepts with which the average
economist seriously contends, the discipline has confined the study of women
to the field of labor economics. Here a nontrivial set of anomolous behaviors
by women (particularly married women) has come to define the economic
approach to gender.[2] This has had two unfortunate consequences. First the
specific role of hierarchy in *creating* a given job mix (the demand side of the

labor market, also known as the social division of labor) is not systematically explored. This issue is not addressed at all by mainstream economists and the dissenting economists have only recently begun exploring this area, through industry case studies. As a result, the demand side of the analysis is much less developed than the supply side.

Second, the social character of gender is conflated with a narrow range of biological differences between men and women. Feminists' efforts to theorize the role of gender in social terms have not been absorbed in mainstream discussions where child rearing is treated as a question of individual tastes and preferences rather than as work whose social imposition is one manifestation of gender hierarchy (Hartmann, 1981). As a result, a broad range of constraints and economic processes escape the consideration of economists, and the econometric focus of standard studies on women's labor supply behavior is subject to diminishing returns. The methods tell us less and less about the dynamics that reproduce, with stunning regularity, women's economic and political inferiority over time and across social systems.

At this point it is useful to clarify what we mean by stratification systems, be they organized on the basis of class, race, sex, physical abilities, or any combination thereof. Stratification systems are social constructions. They are not in any sense biological or natural. They serve as a type of lens through which people are viewed and arranged. Unlike some relatively passive or benign strata (geological, for example) social strata are constructed for the purpose of controlling some groups for the benefit of others. These are neither mere sorting systems nor "efficient" divisions of work or functional distributions of status, but systems of social control. This viewpoint is undoubtedly controversial but will prove useful in challenging the popular ideologies of stratification to which economists have proved surprisingly vulnerable.

The first of these is the doctrine of "separate but equal," struck down by the Supreme Court but still sturdy in the social mythology. One can go to great pains describing the sexual division of labor encasing women in the lowest paid, lowest status jobs, only to hear a remark to the effect that "women get fewer heart attacks because their work is less stressful" or "women like the 'helping' professions" or "women do their work and men do theirs and it all comes out even." "Separate but equal" with respect to sex seems to be a pervasive and socially acceptable attitude (King, 1982). While it is true that given the amount of sexual harassment in the labor force women might indeed find refuge in all-female occupations, there is no disputing the low-wage character of pink-collar jobs. Who would choose this fate if other options were genuinely available?[3]

A second mythology fogging the stratification question is the "nature or nurture" debate. Faced with the statistics on the sexual division of labor, people seem to want to argue whether it indicates a "natural superiority" of one sex over the other in certain areas (such as physical strength) or whether it is all a product of early childhood socialization. Does stratification arise out of innate differences or does it create difference? While certainly more sophisticated than this, the circularity of the nature versus nurture core of the debates is ubiquitous. To overcome this, analogies, while imperfect, are useful; the one that comes to mind is apartheid, primarily because it is another highly structured system of "human difference."

Apartheid is a complex system of stratification based on a plainly artificial definition of differences. In it the minority (white) controlled government dominates the majority of the population in South Africa. While the desired end of the hierarchy of color is control, the purpose of control is the division of work and income so that advantage and power accrue to the white majority. Gender stratification is also a means of control. Obviously it has quite different origins and mechanisms, it is more flexible in certain dimensions, more psychologically rather than physically articulated; but these are differences of degree, not of kind. Each system functions to impose work and distribute resources so that advantage and power accrue to a privileged group.

From this perspective, the sex division of labor results from a gender hierarchy in which women work longer hours for less money. The clearest expression of this is the uncounted, unpriced, and unpaid housework assigned to women in both capitalist and socialist economies. This unequal exchange is also apparent in the wage gap; women working in jobs of comparable worth earn significantly less than men. In each social relational nexus, capitalist and familial, women's contribution to and/or creation of the economy is defined and regarded as something else—as not "economic." This renders their work invisible and we would argue is a key means to forestall demands that it be paid for or that the work itself be shared more equitably.

This chapter is organized to draw attention to this ideological dimension in standard definitions of economic activity and in conceptual choices that dichotomize "public" and "private." This emphasizes the role of economics itself in legitimating the unequal division of work and income to which women are subject. For example, it is commonly argued that women are economically dependent on men. This turns reality on its head, given the abundant evidence that as a group women do more of the socially necessary work than do men. They may be politically inferior but hardly the unproductive wards that the term "economic dependence" implies.

This approach also highlights the work of feminist economic analysis. In it, scholars sought ways to bring women's work into the academy for scrutiny and as a means to critique the main categories of the discipline itself. The work has had simultaneously to construct a body of knowledge about women's work and to explore the mechanisms that hid it from the official histories. Its subject matter is the mechanism of unequal exchange in capitalist and familial relations. It now constitutes a literature that may be referred to as a literature on social production and reproduction. In this chapter, housework will be used as it is used in that literature—as a global referent for the myriad tasks required to produce on a daily and intergenerational basis those resources—

physical and psychological—that permit the ongoing performance of the work that is directly subordinated to capitalist and/or "state" institutions.

In the first section we develop a critique of the conventional linkages made between work and income, focusing on the exclusion of women's unpaid housework and childbearing from formal definitions of income-creating economic activities. In the next section we explore the mainstream approach, with its emphasis on microeconomic or individual decision making, including feminist critiques of the major theoretical models proposed. In the final section we review macroeconomic treatment of occupational segregation and the social reproduction literature and evaluate future prospects and policy issues.

MONEY, WORK, AND POWER

There is more to a woman's place in modern economies than the distinctiveness of her labor supply patterns. The relationships between the work women do, the kind of income it produces (money or directly needed goods and services), and the kind of income they can claim (money or directly needed goods and services) involve a broad range of institutions of which labor markets are only one, and perhaps the least important one at that.

The political dimension of the income-work linkage is exemplified by government policies toward the elderly, the infirm, and the unemployed. Governments provide monetary income to people in these categories and the amounts are independent of current work performed. In fact, when one considers intrafamilial transfer payments, one discovers that over half the population gains income through transfers rather than from paid employment.[4] The work-payment linkage for adult women contrasts sharply with this pattern. Women perform a great deal of socially necessary work but do not receive payment for it. Moreover, there operates a specific and powerful ideology that denies either the necessity or justice of payment for this work. It does so by denying its economic and social character—casting women's work into the realm of personal choice. Thus from the perspective of women, a great deal of the work they are socially expected to perform appears to be outside the economic system.

The treatment of this work in the national accounts and its exclusion from the gross national product (GNP) is the prime example of this mind-set. It is instructive to quote a leading labor force economist, Stanley Lebergott (1964), on the subject of housework:

> There is considerable warrant for considering such work (e.g. housework) as no less real—and far more vital—than work outside the home. However, there would be little analytic value to measures that always showed about 100% of women in the labor force, varying not at all through the business cycle or through time [1964: 56].

The claim here seems to be that certain kinds of work go on whether or not the economy grows. That is, the work is an essential, hence invariant, requirement of the society but not of the economy. Its inclusion, he argues, would provide us with little analytic power in measuring overall economic activity. This is provocative. Women's unpaid work is real economic activity with a purpose, but whose? for whom? This is a mystery indeed. This ambiguity does not stem from mainstream theory, for in it the definition of income-creating, economic activity was set down by Alfred Marshall (1888), who wrote,

> The labor and capital of the country acting on its national resources, produce annually a certain net aggregate of commodities, material and immaterial including services of all kinds. . . . This is the true net annual income of revenues of the country: or, the national dividend [1888: 3].

By firmly identifying production with the creation of utility and including thereby all use values—whether services or physical goods—Marshall established what is termed a "comprehensive definition" of income. It is obvious that under this definition, housework creates income, as suggested by Lebergott. The standard labor supply analysis of the productive value of nonwaged work is an application of this concept to the household. The difficulty is that this definition does not differentiate between monetary forms of income and income in the form of utilities. This body of research assumes that the former is perfectly transformable into the latter.[5] This becomes a major source of confusion in the standard models since their definition of labor force participation is tied to a quite different concept of income.

What Lebergott (1964) was working toward in the argument quoted earlier is a different conceptual universe in which labor force definitions were developed. In it, employment is not defined as *any* utility creating work but only that work which is paid for. This definition embodies the market concept of income. Accordingly, only women who are paid to do housework are considered to be income producing. The unpaid creation of utility is not treated as income. In another twist of logic, however, even this more limited concept of income is not uniformly applied. While housework must meet this criterion, analytically identical forms such as farm production for own use are estimated at market value, and this estimation is included in measures of GNP (Ciancanelli, 1983).

From a feminist perspective, the asymmetric treatment of housework in GNP statistics (and the conflicting conceptions of income that give rise to it) is both cause and effect of women's inferiority. On the one hand, the exclusion of housework from GNP constitutes an official denial that this work is socially necessary and therefore productive of goods and services that contribute to the overall standard of living. On the other hand, it exposes a serious contradiction in the economists' approach to the study of social reproduction. That approach claims that women's specialization in housework maximizes household income (Becker, 1981). But how can income recognized at the microeconomic level not add up to a positive net contribution at the macroeconomic level? Alternatively, if housework does not add to family income (in the Marshallian sense of utility) why does anyone stay home to do it?

Feminist economists all emphasize that housework is part of the social division of labor in which the work of social reproduction gets done, albeit in the guise of family responsibility (Humphries and Rubery, 1984). As such, housework is an extension of the industrial matrix and plays an active role in shaping the investment decisions of capitalists, the kinds of labor processes that are established, and the relative balance of service and manufacturing employment in the macroeconomy.

For example, a rising demand for consumer durables such as refrigerators alters the division of labor both at home and among businesses. Producers of iceboxes and the vendors of ice go out of business while entrepreneurs emerge to manufacture the machines needed to produce refrigerator parts. Women who formerly shopped daily for perishables now find it possible to shop weekly and, with more "free time," can take on additional tasks. Simultaneously the low wages that women command attract investment by profit-seeking firms that manufacture refrigerator components, using women workers, many of whom enter paid employment in order to get the money they need to pay for a refrigerator!

The process of capitalist development can be defined as one in which more and more of the essentials of life—from housing to food to refrigerators—must be bought. Money income becomes the *strategic* income in a household's standard of living. The income produced by housework cannot be used to "buy" a refrigerator and one does not manufacture a refrigerator in one's spare time. Women can, however, work for money and do the housework—including child rearing—*in their spare time*. But consider what an odd denouement that is. The essential work—child care, food preparation, and so forth—is done in spare time while the best part of the day is devoted to work that provides the money needed to pay for the means (e.g., refrigerators) needed in order to work for pay outside the home! One might ask, on what ground do we privilege housework as "essential" and wagework as "added-on," or vice versa? Furthermore what is (and is not) "spare time" for women if both paid work and housework compete for it equally?

In addition, the perception that housework is not income producing reinforces the ideology that monetary income is the only accurate measure of individual productivity. The structured inferiority of housework in capitalist economies conflicts, however, with the fact that the work is socially necessary. The question is, Who will do it and on what terms? In the next section we will explore the treatment of housework in economic models of women's choices as individuals and as members of households.

HOUSEWORK AND GENDER HIERARCHY

The household division of labor refers to sex differences in work patterns within the family. Mainstream and feminist economists have debated forcefully whether these are governed by an altruism that pays off (Lloyd, 1975), a patriarchy that imposes the double day on women (Sargent, 1981; Hartmann, 1981), or a confounding and contradictory synthesis of alliance and domination (Humphries, 1977). These varied interpretations are based on differences in the connections that scholars make between economic activities that are paid for, those that are not paid for (housework), and the economic core imputed to hierarchy itself (capitalism and/or patriarchy).

Whether or not they work outside the home for wages, married women do the bulk of housework or "home production" (the term for housework used in mainstream research). It is in that empirical reality that the debate is rooted. While no one argues that women directly choose an inferior occupational status, mainstream models of women's labor supply are premised on the existence of an alternative available to married women (unpaid labor within the family) for the productive use of their time in addition to paid employment outside the home. This is, in fact, the key theoretical innovation in the discipline of economics with respect to the analysis of women.[6]

Dissenting economists are critical of the implication that this third "option" is freely chosen by the majority of women: They regard housework as socially imposed, the work itself being a critical element in the reproduction of a societywide gender hierarchy. The inexorable burden of this double day of work among highly skilled, professional women suggests that even among the affluent the work is not chosen in any trivial sense. The social reproduction literature asks, Is it not more likely that the majority of women "specialize" in housework for the same reasons that they "specialize" in the pink-collar ghetto: coercion by discriminatory legal and economic structures? To see how the debate developed, it is useful to review the evolution of mainstream models.

The early studies of women's labor supply emphasized a threefold choice facing married women: market work, leisure, and home production (Mincer, 1962; Becker, 1965). In this approach, one looks to individual differences in productivity to understand how women allocate their time among these options. It was argued that choices of time allocation were themselves regulated by the price of one's time calculated as its opportunity cost—that is, the amount of income one might otherwise be producing. Thus when women's market productivity (namely wages) is lower than men's, even if their productivity in household production is identical, both the man and the woman will gain from a trade (e.g., marriage) whereby women specialize in home production and men specialize in market production. As women's own market productivity rises relative to men (e.g., their own market wage rate increases) the household may increase its utility by shifting some of her time from home production to market work, substituting market goods (e.g., restaurant meals) for those produced in the household (e.g., home-cooked meals).

This approach led to greater complexity in cross-sectional studies as scholars included more variables affecting a woman's productivity in the home *relative* to her own productivity in market production. For example, an increase in the market wage of a woman of given education, age, and so on might be offset by an increase in her productivity in the home due to a new baby, a bigger house to take care of, or a gourmet cooking course that increases the value of a home-cooked meal. If her wages rose while her employment pattern remained the same, some economists would infer that her home productivity still exceeded that in the market.

What regulates the choice between household and market production is the price of a woman's time in *real* terms. Does the family gain more income (in Marshall's sense) from a woman's home production or does it gain more income from her market production? Household demand for housework is a demand for particular utilities, and families weigh the cost of purchasing them with money against the other goods they could have had. From this perspective, if she were not at home producing these goods and services, she could be in the labor force earning the money with which to buy some of them (or all, depending on her market wage rate).

The shift in focus from utility maximization to relative productivity in home and market work led, however, to paradoxical results. As the value or productivity of housework is implicitly determined by the value of foregone market wages, it follows that the housework of a lawyer (whose wage rate may be $80/hour) is eight times as valuable as that of a nurse (at a wage rate of $10/hour), even though the housework is technically indistinguishable. Feminist economists are not completely comfortable with the relative productivity argument. Some have challenged whether relative productivity can be the basis of decision making when few are able to formulate estimates of one or both (Ferber and Greene, 1983).

A second critique of this approach (called the New Household Economics) concerns its lack of realism. The original labor supply analysis proposed that women maximized their individual utility (just as men did), gender being composed largely of differences in subjectively formed desiderata including the third option of housework. Becker (1981), however, shifted the analysis from the individual to the household whose utility maximization had to be modeled as the preferences of either everyone ("the family") or no one ("bargained"). But in both cases determining how joint utilities were arrived at posed formidable problems (Nerlove, 1974; Mansur and Brown, 1980; McElroy and Horney, 1981).

Another reason to seek alternative approaches involved the formidable measurement problems researchers faced. For example, in order to estimate the impact of childbearing on the employment decision we need to be able to hold constant other factors such as education and market wages (i.e., the opportunity cost of a woman's time). For market-employed women we have actual wage rates—but for those who are not employed, we have no wage rate; we must assume the opportunity cost of time is identical for both sets of women. This assumption is problematic for many reasons since some of the employed women's earnings are due to work experience, which should not be imputed to the nonemployed women.

Feminist economists have also begun to question the original characterization of women's labor supply behavior on factual grounds. The accuracy of the data reporting the century's trend in the employment of married women has been demonstrated to be an artifact of the data collection procedures of the census (Ciancanelli, 1983; see also Bose, Chapter 10 in this volume). Feminist economic historians have documented very high rates of employment among married women throughout the century, demonstrating that a substantial proportion of married women in urban areas engaged in income-earning activities that conform to current definitions of employment (Klaczyn-ska, 1976; Cantor and Lurie, 1977). Feminist research confirms pre-New Household Economics studies (Jaffee, 1956; Smuts, 1960) of the labor force and imply that few valid correlations can be made between secular increases in the employment of married women and increases in incomes simply because no statistical series yet exists that accurately documents century-long changes in either variable.

Trend data for 1957 to the present, while considerably more accurate than pre-1950s data, do show sharp year-to-year increases; but these data also suffer from confusion in the measurement of income (Ciancanelli, 1985) as well as minor (but widely ignored) enumerator and reporter biases for rural women, urban immigrant women, and minority women.[7]

However, even if the post-1950s data were perfect, most economic researchers view the changes of the last 30 years in the context of a rising long-term trend in women's economic contribution to national income. Were they to view the labor supply patterns of the 1950s and 1960s as exceptional decades of *low* female employment in a century-long pattern of *high* female employment they would have to alter the discipline's focus on the supply side and look at changes in the structure of production.[8]

To overcome some of these difficulties, economists returned to individual decision making by women but within a general model of investment in education and training. In these human capital models, researchers explore the dynamics of occupational choice across the life course. They argue that women choose occupations according to *expected* lifetime labor force participation. Thus initial investment decisions result in differential skill accumulation over the life course and these, in turn, create sex differences in observed occupational distributions. If expected lifetime labor force participation is brief, human capital investments will be low as will the wages earned in market work (Polachek, 1981; Niemi and Lloyd, 1979; see England and McCreary, Chapter 11 in this volume).

This approach suffers from equally serious measurement problems. One can only infer expected lifetime labor force participation from ex post facto labor force participation rates. Occupational outcomes and labor force attachment are so jointly determined in this model that it is impossible to determine which is cause and which is effect (Madden, 1979: 165). Thus the intermittence of participation associated with erosion of skill (or failure to accumulate skill) cannot be shown to be a result of expected lifetime commitments. Since the data are for current occupation, it is unclear whether those who spend a high proportion of time out of the labor force tend to wind up in the low wage occupations or whether they choose these poor jobs in anticipation of a large proportion of time out.

In addition, the human capital investment model suffers from the same theoretical problem that faces all investment models: It must take the fact that the future is unknown and treat it *as if* all future occupational outcomes *are* known in advance. Is it sensible to act as if women's choices are analytically identical to those made in playing poker? If individual women "bet their life" that they will not have to be self-supporting (and therefore do not invest much in their own education), what are the grounds for this risk taking? Must one simply assume that women are less risk averse than men?

Finally, this approach emphasizes that investment in education and the timing of employment both are consequences of women's decision to marry and specialize in home production. Since a woman is free to do otherwise, they would argue, women's unpaid work is best regarded as a functional division of tasks. This analysis is silent, however, on the following questions: How does one explain the ubiquity and generational uniformity in women's expectations? Is it credible to assume that while class differences among men create great divergence in occupational choice, they do not have this effect on women? Can we assume that however different women may be from one another in class terms, they are united in an unshakable belief that the best they can do is to specialize in home production? Does that not at least suggest that their opportunities in paid employment outside the home are very different from those facing men?

These questions expose the model's assumption that individual choice governs life's outcomes; if so, however, the choice theoretic framework must identify the rational grounds for choosing political and economic inferiority. To overcome this dilemma, one must either claim that perceived inferiority is actually "difference" or redefine the commonsense understanding of rationality. The many limitations to mainstream microeconomic models strongly suggest that they offer little scope for analyzing women's oppression. After all, oppression means a lack of choice and refers to coercive ideologies and incentives. Given their interest in structural factors that limit personal choice, feminist scholars have devoted their efforts to the study of macroeconomic phenomena, such as discrimination or labor market segmentation, treating the social division of labor as a strategic force mitigating against more egalitarian arrangements within households. It is to occupational segregation by sex and other market-engineered outcomes that we now turn.

GENDER HIERARCHY IN
THE SOCIAL DIVISION OF LABOR

In spite of decades of very explicit civil rights legislation, our labor force is still characterized by a large wage gap between men and women working in similar occupations even though there has been some increase in the number of women in "male" occupations. (See Table 9.1; see also England and McCreary, Chapter 11 in this volume.)

The stylized facts are quite similar to those publicized decades ago: The majority of working women are in clerical and service occupations. Even where women are in professional or technical occupations, they are usually found in the lowest paid ranks. The occupational map is sex-stratified horizontally as well as vertically.

On the other hand, significant changes have occurred in the numbers of women working outside the home and there is a public perception that women are no longer discriminated against. The extent and meaning of changes in women's occupational status are still difficult to determine. Part of the reason lies in deciding what ought to be compared with what: Do we compare the pay of men and women in similar or comparable occupations, or does demonstration of discrimination require that we compare only men and women in identical occupations? Is the wage gap best measured by the average difference between male and female earnings 20 years ago compared to that found today? Is progress better measured by comparing women's average income 20 years ago to what it is today?

An example may help to clarify the kinds of difficulties researchers encounter. The 1980 Standard Occupational Classification of the Census contained 13 major occupational groups composed of 503 subgroups. If male occupations are defined as those with 20% or fewer jobs held by women, 60% of all occupations are male occupations. Using *this* criteria, sex segregation decreased between 1970 and 1980 as fewer men were employed in male occupations in 1980 than in 1970 (Rytina and Bianchi, 1984: 14). These categories are, however, very broad and include occupations with a great range of jobs. When one moves to finer classifications, subsets of male and female occupations reappear and sex-segregation does not appear to have lessened. The wage gap shows similar problems—narrowing in the 1980s at a broad level of categorization and widening on finer specification. Table 9.1 provides one kind of snapshot of this statistical reality in the social division of labor.

Table 9.1 provides information on incomes earned by men and women in the same occupational groups and within selected occupations in 1984. The

TABLE 9.1

Top Decile Earnings of Men and Women, and Percentage of
Men Earning as Much as the Highest Paid Decile of Women
for Major Occupational Groups and for Selected Occupations,
Full-Time Workers, 1982 Annual Averages

Occupation	Lower Boundary of Top Decile		Percentage of Men Earning at Least as Much as Women's Top Decile
	Men	Women	
Major occupation groups			
Total	$688	$437	37
Professional and technical workers	848	561	37
Managers and administrators except farm	900+[a]	568	40
Salesworkers	790	440	40
Clerical workers	571	386	42
Craft and kindred workers	616	470	29
Operatives, except transport	502	338	43
Transport equipment operatives	569	445	24
Nonfarm laborers	448	355	25
Private household workers	*	197	*
Other service workers	469	295	38
Farm workers	315	285	14
Selected occupations[b]			
Accountants	776	532	39
Secondary school teachers	637	567	18
Sales clerks, retail trade	482	290	37
Assemblers	477	362	40
Cooks, except private household	358	243	34
Checkers, examiners, and inspectors	540	380	45
Bank officers and financial managers	900+[a]	597	46

SOURCE: Mellor (1984: 25, tab. 4).
a. Earnings of $900 or more. Decile boundaries are estimated using linear interpolation of $50- and $100-wide intervals. Since the $900+ interval is open-ended, the boundary cannot be estimated.
b. Occupations in which at least 250,000 of each sex are employed.
*Decile boundary and percentage not estimated where base is under 50,000.

income that men or women need to earn in order to be among the top wage group is compared and the percentage of all men in the occupational group who earn *at least* as much as the elite women earn is given in the adjoining column.

To be among the top 10% of wage-earning professionals, men had to earn at least $688 whereas women had to earn $437. The gap between sales clerks was worse, women having to earn (proportionally) less to be a very well paid sales clerk. In most occupational groups roughly 40% of the men in that occupation earned at least as much as the best paid women. In particular occupations, such as accounting, the pattern continues of a very large proportion of men routinely earning what only 10% of women in that

TABLE 9.2

Median Usual Weekly Earnings of Women and Men,
and Percentage Earning Under $200 and $500 or More
in Major Occupations and in Selected Low- and High-Paying
Occupations, Full-time Workers, 1982 Annual Averages

Occupation	Median Usual Weekly Earnings	Percentage Under $200		Percentage $500 or More	
		Men	Women	Men	Women
Major occupation groups					
Total	$309	12.7	32.7	26.7	6.0
Professional and technical workers	410	3.4	8.8	47.8	15.6
Managers and administrators, except farm	430	3.2	16.2	51.3	14.9
Salesworkers	317	11.8	45.8	32.6	7.5
Clerical workers	248	13.0	30.3	16.5	2.4
Craft and kindred workers	375	7.0	28.4	23.9	7.7
Operatives, except transport	252	16.7	50.7	10.1	1.0
Transport equipment operatives	323	14.4	35.3	16.6	6.8
Nonfarm laborers	243	32.3	47.5	5.9	1.5
Private household workers	111	*	90.7	*	0.3
Other service workers	207	31.9	61.7	7.8	0.8
Farm workers	190	53.8	62.0	1.6	–
Lowest paying occupations[a]					
Waiters	158	36.1	77.5	6.0	–
Food service workers, n.e.c.	169	60.6	75.1	2.8	0.5
Cashiers	176	52.7	66.3	5.4	0.2
Cooks, except private household	180	47.4	76.3	0.3	2.8
Nursing aides, orderlies, and attendants	182	43.2	65.1	2.5	0.1
Farm laborers	184	57.8	63.5	1.0	–
Sales clerks, retail trade	188	34.5	71.0	8.8	1.2
Building interior cleaners, n.e.c.	192	41.0	66.2	3.8	–
Bartenders	196	37.9	65.9	4.6	–
Personal service workers	202	33.2	56.1	7.6	3.1
Highest paying occupations[a]					
Lawyers	626	2.3	3.0	74.8	48.5
Engineers	586	0.4	1.3	71.3	45.0
Computer systems analysts	539	–	4.6	66.9	35.4
Life and physical scientists	519	4.0	11.1	59.1	31.5
Social scientists	518	1.8	2.3	61.8	35.2
School administrators, elementary and secondary	517	0.6	20.7	65.2	28.7
Operations and systems researchers and analysts	508	1.3	2.7	61.6	28.8
Physicians, dentists, and related	507	1.8	7.5	55.2	37.5
Teachers, college and university	499	2.6	6.4	56.1	32.7
Bank officers and financial managers	471	0.7	7.6	63.6	18.2

SOURCE: Mellor (1984: 24, tab. 3).
NOTE: Dashes indicate zero or rounds to zero.
a. Occupations in which at least 50,000 of each sex are employed.
*Percentage not shown where the base is under 50,000 workers.

occupation earn. One observes women's concentration in the lower paid ends of occupations when we examine occupational groups in greater detail. Less than half of the women lawyers earned $500 per week or more; almost 75% of men lawyers earned that. In the lower paying occupations, most women earned below $200 while most men earned more than $200 (see Table 9.2).

The identification of women with low paid work creates seemingly intractable questions: Is secretarial work so low paid because it is a female occupation or did it get to be a low paid occupation once women entered it? Why is it that men enter nursing school and become nursing administrators, enter teaching and become school principals, whereas such is rarely true of women (Reskin, 1984)? Are wages payment for value added or are they an index of social power? Why is it that it is *still* easier to predict a person's occupation and wage level knowing their sex than knowing anything else (Reskin, 1984)?

Mainstream economists have been criticized for generally ignoring sex segregation in labor markets. At best they admit it as an "imperfection," a deviation from the ideal of "perfect competition." In perfect competition, neither workers nor employers exert any power over the wage. An equilibrium price for labor is arrived at in a kind of silent auction of supply price asked and demand price bid (Blau and Jusenius, 1976).

In addition, labor is supposed to be paid in direct proportion to the value it adds to the product: The more productive the worker, the higher the wage. There is no reason, therefore, why women or blacks or anyone else should be concentrated in any one occupation or another except for their differing productivity in these fields. To the mainstream economists a concentration of women in low paid work indicates that women are just not as productive as men (Berch, 1977).

Some mainstream economists have investigated whether theories of market imperfections might be useful in describing sex-segregated labor markets. One school tried to explain women's low wages by arguing that women were "crowded into" a few female-permissible trades, causing an oversupply of these occupations thus pushing down those wages. Crowding theories describe a real phenomenon of imbalance in female labor markets, but they beg the question of what structures the labor markets along gender lines. Usually crowding theories are joined with Becker-type analyses of employer "tastes" for discrimination whose origins are left undiscussed.

Members of the imperfect competition school tried their oligopsonic price discrimination model, which saw a small group of employers profiting from their ability to discriminate by price among different groups of workers based on their different labor market power (Mansur and Brown, 1979). While this theory had a certain intuitive appeal, it also acknowledged that discrimination and segmentation were profitable business tactics. Yet since the model itself was quite unwieldy, it was never particularly popular and little work has been done with it in recent years.

In recent decades economists have acknowledged the existence of discrimination, but by formulating it as a "market imperfection," they do not see it as functional (e.g., profit enhancing). This perspective was developed by radical economists whose theoretical perspective is called labor market segmentation (Gordon et al., 1982). Rather than assume competition, these critics posited a highly balkanized labor market, with strong barriers to entry to the better paid and better prospect jobs. Furthermore, workers are hired in these various sectors *not* according to their intrinsic productivity, but according to gender/race/class-origin profile. While these segmentation models were successful at a descriptive level, they were much less useful on an analytic or policy level. The politics behind these models were too obscure. Why was it women who were cordoned off into the inferior segments? The power analysis was missing.

A unified theoretical framework is proposed by Marxist-feminists in the elaboration of a capitalist-patriarchy theory that viewed discrimination and segmentation as structural features of labor markets and proposed two benefactors of women's oppression—capitalism and patriarchy (Hartmann, 1976; Eisenstein, 1979). In its original formulation, this approach emphasized the economic functions served by a strategic alliance between capitalists and a preexisting system of male power, patriarchy. It was argued that each mutually reinforces the other's social power, at the expense of women, people of color, and other victims of discrimination. How does this work? Occupational segregation is seen as the central device to "divide and conquer" the labor force, a major interest of capitalist firms as this lowers costs and gives individual employers more control over the labor process. Male workers' divided loyalties (to the patriarchy and to their own class interest as workers) tempt them into bargains with capital at the expense of women workers.

Confining women to the most precarious and underpaid sectors of the labor force undoubtedly functions to reproduce both class and gender privileges. Early critiques and extensions of the approach understood certain of the theory's limitations to stem from its functionalist bias—namely, a confusion between history and necessity (Humphries, 1977; Sen, 1980). An associated critique involves the categories of agency in the theory (the patriarchy; the capitalist system) as they assume a supra-historical status as *idea*, into which practically any set of "fact" can be molded into historical proof. For example, the evidence can support a theory of collusion between male trade unionists and capitalists against women or can be used to support a more sympathetic interpretation of trade union limitations (Humphries, 1977; Sen, 1980; Power, 1983).

Since the early formulations of this perspective, a lively debate has been conducted in which competing theories have adopted an overall macro-economic approach whose central conceptual framework is that of social reproduction. This concept evolved as a means to incorporate microeconomic phenomenon (such as the family) into a macroeconomic framework in order to treat gender as a fundamental aspect of the economic system—not simply as a characteristic of individuals (Ciancanelli, 1980). A great number of valuable studies have been conducted shedding light on a range of phenomena from the politics of skill assessment (Cavendish, 1982; Phillips and Taylor, 1980) to the role of gender systems in economic growth and distribution (Picchio del Mercato, 1981).[8]

Three general lines of inquiry are being pursued—one looking at the specific effects of gender on the industrial structure (Craig et al., 1982); another extending Marxian concepts of the industrial reserve army (Power, 1983; Kolko, 1978); and a third seeking to connect the modern construction of gender to the development of the welfare state and the postwar regulation of capitalist economies (Barrett, 1980; Brenner and Ramos, 1984).

Current economic debates reflect the growing tension between feminist researchers whose work emphasizes choice and those whose work emphasizes the structure of women's choices. These tensions are exemplified in the Sears case—a sex discrimination lawsuit brought by the U. S. government against the retail giant Sears, Roebuck and Company. It revolved around the fairly common situation in department store sales where women work selling noncommission small ticket items while men specialize in the more lucrative, big ticket sales of appliances and furniture. The Equal Employment Opportunity Commission (EEOC) built its case on a statistical portrait of employment patterns at Sears from 1973 to 1980. In that period women constituted 75% of the noncommissioned sales force yet received only 40% of the promotions to commissioned sales jobs.

One feminist scholar testified for the EEOC that discrimination was indicated. Another feminist scholar testified that it was not. The disagreement turned on the emphasis given to motives for choosing one type of job or another and the evidence needed to impute choice. The position that discrimination had occurred was argued on the grounds that if Sears women were not promoted in proportion to their presence in the sales force, history pointed to discrimination as the primary reason. This view did not prevail and Sears won the case. The judge in the case drew on the testimony of the feminist who testified for Sears, particularly her argument that women choose jobs not only for salary but to balance family responsibilities with work (New York Times, 1986).

The outcome of the Sears case will frame discussion of women's rights in the near future. It exposes fundamental differences among feminist scholars on the dynamics of gender hierarchy and will inevitably force a deeper examination of both the methods used to demonstrate discrimination and the meaning of the term "equal opportunity" itself. The notion that segregated outcomes in employment provide evidence of unequal opportunities will be debated; separate but equal will inevitably be revived in the social ideology on gender.

Prospects for Transformation

Prognoses for the sex stratification system fall into roughly two categories—the "natural law optimists" and the "interventionist feminists." The former, a mixture of free market types, believe that the labor market of the future will produce sex desegregation on its own (Chavez, 1985). This is supposed to happen in several ways. First, to the extent that access to education and training are equalized, women will no longer enter the job market at a skill disadvantage. The fact that women are traditionally overeducated compared to men hardly seems to matter to these theorists. Second, the whole job structure is supposed to be leaning in the direction of the female dominated "tertiary" sector, with the decline of the male-dominated smokestack industries and the rise of the information economy. Sex desegregation will occur not because women enter male jobs, but because men will be competing for "female" jobs. Of course as soon as this argument is framed in the context of the labor surplus economy of the future, one begins to wonder about women's access to waged work altogether (Berch, 1986).

Hand-in-hand with this transformation of the employment structure will come the rise of the "electronic cottage." Against a backdrop of early twentieth-century industrial outwork for women, the electronic cottage already has a certain *déjà vu* quality (Berch, 1986). Women can combine their unpaid work—child rearing and housework—with some marginally paid work at their home computer terminal. Once it is realized that almost all the test projects on "electronic outwork" use female workers, searching out homebound women in particular, the outlines of a new gender stratification system seem remarkably familiar. Male workers will be recycled into many underpaid, formerly pink-collar jobs while women workers will be herded back into the home, providing a cheap and flexible labor force for the information industries.

The fantasy that high tech will bring an easier future is a mystification of technology with its own gender messages (Grayson, 1985). High tech is supposed to do away with drudgery (the computers will do it), with housework (the robots will do it), even with reproductive work (in vitro conception plus artificial wombs (Arditti et al., 1983); leaving nice clean unisex jobs. But those who analyze the real job outlook are telling a slightly different story. Some experts estimate that growth in "quality jobs" will be small compared to growth in fairly unskilled work of hazardous (waste disposal) or monotonous (machine tending) description. Jobs overall will be scarcer. Some skilled work will be available in this future labor market, and women will compete to get some of those rewarding jobs. Indeed, it is that very prospect that keeps women tugging on their bootstraps to make it. But the carrot is getting smaller, and even if we do not wish to face the prospect, the stick is getting larger. Trying to finance even a small household solely on a female worker's wage is a sure recipe for poverty-line living.[9]

Nevertheless, the high-tech scenario has its female partisans, not because high-tech has offered any special breaks for women, but because it is perceived to be somewhat more gender neutral than the previous modes of production. Although gender stratification has taken very traditional forms in the high-tech industries (men get the hardware to play with, women get the software; men form the computer companies, women work the assembly lines; men do more of the military-funded artificial intelligence work, women do the routine programming in the banks and insurance companies; boys crowd girls off the terminals in elementary schools), it is a new field with new industries, more openings, and more possibilities. How long this door will stay open is another question.[10]

Fortunately, this high-tech scenario is not the only prospect. At the moment, the "feminist interventionist" economic agenda is spearheaded by a drive for "pay equity" or "comparable worth" that could bring radical changes in occupational sex stratification. Pay equity goes much further than the "equal pay for equal [same] work" principle, precisely because it acknowledges that women and men do not do the same work in society and stratification is the rule, not the exception. To achieve any equality in a world already structured around difference it is necessary to engage in some comparability calculus, as employers already do when establishing pay scales. Few economists of any school would argue that the work of a nurse is worth half that of a grounds keeper.

Yet the response from the business community is remarkably disingenuous. Their opposition takes the form of defense of the inviolability of the "free market mechanism," which pay equity would presumably disrupt. Conveniently forgetting that ever since the existence of labor unions and employer associations, no one has ever taken seriously the prospect of labor markets regulated by the invisible hand, opponents tell people that pay equity will destroy the free labor market (Sowell, in Chavez, 1985).

Such claims have little factual basis. Blau (1978) has demonstrated that wages are determined much more by the internal policies of employers than by the operations of "free" labor markets. Bell (1985) recently wrote,

> As all economists recognize, "the market" as a wage setting device fairly bristles with imperfections. This far fetched notion [that the external market is all powerful] . . . disregards the existence of . . . internal wage setting mechanisms . . . [that] are so shrouded in mystery that no appeal to "market force" makes any sense.

In spite of the mathematical elegance of economic models of wage determination, they lack, as Bell so candidly implies, empirical merit. This is due not only to their practical clumsiness but to structural difficulties in gathering the necessary information. Corporations regard their wage setting strategies as proprietary information. Thus the actual deliberations of corporations regarding pay scales and job classifications are not made public unless these are publicly bargained, as is the case for unionized workers, public employees, and the like. It is this reality that forces researchers' use of highly aggregated statistical evidence on the outcomes of industrywide corporate policy (e.g., unequal pay and sex segregation in occupations) to infer discriminatory policies by corporation personnel executives.

Employers are not the only opponents of comparable worth. Large numbers, perhaps even a "silent majority" of Americans, may be quite uncomfortable with women making as much money as men do as this would encroach on men's social power and disturb existing arrangements. In addition, objections to comparable worth are made on analytic grounds. Bell argues that the popularity of the demand masks a lack of clarity in what comparable worth is a remedy for—discrimination or poverty? If it is to remedy discrimination, this suggests current laws against discrimination are inadequate and that the remedy lies in changing the laws or improving their enforcement. If comparable worth is to remedy poverty, it is not particularly suited to the task (Bell, 1985).

Comparable worth cannot be expected to solve the feminization of poverty or equalize income distribution. However, the debate over comparable worth has brought the issue of gender stratification to a broader public, which is an important accomplishment in itself. For unless the sex stratification system can be seen in fundamentally political terms, the belief will persist that inequality between the sexes is a historical legacy instead of a constantly reproduced outcome of a system of class and gender inequality.

What is the future of economic research on gender? Within the discipline of economics, much more work needs to be done to bring work on gender beyond the confines of labor economics and to convince economists that the fields of international trade, public finance, and so forth are not sex neutral. Certainly the investment decisions of multinational corporations are influenced by gender hierarchies and this in turn has serious ramifications for international trade (Elson and Pearson, 1984; Nash and Fernandez-Kelly, 1983). Women's fertility and their accommodation to pronatalist and antinatalist economic environments have important effects on both production and consumption (Youssef, 1982). Certainly the work on technological change requires attention to gender, given the role imputed to women as substitutes for men in standard labor processes (Brenner and Ramos, 1984).

These are examples of the kinds of questions that economists can ask if the assumption of a sex-neutral economy is dropped and if attention is paid to the economic aspects of activities conventionally regarded as private, such as housework. This is no easy task; the profession is monumentally insensitive to the fact that its theories routinely exclude strategic components of economic reality. However, given the power of some economic concepts to help us understand women's situation, the effort to extend the boundaries of economic thinking should be continued.

NOTES

1. Several literature reviews of economists' work on women's economic activities have been done. As the literature has grown, recent reviews have tended to specialize in one aspect or another of the woman question. The most comprehensive one, from a mainstream perspective, is that of Kahne and Kohen (1975). An update of the neoclassical literature on the family is provided by Hannon (1982). Humphries and Rubery (1984) provide a more recent review of the literature on the family that is heavily weighted to labor market segmentation research and Marxist-feminist research.

2. In the late 1950s and early 1960s, Mincer and other labor force scholars observed that the secular trend in women's labor force participation was opposite to that found in cross-sectional studies. Over time, as incomes increased, women's rate of labor force participation increased whereas for a given cross-section of urban women, labor force participation fell as household incomes rose. Men offered more labor as their own wages rose. Married women, however, appeared to do so over time but not to do so at any given point in time. Did women prefer leisure as household incomes rose (the income effect) or did the rising opportunity cost of leisure (i.e., a change in their own wage) encourage them to supply more labor (the substitution effect)?

3. The heightened danger of sexual harassment for women in male-dominated occupations is made quite clear in a remarkable study of the corporate world, "Sexual Harassment: Some See It, Some Won't" (Collins and Blodgett, 1981).

4. The Department of Labor regularly publishes articles on a statistic called the "employment-population ratio." Many regard it as a better comparative statistic than the more widely published labor force participation rates. See *Monthly Labor Review* (May, 1986) for recent data for the United States and other countries. On the concept see Tella (1964).

5. The effect of inflation on the rate of exchange between money and satisfaction (utility) is virtually ignored throughout the New Household Economics. This effect is different from changes in relative prices as it refers to the fact that some utilities can only be purchased with money. In a monetary economy, increasing need for cash caused by increased housing costs, for example, will alter household structures because household members will have to forego the home production of desired utilities in order to work outside the home for cash. Thus the simplest explanation for married women's increased *waged* employment in the 1970s is the need for more money. In retrospect, we know that married women sought paid employment even though the inflation-adjusted wages being offered were declining rather than rising throughout the 1970s. It seems plausible that this reflected at least in part the reality that one cannot pay the rent or the utility bills with one's canned peaches or home-baked cherry pie.

6. It is instructive to review the historical context in which the Mincer and Becker research agenda was constructed. Their early studies were part of efforts by Friedman (1964) and others to establish a positive science of the economy in contrast to what they referred to as the normative emphasis on involuntary employment common in the literature of the 1950s (Gordon et al., 1982). The labor market choices of married women offered a means for exploring the claim that unemployment was largely voluntary and originated in subjective valuations of "time" rather than objective availability of jobs. The first influential study in this genre (Mincer, 1962) explored the effect of marital status on women's labor market behavior. This choice of emphasis was made, one must note, when women's expulsion from factory jobs was well within recent memory and when their exclusion from well-paid corporate jobs was commonplace. In short, a strong ideological component informed the choice of married women as exemplars of voluntary unemployment.

7. The enumeration of immigrant women is difficult where an underground economy exists. Typically, immigrant women help create this untaxed economy given their off-the-books employment as paid housekeepers, cleaning women, and baby-sitters. An excellent overall analysis of this phenomenon is given by Mattera (1985). For an analysis of the structural sources of the underremuneration of women's economic activities see Ciancanelli (1983: chap. 3).

8. There are few published studies, however, that view industrial structure as produced in part by gender hierarchy rather than as something "out there" into which women are fitted. For an alternative approach see Phillips and Taylor (1980).

9. Here are some sample figures: In 1983, the poverty-line income for a family of three (the most typical size of the female-maintained household) was $7,940 per year, but full-time minimum wage earnings for 1983 came to only $6,968 per year (see Rix and Stone, 1984).

10. See the papers from the conference "Women and Computers" held by the MIT Women's Studies Program on May 6, 1985, and the excellent bibliography by Grayson (1985).

REFERENCES

ARDITTI, R. et al. (1983) Test-Tube Babies. New York: Pandora.

BARRETT, M. (1980) Women's Oppression Today. London: Verso Editions.

BECKER, G. S. (1965) "A theory of the allocation of time." Economic Journal 75.

BECKER, G. S. (1981) A Treatise on the Family. Boston: Harvard University Press.

BELL, C. S. (1985) "Will comparable worth work?" Monthly Labor Review (December).

BERCH, B. (1977) "Wages and labour," in Green and Nove (eds.) Economics: An Anti-Text. London: Macmillan.

BERCH, B. (1986) "The resurrection of outwork?" Monthly Review (August).

BLAU, F. (1978) Equal Pay in the Office. New York: Praeger.

BLAU, F. and C. JUSENIUS (1976) "Economists approaches to sex segregation in the labor market," in M. Blaxall and B. Regan (eds.) Women and the Workplace: The Implications of Occupational Segregation. Chicago: University of Chicago Press.

BLAXALL, M. and B. REGAN [eds.] (1976) Women and the Workplace: The Implications of Occupational Segregation. Chicago: University of Chicago Press.

BRENNER, J. and M. RAMOS (1984) "Rethinking women's oppression." New Left Review (March/April).

CANTOR, M. and B. LURIE [eds.] (1977) Class, Sex and the Woman Worker. Westport, CT: Greenwood Press.

CAVENDISH, R. (1982) Women on the Line. London: Routledge & Kegan Paul.

CHAVEZ, L. (1985) "Pay equity is unfair to women." Fortune, March 4.

CIANCANELLI, P. (1980) "Exchange, reproduction and sex subordination among the Kikuyu of East Africa." Review of Radical Political Economics 12: 2.

CIANCANELLI, P. (1983) "Women's transition to wage labor." Ph.D. dissertation, Graduate Faculty of New School for Social Research, New York.

CIANCANELLI, P. (1985) "The social economy and the income creating work of women." Barnard College, New York. (mimeo)

COLLINS, E. and T. BLODGETT (1981) "Sexual harassment: Some see it, some won't." Harvard Business Review (March/April).

CRAIG, C., J. RUBERY, R. TARLING, and F. WILKINSON (1982) Labour Market Structure, Industrial Organization and Low Pay. Cambridge: University Press.

CURTIS, R. (1986) "Households and family in the theory of inequality." American Sociological Review 51, 2.

DALLA COSTA, M. and S. JAMES (1972) The Power of Women and the Subversion of the Community. London: Falling Wall Press.

EISENSTEIN, Z. [ed.] (1979) Capitalist Patriarchy and the Case for Socialist Feminism. New York: Monthly Review Press.

ELSON, D. and R. PEARSON (1984) "The subordination of women and the internationalization of factory production," in K. Young et al. (eds.) Of Marriage and Market. London: Routledge & Kegan Paul.

FERBER, M. and B. BIRNBAUM (1980) "Housework: Priceless or valueless?" Review of Income and Wealth 28, 4.

FERBER, M. and C. GREENE (1983) "Housework vs. marketwork: Some evidence how the decision is made." Review of Income and Wealth 29, 2.

FRIEDMAN, M. (1964) Positive Economics. Chicago: University of Chicago Press.

GORDON, D. et al. (1982) Segmented Work, Divided Workers. New York: St. Martin's.

GRAYSON, L. (1985) The Social and Economic Impact of New Technology 1978-1984: A Bibliography. New York: Plenum.

HANNAN, M. (1982) "Families, markets and social structure." Journal of Economic Literature 20.

HARTMANN, H. (1976) "Capitalist patriarchy and job segregation by sex." Signs 1.

HARTMANN, H. (1981) "The family as the locus of gender, class and political struggle: The example of housework." Signs 6.

HOWE, L. (1977) Pink Collar Workers. New York: Avon.

HUMPHRIES, J. (1977) "Class struggle and the persistence of the working class family." Cambridge Journal of Economics 1.

HUMPHRIES, J. and J. RUBERY (1984) "The reconstruction of the supply side of the labor market: The relative autonomy of social reproduction." Cambridge Journal of Economics 8.

JAFFEE, A. (1956) "Trends in the participation of women in the working force." Monthly Labor Review (May).

KAHNE, H. and A. KOHEN (1975) "Economic perspectives on the role of women in the American economy." Journal of Economic Literature 13.

KING, M. (1982) "The politics of sexual stereotypes." Black Scholar 13, 4-5.

KLACZYNSKA, B. (1976) "Why women work: A comparison of various groups in Philadelphia, 1910-1930." Labor History 17, 1.

KOLKO, G. (1978) "Working wives: Their effects on the structures of the working class." Science and Society 42.

LEBERGOTT, S. (1964) Manpower in Economic Growth: The American Record Since 1800. New York: McGraw-Hill.

LLOYD, C. [ed.] (1975) Sex, Discrimination and the Division of Labor. New York: Columbia University Press.

MADDEN, J. (1979) "Comment on Polachek," in B. Niemi and C. Lloyd (eds.) The Economics of Sex Differences. New York: Columbia University Press.

MANSUR, M. and M. BROWN (1980) "Marriage and household decision making: A bargaining analysis." International Economic Review (February).

MARSHALL, A. (1888) Economics of Industry.

MATTERA, P. (1985) Off the Books. London: Pluto Press.

MCELROY, M. and J. HORNEY (1981) "Nash-bargained household decisions: Towards a generalization of the theory of demand." International Economic Review (June).

MELLOR, E. (1984) "Investigating the differences in weekly earnings of men and women." Monthly Labor Review (June).

MINCER, J. (1962) Labor force participation of married women: A study of labor supply. Report of the National Bureau of Economic Research. Princeton: Princeton University Press.

MINCER, J. and S. POLACHEK (1974) "Family investments in human capital: Earnings of women." Journal of Political Economy (March/April).

NASH, J. and M. FERNANDEZ-KELLY (1983) Women, Men and the International Division of Labor. Albany: SUNY Press.

New York Times (1986) "Of history and politics: Bitter feminist debates." July 6.

NERLOVE, M. (1974) "The new household economics." Journal of Political Economy 82, 2.

NIEMI, B. and C. LLOYD [eds.] (1979) The Economics of Sex Differences. New York: Columbia University Press.

PHILLIPS, A. and B. TAYLOR (1980) "Sex and skill: Towards a feminist economics." Feminist Review 6.

POLACHEK, S. (1981) "Occupational self-selection: A human capital approach to sex differences in occupational structure." Review of Economics and Statistics (February).

POWER, M. (1983) "From home production to wage labour: Women as a reserve army of labour." Review of Radical Political Economics (Spring).

RESKIN, B. [ed.] (1984) Sex Segregation in the Workplace. Washington, DC: National Academy Press.

RIX, S. and A. STONE (1984) "Work," in S. Pritchard (ed.) The Women's Annual.

RUBERY, J. (1978) "Structured labor markets, worker organization and low pay." Cambridge Journal of Economics 2.

RYTINA, N. and S. BIANCHI (1984) "Occupational reclassification and changes in the distribution by gender." Monthly Labor Review (March).

SARGENT, L. [ed.] (1981) Women and Revolution. Boston: South End.

SEN, G. (1980) "The sexual division of labor and the working class family: Towards a conceptual synthesis of class relations and the subordination of women." Review of Radical Political Economics 12: 2.

SMUTS, R. (1960) "The woman labor force: A case study in the interpretation of historical statistics." American Statistical Association Journal (March).

TELLA, A. (1964) "The relation of labor force to employment." Industrial and Labor Relations Review 17, 3.

YOUNG, K., C. WOLKOWITZ, and R. MCCULLOGH [eds.] (1984) Of Marriage and the Market. London: Routledge & Kegan Paul.

YOUSSEF, N. (1982) "The interrelationship between the division of labor in the household, women's roles and their impact on fertility," in R. Anker et al. (eds.) Women's Roles and Population Trends in the Third World. London: Croom Helm.

10   Dual Spheres

CHRISTINE E. BOSE
State University of New York, Albany

I T has long been assumed in both popular culture and much sociohistorical research that beginning in 1800 the U.S. labor force underwent a dramatic process of change often referred to as the "rise and fall of dual spheres"—a male sphere in the labor force and a female sphere at home (also called the public/private split). According to this perspective, the labor force of colonial America was one in which men and women worked side by side in family-based agricultural production. Then, with the rise of industrialization, a radical change is thought to have occurred: Men entered the paid labor force while women remained at home. The period from approximately 1865 to 1890 is described as the height of dual spheres. Finally, in the twentieth century, women are presented as following men into paid work outside of the home.

At the end of the nineteenth century an ideology variously called "the cult of domesticity" or the "cult of true womanhood" became extremely popular and served to justify a drive to achieve dual spheres—the predominance of men in paid work and of women in the home. The training and supervision of children increasingly became women's responsibility rather than a joint male-female activity (Matthaei, 1982). The cult of domesticity elevated the social activity of mothering to an important task and women's homemaking to a profession, albeit a profession whose goal was women's subordination to the needs of the family. Some people even argued that girls and women should be directly trained for these roles. In support of this goal, the home economics education and domestic science movements began at the turn of the century in order to teach efficient housewifery techniques.

Unfortunately for historical accuracy, the dual spheres conceptualization and the ideology of domesticity present a distorted picture of the transformation of the American labor force and obscure the fact that women have *always* worked. But if the existence of dual spheres is not well substantiated, why has the concept been so pervasive?

POLITICAL AND ECONOMIC RAMIFICATIONS

In part, the ideology was a response to competitive capitalist society and an emotional need to keep the home a "haven in a heartless world" (Kessler-

Harris, 1982). But it also served to solidify the new economic structure: Male household heads had to work hard to support a family, since a working wife meant that the husband had failed (Kessler-Harris, 1982). Further, women employed outside the home had to justify themselves even when their families needed the additional income, just at a point when it became harder to find remunerative work to do within the home. Many minority and working class women objected to these new role constraints, and indeed found the new family model unattainable because their families needed their earnings; but the majority of middle-class women supported the ideology. Thus the new domestic code served to sharpen class differences among women (Kessler-Harris, 1982).

The belief in the existence of dual spheres and the cult of domesticity also helped to support the goals of patriarchy or of (white) men in the aggregate (Sokoloff, 1980; Jensen, 1980). Both Sokoloff and Jensen point out that dual spheres was one of the bases on which male unionists argued for women's protective legislation and for the family wage at the beginning of the twentieth century. As described below, the former reduced women's ability to compete for lucrative jobs, and the latter meant that a second income would be unnecessary, thus reinforcing women's dependence on men. The dual spheres concept rationalized viewing the sexes as different but equal, with each heading their own domain (Matthaei, 1982), obscuring the reality that the women's sphere was economically dependent on that of their men. In fact, the cult of domesticity has been revived whenever men feared competition by women for jobs, as in the Great Depression and again after World War II under the guise of the "feminine mystique." It has served as a tool for actively structuring entrance to the labor market.

The development of the cult of domesticity paralleled a rise in racism at the end of the nineteenth century. In 1893 the Supreme Court reversed the Civil Rights Act of 1875, solidifying the South's disfranchisement of blacks and giving sanction to what was an epidemic of lynchings. In 1896, in *Plessy v. Ferguson*, the Court announced its "separate, but equal" doctrine, which sanctified the legal systems of segregation that southern states had been developing. Such discrimination and the pure violence of lynchings forced southern black workers to accept slavelike wages and miserable working conditions (Davis, 1981: 112-117). Thus similar separate-but-equal concepts urged white women to leave the labor force and serve as "mothers of the race," while black men and women were segregated and physically forced into the lowest-paying jobs. Both sexism and racism were used ideologically and structurally to preserve jobs for white males at a time in the late nineteenth century when high immigration rates meant there would be considerable competition for work and again in the twentieth century when jobs were scarce.

The cult of true womanhood had clear economic utility for middle-class white men, and it was this group that had the social power to promote the concept. But if dual spheres did not reflect the reality of all families, what evidence has supported the belief in it?

SOURCES OF THE DUAL SPHERE CONCEPT

There are several sources for the inaccurate descriptions of the U.S. labor force of the period from early industrialization through the development of a modern industrial economy (roughly from 1820 through 1920). First, census methods reduced the enumeration of women's work. The late nineteenth-century definition of gainful employment, focusing on one's usual task, encouraged most married women to indicate their prime employment as housewife even if they were temporarily working for pay.

Second, there were home-based work alternatives that inhibited seeking jobs for which women might be recorded as gainfully employed. Some alternatives brought money into the household, such as caring for boarders or lodgers or doing factory outwork in the home. The equivalent contemporary alternatives would include home day-care, selling Tupperware, Mary Kay cosmetics, or Undercoverwear at house parties, and doing consignment computer work at home. Other women contributed by performing unpaid family work on rural farms or in urban small businesses—a process that continues today. In the latter case, men's self-employment 'hid' the unpaid work of wives and daughters. Although occupation was not recorded in the census until 1850 for free adult males and until 1860 for free adult females (Conk, 1978), these work alternatives would have been socially recognized as women's employment in colonial times, when both men and women engaged in home-based production. Further, since 1940 such roles have been formally recorded by the census when it modified the earlier (1870 to 1930) definitions of employment[1] to include unpaid work in a family business as well as any work for pay regardless of its physical location.[2] Thus from 1870 through 1940 support for the concept of dual spheres was built into the very census categories by which "work" was defined, excluding home-based labor unless it was the major source of income. Use of these categories both reflected the pervasiveness of the ideology of domesticity and provided data that supported the perception of dual spheres. Consequently, what we now consider to be women's dramatic increase in employment since World War II may actually represent both a shift in census definitions and in the locus of women's work so that it is once more classified as such.

Third, throughout the latter half of the nineteenth century socioeconomic differences among women were sharpened and concomitant class and race biases acted to underemphasize female employment. Although the census did record the occupations of slaves, no complete record of their various roles has been preserved (Brown, 1972). After the Civil War both immigrant and black women were much more likely to move in and out of paid employment than were native- born white women, but the census did not tabulate occupations by race until 1890. These losses and omissions allowed historians and demographers to focus on white middle-class patterns and lent more support to the concept of dual spheres than would be possible with the systematic study of working-class and minority women.

These observations, however, do not mean that women's and men's employment patterns were identical. They were not. Many researchers have shown that women's greater share of family responsibilities affect diverse aspects of paid employment, including wages or the choice of full-time work, in a manner not comparable with men, who are less engaged in this "private sphere." However, women's roles were also never as fully separate from the male-dominated productive sphere (Sokoloff, 1980) as popular beliefs imply (Cott, 1977). The purpose of this chapter, then, is to delineate women's actual position in the labor force as it changed over time and to uncover those realities that are hidden by changing census definitions, class and race bias, or the pervasiveness of the dual spheres concept and various domestic ideologies. In so doing, we follow a format of historical periodization organized around changes in women's work rather than a traditional division of historical time by decades or by wars. This new social history approach focuses on the day-to-day lives of ordinary people and how their world was structured, a scholarly perspective that has been greatly enhanced by feminist research on the effects of economic, political, and cultural change on women.

PREINDUSTRIAL WORK

Prior to about 1820 the American economy was based on agriculture; most people lived on farms or in rural areas. Both women and men contributed to the household's operations in an ongoing way, although neither was likely to be earning a salary. Rather, families produced much of what they consumed, and only a few cash purchases for pots and pans, coffee, salt, and the like were necessary. This is usually referred to as a *use-value* and *household* economy, rather than one based on exchange and employment outside of the home. The required monetary income typically came from women's labor in cottage-industry textile work or from selling eggs, butter, or other goods from the home garden. Jensen (1980) documents the variety of this work: Free black and rural white women developed "truck" farming; Mormon women wove rugs; Native American women sold herbs, berries, and nuts and in the West sold flour and cornmeal to travelers, missionaries, and later to the Army; and in the Midwest, German and Scandinavian women sold poultry and frequently worked as midwives.

Historians disagree on the status of women's work in this period, and their ideas can be divided into at least three schools of thought (Matthaei, 1982: 28-29). One group follows earlier research by Clark (1920), Dexter (1924), and

Earle (1895), which stressed that women were able to engage in nontraditional fields such as newspaper publishing, running a tavern, and shopkeeping, and that men were also involved in child rearing through teaching discipline and occupational skills. They conclude that women were released from the sexual division of labor in this era. A second group of historians (Abbott, 1910; Smuts, 1971) takes the opposite point of view, claiming that there was a strict division of labor between men, who were in the fields, and women, who were in the home. This may have been true among the white middle class, but is not evidenced in the lives of black, Native American, or poor white women. A third, compromise, position notes that women labored as hard as men, that men worked in and around the home, and that women's contributions to the household were recognized as essential to the survival of the family. This group claims that the preindustrial period represents a "golden age of equality" that was lost when the nineteenth-century restructuring of work excluded women (Ryan, 1979). Census data are not available for this period and therefore cannot be used to judge the actual degree of occupational inequality or separation of spheres.

On the one hand, we do know that many tasks were assigned on the basis of gender and age, and that women's property rights were circumscribed by law, undermining claims of full gender equality. Indeed, if white women lacked certain rights, black and Native American women had even fewer. Native Americans were driven off their lands as white settlements expanded; and black people were brought against their will to the American South as a source of cheap labor. By the middle of the seventeenth century, the colonies had legal distinctions between blacks and whites that locked Africans into slavery and further deprived them of their rights (Matthaei, 1982). At the same time, the triangular trade between Britain, Africa, and America increased the numbers of black women who worked as slaves.

On the other hand, if the separation of spheres means that women perform domestic labor in the home and men work in a different location for cash, then this situation was also *not* the norm in the colonial era. In fact, rural white and Native American women were more likely than men to be participating in the cash economy.

TRANSITION TO AN INDUSTRIAL ECONOMY

The urban, industrial economy, which eventually replaced the rural and agricultural one, developed slowly and unevenly across the country. As factories were being built in the cities of the northeast, the rest of the country remained predominantly agricultural. During the period from 1820 to 1865, the American economy shifted from one propelled by agriculture to one based on urban industry and commerce. It was not an easy transition. In fact, this whole period is marked by competition between three different systems of organizing labor: self-employment on farms and in the crafts, slavery and indenture, and wagework in factories. Wage labor slowly won this struggle, but until the late nineteenth century most women were outside of the wage economy, contributing instead to the family's financial well-being through unpaid family farm labor or by taking in boarders, doing other people's laundry, and so forth.

Yet, at the beginning of this transition, from 1820 through about 1850, early factory owners sought young farm women as their most likely source of labor. Men who ran their own farms were not available for factory work during much of the year. Accustomed to working outdoors at their own pace, such men were unlikely easily to accept indoor work paced to a machine. In contrast, farm daughters were used to indoor work, and many were also experienced needle workers; they would require less training and were expected to be more accepting of factory work conditions. Although the least essential to the daily operations of a farm, they were, with their mothers, important sources of cash income and their employment was likely to be acceptable, if not necessary, to their families. Further, because of the heavy westward migration of young men, there was a relative surplus of young unmarried women in the industrializing regions (Wertheimer, 1977). Early factories, such as the now famous Lowell Mills, were initially built around the "Waltham system," which promised wholesome dormitory living, religious services, intellectual activity, and a custodial environment for young women employees. This system lasted only as long as there was a shortage of wage-labor and little competition from other textile manufacturers. Thus, although relatively few in number, women were the original wageworkers and the first factory employees. Dual spheres did not exist in this period.

By mid-century, competition from overseas goods resulted in task speed-up and deteriorating conditions of work in American factories (Robinson, 1976). In response, some women workers resorted to wildcat strikes, some returned to the farm, and others moved on to different factories with better conditions. By the 1850s, however, a potentially more docile labor source became available due to the dramatic influx of immigrants, particularly Irish women and men driven by famine, for whom a return to the farm was not an option. Not only did immigrants to the Northeast have little choice other than to sell their labor, but they arrived in such great numbers as to cause an oversupply of labor. One result was a rise in anti-Catholicism on the East Coast and "yellow peril" hysteria on the West Coast. A second outcome was that the New England factory labor force changed from one composed largely of native-born, single farm women to one composed predominantly of urban-based immigrants. As early as 1852, half of all operatives in New England mills were foreign-born women and children (Kessler-Harris, 1982; Hymowitz and Weissman, 1978). Men also joined the ranks of factory workers, particularly in foundries but also in the textile industry.

By the end of the Civil War, women's relative proportion of those employed in manufacturing declined, and the bulk of both native- and foreign-born white women were concentrated in labor-intensive fields ranging from small-goods production to domestic work. Until this point the majority of black women in the United States were slaves, primarily residing in the South, where their labor contributed greatly to the profits of the plantation economy although they themselves received no wages.

This transition period was one in which many social movements flowered and prospered, most notably the abolition movement, culminating in the emancipation of slaves at the end of the Civil War in 1865, and the women's rights movement, with its first national meeting held in Seneca Falls, New York, in 1848. In addition, a popular health movement, religious revivalism, utopian communities, and labor activity were all initiated in mid-century in response to the changes being wrought by industrialization, urbanization, and large-scale immigration.

INDUSTRIALIZATION

From 1865 through 1890 the United States went through a period of rapid industrialization. In 1860, 59% of all workers were employed in farm occupations; but by 1890, 57% were engaged in nonfarm occupations. Between 1860 and 1870 alone large numbers of blacks, especially women, moved from the rural to urban South (Jones, 1985). The expansion of the railroads unified the nation's economy and served as the basis for the growth in commerce. In high school history texts this has been called the era of the "robber baron," when many industrial leaders were able to consolidate their holdings, driving out the competition by any means and creating vast individual fortunes in the process. Cities such as Pittsburgh, based solely on industry (rather than on location close to water), grew rapidly. At the same time, regional economic depressions became commonplace, due to local single-crop dependency, the debt of sharecroppers, and one-industry towns. Beginning in 1880, the rate of immigration doubled and remained high through 1920, turning towns into cities. In many of these cities there were strikes and street demonstrations, as well as factory lockouts, when workers sought to fight the deteriorating conditions imposed on them by an unstable economy and the oversupply of unskilled labor.

This was a difficult time for American women in a number of ways. The separation of productive work from the home was increasing, making it harder for women to combine domestic responsibilities with the newly dominant form of productive work. Single women still worked in shops or factories and in domestic service, but married women were most likely to be employed as home workers. Pushed out of the industrial labor force, they turned to such options as taking in boarders and laundry, or doing factory outwork, often in tenement sweatshops. Women of different ethnic groups tended to enter different trades: German women rolled cigars at home; Italian women manufactured artificial flowers, paper boxes, and hat trimmings; and both Jewish and Italian women sewed at home on coats, dresses, underwear, and other "white goods" (Hymowitz and Weissman, 1978: 200). Black women, as in the pre-Civil War period, worked on the land or as domestic workers in the South, but now the work was for pay. Their occupational options were limited by new segregation laws and by the almost feudal nature of sharecropping.

Because white married women of all classes were primarily involved in homemaking or home-based work, their productive contributions lost social visibility and were less likely to be counted in the census. The amount of *recorded* home-based work involved only 14.1% of all employed women by 1900, including seamstresses, laundresses, and keepers of boardinghouses (Matthaei, 1982). As Anderson (1986) indicates, the Victorian definition of the homemaker obscured her economic function at the same time that men's absence from the home made women's domestic labor less visible. Since men no longer associated the home with work for themselves, it was difficult for them to associate women with work. Further, in a time of surplus labor, families with working women were seen as "greedy" (Kessler-Harris, 1982). Finally, the rise of the cult of true womanhood, defining women's prime role as homemaking and mothering, made it ideologically suspect for women to hold paid jobs. Of course this was not possible for everyone; black women and daughters of immigrants, in particular, accounted for a rather consistent share of the paid labor force. Therefore, class lines became more clearly drawn among women than they had been when the majority of people were engaged in agriculturally related home work or even when the relatively few wage-earning women were primarily white Anglo-Saxons living in New England (Kessler-Harris, 1982).

Among those women who were employed by 1890, 70% were engaged as domestics; black women dominated this job in the South, and young unmarried immigrant women or daughters of immigrants did so in the urban Northeast and West (Katzman, 1978). Another 10% worked in industry, predominantly in textiles. On the whole, women were one-quarter of all nonfarm workers in the United States. Most were young, single and lived with their parents, turning over their pay packets to their family. While 80% were native born, 75% had foreign-born parents. The 1890 census was the first to make a distinction by race in compiling employment data, separating whites from "colored women," including Indians (Native Americans) and some Chinese and Japanese as well as blacks. At that time, 15.8% of all white women were employed, while fully 37.7% of all nonwhite women worked. Of the 975,530 "colored" women in the labor force 39% were engaged in agriculture, 31% were servants, 16% were laundresses, and only 3% were employed in manufacturing or mechanical pursuits, largely due to discrimination against blacks in industry during this period (Brown, 1972). The remaining 11% held a variety of other jobs including seamstress, peddler, waitress, nurse, midwife, and teacher (Matthaei, 1982; Jones, 1985).

THE TURN OF THE CENTURY

The turn of the century marks several changes in the nature of our economy and in women's employment. Social historians refer to the year 1890 as the time of the "closing of the frontier." While no door swung shut, it became increasingly difficult for workers to choose to leave wagework in favor of homesteading. Rather, the numbers of farm workers were steadily declining, dropping from 50% to 30% of the total labor force between 1880 and 1910 (Matthaei, 1982). The first two decades of the century were also ones of high immigration, further increasing the number of workers seeking urban jobs. (Later, after World War I and in the 1920s, immigration laws were changed to cut down this flow.) Perhaps because of reduced economic options and the increased urban labor supply, trade unions had become a relatively strong force by 1900. Although the American Federation of Labor (AFL) recruited among the male-dominated crafts, unskilled women workers began to organize with the help of feminist and socialist groups. Middle-class women joined with working- class women in creating the National Women's Trade Union League in 1903, the only national organization seriously concerned with organizing working women into trade unions. Its members provided strike support, legal counsel, and lobbying for better labor legislation.

The early years of the twentieth century saw many militant labor actions in the female-dominated garment industry, including the 1909 general strike of garment workers in both New York City and Philadelphia and the Lawrence textile strike of 1912, whose theme was "bread and roses" and which was partially organized by the relatively radical Industrial Workers of the World (Wobblies). The New York strike, later called the Great Uprising, transformed the International Ladies' Garment Workers Union (ILGWU) from a small organization into a major labor force, organizing more women into this male-run union than had ever previously been unionized (Hymowitz and Weissman, 1978). The uprising inspired similar actions in other cities, such as Chicago, where a strike ultimately involving 40,000 workers over 14 weeks forced management at one of the factories involved to recognize garment workers rights to collective bargaining.

This was also the period in which reformers, settlement-house workers, and journalists, such as Lincoln Steffens, wrote searing exposés of conditions in factories and tenement sweatshops. The employers called this "muckraking," but reports from state and federal labor bureau investigators documented women's low wages, long hours, and dangerous working environments. The claims of the critics were further substantiated by the disastrous Triangle Shirtwaist Factory fire of 1911 in which 145 women, mostly immigrants, died.

Within American industry, the growth of the retail trade—the basis for a new consumer economy—drew women into "safer" paid employment as sales clerks and "shop girls." Further, the consolidation of corporate capital increased the amount of accounting and clerical work and, consequently, the demand for clerical workers. The typewriter, which had been invented after the Civil War (1873), now found its place in the work world, allowing the creation of the new clerical occupation "typewriter." Corporate managers intended this job to be both more specialized and lower paid than "clerk," an occupation largely occupied by men doing accounting as well as keeping records and writing letters. The new job of typewriter, only later called typist, was intended from the start to be female dominated (Davies, 1974; Glenn and Feldberg, 1977). Its emergence benefited educated middle-class women who now had an option that at least initially paid better than factory work and was considered more respectable because of its white-collar nature. While there is no 1900 data for men and women separately, clerical workers in manufacturing averaged $1,011 per year while other manufacturing wages were $435 yearly. Even as late as 1934 women office workers earned $21.15 per week, while women factory workers received only $14.90 weekly. By the 1940s, however, this clerical wage advantage was gone (Glenn and Feldberg, 1984). These developments in retail and clerical industries led to a gradual increase around 1900 in labor force participation among single, white, native-born women.

The first decade of the century was a period of increasingly complex class, race, and ethnic occupational differentiation and segregation among women. While native-born women were entering clerical and retail jobs, foreign-born white women began to leave domestic work for factory employment, which offered them companionship and comparatively shorter hours. Those who remained in domestic work began to demand contracts, with more regular time off (Katzman, 1978). Black women, however, did not have the option to change jobs since white-collar work was closed to them and only a few southern factories employed black workers. Therefore black women came to dominate the domestic work field, where they had already been pioneers in combining marriage and employment, preferring day work to living in their employers' homes. Thus while class and ethnic differentiation flowed from the increased division of labor in the work force, racial barriers between whites and nonwhites and gender segregation of women and men were often consciously constructed.

In this same period, federal and state labor legislation encouraged occupational segregation of men and women. Protective labor legislation was introduced in the early years of the century, although various state laws were adopted, repealed, and reinstated at different times, and did not always cover the same situations. These laws set minimum wages for women that were lower than men's average wage, required weekly or daily limits on hours, and prohibited night work, employment in particular jobs such as mining and bartending, and employment before and after childbirth (Matthaei, 1982).

The arguments for this legislation indicated that unions could protect men but that women should be protected by the law. Male unionists, who supported protective legislation, invoked the ideology of the cult of true womanhood, in order to support their own claim to a "family wage"—one wage, paid to them which could support a family. They argued that women should be protected from labor exploitation so that they could both bear healthy children and have the time to raise them properly. In retrospect, however, it is clear that another consequence was to limit the types of jobs for which women could be employed. Many single women were eliminated from competing for some of the better-paying jobs, as well as night work—an outcome understood and welcomed by unionists who supported this legislation.

Forms of protective legislation designed to deal with exploitative tenement working conditions gradually abolished homework during the early 1900s. Married women's options were thus also curtailed and many had to rely increasingly on taking in boarders or laundry for additional income. Because unmarried men constituted about two-thirds of the total recent immigrants, the opportunities to do so were great, especially in urban areas. Boarding increased with the process of industrialization, reaching a peak in about 1910, although rates varied by region (Jensen, 1980). A national study of urban areas published in 1892 found that 27% of all wives took in boarders, from which they earned about 43% as much as their husbands' incomes (Jensen, 1980). As the wages of one person could not support a family, one 1912 study in Lawrence, Massachusetts, showed that 90% of all families took in boarders when no children were employed and the husband was the sole wage earner (Kessler-Harris, 1982: 124).

The "turn of the century" period ended with World War I. Although the war spurred the development of industrial technology, it did not have the same lasting effects on increasing women's employment as did World War II (Fox and Hesse-Biber, 1984). Rather, the female work force was reshuffled, drawing women who were already employed into war industries and then returning them to their prior occupational niches, so that by 1920 women's labor force participation was about the same as in 1910. A more significant outcome was to draw many blacks northward in what is known as the Great Migration. Between 1916 and 1921 alone, 5% of southern blacks moved northward in search of jobs. Further, a cultural emphasis on the technological buildup that was part of the war effort had its own impact on the home.

In 1899 the first of a series of conferences on home economics was held in Lake Placid, New York, and served as a "kickoff" for the Home Economics Association and the domestic science movement. The goal of the movement was to bring the industrial model of efficiency into the home, including the adoption of time management principles developed by Taylor. This movement to professionalize housework and the "woman's sphere" was one facet of the cult of domesticity. However, household work was less affected by the myriad new professional tools and appliances, or by the accurately measured movements of scientific management, than by the introduction of utilities such as indoor plumbing, sewage, gas, and electricity, which eliminated much of the physical labor required to run a household (Strasser, 1982; Bose, 1979). Unfortunately, utilities were not completely diffused throughout the country until the 1930s, after originating in wealthy urban areas where residents could afford to subscribe to the new services and where population density made the effort profitable. Thus the increase in women's labor force participation in this century actually *preceded* the availability of technology that might have "liberated women from the home." Further, by the time utilities reached most homes, there were fewer women employed as domestic workers and fewer family members to help out with the housework. The new household technologies ultimately enabled individual housewives to take over the work that several women used to perform, as well as raising expected standards of living. So, just as household size was declining and as utilities eased the labor of household work, the professionalization of housewifery urged wives to take on more of the labor they used to share with other family women (or laundresses) and to increase their output. As a result, the total hours spent on housework did not decline until the 1960s (Vanek, 1974).

In sum, the turn of the century was an eventful period for women's employment. It included events based on the presumed existence of dual spheres for men and women, such as the development of protective legislation and the rise of the domestic science movement. At the same time, those spheres were showing signs of renewed integration through the rising numbers of women entering jobs that could be counted as gainful employment and through the increased labor militancy of women.

THE DEPRESSION

Throughout the 1920s women's rates of gainful employment increased. However, the onset of the Great Depression in 1929 revived the fear that working women were taking jobs away from male household heads. This was actually not true because occupational segregation meant that men would not and did not take over women's clerical or domestic jobs (Milkman, 1976). Rather, many daughters were able to help support their families during the depression because of the availability of such jobs. Their support was necessary because heavy industry, and thus the male labor market, was the first to be hurt by the depression (Milkman, 1976).

Nonetheless, professional women in less segregated jobs and married women in general faced increased obstacles to their employment as the cult of domesticity theme was revived. Wives, rather than young women, were more likely to serve as a reserve army of the unemployed. They "took up the economic slack" by using their unpaid labor in the home to sew more clothes, grow and can more food, take in boarders, or do any other home-based work that would either save money expenditures or bring in cash (Milkman, 1976). However, these types of paid and unpaid productive work in the home were not counted as employment by the census.

Throughout the 1930s an increasing number of women entered the labor force, especially older or young married women without children (Fox and Hesse-Biber, 1984). By the end of the depression decade, New Deal legislation had affected employment conditions. Some of these changes allowed the Congress of Industrial Organizations (CIO) to organize workers along industrial lines, which meant that many more women became union members than had previously been able to under the craft-based AFL. These gradual changes were abruptly transformed by the entry of the United States into World War II in 1941.

WORLD WAR II

The war gave a boost not only to our sagging economy but also to women's employment rates. As millions of men left the full-time labor force to join the armed forces, the government made a conscious effort to draw women into wartime employment through advertisements; needed services such as some industrially based child-care centers were funded by the 1941 Lanham Act. Many women who had previously never worked for pay entered the labor force as the social prohibition against married women's employment was weakened. The ideology of separate spheres was modified to allow women to serve their families and country through employment. Further, women were able to move into skilled, higher paying occupations instead of the unskilled jobs that previously had been the only industrial work available to them. Racial barriers were also lowered as black women were allowed to enter blue-collar industrial employment in large numbers for the first time.

Their wartime work experience had a profound impact on women. When asked in 1944-1945 if they would like to continue working after the war, 75% of the women workers said yes and a full 81% of the women over 45 intended to remain in the paid work force (U.S. Women's Bureau, 1946). However, most women in industrial work were not allowed this choice and were actually fired shortly after the end of the war. In an attempt to encourage women to return to the home and not compete for jobs with returning veterans, magazines and other media reflected a new ideology that Betty Friedan later called the "feminine mystique," an updated version of the cult of true womanhood. And for a few years women's labor force participation rates did drop, in part because many fired women continued to seek the skilled, high-paying jobs they had held during the war (Kesselman, 1987). Eventually, they were forced into more traditionally female occupations in the rapidly expanding clerical and sales sectors. Thus, shortly after the war's end, and in contrast to the events following World War I, women's labor force participation continued to rise. This trend ran counter to the popular ideology that encouraged home-based and consumption-oriented roles for women. However, women in the postwar years were making and selling as well as buying the newly available postwar consumer items.

POSTWAR AND RECENT TRENDS

Since the end of World War II women's labor force participation has steadily risen. However, the aggregate rates hide the changes occurring among different subgroups of women. Older married women aged 45 to 64 years, returning to work after some hiatus, accounted for almost all the increase between 1940 and the mid-1960s. From the mid-1960s on it has been young married mothers aged 20 to 44 years who have accounted for most of the growth in the female labor force. Increases in employment rates have occurred among all but Puerto Rican women, and have been greatest among white women.

The earlier gap between white and black women's labor force participation has almost been closed, with respective rates of 51% and 53% in 1980. The female black-white income and education gaps are also closing. Over the past two decades, due to changes in the distribution of occupations and the influence of the civil rights movement, the occupational segregation of black women has been greatly reduced in the blue-collar trades as well as in white-collar clerical jobs. The former heavy concentration of black women in domestic work has dramatically declined, while there has been a rapid influx into clerical and retail jobs. Between 1940 and 1970, occupational segregation by race among women declined from .62 to .30, or to a point where 30% would have to change jobs in order for black and white women to have the same occupational distribution (Treiman and Hartmann, 1981).

There have also been increasing white-collar job opportunities for Hispanic women, who are still overrepresented among manual operative workers. There is considerable diversity in the experience of Cuban, Puerto Rican, and Mexican-American women, however, with Puerto Rican women having the most unusual labor force patterns. In the 1950s, they had the highest female labor force participation: 39%, as compared to 37% for black women and 28% for white women. By 1970, however, their participation rate had dropped to 30% and only in 1980 did it increase again to 37% still well behind other groups of women. This 20-year decline was primarily the outcome of regional labor market concentration in New York. In 1950, when 83% of Puerto Ricans lived in New York City, there was considerable employment available as operatives in the garment industry; by 1980, 59% of these apparel and textile industry jobs had disappeared and, along with them, Puerto Rican women's best employment opportunities. However, there has been a recent increase in employment among Puerto Rican women as the group has become more geographically dispersed (only about 40% now live in New York City) and as increased levels of education allow them entry into white-collar jobs.

In contrast to Hispanic women, Asian women have relatively high labor force participation and economic status. Yet, as among Hispanics, there is also variation among groups of Asian women (Almquist, 1979; Fox and Hesse-Biber, 1984). Chinese and Japanese-American women are concentrated in clerical jobs, followed by operative, and professional roles. Filipino women are actually most concentrated in professional jobs, particularly in the medical fields; they also have the highest rates of labor force participation for any group of women. Filipino-American women are among the most recent Asians to arrive in the United States. Many of the young women are well educated, while there are relatively few older and less educated Filipino women.

While many groups of racial ethnic women are among the most likely to be employed, other postwar demographic changes have also enhanced the likelihood of women's labor force participation in general. Between 1950 and 1980, the average age of the first marriage for women increased from 20.3 to 22.1 years old, and the proportion of never-married women among those aged 20 to 24 increased from 30% to 45% over the same span (Bianchi and Spain, 1983). This trend has a number of important corollaries. First, women are more able than in the past to complete college education before marrying. Second, childbearing is delayed, and fertility rates decline, as they have done quite consistently since 1963. Third, average household size declines, dropping from 3.37 persons in 1950 to 2.71 persons in 1984. Each of these factors has facilitated women's entry into the paid labor force.

The decline in average household size reflects the growing number of women maintaining both family and nonfamily households, as well as delayed marriage rates. High divorce rates have also added to the rise in household headship among young women. In 1984, 25.4% of white households, 45.7% of black households, and 27.3% of Hispanic households were headed by women (U.S. Department of Commerce, 1985).[3] As women household heads must rely on their own resources and not those of men, their level of paid labor force participation has risen.

The increase in convenience foods heated in a microwave oven, household cleaning services, and dry-cleaning or laundry establishments support this trend, because individual men have less need for a wife to take care of them. Further, since supporting a family is a costly endeavor, Ehrenreich (1983) has argued that men have been fleeing the family in recent years for an unencumbered life-style in which they can purchase household services rather than remaining married. (Ironically, some women responded to this trend by themselves reviving the cult of domesticity through organizations such as Fascinating Womanhood.)

Nonetheless, technology does not increase male contributions to family housework, and studies show that employed married women still do the bulk of these tasks, with husbands only increasing their contribution by about 10% when their wives are employed (Berch, 1982). Women are entering the "male" sphere of paid employment in increasing numbers, but they have not been able to escape the "female" sphere of unpaid housework. Many women now complain that dual spheres have been replaced by two new dualisms: occupational segregation among paid jobs *and* the double day of work in both the labor force and home production.

DUAL SPHERES AND WOMEN'S CONTINUOUS EMPLOYMENT: A DISCUSSION

Our historical review indicates that women have always had a double day of productive work and work for the home. In preindustrial times both men and women worked at home in production of goods for their own use as well as in home maintenance. Currently the location of much productive work is separated from work in the home, but both tasks are now performed by women.

During the intervening period a complex pattern developed. Women were actually the first wageworkers, but by the mid-nineteenth century, factory labor was predominantly male. However, most young urban immigrant and working-class women, as well as most black women, would be engaged in paid labor for a number of years. Once married, it was not uncommon for women to continue to work through home production, much of which was not counted by the census. Because married black women often worked in others' homes, they were more likely than their white counterparts to be recorded as employed. Even during the purported height of dual spheres, many women participated in productive work throughout their lives, but the location of some of that work in the home, in a husband's business, or on a family farm reduced its social visibility. Thus men's and women's spheres were never fully separated, except for some white, native-born, middle-class couples. However, since our predominant historical and demographic accounts have been based on the latter pattern, we have been deprived of a well-rounded view of social history.

Until the rise of feminist research in the 1970s, the male-oriented gatekeepers of historical knowledge did not challenge the older perspective. This may be because the cult of domesticity, the ideological component of the dual spheres concept, had its own independent impact on the labor force, justifying men's family wage and protective legislation demands as well as helping to maintain their jobs in later tight labor markets. It is for this reason that some feminist scholars feel the dual spheres concept has supported patriarchy. Similar separate-but-equal spheres arguments have supported racism. The two ideologies together helped delimit white male competition for high paying jobs.

In the 1980s it is apparent that most women are members of the paid labor force, and it would be difficult to make a dual spheres argument. Men also have less need to keep women dependent in the home to do their housework since such services have become easier to purchase. Further, occupational segregation, which was constant for most of the century and only declined slightly during the 1970s, means that employed women and men generally do not compete for the same jobs. Since men retain the higher paying jobs, segregation constitutes a structural form of patriarchy in the labor force. Thus there is less need for the old dual spheres ideology. Instead, the two spheres that exist now are those of men's jobs and women's jobs, with affirmative action and comparable worth as the two strategies intended to fight this new dualism.

NOTES

1. From 1870 through 1930 employment was defined using the "gainful worker" concept, which included persons at least 10 years old who reported their occupation as employed, whether or not they were working or seeking work at the time of the census. By 1890, an occupation was considered to be "that work upon which a person chiefly depends for support and/or in which he is engaged ordinarily during the larger part of the time" (Ciancanelli, 1983). Although one did not have to work for pay until 1910, housework was always explicitly excluded and enumerator instructions later made it clear that women's homework in taking in boarders and so on was not to be counted as employment unless it provided the majority of her economic support.

2. The 1980 census separates the civilian labor force into two components, the employed and the unemployed. Persons are considered employed if they are 16 years old or over and (1) work for pay during the week of the census survey, (2) work 15 hours or more as unpaid workers in a family business, or (3) have a job but are not working due to illness, bad weather, or vacation. To be counted among the unemployed, one has to be both not working during the survey week and have made specific efforts in the preceding four weeks to find a job. Note that unpaid volunteer work in a charity organization is still excluded from this definition of the labor force.

3. These figures include the 9.1% of white families, 31.3% of black families, and 18.7% of Hispanic families, as well as the 37% of Puerto Rican families with children present.

REFERENCES

ABBOTT, E. (1910) Women in Industry. New York: D. Appleton and Co.

ALMQUIST, E. M. (1979) Minorities, Gender and Work. Lexington, MA: D. C. Heath.

ANDERSON, K. (1987) "A history of women's work in the United States," in S. Harkess and A. Stromberg (eds.) Working Women (2nd ed.). Palo Alto, CA: Mayfield.

BERCH, B. (1982) The Endless Day: The Political Economy of Women and Work. New York: Harcourt Brace Jovanovich.

BIANCHI, S. M. and D. SPAIN (1983) American Women: Three Decades of Change. Bureau of the Census, Special Demographic Analysis # CDS-80-8. Washington, DC: Government Printing Office.

BOSE, C. E. (1979) "Technology and changes in the division of labor in the American home."Women's Studies International Quarterly 2: 295-304.

BROWN, J. C. (1972) "The Negro woman worker: 1860-1890" (1931), pp. 250-252 in G. Lerner (ed.) Black Women in White America: A Documentary History. New York: Pantheon.

CIANCANELLI, P. (1983) Women's Transition to Wage Labor: A Critique of Labor Force Statistics and Reestimation of the Labor Force Participation of Married Women from 1900 to 1930. Ph.D. thesis, Department of Economics, New School for Social Research, New York.

CLARK, A. (1920) The Working Life of Women in the Seventeenth Century. New York: Harcourt, Brace and Howe.

CONK, M. A. (1978) "Occupational classification in the United States census: 1870-1940." Journal of Interdisciplinary History 9, 1: 111-130.

COTT, N. F. (1977) The Bonds of Womanhood: "Women's Sphere" in New England, 1780-1835. New Haven, CT: Yale University Press.

DAVIES, M. (1974) "Women's place is at the typewriter: The feminization of the clerical work force." Radical America 8: 1-28.

DAVIS, A. Y. (1981) Women, Race and Class. New York: Random House.

DEXTER, E. (1924) Colonial Women of Affairs: A Study of Women in Business and the Professions in America Before 1776. New York: Houghton Mifflin.

EARLE, A. M. (1895) Colonial Dames and Goodwives. New York: Houghton Mifflin.

EHRENREICH, B. (1983) The Hearts of Men: American Dreams and the Flight From Commitment. Garden City, NY: Anchor/Doubleday.

FOX, M. F. and S. HESSE-BIBER (1984) Women at Work. Palo Alto, CA: Mayfield.

GLENN, E. N. and R. L. FELDBERG (1977) "Degraded and deskilled: The proletarianization of clerical work." Social Problems 25 (July): 52-64.

GLENN, E. N. and R. L. FELDBERG (1984) "Clerical work: The female occupation," pp. 316-336 in J. Freeman (ed.) Women: A Feminist Perspective. Palo Alto, CA: Mayfield.

HYMOWITZ, C. and M. WEISSMAN (1978) A History of Women in America. New York: Bantam.

JENSEN, J. M. (1980) "Cloth, butter and boarders: Women's household production for the market." Review of Political Economics 12 (Summer): 14-24.

JONES, J. (1985) Labor of Love, Labor of Sorrow: Black Women, Work, and the Family from Slavery to the Present. New York: Basic Books.

KATZMAN, D. M. (1978) Seven Days a Week: Women and Domestic Service. New York: Oxford University Press.

KESSELMAN, A. (1987) "Hidden resistance: Women workers after World War II," in C. Bose et al. (eds.) Hidden Aspects of Women's Work. New York: Praeger.

KESSLER-HARRIS, A. (1982) Out to Work: A History of Wage-Earning Women in the United States. New York: Oxford University Press.

MATTHAEI, J. (1982) An Economic History of Women in America. New York: Schocken.

MILKMAN, R. (1976) "Women's work and the economic crisis: Some lessons from the Great Depression." Review of Radical Political Economics 8 (Spring): 73-97.

ROBINSON, H. H. (1976) Loom and Spindle: Or Life Among the Early Mill Girls (1898). Kailua, HI: Press Pacifica.

RYAN, M. P. (1979) Womanhood in America, from Colonial Times to the Present. New York: New Viewpoints.

SMUTS, R. W. (1971) Women and Work in America. New York: Schocken.

SOKOLOFF, N. J. (1980) Between Money and Love: The Dialectics of Women's Home and Market Work. New York: Praeger.

STRASSER, S. (1982) Never Done: A History of American Housework. New York: Pantheon.

TREIMAN, D. J. and H. I. HARTMANN (1981) Women, Work and Wages: Equal Pay for Jobs of Equal Value. Washington, DC: National Academy Press.

U.S. Department of Commerce (1985) Bureau of the Census, Current Population Reports, Series P-20, No. 398. Household and Family Characteristics. Washington, DC: Government Printing Office.

U.S. Women's Bureau (1946) Bulletin No. 209. Women Workers in Ten War Production Areas and their Postwar Employment Plans. Washington, DC: Government Printing Office.

VANEK, J. (1974) "Time spent in housework." Scientific American 231: 116-120.

WERTHEIMER, B. M. (1977) We Were There: The Story of Working Women in America. New York: Pantheon.

11 Gender Inequality in Paid Employment

PAULA ENGLAND
LORI McCREARY
University of Texas, Dallas

B ETWEEN 1950 and 1985, the proportion of American women in the labor force rose dramatically, from 34% to 55% (U.S. Department of Labor, 1983: 11, 1985). By 1985, 53% of married women with children under 6 years old and 51% of married women with children under 3 years old were in the labor force (U.S. Department of Labor, 1985). As more women enter paid employment, gender inequality in this sphere becomes an ever more important issue. In this chapter we examine three aspects of gender differentiation in paid employment in the United States: what jobs individuals hold, their earnings, and the nonmonetary rewards they receive from their work. Where information is available, we note differences between the experiences of black and white women. In examining these topics, we draw on sociology, economics, and psychology.

THE SEX SEGREGATION OF JOBS

A major form of gender differentiation is the segregation of jobs by sex. Men and women generally hold different jobs requiring different kinds of skills. This segregation is attended by a sex gap in pay, with most "male jobs" offering higher earnings than most "female jobs."

Trends in Segregation

Most studies have measured segregation with the index of dissimilarity (Duncan and Duncan, 1955; England, 1981) applied to the census detailed occupational categories. The index reveals the minimum percentage of men or women that would have to change occupations in order for each sex to be

---

AUTHORS' NOTE: We would like to thank Katherine Donato, Deb Figart, Janice Madden, Barbara Reskin, Patricia Roos, and the editors for helpful comments.

represented in each occupation in the same proportion they are of the labor force as a whole. England's (1981) compilation of findings from a number of studies describes changes in occupational segregation up to 1970. (The studies evaluated used varied procedures for dealing with occupations' differing sizes and the changes in census occupational categories over time.) England estimated that occupational segregation declined 3 to 4 points (on the 100-point scale) in the first decade of the century and 1 to 2 points in the 1910s, then showed an increase of 1 to 2 points in the 1920s. Studies conflict in their conclusions about trends in the 1930s, but concur that the 1940s brought a drop in segregation of about 6 points. Apparently some women who entered traditionally male jobs during the war kept them after the war, even though many women in nontraditional jobs were fired to make room for returning war veterans. Segregation increased 2 points during the return to traditionalism of the 1950s, then decreased 3 to 4 points during the 1960s. (Conclusions are especially hard to draw for the 1960s because of methodological problems; see England, 1981.) Blau and Hendricks (1979) link the decline in segregation during the 1960s to the entry of men into teaching and social work, and to women becoming real estate salespersons, door-to-door peddlers, postal clerks, and ticket agents. To summarize, the twentieth-century trends in occupational segregation up until 1970 were sporadic though there was some net decline. If the most detailed census occupational categories are utilized, the index for 1970 stood at about 60. This value means that at least 60% of either men or women would have had to change to occupations dominated by persons of the other sex to integrate all occupations.

A substantial decline in occupational segregation was finally observed during the 1970s, as shown in Table 11.1 (Beller, 1984). This decline averaged a rate almost twice the rate of change for the 1960s (Beller, 1984; Bianchi and Rytina, 1986). Most of the decline in the 1970s came from women entering male jobs. The 1970s saw an increasing number of women becoming accountants, bank officers, financial managers, and janitors. These changes contributed heavily to the decline in occupational segregation. Other male-dominated occupations that increased their representation of women by at least 10 percentage points during the 1970s include computer programmers, personnel and labor relations professionals, pharmacists, drafters, radio operators, public relations professionals, office managers, buyers and purchasing agents, insurance agents, real estate agents, postal clerks, stock clerks, ticket agents, typesetters, bus drivers, animal caretakers, and bartenders (Beller, 1984). The decline in segregation was much greater among younger than among older cohorts, and in professional occupations than in occupations as a whole. A decline in sex differences in college majors also occurred during the 1970s (Beller, 1984; Jacobs, 1985).

The overall decline in occupational segregation in the 1970s was as great for men and women of color as for whites (see Table 11.1). However, the decline in sex segregation experienced by nonwhites within professional occupations

TABLE 11.1
Degree of Occupational Sex Segregation for
All Occupations and Professional Occupations,
1972 to 1981, for Whites and Nonwhites

| | Index of Segregation by Sex | | | | | |
| | All Occupations | | | Professional Occupations | | |
	1972	1977	1981	1972	1977	1981
Whites	68.4	65.0	62.1	60.1	54.7	50.8
Nonwhites	68.0	63.3	59.4	51.6	50.0	48.9

SOURCE: Adapted from Beller (1984: 20).
NOTE: The segregation index used is the "index of dissimilarity" weighted by the size of occupations. The computations are from 262 three-digit 1970 census occupational categories (including 59 professional occupations).

was smaller than for whites, though nonwhites started the decade with a lower level of sex segregation in professional occupations than did whites. By 1981 the degree of sex segregation for both professional occupations and all occupations was scarcely different for white persons and persons of color. What Table 11.1 does not reveal is that black females and black males are both more likely than same-sex whites to be in predominantly female occupations (Malveaux, 1982; Rosenfeld, 1984), and blacks of both sexes are underrepresented in professional jobs.

We think of "jobs" as specific occupations with a specific establishment (and, hence, within a specific industry). Such jobs would be the most meaningful categories across which to compute a measure of the segregation in the U.S. economy. Unfortunately, such data are not available. Thus the studies above considerably understate the full extent of job segregation, since men and women in mixed-sex occupations often work in different industries (Oppenheimer, 1970; Reskin and Hartmann, 1985) and firms (Blau, 1977). For example, bookkeepers in some firms are all women, while other firms hire all men for the job. A rough idea of the extent of this overstatement can be seen from Bielby and Baron's (1984) data on 393 establishments in California. Using the job categories used by each firm (generally more detailed than the three-digit census categories), they found that less than one-fifth of the establishments had segregation indexes lower than 90! Many establishments had no mixed-sex jobs, but even among those that did, the mean segregation index was 84. This is much higher than figures for occupational segregation considered above.

But what are the *trends* in the sex segregation of these more detailed categories of jobs? Unfortunately we have little information on this. Biebly and Baron's (1984) data permit a rough look at possible changes in job segregation. This is possible because some of the establishments in their sample had data collected at two points in time, generally once in the mid-1960s and once in the early 1970s. They found no evidence of change in the extent of segregation between the two time points. Yet because their data did not cover the late 1970s and are not a representative sample, this finding does not preclude the possibility that job segregation by sex declined along with occupational segregation in the 1970s. We simply do not know.

One cautionary note to the conclusion that job segregation declined in the 1970s comes from case studies of occupations that recently began integrating by sex. Reskin and Roos (1985) point to many cases where there has been occupational desegregation but not job desegregation. That is, women and men in a newly integrated occupation may often work for different establishments, sometimes in different industries. For example, many women became pharmacists in the 1970s, but the women are concentrated in hospitals while the men usually work in retail stores where pay scales are higher. Bus driving has become integrated, but many women are part-time bus drivers for school districts while men have the more lucrative jobs as city bus drivers. The increase in female bakers has added women to the automated process of making cakes and cookies, while men still dominate the less automated and more highly paid tasks of making bread. Women are also becoming systems analysts. Yet women are apt to work in hospitals, banking and insurance, while male systems analysts are more likely to work in more highly paid manufacturing industries.

An occupation's desegregation may not always be a positive step for women since women sometimes first enter a male field just as it is being phased out or deskilled (Reskin and Roos, 1985). For example, women have become insurance adjusters and examiners just at the time when jobs require more routinized date entry at an indoor terminal and fewer trips into the field (Reskin and Roos, 1985). When AT&T signed a consent decree with the government in order to avoid a lawsuit over sex discrimination, the company promised to open male craft jobs to women. But they often moved women into the very jobs scheduled for reductions in force because of technological changes (Hacker, 1979). Other historical examples of women entering jobs as they are degraded include women's entrance into clerical work and school teaching as these jobs were routinized, decreased in their autonomy, and detached from mobility ladders (Strober and Best, 1979; Strober, 1984).

In summary, what can we conclude regarding trends in segregation? Occupational classifications measure the function or task people perform. Occupational segregation increased and decreased sporadically throughout the century, with some net decline between 1900 and 1970, and then a faster pace of decline during the 1970s. But we do not have data on whether segregation in jobs (defined by cross-classifying occupations and firms) has also decreased in the 1970s. Doubts about this are fueled by evidence that some of the occupational integration has led to new patterns of resegregation within occupations in which the jobs women perform involve less authority, autonomy, and pay than those of men. Our conjecture is that some desegregation in jobs is occurring and will continue, particularly at the managerial and professional level, but that the pace of desegregation of jobs is slower than that of occupations.

Explanations for Segregation

To explain persistence and change in occupational segregation, four major factors are important: gender role socialization, human capital, discrimination, and structured mobility ladders.

Socialization and segregation. Children anticipate sex-typical jobs by a very early age (Looft, 1971; Nemerowicz, 1979; Marini and Brinton, 1984). Theories that attempt to explain how this socialization occurs include reinforcement and cognitive learning theories from psychology, and a feminist revision of psychoanalytic theory from sociology. Cognitive learning theory (Kohlberg, 1966) posits that children learn to distinguish males and females, and thereafter infer from the sex differentiation they observe among adults (in the media and in real life) that this is the way things are and should be. By contrast, reinforcement theory focuses on socialization that proceeds from reward and punishment rather than from observation alone (Stockard and Johnson, 1981: 180-187). Adults and peers reward girls for traditionally female behavior and aspirations, while rewarding boys for things associated with males. Boys are especially likely to evoke disapproval if they behave in "girlish" ways (Maccoby and Jacklin, 1974: 328, 339). Both of these psychological theories help explain occupational choices that arise through learning what types of jobs are expected for each sex. They also suggest indirect effects of socialization on job choices that arise because socialization encourages skills and values more consistent with jobs typical for one's sex.

An important revision of psychoanalytic theory by the sociologist Chodorow (1978) sheds more light on the second of these processes, the way in which males and females learn orientations consistent with different jobs. Chodorow argues that much about sex differentiation flows from the fact that almost all children are cared for by women, not men. As a result of being reared by a parent of the opposite sex, males become more individuated than females. This is because defining themselves as males requires psychological separation from—rather than identity with—their opposite-sex caretaker. Indeed, because young boys have little chance directly to observe adult male behavior, they often come to define maleness as a rejection of femaleness, leading to a need to dominate and deprecate females in order to maintain their own identity. In contrast, such psychological separation is not required for females to gain gender identity, so females retain more permeable psychological boundaries that encourage parenting, emotional closeness, empathy, and altruism. We suggest that this helps explain why many women are attracted to the helping professions, such as social work, counseling, teaching, and nursing, and why men are attracted to jobs that involve authority.

In thinking about the occupational preferences people state, it is useful to distinguish between tastes, norms, and responses to anticipated discrimination. All of these affect occupational outcomes. Economists define tastes as that part of the variance in stated or revealed preferences that arises from things other than the economic constraints of prices and one's income (Schultz, 1981: 151-152). Economists often talk of tastes as if they represented individual free choices, but the preferences that economists call tastes may also be influenced by social forces such as norms and the position one holds. The sociological concept of norms refers to internalized notions of what one ought to do arising from the sort of social constraint envisioned in Durkheim's "conscience collective" (Giddens, 1971: 86-94, 105-118) and Freud's superego (Hall, 1954). An example is our awareness of what behavior is thought appropriate for men and women in our culture or subculture. Sociologists have also shown that the characteristics of the job one holds affect one's psychological traits (Kohn and Schooler et al., 1983) and thus presumably one's preferences. Knowledge about sex discrimination by employers also affects occupational preferences since there is little point in preparing for a job if one does not expect to be hired for it.

Unfortunately, our data on sex differences in stated preferences do not allow us to distinguish between all of these components. However, by noting the difference in the degree of sex differentiation between the occupations individuals state that they would like to have (aspirations) and those they say they expect to have (expectations), we can get a rough notion of the economic or social constraints individuals anticipate if they choose a job atypical for their sex. Marini and Brinton (1984) review evidence that most girls aspire to female jobs, but fewer of them *expect* to work in male jobs than *aspire* to these nontraditional jobs. Even more direct evidence of either economic or social constraint comes from a study reporting that 34% of the girls surveyed thought sex to be a barrier to getting jobs (Bachman et al., 1980). Thus it is important to remember that stated job preferences are not exogenous to what goes on in labor markets. There supply-side measures are often influenced by social constraints as well as by the economic constraint of the anticipation of discrimination in labor markets.

Some feminist scholars have questioned the importance of sex role socialization for the sex segregation of jobs and other forms of gender inequality, using arguments that are at once structuralist and materialist (Kanter, 1977; Lorber et al., 1981; Chafetz, 1984). Their contention is that the actual positions men and women hold determine ideas about proper sex roles, not vice versa. In rejecting the possibility that socialized ideas can affect the jobs women get, these scholars espouse a kind of materialism that has also appeared in feminist theories of patriarchy (e.g., Hartmann, 1976) as well as in socialist-feminist theories (see relevant portions of Jaggar and Rothenberg, 1984). In our view, the material and ideal have *reciprocal* effects, as do individual and structural realities. Recognizing the effects of socialization is a part of understanding such reciprocal effects.

Some writers criticize notions of sex role socialization because, to them, stating that the desire to hold traditional roles is internalized through women's socialization is tantamount to "blaming the victim." We think that this criticism is well taken in relation to views that ignore the role of anticipation of social and economic constraints in the socialization process, see socialization as insulated from employment realities, and argue that attempts to change segregation must begin with changing the deliberate socialization practices adults direct toward children. But this is not the view one gets from much of the literature on socialization reviewed here. This literature has distinguished between aspirations and expectations, and been sensitive to the possibility that what started as a constrained expectation about what is possible may in time come to be felt as an aspiration. Indeed, a striking feature of the cognitive development theory is its implication that children's job preferences will change only when adults are actually found in a range of non-sex-typed jobs, not merely when adults change their intentional reinforcement practices. This is because segregation among adults is the data children learn cognitively and often convert to preferences. If we keep these caveats in mind, theories of socialization do not blame the victim. Rather, they show socialization to be part of the web of reciprocal determination between sex differentiation in paid employment (some of which results from demand-side discrimination) and gender roles in the household (England and Farkas, 1986). In this view, supply-side preferences depend in part on demand-side discrimination, and vice versa. Although this holistic view has been more common among sociologists, a number of economists have also begun to recognize the implications for job preferences of feedback effects from employment discrimination (e.g., Weiss and Gronau, 1981; Blau, 1984).

Although we believe gender role socialization to have important effects, a number of research findings caution us from overemphasizing the role of socialization to the exclusion of other factors. Despite the overall level of segregation, middle-aged women made quite a few moves into and out of predominantly male occupations during the 1970s (Jacobs, 1987; Rosenfeld, 1984). Further, the correlations between the sex composition of young women's occupational preferences and their later jobs, while positive, are quite low—about .25 (Jacobs, 1987). If early socialization explained most of segregation, we would expect higher correlations than this. It is also incorrect to see the decline in segregation since 1970s as resulting from changes in sex role socialization of children since most women entering the labor force in the 1970s were raised in the traditional social climate of the 1950s.

Human capital and segregation. Economists' theory of human capital argues that individuals have higher earnings if they make investments in themselves that increase their productivity. Human capital can appreciate in value through the investments of education or on-the-job learning. One's job-relevant human capital can also depreciate through obsolescence or nonuse, as when a homemaker is out of the labor force.

Table 11.2 shows that in the 1950s women in the labor force had more education than men, but more recently men and women have had an equal median of 12.7 years of education. Men do hold more bachelor's and graduate degrees than do women, but more males than females are high school dropouts. Thus average educational attainment is virtually the same for men and women, but men's variance is greater, with more men on both the high and low ends of the distribution and more women in the middle. Since male and female medians on educational attainment do not differ, it is impossible to explain job segregation by sex as a result of sex differences in average amounts of this form of human capital. The different variances of the male and female educational distributions may affect job segregation somewhat, though this cannot account for women's concentration in lower paying jobs.

Men and women differ substantially in their average employment experience. One 1976 national survey showed that white females had 14 years of employment experience, which was 69% of the 20 years averaged by white males. The experience gap was smaller for blacks; black women averaged 16 years of experience, or 85% of the 19 years averaged by black men. (These numbers were computed from Corcoran and Duncan, 1979: tab. 1, from the Panel Study of Income Dynamics.) Given women's lesser experience, the paucity of women in male jobs may result in part from the lack of women with as many years of relevant experience as are required to enter these jobs. Yet, this does not appear to be a *major* factor in segregation. Evidence for this comes from studies showing that women with continuous experience are not more apt than other women to be employed in predominantly male occupations (England, 1982; Daymont and Statham, 1983; Corcoran et al., 1984). Nor are women's ages or number of children (which might index anticipated experience) correlated with the percentage female in their occupations (Daymont and Statham, 1983; Rosenfeld, 1984). Furthermore, extensive sex segregation exists in entry-level positions, where neither males nor females have any experience (Green, 1983; Greenberger and Steinberg, 1983). If segregation occurs before either men or women have any experience, and even women with extensive job experience are apt to be in female jobs, the lesser experience of women cannot be a principal cause of sex segregation. It may, however, explain the absence of women from jobs at the top of those few lengthy promotion ladders that have an appreciable number of women in the jobs at their base.

A more sophisticated application of human capital theory offers an explanation of segregation that emphasizes lifetime plans, wage depreciation while women are at home, and wage appreciation while on the job. Polachek (1979, 1981, 1985) has proposed a supply-side explanation for sex segregation that emphasizes the depreciation of human capital while one is a homemaker. Wage depreciation occurs if a woman has a lower real wage rate upon

TABLE 11.2
Median Years of School Completed by Men and Women
in the Labor Force, for Whites and Blacks, 1952 to 1983.

	1952	1959	1969	1979	1983
All Races					
Women	12.0	12.2	12.4	12.6	12.7
Men	10.4	11.5	12.3	12.6	12.7
Whites					
Women	12.1	12.2	12.4	12.6	12.7
Men	10.8	11.8	12.4	12.7	12.8
Blacks					
Women	8.1	9.4	11.9	12.4	12.6
Men	7.2	8.1	10.8	12.2	12.4

SOURCE: Adapted from J. O'Neill, "The trend in the male-female wage gap in the United States." Journal of Labor Economics 3, no. 1 (January 1985): S99. Reprinted by permission. The University of Chicago Press.
NOTE: Data are for persons 18 years old and over for 1952 to 1969, and for persons 16 years old and over for 1979 and 1983. For 1952 to 1969 "black" refers to all nonwhites (including Asians); in 1979 and 1983 it refers only to blacks.

returning to paid employment than she had when she quit her job to take up full-time homemaking. Polachek argues that certain occupations entail greater risks of depreciation than others, and that women who plan intermittent employment will maximize lifetime earnings by choosing occupations with low depreciation penalties. Since most men plan continuous employment, they do not have this incentive to choose occupations with low depreciation rates. Thus Polachek argues that sex differences in plans for employment continuity lead to sex differences in the job choices that maximize men's and women's lifetime earnings and, hence, to segregation. Polachek's hypothesis regarding the lesser depreciation of female jobs has not been supported by either cross-sectional (England, 1982, 1984) or longitudinal analyses (Corcoran et al., 1984). That is, the amount of wage depreciation suffered by women while out of the labor force is no greater in occupations containing mostly men than in female occupations. Thus women have no *pecuniary* motive to select female occupations.

Another claim of human capital theory is that women who anticipate spells of homemaking will make more money if they choose jobs with low rates of wage appreciation due to experience. At first glance it is hard to understand why anyone would prefer lower pay increases with experience. But human capital theory asserts that, other things being equal, jobs that provide more on-the-job training and thus steeper wage increases will have lower starting wages. In this view, accepting lower starting wages is the way the employee shares in the cost of the training that leads to the higher wage. If this is true, a person choosing a job faces a trade-off between starting salary and wage appreciation. Thus women who plan to drop out of the labor force soon will be more likely (than men or women who plan more continuous employment) to make the trade-off in favor of higher starting wages. This is because they will not be employed long enough to realize much advantage from wage appreciation. The general claim of human capital theorists that there is a trade-off between starting wage and wage appreciation may have some merit. However, the evidence does not support their deduction that this explains segregation. Rather, the data show that, even holding education constant, male occupations offer women higher starting wages than do female occupations (England, 1984). This being the case, we cannot say that women maximize earnings by choosing female jobs. (It is clear that males gain by choosing male jobs.) Thus both versions of human capital theory that attempt to show that it is *financially* rational for women to choose female occupations have little evidence to support them.

Despite these weaknesses, human capital theory is helpful in explaining the *decline* in segregation in the 1970s, although it provides only part of the story. The increase in the continuity of employment now expected by young women makes the lifetime monetary penalty for choosing a female job greater than ever, since male jobs generally pay more at every level of education and experience. Counter to Polachek's contention, women have always paid a financial price for choosing the female occupations encouraged by their socialization. But, consistent with the spirit of Polachek's view, this price was less for women than for men precisely because women anticipated fewer years of employment. This cost to women of choosing a female job—and the implied motive to choose a male job—has been raised even higher by women's shift toward more continuous employment. Thus the most recent cohort of female entrants to employment has a greater pecuniary motivation than any previous cohort to defy the dictates of their socialization and choose a male occupation that yields higher lifetime earnings. According to the data on trends in segregation we reviewed above, women are doing so in increasing numbers.

Discrimination in hiring, placement, and promotion. Discrimination by employers has historically been an overtly acknowledged factor in job segregation by sex. The major theories of discrimination emphasize tastes, error, statistical generalization, and group collusion as determinants of discrimination. We review these below and suggest that the various types of discrimination may work together to affect sex segregation. (For another review of these models, see Blau, 1984.)

Becker (1957) coined the term "taste discrimination" to refer to a preference for not hiring members of a particular group. Although he was discussing race discrimination, the idea can be applied to sex segregation by positing that employers have tastes against hiring women to fill male jobs (or men to fill female jobs). Becker defined a taste as something one is willing to pay to indulge. Employers with discriminatory tastes may differ in how much money they are willing to lose to avoid hiring women or, equivalently, how much women would have to lower their asking wage in order for the pecuniary gain of getting cheaper labor to counterbalance the employer's distaste for hiring women. This is why, to economists, there is an inextricable link between discrimination in wages and in access to positions. Discriminatory "tastes" may be determined by sex role socialization. Indeed, Becker presented his theory as explaining only the economic consequences of tastes; determinants of tastes, he felt, must be explained by sociologists or psychologists (Becker, 1957: 1).

What Becker would call tastes for sex discrimination, sociologists are more apt to call patriarchal cultural "norms" that themselves arise out of prior discrimination. These discriminatory tastes or norms may reside in employers, or the employers may engage in discrimination in response to their employees or customers. For example, male workers may require a higher wage to work with women. Or men may lower their productivity by various forms of sabotage when employers hire women into "their" niches (Bergmann and Darity, 1981). It seems likely that employers who do not themselves have discriminatory tastes would take into account their male employees' preferences for discrimination only in those jobs where the employer already made a significant investment in on-the-job training of men. Were it not for this training, and the incentive it gives employers not to replace these workers once they are trained, employers without discriminatory tastes would respond to such wage demands or sabotage of productivity on the part of male workers by firing the men and hiring women. (For a discussion of the "implicit contract" features of jobs involving significant investments in training, see England and Farkas, 1986: chap. 6.)

"Error discrimination" occurs where employers do not have discriminatory tastes, but they erroneously underestimate the potential productivity of average women in men's jobs and therefore will not hire women in these jobs (or will not hire them unless they will work for less than men will). Employers may also hesitate to hire the occasional man seeking entrance to a female job because of an underestimation of men's average productivity in the female job.

A more subtle notion underlies the model of "statistical discrimination." This type of discrimination results from a combination of real *group* differences in productivity-linked qualifications and information costs that prevent employers from measuring prospective productivity directly. (Some authors such as Blau, 1984, include what we have called "error discrimination" under the rubric of statistical discrimination. We believe the two have distinct theoretical implications.) Thus, some hiring, placement, or promotion decisions are based on differences between male and female averages on predictors of productivity. For example, most employers probably know that, on average, women have developed less mechanical knowledge than men. So they may decide not to hire any women in positions requiring mechanical knowledge, screening out even those atypical women with extensive mechanical skills. Or, if women have higher turnover rates than men,[1] an employer may resist hiring women in jobs where they must provide expensive training, thus screening out even those women who would have stayed for decades. Since men and women have overlapping distributions on virtually all characteristics of interest to employers, the use of sex as a decision rule guarantees that many hires will not be optimal. In this sense it involves some errors in individual cases, but it differs from error discrimination in that the employers are correct about the *group* differences in means when they engage in statistical discrimination. Statistical discrimination may be economically rational for employers in the absence of better cost-effective ways to infer the future productivity of applicants (Phelps, 1972; Spence, 1974). For example, it would be expensive to test applicants' ability as auto mechanics.

Another sort of discrimination discussed by sociologists as well as economists involves the collusion of individuals within a group. Since the discrimination entails a group acting monolithically rather than as competing individuals, it is discussed by economists within monopoly (or monopsony) models. Madden's (1973) monopsony model and Hartmann's (1976) and Strober's (1984) theories of patriarchy all see women as being kept out of good jobs by collusion among men—as husbands, employers, legislators, and workers. It is clear that such a "cartel" or "gentlemen's agreement" benefits men as a group at the expense of women as a group. Indeed, it should be clear that members of any group (e.g., whites, Catholics, heterosexuals, or even those with brown eyes) will make relative gains if they can exclude nonmembers from opportunities.

A variant of the monopoly model is the Marxist notion of "divide and conquer." This conception holds that employers segment their work force into noncompeting groups to keep workers from organizing cohesively enough to bargain, strike, or engage in more radical political action (Gordon, 1972: 71-78; Edwards et al., 1975: xiii-xiv; Bonacich, 1976; Bowles and Gintis, 1976: 184; Humphries, 1976; Reich, 1981; Stevenson, 1986). It is clear that every employer has a material interest in segmenting workers, but the theory does not provide an explanation of why race, ethnicity, sex are chosen most often as the cleavages to exploit, and why white males are the favored group. It is the fact that white male employers generally segment workers by colluding with white male workers that makes the divide-and-conquer model of discrimination fall under the broader category of monopoly models.

Economists point out that monopolies are inherently unstable because their members have an individual incentive to be a "free rider" by cheating on the group collusion. An example of such cheating would be a male employer who cannot resist hiring exclusively women into traditionally male jobs when women can be hired for less precisely because other male employers are following the gentleman's agreement to discriminate. If it were possible to avoid detection and sanctions, cheating in the monopoly so as to hire cheaper labor while the rest of the monopoly stayed in force would be the individually maximizing strategy. Yet, cheating on the group monopoly by not dis-criminating is not always economically rational; it is individually rational only if the cheating does not draw sanctions or lead others to follow suit, thus ending the monopoly. Such indeterminacy in what is individually rational arises because each individual employer is not sure of the probability that his free riding behavior will be noticed, the probability this will bring down the cartel by encouraging others to do likewise, the probability that the group will take sanctions against him, and the severity of such sanctions. In such an uncertain situation, nonpecuniary group loyalties may also help to hold monopolies together. But being willing to take a risk on a monopoly because of nonpecuniary group loyalties amounts to a form of taste discrimination. Nonetheless, if we see the monopoly model this way, it suggests that pecuniary motives and nonpecuniary group loyalties are often blended in discrimination and, thus, that the monopoly model cannot be as completely materialistic a theory as its proponents contend.

Although economists originated the models of discrimination discussed above, economists have also been most skeptical about the existence of discrimination. This is because neoclassical economists believe that discrimina-tion will erode in competitive labor markets. (By "competitive labor markets" economists mean that there are a number of employers who are potential buyers for each type of labor, so that employees have at least some choice between employers.) The logic of why discrimination should erode is similar for each of the types of discrimination we have discussed. To explore this logic, we consider the situation where some employers will not hire women in "male" jobs, or will only hire them at a wage rate lower than paid to the males. If the discrimination is based on employers' tastes, and there is some dispersion in tastes across employers, then those employers with the least discriminatory tastes will begin to hire women. These employers will find that women are a bargain because other employers' discriminatory acts have lowered the wage that women will accept. Since the employers hiring women have relatively low labor costs, they will be at an advantage in competitive product and capital markets, and thereby gain an increasing share of the product and labor market in their industry. As employers who will not hire women lose market share or go out of business, women's job distributions should eventually converge with men's. And since few hiring discriminators are left, women should no longer need to offer to work at a lower wage than men to get hired.

A similar logic applies to the erosion of the other types of discrimination. In the case of error discrimination, employers who do not have erroneous estimates of male and female average abilities for particular jobs will get labor at a bargain price and can thus come to represent a larger share of their markets in a competitive environment. Also, error discrimination should be self-correcting if discriminators observe the success of firms that do not discriminate.

The concept of statistical discrimination has had great appeal to economists because it seems more likely than other types of discrimination to be able to persist in competitive markets, thus explaining the seeming anomaly of discrimination. Unlike taste or error discrimination, it is rational in pecuniary terms for employers to engage in statistical discrimination if its degree of "unexplained variance" in predicting productivity incurs less cost than the expense of developing and administering new screening instruments to gain predictive power. These information and transaction costs exist because of limitations in the "technology" of personnel administration. On the surface it appears that there is no pecuniary advantage to ceasing statistical discrimination, as there is for taste or error discrimination. Why would an employer want to abandon a cheap method of estimating productivities when it is expensive to develop screening devices that allow one to find those individuals whose productivities are above the average of their racial and sexual groups? If an employer develops new screening devices that increase the predictive power of screening techniques the employer gains in two ways. First, a more productive work force is hired, the benefits of which may exceed the cost of the new screening devices. Second, the new screening devices allow an employer to hire those whom others discriminate against but whose productivities are above the average for their race or sex. They can be hired for relatively low wages since their labor has been cheapened by the other employers' statistical discrimination against them. In competitive markets, the advantage of finding more sensitive screening instruments than sex will lead those who do so to gain at the expense of those who do not, much as with taste and monopoly discrimination. Yet it remains an empirical question whether the costs of developing and administering more accurate screening devices exceed the benefits; and it is this calculation on which the erosion of statistical discrimination depends. We conclude that statistical discrimination, like other forms of discrimination, is subject to market pressures encouraging its erosion, but it is more tenacious than other forms to the extent that it is costly to overcome the information and transaction costs that are its cause.

In the case of monopolistic collusion, the mechanism through which discrimination may erode is the temptation of individual employers to break out of the cartel and take advantage of cheaper labor. Thus there is tension in every monopolistic collusion in that employers with the lowest aversion to the risk of sanctions or destroying the cartel may begin to subvert the monopoly. Yet whether this will occur remains an empirical question given the indeterminacy of whether it is individually rational to uphold the monopoly or to try to get away with being a free rider.

These theoretical arguments suggest that market forces should tend to erode discrimination, and we agree that they push in this direction. Yet there is considerable evidence that sex discrimination has been and remains an important cause of sex segregation, although anecdotal evidence suggests some diminution since the early 1970s. In part, the reduction of discrimination has been due to enforcement of Title VII of the Civil Rights Act and federal requirements for affirmative action (Beller, 1979, 1982a, 1982b; Leonard, 1984; U.S. Department of Labor, 1984; Burstein, 1985). Some reduction has probably resulted from the operation of market forces. But even today there is evidence of sex discrimination in hiring, placement, and promotion.

Industrial and social psychologists have taken the most direct approach to documenting sex discrimination in hiring, placement, and promotion. Using surveys or experiments involving present and prospective managers, they find that men are often preferred to equally qualified women for traditionally male positions (Rosen and Jerdee, 1974, 1978; Levinson, 1975; Rosen, 1982). Sociologists Bielby and Baron (1986) find substantial evidence of discrimination in the statements and practices of California manufacturers.

How can we reconcile this persistence of discrimination with economists' arguments that it should erode in competitive markets in the long run? We think the answer is deceptively simple: The long run may be extremely and even infinitely long, particularly because of feedback effects that cross the boundary between employment and households. These feedback effects mean that discrimination may affect choices made in the household, and these choices may create discrimination anew before it has had time to erode completely. For example, if women are discriminated against, fewer females will aspire to or train for male jobs (knowing that they are unlikely to get them), more couples will specialize with the wife doing household work and the husband doing paid work, more educational and geographical investments will be made in male careers, and traditional socialization will continue to seem rational to parents. These developments will reinforce stereotypical notions about men and women that create tastes or norms in favor of discrimination and allow correct statistical calculations that suggest that fewer women than men are suited for male jobs. These feedback effects create *new* discrimination (as well as supply-side sex differentials), working at cross-purposes with competitive market forces that erode discrimination. Their existence makes it indeterminate whether the market forces eroding discrimination will prevail or not. Economists have often ignored these feedback effects, seeing household behavior and tastes as exogenous to employment discrimination. Other economists acknowledge that feedback effects may slow the erosion of sex differentials (Arrow, 1973, 1976; Bergmann, 1976; Ferber and Lowry, 1976; Strober, 1976; Blau, 1977, 1984; Weiss and Gronau, 1981).

Structured mobility ladders in internal labor markets. Mobility ladders within a firm have been emphasized by theories of internal labor markets. They cannot explain segregation in entry-level jobs, but they explain a great deal about the persistence of segregation as employees move up job ladders. Once segregation has occurred at jobs that are ports of entry to firms—whether from discrimination or socialization—the segregation will be perpetuated within a firm because both the training provided and the mobility opportunities depend more on the ladder to which one's entry job is attached than on the personal characteristics one brought to the work place. Thus, the existence of structured mobility ladders in internal labor markets can carry much of the segregation found in entry-level jobs into the future without a need for further overt discrimination (Roos and Reskin, 1984). Many women (and some men) are in dead-end jobs with no mobility prospects; other workers are usually either on a "female ladder" or a "male ladder," and the female ladders are generally shorter. Thus most studies find that men increase status and earnings with experience to a greater extent than women do (Sorensen, 1975; Wolf and Rosenfeld, 1978; Corcoran and Duncan, 1979; Kelley, 1982) because they are in jobs attached to longer mobility ladders, in which each job provides training for the next and in which there is often an implicit contract specifying wage increases over time. (For a discussion of implicit contracts see England and Farkas, 1986: chap. 6.)

THE GENDER GAP IN PAY

Trends

Recent trends in the gender gap in pay for blacks and whites are shown in Table 11.3. The data pertain to usual weekly earnings of full-time wage and salary workers. Full-time is defined as those working at least 35 hours per week. But since hours worked vary considerably even among those who work 35 or more hours per week, with men averaging more hours than women, the table also provides the ratio of female to male median earnings adjusted for hours worked. Whether adjusted for hours or not, Table 11.3 shows that white women's relative earnings have improved since 1978. Other researchers have used slightly different data and have also found declines in the sex gap in pay among whites starting in the late 1970s or early 1980s (Blau and Beller, 1984; Smith and Ward, 1984). This decline in the gender gap in pay among whites comes after decades of being nearly constant. The large size of the remaining gap still must be recognized.

Trends are quite different for the relative status of black women. Black women are still the lowest earning group, but their earnings relative to other groups improved quite consistently throughout the 1960s and 1970s (Smith, 1979; O'Neill, 1985: S94, S98). By 1983, the median of usual weekly earnings of full-time black women workers was 83% of that of black men and over 90% of that of white women (O'Neill, 1986: S93, n. 3, S94). Some scholars have urged caution in interpreting data suggesting an improvement in black women's occupational status, such as their increased entry into professions (Collins, 1983; Higginbotham, 1985; Sokoloff, 1985). In particular, they point out that a high proportion of the increase in professional employment

TABLE 11.3

Female/Male Ratios of Usual Weekly Earnings of
Full-Time Workers, for Blacks and Whites, 1967 to 1983

| | Ratios Unadjusted for Hours per Week | | Ratios Adjusted for Hours per Week | |
	Whites	Blacks	Whites	Blacks
May 1967	.608	.700	.676	.738
May 1971	.607	.707	.669	.747
May 1973	.606	.718	.669	.756
May 1975	.613	.751	.672	.789
May 1977	.606	.731	.669	.775
1979, annual average	.611	.747	.673	.790
1981, annual average	.635	.775	.694	.817
1983, annual average	.646	.790	.703	.832

SOURCE: Adapted from J. O'Neill, "The male-female wage gap in the United States."
Journal of Labor Economics 3, no. 1 (January 1985): S95. Reprinted by permission.
©The University of Chicago Press.
NOTE: All data pertain to full-time wage and salary workers, 16 years old and over. How-
ever, since hours worked vary considerably within full-time workers (defined as those who
work at least 35 hours per week), ratios are also provided that adjust for hours worked.
From 1967 to 1977 "blacks" refers to all nonwhites; thereafter it refers only to blacks.

for black women has been in public sector jobs where they serve poor, often
black clientele and where their jobs may be lost in the current climate of fiscal
austerity. However, claims of a rise in black women's socioeconomic status
based on earnings data are less likely to be misleading. They may be
misleading for the 1960s insofar as the increase in Aid to Families with
Dependent Children (AFDC) payments and ease of eligibility took some of
the lowest earning black women out of employment altogether and, thus, out
of relative wage comparisons. However, in the 1970s, AFDC payments
decreased after adjustment for inflation (Preston, 1984), so this cannot
account for the improvement in black women's relative earnings in the 1970s.

Explanations of the Gender Gap in Pay

What explains the gender gap in pay? We will divide our discussion into
what sociologists have termed "individual" and "structural" factors. In
examining individual explanations of the sex gap in pay, we shall consider the
extent to which sex differences in indicators of human capital contribute to
the sex gap in pay and to the gap between the pay of black women and other
groups. Under the rubric of structural explanations, we will consider the
extent to which men and women's concentration in jobs with different
characteristics can explain the portion of the sex gap that remains after sex
differences in human capital are controlled.

Human capital and the gender gap in pay. The most exhaustive analysis of
the contribution of human capital to race and sex gaps in pay is provided by

Corcoran and Duncan (1979). Their study is unusual in its detailed indicators of human capital. Because of this feature, and their inclusion of both full and part-time workers, we discuss their findings, presented in Table 11.4, in some detail.

Corcoran and Duncan (1979) used a standard technique for decomposition of the earnings gap between race and sex groups. First, they used multiple regression to estimate separate equations for four groups: white males, white females, black males, and black females. Each equation regressed the natural logarithm of hourly wage on the full list of indicators of human capital presented in Table 11.4. The gap in log wage between any two groups can be divided into portions resulting from (1) differences between the groups in means in the independent variables, (2) differences between the groups in the rates of return (slopes) they receive to each type of human capital (e.g., what gain there is for each additional year of education or experience), (3) net effects of group membership (represented by the difference in intercept of the groups' equations) which indicate group differences in pay when all other included variables are controlled, and (4) a residual interaction effect between means and slopes, which is small and of little substantive interest. (See Jones and Kelley, 1984, for discussion of this methodology.)

Corcoran and Duncan (1979) found that the regression slopes—the rates of return to different types of human capital—were not terribly different for the four race-sex groups. Thus their analysis focuses only on the contribution made by average differences between groups on the independent variables to the gaps between groups in pay. We can assume that most of the unexplained component is the net effect of group membership (the intercept term discussed above), and thus indicates the effect of being a white male, white female, black male, or black female. Their results confirm earlier findings that the overall rates of return to experience are higher for white males than other groups. But when experience was divided into subcomponents according to whether the experience was the one's current employer and whether it involved on-the-job training, rates of return for the subcomponents did not differ greatly by group. This implies that the overall group differences in rates of return to experience come from groups spending different proportions of their employed years in different types of experience. For example, men are likely to have a higher portion of their experience in a job that provides on-the-job training and men have more of their total experience with their current employer. (We discuss what this suggests about discrimination below.)

Table 11.4 shows the extent to which mean differences between groups on indicators of human capital contribute to the pay gap between each group and while males. The size of a variable's contribution to this gap depends on the size of the mean difference between the two groups on the variable and the extent to which the variable affects earnings (i.e., the slope). (We report results using the higher earning group's slopes. However, Tables 11.4 and 11.5 also provide estimates using the lower earning group's slope in parentheses.) Years

TABLE 11.4

Percentage of 1975 Wage Gap Between White Men and Other

Groups Accounted for by Indicators of Human Capital

	Black Men		White Women		Black Women	
Years out of labor force since completing school	0	(0)	6	(5)	3	(−3)
Years of work experience before present employer	2	(6)	3	(1)	1	(−1)
Years with current employer prior to current position	5	(4)	12	(11)	7	(5)
Years of training completed on current job	15	(22)	11	(17)	8	(14)
Years of posttraining tenure on current job	−4	(−5)	−1	(−1)	−1	(1)
Proportion of total working years that were full-time	0	(−1)	8	(7)	4	(2)
Hours of work missed due to illness of others in 1975	−1	(1)	−1	(0)	−2	(−1)
Hours of work missed due to own illness in 1975	−1	(−1)	0	(0)	−1	(0)
Placed limits on job hours or location	0	(1)	2	(1)	1	(−1)
Plans to stop work for nontraining reasons	−1	(−1)	2	(1)	1	(2)
Formal education (in years)	38	(43)	2	(2)	11	(15)
Percengage of total gap explained by human capital	53	(71)	44	(45)	32	(32)
Percentage of total gap unexplained by human capital	47	(35)	56	(55)	68	(68)

NOTE: The decomposition calculates what percentage of the total gap in natural log of hourly earnings between white men and each other group arises because of group differences in means on the independent variables, assuming the white male slopes. (The percentages in parentheses are alternate estimates arrived at by using the lower earning group's slopes.) The total gap is adjusted for whether individuals live in the South and the size of the largest city they live near. Adapted and computed from Corcoran and Duncan (1979: tab. 1.)

of formal education explain a sizable portion of the pay gap between white men and both black men (38%) and black women (11%). On the other hand, since white men and white women differ little on years of formal education, this factor explains very little (2%) of the white sex gap in pay. (Indeed, as we saw in Table 11.2, in many data sets men have no more education than women, on average.)

A striking implication of Table 11.4 is the amount of the higher earnings of white men that comes from having more experience with their present employer, particularly in periods during which the employer was providing training. This last factor explains 11% of the gap between white men and white women, and 8% of the gap between white men and black women.

Table 11.4 also shows that women's current wages suffer in relation to men's because more of women's past years of experience were in part-time jobs. This accounts for 8% of the sex gap in pay among whites, implying that there is less wage *growth* in part-time than full-time jobs (see also Corcoran et al., 1984). However, to their surprise, Corcoran and Duncan (1979) found that women's *current* hourly wage is not adversely affected by presently being in a part-time rather than full-time job, thus this variable was dropped from the analysis and does not appear in Table 11.4.

White women have also suffered some small amount of human capital depreciation while out of the labor force. This is shown by the net effects of years out of the labor force on wages. This factor explains 6% of the gap between white men and white women but has little effect for blacks. The effects of other variables are very small. To summarize Table 11.4, measures of human capital explain 44% of the pay gap between white men and white women and 32% of the gap between white men and black women.

In Table 11.5 we have used Corcoran and Duncan's means and slopes to compute a decomposition that highlights the position of black women vis-à-vis white women (to see effects of race) and vis-à-vis black men (to see effects of sex). This contrasts with analysis in Table 11.4 in which black women were compared to white men, so that effects of race and sex and their interaction were lumped together in one comparison. The findings are striking in the stark contrast between the sizes of the race and sex effects. Overall (when negative and positive components are added together), a much smaller proportion of the sex gap in pay between black women and men is explained by human capital than is explained for the gap between black and white women. In particular, black women's higher average education than black men's makes a negative contribution to the sex gap in pay among blacks. That is, if black women had the low educational average of black men, the pay gap would actually increase. In contrast, education makes a large contribution to the pay gap between black and white women. Compared to white women, black women have relatively favorable levels on some of the experience variables, such as years with current employer and proportion of total working years that were full-time. But the factor that explains most of the gap between black and white women is the higher levels of schooling of white women. Table 11.5 suggests that, at present, black women are currently more affected by sex discrimination than race discrimination. However, race rather than sex discrimination is undoubtedly at the historical root of the race differences in schooling that contribute to the pay differences between black and white women.

How should we interpret these findings of how much group differences in human capital contribute to group differences in earnings? Some analysts interpret the share of the gap explained by human capital as resulting from supply-side differences in groups' skills and motivations, and the portion of the gap unexplained by human capital as explained by demand-side discrimination in wages or in access to high paying jobs. As an approximation, this is a reasonable interpretation, but it can be misleading in several ways,

TABLE 11.5
Percentage of 1975 Wage Gap Between Black Men and
Women and Between Black and White Women
Explained by Indicators of Human Capital

	Black Women and Black Men		Black Women and White Women	
Years out of labor force since completing school	10	(−7)	−8	(14)
Years of work experience before present employer	0	(−3)	−3	(3)
Years with current employer prior to current position	7	(6)	−12	(−12)
Years or training completed on current job	2	(2)	1	(2)
Years of posttraining tenure on current job	2	(−2)	−4	(3)
Proportion of total working years that were full time	16	(4)	−10	(−6)
Hours of work missed due to illness of others in 1975	2	(−1)	3	(−5)
Hours of work missed due to own illness in 1975	0	(0)	3	(−2)
Placed limits on job hours or location	−3	(1)	−3	(−6)
Plans to stop work for nontraining reasons	3	(5)	−1	(7)
Formal education (in years)	−16	(−20)	76	(97)
Percentage of total gap explained by human capital	25	(−15)	43	(95)
Percentage of total gap unexplained by human capital	76	(115)	56	(5)

NOTE: The decomposition calculates what percentage of the total gap in the natural log of hourly earnings between the two groups arises because of group differences on the independent variables, assuming the slopes of the higher earning groups, black men in column 1 and white women in column 2. (The percentages in parentheses are alternate estimates arrived at by using the lower earning group's slopes.) The total gap is adjusted for whether individuals live in the South and the size of the largest city they live near. Computed from Corcoran and Duncan (1979: tab. 1).

discussed below (see also Blau, 1984: 127-133).

Neoclassical economists are often skeptical about the existence of discrimination, because they believe it should erode in competitive markets, as we discussed above. Since they view discrimination as a theoretical anomaly they have been quite inventive in pointing out ways in which the proportion of the gap in pay unexplained by measures of human capital may overestimate discrimination by employers. They point out that any group differences in forms of human capital that have gone unmeasured in the analysis may explain some of the residual portion of the gap. Yet the argument that the portion of the pay gap unexplained by indicators of human capital represents discrimination gets stronger as the number and quality of such indicators in the data increase. The Corcoran and Duncan (1979) study is much less vulnerable to this critique than most because of the many indicators of human capital employed. Yet, even here, group differences in the quality of schooling or in motivation to maximize earnings might be omitted variables that explain some of the group differences in pay.

On the other hand, some portion of the gap in pay explained by human capital may arise because of past discrimination, and thus the portion of the gap unexplained by human capital only estimates current discrimination, not all the discrimination this sample of people have ever experienced. One cause of this is the endogeneity of human capital investment because of the feedback effects we discussed above. The choices people make about how much education or job experience to get may be influenced by how much discrimination against their group they observe in the labor market. In addition the investments in human capital of one generation of children may vary according to the race or sex discrimination experienced by their parents' generation. In this way, past discrimination by employers may affect the human capital investment of minorities and women such that some of the pay gap explained by present human capital differences is actually a function of past discrimination.

The portions of wage gap unexplained by human capital may also underestimate discrimination by the current employers because employer's discrimination can affect how much investment in on-the-job training will be undertaken for different groups of workers. Human capital theorists generally assume that, other things being equal, pay levels start lower in jobs where training is provided, but earnings trajectories will slope more steeply upward as productivity reflects this training. They also assume that individuals choose between jobs providing more or less training on the basis of how long they plan to stay in the labor force and their personal tendency to defer gratification (which economists call a discount rate). However, it is equally possible that employers discriminate in not assigning women and blacks to jobs where training is to be provided, or that they avoid providing training in jobs once these jobs are filled by women or minorities. Thus the large effects on the pay gap that Table 11.4 shows as explained by years of on-the-job training may reflect either different job choices by groups or discrimination in assignment to training, or a combination of both.

Structural explanations of the gender gap in pay. The "new structuralism" in sociology has shifted attention from how the characteristics of individuals affect their pay to an examination of those characteristics of job slots that determine rewards. The thrust of such research has been to demonstrate that certain structural locations (defined in terms of occupational, industrial, and firm characteristics) affect the rewards received by employees, net of their human capital. This sociological work builds on notions of segmented labor markets introduced by economists of the institutionalist school (e.g.,

Doeringer and Piore, 1971). The persistence of such structural effects is an anomaly for the neoclassical economic model, since mobility between sectors should eventually erode portions of pay gaps between sectors not explained by human capital. But the evidence for these effects is mounting. Such research helps us to understand the sex gap in pay, if accompanied by evidence that women are disproportionately employed in positions whose structural characteristics lead to low pay. Some researchers have seen structural explanations of the sex gap in pay as implying sex discrimination in access to jobs (e.g., Coverman, 1986). We prefer to distinguish between questions about whether discrimination explains women's job placements, and whether structural characteristics of the jobs men and women hold explain some of the sex gap in pay. The latter can be true regardless of whether women chose or were confined to their jobs once we recognize that individuals consider more than earnings when choosing a job. In the discussion that follows, we summarize the structural dimensions that have been found important in explaining the gender gap in pay.

We can think of the skill requirements of jobs as structural characteristics. Using measures of occupations' skill demands taken from the U.S. Department of Labor's Dictionary of Occupational Titles, Roos (1981) and England et al. (1982) examined the question of how much the differential distribution of men and women across occupations by their skill levels contributes to the sex gap in pay. Both analyses found that the skill levels of jobs explained virtually none of the gap. The only factor that stood out as important was the amount of on-the-job training provided (England et al., 1982). Women are disproportionately in jobs that do not provide such training, as we also saw in the individual analyses of Corcoran and Duncan (1979; see also Hoffman, 1981). This means that women are less often in jobs where employers are investing in the employees' human capital by providing training. Employer's incentives to honor an "implicit contract" to increase rewards as experience increases are greater where the employers have something to lose if employees quit because the employers have provided firm-specific training (England and Farkas, 1986: chap. 6), and we see that women are often not in jobs with implicit contract features.

The sex composition of occupations appears to exert an independent effect on earnings (Treiman and Hartmann, 1981; England et al., 1982). That is, net of the skill requirements of jobs and the human capital of their incumbents, jobs pay less when the workers are mostly women. This is the sort of wage discrimination at issue in "comparable worth" (Treiman and Hartmann, 1981; England and Norris, 1985a, 1985b). It is a form of wage discrimination different from lack of equal pay for equal work.

To say that the wages in women's jobs are low because women do the work is to say that, *ceteris paribus*, the jobs pay less than the same jobs would pay if they were done by men. One way to ascertain whether this type of wage discrimination is operating is to uncover what policies, explicit or implicit, determine the wage levels of jobs and then to test whether jobs populated by women systematically pay less than one would expect them to on the basis of other characteristics of the jobs that are criteria of wages in the operative policies. This is a "policy-capturing" or "hedonic" approach. Hypotheses about the operative policies (and the forces external to the employer they reflect) may come from economics, sociology, psychology, or other disciplines.

This conceptualization of comparable worth is best operationalized in a multiple regression analysis. The analysis usually takes jobs rather than individuals as the units of analysis (or it may take individuals as cases and enter job characteristics as contextual variables). The dependent variable is jobs' wages, and independent variables include characteristics of jobs that may affect jobs' wages. For example, measure of the educational and skill requirements, functional importance, or physical capital associated with the job may be entered. The sex composition of jobs (usually measured as percentage female) is entered as the independent variable, whose coefficient measures wage discrimination against female jobs. Indeed, we operationally define the sort of discrimination at issue in "comparable worth" as the presence of a net effect of sex composition on jobs' wages in a properly specified wage function. If women choose or are discriminatorily confined to jobs that would be low paying quite apart from their sex labels, these differentials in wages will *not* be included in this measure of discrimination as long as equations include adequate control variables.

England et al. (1982) present a policy-capturing analysis that captures employers' wage setting policies fairly well, as indicated by an R^2 of .75 for the female regression and .77 for the male regression. Each 1% female in an occupation was found to have a net depressing effect on annual earnings of $30 for males and $17 for females. This means that the difference between the median annual earnings in two occupations comparable on their skill demands but differing in that one is 100% female and one is 100% male is $1,682 for women and $3,005 for men. The net effect of this is to lower women's earnings in relation to men's for reasons quite apart from the skill requirements of their occupations. England et al. (1982) further estimate that these effects of jobs' sex composition that measure wage discrimination against female occupations accounted for almost one-third of the sex gap in earnings between full-time year-round male and female employees in 1970. Several other studies have found evidence of such wage discrimination in economywide analyses of comparable worth (McLaughlin, 1978; England and McLaughlin, 1979; Treiman and Hartmann, 1981: 28-30). Future research should assess whether the net effect of sex composition remains when more detailed control variables (including industrial characteristics) are included.

Women also tend to work in low paying industries. Beck and his colleagues (1980) have shown that women are less apt to work in "core" industries than men. Hodson and England (1986) explored the question of which of the separate dimensions of industrial structure are related to the sex gap in pay. They found that about 15% of the gender gap in pay is explained by the fact that more women than men are employed in jobs with low industry unionization rates and low capital intensity (hence high labor intensity). For example, many blue-collar women work in the production of electronics and textiles, while blue-collar men are more apt to produce autos or steel in unionized jobs involving heavy machinery. Hodson and England (1986) found other dimensions of industrial structure such as the oligopoly and profit levels of industries unrelated to the sex gap in pay.

GENDER AND NONMONETARY JOB REWARDS

How do women and men differ in their experience of nonmonetary (nonpecuniary) rewards from jobs? And what does this tell us about the overall distribution of job rewards between men and women? To explore these questions, we look at sex differences in levels and determinants of job satisfaction. We also examine sex differences in "occupational values"—what things prospective employees say they are seeking in jobs. Finally, we consider two distinct theoretical interpretations of these findings—one from social psychology and one from economics.

The fact that jobs have nonmonetary rewards makes it difficult to answer the most basic question about gender inequality in employment, to wit, whether women receive less overall reward for their jobs. When the only reward to be considered is earnings, the answer is clearly yes. But when we consider nonmonetary rewards as well, the answer is less clear. If women receive more nonpecuniary rewards from employment than men, then the overall rewards of the sexes from employment might be equal. However, we will also present what we regard as compelling arguments from social psychology suggesting that women receive fewer rewards overall.

Research on job satisfaction has generally found only very small, if any, sex differences in the overall level of job satisfaction reported by men and women (Hulin and Smith, 1964; Glenn et al., 1977; Sauser and York, 1978; Penley and Hawkins, 1980; Smith and Plant, 1982; Crane and Hodson, 1984; Darcy et al., 1984). After controls for various job characteristics, a number of studies have found that a small sex difference in favor of men disappeared (Crane and Hodson, 1984; Sauser and York, 1978; Brief and Oliver, 1976), or occasionally turned to women's advantage (Tsui and Gutek, 1984; Darcy et al., 1984). But the main conclusion is that whether statistical controls are included or not, there is little sex difference in reported job satisfaction.

Is the job satisfaction of men and of women affected by different job characteristics and rewards? Some studies have approached this question by using multivariate analysis to discern what characteristics of jobs explain variance across individuals in their job satisfaction, and how the effects vary by sex. Research on occupational values has approached the question by asking men and women what they are looking for in jobs. The multivariate studies have found that women's satisfaction is more affected by their earnings than is men's (Glenn and Weaver, 1982; Crane and Hodson, 1984). It is hard to know what to make of this since surveys of graduating students still find that males express a greater importance on choosing a job that pays well than do women (Lueptow, 1980; Peng et al., 1981; Herzog, 1982). It has also been found that men's job satisfaction is more affected by autonomy and authority (Glenn and Weaver, 1982) and promotion possibilities (Crane and Hodson, 1984; Murray and Atkinson, 1981) than is women's. These findings concur with data on expressed differences in occupational values of men and women (Leuptow, 1980: Peng et al., 1981; Herzog, 1982). The literature on determinants of job satisfaction and on occupational values also agrees in finding that women care more about relationships with coworkers than do men (Lueptow, 1980; Murray and Atkinson, 1981; Peng et al., 1981; Herzog, 1982). Research on occupational values finds women more interested than men in helping people (Leuptow, 1980; Peng et al., 1981; Herzog, 1982); but whether this job attribute actually affects women's satisfaction has not been tested.

Two theoretical frameworks offer ways of viewing these findings. The first comes from economics. Neoclassical economists have grappled with the fact that human capital models never explain even half of the earnings gap between men and women. Most have avoided interpretations emphasizing discrimination because of the belief that discrimination should erode in competitive markets. Thus some have responded to the anomaly by arguing that women may place more importance on the nonpecuniary satisfactions of work, trading off more earnings for these satisfactions than men do. This is especially likely when women see themselves as "secondary breadwinners"; thus if it has any validity at all, we would expect this hypothesis to apply to white women much more than black women, who are more likely to rear children without husbands or to have husbands with low earnings.

One variant of this economic argument is to view psychological dispositions on which men and women differ as kinds of "human capital" and to show that differences in these dispositions statistically explain some of the sex difference in earnings (Filer, 1983). Investing in kinds of human capital that have a lower payoff to earnings (e.g., nurturant skills) then becomes an indulgence in a nonpecuniary work reward. Closely related to this is the neoclassical critique of the doctrine that employers engage in comparable-worth wage discrimination against female jobs. The critique states that jobs differ in their nonpecuniary attractions, men and women differ in their tastes for various nonpecuniary job amenities, and women may be willing to trade off earning for sex-typical work (Killingsworth, 1984). In a third variant of this view Becker (1985) has argued that women may sacrifice some earnings in order to be able to hold jobs requiring less intense effort so they can conserve energy for their family responsibilities. It is possible, therefore, to view the requirement for less physical, cognitive, or emotional effort as a nonmonetary job reward that women will forego wages to gain.

Economists generally forego making interpersonal utility comparisons (Hirshleifer, 1976: 54-64). Thus they are disinclined to interpret answers to questions about subjective experiences of job satisfaction or effort as indicative of "who is getting more utility" out of employment. Yet the commonsense translation of their efforts to show that women trade nonpecuniary for pecuniary rewards would seem to be that women's and men's overall utility from jobs are equal. And they might claim some support for this view via the following reasoning: If job satisfaction measures utility from both monetary and nonmonetary rewards of a job, then, given women's lower earnings, the nearly equal levels of job satisfaction reported by the sexes suggest that women get more nonmonetary rewards than do men from their jobs. Whether this is true to an extent that compensates for their lower pay is another question.

There is a social-psychological interpretation of the evidence considered above that leads to a different conclusion—that women's overall rewards from employment are lower than men's. Equity theory posits that arrangements are seen as fair when the ratio of inputs to outputs is equal across individuals. Research in this tradition has assumed that individuals make rough interpersonal utility comparisons, and examined how individuals choose the social or temporal comparisons by which they make equity judgments (Berger et al., 1972; Crosby, 1982). A uniform finding is that women have lower internal standards of "personal entitlement," and that, in the absence of clear external comparison standards, they tend to think they deserve fewer rewards than men who have performed similarly, in part because they underestimate their own abilities or performance (Berger et al., 1972; Crosby, 1982; Colwill, 1982; Major et al., 1984; Bielby and Bielby, 1985). This suggests that women may evaluate their jobs in comparison with the jobs other women have, thus reporting satisfaction equal to that of men even when their overall rewards (and possibly even their nonpecuniary rewards alone) are lower than men's (Crane and Hodson, 1984). The ability to have a non-sex-specific basis of comparison is impeded by the extreme level of job segregation. Thus, counter to the arguments of economists, women may get less nonpecuniary satisfaction than men from their jobs. Further evidence for this comes from psychological evidence suggesting that men consider it more psychologically painful to do "female" activities than females find "male" activities (Maccoby and Jacklin, 1974: 328), which suggests that men may derive more nonmonetary utility from sex-typed job placements than do women.

But what of Becker's hypothesis that women have the nonpecuniary advantage of jobs requiring less effort? Bielby and Bielby (1985) have tested this hypothesis and found the evidence does not support it. They analyzed data from a national survey that asked respondents how "hard" their jobs require them to work, how much "effort, either physical or mental" their jobs require, and how much "effort" they put into their jobs "beyond what is required." Women reported slightly more effort than men, and the difference increases rather than decreases when human capital and household responsibility are controlled in a regression analysis. Given the social psychological experiments mentioned above that suggest that women tend to underestimate their performance, this is strong evidence against Becker's hypothesis. In summary, it is hard to determine which sex receives more nonmonetary rewards from paid employment, but the evidence suggests that women's overall rewards are lower.

CONCLUSION

In surveying gender inequality in paid employment, we have focused on what jobs men and women hold, their earnings, and their nonmonetary rewards from employment. We have stressed throughout that one cannot reduce explanations of gender inequality to simplistic one-factor stories attributing everything to supply-side household decisions or to demand-side structure and discrimination. Nor can we reduce explanations to either ideal or structural/material factors. Rather, reciprocal effects are operative, with feedback effects cycling back and forth between them. These feedback effects have often operated to preserve sex discrimination and differentials, even where market forces tend to erode them. Yet once substantial change begins, as it has in some aspects of gender inequality, these changes will be magnified by these same feedbacks.

We expect that future cohorts of women will continue to make wage gains relative to men. There are two basic sources of these gains. First, differences in labor force experience explain some portion of the sex gap in pay. But until recently, the gap between the average experience of employed men and women had not decreased, since the propensity of women to stay employed longer was being offset by the continued entrance of women with little experience (Smith and Ward, 1984). This bottleneck cleared around 1980, and women's relative experience is now increasing, thus increasing women's relative wages. Second, thanks to reduced hiring discrimination and less traditional job choices by women, women have moved increasingly into predominantly male jobs, which have always paid better. This raises the wages of those women entering the "male jobs," and it may also indirectly produce upward pressure on the wages of traditionally female jobs by lessening the supply of labor to those jobs. These declines in segregation will likely continue and become self-reinforcing since they provide employers with evidence that women perform well in jobs nontraditional for them and also provide less sex-differentiated cognitive inputs to children's socialization.

On the other hand, two factors mitigate against continued decreases in the sex segregation of jobs and the sex gap in pay. The first is the decrease in resources for enforcement of discrimination laws brought about by the Reagan administration and the longer-term effects of Reagan's appointment of conservative judges. These developments are particularly likely to slow the pace of desegregation where it is less well established—for example, in predominantly male blue-collar jobs. This will be especially detrimental to working-class women. Another factor hindering women's progress toward equality in jobs and pay is the fact that most women still do the lion's share of household work even when employed full-time (England and Farkas, 1986: 94-99). Unless women can negotiate a more equal sharing of household work with men, it is unlikely that the sex gap in pay will be eradicated (Coverman, 1983).

Nonetheless, we expect that increased female employment experience and entrance into traditionally male jobs will raise women's relative wages. But we are less certain that the underpayment of predominantly female jobs relative to their educational and skill requirements will cease. That is, we believe the future of "comparable worth" to be quite uncertain. Barring new legislation, the usefulness of Title VII in combating this form of discrimination hinges on future court decisions. Trends in the relative wages of predominantly female occupations may also depend on whether workers in these occupations unionize, or whether the political movement to raise the pay of female jobs in the public sector has a spillover effect in private sector wages. As always, the future is uncertain.

NOTE

1. Actually the evidence is mixed on whether women have higher turnover rates than men (Price, 1977: 40; Viscusi, 1980; Blau and Kahn, 1981; Osterman, 1982; Haber et al., 1983; Shorey, 1983). Part of the difficulty is deciding whether one's human capital and the characteristics of one's job are exogenous to plans for turnover and thus should be statistically controlled. Studies using such controls generally do not find sex differences in turnover. However, if turnover plans influence job choices then job level should not be controlled. Studies not using such controls have had mixed findings.

REFERENCES

ARROW, K. (1973) "The theory of discrimination," pp. 83-102 in A. H. Pascal (ed.) Racial Discrimination in Economic Life. Lexington, MA: D. C. Heath.

ARROW, K. (1976) "Economic dimensions of occupational segregation: Comment I," pp. 233-237 in M. Blaxall and B. Reagan (eds.) Women and the Workplace. Chicago: University of Chicago Press.

BACHMAN, J. G., L. D. JOHNSTON, and P. M. O'MALLEY (1980) Monitoring the Future: Questionnaire Responses from the Nation's High School Seniors. Ann Arbor: Institute for Social Research, University of Michigan.

BECK, E. M., P. HORAN, and C. TOLBERT, II (1980) "Industrial segmentation and labor market discrimination." Social Problems 28: 113-130.

BECKER, G. (1957) The Economics of Discrimination. Chicago: University of Chicago Press.

BECKER, G. (1985) "Human capital, effort, and the sexual division of labor." Journal of Labor Economics 3: S33-S58.

BELLER, A. (1979) "The impact of equal employment opportunity laws on the male/female earnings differential," pp. 304-330 in C. Lloyd et al. (eds.) Women in the Labor Market. New York: Columbia University Press.

BELLER, A. (1982a) "The impact of equal employment opportunity policy on sex differentials in earnings and occupations." American Economic Review, Papers and Proceedings 72 (May): 171-175.

BELLER, A. (1982b) "Occupational segregation by sex: Determinants and changes." Journal of Human Resources 17: 371-392.

BELLER, A. (1984) "Trends in occupational segregation by sex and race, 1960-1981," pp. 11-26 in B. Reskin (ed.) Sex Segregation in the Workplace. Washington, DC: National Academy Press.

BERGER, J., M. ZELDITCH, Jr., B. ANDERSON, and B. COHEN (1972) "Structural aspects of distributive justice: A status value formulation," pp. 119-146 in J. Berger et al. (eds.) Sociological Theories in Progress, Vol. 2. Boston: Houghton Mifflin.

BERGMANN, B. (1976) "Reducing the pervasiveness of discrimination," pp. 120-141 in E. Ginzberg (ed.) Jobs for Americans. Englewood Cliffs, NJ: Prentice- Hall.

BERGMANN, B. and W. DARITY (1981) "Social relations in the workplace and employer discrimination." Industrial Relations Association 33rd Annual Proceedings: 155-162.

BIANCHI, S. and N. RYTINA (1986) "The decline in occupational sex segregation during the 1970s: Census and CPS comparisons." Demography 23: 56-59.

BIELBY, W. and J. BARON (1984) "A woman's place is with other women: Sex segregation within organizations," pp. 27-55 in B. Reskin (ed.) Sex Segregation in the Workplace, Washington, DC: National Academy Press.

BIELBY, W. and J. BARON (1986) "Men and women at work: Sex segregation and statistical discrimination." American Journal of Sociology 91: 759-799.

BIELBY, D. and W. BIELBY (1985) "She works hard for the money: Household responsibilities and the allocation of effort." Presented at the annual meetings of the American Sociological Association, Washington, DC, August.

BLAU, F. (1977) Equal Pay in the Office. Lexington, MA: D. C. Heath.

BLAU, F. (1984) "Occupational segregation and labor market discrimination," pp. 117-143 in B. Reskin (ed.) Sex Segregation in the Workplace. Washington, DC: National Academy Press.

BLAU, F. D. and A. H. BELLAR (1984) "Trends in earnings differentials by sex and race: 1971-1981." Presented at the annual meetings of the American Economic Association, Dallas.

BLAU, F. and W. HENDRICKS (1979) "Occupational segregation by sex: Trends and prospects." Journal of Human Resources 12: 197-210.

BLAU, F. and L. KAHN (1981) "Race and sex differences in quits by young workers." Industrial and Labor Relations Review 34: 563-577.

BONACICH, E. (1976) "Advanced capitalism and black-white relations in the U.S.: A split labor market interpretation." American Sociological Review 41: 34-51.

BOWLES, S. and H. GINTIS (1976) Schooling in Capitalist America. New York: Basic Books.

BRIEF, A. P. and R. L. OLIVER (1976) "Male-female differences in work attitudes among retail sales managers." Journal of Applied Psychology 61: 526-528.

BURSTEIN, P. (1985) Discrimination, Jobs, and Politics: The Struggle for Equal Employment Opportunity in the United States Since the New Deal. Chicago: University of Chicago Press.

CHAFETZ, J. (1984) Sex and Advantage. Totawa, NJ: Rowman & Allanheld.

CHODOROW, N. (1978) The Reproduction of Mothering. Berkeley: University of California Press.

COLLINS, S. (1983) "The making of the black middle class." Social Problems 30: 369-382.

COLWILL, N. (1982) The New Partnership: Women and Men in Organizations. Palo Alto, CA: Mayfield.

CORCORAN, M. and G. DUNCAN (1979) "Work history, labor force attachment, and earnings differences between the races and sexes." Journal of Human Resources 14: 3-20.

CORCORAN, M., G. DUNCAN, and M. PONZA (1984) "Work experience, job segregation, and wages," pp. 171-191 in B. Reskin (ed.) Sex Segregation in the Workplace. Washington, DC: National Academy Press.

COVERMAN, S. (1983) "Gender, domestic labor time, and wage inequality." American Sociological Review 48: 623-637.

COVERMAN, S. (1985) "Explaining husbands' participations in domestic labor." Sociological Quarterly 26: 81-97.

COVERMAN, S. (1987) "Sociological explanations of the male-female wage gap: Individualist and structuralist theories," in A. Stromberg and S. Harkess (eds.) Women Working. Palo Alto, CA: Mayfield.

CRANE, M. and R. HODSON (1984) "Job satisfaction in dual career families: Gender differences in the effects of job and family characteristics and personal expectations." University of Texas-Austin. (mimeo)

CROSBY, F. (1982) Relative Deprivation and Working Women. New York: Oxford University Press.

DARCY, C., J. SYROTUIK, and C. M. SIDDIQUE (1984) "Perceived job attributes, job satisfaction, and psychological distress: A comparison of working men and women." Human Relations 37: 603-611.

DAYMONT, T. and A. STATHAM (1983) "Occupational atypicality: Changes, causes, and consequences," pp. 61-76 in L. B. Shaw (ed.) Unplanned Careers: The Working Lives of Middle Aged Women. Lexington, MA: D. C. Heath.

DOERINGER, P. and M. PIORE (1971) Internal Labor Markets and Manpower Analysis. Lexington, MA: D. C. Heath.

DUNCAN, O. D. and B. DUNCAN (1955) "A methodological analysis of segregation indices." American Sociological Review 20: 200-217.

EDWARDS, R., M. REICH, and D. GORDON [eds.] (1975) Labor Market Segmentation. Lexington, MA: D. C. Heath.

ENGLAND, P. (1981) "Assessing trends in occupational sex segregation, 1900-1976," pp. 273-295 in I. Berg (ed.) Sociological Perspectives on Labor Markets. New York: Academic Press.

ENGLAND, P. (1982) "The failure of human capital theory to explain occupational sex segregation." Journal of Human Resources 17: 358-370.

ENGLAND, P. (1984) "Wage appreciation and depreciation: A test of neoclassical economic explanations of occupational sex segregation." Social Forces 62: 726-749.

ENGLAND, P., H. CHASSIE, and L. McCORMACK (1982) "Skill demands and earnings in female and male occupations." Sociology and Social Research 66: 147-168.

ENGLAND, P. and G. FARKAS (1986) Households, Employment, and Gender: A Social, Economic and Demographic View. New York: Aldine.

ENGLAND, P. and S. D. McLAUGHLIN (1979) "The sex segregation of jobs and the male-female income differential," pp. 89-213 in R. Alvarez, K. Lutterman, and Associates (eds.), Discrimination in Organizations. San Francisco: Jossey-Bass.

ENGLAND, P. and B. NORRIS (1985a) "Comparable worth: A new doctrine of sex discrimination." Social Science Quarterly 66: 629-643.

ENGLAND, P. and B. NORRIS (1985b) "Comparable worth: Rejoinder to Quester and Utgoff." Social Science Quarterly 66: 650-653.

FERBER, M. A. and H. M. LOWRY (1976) "The sex differential in earnings: A reappraisal." Industrial and Labor Relations review 29: 377-387.

FILER, R. (1983) "Sexual differences in earnings: The role of individual personalities and tastes." Journal of Human Resources 18: 82-99.

GIDDENS, A. (1971) Capitalism and Modern Social Theory. New York: Cambridge University Press.

GLENN, N., P. TAYLOR, and C. WEAVER (1977) "Age and job satisfaction among males and females: A multivariate, multisurvey study." Journal of Applied Psychology 62: 789-793.

GLENN, N. and C. WEAVER (1982) "Further evidence on education and job satisfaction." Social Forces 61: 46-55.

GORDON, D. (1972) Theories of Poverty and Unemployment. Lexington, MA: D. C. Heath.

GREEN, G. (1983) "Wage differentials for job entrants, by race and sex." Ph.D. dissertation, Department of Economics, George Washington University.

GREENBERGER, E. and L. STEINBERG (1983) "Sex differences in early labor force experience: Harbinger of things to come." Social Forces 62: 467-487.

HABER, S. E., E. J. LAMAS, and G. GREEN (1983) "A new method for estimating job separations by sex." Monthly Labor Review 106: 20-27.

HACKER, S. (1979) "Sex stratification, technology, and organizational change: A longitudinal analysis." Social Problems 26: 39-57.

HALL, C. (1954) A Primer of Freudian Psychology. New York: World.

HARTMANN, H. (1976) "Capitalism, patriarchy, and job segregation by sex," pp. 137-170 in M. Blaxall and B. Reagan (eds.) Women and the Workplace. Chicago: University of Chicago Press.

HERZOG, A. R. (1982) "High school students' occupational plans and values: Trends in sex differences 1976 through 1980." Sociology of Education 55: 1-13.

HIGGINBOTHAM, E. (1987) Employment for Professional Black Women in the Twentieth Century, in C. Bose and G. Spitze (Eds.), Ingredients for Women's Employment Policy. Albany: SUNY Press.

HIRSHLEIFER, J. (1976) Price Theory and Applications. Englewood Cliffs, NJ: Prentice-Hall.

HODSON, R. and P. ENGLAND (1986) "Industrial structure and sex differences in earnings." Industrial Relations 25: 1.

HOFFMAN, S. (1981) "On-the-job training: Differences by race and sex." Monthly Labor Review (July): 34-36.

HULIN, C. L. and P. C. SMITH (1964) "Sex differences in job satisfaction." Journal of Applied Psychology 48: 88-92.

HUMPHRIES, J. (1976) "Women: Scapegoats and safety valves in the great depression." Review of Radical Political Economics 8: 98-121.

JACOBS, J. (1983) "The sex segregation of occupations and women's career patterns." Ph.D. dissertation, Department of Sociology, Harvard University.

JACOBS, J. (1985) "Trends in sex-segregation in American higher education, 1948-80," in L. Larwood et al. (eds.) Women and Work: An Annual Review, Vol. 1. Newbury Park, CA: Sage.

JACOBS, J. (1986) "Occupational sex typing: Change in young women's aspirations and occupations." Presented at the annual meetings of the Southern Sociological Society, April.

JACOBS, J. (1987) "The sex typing of aspirations and occupations: Instability during the careers of young women." Social Science Quarterly 68: 122-137.

JAGGAR, A. and P. ROTHENBERG (1984) Feminist Frameworks. New York: McGraw-Hill.

JONES, F. L. and J. KELLEY (1984) "Decomposing differences between groups: A cautionary note on measuring discrimination." Sociological Methods and Research 12: 323-343.

KANTER, R. (1977) Men and Women of the Corporation. New York: Basic Books.

KELLEY, M. (1982) "Discrimination in seniority systems: A case study." Industrial and Labor Relations Review 36: 40-55.

KILLINGSWORTH, M. (1984) "Statement on comparable worth." Testimony before the Joint Economic Committee, U.S. Congress, April 10.

KOHLBERG, L. (1966) "A cognitive developmental analysis of children's sex-role concepts and attitudes," pp. 82-173 in E. Maccoby (ed.) The Development of Sex Differences. Stanford, CA: Stanford University Press.

KOHN, M. L. and C. SCHOOLER, with J. MILLER, K. MILLER, C. SCHOENBACK, and D. SHOENBERG (1983) Work and Personality: An Inquiry into the Impact of Social Stratification. Norwood, NJ: Ablex.

LEVINSON, R. (1975) "Sex discrimination and employment practices: An experiment with unconventional job inquiries." Social Problems 22: 533-543.

LEONARD, J. S. (1984) "Impact of affirmative action on employment." Journal of Labor Economics 2: 439-463.

LOOFT, W. (1971) "Sex differences in the expression of vocational aspirations by elementary school children." Developmental Psychology 5: 366.

LORBER, J., et al. (1981) "On the reproduction of mothering: A methodological debate." Signs 6: 482-514.

LUEPTOW, L. B. (1980) "Social change and sex-role change in adolescent orientations toward life, work, and achievement: 1964-1975." Social Psychology Quarterly 43: 48-59.

MACCOBY, E. and C. JACKLIN (1974) The Psychology of Sex Differences. Stanford CA: Stanford University Press.

MADDEN, J. (1973) The Economics of Sex Discrimination. Lexington, MA: D. C. Heath.

MAJOR, B., D. MCFARLIN, and D. GAGNON (1984) "Overworked and underpaid: On the nature of gender differences in personal entitlement." Journal of Personality and Social Psychology 47: 1399-1412.

MALVEAUX, J. (1982) "Recent trends in occupational segregation by race and sex." Presented at the Workshop on Job Segregation by Sex, National Academy of Sciences, Washington, DC, May.

MARINI, M. and M. BRINTON (1984) "Sex typing in occupational socialization," pp. 192-232 in B. Reskin (ed.) Sex Segregation in the Workplace. Washington, DC: National Academy Press.

McLAUGHLIN, S. D. (1978) "Occupational sex identification and the assessment of male and female earnings inequality." American Sociological Review 43: 900-921.

MURAY, M. and T. ATKINSON (1981) "Gender differences in correlates of job satisfaction." Canadian Journal of Behavioral Science 13: 44-52.

NEMEROWICZ, G. (1979) Children's Perceptions of Gender and Work Roles. New York: Praeger.

O'NEILL, J. (1985) "The trend in the male-female wage gap in the United States." Journal of Labor Economics 3: S91-S116.

OPPENHEIMER, V. (1970) The Female Labor Force in the United States. Berkeley: University of California Press.

OSTERMAN, P. (1982) "Affirmative action and opportunity: A study of female quit rates." Review of Economics and Statistics 64: 604-612.

PENG, S. S., W. B. FETTERS, and A. J. KOLSTAD (1981) High School and Beyond: A Capsule Description of High School Students. Washington, DC: National Center for Education Statistics.

PENLEY, L. and B. HAWKINS (1980) "Organizational communication, performance, and job satisfaction as a function of ethnicity and sex." Journal of Vocational Behavior 16: 368-384.

PHELPS, E. (1972) "The statistical theory of racism and sexism." American Economic Review 64: 59-61.

POLACHEK, S. (1979) "Occupational segregation among women: Theory, evidence, and a prognosis," pp. 90-122 in C. Lloyd (ed.) Sex Discrimination, and the Division of Labor. New York: Columbia University Press.

POLACHEK, S. (1981) "Occupational self-selection: A human capital approach to sex differences in occupational structure." Review of Economics and Statistics 58: 60-69.

POLACHEK, S. (1985) "Occupational segregation: A defense of human capital prediction." Journal of Human Resources 20: 437-440.

PRESTON, S. (1984) "Children and the elderly: Divergent paths for America's dependents." Demography 21: 435-458.

PRICE, J. L. (1977) The Study of

REICH, M. (1981) Racial Inequality: A Political Economic Analysis. Princeton, NJ: Princeton University Press.

RESKIN, B. and H. HARTMANN (1985) Women's Work, Men's Work. Washington, DC: National Academy Press.

RESKIN, B. and P. ROOS (1987) Status Hierarchies and Sex Segregation, pp. 3-21 in C. Bose and G. Spitze (eds.), Ingredients for Women's Employment Policy. Albany: SUNY Press.

ROOS, P. (1981) "Sex segregation in the workplace: Male-female differences in returns to occupation." Social Science Research 10: 195-224.

ROOS, P. and B. RESKIN (1984) "Institutional factors contributing to sex segregation in the workplace," pp. 235-260 in B. Reskin (ed.) Sex Segregation in the Workplace. Washington DC: National Academy Press.

ROSEN, B. (1982) "Career progress of women: Getting in and staying in," pp. 70-99 in H. J. Bernardin (ed.) Women in the Work Force. New York: Praeger.

ROSEN, B. and T. H. JERDEE (1974) "Effects of applicant's sex and difficulty of job on evaluations of candidates for managerial positions." Journal of Applied Psychology 59: 511-512.

ROSEN, B. and T. H. JERDEE (1978) "Perceived sex differences in managerially relevant behavior." Sex Roles 4: 837-843.

ROSENFELD, R. (1984) "Job changing and occupational sex segregation: Sex and race comparisons," pp. 56-86 in B. Reskin (ed.) Sex Segregation in the Workplace. Washington, DC: National Academy Press.

SAUSER, W. and C. M. YORK (1978) "Sex differences in job satisfaction: A re-examination." Personnel Psychology 31: 537-547.

SCHULTZ, T. P. (1981) Economics of Population. Reading, MA: Addison-Wesley.

SHOREY, J. (1983) "An analysis of sex differences in quits." Oxford Economic Papers 35: 213-227.

SMITH, D. and W. PLANT (1982) "Sex differences in the job satisfaction of university professors." Journal of Applied Psychology 67: 249-251.

SMITH, J. (1979) "The convergence to racial equality in women's wages," pp. 173-215 in C. Lloyd et al. (eds.) Women in the Labor Market. New York: Columbia University Press.

SMITH, J. and M. WARD (1984) Women's Wages and Work in the Twentieth Century. R-3119-NICHD. Santa Monica, CA: Rand.

SOKOLOFF, N. (1985) "The increase of black and white women in the professions: A contradictory process." Presented at the Conference on Ingredients for Women's Employment Policy, State University of New York, Albany, April 19-20.

SORENSEN, A. (1975) "The structure of intragenerational mobility." American Sociological Review 40: 456-471.

SPENCE, M. (1974) Market Signaling. Cambridge: Harvard University Press.

STEVENSON, M. (1986) "The persistence of wage differences between men and women: Some economic approaches," in A. Stromberg and S. Harkess (eds.) Women Working. Palo Alto, CA: Mayfield.

STOCKARD, J. and M. JOHNSON (1981) Sex Roles. Englewood Cliffs, NJ: Prentice-Hall.

STROBER, M. (1976) "Toward dimorphics: A summary statement to the Conference on Occupational Segregation," pp. 293-302 in M. Blaxall and B. Reagan (eds.) Women and the Workplace. Chicago: University of Chicago Press.

STROBER, M. (1984) "Toward a general theory of occupational sex segregation: The case of public school teaching," pp. 144-156 in B. Reskin (ed.) Sex Segregation in the Workplace. Washington, DC: National Academy Press.

STROBER, M. and L. BEST (1979) "The female/male salary differential in public schools: Some lessons from San Francisco, 1879." Economic Inquiry 17: 218-236.

TREIMAN, D. and H. HARTMANN (1981) Women, Work, and Wages: Equal Pay for Jobs of Equal Value. Washington, DC: National Academy Press.

TSUI, A. and B. GUTEK (1984) "A role set analysis of gender differences in performance, affective relationships, and career success of industrial middle managers." Academy of Management Journal 27: 619-635.

U.S. Department of Labor (1984) Employment Patterns of Minorities and Women in Federal Contractor and Noncontractor Establishments, 1974-1980: A Report of the Office of Federal Contract Compliance Programs. Employment Standards Administration. (mimeo)

U.S. Department of Labor (1985) "Labor Force activity of mothers of young children continues at record pace." News, September 19.

VISCUSI, W. K. (1980) "Sex differences in worker quitting." Review of Economics and Statistics 62: 388-398.

WAITE, L. (1981) U.S. Women at Work. Washington DC: Population Reference Bureau.

WEISS, Y. and R. GRONAU (1981) "Expected interruptions in labour force participation and sex-related differences in earnings growth." Review of Economic Studies 58: 607-619.

WOLF, W. and R. ROSENFELD (1978) "Sex structure of occupations and job mobility." Social Forces 56: 823-844.

IV

GENDERED WORLDS

12 She Works Hard for a Living: Gender and Class on the Job

MYRA MARX FERREE
University of Connecticut

W OMEN have always worked, as the title of Alice Kessler-Harris's (1981) celebrated overview of the history of American women's labor proclaims. The women of the working class have carried particularly heavy burdens of labor for both their employers and their families. This daily struggle has typically been considered of little academic interest in comparison to the work men do or even the achievements of elite women. However, as the feminist perspective has widened to take in the significance of race and class as well as gender, the importance of understanding the labor of ordinary working women has begun to be recognized (see Harkess, 1985). Their own perceptions of their work and the meaning it holds for them present an important viewpoint on these intersecting systems of stratification.

In recent years feminist social historians have rescued from invisibility the unpaid and poorly paid labors of women on farms and in factories of the past. They have highlighted women's struggles for better working and living conditions, a less exploitive wage, more self-determination, and respect on the job and in the home (Kessler-Harris, 1982; Cantor and Laurie, 1977; Matthaei, 1982). One important insight into the authentic history of women provided by this research is the centrality of women's efforts to support themselves and their families and to resist victimization by employers and husbands. This perspective needs now to be carried forward into the present.

Awareness of women's history of resistance should make us wary of terminology for women's work today that describes all nonstereotypical behavior as nontraditional. Labeling such actions "nontraditional" not only denies the history of women's resistance but also supports an ideology that deems "progress" and "modernization" the impersonal agents of women's emancipation and neglects the importance of women's actions on their own

AUTHOR'S NOTE: Particular thanks are due to Elaine J. Hall for her assistance in preparation for this chapter, and to Nancy Andes, Christine Bose, Beth Hess, and Jane Wilkie for their suggestions of how to improve it.

behalf. Finally, the labeling of women's nonconforming behavior as "nontraditional" prompts a confusion between recent changes in women's working lives and improvement in their life chances. Change is a common theme in women's collective employment history, but real advances are harder to identify.

Even a brief historical survey makes the many transformations of women's work obvious: the nineteenth-century move from farm to city and the lessening significance of domestic production of goods (Matthaei, 1982; Strasser, 1982); the decline in numbers of domestic servants and the growing racial segregation of that occupation from 1900 to 1960 (Katzman, 1981; Palmer, 1984; Rollins, 1985); the sharper differentiation of clerical from managerial work in the 1920s and the increasing gender segregation of these jobs (Glenn and Feldberg, 1984; Kanter, 1977); the post World War II growth in mass consumption, the concomitant expansion of retail sales and service positions, and the de-skilling of this work (Braverman, 1974; Benson, 1984); the emerging global division of labor (Fuentes and Ehrenreich, 1983; Nash and Fernandez-Kelly, 1983). But as women's work has changed in site and substance, the significance of gender stratification remains. Women have repeatedly entered "nontraditional" jobs only to discover that the rewards and opportunities attached to them continued to be structured by gender as well as class and race.

This chapter examines contemporary studies of women as workers who act on their interests within structures that segregate and subordinate them. The primary focus is on nonelite women, women who commonly have to struggle with the class and race relations that restrict their lives as well as with the limitations of the gender hierarchy. As will be seen, women value and guard their ability to choose, even when the range of options open to them is severely limited (see Gerson, 1985; Rosen, forthcoming). The choices they make today, as in the past, include resistance to conventional authorities and expectations as well as acceptance of such demands. Their options may only be between the intensified domestic labor needed to make their husbands' paycheck stretch a little further or a low-wage job to make ends meet, or between enduring a boss's harassment or accepting a period of unemployment. Nonetheless, as this chapter will show, these choices matter even when they are limited in scope.

Once it is recognized that nonconventional behavior is not found exclusively or even predominantly in occupations once nontraditional for women, it is possible to develop a broader picture of the ways in which women resist the expectations of male-defined society. But nonconforming behavior is not the only option women see as expressing their own interests, and an exclusive emphasis on resistance would be as one-sided as a picture of women as passive and compliant.

In this context, it is crucial to explore what the much heralded expansion of women's labor force participation actually implies for the women who are the primary constituents of this change. Where are most women working, and what does their work mean to them? This chapter begins by testing the image of dramatic change suggested by the higher levels of women's participation in paid employment against the continuing reality of segregation. The following three sections then examine the experiences of women in the sex-segregated occupations where most women work rather than highlighting the few women in atypical occupations as the media and sociology more typically have done. The first of these sections focuses on the job experiences of women in the female- sex-typed professions of teaching and nursing, which in 1985 together accounted for 59% of all women in the professions (U.S. Department of Labor, 1986). The second explores the vast female ghetto of clerical work, where one in three women are employed. The third highlights women's experience on factory assembly lines, particularly in the electronics and garment industries, which are the major employers of women worldwide.

The next three sections focus on the dynamics of segregation and change in particular areas. The first explores the processes by which women enter jobs from which they have previously been excluded, particularly in blue-collar skilled craft occupations, and what rewards and costs they experience as a result. The second of these sections looks at the significance of women's relationships with other women on the job as components of women's work culture. The concept of work culture can illuminate both the interpersonal rewards of segregated work and the forms of resistance found there. Finally, the continuing responsibility of women for the vast majority of housework and child care and the recognition of these activities as work prompts a closer examination of the nature of this unpaid occupation and its relation to paid work. The three sections describing where women work and the latter three sections exploring what work means to them are then drawn into a concluding section on the significance of class for understanding gender relations.

THE MYTH OF THE TRANSFORMED LABOR FORCE

Because women have continually entered nontraditional areas of work to find them not quite the source of independence they once thought, the supposed liberation implied by the "subtle revolution" of women's expanding labor force participation demands critical examination (Smith, 1979). A higher proportion of women are indeed working in the paid labor force. As of 1985, a clear majority of women (54%) were in the paid labor force, as were 51% of married mothers of children under 3 years old, the latter up from only 26% in 1970 (U.S. Department of Labor, 1986). Single-parent mothers, an increasing proportion of the total, are more likely to be employed in general (61% are) but are less likely to have a job if there is a child under 3 at home (45% employed), presumably because of the unavailability of affordable child care (Hayghe, 1986).

If women now drop out of the labor force at all, it is not so much at marriage as at the birth of the first child (Oakley, 1980), and fewer are leaving even at that point. In 1985, half (49%) of all mothers and two-thirds (64%) of black mothers of infants under 1 year old were employed (Hayghe, 1986). If women do drop out, reentry is quick and increasingly certain. Slightly over two-thirds of married mothers of school-aged children, black and white alike, were employed, as were approximately 80% of single-parent mothers of school-aged children.

This does not mean, however, that most women participated in paid employment as year-round, full-time workers. Sokoloff (1987b) estimates that in 1983 only 45% of the women with jobs were employed both year-round and full-time. Among mothers of preschoolers, 47% of blacks but only 31% of whites worked full time, year round (Hayghe, 1986). While the year-round full-time woman worker earns about 60% of what her male counterpart does, working women in general earn far less. The average annual earnings of all women with paid jobs in 1983 was only $8,230, thus underlining women's continuing dependence on marriage for economic survival (U.S. Bureau of the Census, 1985).

Second, the expansion of women's paid employment has occurred in a strongly gender-segregated labor market, and most women who have entered or reentered paid employment in recent years have done so in occupations held primarily by women. In 1980, a majority (54%) of all working women were in occupations dominated by their sex and one-quarter worked in the 22 occupations that were over 90% female, compared to three-eighths of male workers who were in the 165 occupations that were 90% or more male (Reskin and Roos, 1987). Further, jobs held by individuals within occupations (e.g., computer programmer, retail sales clerk) are segregated by industry and firm so that few companies employ both men and women to do the same work (Bielby and Baron, 1984), and women are concentrated in the less well paying firms (Talbert and Bose, 1977).

Third, the structure of the economy itself relies on gender as a social construct that not only legitimates the assignment of certain jobs to women but rewards these jobs according to different rules. The taboo on women doing men's work and men doing women's is clearly evident in the contemporary work force (Reskin, 1984; Burris and Wharton, 1982), and sex-typed jobs have quite distinct wage structures. The female-sex-typed occupations pay low wages even for year-round, full-time work (Reskin, 1984). Features of skill, experience, and responsibility that are rewarded in the jobs typically held by men are often overlooked or undercompensated in female-sex-typed jobs (Treiman and Hartmann, 1981).

Seeing the higher levels of women's labor force participation as an indication of women's progress toward equality with men is simply wishful thinking if these other important features of women's work experience are ignored. Such misperceptions have contributed, for example, to the feminization of poverty (Pearce and McAdoo, 1981; Marciano, 1986). Judges and ex-husbands often accept the myth of women with paid jobs as financially independent. Thus women heading households are assumed neither to need nor deserve alimony or child support because they are employed or employable (Weitzman, 1986). Besides overlooking the significant contributions of unpaid housework and child care women made to the economic well-being of the family during the marriage—and even employed wives are in almost all cases responsible for this work—this attitude takes for granted that the paid jobs available to women are adequate to support a family. Unfortunately, the wages available to women in most sex-segregated jobs fall far short of this standard (Pearce and McAdoo, 1981; Shortridge, 1984).

One response to women's currently insufficient earnings is to encourage women to aspire to be economically independent, to seek out careers in male-dominated or mixed-sex occupations, and to maintain continuous full-time labor force participation. This advice assumes that women's difficulties lie with them as individuals and that insofar as individual women succeed in approximating the middle-class male career model they can legitimately expect to be treated by employers as if they were men. But greater attention to class and race along with gender makes clear that this can only be a solution for an elite. Structurally, only those women who already have class and race advantages and who avoid the gender-based social costs of marriage and motherhood can expect to succeed under these rules.

The crucial issue for most women is not how well they can conform to achievement norms established for white male professionals, but how they can attain a living wage in a gender- and race-segregated economy. Despite this, the mass media hold up exceptional women professionals as models, as the "superwomen" who "have it all" in the present economic structure (Ferree, 1987). Recognizing that they cannot meet this standard, many women come to believe that they are not entitled to equal treatment.

Because superwomen are so pervasive in the media, it is worth noting just how uncommon these women are in reality. In 1983, only slightly more than one percent (1.13%) of all employed married women and less than 12% of all women in professional jobs were in the the high status, male-dominated professions (Benenson, 1984: 21; U.S. Department of Labor, 1986). Only 8% of women with full-time jobs earned $25,000 in 1983, compared to 33% of male workers (U.S. Department of Labor, 1984: A-22). Moreover, several studies suggest that only about 60% of women in management careers ever marry and have children, compared to over 90% of women in general (Hewlett, 1986: 407). Among college-educated married women over 30, nearly a quarter (23%) of those earning 25% or more of the total family income had no children at all, compared to only 7% of otherwise similar women earning a smaller share of family income (National Center for Health Statistics, 1982).

In short, most women workers are quite unlike the media stereotype of the woman in an elite career who has it all, both on the job and at home. They are typically in segregated jobs with depressed wages, and rely on marriage as well as employment to maintain their income above poverty. Given this reality, we can better understand what work means for women by examining three major occupational categories and the work conditions women experience there.

TEACHERS AND NURSES

These two professions, poorly paid though they are, have long defined the top of the female-sex-typed job structure and thus have been the focus of many girls' career aspirations. They are customarily considered "good jobs for a woman" because of their unusual hours, demand for interpersonal skills, and relatively steady employment prospects. In fact, 96% of all nurses and 84% of elementary teachers are women (U.S. Department of Labor, 1985), proportions that have remained relatively constant for the past 20 years. These are also fields that continue to grow—the absolute number of women nurses rose from 904,000 in 1974 to 1.7 million in 1985 (Berch, 1982; U.S. Department of Labor, 1986). In fact, teaching and nursing are the only two professional jobs among the 20 occupations expected to show the greatest increases between 1978 and 1990 (Leon, 1982).

These occupations are also considered "semiprofessions," however, particularly because of their lack of autonomy (Etzioni, 1969). Unlike doctors and lawyers, teachers and nurses have no control over accreditation, do not set their own fees, have little latitude in how they do their work, and are closely supervised. Stevenson notes that

> nursing is called a "profession," but in fact nurses are employees of hospitals [while] physicians are in partnership with hospitals . . . [doctors] admit "their" patients to hospitals for service according to physician's orders. The physician is also a boss. The physician writes the "orders" and expects them to be implemented [1981: 9].

Doctors also expect nurses' subordination to be manifest in routinely deferential behavior, even to correcting physician's mistakes without challenging their authority. Teachers are the employees of school systems and are directly supervised by school administrators (80% male) to whom they must submit lesson plans (Parelius and Parelius, 1978). Both teachers and nurses are exceptionally poorly paid considering the education, skill, and experience demanded by their jobs.

Not surprisingly, both elementary school teaching and nursing are occupations with high attrition rates—some estimates suggest that one in three women with a nursing degree works in a nonnursing job—as women discover the rewards are not commensurate with the work. Leaving the occupation is one form of resistance, but it is costly for women who have invested in acquiring educational credentials they will no longer use. Women who remain teachers and nurses are increasingly unionizing and bargaining collectively for improved pay and work conditions; indeed such professional unions are one major source of growth in a period of decline for unions.

However, these occupations, like the other female-dominated professions such as librarian and social worker, are disproportionately concentrated in the public sector, where unions alone may not suffice. Cutbacks in funding have significantly reduced the quality and quantity of jobs. Thus women professionals also face a battle to maintain public support for schools and social service agencies (Erie et al., 1983). Pay equity, or comparable worth, is an effort to reduce the discrimination against jobs typically held by women that relies at times on collective bargaining and at times on legislation regarding the wages of public sector jobs (Steinberg, 1983). Because women professionals are so heavily concentrated in public employment, voting and other forms of political action are a way for women to change the conditions of their jobs to better reflect the importance of their work.

The problems of low pay and restricted opportunity are exacerbated for minority women, who have only recently begun to hold more than a tiny number of professional jobs (Sokoloff, 1987a; Higginbotham, 1987). While the Jim Crow system in the South allowed some black women access to teaching jobs in segregated schools, northern schools did not usually employ black teachers and few black women were permitted into nursing in hospitals anywhere in the country (Higginbotham, 1987). Even today, black women professionals are largely employed in positions dealing with black clients, typically in the poorer public schools and city hospitals (Higginbotham, 1987). The large percentage increases of black women in the professions lauded in the media were produced because the initial base was so small that only small increases in absolute numbers were needed to double or triple their representation. Overall, black women are still greatly underrepresented, constituting only 2.2% of all professionals in 1979 (up from 0.6% in 1966; Sokoloff, 1987a).

CLERICAL WORK

More women are working in clerical occupations than in any other occupational group; approximately one in three employed women holds a clerical job (Glenn and Feldberg, 1984). While at the end of World War I women saw working "in business" as a new opportunity (see Gluck, 1976: 77-81) and the mass media worried about the effects of the office on women's morality, today secretarial work is the job to which any woman who can type is steered. The jobs in today's offices however bear only a passing resemblance to the work of yesterday's "business girl."

Clerical jobs have been increasingly divided and specialized as the size of corporations has grown. Routine clerical information processing also expanded as formerly elite services such as banking and insurance came into more widespread use. Fewer clerical workers have the one-on-one relationship with an individual boss that the image of secretary still conjures up (Braverman, 1974). Along with these changes came a decline in clerical wages, so that although office workers earned more than factory workers at the turn of the century, by 1940 this was no longer true. Women office workers, who had been earning 84% of a male factory worker's wage in 1939, were receiving only 70% as much in 1980 (Glenn and Feldberg, 1984).

These changes in the nature of clerical work were already well established as the computerization of the office began. Electronic data processing was widely heralded by managers as improving productivity, reducing monotony, and expanding worker's skills (see Carter, 1987), but it was typically introduced in a fashion that instead turned the office into a paper-handling factory (see Murphree, 1984; Machung, 1984) and increased the routinization of women's work. The first industries to make extensive use of computers, banking and insurance, often constructed large data-processing divisions in cavernous rooms in which women worked on video display terminals where every keystroke was monitored and strict productivity standards enforced (Carter, 1987). The similarities with factory work are striking; even the loss of jobs to low-wage workers overseas has its parallels here, as cheap telecommunications allow banks to export checks for processing in the West Indies and other poor countries (see Business Week, March 15, 1982, cited in Roos and Reskin, 1984). In the United States, word processing is also being sent out to be done at home at piece rates on leased machines as garment manufacturing once was (New York Times, May 20, 1984, cited in Roos and Reskin, 1984). The routine work in office backrooms is increasingly being done by black and other minority women (Murphree, 1984).

Indeed, there is evidence of increasing race stratification within clerical occupations overall (U.S. Department of Labor, 1985: 20-21). Black and other minority women, who were only able to enter clerical occupations in any numbers after 1966, are typically still restricted to the lower-level clerical jobs. For black women under 35, clerical work is now the dominant occupation, as it has long been for white women, but their jobs are disproportionately the increasingly routine and factory-like ones. One study notes that "automation is eliminating precisely those jobs (routine keyboarding, filing) in which black women are present in significant numbers" (U.S. Department of Labor, 1985: 21). More skilled clerical jobs are being moved to the suburbs to take advantage of a more highly educated work force whose members are less likely to be the sole support of their families (U.S. Department of Labor, 1985: 22; Appelbaum, 1987). Black clericals, like black professionals, are also disproportionately likely to work for the government rather than private employers (Wilkie, 1985) and to face losing jobs because of budget cuts.

Appelbaum's study of the insurance industry (1987) and Murphree's of legal secretaries (1984) both indicate that computerization has had some paradoxical effects. Although a relatively few clerical workers (typically white and college educated) have seen their skills and responsibilities expand in the electronic office, access to these new customer service and paralegal jobs is not typically from other clerical positions in the office. While clerical work once led to lower professional jobs, the mobility chances of clerical workers, along with the quality of their jobs, are being substantially reduced in the computerized office (Appelbaum, 1987). Black women use computers, but they are rarely able to use them to move up in the organization (Glenn and Tolbert, 1987).

Computerization may have been introduced to increase management control over productivity, but some women are also finding that it can increase the power they bring to bear. Sacks (1984), in a study of mostly black ward secretaries in a southern hospital, found that the women used their monopoly over knowledge of how patient information was stored on the computer to win a strike. Carter's (1987) study of university clerical workers found that the women in decentralized offices used word-processing systems to simplify tasks they found unpleasant and reduce stress, in contrast to workers in the large, centralized data-processing offices who had little ability to control the conditions of their work and found that the computer made their work stressful and boring.

In general, the clean office environment tends to disguise just how stressful and unpleasant most clerical jobs are. A large West German study of factory and office workers reports, for example, that clerical workers were the most dissatisfied with their jobs, complaining particularly of having to pay sustained attention to avoid errors although the work was boring and the distraction level high. Factory workers, in contrast, could daydream to cope with the monotony of their jobs (Lappe, 1981; Schoell-Schwinghammer, 1979). O'Farrell and Harlan (1984) and Schreiber (1979) in the United States also found clerical workers less satisfied with their work than were women in male-sex-typed craft jobs in the same company. The Framingham Heart Study found the highest levels of stress and stress-related heart disease among workers who had more than one person making work demands on them and little control over the pacing of their own work, both of which were seen as characteristic of clerical work (Pappas, 1986).

In sum, it is important to remember that clerical work is not one occupation, but many. The differentiation among clerical jobs is increasing, along with race and class segregation within the occupational group. The problems that are faced will be different for the women who are doing the most rule-bound, repetitive work than for those who are doing work that is essentially managerial and called clerical primarily because of the gender of the employee.

FACTORY WORK

In contrast to clerical work, women's work on the assembly lines of the world is remarkably uniform. From the earliest days of the industrial revolution, farmers' daughters were sought as cheap labor in the factories, particularly in textile and garment manufacturing (Kessler-Harris, 1982). Women from the farms of England and New England were subsequently replaced by peasant women migrating from Italy, Ireland, Russia, and Greece. This continues today, although the farms now are more likely to have been in the Azores, the Philippines, Puerto Rico, or the West Indies (Sacks, 1984). Factory work is particularly likely to be consigned to immigrant women: Turkish women in West Germany, Jamaicans and Indians in England, Portuguese, Hispanic, and Asian women in the United States. Despite heavy losses of such jobs to lower-wage countries, factory work for U.S. women is also still heavily garment manufacturing; sewer/stitcher is the eleventh largest occupation for women in the United States, and one in four women factory workers is employed in the garment industry (U.S. Department of Labor, 1986). Electronics assembly has now joined in exploiting this same pool of economically vulnerable women workers.

Several studies done in different countries present a remarkably consistent picture of life on the assembly line in which several key features stand out. First, the work women do is very skilled even though it is officially labeled unskilled and paid accordingly. Lamphere, doing participant observation in a New England factory, found she was expected to set sleeves in 76 dozen shirts a day just to make the minimum wage (1984: 250); it took most women months to learn to work this fast and even longer before they could "make money" on piece rates by performing even faster. Cavendish, a participant observer in England, noted the complex skills expected of women on the assembly line actually took longer to acquire than those of the male skilled workers (1982).

The men in these factories also had significantly better working conditions. Their jobs allowed them to interrupt their work for an occasional cigarette, to move around more freely, and to slow down sometimes without financial penalty, while the women lost money every second they were not working at top speed (Cavendish, 1982; Rosen, 1987; Coyle, 1982). Women are disproportionately concentrated in jobs that demand a pace faster than an operation per minute—that is, the most stressful and dissatisfying assembly line work (Lappe, 1981; Schoell-Schwinghammer, 1979).

Despite this, women factory workers report considerable satisfaction with other aspects of their work. Being able to earn more money than they could otherwise is an important reward. Even when the pay is not objectively very much, these workers often have few if any other alternatives (Lamphere, 1984; Weiner and Green, 1984). For other workers, fortunate enough to be in unionized shops, earnings are greater in the factory than they would be in an office or restaurant (Rosen, 1987). Psychological rewards are also important, even though they come mixed with costs (Becker-Schmidt et al., 1984; Ferree, 1976). The ambivalence of women factory workers toward their jobs reflects both satisfaction of being able to do their difficult jobs well and anger at having their skills exploited (see Ferree, 1985, for a fuller discussion).

The resistance of women workers to employer demands is another common theme in the factory studies. Contrary to the stereotype of working-class and immigrant women as a docile work force, these women actively resist speed ups and other attacks on their wages and working conditions (Lamphere, 1984; Coyle et al., 1984; Frankel, 1984; Shapiro-Perl, 1984; Hoel, 1982; Cavendish, 1982). Some resistance is simply part of the daily routine of struggle on the shop floor (e.g., Lamphere, 1984), while in other cases it involves organizing a union (e.g., Coyle et al., 1984) or staging a walkout or strike (e.g., Cavendish, 1982). Women on the global assembly line are neither so family-oriented that they are indifferent to the conditions of their paid job nor so effectively socialized into passivity that they are unwilling to express their anger and act assertively when necessary.

Another common theme, however, is the way in which employers take advantage of the women's needs both to earn an income and to care for their children. Because there are few if any social services to make the domestic burden more manageable, women are forced to negotiate individually for working conditions they can handle. Thus an "understanding employer" who allows women occasionally to take time off to care for sick children (without pay, of course, but also without being fired for absenteeism) is a necessity for these women (Freeman, 1982). The paternalism involved in such individual arrangements can be used to hamper unionization, both by making women grateful to their employers for being so "accommodating" and by threatening to revoke such "special treatment" in the rules negotiated under the contract (Eckart et al., 1979; Rosen, 1987; Fernandez-Kelly, 1984). Employers who depend on a female labor force may also offer collective benefits that are cheap for them (nonstandard hours such as "mother's shifts" or on-site child care) that make their workers unwilling to risk their jobs even for the prospect of higher pay. This structural dependence of working mothers on their employers should not be confused with an attitude of indifference to unions or to their own interests.

A final commonality found in these studies is the racial and ethnic diversity of the female factory work force and how this is used by employers to keep workers apart. Newer immigrant groups or ethnic minorities are often settled in the most demanding and poorly paid jobs in the plant (Rosen, 1987; Cavendish, 1982; Eckart et al., 1979) and in the least desirable factories (Rosen, 1987). Women were often hired on the recommendation of workers already in the job, which not only contributed to the segregation by ethnic group but also strengthened the paternalistic tie between workers and their employer (Hoel, 1982; Fernandez-Kelly, 1984). Equally common, however, in these accounts are the women's own efforts to overcome such divisions. New immigrants, often perceived as rate-busters, are schooled to common production norms (Lamphere, 1984), and shared social activities are also used to reduce destructive competition between individuals and groups (Cavendish, 1982; Zavell, 1985).

In sum, the limited occupational options available to women factory workers render them a highly exploitable work force. This, rather than supposedly feminine attributes of passivity and dependence, forces them to accept low pay for their skilled labor and hard working conditions. However, women also find ways to resist, which sometimes involves unions. Particularly in the newer electronics assembly lines, women are beginning to organize to prevent health risks that are increasingly being identified there (see Fuentes and Ehrenreich, 1983; Spake, 1986). Even as they fight these conditions, ever more employers are fleeing to the Third World, creating new groups of exploited women workers abroad and devastating losses of jobs at home (Rosen, 1987).

For factory women, unemployment can be a particularly serious problem. The economic costs to women of losing a factory job seem to be greater than those men suffer. Snyder and Nowak (1984) found that one or two years after losing their jobs 41% of women (vs. 58% of men) had found alternate employment; nearly half (47%) of the reemployed men were able to stay craft workers or operatives but only 15% of the women could. The vast majority (70%) were forced into sales or service jobs in which they were able to earn only half of what they did in the factory (Snyder and Nowak, 1984). Thus these women's feelings of vulnerability and dependence are no figment of their imaginations. The psychological costs of unemployment for women, most of whom have worked for pay and contributed to the economic support of their families virtually all of their lives, are not only very significant (Voydanoff, 1983; Snyder and Nowak, 1984; Perrucci et al., 1985), but are unacknowledged by policymakers, the media, and often the women's own families. While life on the assembly line is hard, most of these women clearly do not prefer to leave the labor force for a life of full-time housework, and they rely on the psychological as well as the economic rewards of their jobs (Rosen, 1987; Shamir, 1985).

To summarize briefly the three previous sections we can note that women in female-sex-typed occupations are not without ambition and do not passively accept discrimination and the devaluation of their jobs. But the alternatives open to them are seriously limited by class and race as well as by their gender. Within the range of options open to them, the jobs they have contribute psychologically as well as financially to their lives; women fear losing these jobs. Their struggle to improve their pay and work conditions takes place within a context in which the jobs themselves are threatened by budget cuts, automation, and employer flight to low-wage countries. To better understand what jobs mean to women, we turn now to consider some of the internal dynamics of three different work places: male-sex-typed jobs, female-sex-typed jobs, and unpaid work at home.

DESEGREGATING BLUE-COLLAR JOBS

For some women the rewards of work may be substantially greater in jobs that have been customarily reserved for men. The progress women have made in entering the male-dominated elite professions has been substantially greater in recent years than their success in entering male-dominated blue-collar jobs. While percentage of women has gone from 7% to 17% of doctors, 4% to 18% of lawyers, and even .8% to 6.8% of engineers between 1960 and 1985, the proportion of women carpenters has risen from only .3% to 1.2% in the same period (U.S. Bureau of the Census, 1960, 1980; U.S. Department of Labor, 1986).

There are several reasons for this difference. First, access to the elite professions is controlled primarily by educational credentialing, and university admissions have been influenced directly by the civil rights and women's movements (see Haignere, 1981, for the case of medical schools). Access to skilled craft jobs is via union apprenticeship and shop floor selection, which are less publicly visible processes. Second, the relative size of the crafts compared to the professions makes any change process slower. Since there are two and a half times as many carpenters as doctors, the absolute number of new women needed in the occupation to produce a similar proportional change is considerably greater (U.S. Department of Labor, 1986). Third, the male-sex-typed professions have expanded while the male crafts have not. For example, the total number of lawyers nearly tripled between 1970 and 1985, and the number of women lawyers increased tenfold, but the construction trades continue to employ about the same number of people as 15 years ago. Finally, the ideological basis of gender segregation in the elite professions is the belief in sex differences in intelligence, while the legitimation of gender segregation in blue-collar jobs is primarily the belief in sex differences in strength and hence in the ability to do the work demanded. The former belief has not disappeared but is certainly reduced in scope and salience (see Sayers, 1982), while the latter remains very strong.

Additionally, women both in the professions and in the crafts face a variety of forms of male resistance to gender integration. Roos and Reskin (1984) outline three basic forms: internal resegregation within a nominally integrated occupation; male flight from desegregating jobs, producing resegregation along new lines; and direct resistance in the form of new barriers to entry or harassment of new entrants. Changes in economic opportunities and occupational structures greatly affect men's willingness and ability to engage in any of these strategies. Thus jobs that are being deskilled by the introduction of new technologies or changes in the organization of work may be seen as particularly appropriate for women to enter, while men who are nominally in the same occupation have the more rewarding jobs (see Carter and Carter, 1981; Donato and Roos, 1987; Reskin and Roos, 1987; O'Farrell and Harlan, 1984).

In blue-collar jobs, both direct resistance and resegregation are much in evidence. Hacker (1979), Schreiber (1979), Remy and Sawers (1984), and Deaux and Ullman (1983) all describe management responses to court-mandated affirmative action plans that indicate how such programs may be effectively circumvented on the shop floor. In some cases, women were funnelled into precisely those lower-level craft jobs that were already being deskilled by new technology and were soon to be eliminated entirely, such as phone installer (Hacker, 1979; Schreiber, 1979). Managers also used union-mandated seniority lists to place women in positions where they would be particularly vulnerable to layoffs. In a study of job histories conducted for a sex discrimination case, I found women industrial painters being promoted to new job categories just before layoffs from these jobs began (Ferree, n.d.; see Remy and Sawers, 1984, for examples in meatpacking). In general, the very recent access of women to these blue-collar jobs means that little job protection is available in cases of economic downturn. Deaux and Ullman (1983) found that virtually all the positions women had attained in the steel industry in the 1970s were eliminated by the early 1980s.

There is also considerable evidence that stereotyping guides the resegregation of some blue-collar work. Women who have entered formerly all-male factories find themselves being disproportionately assigned to janitorial work, even though this work is hard, heavy, and hot (Deaux and Ullman, 1983; Padavic and Reskin, 1986; Ferree, n.d.). Despite its high physical demands, this work is less well paid and of lower status than most of the factory jobs with equal skill levels (e.g., mechanics' helper, driver, painter). Women clearly like these cleaning jobs less than the other male-sex-typed factory work they enter, even though the high pay relative to most female-sex-typed jobs makes women stay in them (Deaux and Ullman, 1983; see Padavic and Reskin, 1986). Job training programs also tend to place women in the lowest paying and most sex-typed jobs, even when trainees have experience in and have expressed a preference for male-sex-typed work (see Waite and Berryman, 1984, on the CETA program).

Women entering formerly all-male jobs and work places also frequently experience sexual and other forms of harassment from their male coworkers (Gruber and Bjorn, 1982; Walshok, 1981; O'Farrell and Harlan, 1982). While the harassment clearly has a negative impact on women's satisfaction with their work and desire to stay in the job, it is typically outweighed by their greater satisfaction with the high pay and varied work content of these jobs (O'Farrell and Harlan, 1982; Deaux and Ullman, 1983; Gruber and Bjorn, 1982; Walshok, 1981). Thus the women not only report that they are satisfied with their jobs in these male-dominated fields but seem willing to fight their employers and their male coworkers, if necessary, to keep them.

WOMEN'S WORK CULTURE

Because most women continue to work in female-sex-typed jobs, they also work primarily with other women. The ties among women created in the work place, and the conflicts between women also generated there, reflect structural demands for cooperation, competition, and subordination, as well as the women's own efforts to resist these demands (Becker-Schmidt et al., 1984; Sacks, 1984). These connections and conflicts form an important part of women's work experience.

Studies of several different occupations have shown some interesting commonalities in women's work culture. Studies of clerical (Goldberg, 1983; Glenn and Feldberg, 1984), restaurant (Creighton, 1982), and factory workers (Cavendish, 1982; Lamphere, 1984; Fernandez-Kelly, 1984; Zavella, 1985) have all noted that women make a point of celebrating family events, such as births and engagements, with parties and gifts for their coworkers. Women workers also share stories and photographs that help make their personal lives less private and highlight common features of their experience despite the diversity of class and ethnicity that is found in these work places. With their coworkers women affirm their common status as women and as workers and look for equal respect for both aspects of their lives (Goldberg, 1983). They also make efforts to overcome racial or ethnic animosities that interfere with their ability to achieve the cooperation they need to do their jobs effectively and to resist speed ups (Lamphere, 1984; Shapiro-Perl, 1984; Cavendish, 1982).

The resultant work culture blurs the boundaries between friendship and work relations (Creighton, 1982). In cases where hiring has been done by recruiting friends and relatives of employees (e.g., Fernandez-Kelly, 1984; Hoel, 1982) or where a single employer dominates a community (e.g., Bryant and Perkins, 1982) the overlap between kinship and work ties will also be high from the start. The close occupational community that results can be a source of satisfaction, though one that is often exaggerated in descriptions of women's work (O'Farrell and Harlan, 1984). It may also have paradoxical effects on women's willingness to unionize and to sustain a strike over time. Fear of risking friendships over differences of opinion about the efficacy of joining a union may impede organizing (Creighton, 1982), but once organized these same friendships and kin ties help maintain militancy (Turbin, 1984; Ladd-Taylor, 1985; Sacks, 1984).

In contrast to the solidarity evident in lateral ties among women, the conflict between women workers and women bosses is apparently heightened when this status division falls along racial lines. Several sensitive studies of domestic workers have shown the diversity of ways in which white women employers deny the common gender status they share with their maids as part of their general failure to respect their nonwhite employee as a human being (Dill, 1980; Kaplan, 1984; Glenn, 1987; Rollins, 1985). Pretending that the employer's family is the only family the domestic worker has, for example, facilitates making demands for weekend or night work. When the domestic worker's family is recognized, it is often a means of symbolically affirming its subordination and of keeping her wages down, as when the employer compensates extra work with leftover food or castoff clothing. Although both housewife and servant are actually subordinated to the male head of household, the female employer tries to improve her own status at the domestic worker's expense through impressing her husband with an exaggeratedly perfect standard of cleanliness or by displays of arbitrary authority. Rather than shared work, the labor of housework becomes divided into "management" and actual performance, and the female employer attempts to appropriate the credit for knowing how the tasks should be done while denying and demeaning the actual expertise of the domestic worker.

Racial and ethnic cleavages are used to facilitate this process of differentiation in the face of the gender-based assignment of responsibility for housework that the women actually have in common. Stereotyping is perpetuated by the female employer's desire not to know about the employee's family life, just as it is broken down on the factory floor by the women workers' shared celebrations of life events. The actual powerlessness of the female employer is particularly evident to the domestic worker when she is incapable of preventing her husband from sexually harassing "her" employee, a problem that certainly did not end with the demise of slavery. In this situation, and presumably in others where women supervise other women on behalf of men (such as typing pools), this derivative female authority is often exercised in particularly demeaning ways, perhaps as an effort to disguise its limited scope (see Kanter, 1977).

In sum, the contrast between the racial solidarity evident in many factories and offices and the exploitation of the ethnic cleavage in domestic work highlights the fact that sisterhood among women is not automatic. Achieving solidarity among women rests in part on structures that promote real economic and social equality and in part on the active strategies of women workers to affirm their commonalities.

HOUSEWORK: A LABOR OF LOVE?

Awareness of domestic work as a point of conflict between affluent white women and women of racial and ethnic minority groups also suggests greater caution in generalizing about women's attitudes toward housework. Palmer (1984) suggests that black women historically were likely to see housework primarily as a skilled craft, and to struggle to get these skills formally certified and to control access to the craft, thereby increasing their pay and respect. White women, in contrast, tended to see housework in terms of science and management and to try to improve their status by rationalizing and regulating the work, even when the only persons they were managing were themselves. This latter perspective on housework dominates the historical accounts of the transformation of women's work in the home in the age of industrialization (Strasser, 1982; Cowan, 1983).

Despite possible changes in women's attitudes toward housework, the historical continuity in women's actual responsibility for housework is exceptionally high. Even though the tasks have changed and the amount of arduous physical labor has declined, the total time women actually spend on housework has remained relatively constant from the 1920s to the present (Vanek, 1979). Hours devoted to physical care of children have, of course, decreased along with the number of children, but as with housework, increased demands for higher standards of achievement have tended to keep the total time spend in child care high. Both housework and child care also remain overwhelmingly the woman's responsibility, as studies repeatedly show women doing virtually all the traditionally female tasks around the home (or about 80% of the total housework) as well as the child care (Meissner et al., 1975; Walker and Woods, 1976; Berk, 1985; Michelson, 1985).

Most of the current evidence also shows no indication that men are taking on any significant proportion of the housework and child care when their wives are employed, even full time (Berk, 1985; Michelson, 1985; Hess and Sussman, 1985), although some researchers have found indications that some men are doing more, at least under certain conditions (Pleck, 1979; Staines and Pleck, 1983; Huber and Spitze, 1981; Hood, 1983; Ferree, 1987). Families that manage child care by working alternate shifts and couples with more equal earnings are more likely to experience an increase in husband's domestic work. In almost all cases, only full-time employment among wives had any impact on men's chores, and even then the actual increases seem quite modest.

Women's experience of housework as work flatly contradicts the classic functionalist equation of work in the home with expressive activity and work for pay with instrumental task-oriented behavior (Parsons and Bales, 1956). Women's concerns with housework are often those common to any work experience: The rewarding elements of autonomy and intrinsic satisfaction with doing a hard job well are mixed with negative aspects such as monotony, fragmentation of tasks, and excessive stress (Ferree, 1985). While some critics have proposed reducing dissatisfaction by making housework a paid job (e.g., Leghorn and Warrior, 1975), others locate the roots of women's ambivalence in the nature of the work itself, its significance as a source of pride and identity as well as symbolic subordination, and the structural dependence of housewives on the person (or state) that provides the income that makes it possible (Becker-Schmidt et al., 1984; Eckart et al., 1979; Ferree, 1980; Lopate, 1974).

Rather than simply liking or hating housework, most women seem to find it sometimes a welcome refuge from some of the more unpleasant aspects of capitalist work relations: One knows the people for whom one is producing, the work process is more self-regulated, and there may be respect and appreciation expressed for the quality of one's work. Conversely, these same elements may sometimes be largely lacking from housework, and it has particular stresses of its own, including the lack of financial recognition as work, the unending nature of the responsibilities, and the absence of close coworkers (see also Ferree, 1976, 1980, 1985).

Despite such problems, studies of working-class women conducted over the past 30 years consistently show relatively high levels of actual employment as well as considerable interest in working for pay among women who work at home full time (e.g., Komarovsky, 1962; Gavron, 1966; Berger, 1968; Rubin, 1976; Ferree, 1976; Becker-Schmidt et al., 1984), even though the demeaning yet demanding character of the jobs available to working-class women would seem to make a preference for housework seem reasonable, perhaps even inevitable (see Ferree, 1984). Instead, these women largely feel ambivalent about both their paid and unpaid work. Their contradictory emotions—pride and pleasure as well as dismay and anger—are not readily translated into "work commitment" (Levitan and Johnson, 1982) or its opposite. For example, looking forward to "someday" being able to quit may, like the prospect of retirement for blue-collar men, be a way of dealing with the stress of daily labor (Eckart et al., 1979), even when the idea of "sitting home" for the rest of their lives may be quite unappealing (Ferree, 1976; Gavron, 1966; Rosen, 1987). Full-time housework, like the paid jobs available, has strongly negative features as well as unique rewards (Luxton, 1980).

Despite women's ambivalence toward housework, the division of labor in the home is sometimes studied as if it were a simple indicator of the balance of power in the family (e.g., Hartmann, 1981; see Berk, 1985: chap. 1). While this is surely an oversimplification, it is also true that power relations do affect who does the housework. There is some evidence, for example, that how much housework men take on is more influenced by the relative equality of earnings between husband and wife than by their ideological support for women's equality (Heer, 1958; Hiller, 1980). This would mean that working-class women are at least as likely to be able to achieve a somewhat more egalitarian division of labor in the home as middle- or upper-middle-class women.

CLASS, GENDER, AND WOMEN'S EMPLOYMENT

Recent years have seen a move away from dichotomous "job" and "gender" models of work for men and women, respectively, and toward a more integrated picture of paid work and family responsibilities for both (see Feldberg and Glenn, 1979; Pleck, 1985; Berheide and Chow, 1983). However, the implicit model of households used in much of this research remains biased toward the atypical woman in one of the elite professions. This model pervades both the social sciences and the mass media, and it distorts our thinking about the meaning of paid employment for women (Benenson, 1984). Because women's on-the-job experiences are treated as unequivocally positive and housework as unidimensionally burdensome, it is assumed that a more supportive relationship at home would remove the last obstacles ("role conflict" and "the double day") to women's total enjoyment of full-time careers. This in turn is taken to be the hallmark of the nontraditional, even "liberated," woman. Since it is the woman in an elite career who is seen as exemplifying independence and innovation, the real changes that most working women are experiencing are ignored or trivialized (e.g., Harding, 1981).

As Benenson (1984) also points out, this model treats behavior that violates stereotypes of femininity as an elite innovation that might gradually diffuse downward rather than as one of the ways in which working-class women and women of color have always coped with the difficulties of their lives. Such women have never had the luxury of conforming to white middle-class ideals, either of paid employment or of housework. Ordinary women in sex- and race-segregated jobs have always had to innovate strategies for combining both forms of labor, for resisting the demands of husbands and employers, for redefining femininity to reflect the realities of their lives, including celebrating the strength and skills of women. For such women, calling behavior that better accords with feminist ideals of independence and accomplishment "nontraditional" flies in the face of the historical record and distorts the picture of their working lives today.

The class-biased model of employment prevalent in the social sciences also tends to compare working-class women not to working-class men, but to those women in the professions who most closely conform to male professionals in their career orientation and commitment. Placing career needs and goals in central position is then often taken as a model of independence for women, and working-class women are seen as deficient. The real economic dependencies of being a wage earner are thus overlooked, as are the ways in which families may be able to cooperate to resist the demands of employers (Rapp, 1982). As we have seen, most women workers need to rely on their families in order to sustain their lives and continue to work, but family additionally provides most of the rewards that make work meaningful, for men as well as for women.

However psychologically important, most women's jobs are not careers. As Komarovsky put it, "a good job is a means to a good living, but achievement in a specialized vocation is not the measure of a person's worth, not even for a man" (1962: 57). Blue-collar women are proud of their accomplishments on the job and they are proud of their role as family providers, alone or in conjunction with their husbands (Walshok, 1981; Rosen, 1987). Working-class women see their work as something good for them as well as their families (Rubin, 1981) and define themselves as breadwinners even when they have husbands who also support the family (Rosen, 1987). Despite all this, they clearly do not have the same kind of work commitment that professional women have—and they should not be expected to acquire it just to measure up to a class-biased standard of "nontraditionality."

However, social policy, guided by the fictitious dichotomy between women who want to work and women who have to work, is typically directed at ensuring women a "choice" and so protecting them from the presumably evil necessity of employment. This perpetuates the notion that it is the male alone who is responsible for financial support, even if he does not much like his job either. Exploitation is assessed not from the characteristics of women's work itself, which is rarely studied, but from the simple fact of women's employment at all (Feldberg and Glenn, 1979). Women stuck in bad jobs are not seen as entitled to better work conditions but as needing to be "protected" from working for pay at all (e.g., Kreps, 1972).

Women are active today, as they have been throughout the history of this country, in trying to make a better life for themselves as well as for their families. In this effort they primarily need to improve the conditions of their jobs, not to have the illusion of choice thrust upon them. The feminist movement will have to be much more active in policy areas such as affordable child care and equitable wages for part-time workers if it wishes to be a real representative of all women's interests. Social science research will also have to change some of its basic concepts if its theories are to provide adequately for the experiences of working-class women and women of color. Such women may be unconventional, but they are hardly nontraditional. Instead, the tradition of resistance, strong in many black and working-class families, is an important resource for women who are seeking not merely change but a lasting improvement in their status. By adopting a perspective on women's work that highlights these experiences, social science research may develop insights that may be of some use to women in these struggles.

REFERENCES

APPELBAUM, E. (1987) "Technology and the redesign of work in the insurance industry," in B. Wright et al. (eds.) Transformations: Women, Work and Technology. Ann Arbor: University of Michigan Press.

BECKER-SCHMIDT, R. (1980) "Widerspruechliche Realitaet und Ambivalenz: Arbeitserfahrungen von Frauen in Fabrik und Familie." Koelner Zeitschrift fuer Soziologie und Sozialpsychologie 32: 705-725.

BECKER-SCHMIDT, R., G. A. KNAPP, B. SCHMIDT (1984) Eines ist zu weing—Beides ist zu viel. Bonn: Verlag Neue Gesellschaft.

BENENSON, H. (1984) "Women's occupational and family achievement in the U.S. class system: A critique of the dual-career family analysis." British Journal of Sociology 35, 1: 19-41.

BENSON, S. (1984) "Women in retail sales work: The continuing dilemma of service," pp. 113-123 in K. Sacks and D. Remy (eds.) My Troubles Are Going to Have Trouble with Me: Everyday Trials and Triumphs of Women Workers. New Brunswick, NJ: Rutgers University Press.

BERCH, B. (1982) The Endless Day: The Political Economy of Women and Work. New York: Harcourt Brace Jovanovich.

BERGER, B. (1968) Working Class Suburb: A Study of Auto Workers in Suburbia. Berkeley: University of California Press.

BERHEIDE, C. W. and E. CHOW (1983) "The interdependence of family and work: Some models and proposals." Presented at the American Sociological Association meetings, Detroit, Michigan.

BERK, S. (1985) The Gender Factory: The Apportionment of Work in American Households. New York: Plenum.

BERRYMAN, S. and L. WAITE (1987) "Young women's choice of occupations non-traditional for their sex," in C. Bose and G. Spitze (eds.) Ingredients for Women's Employment Policy, Albany: SUNY Press.

BIELBY, W. and J. BARON (1984) "A woman's place is with other women: Sex segregation within organizations," pp. 27-55 in B. Reskin (ed.) Sex Segregation in the Workplace: Trends, Explanations, Remedies. Washington, DC: National Academy Press.

BLAU, F. (1984) "Women in the labor force: An overview," pp. 297-315 in J. Freeman (ed.) Women: A Feminist Perspective. Palo Alto, CA: Mayfield.

BRAVERMAN, H. (1974) Labor and Monopoly Capital. New York: Monthly Review Press.

BRYANT, C. and K. PERKINS (1982) "Containing work disaffection: The poultry processing worker," pp. 199-212 in P. Stewart and M. Cantor (eds.) Varieties of Work Experience. Newbury Park, CA: Sage.

BURRIS, V. and A. WHARTON (1982) "Sex segregation in the US labor force." Review of Radical Political Economics 14: 43-56.

CANTOR, M. and B. LAURIE (1977) Class, Sex and the Woman Worker. Westport, CT: Greenwood.

CARTER, V. (1987) "Office technology and relations of control in clerical work organization," in B. Wright et al. (eds.) Women, Work and Technology: Transformations. Ann Arbor: University of Michigan Press.

CARTER, M. and S. CARTER (1981) "Women's recent progress in the professions, or women get a ticket to ride after the gravy train has left the station." Feminist Studies 7 (Fall): 476-504.

CAVENDISH, R. (1982) Women on the Line. Boston: Routledge & Kegan Paul.

COWAN, R. S. (1983) More Work for Mother: The Ironies of Household Technology from the Open Hearth to the Microwave. New York: Basic Books.

COYLE, A. (1982) "Sex and skill in the organization of the clothing industry," pp. 10-16 in J. West (ed.) Work, Women and the Labour Market. London: Routledge & Kegan Paul.

COYLE, L., B. HERSHATTER, and E. HONIG (1984) "Women at Farah: An unfinished story," pp. 227-277 in J. Jensen and L. A. Davidson (eds.) A Needle, a Bobbin, a Strike: Women Needleworkers in America. Philadelphia: Temple University Press.

CREIGHTON, H. (1982) "Tied by double apron strings: Female work culture and organization in a restaurant," Insurgent Sociologist 11, 3: 59-64.

DEAUX, K. and J. ULLMAN (1983) Women of Steel: Female Blue-Collar Workers in the Basic Steel Industry. New York: Praeger.

DILL, B. T. (1980) "The means to put my children through: Childrearing goals and strategies among black female domestic servants," pp. 107-123 in L. Rodgers-Rose (ed.) The Black Woman. Newbury Park, CA: Sage.

DONATO, K. and P. ROOS (1987) "Gender and earnings inequality among computer specialists," in B. Wright et al. (eds.) Women, Work and Technology: Transformations. Ann Arbor: University of Michigan Press.

ECKART, C., U. JAERISCH, and H. KRAMER (1979) Frauenarbeit in Familie und Fabrik, Forschungsbericht des Institutes fuer Sozialforschung. Frankfurt a/M: Campus Verlag.

ERIE, S., M. REIN, and B. WIGET (1983) "Women and the Reagan revolution: Thermidor for the social welfare economy," pp. 94-119 in I. Diamond (ed.) Families, Politics and Public Policy. New York: Longman.

ETIZIONI, A. [ed.] (1969) The Semi-Professionals and Their Organization: Teachers, Nurses, Social Workers. New York: Free Press.

FELDBERG, R. and E. GLENN (1979) "Male and female: Job versus gender models in the sociology of work." Social Problems 26: 524-538.

FERNANDEZ-KELLY, M. P. (1984) "Maquiladoras: The view from the inside," pp. 229-246 in K. Sacks and D. Remy (eds.) My Troubles Are Going to Have Trouble With Me: Everyday

Trials and Triumphs of Women Workers. New Brunswick, NJ: Rutgers University Press.

FERREE, M. M. (1976) "Working-class jobs: Paid work and housework as sources of satisfaction." Social Problems 23, 4: 431-441.

FERREE, M. M. (1980) "Satisfaction and housework: The social context," pp. 89-112 in S. F. Berk (ed.) Women and Household Labor. Newbury Park, CA: Sage.

FERREE, M. M. (1984) "Sacrifice, satisfaction and social change," pp. 61-79 in K. Sacks and D. Remy (eds.) My Troubles Are Going to Have Trouble With Me: Everyday Trials and Triumphs of Women Workers. New Brunswick, NJ: Rutgers University Press.

FERREE, M. M. (1985) "Between two worlds: German feminist approaches to working class women and work." Signs 10, 3: 517-536.

FERREE, M. M. (1987) "The superwoman syndrome," in C. Bose et al. (eds.) Hidden Aspects of Women's Work. New York: Praeger.

FERREE, M. M. (n.d.) Unpublished Report to Connecticut Women's Education and Legal Fund.

FOX, M. F. and S. HESSE-BIBER (1984) Women at Work. Palo Alto, CA: Mayfield.

FRANKEL, L. (1984) "Southern textile women: Generations of survival and struggle," pp. 39-59 in K. Sacks and D. Remy (eds.) My Troubles are Going to Have Trouble With Me: Everyday Trials and Triumphs of Women Workers. New Brunswick, NJ: Rutgers University Press.

FREEMAN, C. (1982) "The 'understanding' employer," pp. 135-153 in J. West (ed.) Work, Women and the Labour Market. London: Routledge & Kegan Paul.

FUENTES, A. and B. EHRENREICH (1983) Women in the Global Factory. New York: Institute for New Communications.

GAVRON, H. (1966) The Captive Wife: Conflicts of Housebound Mothers. London: Routledge & Kegan Paul.

GERSON, K. (1985) Hard Choices: How Women Decide about Work, Career, and Motherhood. Berkeley: University of California Press.

GLENN, E. N. (1987) "Labor migration and women's household work: Japanese-American women in the pre-war period," in C. Bose and G. Spitze (eds.) Ingredients for Women's Employment Policy. Albany: SUNY Press.

GLENN, E. and R. FELDBERG (1984) "Clerical work: The female occupation," pp. 316-336 in J. Freeman (ed.) Women: A Feminist Perspective. Palo Alto, Ca: Mayfield.

GLENN, E. and C. TOLBERT (1987) "Technology and emerging patterns of stratification for women of color: Race and gender segregation in computer occupations," in B. Wright et al. (eds.) Women, Work, and Technology: Transformations. Ann Arbor: University of Michigan Press.

GLUCK, S. [ed.] (1976) From Parlor to Prison: Five American Suffragists Talk About Their Lives. New York: Vintage.

GOLDBERG, R. (1983) Organizing Women Office Workers: Dissatisfaction, Consciousness, and Action. New York: Praeger.

GRUBER, J. E. and L. BJORN (1982) "Blue-collar blues: The sexual harassment of women auto workers." Work and Occupations 9, 3: 271-298.

HACKER, S. (1979) "Sex stratification, technological and organizational change: A longitudinal case study of AT&T." Social Problems 26: 539-557.

HAIGNERE, L. (1981) "Admission of women to medical schools: A study of organizational response to social movement and public policy pressures." Ph.D. dissertation, University of Connecticut, Storrs.

HARDING, S. (1981) "Family reform movements: Recent feminism and its opposition." Feminist Studies 7(1): 57-76.

HARKESS, S. (1985) "Women's occupational experiences in the 1970s: Sociology and economics." Signs 10, 3: 495-516.

HARTMANN, H. (1981) "The family as the locus of gender, class, and political struggle." Signs 6, 3: 366-394.

HAYGHE, H. (1986) "Rise in mothers' labor force activity includes those with infants." Monthly Labor Review 109, 2: 43-45.

HEER, D. (1958) "Dominance and the working wife." Social Forces 36, 4: 341-347.

HESS, B. and M. SUSSMAN (1984) Women and the Family: Two Decades of Change. New York: Hayworth Press.

HEWLETT, S. (1986) A Lesser Life: The Myth of Women's Liberation in America. New York: Morrow.

HIGGINBOTHAM, E. (1987) "Employment for black professional women in the twentieth century," in C. Bose and G. Spitze (eds.) Ingredients for Women's Employment Policy. Albany: SUNY Press.

HILLER, D. (1980) "Determinants of household and childcare task-sharing." Presented at the American Sociological Association meetings, New York.

HOEL, B. (1982) "Contemporary clothing 'sweatshops': Asian female labour and collective organization," pp. 80-98 in J. West (ed.) Work, Women and the Labour Market. London: Routledge & Kegan Paul.

HOOD, J. (1983) Becoming a Two-Job Family. New York: Praeger.

HUBER, J. and G. SPITZE (1981) "Wives' employment, household behaviors, and sex-role attitudes." Social Forces 60: 150-169.

KANTER, R. M. (1977) Men and Women of the Corporation. New York: Basic Books.

KAPLAN, E. B. (1984) "Competition, struggle, and strife: The domestic worker and the housewife." Presented at the American Sociological Association meetings, San Antonio, Texas.

KATZMAN, D. (1981) Seven Days a Week: Women and Domestic Service in Industrializing America. Urbana: University of Illinois Press.

KESSLER-HARRIS, A. (1981) Women Have Always Worked. Old Westburg, NY: Feminist Press.

KESSLER-HARRIS, A. (1982) Out to Work: A History of Wage-earning Women in the United States. New York: Oxford University Press.

KOMAROVSKY, M. (1962) Blue Collar Marriage. New York: Random House.

KREPS, J. (1972) "Do all women want to work?" pp. 225-238 in L. K. Howe (ed.) The Future of the Family. New York: Simon & Schuster.

LADD-TAYLOR, M. (1985) "Women workers and the Yale strike." Feminist Studies 11, 3: 465-489.

LAMPHERE, L. (1985) "Bringing the family to work: Women's culture on the shop floor." Feminist Studies 11, 3: 519-540.

LAMPHERE, L. (1984) "On the shop floor: Multi-ethnic unity against the conglomerate," pp. 247-263 in K. Sacks and D. Remy (eds.) My Troubles Are Going to Have Trouble With Me: Everyday Trials and Triumphs of Women Workers. New Brunswick, NJ: Rutgers University Press.

LAPPE, L. (1981) Die Arbeitssituation erwerbstaetiger Frauen: Geschlechtsspezifische Arbeitsmarktsegmantation und ihre Folgen. Frankfurt a/M: Campus Verlag.

LEGHORN, L. and B. WARRIOR (1975) The Houseworker's Handbook. Cambridge, MA: Women's Center.

LEON, C. (1982) "Occupational winners and losers, 1972-80." Monthly Labor Review (June): 18-28.

LEVITAN, S. and C. JOHNSON (1982) Second Thoughts on Work. Kalamazoo, MI: Upjohn Institute.

LOPATE, C. (1974) "Pay for housework?" Social Policy 5 (Sept./Oct.): 27-31.

LUXTON, M. (1980) More Than a Labor of Love: Three Generations of Women's Work in the Home. Toronto: Women's Educational Press.

MACHUNG, A. (1984) "Word processing: Forward for business, backward for women," pp. 124-139 in K. Sacks and D. Remy (eds.) My Troubles Are Going to Have Trouble With Me:

Everyday Trials and Triumphs of Women Workers. New Brunswick, NJ: Rutgers University Press.

MARCIANO, T. (1986) "Why did poverty 'feminize' when women have always been poor?" Presented at the American Sociological Association meeting, New York.

MATTHAEI, J. (1982) An Economic History of Women in America. New York: Schocken.

MEISSNER, M., E. HUMPHRIES, S. MEIS, and W. SCHEU (1975) "No exit for wives: Sexual division of labor and the cumulation of household demands." Canadian Review of Sociology and Anthropology 12: 424-439.

MICHELSON, W. (1985) From Sun to Sun: Daily Obligations and Community Structure in the Lives of Employed Women and their Families. Totowa, NJ: Rowman & Allenheld.

MURPHREE, M. (1984) "Brave new office: The changing world of the legal secretary, " pp. 140-159 in K. Sacks and D. Remy (eds.) My Troubles Are Going to Have Trouble With Me: Everyday Trials and Triumphs of Women Workers. New Brunswick, NJ: Rutgers University Press.

NASH, H. and M. P. FERNANDEZ-KELLY (1983) Women, Men and the Division of Labor. Albany: SUNY Press.

National Center for Health Statistics (1982) "Working women and childbearing: United States." National Survey of Family Growth 23: 9. U.S. Department of Health and Human Services. Washington, DC: Government Printing Office.

O'FARRELL, B. and S. HARLAN (1982) "Craftworkers and clerks: The effect of male coworker hostility on women's satisfaction with non-traditional jobs." Social Problems 29, 3: 252-265.

O'FARRELL, B. and S. HARLAN (1984) "Job integration strategies: Today's programs and tomorrow's needs," pp. 267-291 in B. Reskin (ed.) Sex Segregation in the Workplace: Trends, Explanations, Remedies. Washington, DC: National Academy Press.

OAKLEY, A. (1980) Women Confined: Toward a Sociology of Childbirth. New York: Schocken.

PADAVIC, I. and B. RESKIN (1986) "Supervisors as gatekeepers: Supervisors' role in the sex segregation of jobs." Presented at the American Sociological Association meetings, New York.

PALMER, P. (1984) "Housework and domestic labor: Racial and technological change," pp. 80-93 in K. Sacks and D. Remy (eds.) My Troubles Are Going to Have Trouble With Me: Everyday Trials and Triumphs of Women Workers. New Brunswick, NJ: Rutgers University Press.

PAPPAS, N. (1986) "Secretary is classic case of low control over job." Hartford Courant, April 7.

PARELIUS, A. and R. PARELIUS (1978) The Sociology of Education. Englewood Cliffs, NJ: Prentice-Hall.

PARSONS, R. and R. F. BALES (1956) Family, Socialization and Interaction Process. New York: Free Press.

PEARCE, D. and H. McADOO (1981) Alone and in Poverty: Women and Children. Washington, DC.

PERRUCCI, C., R. PERRUCCI, D. TARG, and H. TARG (1985) "Impact of plant closings on workers and the community," in I. Simpson and R. Simpson (eds.) Research in the Sociology of Work, Vol. 3. Greenwich, CT: JAI Press.

PLECK, J. (1979) "Men's family work: Three perspectives and some new data." Family Coordinator 28: 481-488.

PLECK, J. (1985) Working Wives/Working Husbands. Newbury Park, CA: Sage.

RAPP, R. (1982) "Family and class in contemporary America: Notes toward an understanding of ideology," pp. 168-187 in B. Thorne with M. Yalom, Rethinking the Family. New York, NY: Longman.

REMY, D. and L. SAWERS (1984) "Economic stagnation and discrimination," pp. 95-112 in K. Sacks and D. Remy (eds.) My Troubles Are Going to Have Trouble With Me: Everyday Trials and Triumphs of Women Workers. New Brunswick, NJ: Rutgers University Press.

RESKIN, B. (1984) Sex Segregation in the Workplace: Trends, Explanations, Remedies. Washington, DC: National Academy Press.

RESKIN, B. and P. ROOS (1987) "Status hierarchies and sex segregation," in C. Bose and G. Spitze (eds.) Ingredients for Women's Employment Policy. Albany: SUNY Press.

ROLLINS, J. (1985) Between Women: Domestics and Their Employers. Philadelphia: Temple University Press.

ROOS, P. and B. RESKIN (1984) "Institutional factors contributing to sex segregation in the workplace," pp. 235-260 in B. Reskin (ed.) Sex Segregation in the Workplace: Trends, Explanations, Remedies. Washington, DC: National Academy Press.

ROSEN, E. (1981) "Hobson's choice: Employment and unemployment among factory workers in New England." Report to the U.S. Department of Labor. Washington, DC: Government Printing Office.

ROSEN, E. (1987) Bitter Choices: The Impacts of Layoffs on Blue Collar Women. Chicago: University of Chicago Press.

RUBIN, L. (1976) Worlds of Pain: Life in the Working Class Family. New York: Basic Books.

RUBIN, L. (1981) "Why should women work?" Working paper, Center for the Study, Education, and Advancement of Women, University of California, Berkeley.

SACKS, K. (1984) "Computers, ward secretaries and a walkout in a Southern hospital," pp. 173-190 in K. Sacks and D. Remy (eds.) My Troubles Are Going to Have Trouble With Me: Everyday Trials and Triumphs of Women Workers. New Brunswick, NJ: Rutgers University Press.

SACKS, K. and D. REMY [eds.] (1984) My Troubles Are Going to Have Trouble With Me: Everyday Trials and Triumphs of Women Workers. New Brunswick, NJ: Rutgers University Press.

SAYERS, J. (1982) Biological Politics: Feminist and Anti-feminist Perspectives. London: Tavistock.

SCHOELL-SCHWINGHAMMER, I. (1979) Frauen in Betrieb: Arbeitsbedingungen und Arbeitsbewusstsein. Frankfurt a/M: Campus Verlag.

SCHREIBER, C. T. (1979) Changing Places: Men and Women in Traditional Occupations. Cambridge: MIT Press.

SHAMIR, B. (1985) "Sex differences in psychological adjustment to unemployment and reemployment." Social Problems 33, 1: 67-79.

SHAPIRO-PERL, N. (1984) "Resistance strategies: The routine struggle for bread and roses," pp. 193-208 in K. Sacks and D. Remy (eds.) My Troubles Are Going to Have Trouble With Me: Everyday Trials and Triumphs of Women Workers. New Brunswick, NJ: Rutgers University Press.

SHORTRIDGE, K. (1984) "Poverty is a woman's problem," pp. 492-501 in J. Freeman (ed.) Women: A Feminist Perspective. Palo Alto, CA: Mayfield.

SMITH, R. (1979) The Subtle Revolution: Women at Work. Washington, DC: Urban Institute Press.

SNYDER, K. and T. NOWAK (1984) "Job loss and demoralization: Do women fare better than men?" International Journal of Mental Health 13: 92-106.

SOKOLOFF, N. (1987a) "The increase of black and white women in the professions: A contradictory process," in C. Bose and G. Spitze (eds.) Ingredients for Women's Employment Policy. Albany: SUNY Press.

SOKOLOFF, N. (1987b) "What's happening to women's employment: Issues for women's labor struggles in the 1980s," in C. Bose et al. (eds.) Hidden Aspects of Women's Work. New York: Praeger.

SPAKE, A. (1986) "High-tech disease: Is this a new American nightmare?" Ms. 14, 9: 35-42, 93-95.

STAINES, G. and J. PLECK (1983) The Impact of Work Schedules on the Family. Ann Arbor, MI: ISR Press.

STEINBERG, R. (1983) "The political economy of comparable worth." Presented at the annual meeting of the Eastern Sociological Society.

STEVENSON, J. (1981) "The nursing profession: From the past into the future." National Forum 61: 9-10.

STRASSER, S. (1982) Never Done: A History of American Housework. New York: Pantheon.

TALBERT, J. and C. BOSE (1977) "Wage-attainment processes: The retail clerk case." American Journal of Sociology 83: 403-424.

TREIMAN, D. and H. HARTMANN (1981) Women, Work and Wages: Equal Pay for Jobs of Equal Value. Washington, DC: National Academy Press.

TURBIN, C. (1984) "Reconceptualizing family, work and labor organizing: Working women in Troy, 1860-1890." Review of Radical Political Economics 16, 1: 1-16.

U.S. Bureau of the Census (1960) Volume 1: Characteristics of the Population. Part 1: United States Summary. Table 201: Detailed Occupations. Washington, DC; Government Printing Office.

U.S. Bureau of the Census (1980) Volume 1: Characteristics of the Population. Part 1: United States Summary. Chapter D: Detailed Population Characteristics. Section A: United States. Table 201: Detailed Occupations. Washington, DC: Government Printing Office.

U.S. Bureau of the Census (1985) Money Income of Households, Families and Persons. P-60, No. 146. April Table, 55. Washington, DC: Government Printing Office.

U.S. Department of Labor (1978) Employment and Earnings 25, 1 (January): 153.

U.S. Department of Labor (1985) Women and Office Automation: Issues for the Decade Ahead. Women's Bureau. Washington, DC: Government Printing Office.

U.S. Department of Labor (1986) Employment and Earnings (January): tab. 22, 175-9.

VANEK, J. (1979) "Time spent in housework," in N. Cott and E. Pleck (eds.) A Heritage of Her Own. New York: Simon & Schuster.

VOYDANOFF, P. (1983) "Unemployment and family stress," pp. 239-250 in H. Z. Lopata and J. Pleck (eds.) Research in the Interweave of Social Roles: Families and Jobs. Greenwich, CT: JAI Press.

WAITE, L. and S. BERRYMAN (1984) "Occupational desegregation in CETA programs," pp. 292-313 in B. Reskin (ed.) Sex Segregation in the Workplace: Trends, Explanations, Remedies. Washington, DC: National Academy Press.

WALKER, K. and M. WOODS (1976) Time Use: A Measure of Household Production of Goods and Services. Washington, DC: American Home Economics Association.

WALSHOK, M. (1981) Blue-Collar Women: Pioneers on the Male Frontier. Garden City, NY: Anchor/Doubleday.

WEINER, E. and H. GREEN (1984) "A stitch in our time: New York's Hispanic garment workers in the 1980s," pp. 278-294 in J. Jensen and L. Davidson (eds.) A Needle, a Bobbin, a Strike: Women Needleworkers in America. Philadelphia: Temple University Press.

WEITZMAN, L. (1986) The Divorce Revolution: The Unexpected Social and Economic Consequences for Women and Children in America. New York: Free Press.

WEST, J. (1982) Work, Women and the Labour Market. London: Routledge & Kegan Paul.

WILKIE, J. (1985) "The decline of occupational segregation between black and white women." Research in Race and Ethnic Relations 4: 67-89.

ZAVELLA, P. (1985) "'Abnormal intimacy': The varying work networks of Chicana cannery workers." Feminist Studies 11, 3: 541-557.

13 Gender and the Family

EVELYN NAKANO GLENN
State University of New York, Binghamton

I N the current climate of "family crisis" the question of women's place in the family has emerged as *the* central issue for feminists and antifeminists alike. Conservatives view such trends as rising divorce rates, illegitimacy, cohabitation, and family violence with alarm, seeing in them the breakdown of the family—or at least of their ideal of the family, in which women's constant presence and attention are what make the family possible. Because feminists view the traditional family as problematic for women, its possible erosion is not a major worry. Rather, their concern is the continued gender inequities despite the many changes in household forms, domestic law, and economic relationships. The contradictory pressures women face as a result of change, especially the problems of managing both employment and domesticity, have given feminists added impetus to examine critically the family and women's relationship to it.

Explicating this relationship is essential to the overall enterprise of feminist reconstruction of theory and research for both logistical and substantive reasons. Women are so closely identified with family in popular and scholarly thought that reconceptualizing gender necessarily requires rethinking kinship, household, and domesticity. The substantive reason is that the family is the primary institution for organizing gender relations in society. It is where the sexual division of labor, the regulation of sexuality, and the social construction and reproduction of gender are rooted. Gender hierarchy is created, reproduced, and maintained on a day-to-day basis through interaction among members of a household.

In a real sense, then, the debate about women's place in the family is actually a debate about women's place in society. We cannot comprehend women's subordination in the labor market without taking into account the organization of household labor and the primary responsibility women carry for domestic maintenance. Nor can we understand the exclusion of women from centers of public political power without referring to their encapsulation within the family.

The assumption of women's centrality to the family (in contrast to their presumed marginality in nonfamilial institutions) has not, however, eased the task of reconstruction. Seeing women as integral to the family is very different from placing women's experience at the center of the analysis or from recognizing gender as a basic structural feature of families. As I will argue in the next section, social science thinking about the family has been male centered. The paradigms used to model the family have been framed in male language and reflect male thought, thus distorting women's experiences and disguising the gendered nature of family experience.

In some ways the centrality accorded women has actually complicated the task of feminist reconstruction. Women are virtually equated with family. Their existence is so fused with and embedded in the family that it has been difficult to extract them as individuals—as persons acting not only within the family but also outside of it. While men are seen as actors in a variety of settings, women are seen only in relation to this one context. Yet it is only when we conceptually separate women from the family that we can ask these important questions: What do women do in the family? What do families do for and to women? (See Bridenthal, 1982; Smith, 1979.)

Feminist thinkers therefore have had to disentangle themselves from existing categories of thought while simultaneously moving women's experience to center stage; that is, to both challenge basic paradigms and to develop alternative questions and conceptualizations.

This chapter is organized around a sequence of three questions and subquestions: (1) How have social scientists thought about the family? What do these dominant paradigms omit and what kinds of distortions do they foster? (2) How are feminists rethinking the family? To what kinds of topics and issues do they systematically draw our attention? What concepts do they generate that are useful in understanding women's experiences? (3) What further challenges does feminist reconstruction of family face? How can feminists develop an inclusive perspective that incorporates the variation in women's experience by race and class?

PREVAILING THOUGHT

According to Bridenthal (1979) the formal academic study of the family is a comparatively recent phenomenon, coming to conscious attention only when perceived as a problem. This occurred in the nineteenth century, when rapid economic and social change in Europe threatened to unravel the social fabric. The shift from household production to individual wage labor robbed the working-class family of its central mission and eroded traditional relations of authority. Individual households responded in varying ways, and some families disintegrated. This context, one of concern over the integrity of the family, may help explain the particular assumptions and themes that pervade the academic literature.

In whatever guise, family is writ large as *the* Family, a fixed unchanging and singular entity. This entity is defined as a "bounded set of people" (the nuclear unit), responsible for child rearing (domesticity), sharing residence (home), and tied together by affective bonds (love; Collier et al., 1982). Its basic features are sometimes attributed to biology (e.g., women's procreative capacity) but more often to social function (e.g., the need to socialize children to fulfill adult roles). Even when family change in response to societal change is recognized, it is still viewed as a singularity: the modern nuclear family as the product of a single, linear evolutionary trend.

The family is conceived as a united entity ruled by consensus; its interests are synonymous with the interests of individual members. Hence demographers refer to "family decisions" about limiting family size. This characterization ignores the conflict and inequality underlying such decisions and ignores the long history of struggle between men and women over reproduction (Ross, 1979). Reifying the family is another way of perpetuating the image of unity and consensus. Historians speak about the "family's adjustment" to industrialization and about working-class "family strategies" for coping with a wage labor system (e.g., Hareven, 1982; Anderson, 1971). The family here is portrayed as an agent, independent of the individuals who constitute it. This assumes that men and women have the same goals and the same stakes in maintaining particular household forms.

The family is seen as a bounded sphere, distinct and separate from nonfamily. The concept of a private-public split and the notion of the family as a "haven in a heartless world" reflect this dichotomization. These ideas make sense only if we assume there are clear boundaries between family and the "outside" world. They also imply a differentiation between how the family operates and how the rest of the world (especially the market) operates. Characteristics of the family are cast in opposition to those presumed to characterize nonfamilial institutions. Thus, for example, relations in the family are described as cooperative, altruistic, and not goal oriented, while relations outside are said to be competitive, mercenary, and aimed at gain.

Equally important as what is said about the family is what is not said, what is missing or overlooked in prevailing thought. Much of the thinking about the family is characterized by a systematic lack of attention to underlying structures of gender, despite ritual lip service. As Ross (1979) notes, Mark Poster (1978) states in his *Critical Theory of the Family* that gender and age are two fundamental axes of the family, but devotes most of his discussion to parent-child relations without regard to gender. More often, gender is submerged by gender-neutral language. Breines and Gordon (1983) point out that much of the literature on family violence fails to incorporate gender as an integral part of the analysis, despite its being the single most important structural feature of the phenomenon. The use of terms such as "family violence" or "spouse abuse" conjure up the image of members equally abusing other members, when, in reality, women are overwhelmingly the victims. In discussions of generational relations and socialization, the gender neutral term "parent" is frequently used even though only the mother or father is being studied, thus obscuring certain gender assumptions. When socialization is involved, "parent"typically means mother; but when generational relations, especially over property or authority, are discussed, "parent" means father and "child" means son (e.g., Lasch, 1977).

Similarly, thinking about the family fails to incorporate systematic analyses of race, ethnicity, and class. The significance of variation in the structure and meaning of family among different race and class segments goes unrecognized. Instead, the perspective of one particular class and race segment, the white middle class, defines what is universal. When family life in other social segments is studied, other forms are seen as variant. Thus studies of working-class families always involve an explicit or implicit comparison with the middle class, while studies of "The Family" (i.e., the middle class family) do not require a comparative referent. For the most part research on racial ethnic families is "ghettoized," and findings from these studies are not considered relevant to understanding the generic family. The findings do not force a revision or reformulation of the basic paradigms, and consequently these models fail to "fit" the experience of racial ethnic and working-class women.

DOMINANT PARADIGMS

To illustrate how these themes are expressed in specific theoretical treatments, I turn to a critical examination of three of the most widely used frameworks: structural functionalism, exchange theory, and interactionism. These frameworks perpetuate in one way or another a monolithic model of the family. They assume consensus and continuity and obscure the significance of variation in family forms and of conflict and inequality as features of family life.

Structural functionalism. Even though functionalism has supposedly fallen out of favor, it remains the dominant and most prevalent social science perspective on the family. It is the perspective that most explicitly asserts the immutability of the family. Functionalist anthropologists, ranging from Malinowski (1913) to Murdock (1949) proclaimed the conjugal family to be universal on the grounds that it fulfills universal human needs. Feminist anthropologists such as Collier et al. (1982) point out the circularity of functionalist reasoning: It uses the *existence* of an institution to infer its necessity. Moreover, even its existence as a universal form is doubtful. The anthropological literature is replete with the variety of arrangements, other than the conjugal family, that exist for carrying out basic tasks, such as child rearing and household work. Even Murdock (1949) conceded that the actual conformation of the conjugal unit varies greatly, being most often embedded in a larger residential or domestic unit.

Sociological functionalism does not pose The Family as a universal, but does make it seem inevitable in modern industrial societies. Thus, for example, Goode (1963) argued that the prevalance of the conjugal form in Europe and North America (an assertion based on general observation rather than empirical evidence) was evidence of a "fit" between the conjugal family and the requirements of an industrial economy for a mobile labor force.

Goode's thesis follows Parsons's (1943, 1955) argument for the "necessity" of a particular form of the conjugal family: the co-residential unit of a breadwinner father, homemaker mother, and dependent children. Parsons makes two related observations about the modern family: The conjugal unit is "relatively isolated" from extended kin, and most of its former functions have been taken over by other more specialized institutions. Those that remain are socioemotional in nature: the socialization of children and stabilization of adult personalities. Because of its smallness and intimacy, the conjugal family was particularly well suited to carry out these socioemotional functions. Within the conjugal unit, Parsons posited two main structural features: a hierarchy of gender and age, and task specialization. The conjugal family had evolved a functional role differentiation in which men specialized in instrumental activity, tasks that linked the family to outside institutions, particularly through men's occupations, while women assumed responsibility for expressive activity, the socialization and stabilization tasks that were its main function. This division into nonoverlapping, complementary roles promoted harmony among members and ensured that the family acted in a unified fashion in relation to outside institutions. Parsons acknowledged that housewives suffered from the lack of meaningful work and loss of self-esteem because of the devaluation of "expressive" work, but he concluded the division of labor was nonetheless necessary for the smooth functioning of the family and of society as a whole. The implications of the conflicting interests of men and women remain unexamined.

Parsons's account has been extensively criticized on a number of grounds. At the most obvious level, his thesis reproduced and legitimated conventional attitudes about women's place that prevailed at the time he formulated his account (Friedan, 1963). It also reflects the author's own narrow class (professional) and ethnic/race (Anglo) perspective. Further, Parsons's dichotomization glosses over the complexity of behavior and, in Thorne's words, "falsely assumes that expressive and instrumental activities are mutually exclusive" (1982: 8). Parsons was apparently unaware of what women actually do as homemakers: Anyone who observed what they do would be hard pressed to classify specific activities, such as buying, preparing, and serving food, as unambiguously expressive or instrumental. Furthermore, in the course of her duties, it is the housewife who becomes the major link between the family and outside institutions ranging from the schools to the health care system (Weinbaum and Bridges, 1976). Perhaps the most serious problem is that conceptualizing women's domestic tasks as expressive obscures the fact that these activities contribute to the economic well-being of the family and raises its standard of living (Barrett, 1980: 188).

The functionalist approach to the family has had more widespread implications, shaping the conceptualization of gender throughout sociology. Much research on gender is still cast in the language of roles (e.g., the male role, the female role, sex roles, sex role socialization). This approach locks men and women into seemingly immutable positions. As Ellen Ross (1979: 188) notes, roles "provide the building blocks of the harmonious families and societies which functionalism posits; they are thus pieces of a static and conflict-free social picture." Further, as Stacey and Thorne (1985) observe,

> The notion of "role" focuses attention more on individuals than on social structure, and implies that "the female role" and the "male role" are complementary (i.e. separate or different but equal). The terms are depoliticizing; they strip experience from its historical and political context and neglect questions of power and conflict. It is significant that sociologists do not speak of "class roles" or "race roles" [1985: 307].

Exchange theory. Exchange theory has had wide currency in political science, economics, social psychology, and sociology as a general model for human behavior. In this paradigm, the free market is the template for all social relationships. Individuals interact out of their need or desire to obtain valued ends at the lowest cost.

The exchange paradigm has been widely use in family research, particularly in descriptions of courtship and mate selection, and in studies of power and decision making in marriage.[1] An example of the former is Blau's amazing discussion of the courtship market. Taking a blatantly masculinist line, Blau says men begin the process of mate selection by comparison shopping before deciding to associate with a woman. Once courtship is initiated, men and women maneuver to strike the best possible bargain. The commodities to be exchanged consist of "sexual favors" on her part and "firm commitments" (the promise of marriage) on his part. Perhaps the best-known application of the exchange model to marital relations is Blood and Wolfe's "resource theory" of marital power. These authors hypothesized that the extent of resources controlled by husbands and wives determined their relative influence over major decisions. Thus, for example, Blood and Wolfe predicted that employed wives would have greater power than nonemployed wives (for review and critique of the marital power literature, see Safilios-Rothchild, 1970; Gillespie, 1971).

As a general model of social relationships, exchange theory has been criticized for being reductionist, ahistorical, and conservative. Marxists in particular view it with a jaundiced eye, observing that its prevalence in Western social science is logical given its congruence with capitalist ideology (Osmond, 1986). The model also performs important ideological functions.

The language of "free choice" obscures relations of domination. By explaining outcomes as the product of differences in human capital, it justifies and rationalizes inequality.

Unlike functionalism, exchange theory recognizes, and in fact posits, differences in interests and power among family members. However, it accepts power as a "given" and does not question the origin of differences in power. People are portrayed as "free" to make choices in their own best interest, without consideration of how differences in power shape choices and set limits on the ability to act in one's own best interest. By conceptualizing power as reciprocal and relational, exchange theory draws attention away from the hierarchical and asymmetrical nature of power. In the words of one theorist, the language of exchange theory depicts exchange relations as "cooperative, positive, beneficial, voluntary, and pleasant" rather than as "conflictful, negative, exploitative, coercive, and unpleasant from the stand-point of the one who is influenced" (Baldwin, 1978).

Feminist critics have sharpened and extended these lines of criticism and also opened up new ground. Nancy Hartsock (1983) demonstrates how the market model embodies not only capitalist ideology but also patriarchal (masculinist) concepts of social structure and social relationships. Assuming that the glue holding people together is little more than individual desire for gain, and with each party in an exchange jockeying for advantage, the individual stands very much alone and in hostile relation to clearly separated others. The existence of community is thus rendered problematic.

According to Hartsock (1983), this model embodies a dualistic male mode of thought. Not only is the individual separated from others, but rationality from emotion and mind from body. Hartsock posits an alternative female-centered epistemology, deduced from women's writings on power, that conceives of the self as embedded in a social nexus, with power deriving from connections. Female thought is nondualistic and able to encompass contradictions. In short, Hartsock argues male and female thought involve different ways of knowing.

Hartsock traces the origins of these differences to the sexual division of labor that assigns to women the responsibility for rearing both males and females. Drawing on Nancy Chodorow's (1978) work, Hartsock argues that this arrangement means that boys must learn to individuate and separate their selves from others (initially because of having to distinguish self from mother) while girls' identity formation emphasizes fusion or connectedness with others. The daily lives of men and women further reinforce these differences. The abstraction of men from the concrete details of daily living strengthens their dualistic orientation. In contrast, women's immersion in domestic maintenance and child care requires them to deal constantly with the concrete, reinforcing the tendency toward a sense of connectedness to the material and social world.

Whether one agrees with her analysis of the nature and sources of men's and women's consciousness, one has to take seriously Hartsock's basic thesis of an intimate connection between gender and the construction of knowledge. If we do, we soon realize that we cannot simply modify categories from existing male-centered theories in order to arrive at a feminist conception of the family. Rather, we need to begin with an analysis of the family from the perspective of women and their experiences. Only by grounding our theories in women's experiences can we derive concepts and categories that encompass and make sense of women's realities.

Interactionism. How then to proceed in grounded inquiry? At first blush, the interactionist tradition seems to offer a means of arriving at a feminist epistemology. Interactionism focuses on the "subjective" realities that are the basis of individual action: meaning, identity, and definitions of situations. These realities are not mere reflections of some objective external reality but are actively constructed as people interact with their material and social world. Reality is thus relativistic; its definition grows out of the dialectical relation between the self and the environment. This conception leads us to consider the possibility of multiple realities. In the case of the family, our attention is directed to the contradictory and conflicting realities experienced by men and women, and by adults and children.

When family researchers have taken the rare step of interviewing both husbands and wives, they have discovered that spouses give quite discrepant accounts of the same events. Some time ago, Safilios-Rothschild (1969) wrote of "'two realities,' the husband's subjective reality and the wife's subjective reality—two perspectives which do not always coincide. Each spouse perceives 'facts' and situations differently according to his (sic) own needs, values, attitudes and belief." Jessie Bernard (1972) in *The Future of Marriage* takes the idea a step further, describing every marital union as consisting of two marriages, "his" and "hers," rooted in men's and women's different structural realities. Lillian Rubin (1976) describes the contrasting interpretations and accounts that working-class husbands and wives provide about every stage of marriage, differences that grow out of divergence in their early socialization, their internalization of gender ideologies, including definitions of masculinity and femininity, and their differing relation to paid work and the larger economic system.

None of these three feminist writers explicitly adopts an interactionist framework. Writers who subject marital relations to explicit interactionist or phenomenological analyses are not so concerned with conflicting definitions and meanings, as with the process by which individuals cooperate to create a consensual reality. In their classic article "Marriage and the Construction of Reality" Berger and Kellner (1964) assume that interaction in marriage is aimed at building and stabilizing individual identities. Through "conversations" newly married spouses, who come to the marriage with separate individual biographies, collaborate to construct a new mutually shared reality. Such construction leads to a retrospective redefinition of each spouse's past identities consistent with the new reality. The new identities are experienced not as conscious alterations but as "discoveries" of characteristics that were always there. A shared reality is not achieved once and for all but "goes on being redefined not only in the marital interaction itself but also in the various maritally based group relations into which the couple enters" (1964: 171). Extending Berger and Kellner's analysis to the process of divorce, Vaughan (1985) describes the interaction leading to divorce as a reversal of the marital interaction—that is, as a process of uncoupling in which a couple starts with a shared reality and gradually negotiate separate realities.

Does this kind of analysis help us view the family through women's eyes? Does it draw attention to the way gender shapes people's experience of the family? More generally, does this approach lend itself to the construction of feminist epistemology? Some answers are suggested by Nancy Mandell's (1984) critique of Mead's philosophy, a critique that is relevant to interaction-ist and phenomenological thought generally. Mandell argues that Mead's emphasis on "intelligent action" is grounded in a male model of rationality. Mead ignores emotion, power, inequality, and diversity in gesture and language. These elements are certainly missing or subdued in Berger and Kellner and Vaughan's accounts. The downplaying of power, conflict and inequality and the emphasis on consensus is evident in Vaughan's conclusions about the uncoupling process. She states that despite the presence of conflict, "Patterns of caring and responsibility that emerge between the partners in coupling are not easily dispelled, and in many cases persist throughout the uncoupling process and after" (Vaughan, 1983). Thus we find, as was the case with exchange theory, that an interactionist perspective largely obscures the asymmetry in relations between men and women.

The omission leads to a benign view of social relationships that ignores the capacity of dominant groups to control interaction and to impose their definitions of reality. It can be readily observed in a variety of situations that subordinates (women, servants, racial minorities) must be more sensitive to and responsive to the point of view of superordinates (men, masters, dominant racial groups) than the other way around. If, indeed, dominant groups have the capacity to compel subordinates to accept an imposed version of reality, it follows that even allowing women to describe their own experiences of marriage and family does not necessarily lead us to female-centered categories and concepts. We must consciously seek to understand how gender hierarchies and structures of subordination systematically affect interaction and definitions of reality.

FEMINIST RETHINKING

As suggested in the previous section, scholarly attention is paid to the family only when it is seen as problematic. In the nineteenth century, European academic study of the family was stimulated by the disjunctions brought about by industrialization. Thus the central issue was the relation of the family to the economic system. How does the organization of production and reproduction in the broader society affect production and reproduction within the household? This is the question Marx and Engel asked as they observed the increasing impoverishment of the working-class family in England (Engels, 1968). For traditionalists, such as Frederic Le Play, the concern was maintaining some balance between the group cohesion that characterized preindustrial society and the rising individualism in industrial society that threatened to tear the family apart (Le Play, 1982).

For feminists the problem is women's oppression, and their focus on the family grows out of the conviction that the family is the fundamental vehicle for creating and maintaining women's oppression. Feminists suggest two interlocking structures of subordination: The first grows out of women's positions as wives and mothers, which enmesh them in relations of subordination and lock them into stereotyped domestic and service behavior. The second structure emerges from the socialization process in the family whereby children internalize male and female attributes and attitudes, and transmit them to their own children, thus perpetuating relations of gender domination and subordination.

The idea of family as oppressive is not new, of course. Feminists have drawn on critical streams of thought in Marxism and radical psychology. Marx and Engels studied the family as a historical phenomenon, whose form changes with changes in the modes of production. Their analysis suggests that new forms would evolve in the future that would liberate women and children, contingent on a major change in the ownership and organization of production. Engels's analysis of women's domestic enslavement has stimulated many contemporary feminist analyses of housework, while Marx and Engels's discussion of the distinctions between the bourgeois and proletarian household has influenced feminist treatments of class differences.

The radical psychology movement (led by Laing, 1967, 1972; Laing and Esterson, 1964) attacked relations within the conjugal family, which were portrayed as destructive to its members. What began as a search for the roots of insanity in bad family relations ended in the discovery that even normal families were pathogenic. Radical psychology's negative appraisal of parent-child relations, its highlighting of the role of power and coercion, and its recognition of how ideologies of family harmony mystify experience were important influences on feminist thinking.

Neither Marxian nor radical psychology's criticism, however, sufficiently separates women from the family. The psychological perspective implies that, because women are the primary parenting agents, they are the main perpetuators of oppression. This grossly distorts actual power relations in the family, overlooking the ways in which women are disproportionately constrained and affected by the oppressive features of families.

Although feminists draw on Marxist and radical psychological critiques, intellectual currents are secondary to analyses based on personal, grounded experience. Indeed, initial misgivings about the family in the early days of the "second wave" of feminism were voiced as middle-class women became conscious of the discrepancy between the ideology of domesticity and their own personal experiences as wives and mothers. Because of this disjunction, women lacked labels to describe their experiences; hence Friedan (1963) called the distress suffered by middle-class housewives the "problem that had no name." These early formulations focused almost exclusively on women's personal feelings of isolation, depression, and worthlessness.

At the same time, because feminist analysis is rooted in personal experience, oppression is not treated as monolithic. Stanley and Wise (1983) argue that many women distinguish between the family as an institution and *their* family. "The family" is oppressive; "their family" may or may not be. These women want "the family" to change, but don't want to give up "their family." Such thoughts should be seen not as false consciousness but as reflections of the actual contradictions women confront. Thorne (1982) makes a related point when she notes a basic ambivalence underlying much feminist thinking, which, on the one hand, extols individualism and equity and, on the other, nurturance and support. Thus many feminists celebrate the womanly qualities fostered in the family and use what they see as the positive character- istics of kinship-based relations to critique the man-made world of the market. The point of these observations is that families may not be experienced as uniformly oppressive; the extent to which they are varies for different women and for particular women from one time to another. The touchstone for feminist analysis must, in any case, be women's own experiences, however complex and contradictory.

By rooting analyses in women's experience and in an awareness of the varied nature of that experience, feminists have sought to reclaim the family *for* women. They have challenged the monolithic view of the family and helped women to break *out* of the family so that their experiences can be examined separately. They have done this by *decomposing* the family—that is, breaking the family into constituent elements so that the underlying structures are exposed. In doing so, feminists have brought into relief three aspects of that structure: ideologies that serve to mystify women's experiences as wives and mothers; hierarchical divisions that generate conflict and struggle within families; and the multiple and dynamic interconnections between households and the larger political economy.

IDEOLOGY: MOTHERHOOD AND MOTHERING

Perhaps no area of family life is more laden with ideological baggage than that surrounding women's roles as mothers. Though seemingly tied to biological givens—women's unique capacity for childbearing and lactation—

mothering in fact varies temporally and geographically. As distinct from mothering,[2] "motherhood" is a social construction, one that has mystified the experience of mothering and interfered with our ability to find out what mothers actually do and how they feel about it.

Thus a questioning of motherhood has been one of the central thrusts of feminist reconstruction (e.g., Rich, 1976; Feminist Studies, 1978; Chodorow, 1978). Feminists have uncovered the historical specificity of the concept of motherhood as women's chief vocation and primary identity. This concept developed among the white bourgeoisie in Western Europe and North America with the rise of industrialization, as the transfer of manufacture out of the household gave rise to a new ideology of domesticity and womanhood (e.g., Welter, 1966; Lerner, 1969; Degler, 1980). The split between publicly organized production and privately organized consumption and reproduction was reified in the doctrine of separate spheres. A "natural" division of labor was posited, with men ruling the "public" sphere of economy and polity, while women and children inherited the shrinking and narrow "private" sphere of the household.

This period also saw the rise of *social childhood*. Childhood came to be seen as a special and valued period of life, and children were depicted as innocent, dependent beings in need of prolonged protection and care. This new construction of childhood required a complementary conception of motherhood as serious responsibility, one that required total and exclusive devotion. Women were deemed naturally suited for child care because of their innate qualities of nurturance, self-sacrifice, moral purity, and narrowness of purpose.

The extent to which women and families acted out the norms prescribed in the ideology cannot be verified. What is clear is that these norms were appropriate for only a very limited subgroup within a narrow time period, namely the European and American bourgeoisie of the last 200 years. Such prescriptions were largely irrelevant for the majority of working-class families and women—native whites, immigrants, Afro-Americans and other racial ethnics—in the last century and the present. For these groups, the ideal of full-time motherhood, even if desired, was unattainable. Men in these families rarely earned a "family wage," and women had to combine income earning activities in and out of the home with child care and domestic labor (Degler, 1980; Smuts, 1971; Lerner, 1969; Jones, 1984; Dill, 1986; Higginbotham, 1983; Kessler-Harris, 1982.) Even within comparable income levels, women in different ethnic groups adopted varying strategies for combining mothering and income earning; thus, for example, Italian women preferred to remain at home, sending children out to work, while Afro-American women were more likely to keep children in school while going out to work themselves (Pleck, 1979).

Women of color were not accorded the respect and social support for the mother role that white middle-class women received. Racist ideology triumphed over sexist ideology: Women of color were not deemed to be truly women, exempting them from the protective cloaks of feminine frailty or womanly morality. Their roles as workers took precedence; thus, black, Mexican-American, and Japanese-American domestic servants were expected to devote long hours to taking care of their mistress's households and children, while leaving their own offspring in the care of others (Lerner, 1973; Garcia, 1980; Glenn, 1986).

Yet despite their limited social base, norms based on the conception of motherhood as a full-time vocation have shaped thinking about women and mothering. Women who could not or did not fit the model were judged deviant. Even the large-scale movement of white women into the labor force after World War II did not dislodge motherhood from its position as women's primary responsibility. Rather, employed mothers and wives found themselves in the now-familiar dilemma of the double day. Nonetheless, the fact that most women today are juggling "two jobs" has eroded the notion of motherhood as a full-time and exclusive responsibility.

The ideology of motherhood has served an important mystifying function in capitalist society, simultaneously glorifying motherhood and marginalizing mothering (Bridenthal, 1982; Mitchell, 1971). Regardless of their actual maternal status, all women have been shackled to the role (since if they are not now mothers, they were, will, or should be) and their opportunities in activities other than mothering restricted: If motherhood is their inevitable fate, then other activities, including income earning ones, interfere with full-time devotion to the role. Moreover, because children's development is seen as totally contingent on the quality of mothering they receive, mothers are held to impossibly high standards and made to feel guilty for less than perfect outcomes. The other side of being idealized is that mothers are blamed for all the problems and ills of their children, even into adulthood. In one direction, they are accused of being neglectful and insufficiently loving (Fraiberg, 1977) and in the other of being smothering and over-protective (Levy, 1943; Wiley, 1942; Liz et al., 1965; Reingold, 1964; Lasch, 1977).

Piercing this ideology requires a challenge to the inevitability of mothering. Giving women the choice *not* to mother has been a major focus of the contemporary women's movement. The issue of choice lies at the heart of the struggle for access to birth control, abortion, and forms of sexual expression separated from reproduction. It also lies at the core of the fight to obtain equality in the labor market, politics, and other arenas beyond the family.

Viewing motherhood as a social construction has in turn led feminists to question the organization of mothering in Western industrial societies. They charge that the mothers in these societies are encapsulated in their roles, and left isolated, overburdened, and unsupported—conditions that distort the mother-child relation and inflict long-term damage on women and their children. In the minds of some feminist critics of American motherhood, isolation engenders frustration and rage that lead mothers to become the oppressors or destroyers of their own children, particularly daughters (Dinnerstein, 1976; Friday, 1977; Lazarre, 1986). Although she does not share this apocalyptic vision, Nancy Chodorow (1978), in her influential book *The Reproduction of Mothering*, suggests some negative consequences of a sexual division of labor that assigns women primary responsibility for infant and child care. Having female caretakers creates different developmental experiences for girls and boys that result in distorted adult personalities. Men undervalue connections with others, while women are overly concerned with relationships. A more disturbing implication of Chodorow's analysis is that males are encouraged—indeed, required—to devalue women in order to develop a masculine self-identity.

In precapitalist societies, parenting is much less vested in the biological mother and, not coincidentally, is also accorded greater centrality (see Rosaldo and Lamphere, 1974; Reiter, 1975). Child care is carried on in conjunction with other activities and is shared by kin and nonkin, so that mothers are not isolated. This organization of parenting, one that spreads the responsibility to the larger kin group or society as a whole, is built into the organization of preindustrial societies, and some socialist states have attempted to achieve it through conscious design (see Jancar, 1978; Lapidus, 1979; Stacey, 1983; Diamond, 1983; Holter, 1984). Examples include policies designed to encourage male involvement in child care (e.g., by granting parental leaves to fathers as well as mothers); to ease the burden on women (e.g., by establishing flexible work hours); and to provide nonkin child care arrangements (e.g., by funding nurseries and day care centers).

An additional critique of the mystique of motherhood emerges in some feminist accounts. The mystique implies that the mother alone holds her children's fate in her hands. This view of the all-powerful, all-giving mother greatly distorts her actual power to shape her children's lives. It reduces mothers to one dimension, ignoring the fact that they have activities, interests, needs, and relationships apart from mothering. Even in our own society, what has been termed "social reproduction" is not exclusively carried out by mothers. Nurturance may be shared among female kin, a predominant pattern among some groups (e.g., Stack, 1974). Nor is social reproduction limited to the kin group. A variety of institutions—including schools, welfare agencies, the media, and health care organizations—are involved in social reproduction (Bridenthal, 1979). Feminists have typically focused on the negative side of this situation, seeing mother's work as distorted by the conditions imposed by a patriarchal and capitalist social order. Women are given the responsibility of mothering but are deprived of the power to determine the actual conditions of mothering. Feminist scholars have pointed to the increasing control of these conditions by male professionals and "experts" (Ehrenreich and English, 1978). Two areas of particular concern have been the way in which the medical system has structured the childbirth process to enhance physician control and profits, and the way in which the welfare system regulates the lives of women with dependent children so that mothers have little ability to plan their children's future.

Quite a different perspective on the limits of mothering is offered by Chodorow and Contratto (1982) in their essay, "The Fantasy of the Perfect Mother." They suggest that many feminist writers, whether they celebrate mothering (Rossi, 1979; Rich, 1976) or decry it (Friday, 1977; Dinnerstein, 1976), share with conservative writers, such as Fraiberg (1977), a larger-than-life image of the mother. Though these scholars recognize that structural conditions shape mothering, they have not escaped the vision that underlies the myth: the image of mothers as omnipotent and potentially perfect and of infants as passive and totally needy. Chodorow and Contratto (1982) argue that feminists need to abandon these fantasies and embrace a more interactive, complex, realistic view of mothers and children. To do this they need to look at the actual practice of mothering and to listen to mothers' own voices, a task that has barely been begun (see Ruddick, 1980).

POWER AND INEQUALITY: THE DIVIDED FAMILY

A second prong of feminist efforts to decompose the family challenges the concept of the family as an entity with unitary interests by exposing hierarchical divisions within the family that produce different and conflicting interests among members.

The theme of family unity runs as a consistent thread in popular, prescriptive, and legal thought. Although the assumption of common interests is ancient, the sentimentalization of the family as a domestic refuge is a nineteenth-century development that has perpetuated the myth of family harmony. Berg (1978) claims that industrialization and urbanization increased men's insecurity; the concept of the family as a domestic haven arose to satisfy their cravings for control and security. Thus the image of the family was cast in direct opposition to that of the outside world. While acknowledging that authority resided with the father/husband, the myth assumed that he ruled by consensus; in general, stronger members (husbands/fathers/mothers) could be trusted to protect the interests of their dependents (wives/children). Today, when increased divorce and other evidence of conflict make it difficult to maintain the image of the unified family, the ideal persists in the form of nostalgia for a mythical past when families were unified and harmonious (Skolnick and Skolnick, 1986).

It is worth noting that the myth of family unity has coexisted with a seemingly contradictory belief in individualism. How is this possible? As the above discussion of the father's authority suggests, the answer is that the "family's interest" is defined as synonymous with the husband/father's interest.[3] Thus the fiction of a unitary family interest disguises not only conflict but also male dominance, and legitimates the primacy of husband/father's interest over those of other members.

Feminists have been among critics who have challenged the ideal of malecentered family unity. They were among the first to identify family violence as such a pervasive phenomenon that it constituted a "normal" feature of family life (Pagelow, 1981; Dobash and Dobash, 1979; Chapman and Gates, 1978). Despite its long historical roots, wife-battering was not recognized as a social problem until the late 1960s, and its discovery can be almost totally credited to feminist activists, who began establishing services and shelters for battered women in the 1970s (Tierney, 1982). Feminist efforts to put an end to wife- and child-battering and to aid victims have done more to challenge the myth of unitary family than any other issue. Feminists have had to wage battles with a legal system that fails to protect women and children because it maintains the fiction of family unity, even in the face of evidence of conflict. Thus in 1906 the Supreme Court ruled that to allow wives to sue their husbands for physical abuse would destroy the "harmony" of the family. Although laws no longer protect husbands from prosecution, enforcement has favored keeping the family intact over ensuring the safety of wives and children.

Although significant strides have been made in providing support and assistance to battered women, making it easier for them to leave abusive partners, many feminists feel these solutions are superficial. The structural root of family violence, gender inequality, remains untouched. Violence has long been a weapon of patriarchy, according to Dobash and Dobash (1979), who trace a history of violence directed against women who transgressed community mores. English common law granted husbands the right to "chastise" their wives, and current cultural prescriptions still lead men to feel they need to control "their" women. Inequality outside the family, especially in the labor market, ensures women's economic dependence. Dependency and the lack of other options impel many women to remain in abusive relationships.

Some feminists have also addressed the issue of child abuse, seeing the two forms of violence as closely connected. Whether or not they are closely related may require further study (Breines and Gordon, 1983), but it is clear that both are profoundly gendered phenomena. Mothers are the parents who most frequently inflict abuse, a fact that raises some discomfort. It should be kept in mind that mothers have more opportunities to be abusive because they spend the most time caring for children. Feminist analysis has tended to treat abusive mothers as victims, overwhelmed by the pressures of isolated motherhood. Chodorow and Contratto (1982) argue that feminists have been concerned with describing and understanding the motivations underlying maternal violence, but have been slow to condemn it, to work to eliminate it, and to protect the victims. Perhaps one reason we have had trouble contending with maternal violence is that we often perceive the interests of mother and child as fused. Yet if we accept the idea that differences in power and conflicting interests between husbands and wives are a factor in wife-battering, then we ought to recognize that power differences and conflicting interests between mothers and children may be factors in maternal violence.

Feminist decomposition begins with what is hidden by the concept of family as a unified, harmonious entity: the hierarchical divisions of the family along gender and generational lines. Thus feminist analyses lead to a fundamentally different concept of the family, the family as the locus of gender and generational conflict. Because of inequities in power and resources, the interests of individual members differ.

Feminist analyses have focused on searching for the origins or causes of gender hierarchy. The concept of patriarchy—most broadly conceived as a material and ideological system of male domination over women—has evolved to account for gender inequality both in and out of the family. The nature of patriarchy, its origins and construction, and the means by which it is maintained have been subject to varying interpretations. Juliet Mitchell (1971) argued that it is necessary to discuss the family not as an undifferentiated entity but as composed of separate structures that may in the future be decomposed into different patterns. She identified four underlying structures: sexuality, production, reproduction, and socialization of children. Other analysts have offered other categories. A review of feminist writing suggests the centrality of at least three structures: sexuality, productive and reproductive labor, and redistribution.

Sexuality. Feminist writers have long recognized male-imposed restrictions on female sexuality as an essential element in women's oppression. The origins of men's control of women's bodies and the ways in which that control articulates with other systems of domination have been widely debated. Engels (1972) traced the origins of male sexual control to the rise of private property associated with settled agriculture, a mode of production that created surplus. Men became concerned with preserving property and transmitting it to heirs, whose legitimacy could be ensured only by restricting women's sexuality. According to Engels, the imposition of monogamous marriage and of father-right (patrilineal inheritance) represented the historical defeat of the female sex and their establishment as a subordinate class. Gayle Rubin (1974) was dissatisfied with Engels's formulation, reasoning that oppression of women and control of female sexuality predated private property. In a complex formulation that I will not recapitulate here, she argues that control of female sexuality is a byproduct of universal kinship arrangements that give men rights to engage in exchange with other men to obtain women for marriage. Since women are the ones who are exchanged, female sexuality of necessity is defined as one that is responsive to others, and, of course, heterosexual. In another influential reconstruction, Shulamith Firestone (1971) argues that female subordination, including sexual enslavement, can be traced ultimately to biology. The biological difference between the sexes—women bear children—leads to a sexual division of labor that is the root of women's oppression. Liberating women, therefore, requires freeing them from biological tyranny. Sexuality must be separated from procreation, technologically and politically: Women must seize control of their bodies. For Firestone, liberation means total sexual freedom.

Still other writers, especially radical feminists, view male control of female sexuality, including compulsory heterosexuality, not just as one axis in an overall system of oppression but as the *root* of male domination (e.g., Rich, 1976, 1979; Daly, 1978; Barry, 1985). In these accounts men's view of women as primarily sexual beings, and the establishment of heterosexual intercourse as the norm, means that women's fulfillment is dependent on sexual and emotional relationships with men. In arguing against heterosexuality as the primary mode of sexual expression, radical feminists draw on evidence that female orgasm is produced by clitoral stimulation that is not usually provided through heterosexual intercourse. If this is true, the implication is that women are deceived or compelled in some way to participate in heterosexual intercourse. Atkinson (1984) and others have stressed ideologies of love and romance that cloak male domination. Whatever the role of ideology, radical feminists believe that force ultimately buttresses male control of women's sexuality: violence and the threat of violence (see Barry, 1985). Thus rape, imposed heterosexuality, wife-battering, forced sterilization, limitations on access to birth control and abortion are all pieces of patriarchal control of women's bodies, as noted in other chapters in this volume.

According to all these analyses of sexuality, liberation of women requires their sexual liberation, which means untying sexual activity from procreation, freeing women from one-sided monogamy, and allowing them to pursue sexual gratification outside of heterosexual intercourse.

Productive and reproductive labor. While radical feminists stress sexual controls as the root of subordination, Marxist feminist focus on control of labor, whether productive or reproductive. Production and reproduction are structured by the interaction of capitalism with patriarchy, a system that is analytically separate from and predates capitalism. Sokoloff (1980) defines patriarchy as a material and ideological system that allows men to control and disproportionately benefit from women's labor.

Patriarchy ensures that women perform a disproportionate share of unpaid labor in the home and are relegated to a secondary position in the labor market. Men benefit in two ways. First they receive a disproportionate share of services performed by wives. Second, they monopolize better jobs and are paid on a separate and higher wage scale.

Because housework exacts so much effort and time from women, it has been a major topic for feminist research and theorizing (for reviews and histories, see Glazer, 1976; Ferree, 1983; Oakley, 1974a, 1974b; Strasser,

1982). As a result, it is now taken seriously as a form of labor that produces value and is central to the larger economy, connections that will be discussed in the next section. Studies of household division of labor have documented the significance of domestic labor as an arena for gender struggle:

(1) The sheer number of hours women spend on housework is large, and the total for all women probably exceeds the number of hours all workers spend in paid employment, while the value of housework (calculated as the wages that would have to be paid to replace the wife's services) exceeds the total paid in wages for all current employees (Chase Manhattan Bank, 1972; Glazer, 1976).

(2) Average hours spent in housework by unemployed wives has not decreased despite technological and social changes (Vanek, 1974; Oakley, 1974b). The allocation among different activities has changed; for example, fewer hours are spent in preparing meals, but more time is spent on shopping and running errands. This indicates that the kind of labor involved has changed but that the total amount has not (Vanek, 1974).

(3) There seems to be an irreducible minimum of time (around 20 hours a week) married women spend on housework (Morgan, 1978). The hours increase sharply when children, especially young children, are present, rising by various estimates up to 70 hours a week (Morgan, 1978; Walker and Woods, 1976).

(4) Women do about 70% of all domestic labor, while men perform around 15%, with children providing the remaining 15% (Walker and Woods, 1976). Men's hours do not increase in proportion to expanded need as women's hours do; for example, the presence of small children only slightly increases men's hours (Walker and Woods, 1976; Morgan, 1978; Geerkin and Gove, 1983).

(5) The hours contributed by men do not increase markedly when their wives are employed. Women spend somewhat less time on housework, however, so men's proportionate share increases (Meissner et al., 1975; Robinson et al., 1976; Geerken and Gove, 1983).

(6) Men probably create more housework than they contribute. That is, the presence of a man in the household is associated with an increase in hours women devote to housework that is greater than the average hours men contribute to the household (evidence reviewed by Hartmann, 1981). The result is what Richard Curtis (1986: 179) calls the paradox of housework: "Men can receive from their wives a market value of housework that is greater than their own incomes, yet housework is only a portion of what the wife contributes in order to have a partial claim on that income." For Hartmann (1981) the historical inequities in the labor contributed by men and women, the inelasticity of men's contribution, and a recent slight rise in men's proportional contribution are evidence of ongoing conflict over housework, with women struggling to gain greater equity and men to maintain status quo.

Redistribution. In addition to being the unit for pooling domestic labor, families organized as households are also the unit for redistribution of resources. Individual workers earn income and then bring it into the household, where it is then converted into goods and services for family consumption (Curtis, 1986). Redistribution provides for the support of non-income-producing members (primarily children, but possibly full-time house-wives and elderly kin). It is fairly evident that the rules or norms regulating redistribution in the household are not the same as those regulating redistribution in larger organizations, including work organizations. Humphries (1977) characterized the family as operating as a primitive commune, sharing more or less equally according to need rather than according to economic productivity. It was this communal redistribution that explained the continuing relevance of the working-class family and accounted for its resistance to the atomizing impacts of the individual wage labor system.

Humphries (1977, 1979) romanticizes the working-class family and pays insufficient attention to inequities in redistribution. Not only do men benefit from women's domestic labor, they also claim a greater share of resources, irrespective of who brings them into the household. In times of food shortage, for example, men consume more food and better food than do women (see Oren, 1973). In times of surplus, they control discretionary spending (Rubin, 1976). In short, as Spalter-Roth (1985) suggests, men have traditionally enjoyed a higher standard of living than women in their own households, and women and children may live in poverty even when total family income is above the poverty line (Pahl, 1983).

Yet the general point that Humphries makes, that family redistribution reflects different assumptions than distribution in the larger economy, is essentially correct. Although I earlier criticized market-based exchange theory, I find Curtis's (1986) discussion of inequality in redistribution in exchange terms useful for thinking about the issue. He suggests that redistribution of resources in the family follows (though not exclusively) rules of social exchange rather than those of the marketplace. In contrast to the explicit and enforceable agreements characterizing economic exchanges, nonmarket social exchange entails supplying benefits that create diffuse future obligations whose nature is not specified in advance.

This does not mean that redistribution within the family is equitable. Redistribution processes in the family may be as important as inequities in distribution (e.g., differences in men's and women's wages) in sustaining intrafamilial inequality. Power structures in the family ensure male control of redistribution. Authority (i.e., legitimate power to command resources) is essential to patriarchy. For the most part, unequal redistribution occurs without overt conflict because members accept male privilege. Moreover, even when individual members oppose the arrangements or are dissatisfied, external organizations support male authority and thereby weaken opposition within the family. As Curtis states, "Throughout history men have used 'social' rules of exchange to reduce women, children, and other men to conditions of dependence and helplessness incomparable to any instance of purely contractual inequality" (1986: 179).

Although feminist analyses of sexuality, labor, and redistribution differ about the primary source of gender hierarchy, they share the view that power and inequality are inherent features of family structure. They also project a view of women as actively engaged in a struggle for greater equality rather than as objects or passive targets of oppression. As ethnographic and qualitative accounts have revealed, systems of inequality establish their own dialectic; in the family there is an ongoing shifting of power and resources, as men struggle to maintain domination while women struggle to circumvent men's control and carve out areas of autonomy (e.g., Whitehead, 1976; Glenn, 1980).

HOUSEHOLDS AND THE POLITICAL ECONOMY: QUESTIONS OF RACE AND CLASS

Through scholarship and research, feminists have sought a more complex understanding of the family's relationship to the economy and the state, and how such relationships vary over different historical periods by race and class. Yet systematically incorporating hierarchies of race and class into feminist reconstruction of the family remains a challenge, a necessary next step in the development of theories of family that are inclusive of all women.

Rayna Rapp (1982) frames the issue beautifully when she describes a prototypical feminist meeting in which one speaker (presumably white and middle class) stands up and calls for the abolition of the nuclear family on the grounds that it oppresses and degrades women; another speaker, usually Third World, asserts that the first speaker represents a typically white middle-class point of view and that other women need their families for survival and support. Rapp suggests that both women are in a sense right and that they are not talking about the same thing when they say family.

A corresponding rift has grown among scholars between those who emphasize stratification within the family and the subordination of women, as explicated above (e.g., Harmann, 1981), and those who emphasize the family and kin network as a resource in the struggle for survival of working-class and racial ethnic people (e.g., Humphries, 1977). As in the previous case, both positions are partially correct, focusing on one side of a fundamental dualism in women's lives. The family is simultaneously an important source of emotional and material support and a source of oppression. How that contradiction gets played out and which side of the contradiction is most salient are shaped by larger systems of domination and subordination. Thus different groups of women experience the contradiction differently because the relationship of the family to the political economy varies by race, class, and family formation.

Variation in household boundaries. Historians charting the development of the modern Western family have described a trend of increasing privatization of the household over the past 500 years (Laslett, 1973). In premodern

Europe the conduct of business in the home, the presence of nonfamily members, such as servants, apprentices, and visitors, and the design of domestic architecture (e.g., the lack of hallways and special purpose rooms) precluded privacy and blurred household boundaries (Aries, 1963; Laslett, 1973). Demos (1970) noted these same features in the American colonial household and observed that families performed many functions, such as criminal correction and vocational training, that would be considered public today. The other side of the coin was that through the courts the community oversaw the household and intervened in what today would be considered private family matters.

Besides the transfer of production from the household, the change that contributed most to privatization was the shrinking size of households. This shrinkage was not due to a decline in extended kin households, since historical demographers have amassed evidence that, contrary to popular myth, households in Western Europe and North America have been predominantly conjugal for several centuries (P. Laslett, 1972, 1977; Anderson, 1971; Katz, 1975; Blumin, 1975; B. Laslett, 1975, 1977). Rather, the decline stems from a decrease in such nonfamily members as servants and boarders, reduced fertility, and the increase in young adults and older adults residing alone (Kobrin, 1976). Some feminists have argued that the situation of women in modern Western societies, often isolated as housewives and mothers, compares unfavorably with that of women in societies where they are closely associated with other women and can form a collective woman-centered consciousness because the family group is larger and more integrated into political and economic life (see Rosaldo and Lamphere, 1974).

Though the increase in smaller, more isolated households represents the overall historical trend, historians have also documented considerable variation in household forms by ethnicity and class (Glasco, 1975; Gutman, 1976; Furstenberg et al., 1975; Modell and Hareven, 1973; Hareven, 1982; McLaughlin, 1971; Goldin, 1981; DuBois, 1967). These variations reflect differences in families' and individual members' relation to production and their position in the labor system.

The existence of widespread variation suggests that it is not so much the *fact* of isolation but the cultural *ideal* of the autonomous self-supporting family that is problematic. The independent family is a race- and class-biased social construct, one that obscures class differences and the interpenetrating relations among the family, institutions of production, and the state. This ideal places families "under cultural constraints to *appear* as autonomous and private" (Rapp, 1982). Yet the extent to which nuclear units can rely primarily on their own resources varies a great deal by class.[4]

The ideal is premised on a conjugal household in which men hold authority and women are economically dependent and responsible for nurturance. It also presupposes a larger social, political, and economic context that supports the integrity of the household as a private economic unit and an ideological system that recognizes and legitimates women's domestic role. For many groups of women in various historical circumstances, these assumptions are invalid or only partially valid.

The ability of most working-class families to be economically self-sufficient is limited by the uncertainties of wage labor as a source of support. Low wages and periodic unemployment among the black ghetto families studied by Stack (1974) made the conjugal unit a shaky base for survival. Most of the families survived through a combination of low-paid jobs, welfare, and pooling of services and goods among several female-related households. In such circumstances, household and kinship relations take forms that differ from the self-contained nuclear model; male authority and female dependence are muted, while kinship ties among women take precedence over the conjugal tie. Women-centered kin networks that cooperate in domestic tasks have been found in a wide variety of working-class settings: in a white working-class district in East London (Young and Willmott, 1962); among second-generation Japanese-Americans in Seattle (Yanagisako, 1977); and among black ghetto residents in the Midwest (Stack, 1974). In general, extended kin arrangements seem to be more prevalent among some ethnic groups, such as Chicanos (Sena-Rivera, 1979) and blacks (Martin and Martin, 1978). However, even this characterization is too simplistic in that a variety of household formations may be found within specific communities (see Hannerz, 1969). For example, Valentine (1978) found relatively little evidence of kin-based networks in the black community she studied, but she was struck by the extent to which residents' time and energy were completely absorbed by the effort of making a living in an economy that provided no reliable legal means of support. Most families engaged in a constant round of labor, piecing together income from jobs, hustling (semilegal or illegal activity), welfare, and informal market work. For Valentine's families, the household was in no way isolated or protected from the outside world.

Work and labor systems. Regardless of class, all families are profoundly shaped by the demands and exigencies of making a living. Yet the connections between work and family life are often obscure, hidden by what Kanter (1977) calls the "myth of separate worlds." As production was transferred out of the household, work organizations perpetuated the myth as a way of reducing the influence of the family and increasing external control over individual workers. The family was considered a rival for workers' loyalty and its authority competed with that of the work organization. Instituting rules and norms that excluded family considerations from the work place (e.g., "Don't bring your family problems to work") was one strategy for ensuring loyalty and compliance, at least during working hours.

Apparently the myth of separate worlds is effective ideologically; re-searchers have found that men typically report very little carryover from job to home, even when the connection is obvious to an outside observer. The families of middle-level corporate managers studied by Margolis (1979) were deeply penetrated by the demands of the husbands' jobs. The corporation required frequent loyalty tests, which the men passed by working long hours and accepting frequent uprooting. Constant relocation severed community and extended kin ties, and made them almost completely dependent on the corporation for a sense of identity. Wives' lives were also absorbed since they had to bear the brunt of maintaining a supportive environment at home and dealing with the emotional and practical upheavals generated by each move. Their own career concerns had to be sacrificed for the sake of the husband's. Interestingly, most of the managers denied that transfers harmed their wives or children, even though Margolis noticed that most of them described one or more of their children as "loners." By seeing their child's withdrawal from friendships as due to personality, they avoided feeling guilty about the harm inflicted on their children by their own subservience to the corporation.

Working-class men in routinized jobs also experience a sharp discontinuity between work and private life. Chinoy (1955) found that as their tenure on the job lengthened, male assembly-line workers resigned themselves to nonmobility, withdrew interest from the job, and invested their energies into their "real lives" outside of work. Yet, as numerous studies show, the job has a long arm, reaching out to affect husband-wife relations, child socialization, and quality of family life (Rubin, 1976; Kohn, 1969; Piotrokowski, 1980).

The blue-collar men in Rubin's study had little authority or autonomy at work and their wages were not sufficient to support the family at a level that marked them as successful breadwinners. These conditions, combined with their internalization of ideals that define masculinity in terms of authority and economic success, may explain why these husbands demanded compliance to their authority at home and felt threatened by their wives' outside employment.

Since the nineteenth century, white working families have struggled to survive in a wage labor system that threatened to atomize the family. Family members have worked under conditions that endangered their own life and health and that threatened future reproduction.

People of color faced even more unfavorable conditions of work and have had to struggle to maintain personal life in a context that is not supportive of —and often actively hostile to—the institutions of their community, including the family. Asian-Americans, blacks, and Hispanics were incorporated or brought into the United States primarily to provide cheap and malleable labor. Their usefulness was calculated primarily in terms of their contributions as individual units of labor. Capitalists and the state could save costs by contributing as little as possible to reproduction; the trick was to pay only enough to maintain the prime worker. This was done by excluding nonproductive family members, such as children and women (as in the case of Asian-Americans) or by exploiting the marginal productivity of dependents (as in the case of migrant Mexican farm workers). Under such conditions, creating and maintaining some semblance of personal life was a heroic feat.

The organization of domestic labor. The connection between the family and the economy runs in the other direction as well, in that work performed in and on behalf of the household is also "public" labor. The encapsulation of housework within the family long prevented us from understanding its public significance, and its idealization as a "labor of love" prevented us from realizing its contribution to the economy. Socialist feminists were among the first to point out the connection between housework and the larger system of production. Early socialist feminist analyses (e.g., Benston, 1969; Dalla Costa, 1972) focused primarily on how domestic labor was shaped by the needs of industrial capital. Housework was seen as furthering capitalist interests in two ways. First, housework helps to shore up the market. Privatizing housework generates a large market for goods. Delegating the work to one person whose primary duty is to maintain the household creates a segment of almost full-time consumers. Bridges and Weinbaum (1976) conceive of housework as "the other side of the pay check." As wageworkers, men and women produce goods and services for the market in exchange for wages; as housewives, women convert those wages back into goods and services that are needed by the family. Women's domestic labor is thus basically consumption work; shopping, negotiating for services, then performing whatever labor is necessary to turn them into a form that can be consumed (e.g., preparing food into a meal).

The second way housework supports capitalism is by maintaining the labor force. Housework has been labeled "reproductive labor"—that is, labor that maintains the current labor force (by providing meals, clean clothes, and ego support for the male worker) and creates the next generation of workers (by nurturing and socializing children). This labor is unrecognized, unpaid, and taken for granted (Ferree, 1983). In a market economy it has no exchange value and is therefore devalued.[5]

This line of analysis argues that capitalism and patriarchy not only shape wage labor but also domestic labor. It follows that the material and social conditions of that labor differ by class, but discussions of these variations tend to be scattered and unsystematic. Oakley (1974b) notes that the technological and material conditions of working-class homes make housework arduous. She also remarks on differential attitudes toward housework by class, with working-class women expressing more positive attitudes than their middle-class counterparts about being housewives. She speculates that this is because their alternatives (routine, low paying jobs) are even less attractive. Ferree (1983) suggests an important difference in the "content" of working-class and middle-class women's domestic labor. She identifies two types of activities within housework: material production (or reproduction) and status production. Material production (e.g., stretching the food budget) is the focus of working-class women's domestic labor, while status production (e.g., home decoration, entertainment) is a larger component of middle-class women's labor at home.

An analysis of Chicana, Chinese-American, and Afro-American women's history suggests other variations in women's domestic labor and a need to broaden the definition of reproductive labor even further (Glenn, 1985; Dill, 1986). In situations of racial exploitation, as described in the previous sections, subordinate groups find their cultural and family systems are targets for dominant group control. This is because the family is a major instrument of legal and political power and the primary vehicle for socializing children—teaching them their place in society and reproducing social relationships. To ensure domination, the dominant group also must act to control or manage family formation within the subordinate culture.

The family is, however, a double-edged sword. It is also the subordinate group's main resource in its struggle against dominant group control. The family provides an alternative value system and is the main institution for socializing children to resist dominant group culture and authority. Because of their central position in maintaining the family, women play a critical role in the defense of the family and indigenous cultures. Under conditions of racial domination, women's "domestic" labor is both more arduous (e.g., striving to maintain health under primitive conditions and with insufficient income) and more essential (e.g., teaching children to survive in a racist society.) Angela Davis's (1971) essay on women's role in slave communities was an early expression of this concept of the racial-ethnic family. She argues that women's work in maintaining the household and socializing children was the only labor that was not directly appropriated by the slavemaster. Moreover she sees women's defense of the family as part of the larger pattern of resistance to slavemaster control. Minna Caulfield (1974) applies a similar conception of indigenous family system under conditions of imperialist domination (which covers both external colonies and minority communities in the United States), which she describes as "cultures of resistance":

> We must look not only at the ways in which the colonizer acts to *break down* family solidarity, but also the ways in which the colonized—women, men and children—act to *maintain, consolidate and build anew* the basic units in which children can grow and be enculturated in the values and relationships that are independent of and in opposition to the imperial culture [1974: 73].

The varying forms of households, relations to labor systems, and organizations of domestic labor that result from different historical circumstances of specific groups leads to different experiences of family. Women view the "tangle of love and domination" from many different angles. While many (white middle-class) feminists experience the family (conjugal, male-dominated) as oppressive, many (minority and/or working-class) feminists are more concerned about threats to the integrity of their families (often extended, female-centered).

Considerable debate has been generated over the meaning of working-class women's efforts on behalf of the family wage and Afro-American women's support for male authority in the black household. The usual interpretation is that these women were acting against their own interests because they have internalized ideologies of "women's place." This explanation relies on "false consciousness" for the seeming contradiction between women's interests as a gender and their support for policies that may further institutionalize women's dependence. An understanding of the historical experiences of specific groups, however, can reveal the "rationality" of these women's responses. Such an understanding is essential if we are to bridge the divisions among us.

NOTES

1. The language of exchange creeps into accounts of husband-wife relations even where the research as a whole is not framed in the paradigm. Hence Hiller and Philliber (1986: 191) discuss contemporary division of labor in these terms: "The underlying issue for individual spouses is equity and fairness in the distribution of *costs* and *rewards* within a relationship. With a majority of wives employed in the United States, a new definition of an equitable role *bargain* is emerging which suggests men should take a more active role in housekeeping and childcare." Hiller and Philliber use this "rational" language despite their findings that indicate no such equitable bargain in terms of actual division of labor.

2. A good working definition of mothering is provided by Sara Ruddick (1980), who uses the term to refer to an array of activities aimed at preserving life, fostering growth, and molding an acceptable person.

3. The definition of husband's interests as synonymous with the family's interests has long historical roots; for example, under the common law doctrine of coverture women's identity merged with that of her husband upon marriage (see Baron, Chapter 17 in this volume). Legal reforms over the past century have increased the rights of individual family members, freeing them from family authority. However, sociological thinking about the family still retains the fiction of unitary interests. Geerken and Gove (1983), for example, suggest that husbands are the spokesmen for the larger family interest while wives represent a narrower, presumably personal, interest.

4. The ideal of the autonomous, self-supporting family is based on the norm of the middle-class family that has a male head of household, a stable income, and some property or savings as cushions; but even among this class segment, independence is more myth than reality. When their material needs exceed their own resources, middle-class people turn to nonfamilial institutions, such as banks, and insurance funds or other nonkin sources closed to the poor.

5. Suggestions for deprivatizing housework so that it is not oppressive have included turning housework into public production, for example, by establishing communal kitchens and paying women for cooking, or recognizing and rewarding women for the work they do in the home by paying them wages. Besides pointing to practical obstacles to such arrangements, some feminists have raised analytic objections to focusing exclusively on the structure of homemaking. For marxist feminists such solutions do not adequately take into account the complex and mutually reinforcing relationship between the household and the labor market. From this perspective, moving housework into public production and paying women for performing it will not lead to equality as long as women are disadvantaged in the labor market. The unequal division of household labor is supported by and helps maintain women's subordination in the labor market; in turn, women's subordination in the labor market keeps women economically dependent on men and therefore reinforces the unequal division of labor in the family. Thus any change in the

organization of household work requires a change in the organization of paid employment. Both systems must be restructured for women to achieve equality.

REFERENCES

ANDERSON, M. (1971) Family Structure in Nineteenth Century Lancashire. Cambridge: Cambridge University Press.

ARIES, P. (1963) Centuries of Childhood. New York: Vintage.

ATKINSON, T.-G. (1984) Amazon Odyssey. New York: Links Books.

BALDWIN, D. A. (1978) "Power and social exchange." American Political Science Review 72: 1229-1242.

BARRETT, M. (1980) Women's Oppression Today. London: Verso.

BARRY, K. (1985) Female Sexual Slavery. New York: New York University Press.

BENSTON, M. (1969) "The political economy of women's liberation." Monthly Review (September): 13-25.

BERG, B. (1978) The Remembered Gate: Origins of American Feminism. New York: Oxford University Press.

BERGER, P. L. and H. KELLNER (1964) "Marriage and the construction of reality." Diogenes 46: 1-32.

BERK, R. A. and S. F. BERK (1979) Labor and Leisure at Home: Content and Organization of the Household Day. Newbury Park, CA: Sage.

BERNARD, J. (1973) The Future of Marriage. New York: Bantam.

BLASSINGAME, J. W. (1972) The Slave Community: Plantation Life in the Antebellum South. New York: Oxford University Press.

BLAU, P. (1964) Exchange in Social Life. New York: John Wiley.

BLOOD, R. O. and D. M. WOLFE (1960) Husbands and Wives. New York: Free Press.

BLUMIN, S. M. (1975) "Rip Van Winkle's grandchildren: Family and household in the Hudson Valley, 1800-1860." Journal of Urban History 1: 293-315.

BORIS, E. and P. BARDAGLIO (1983) "The transformation of patriarchy: The historic role of the state," pp. 70-93 in I. Diamond (ed.) Family, Politics and Public Policy: A Feminist Dialogue on Women and the State. New York: Longman.

BREINES, W. and L. GORDON (1983) "The new scholarship on family violence." Signs 8: 490-531.

BRIDENTHAL, R. (1979) "Examining family history: Family and reproduction," Feminist Studies 5: 189-195.

BRIDENTHAL, R. (1982) "The family: The view from a room of her own," in B. Thorne with M. Yalom (eds.) Rethinking the Family: Some Feminist Questions. New York: Longman.

BROWN, C. (1981) "Mothers, fathers and children: From private to public patriarchy," pp. 239-269 in L. Sargent (ed.) Women and Revolution: A Discussion of the Unhappy Marriage of Marxism and Feminism. Boston: South End.

CAULFIELD, M. D. (1974) "Imperialism, the family and cultures of resistance." Socialist Revolution 20: 67-85.

CHAPMAN, J. R. and M. G. GATES [eds.] (1978) The Victimization of Women. Newbury Park, CA: Sage.

Chase Manhattan Bank (1972) What Is a Wife Worth? New York: Author.

CHINOY, E. (1955) Automobile Workers and the American Dream. New York: Random House.

CHODOROW, N. (1978) The Reproduction of Mothering. Berkeley: University of California Press.

CHODOROW, N. and S. CONTRATTO (1982) "The fantasy of the perfect mother," pp. 54-75 in B. Thorne with M. Yalom (eds.) Rethinking the Family. New York: Longman.

COLLIER, J., M. Z. ROSALDO, and S. YANAGISAKO (1982) "Is there a family? New anthropological views," pp. 25-39 in B. Thorne with M. Yalom (eds.) Rethinking the Family: Some Feminist Questions. New York: Longman.

CURTIS, R. (1986) "Household and family in theory on inequality." American Sociological Review 51: 168-183.

DALLA COSTA, M. (1972) "Women and the subversion of the community," in M. Dalla Costa and S. James, The Power of Women and the Subversion of the Community. Bristol: Falling Wall Press.

DALY, M. (1978) Gyn/Ecology: The Metaethics of Radical Feminism. Boston: Beacon.

DAVIS, A. (1971) "Reflections of the black woman's role in the community of slaves." Black Scholar 3, 4: 3-15.

DEGLER, C. N. (1980) At Odds: Women and the American Family from the Revolution to the Present. New York: Oxford University Press.

DEMOS, J. (1970) A Little Commonwealth. New York: Oxford University Press.

DIAMOND, I. [ed.] (1983) Family, Politics and Public Policy: A Feminist Dialogue on Women and the State. New York: Longman.

DILL, B. T. (1980) "The means to put my children through: Childrearing goals and strategies among black female domestic servants," pp. 107-124 in L. F. Rodgers-Rose (ed.) The Black Woman. Newbury Park, CA: Sage.

DILL, B. T. (1986) "Our mother's grief: Racial ethnic women and the maintenance of families." Research Paper, Center for Research on Women, Memphis State University.

DINNERSTEIN, D. (1979) The Mermaid and the Minotaur. New York: Harper & Row.

DOBASH, R. E. and R. DOBASH (1979) Violence Against Wives: A Case Against the Patriarchy. New York: Free Press.

DUBOIS, W.E.B. (1899) The Philadelphia Negro (1967). New York: Shocken.

EHRENREICH, B. and D. ENGLISH (1978) For Her Own Good: 150 Years of Experts' Advice to Women. Garden City, NY: Anchor/Doubleday.

ENGELS, F. (1968) The Conditions of the Working Class in England (trans. and ed., W. O. Henderson and W. H. Chaloner). Stanford: Stanford University Press.

ENGELS, F. (1972) The Origins of the Family, Private Property and the State, 1884 (ed. with an introduction, E. Leacock). New York: International Publishers.

Feminist Studies (1978) "Special Issue: Toward a Feminist Theory of Motherhood." No. 2.

FERREE, M. M. (1983) "Housework: Rethinking the costs and benefits," pp. 148-167 in I. Diamond (ed.) Family Politics and Public Policy: A Feminist Dialogue on Women and the State. New York: Longman.

FIRESTONE, S. (1970) The Dialectic of Sex. New York: Morrow.

FRAIBERG, S. (1977) Every Child's Birthright: In Defense of Mothering. New York: Basic Books.

FRIDAY, N. (1977) My Mother/Myself. New York: Delacorte.

FRIEDAN, B. (1963) The Feminine Mystique. New York: Norton.

FURSTENBERG, F. F., Jr., T. HERSHBERG, and J. MODELL (1975) "The origins of the female-headed black family: The impact of the urban experience." Journal of Interdisciplinary History 6: 211-233.

GARCIA, M. T. (1980) "The Chicana in American history: The Mexican women of El Paso, 1980-1920—a case study." Pacific Historical Review 49: 315-337.

GEERKEN, M. and W. R. GOVE (1983) At Home and At Work: The Family's Allocation of Labor. Newbury Park, CA: Sage.

GENOVESE, E. (1974) Roll, Jordan, Roll: The World the Slaves Made. New York: Vintage.

GILKES, C. (1980) "Holding the ocean back with a broom: Black women and community work," pp. 217-233 in L. F. Rodgers-Rose (ed.) The Black Woman. Newbury Park, CA: Sage.

GILLESPIE, D. (1971) "Who has the power? The marital struggle." Journal of Marriage and the Family 33: 445-458.

GLASCO, L. A. (1975) "The life cycle and household structure of American ethnic groups: Irish, Germans and native-born white in Buffalo, New York, 1855." Journal of Urban History 1: 364-399.

GLAZER, N. (1976) "Review essay: Housework." Signs 1: 905-922.

GLENN, E. N. (1980) "The dialectics of wage work: Japanese American women and domestic service, 1905-1940." Feminist Studies 6: 432-471.

GLENN, E. N. (1985) "Racial ethnic women's labor: The intersection of race, gender and class oppression." Review of Radical Political Economics 17, 3: 86-109.

GLENN, E. N. (1986) Issei, Nisei, Warbride: Three Generations of Japanese American Women in Domestic Service. Philadelphia: Temple University Press.

GOLDIN, C. (1981) "Family strategies and the family economy in the late nineteenth century," pp. 277-310 in T. Hershberg (ed.) Philadelphia: Work, Space, Family and Group Experience. New York: Oxford University Press.

GOODE, W. (1963) World Revolution and Family Patterns. New York: Free Press.

GREVEN, P. (1970) Four Generations: Population, Land and Family in Colonial Andover, Massachusetts. New York: Cornell University Press.

GUTMAN, H. G. (1976) The Black Family in Slavery and Freedom, 1750-1925. New York: Pantheon.

HANNERZ, U. (1969) Soulside: Inquiries into Ghetto Culture and Community. New York: Columbia University Press.

HAREVEN, T. K. (1982) Family Time and Industrial Time: The Relation Between the Family and Work in a New England Industrial Community. Cambridge, MA: Harvard University Press.

HARTMANN, H. (1981) "The family as a locus of gender, class, and political struggle: The example of housework." Signs 6: 366-394.

HARTSOCK, N. (1983) Money, Sex and Power: Toward a Feminist Historical Materialism. New York: Longman.

HIGGINBOTHAM, E. (1983) "Laid bare by the system: Work and survival for black and Hispanic women," in A. Swerdlow and H. Lessinger (eds.) Class, Race and Sex: The Dynamics of Control. Boston: G. K. Hall.

HILLER, D. V. and W. W. PHILLIBER (1986) "The division of labor in contemporary marriage: expectations, perceptions, and performance." Social Problems 35: 191-201.

HOLTER, H. (1984) Patriarchy in a Welfare State. Oslo: Universitetsforlaget (distributed by Columbia University Press).

HUMPHRIES, J. (1979) "The working class family, women's liberation and class struggle: The case of nineteenth century British history." Review of Radical Political Economics 9: 25-41.

HUMPHRIES, J. (1977) "Class struggle and the persistence of the working class family." Cambridge Journal of Economics 1: 241-258.

JANCAR, B. W. (1978) Women Under Communism. Baltimore, MD: Johns Hopkins University Press.

JONES, J. (1984) Labor of Love, Labor of Sorrow: Black Women, Work and the Family from Slavery to the Present. New York: Basic Books.

KANTER, R. (1977) Work and Family in the United States: A Critical Review and Agenda for Research and Policy. New York: Russell Sage Foundation.

KATZ, M. (1975) The People of Hamilton, Canada West. Cambridge, MA: Harvard University Press.

KESSLER-HARRIS, A. (1982) Out to Work: A History of Wage-Earning Women in the United States. New York: Oxford University Press.

KOBRIN, F. E. (1976) "The fall in household size and the rise of the primary individual in the United States." Demography 31: 127-138.

KOHN, M. (1969) Class and Conformity. Homewood, IL: Dorsey Press.

LADNER, J. A. (1971) Tomorrow's Tomorrow: The Black Woman. Garden City, NY: Doubleday.

LAING, R. D. (1967) The Politics of Experience and the Bird of Paradise. Harmondsworth: Penguin.

LAING, R.D. (1972) The Politics of the Family and Other Essays. New York: Random House.

LAING, R. D. and A. ESTERSON (1964) Sanity, Madness and the Family. Harmondsworth: Penguin.

LAPIDUS, G. W. (1979) Women in Soviet Society. Berkeley: University of California Press.

LASCH, C. (1977) Haven in a Heartless World. New York: Basic Books.

LASLETT, B. (1973) "The family as public and private institutions: An historical perspective." Journal of Marriage and Family 35: 480-492.

LASLETT, B. (1975) "Family membership, past and present." Social Problems 25: 476-490.

LASLETT, B. (1977) "Social change and the family: Los Angeles, California, 1850-1870." American Sociological Review 42: 269-291.

LASLETT, P. (1972) Household and Family in Past Time. Cambridge: Cambridge University Press.

LASLETT, P. (1977) Family Life and Illicit Love in Earlier Generations. Cambridge: Cambridge University Press.

LAZARRE, J. (1986) The Mother Knot. Boston: Beacon.

LE PLAY, F. (1982) Frederic Le Play on Family, Work and Social Change (ed., C. Silver). Chicago: University of Chicago Press.

LERNER, G. (1969) "The lady and the mill girl: Changes in the status of women in the age of Jackson." American Midcontinent Studies Journal 10: 5-15.

LERNER, G. [ed.] (1973) Black Women in White America: A Documentary History. New York: Vintage.

LEVY, D. (1943) Maternal Overprotection. New York: Columbia University Press.

LEWIS, J. (1980) The Politics of Motherhood: Child and Maternal Welfare in England, 1900-1939. Montreal: McGill-Queens University Press.

LEWIS, J. [ed.] (1986) Labor and Love: Women's Experiences of Home and Family, 1850-1940. London: Basil Blackwell.

LIDZ, T., S. FLECK, and A. R. CORNELISON (1965) Schizophrenia and the Family. New York: International Universities Press.

LUKER, K. (1984) Abortion and the Politics of Motherhood. Berkeley: University of California Press.

MALINOWSKI, B. (1913) The Family Among the Australian Aborigines. London: University of London Press.

MANDELL, N. (1984) "Where are the women? The tradition of G.H. Mead." Presented at the meetings of the American Sociological Association, San Antonio, Texas.

MARGOLIS, D. R. (1979) The Managers: Corporate Life in America. New York: Morrow.

MARTIN, E. P. and J. M. MARTIN (1978) The Black Extended Family. Chicago: University of Chicago Press.

McLAUGHLIN, V. Y. (1971) "Patterns of work and family organization: Buffalo's Italians." Journal of Interdisciplinary History 2: 299-314.

MEISSNER, M., E. W. HUMPHREY, S. M. MEISS, and W. J. SCHEU (1975) "No exit for wives: Sexual division of labor and the cumulation of household demands." Canadian Journal of Sociology and Anthropology 12: 424-459.

MITCHELL, J. (1971) Women's Estate. New York: Pantheon

MODELL, J. and H. TAMARA (1973) "Urbanization and the malleable household: An examination of boarding and lodging in American families." Journal of Marriage and the Family 35: 467-479.

MORGAN, J. N. (1978) "A potpourri of new data gathered from interviews with husbands and wives," pp. 367-401 in G. J. Duncan and J. N. Morgan (eds.) Five Thousand American Families: Patterns of Economic Progress, Vol. 6, Accounting for Race and Sex Differences in Earnings and Other Analysis of the First Nine Years of the Panel Study of Income Dynamics. Ann Arbor: University of Michigan, Institute for Social Research.

MURDOCK, G. (1949) Social Structure. New York: Macmillan.

OAKLEY, A. (1974a) Woman's Work: The Housewife, Past Present. New York: Pantheon.

OAKLEY, A. (1974b) The Sociology of Housework. New York: Pantheon

OREN, L. (1973) "The welfare of women in laboring families: England, 1860-1950." Feminist Studies 1: 107-125.

OSMOND, M. (1986) "Radical-critical theories," in M. Sussman and S. Steinmetz (eds.) Handbook of Marriage and Family. New York: Plenum.

PAGELOW, M. (1981) Woman-Battering: Victims and Their Experiences. Newbury Park, CA: Sage.

PAHL, J. (1983) "The allocation of money and the structuring of inequality within marriage," Sociological Review, 31(2) 237-262.

PARSONS, T. (1943) "The kinship system of the contemporary United States." American Anthropologist 45: 22-38.

PARSONS, T. (1955) "The American family: Its relation to personality and to the social structure," pp. 3-33 in T. Parsons and R. F. Bales (eds.) Family, Socialization, and Interaction Process. New York: Free Press.

PIOTRKOWSKI, C. S. (1980) Work and the Family System. New York: Free Press.

PLECK, E. (1979) "A mother's wages: Income earning among married Italian and Black women, 1896-1911," pp. 343-366 in N. F. Cott and E. H. Pleck (eds.) A Heritage of Her Own: Toward a New Social History of American Womanhood. New York: Touchstone.

PLECK, J. (1979) "Men's family work: Three perspectives and some new data." Family Coordinator 28: 481-488.

POSTER, M. (1978) Critical Theory of the Family. New York: Seabury Press.

RAPP, R. (1982) "Family and class in contemporary America: Notes toward an understanding of ideology." Science and Society 42: 278-300.

REINGOLD, J. C. (1964) The Fear of Being a Woman: A Theory of Maternal Destructiveness. New York: Grune & Stratton.

REITER, R. R. [ed.] (1975) Toward an Anthropology of Women. New York: Monthly Review Press.

RICH, A. (1979) On Lies, Secrets and Silence. New York: Norton.

RICH, A. (1976) Of Woman Born: Motherhood as Experience and Institution. New York: Norton.

ROBINSON, J., T. JUSTER, and F. STAFFORD (1976) America's Use of Time. Ann Arbor: Institute for Social Research, University of Michigan.

ROSALDO, M. Z. and L. LAMPHERE [eds.] (1974) Woman, Culture and Society. Stanford: Stanford University Press.

ROSS, E. (1979) "Examining family history: Women and family." Feminist Studies 5: 181-189.

ROSSI, A. (1979) "A biosocial perspective on parenting." Daedalus 106, 2: 1-31.

RUBIN, G. (1974) "The traffic in women: Notes on the 'political economy' of sex," pp. 157-210 in R. Reiter (ed.) Toward an Anthropology of Women. New York: Monthly Review Press.

RUBIN, L. (1976) Worlds of Pain. New York: Basic Books.

RUDDICK, S. (1980) "Maternal thinking." Feminist Studies 6: 343-367.

SAFILIOS-ROTHSCHILD, C. (1969) "Family sociology or wives' family sociology? A cross-cultural examination of decision-making." Journal of Marriage and the Family 31, 2: 290-301.

SAFILIOS-ROTHSCHILD, C. (1970) "The study of family power structure: A review of 1960-1969." Journal of Marriage and the Family 32: 539-552.

SENA-RIVERA, J. (1979) "Extended kinship in the United States: Competing models and the case of la familia Chicana." Journal of Marriage and the Family 41, 1: 121-130.

SKOLNICK, A. and J. H. SKOLNICK (1986) "Introduction," pp. 1-18 in A. Skolnick and J. H. Skolnick (eds.) Family in Transition. Boston: Little, Brown.

SMITH, D. (1979) "A sociology for women," in J. A. Beck and E. T. Beck (eds.) The Prism of Sex. Madison: University of Wisconsin Press.

SMUTS, R. (1971) Women and Work. New York: Schocken.

SOKOLOFF, N. (1980) Between Money and Love. New York: Praeger.

SPALTER-ROTH, R. (1985) "Dollars, dirt and time alone: Struggles over living standards in dual career households." Presented at the meetings of the Society for the Study of Social Problems, Washington, DC.

STACEY, J. (1983) Patriarchy and Socialist Revolution in China. Berkeley: University of California Press.

STACEY, J. and B. THORNE (1985) "The missing feminist revolution in sociology." Social Problems 32, 4: 301-316.

STACK, C. B. (1974) All Our Kin: Strategies for Survival in a Black Community. New York: Harper & Row.

STANLEY, L. and S. WISE (1983) Breaking Out: Feminist Consciousness and Feminist Research. London: Routledge & Kegan Paul.

STAPLES, R. and A. MIRANDE (1980) "Racial and cultural variations among American families: A decennial review of the literature on minority families." Journal of Marriage and the Family 42: 887-903.

STRASSER, S. (1982) Never Done: A History of American Housework. New York: Pantheon.

SZALAI, A., P. CONVERSE, P. FELDHEIM, E. SCHEUCH, and P. STONE [eds.] (1972) The Use of Time: Daily Activities of Urban and Suburban Populations in Twelve Countries. The Hague: Mouton.

THORNE, B. (1982) "Feminist rethinking of the family: An overview," pp. 1-24 in B. Thorne with M. Yalom (eds.) Rethinking the Family: Some Feminist Questions. New York: Longman.

TIERNEY (1982) "The battered woman movement and the creation of the wife-beating problem." Social Problem 29(3): 207-220.

VALENTINE, B. L. (1978) Hustling and Other Hard Work. New York: Free Press.

VANEK, J. (1974) "Time spent in housework." Scientific American (November): 116-129.

VAUGHAN, D. (1985) "Uncoupling: The social construction of divorce," pp. 429-439 in J. Henslin (ed.) Marriage and Family in a Changing Society. New York: Free Press.

WALKER, K. E. and M. E. WOODS (1976) Time Use: A Measure of Household Production of Family Goods and Services. Washington, DC: American Home Economics Association.

WEINBAUM, B. and A. BRIDGES (1971) "The other side of the paycheck: Monopoly capital and the structure of consumption." Monthly Review 28: 88-103.

WELTER, B. (1966) "The cult of true womanhood: 1820-1860." American Quarterly (Summer): 151-171.

WHITE, D. G. (1983) "Female slaves: sex roles and status in the antebellum south." Journal of Family History 9: 248-261.

WHITEHEAD, A. (1976) "Sexual antagonism in Herefordshire," pp. 169-203 in D. L. Barker and S. Allen (eds.) Dependence and Exploitation in Work and Marriage. New York: Longman.

WILSON, E. (1977) Women and the Welfare State. London: Tavistock.

WYLEY, P. (1942) Generation of Vipers. New York: Farrar, Rinehart.

YANAGISAKO, S. J. (1977) "Women-centered kin networks in urban bilateral kinship." American Ethnologist 4: 207-226.

YOUNG, M. and P. WILLMOTT (1962) Family and Kinship in East London. Baltimore: Penguin.

ZARETSKY, E. (1976) Capitalism, the Family and Personal Life. New York: Harper.

ZARETSKY, E. (1982) "The place of the family in the origins of the welfare state," pp. 188-224 in B. Thorne with M. Yalom (eds.) Rethinking the Family: Some Feminist Questions. New York: Longman.

14　Women's Family Roles in Life Course Perspective

HELENA Z. LOPATA
Loyola University of Chicago

HOW do contemporary American women perceive and assign priorities to the various roles they occupy in the family dimension throughout their lives? Does "mother" outrank "wife"? When is "daughter" most salient? What are the components of the "grandmother role"? These and many other questions immediately direct our attention to the complexity of the subject. Interestingly enough, such queries are rarely posed for men although they, too, have patterned relationships with parents, offspring, siblings and spouse. The major focus of the lives of men is their occupational and political roles. Yet the centrality of family roles for women is taken for granted, despite current trends in labor force participation, rising age at first marriage, delayed childbearing, and current low fertility rates (see Glenn, Chapter 13 in this volume).

Curiously, even given the emphasis on women in family research, little attention has been paid to shifts over the life course in the hierarchy of women's family commitments. This chapter attempts to remedy this omission by examining recent research data in the context of the emergent life course perspective and social change. We shall see how, from girlhood to widowhood in old age, female lives are constrained by the gender stratification system and its consequences for self-concept and life changes.

But first we must address some important definitional concerns. Although the term "social role" has often been used carelessly as indicating status, set of expectations, or stereotype, it is defined here as a set of patterned, interrelated social relations between a social person and members of the social circle, involving duties and personal rights (Lopata, 1964, 1966, 1971; Lopata et al., 1984).[1] A person enters a social role with characteristics deemed necessary for adequately discharging such duties and receiving such rights. The rights are the actions and objects contributed by circle members in order to enable the person to perform the role in the agreed upon manner. The social circle contains everyone with whom the person interacts in the role. Thus the role involves not only tasks but also a flow of relations through which mutual goals are met.

A second definitional distinction involves the concept of gender identity. A human being is assigned sex identification at birth on the basis of biological characteristics. In all societies this identification is extremely important and, through socialization, is translated into a pervasive gender identity carried through life and influencing social roles available to the individual and the manner in which common roles are performed (Bernard, 1975: 64; Lopata and Thorne, 1978). There are *no* sex roles, only gender identities that influence how others act toward the social person in various roles, how the person sees herself or himself, and how status is allocated. Typically, gender forms a dichotomized status structure, with the lower status position assigned to women (Bernard, 1981b; Laws, 1979). In a society such as America, characterized by diffuse status clusters (decrystallization), gender is only one criterion for location in various status hierarchies. An upper class woman might be given higher status than a lower class man. Yet gender identity remains an important feature of self-concept, role selection, and relations within roles, as gender relations are based on a sexual division of labor that maintains male dominance.

At any life stage, a person is involved in a cluster of social roles that change over time, old ones having been dropped, new ones prepared for through anticipatory socialization and entered, willingly or not. Sociologists analyze role clusters in two ways: in terms of social life space and as a hierarchical system developed by the person. The social life-space perspective attends both to number of institutions contained in the cluster—institutional multidimensionality—and to the number of roles in a single institution—dimensional richness or poverty. People whose role cluster embraces several institutions are less focused on any one dimension than are those whose cluster is more limited. Multidimensional role clusters are often associated with psychological well-being (Baruch, 1984; Long and Porter, 1984) and individual autonomy (Coser, 1975).

The hierarchical system refers to the importance the person herself or himself assigns to each role within the cluster. Most people do not differentiate among their roles the way sociologists do, but they are more or less conscious of the priorities they assign to various roles when conflicts occur. The hierarchical structure of the role cluster is modified throughout life, as a person enters (or exits) from valued roles (Lopata and Barnewolt, 1984).[2] Figures 14.1 and 14.2 illustrate both the life-space and the hierarchical arrangement of role clusters.

This chapter is devoted to the examination of the life-course involvement and changes in the hierarchical positions assigned by women to the social roles in only one dimension of their role cluster, the family dimension. For example, one study of American urban women in their middle years of life found them, not surprisingly, most strongly committed to the roles that they currently occupied. Additionally, the most likely to place highest value on the role of mother is the woman without competing major roles of wife or

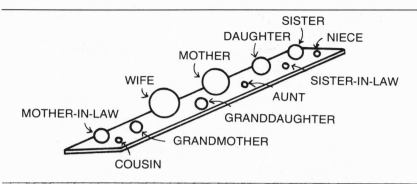

Figure 14.1   A Single Dimension of an Adult Woman

employee (Lopata and Barnewolt, 1984: 92). The role of wife is ranked as either the first or the second most important, depending on the presence or absence of young children. This is not surprising, due to the simplicity of the roles in the family dimension of American women relative to those in other societies. Thus the single role of wife is usually seen as of much greater significance to American women living in small nuclear families than to a member of an Indian joint family, although there are important variations in our society on the basis of race and social class. Let us now follow the shifting hierarchy of family roles across the life course.

BECOMING AND BEING A GIRL, AND THEN A WOMAN

The birth and acceptance of a child activates a number of potential roles such as mother, father, brother, sister, grandmother, grandfather. These sets of relations are shaped by cultural ideals based on gender, initiating a very complex system of socialization by significant others who already have a picture of what a girl and a woman should be like and who try to ensure that the product will conform to the image. However, each culture allows, even encourages, individual diversity within the boundaries of the image. Not all girls are seen as alike or expected to grow into the same kind of woman. In addition, there are racial, ethnic, class, and other subcultural variations on the dominant norms (Elkin and Handel, 1984). In the process of becoming and being a woman, the girl will enter and exit a sequence of social roles, which also change across time or in response to particular historical events such as the Great Depression (Elder, 1974; Hareven, 1978).

To a greater degree than for men, biological changes set parameters to stages in the life course of women, sometimes with dramatic turning points

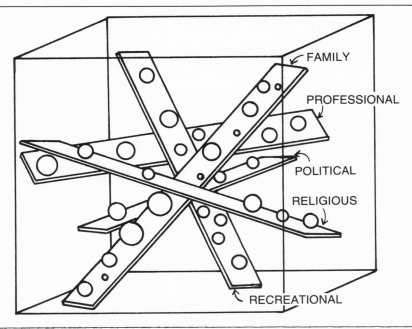

Figure 14.2   A Multidimensional Life Space With Varied Richness of Institutional
                 Dimensions

(Bernard, 1975a; Laws and Schwartz, 1977; Rossi, 1968). In societies that emphasize the reproductive contributions of women, stages of life are divided into premenarchical, childbearing, and postmenopausal (Bernard, 1975a: 100). Modern feminists have documented how wasteful such an emphasis is in modern American society, in which less than one-fourth of the woman's life course is actually involved in childbearing and rearing, if she enters the role of mother at all, and in which other role involvements are also necessary (Ehrenreich and English, 1979; Freidan, 1963; Huber and Spitze, 1983).

The chronological ages and signals of turning points vary considerably across cultures and time. American culture contains many contradictory and changing images of the role clusters and transitions of women. Although traditional socialization practices aimed young women toward being good, or at least adequate, mothers and, secondarily, wives, there have been few structural supports for motherhood, especially if the woman is not currently married. There are, however, many ideological supports and pronatalist policies that encourage motherhood (Rich, 1976). The feminist movement and young women themselves have increasingly stressed the importance of involvement in, and commitment to, roles outside of those of wife-mother-homemaker (Lopata et al., 1985). Increasing proportions of American urban women are preparing for work roles through education and job training, and are delaying marriage and parenthood on the assumption that these would interfere with their life in the public sphere. Other women have fewer choices in when and how they mix family and nonfamily roles.

At present, however, the wife-mother-homemaker subcluster is interwoven with the student-worker-career woman subcluster only with difficulty even for middle-class white women during the crucial 15 to 20 years of their life span (Troll et al., 1977). Two important changes will have to take place in order to free up the life course of American women: opening up the social structure to variety and flexibility in the involvements of both men and women, and modification of socialization of both genders to encourage such involvements. If we assume that most women will spend the major part of their lives in paid occupations, the foundation of commitment to a multidimensional life must be established early and reinforced by the educational system. Those who wish to withdraw from paid employment during childbearing years, or who want to combine both subclusters, will at least have flexibility built into their personal resources if societal cooperation is extended to the provision of assistance such as is currently available in other countries. The dichotomy of choice between home life and public life now presented to both women and men needs to be erased.

In spite of continuing inflexibility in the societal economic structure, especially in the scheduling of paid work, our study of women aged 25 to 54 in an American urban center indicates great heterogeneity in life patterns and decrystallization of status packages (Lopata et al., 1985). Reflecting the national picture, younger women are combining different roles in more varied ways than was true of their older counterparts. The influence of social background characteristics has declined. Many have returned to school (43%), enrolled in job training programs, or changed occupations. They are entering and exiting marriage at all stages of the life span, delaying childbearing and often combining child rearing with employment. Some have even planned it this way, entering occupational preparation with greater commitment to the world of work outside of the home than was true of prior generations. Others are "displaced homemakers" who had not planned on losing the support of a husband through desertion, separation, divorce, or widowhood. Yet others purposely ended an unsatisfactory marriage and many are in second or even third marriages, with all the complications of blended families.

Aging brings additional problems of identity and opportunity, with changes in body appearance and abilities (Rossi, 1985). Widowhood faces women oftener than men. Retirement is experienced by workers of either gender. In a society so focused on motherhood, wifehood, and occupations, the loss of valued roles in old age might be seen as the inevitable and even welcome "disengagement" (Cumming and Henry, 1961), but research shows that other roles can increase in importance (Lopata, 1979). Friendship, neighboring, church membership, club and community involvement can be very meaningful and entered into without feelings of guilt for "neglecting" the roles defined in the culture as most important to women. A lack of viable family or occupational roles does not, therefore, necessarily lead to social isolation.

Turning now to a life course analysis of major family roles of women in the United States today, we will examine the roles of daughter, sister, wife, mother, mother-in-law, stepmother, and grandmother.

DAUGHTER

The role of daughter has the longest duration and probably the greatest change of all roles performed by a woman. One is a daughter to parents as a couple, to one's mother, and to one's father, with variations on the theme in all three relationships. The role contains everyone with whom the girl/woman interacts because she is a daughter. The content of the social circle varies over time, as do the role clusters of all persons involved. Daughters, like sons, have obligations to their siblings that are really duties to the parents—not to fight or hurt the other, to "be polite," help with activities, defend against harm from others, and so forth. In some families the daughter is the major contributor to the mother's work in the home and care of other family members; in other households she may be the "princess," receiving all the benefits of childhood and young adulthood through which the parents live vicariously. Each society and social class has its own norms concerning the duties of a daughter to the parents, not identical to the rights and duties of sons, such as help with housework in a gender-segregated manner or being a confidant and companion (Lopata, 1979).

If the way fathers and mothers socialize their sons and daughters varies on all levels, then daughters at even early ages are supposed to distinguish the father from the mother and respond differently to their actions (Lengermann and Wallace, 1985; Pleck and Pleck, 1980). Doctors and other "experts" are available if the child does not respond in the expected ways (Ehrenreich and English, 1979). Above all, the daughter should grow up in a manner that validates her mother as a good mother (Ruddick, 1982). In our society, daughters are supposed to look pretty, yet crawl and move with agility, walk and talk at the right age or even earlier than Spock (1957) and other experts predict. Daughters of ministers, psychiatrists, professors, and politicians are especially obligated to behave in an exemplary manner since they are allegedly imbued with special abilities or have a visible public family image to protect.

The early mother-daughter relationship has received much attention from feminist scholars (Chodorow, 1978; Hirsch, 1981; Rich, 1976) which we will examine when discussing the role of mother. The changing relations between adolescent and adult daughters and their mothers as they go through transitions in their "linked lives" has been analyzed by Fisher (1986). Over time the daughters take away from the mother the right to decide their life paths. Sometimes the shift in rights and duties is accomplished only after constant pushing or active rebellion on the part of the daughter. The oldest daughter is frequently the pioneer or forward scout in this battle for independence. The thrust is aimed at the parent most representative of the family norms. Sometimes the parent forces changes in the relationship, for example, demanding greater assistance in the role of homemaker. The problem during adolescent years is thus one of push and pull, of "holding on and letting go" on the part of both the daughter and the mother (Fisher, 1986). Sooner or later, the daughter must "launch herself" and establish her own life relatively independent of the mother and father.

There is some evidence that the daughter is drawn again to her mother when she herself becomes a mother (Fisher, 1986). At that time the daughter is "settled in" and shares many experiences, turning to the mother for advice and help with child care. She often changes her perspective on her own childhood and understands better her mother's behavior toward her; "the hierarchical nature of their relationship becomes less problematic" (Fisher, 1986: 126). Both are "role colleagues" and share a focus on the young child. Thus the mother becomes a source of support for the daughter (Baruch et al., 1983). This relative symmetry, or less bothersome version of asymmetry, may last for years. Among American blacks, daughters appear to have a right to tolerance and support from their own mothers even in bearing and rearing children out of wedlock (Ladner, 1971; Staples and Mirande, 1980).

The duties of the daughter toward her mother tend to change and even increase as the parents age. These are both emotional and service oriented (Lopata, 1973, 1979). The amount and type of support provided by the daughter depend on many factors on both sides of the relationship: the competing roles in the daughter's cluster and the ease with which she is able to provide supports, and the self- and other-defined needs and alternative resources available to the parent.

The most frequently studied aspects of the role of adult daughter focus on the stage at which parents can no longer fully care for themselves. An expanding professional and public interest in the problems and solutions facing daughters of the frail elderly follows the demographic realities of an aging society. Women live longer than men, and the age group of 85 and older is the fastest growing segment of the older population. Without public supports for their well-being, the burden of care for the very old and ill parents will fall on their offspring.

And it is the daughter who is usually the most important supplier of supports to aging parents and especially to widowed mothers (Lopata, 1979; Shanas, 1980). Sons render fewer and quite gender-segregated supports, such as household repairs or advice in business matters. That is, the gender division of labor within the family extends across the life course. One daughter is usually more active than other offspring, although the process of selection that ensures that she lives within easy contact distance and is available for support is often complex. According to Stueve and O'Donnell (1984), variations in the involvement of adult daughters with elderly parents depend on timing of events in the lives of both generations, the relationship between them, social class, and the presence of competing roles such as job or family.

Caring for a parent can lead to conflict within the daughter's role cluster. Her husband and children can resent the time and energy, or the money and other expenditures, that a daughter contributes to the parents. She, in turn, can deeply resent the failure of others to understand the depth of her sense of obligation. Paid employment may further shorten the time available to a woman to spend with her mother and/or father (Finch and Groves, 1983).

The final duty of a daughter is to keep alive the social person of a deceased parent. Immortality is ensured in some cultures mainly by the action of sons rather than daughters—which is one reason why sons are so desired in these cultures—but it is daughters and daughters-in-law in modern America who are expected to transmit family memories to the next generations.

The special case of the daughter-in-law is an interesting one and also varies from society to society. Rather than becoming the daughter, she is frequently seen as an adjunct to the son, helping him fulfill his obligations to his parents. In some cultures, the daughter drops all or most of her ties to her own parents and fully enters the family of the husband. In such cases she may replace the in-laws' own daughters who have left to join their husband's families. In our society, the daughter-in-law is the primary caregiver in the household where a son has assumed responsibility for the ill or very old parent.

SISTER

A sister (and brother) is often obliged not only to protect younger siblings but also to ensure that they behave in a manner that will not damage their reputation. Gender, birth order, and the number of siblings influences their relationship, as parents typically assign tasks along age and gender lines (Brody and Steelman, 1985). In extreme situations, such as the absence of the mother, sisters have taken over the role of parent. A variety of circumstances determine whether they see this as part of the role of sister or of daughter—that is, whether they act out of concern for the siblings rather than obedience to the older generation. Sisters are often asked to stand up at sibling's weddings and to serve as godmothers to nieces and nephews.

In the American middle class, sibling groups tend to disperse in adulthood; whereas the constrictions of life among the less affluent, and especially in the underclass, result in a continued cycle of interdependence. Stack (1974) found that poor black women even developed fictive brothers and sisters in an effort to guarantee service and emotional support.

However, and in spite of earlier claims that the extended family is active in the support systems of the elderly (Sussman, 1962; Litwak, 1965), later research (Lopata, 1979; Shanas, 1980) finds that siblings are not important sources of support. Brothers and sisters appear at the time of the funeral and occasionally as people to whom a widow turns in times of crisis, but they are absent from the daily life and support networks of urban widows (Lopata, 1973, 1979). Also absent are nieces and nephews. It may be that the early sibling rivalry prevents closeness once adulthood frees people from obligations to brothers and sisters. Geographic and socioeconomic dispersal may make contact difficult except for special occasions. The death of the parents cuts another connecting link. Similar findings of an "overheralded" kin network are reported by Gibson (1982) and Lee (1980).

WIFE

Of signal importance in American society is the role of wife, its significance stemming from the absence of a joint or stem family and the relative independence of each nuclear unit, mate selection by choice, and the availability of divorce to end unsatisfactory relations. "Almost every adult in the United States eventually marries" (Cherlin, 1981: 9), but there are signs that people are now postponing entry into this role, and some are even rejecting it entirely. Ehrenreich (1984), for example, claims that men are decreasingly interested in supporting a wife and children, while some women are focusing on careers.

Entrance into the role of wife is a complicated process. Americans typically select their mate from a pool of eligibles acceptable to parents, usually within the same social class, racial, and often religious subgroup, although the parents have little direct influence on the choice (Cherlin, 1981). Laws (1979) defines courtship, traditional and even current, as a dance or series of steps, with cohabitation being added in recent times (Skolnick, 1983).

Becoming a wife modifies existing relations, pulls together a new social circle, and generally requires a new construction of reality (Berger and Kellner, 1970). Even if the daughter were already living independently of the parents, her marriage changes their relationship because of her new social position as well as the addition of the husband to the interaction. Friendships are also transformed; still-unmarried friends tend to be seen less frequently, as leisure time becomes devoted to couple companionate relations (Lopata, 1975, 1979). Single companions tend to be seen as a "threat to married people" (Duberman, 1975; see also Stein, 1976, 1977). In addition, attempts are made to develop symmetrical friendships, each member of each couple liking one another. In American society, one suspects that the wife is more involved in the process of constructing the reality of the marriage than is the husband, whose identity is based on occupational rather than marital status. Bernard

(1972: 42) refers to the "shock theory of marriage" for women and states that "dwindling into a wife" takes time and much greater adjustment than becoming a husband requires of a man. The wife drops her birth name and becomes Mrs. John Brown. This shift connects her now to him, not to her parents. Chapman and Gates (1977) show that, although laws defining a wife in British common law terms adopted in America have undergone change, there are still legal disadvantages to wifehood. Full partnership in marriage requires further legislative reforms, which are only slowly evolving (Krauskopf, 1977). Even the new community property laws have proven detrimental to many women.

Women interviewed in the Chicago area in the 1950s and 1960s explained that marriage changed them from an "irresponsible girl" to a settled woman. Yet other aspects of life can remain fairly unchanged; newly married women today usually continue their involvement in jobs and some homemaking tasks are often shared although the wife still performs the bulk of the household work. If a couple had been living together before marriage, the identity shift does not necessarily bring changes in daily routines (DeMaris and Leslie, 1984; Macklin, 1977). Of course, age at marriage and prior roles and relations are important factors in the degree to which entry into marriage changes one's self-concept and relationships.

Much of the literature on husbands and wives has focused on the power relationship between them and the processes of negotiation involved in its maintenance and shifts (Blood and Wolfe, 1960; Safilios-Rothschild and Dikjers, 1980). In general, access to nonfamily roles and resources enhances the power of one partner (usually the husband) over the other. In modern middle-class marriages, the power of the wife is reduced if and when she withdraws from a multidimensional life into confinement in the home with newborn children. If the woman is then a full-time homemaker, her life and identities become increasingly different from those of the husband who remains linked to the world of work. The role of wife loses some of its importance in the role cluster of the new mother (Lopata and Barnewolt, 1984). Although most women expect the role of wife to return to its primary position after the children are grown, the husband is often jealous of the child and feels relatively neglected. Thus there is conflict between the role of mother and that of wife, in addition to major life changes for the woman from her prior involvements and self-concepts. Parenthood is often described as creating a "crisis" for both mother and father and for the marital relation (Dyer, 1963; Rossi, 1968).

Women who are full-time homemakers and whose husbands are in white-collar jobs may become involved in what Hanna Papanek (1973) calls a "two-person single career"—that is, the wife functions as the back-up person assisting the husband's career. This usually happens in midlife rather than early in the marriage, when the husband has not achieved visibility in his world and the wife is still deeply involved with the role of mother. Papanek

(1979) also draws our attention to family status production work.

Seen comparatively and historically, the two-person career is not uncommon if we broaden the concept of career to include any significant role or sequence of roles demanding high levels of commitment in "greedy institutions" (Coser, 1974). It is difficult for anyone without a supportive partner— supportive not only psychologically but actively—to reach and maintain a job in the high rungs of American professional and business worlds. This may be one reason women have problems moving up the management ladder, since they lack such supports. The wife as back-up person is less visible than the man, since he is the public representative of the role, carries the job title, and does most of his work in the employing organization. Thus it is his career that absorbs the energies of both partners. She may be the "power behind the throne" but he is the king and is paid directly while her rewards are indirect and vicarious (Lipman-Blumen and Leavitt, 1976). Wives contribute to the husband's occupational career in four major ways: (1) in how they perform the homemaker role, (2) in status production work, (3) "stroking" or emotional support, and (4) in direct involvement in the social circle of the husband's job.

The first work area consists of an overlap between the role of homemaker and that of wife. Although it is possible for a wife not also to be a homemaker, most are, and contribute to their husband's job performance by cutting the time it would take him to prepare his food, maintain his clothing and living space, and find objects necessary to his life-style, by providing a functioning household, and by ensuring that the children and others do not interfere while he recuperates from the strain of his job (Dulles, 1965; Finch, 1983; Lopata et al., 1980; Papanek, 1979). In other words, if she were not in the role of homemaker, he would have to do all this himself or hire others. If he were not in the home, she would not have to perform these tasks.

Status production work for women married to "important" men consists of efforts at enhancing community visibility through club work, voluntary activities and friendships, socializing the children and younger wives into appropriate demeanor and life-style, in addition to maintaining a home and social life commensurate with their class positions (Ostrander, 1984; see also Veblen, 1925). Daniels (1985, 1987) discusses the importance of social skills to women volunteers maintaining the family's status in the community.

Somewhere between status production work and direct involvement with the husband's occupation stand the activities designated by Bernard (1972) and developed by Ostrander (1984: 39) as having a stroking function. They consist of "showing solidarity, giving help, rewarding, agreeing, understanding and passively accepting." The literature on wives of managers stresses the need to "hang loose" and not become committed to a social role, relationship, or community too strongly, in view of frequent career-related geographic transfers (Margolis, 1979; Seidenberg, 1973). Such transfers require packing and unpacking of physical objects and the creation of a new home, as well as the social establishment of the family in a new community (Bucher, 1977).

Such transfers also entail personal stress and loneliness until new relations are developed and make it impossible for many wives to even consider maintaining a career.

The work a wife does to help the husband directly with his job and as an active participant in his social circle varies with the demands and opportunities to be so involved. An earlier study of full-time homemakers (Lopata, 1971) found great social class variations in how women perceive their influence on the husband's career, ranging from nagging him to work harder on the part of the least educated wives, through maintenance of a cooperative household, to direct involvement by the more educated wives of men in business and professional occupations.

There is a voluminous literature attesting to the importance of a wife's contribution to the careers of men in high status jobs—as army officers (Shae, 1941), physicians or professors (Fowlkes, 1980), or corporate executives (Kanter, 1977; Margolis, 1979; Seidenberg, 1973; Vendervelde, 1979). Many a preface to a scholarly book contains an acknowledgment to the wife for typing the manuscript and for ideas, as well as stroking support; and recent consciousness-raising has pushed some authors to admit coauthorship. Still, let us not minimize the importance of typing, especially before the introduction of the personal computer! There is no comparable literature dealing with lower status male occupations, possibly because they do not require direct involvement on the part of the wife. Lopata et al. (1980) found that middle-aged women claimed to be giving much more direct support to their husband in his job that they received from him. Again, this may be because most women's jobs do not require activity away from the place of employment. According to many studies, whether or not a woman is employed makes little difference in how much "help" in homemaking tasks she perceives receiving from her husband, or in how much help he expects of her, according to many studies (see, for example, Berk, 1980).

Assisting with the husband's career is linked to his need to fill "the good provider" role that Bernard (1981a: 2) defines as a specialized male role that "seems to have arisen in the transition from subsistence to market—especially money—economics that accelerated with the industrial revolution." The good provider should be able to support an unemployed wife and children, and employers claim to be providing a "family wage" on that basis. Wives in the labor force are assumed to need only token wages to supplement the husband's income. This applies at all class levels (see Bose, Chapter 10 in this volume).

Although the duties of the role of wife are complex, so are the rights. If she is not to earn her own subsistence, she should be economically supported. She has a right to expect that her activities as a wife and as a homemaker will be recognized and that the man of the family will do his part in maintaining the household. Our society expects husbands to show love to wives and to engage in social activities with them.

One of the rights assumed to accompany the role of wife in modern America is the guarantee of physical safety and absence of physical violence. This right did not exist in America's past and does not exist in all parts of the world (Pleck, 1983). Public and scientific attention has recently been drawn to the prevalence of wife-beating, which, while widely deplored, is also "normalized" and legitimated in many ways (Gelles, 1974; Straus et al., 1980). Research on violence in the family, summarized by Gelles (1980) suggests the following causal factors: (1) the cycle of violence (people abused as children tend to become abusers in adulthood), (2) low socioeconomic status, (3) stress, especially that brought about by unemployment of the husband and financial problems, and (4) social isolation. Alcohol is a frequent accompanying factor, as is generally low social integration in the community, including the church (Walker, 1979). More general, cultural supports are analyzed by Sheffield (Chapter 6 in this volume).

Of equal interest to social scientists is the willingness of the abused wife to return to the husband. Those who did so were usually unemployed, had nowhere else to go, and thought they could reform the abuser through love (Strube and Barbour, 1984: 837). The absence of alternatives leading to a feeling of entrapment, low self-concept, or self-blame for the attack are powerful factors keeping a wife with an abusive husband. The lack of economic supports and habituation to a long-term relation as well as the presence of children makes many women feel there are no alternatives to even a miserable marriage (see also Rubin, 1976).

Another right expected by modern wives is the absence of a double standard in extramarital relations. However, there is every indication that equality in involvement in or abstention from such relations among monogamous couples is far from being achieved, although there appears to be an increase in the frequency with which wives report extramarital relations, a tendency long indulged by husbands (Hunt, 1966, 1974, 1977; Neubeck, 1969; Reiss et al., 1980; Saunders and Edwards, 1984; Thompson, 1984). Some of the decline of the double standard may reflect increased opportunities on the part of employed wives.

Generally speaking, the latter years of marriage, not just in the postparental but also in the postretirement period, tend to be calmer and more enjoyable assuming there are no serious health or economic problems. If the couple has stayed together, it has completed prior "unfinished business," the children are grown and out of the way. Remaining problems are habitual ones, as couples continue the arguments that have both separated and bound them over three or four decades.

The rights of both husbands and wives include care during illness and disability. In actuality, it is usually the wife who cares for the husband since he tends to be older in age and since women tend to outlive men. Caring for a disabled spouse requires a great deal of work, often for years and with little outside assistance, because professionals assume that such action is "natural" and older women are often loath to seek formal services (Finch and Groves, 1983; Oliver, 1983).

VESTIGES OF THE ROLE OF WIFE
IN DIVORCE AND WIDOWHOOD

Women may experience a transformation in the role of wife through desertion, separation, divorce, and widowhood. Temporary separations are not uncommon where one spouse, usually the husband, has had to leave home for economic, political, or religious reasons. Men travel for business as merchants or consultants; they are absent during wars or as prisoners (Lowenstein, 1984; McCubbin and Dahl, 1975; Pearlin and Schooler, 1978), or as guest workers and advance immigrants (Lopata, 1976). The role of wife is dramatically changed by the absence of the husband, since personal interaction and the exchange of duties and rights are temporarily suspended. Some obligations remain, such as refraining from "infidelity," the maintenance of the household for the return of the traveler, and usually some form of correspondence providing news of the home and family.

Permanent separation or divorce influences the role of wife along many dimensions in varying degrees. The role is usually not totally withdrawn: In-laws may still be seen, even exhusbands may have contacts due to legal or other obligations, particularly if children are involved. The degree of disorganization created by the break in the marriage depends on the centrality and salience of the role in the life of the wife; her dependence on her husband for various supports; the timing, in terms of stage in the life course; the circumstances surrounding the divorce (e.g., who initiated it and how sudden the onset); the effect of the situation on the wife's other's roles, such as that of mother, homemaker, or friend; the amount of stigma; other attitudes toward the couple; and the alternative roles and relations available to the wife (Lipman-Blumen, 1977).

Permanent separations—that is, those designed to end the relationship—are common in all modern societies. In the United States, the proportion of marriages that end in divorce are one in two for persons entering marriage since 1973 (Cherlin, 1981), although the divorce rate appears to have leveled off in the 1980s due to later age at marriage (National Center for Health Statistics, 1985). Rates of marital dissolution from all causes, however, are much higher for blacks than for whites, so that black women spend fewer years in the role of wife than do their white age peers.

Marriages are also dissolved by death, although less frequently compared to divorce today than in the past. There are some similarities between divorcees and widows (Kitson et al., 1980). Both types of women go through grief for the past and express loneliness. Divorcees experience greater stigma and often have less social support, but both must rebuild the support systems and networks in the absence of the husband and those people who entered the woman's social circles because of his presence. Divorcees, however, have different memories of their spouses and their past, while widows tend to idealize the late husband, often to the point of sanctification (Lopata, 1981; Kitson et al., 1980). Placing the dead husband in the position of saint removes from his spirit mortal jealousies and criticisms, and distances him from ongoing life. However, it can create strains with people who had known him and prevent relations with living men who can not measure up to the late husband's image.

There is considerable debate over the consequences for the wife of the circumstances surrounding the husband's death, such as her age when it occurs, the manner of death, the way the wife hears of it and initially deals with it, and related events that she must handle. Younger, "off-time" widows face different, possibly more traumatic effects than do other women (Glick et al., 1974). Neugarten (1968) suggests that people go through a "rehearsal for widowhood" as they grow older and watch their friends go through the real thing, which lessens the effects of the death of their own husband. Whatever the variations of the effects of sudden versus lingering, off-time or on-time death, it is almost invariably traumatic even if it also results in relief.

Americans believe that people marry for love, that they are important to each other, and that marriage either meets their needs or is terminated. Thus, when a spouse dies, the survivor is expected to feel the loss and go through the rituals of mourning and grief. The rituals themselves have become minimized in this society (Gorer, 1967). People suffering, dying, and grieving tend to be avoided when possible (Glaser and Strauss, 1965), and those coming into contact with the dying person and the survivors usually do not know how to handle the situation. The widow herself may not know how to put others at ease, or she may be too concerned with her own emotions to even want to make that effort. Grief work involves "emancipation from the bondage of the deceased, readjustment to the environment in which the deceased is missing and the formation of new relationships," (Lindemann, 1944: 43). To this we can add the task of reconstructing reality, including the self. Typically, a widow is allowed a limited period to recover from the shock, "gather herself together," and then proceed with "normal" activities. But daily life continues with its problems at a time when the survivor is unable to deal with any but her own emotional trauma. Many immediate situations facing the widow provide, or reinforce, her feelings of incompetence. The prior division of labor has suddenly fallen apart, and the woman finds herself unable to take on the tasks and relationships previously managed by the husband. Many of these tasks may fall outside the widow's area of competence, leading to some bewilderment and resentment. In general, better educated and more multidimensional women are best able to restructure life following the period of heavy grief.

Loneliness can be a major problem for wives who had grown accustomed to the husband (Lopata, 1969, 1979). The widow misses the husband as a love object, as someone who treated her as a love object, and someone who treated her as an important person—even if only to argue with—a sexual companion, a social companion, an escort in public places, a partner in couple companionate interaction with other married friends, a person around whom work and time are organized, and as someone simply "there." Widows also miss the status of being a wife, and the wife of that particular husband, with its accompanying life-style.

The effect of the dissolution of a marriage on the woman's self-concept bears further discussion (Lopata, 1984). To the extent that she went through a process of reconstruction of reality while becoming and being a wife, she must restructure it again after she loses that role, a need felt more strongly by middle-class than working-class women (Lopata, 1984). The widows in our studies who were highly dependent on the marriage went through a period of feeling in "limbo" with "no place to go" in terms of their sense of self. They could no longer identify themselves as wives, could not go back to being "girls," and did not want to build an identity around the negative concept of widow. Occupationally involved women often reported less displacement in widowhood, as did those embedded in neighborhood or kin networks. Younger widows are more apt to report change and to modify their lives, especially if not limited by the presence of small children and/or the absence of economic resources.

REENTRANCE INTO THE ROLE OF WIFE

For many women, divorce and widowhood may be opportunities to start a new life (Lipman-Blumen, 1977). The role of wife may be reentered with another person, as most divorces occur early in the marriage (Cherlin, 1981: 26) and not all widows are old when the husband dies. "About five out of six men and about three out of four women remarry after a divorce" (Cherlin, 1981: 29). Widows are less fortunate, since there are almost 10 times as many women in that marital status as men (Lopata, 1979). Divorced men prefer not to date or to marry widows (Hunt, 1966) and men tend to marry even younger women the second time around, while there are few older men for the widows (Lopata, 1973; McKain, 1969: 15). The older the widow or the divorcee, the lower her probability of remarriage.

Some widows choose not to remarry, giving several reasons besides their newly found independence, such as fear of having once again to care for an ailing spouse or the feelings that no man can replace the sanctified deceased. Other barriers include the possibility of jeopardizing her inheritance through remarriage, especially in states with community property laws (Prager, 1982). In addition, children of the former marriage may not want to see their mother reenter the role of wife, from either emotional or monetary concerns.

Younger women who reenter the role of wife frequently create complex family structures, with the addition of new sets of relatives. The role of wife must be adjusted to those of stepmother, new in-law, former wife, wife to the father of the children, and so forth. Expectations of marriage may be more realistic the second or third time around. Simultaneously, the emotional aftermath of the prior experiences may interfere with adjustment to the new roles. Remarriages have a slightly higher chance of divorce than first marriages (Cherlin, 1981).

The role of wife is inevitably different the second time since the personalities and life patterns have changed. The people are older and their role clusters different. According to McKain (1969) most people who enter marriage in the retirement years have very clear ideas of requirements of a potential partner. "Successful" remarriages provide companionship and security as well as affection.

MOTHER

The role of mother, in all its depth and vicissitudes, can be entered through giving birth, adoption, or marriage to a child's father. The duties and rights of motherhood vary considerably by society, the location of the mother in it, her characteristics (e.g., age, race, marital status, sources of support), and characteristics of the child (e.g., gender, birth order, physical condition, and behavior). Mothers of future kings perform this role differently and in different social circles than do mothers of children destined to repeat a peasant life-style. That mothers parent very differently than fathers may be attributed to both physiological and social factors, and this attribution is the subject of a lively debate among feminist scholars (Chodorow, 1978; Lorber et al., 1981; Rossi, 1985).

Motherhood is always more than a biological event. Why women are willing to become mothers is a question answered by Chodorow (1978) with the help of psychoanalytic theory, by Lorber and Coser from a sociological point of view, and by Rossi with reference to the interplay between biology and social structure (see Lorber et al., 1981). Although medical advances have enlarged the potential for choice over whether and when to have children, societies vary in whether or not such action is encouraged. For the most part, women's decisions are constrained by policies created and maintained by men for political, economic, or religiously guided goals. Thus fertility is mandated in Romania but suppressed in the People's Republic of China.

In contrast to other modern societies, American governments provide minimal assistance to families (Kamerman, 1984). It was not until the 1909 White House Conference on the Care of Dependent Children that Americans decided that a mother is better suited to care for her children than are alms-houses, orphanages, workhouses, or foster parents (Leff, 1973; Lopata and Brehm, 1986). The type of help provided to mothers depends on the societal definition of who is "worthy." There are still two tiers of support. The Social Security system separates the "deserving" mothers—those whose husbands are disabled or dead—from the stigmatized recipients of Aid to Families with Dependent Children (i.e., welfare mothers) who have children out of wedlock or whose husband is absent through divorce, desertion, or imprisonment. In addition, federal, state, and local governments retain the right to judge the behavior of mothers toward their children in cases of neglect or sexual and physical abuse (Handel, 1982; Pfohl, 1978).

Americans still have mixed feelings about many aspects of mothering. There is no nationwide program of sex education for the young; effective contraceptives are not freely or easily available; and there is widespread, often violent, opposition to abortion. Yet these same "pro-life" forces refuse to support policies for assisting mothers to rear the children thus produced.

In fact, the rights and duties of the role of mother in this society are bound up with the idealized image of the "perfect" family of the 1950s, in spite of the fact that the image was not real even then and may characterize fewer than 10% of U.S. households today. The 1950s were also a unique period in American history (Cherlin, 1981; Skolnick, 1983). The utopian family of that time consisted of a breadwinning husband/father, a full-time homemaking mother with two children of whom they were the natural parents in a suburban home with Spot, the dog (Skolnick, 1983). The mother constantly worried that her family was not perfect enough, hiding problems and assuming that no one else had them. It is only in the past two decades that this mystique has been rigorously examined, due in part to the new feminist movement and in part to actions by individual women based on their own experience. Recognition of family violence and the frequency of divorce demonstrate that the roles of wife and husband, mother and father, are difficult ones requiring constant negotiation and change. It is also now apparent that the roles of wife and mother are not inevitably joined. However, the organization of social life around the assumption that a woman who enters the role of mother will inevitably be economically supported by the father has led to the feminization of poverty. As summarized by Kamerman (1984: 250),

> Single-parent, female headed families constitute almost half of all poor families in the United States in 1982. Even though they are only about one-fifth of all families with children, they represent more than half (53 percent) of all poor families with children. Furthermore, not only are female-headed families with children disproportionately at risk of poverty in the United States, but also the percentage that are poor has increased significantly in the last few years.

Becoming a mother is a complex experience (Oakley, 1979; see also Lopata, 1971) requiring reconstruction of reality, redefinition of the world and of the self. It is quite different for a young woman who does not combine it with the role of wife than for one who has an active husband with whom to share child rearing. Entering motherhood at a very young age, without the support of a husband has important consequences for other social roles such as student and employee (Chilman, 1980). Yet the numbers of unwed mothers have increased dramatically in recent years, for both white and nonwhite women, especially teenagers (Cherlin, 1981). The society has not provided supports for such women in the past, and now there are only a few school systems that help the young mother at least complete her education and sometimes find a job (Genovese, 1983). Actually, research has shown that in the black community unmarried young mothers are better off in terms of social supports than are married ones, as the kinship network provides help in the absence of a husband (Staples and Mirande, 1980; see also Ladner, 1971).

Feminist literature is currently reexamining mothering, in all of its gendered richness. Rossi (1985) argues for the "naturalness" of maternal feelings, while Ruddick (1982) proposes that the daily activities of mothering produce a special frame of "maternal thinking." Chodorow and Contratto (1982) criticize some psychological themes in recent feminist literature that have created a "fantasy of the perfect mother" who is all powerful in influencing the outcome for her offspring. The idea of an all-powerful mother generates fear and a recurrent tendency to blame her for all kinds of failure. The controversy around Chodorow's (1978) thesis in *The Reproduction of Mothering* stems in part from its psychoanalytical explanation of gender differences as linked to the process of separation from the mother (the first intense attachment for both girls and boys). Boys, by virtue of their different gender, can and must separate sharply, suppressing their relatedness. Girls, because they share a gender identity with their mothers, separate less sharply or completely, developing a personality founded on relatedness, and thus reproducing motherhood from one generation to another as long as child rearing is the exclusive task of women. Lorber et al. (1981) point to the social and cultural rewards of motherhood, while Huber (1980) suggests that such rewards are more symbolic than real in the United States. Clearly mothering has been ambiguously perceived in our society and among feminist writers (Chodorow and Contratto, 1982).

The insistence that mothers should be the exclusive caregivers of their children, available for emergencies as well as for such routine duties as attending teacher conferences and keeping doctors' appointments, creates a very strong probability of role conflict if roles outside the home require prolonged involvement. It is interesting to note that only recently has there been any literature focusing on role conflict for the man who is both a father and an employee. Schools have not as yet adjusted to working mothers, feeling free to release students early or to cancel classes entirely. Seldom does one hear of fathers leaving their jobs so that the children will be supervised at home, a gender bias currently being examined by feminist scholars (Thorne and Yalom, 1982).

The role of mother changes as the children grow, develop new skills and knowledge, add new social roles and modify social circles. Although role relations are strongly influenced by the presence of other people in the household, there is little evidence that the physical care of the offspring is eased by them, especially if they are men. Other women, relatives or someone in a lesbian relation with the mother, are often of greater help. Homosexual parenting remains an interesting but understudied subject (Blumstein and Schwartz, 1983).

Early analyses of the role of mother concluded that the "empty nest" stage when children start leaving home can produce depression. Bart (1973) found that middle-class women who were so severely depressed that they had to be hospitalized were responding to the loss of their central identity as mothers— the basis of their gendered selves—and were without other salient roles upon which to focus the same amount of affect and effort. Recent research suggests, however, that most women experience their middle years very positively, with enhanced feelings of well-being, relief at having survived child rearing, and excitement over new options (Baruch et al., 1983).

Focus on the duties and problems of motherhood in modern America often leads to a neglect of the rights and rewards of the role. At the same time, idealization of motherhood obscures the essential subordination of women in the gender stratification system. Early leaders of the new feminist movement tended toward a negative view of motherhood, feeling that it restricts women too much, especially as now organized (Chodorow and Contratto, 1982). More positive views are currently emerging as research documents the importance of children, especially daughters, as suppliers of all kinds of support in later life (e.g., Lopata, 1973, 1979). Nevertheless, a role as complex and persistent as that of mother will continue to generate tensions—limiting and expanding one's experience and sense of efficacy, combining responsibilities and rewards in an ever-changing matrix, evading easy categorization.

MOTHER-IN-LAW, STEPMOTHER, AND GRANDMOTHER

The role of mother typically involves the process of becoming and being a mother-in-law, an uncomfortable one evidenced by the crudity of mother-in-law jokes. These can be as easily interpreted in terms of the structural ambiguity of the role and the generalized disdain of older women, as by the Freudian model usually applied by male commentators (Bernard, 1975: 141).

When a woman marries a previously married man she often also assumes the role of stepmother, with its unique level of involvement and affective tones. In modern America, in contrast to other societies and our past, stepmotherhood more often occurs after divorce rather than the death of the birth mother. In addition, because of the custody trends, most stepmothers do not have full-time or total mothering rights or duties. The child from the previous marriage is still attached to her or his mother and often resentful of the new unit her or his father has created. Loyalties still rest elsewhere, even if the father's remarriage resulted in geographical mobility. "His," "hers," and "their" children vie for attention. The stepmother also has to fight the stereotype of the mean mother of the Cinderella story.

Most mothers will also become grandmothers, though at increasingly later ages as children delay marriage. Conversely, longer life expectancy adds to the likelihood of becoming a great-grandparent. Grandparenting varies greatly by the ages of all three generations (Robertson, 1977). Relatively young grandmothers may not have much time for child care when the third generation is young, but older grandchildren may be a source of both pleasure and problems, especially in the case of coresidence. The role has many advantages: The relation does not carry with it the onus of responsibility for the grandchild's future, it is freed of many emotionally grating conflicts, and it is intermittent in interaction since few older people live in three-generation families for an extended period.

SUMMARY AND CONCLUSIONS

This chapter has examined some aspects of the life course of major family roles of women. The emphasis has been on American women and mainly on white, nonethnic families. The theme, however, is one of great diversity even without these basic variations.

Recent research and theoretical analyses have certainly reexamined some of the assumptions about women and their family roles. The "feminine mystique" (Friedan, 1963) of the post-World War II era embodied an unidimensional image of gender "normalcy"—of girls and women wholly committed to family roles and to an idealized version of the content of these roles. Daughters were to learn from mothers how to be future mothers themselves, with other commitments, especially those outside of this institutional dimension, seen as only temporary. Being identified as a girl at birth, the future wife and mother was expected to conform to traditional images of behavior and the self. Gender functioned as a pervasive identity in the selection of all roles, and relations within these.

Feminists and others have since drawn attention to the falseness of these images of the American family. Many women had to continue paid employment even after marriage and motherhood because they needed the money. Divorce, followed by the failure of former fathers to pay court-ordered child support, led many a woman into poverty or the need to care for a child while at the same time making money for their support.

The role of wife fell under sociological examination as women began demanding greater rights in marriage and gained more power from being more educated and directly involved in the world of work outside of the home.

At the same time, work in the home was reexamined, showing how much it contributes to the husband's career and the status of the family.

The isolated nuclear family has been shown to be quite connected to the community, often through the activities of the homemakers who serve as a link between the home and its resources. Research has also shown, however, that regardless of paid or unpaid work outside of the home, family members do not typically share work inside of the home.

Sexual stratification and its influence on women's family roles and on the resources available to them have also come under critical examination, as it socializes girls to accept the male-dominated world, the differential treatment of girls and boys, and the scheduling of life events, both daily and across the life course. The refusal to accept women's household work as valuable has resulted in dependency on an income-earning man, the father and then the husband. Social security and the possibility of earning an income, albeit inferior to that earned by a man for the same work, have at least freed older women from dependence on their children and enabled independent living in later life.

Although there is increasing research on role conflict for women who try to be committed to roles in several institutional dimensions, we really need more knowledge about various ways in which this conflict is resolved. We also need to know more, preferably through longitudinal studies, of the sociopsychological interior of the family as it changes over its own cycle of growth and contradiction. Family sociology has been called "women's sociology" because it is assumed to be their special province, but this assumption is beginning to be revised.

More knowledge is also needed concerning the relation between women's family roles and the scheduling of the economic sphere of life. Equally important is research on the ways in which each of the major roles of women in the family are affected by variations in family form, social mobility, the addition and removal of family members through separation, divorce, and death. Nor can we ignore the effect of household composition on all roles. For example, how is the family dynamic influenced by the presence of all girls or all boys?

It is interesting that so much attention is devoted to the family roles of women in the few years they are mothers of young children and how little really is known about them in the decades that follow, when that role recedes in salience. Who are the husband-focused women? How does the role hierarchy change over time, with the addition, removal, or substitution of circle members? There are many questions still unanswered, and many not even defined. However, family literature is at least beginning to free itself of the stereotypes of a family and women's family roles that never did really exist. The hope is that new stereotypes, such as of the woman who "has it all," are not substituted.

NOTES

1. This use of social role was developed by Znaniecki (1965). I have found it much more useful than any other version of the concept.
2. This chapter refers to four studies of American women, all conducted in metropolitan Chicago. The first, consisting of interviews with married full-time homemakers who had at least one pre-high-school child, started in 1956 and extended to 1965. Two widowhood studies, one of role changes and the other of support systems, followed. Finally, the latest study was conducted in the late 1970s and involved a weighted sample of 1,877 women aged 25 to 54. It focused on their changing commitments to work and family roles and was funded by the Social Security Administration (Contract #SSA 600-75-0190). Dr. Henry Brehm was the SSA project officer; Helena Z. Lopata, the principal investigator; and Kathleen Fordham Noor, deputy director. Thanks go to the staff of the Survey Research Laboratory of the University of Illinois, Chicago, campus and the members of the Center for Comparative Study of Social Roles, Loyola University of Chicago.
3. The literature concerning the conflict between the roles of mother and employee for women is so extensive it is impossible to cover it here.

REFERENCES

ANDRE, R. (1982) Homemakers. Chicago: University of Chicago.

BART, P. (1973) "Portnoy's mother's complaint," pp. 222-228 in H. Z. Lopata (ed.) Marriages and Families. New York: Van Nostrand.

BARUCH, G. (1984) "The psychological well-being of women in middle years," pp. 161-180 in G. Baruch and J. Brooks-Gunn (eds.) Women in Midlife. New York: Plenum.

BARUCH, G., R. BARNETT, and C. RIVERS (1983) Lifeprints. New York: McGraw-Hill.

BERGER, P. and H. KELLNER (1970) "Marriage and the construction of reality: An exercise in the microsociology of knowledge," pp. 50-73 in J. Dreitzel (ed.) Patterns of Communicative Behavior. London: Collier-Macmillan.

BERK, S. F. [ed.] (1980) Women and Household Labor. Newbury Park, CA: Sage.

BERNARD, J. (1972) The Future of Marriage. New York: Bantam.

BERNARD, J. (1975) Women, Wives, Mothers. Chicago: Aldine.

BERNARD, J. (1981a) "The good-provider role: Its rise and fall." American Psychologist 36, 1: 1-12.

BERNARD, J. (1981b) The Female World. New York: Free Press.

BLOOD, R. O., Jr., and D. M. WOLFE (1960) Husbands and Wives. New York: Free Press.

BLUMSTEIN, P. and P. SCHWARTZ (1983) American Couples. New York: Morrow.

BRODY, C. and L. C. STEELMAN (1985) "Sibling structure and parental sex-typing of children's household tasks." Journal of Marriage and the Family 27, 2: 265-273.

BUCHER, J. D. (1977) "Moving." Redbook Magazine 60, 146 & 148.

CHAPMAN, J. R. and M. GATES (1977) Women Into Wives: The Legal and Economic Impact of Marriage. Newbury Park, CA: Sage.

CHERLIN, A. J. (1981) Marriage, Divorce, Remarriage. Cambridge, MA: Harvard University Press.

CHILMAN, C. S. (1980) "Social and psychological research concerning adolescent childbearing: 1970-1980." Journal of Marriage and the Family 42, 4: 793-805.

CHODOROW, N. (1978) The Reproduction of Mothering: Psychoanalysis and the Sociology of Gender. Berkeley: University of California Press.

CHODOROW, N. and S. CONTRATTO (1982) "The fantasy of the perfect mother," pp. 54-75 in B. Thorne with M. Yalom (eds.) Rethinking the Family. New York: Longman.

COSER, L. (1974) Greedy Institutions. New York: Free Press.

COSER, R. L. (1975) "The complexity of roles as a seedbed of individual autonomy," pp. 237-263 in L. A. Coser (ed.) The Idea of Social Structure. New York: Harcourt Brace Jovanovich.

CUMMING, E. and W. HENRY (1961) Growing Old. New York: Basic Books.

DANIELS, A. K. (1985) Invisible Careers: Women Community Leaders in the Volunteer World. Chicago: University of Chicago Press.

DANIELS, A. K. (1987) "Good works and good times: The place of sociability in the work of women volunteers." Social Problems 23, 4: 363-374.

DEMARIS, A. and G. R. LESLIE (1984) "Cohabitation with the future spouse: Its influence upon marital satisfaction and communication." Journal of Marriage and the Family 46, 1: 77-84.

DUBERMAN, L. (1975) The Reconstituted Family. Chicago: Nelson Hall.

DULLES, F. R. (1965) A History of Recreation: America Learns to Play. New York: Appleton-Century-Crofts.

DYER, E. D. (1963) "Parenthood as crisis: A re-study." Marriage and Family Living 25 (May): 196-201.

EHRENREICH, B. (1984) Hearts of Men: American Dreams and the Flight from Commitment. Garden City, NY: Anchor/Doubleday.

EHRENREICH, B. and D. ENGLISH (1979) For Her Own Good: 150 Years of Experts' Advice to Women. Garden City, NY: Anchor/Doubleday.

ELDER, G. (1974) Children of the Great Depression. Chicago: University of Chicago Press.

ELKIN, F. and G. HANDEL (1984) The Child and Society. New York: Random House.

FINCH, J. (1983) Married to the Job. London: Allen & Unwin.

FINCH, J, and D. GROVES [eds.] (1983) A Labor of Love: Women, Work and Caring. London: Routledge & Kegan Paul.

FISHER, L. (1986) Mothers and Daughters.

FOWLKES, M. R. (1980) Behind Every Successful Man. New York: Columbia University Press.

FREIDAN, B. (1963) The Feminine Mystique. New York: Norton.

GELLES, R. J. (1980) "Violence in the family: A review of research in the seventies." Journal of Marriage and the Family 42, 4: 873-885.

GELLES, R. J. (1987) The Violent Home. Newbury Park, CA: Sage.

GENOVESE, R. [ed.] (1983) Families and Change. South Hadley, MA: Bergin & Garvey.

GIBSON, G. (1972) "Kin family networks: Overheralded structure in past conceptualizations of family functioning." Journal of Marriage and Family 34 (February): 13-34.

GLASER, B. and A. STRAUSS (1965) Awareness of Dying. Chicago: Aldine.

GLICK, I., R. WEISS, and C. M. PARKES (1974) The First Year of Bereavement. New York: John Wiley.

GORER, G. (1967) Death, Grief and Mourning. Garden City, NY: Anchor/Doubleday.

HANDEL, G. (1982) Social Welfare in Western Society. New York: Random House.

HAREVEN, T. K. [ed.] (1978) Transitions. New York: Academic Press.

HESS, B. B. (1985) "Aging policies and old women: The hidden agenda," pp. 319-331 in A. S. Rossi (ed.) Gender and the Life Course. Chicago: Aldine.

HIRSCH, M. (1981) "Mothers and daughters." Signs 7, 1: 200-222.

HOCHSCHILD, A. R. (1973) The Unexpected Community. Englewood Cliffs, NJ: Prentice-Hall.

HUBER, J. (1980) "Will U.S. fertility decline toward zero?" Sociological Quarterly 21, 4: 481-492.

HUBER, J. and G. SPITZE (1983) Sex Stratification: Children, Housework and Jobs. New York: Academic Press.

HUNT, M. (1966) The World of the Formerly Married. New York: McGraw-Hill.

HUNT, M. (1974) Sexual Behavior in the 1970s. Chicago: Playboy.

HUNT, M. (1977) "The affair," pp. 407-425 in J. P. Wiseman (ed.) People as Partners. San Francisco: Canfield.

KAMERMAN, S. B. (1984) "Children and poverty: Public policies and female-headed families in industrialized countries." Signs 10, 2: 249-270.

KANTER, R. M. (1977) Men and Women of the Corporation. New York: Basic Books.

KITSON, G., H. Z. LOPATA, W. HOLMES, and S. MEYERING (1980) "Divorceés and widows: Similarities and differences." American Journal of Orthopsychiatry 50, 2: 291-301.

KRAUSKOPF, J. M. (1977) "Partnership marriage: Legal reform needed," pp. 93-121 in J. Roberts and M. Gates (eds.) Women Into Wives: The Legal and Economic Impact of Marriage. Newbury Park, CA: Sage.

LADNER, J. (1971) Tomorrow's Tomorrow: The Black Woman. Garden City, NY: Doubleday.

LAWS, J. L. (1979) The Second X: Sex Role and Social Role. New York: Elsevier.

LAWS, J. L. and P. SCHWARTZ (1977) Sexual Scripts. Hinsdale, IL: Dryden Press.

LEE, G. R. (1980) "Kinship in the seventies: A decade review of research and theory." Journal of Marriage and the Family 42, 4: 923-934.

LEFF, M. H. (1973) "Consensus for reform: The mother's-pension movement in the progressive era." Social Service Review 47 (September): 397-417.

LENGERMAN, P. M. and R. A. WALLACE (1985) Gender in America. Englewood Cliffs, NJ: Prentice-Hall.

LIPMAN-BLUMEN, J. (1977) "A crisis perspective on divorce and role change," pp. 233-258 in J. Roberts and M. Gates (eds.) Women Into Wives: The Legal and Economic Impact of Marriage. Newbury Park, CA: Sage.

LIPMAN-BLUMEN, J. and H. LEAVITT (1976) "Vicarious and direct achievement patterns in adulthood." Counselling Psychiatrist 6, 1: 26-32.

LINDEMANN, E. (1944) "Symptomology and management of acute grief." American Journal of Psychiatry 101, 1: 141-148.

LITWAK, E. (1965) "Extended kin relations in an industrial democratic society," pp. 290-325 in E. Shanas and G. Streib (eds.) Social Structure and the Family. Englewood Cliffs, NJ: Prentice-Hall.

LONG, J. and K. L. PORTER (1984) "Multiple roles of midlife women: A case of new directions in theory, research and policy," pp. 109-159 in G. Baruch and J. Brooks-Gunn (eds.) Women in Midlife. New York: Plenum.

LOPATA, H. Z. (1984) "The self-concept, identities and traumatic events: The death of a husband." Presented at the International Conference on Self and Identity, Cardiff, Wales, July 9-13.

LOPATA, H. Z. (1981) "Widowhood and husband sanctification." Journal of Marriage and the Family 43, 2: 439-450.

LOPATA, H. Z. (1979) Women as Widows: Support Systems. New York: Elsevier.

LOPATA, H. Z. (1976) Polish Americans: Status Competition in an Ethnic Community. Englewood Cliffs, NJ: Prentice-Hall.

LOPATA, H. Z. (1975) "Couple-companionate relationships in marriage and widowhood," pp. 119-149 in N. Glazer-Malbin (ed.) Old Families/New Families. New York: Van Nostrand.

LOPATA, H. Z. (1973) Widowhood in an American City. Cambridge, MA: Schenkman.

LOPATA, H. Z. (1971) Occupation: Housewife. New York: Oxford University Press.

LOPATA, H. Z. (1969) "Loneliness: Forms and components." Social Problems 17, 2: 248-262.

LOPATA, H. Z. (1966) "The life cycle of the social role of housewife." Sociology and Social Research 51: 5-22.

LOPATA, H. Z. (1964) "A restatement of the relation between role and status." Sociology and Social Research 49, 1: 58-68.

LOPATA, H. Z. and H. BREHM (1986) Widows and Dependent Wives: From Social Problem to Federal Policy. New York: Praeger.

LOPATA, H. Z., D. BARNEWOLT, and C. A. MILLER (1985) City Women: Work, Jobs, Occupations, Careers, Vol. 2: Chicago. New York: Praeger.

LOPATA, H. Z., D. BARNEWOLT, and K. NORR (1980) "Spouses contributions to each other's roles" pp. 111-141 in F. Pepitone-Rockwell (ed.) Dual-Career Couples. Newbury Park, CA: Sage.

LOPATA, H. Z. and B. THORNE (1978) "On the term 'sex roles.'" Signs 3, 3: 718-721.

LORBER, J., R. L. COSER, A. S. ROSSI, and N. CHODOROW (1981) "On the Reproduction of Mothering: A methodological debate." Signs 6, 3: 482-514.

LOWENSTEIN, A. (1984) "Coping with stress: The case of prisoner's wives." Journal of Marriage and the Family 46, 3: 699-708.

MACKLIN, E. D. (1977) "Unmarried heterosexual cohabitation on the university campus," pp. 33-51 in J. Wiseman (ed.) People as Partners. San Francisco: Canfield.

MARGOLIS, D. R. (1979) The Managers: Corporate Life in America. New York: William Morrow.

McCUBBIN, H. I. and B. DAHL (1975) "Residuals of war: Families of war and servicemen missing in action." Journal of Social Issues 31, 4: 95-109.

McKAIN, W. (1969) Retirement Marriage. Storrs: Storrs Agricultural Experimental Station, University of Connecticut.

National Center for Health Statistics (1985) Vol. 33, No. 12 (March).

NEUBECK, G. [ed.] (1969) Extra-Marital Relations. Englewood Cliffs, NJ: Prentice-Hall.

NEUGARTEN, B. (1968) Middle Age and Aging. Chicago: University of Chicago Press.

OAKLEY, A. (1979) Becoming a Mother. London: Martin Robertson.

OLIVER, J. (1983) "The caring wife," pp. 72-88 in J. Finch and D. Groves (eds.) A Labour of Love: Women, Work and Caring. London: Routledge & Kegan Paul.

OSTRANDER, S. (1984) Women of the Upper Class. Philadelphia: Temple University Press.

PAPANEK, H. (1979) "Family status production: The 'work' and 'non-work' of women." Signs 4, 4: 775-781.

PAPANEK, H. (1973) "Men, women and work: Reflections on the two-person career." American Journal of Sociology 78 (January): 852-872.

PEARLIN, L. and C. SCHOOLER (1978) "The structure of coping." Journal of Health and Social Behavior 19: 2-21.

PFOHL, S. (1978) "The 'discovery' of child abuse." Social Problems 24, 3: 310-323.

PLECK, E. (1983) "The old world, new rights and the limited rebellion: Challenges to traditional authority in immigrant families," pp. 91-112 in H. Z. Lopata and J. H. Pleck (eds.) Research on the Interweave of Social Roles: Jobs and Families. Greenwich, CT: JAI Press.

PLECK, E. H. and J. H. PLECK (1980) The American Man. Englewood Cliffs, NJ: Prentice-Hall.

PRAGER, S. W. (1982) "Shifting perspectives on marital property law," pp. 111-130 in B. Thorne with M. Yalom (eds.) Rethinking the Family. New York: Longman.

REISS, I., R. E. ANDERSON, and G. C. SPONAUGLE (1980) "A multi-variate model of the determinants of extramarital sexual permissiveness." Journal of Marriage and the Family 42 (May): 395-411.

RICH, A. (1976) Of Women Born: Motherhood as Experience and Institution. New York: Norton.

ROBERTSON, J. (1977) "Grandmotherhood: A study of role conceptions." Journal of Marriage and the Family 39, 1: 165-174.

ROSSI, A. (1985) "Gender and parenthood," pp. 161-191 in A. S. Rossi (ed.) Gender and the Life Course. Chicago: Aldine.

ROSSI, A. (1968) "Transition to parenthood." Journal of Marriage and the Family 30 (February): 26-39.

RUBIN, L. B. (1976) Worlds of Pain: Life in the Working Class Family. New York: Basic Books.

RUDDICK, S. (1982) "Maternal thinking," pp. 76-94 in B. Thorne with M. Yalom (eds.) Rethinking the Family. New York: Longman.

SAFILIOS-ROTHCHILD, C. and M. DIJKERS (1980) "The roles of Greek husbands and wives: Definitions and fulfillment," pp. 139-166 in H. Z. Lopata et al. (eds.) Research on the Interweave of Social Roles: Women and Men, Vol. 1. Greenwich, CT: JAI Press.

SAUNDERS, J. M. and J. N. EDWARDS (1984) "Extramarital sexuality: A predictive model of permissive attitudes." Journal of Marriage and the Family 46, 4: 825-835.

SCANZONI, L. D. and J. SCANZONI (1981) Men, Women and Change. New York: McGraw-Hill.

SEIDENBERG, R. (1973) Corporate Wives—Corporate Casualties. New York: American Management Association.

SHAE, N. (1941) The Army Wife. New York: Harper.

SHANAS, E. (1980) "Older people and their families: The new pioneers." Journal of Marriage and the Family 42 (February): 9-15.

SKOLNICK, A. (1983) Intimate Environment: Exploring Marriage and the Family. Boston: Little, Brown.

SPOCK, B. (1957) Baby and Child Care. New York: Cardinal.

STACK, C. (1974) All Our Kin. New York: Harper & Row.

STAPLES, R. and A. MIRANDE (1980) "Racial and cultural variations among American families: A decennial review of the literature on minority families." Journal of Marriage and the Family 42, 4: 887-903.

STEIN, P. (1977) "Singlehood: An alternative to marriage," pp. 382-396 in P. J. Stein et al. (eds.) The Family. Reading, MA: Addison-Wesley.

STEIN, P. (1976) Single. Englewood Cliffs, NJ: Prentice-Hall.

STRAUSS, M., R. GELLES, and S. STEINMETZ (1980) Behind Closed Doors: Violence in the American Family. Garden City, NY: Doubleday.

STRUBE, M. and L. BARBOUR (1984) "Factors related to the decision of leave an abusive relationship." Journal of Marriage and the Family 45, 4: 785-793.

STEUVE, A. and L. O'DONNELL (1984) "The daughter of aging parents," pp. 203-225 in G. Baruch and J. Brooks-Gunn (eds.) Women in Midlife. New York: Plenum.

SUSSMAN, M. (1962) "The isolated nuclear family: Fact or fiction," pp. 49-57 in R. Winch et al. (eds.) Selected Studies in Marriage and the Family. New York: Holt, Rinehart & Winston.

THOMPSON, A. P. (1984) "Emotional and sexual components of extramarital relations." Journal of Marriage and the Family 1 (February): 35-42.

THORNE, B. with M. YALOM (1982) Rethinking the Family: Some Feminist Questions. New York: Longman.

TROLL, L., J. ISRAEL, and K. ISRAEL (1977) Looking Ahead: A Woman's Guide to the Problems and Joys of Growing Older. Englewood Cliffs, NJ: Prentice-Hall.

VENDERVELDE, M. (1979) The Changing Life of the Corporate Wife. New York: Mecox.

VEBLEN, T. (1925) The Theory of the Leisure Class. London: Allen & Unwin.

WALKER, L. (1979) The Battered Woman. New York: Harper & Row.

WEITZMAN, L. (1985) The Divorce Revolution. New York: Free Press.

ZNANIECKI, F. (1965) Social Relations and Social Roles. San Francisco: Chandler.

15 Women and Religion

SHEILA BRIGGS

I NTERPRETING the social formations of women and religion in
contemporary North America, I focus on the feminist religious
movements among both women who remain in the Jewish and
Christian traditions and those who develop new forms of spirituality.
Feminist religious movements are embedded in the crucial experiences that *all*
women bring to their spiritual commitments. Many women reject any
religious involvement at all, while many others participate in conservative and
patriarchal religious bodies, but the common experiences of gender that
inform these two options lie at the root of religious feminism.

THE CHALLENGE OF FEMINISM

A feminist critique of religion was inevitable with the reemergence of a
powerful women's movement in the 1960s. Religion in Western countries had
long been a primary, indeed, many would argue, the major cultural reinforcer
of modern industrial patriarchy. In fact, the once pervasive and controlling
influence of the Christian churches over all aspects of social and political
behavior shrunk in the last two centuries to the role of guardian of marriage,
family, and the home. Religion itself had acquired a "feminine" character: It
cared for and nurtured those too tired or abused or weak to grapple with the
harsh realities of the world, and much of religion's succor was provided (and
still is) by the unpaid work of women in the voluntary welfare organizations of
church and synagogue. The cult of domesticity in the nineteenth century
always had religious undertones: The home had become a religious sanctuary
and the church a second home and family. In contrast, whenever women
demanded equal employment opportunities and remuneration, a fair division
of labor outside and inside the home, reproductive rights and the end of the
social control of women's sexuality, they began to challenge the religious
legitimation of patriarchal gender roles and household arrangements.

The women's movement has provoked an enduring crisis for churches and
synagogues. Feminism threatens the authority of religious institutions in the
one area of social life and public policy where they continue to receive a

hearing: marriage, family, and issues of sexual morality. Religious leaders, whose voices have long been discounted in foreign or economic policy, have been consulted at the highest levels of policymaking in these three areas. In Britain the legalization of abortion became possible only when a majority of the Anglican bishops consented to passage of the Abortion Law Reform Act of 1967. The opposition of Roman Catholic Church authorities to abortion is viewed by the Reagan administration as a major advantage in its own antichoice campaign and in the election of conservative Republican candidates. Yet, when the Catholic bishops of the United States draft a severely critical pastoral letter on the economy, neither the U.S. Treasury nor Republican candidates are threatened.

Feminism not only represents a challenge to the influence of religious institutions in the wider society, but also to their internal authority. Women account for the majority of church members. The perception of the Christian churches as the moral custodians of social policy on marriage, family, and sexuality has been buttressed by these being considered "women's issues." The churches, it has been assumed, prepare women for their special responsibility for the "woman's sphere" of home and family, and then mirror these concerns for the larger society. As increasing numbers of Christian women question (and in many cases reject) the moral tutelage of the churches in these areas, the church no longer appears an effective agent for the social control of women.

I am not arguing that there has been a wholesale feminization of religion during the last two centuries. On the contrary, until the reemergence of feminism in religious as well as secular contexts during the 1960s, religious leadership was in male hands; and formal religious discourse (theology) was not only conducted in a conventionally masculine tone, but also reflected the experiences, values, and self-images of men. Indeed, the genesis of the movement known as feminist theology lay in the recognition of the male bias in religious discourse. As early as 1960, Valerie Saiving contended that Christian theology neglected female experience and, in applying the categories gained from reflection on male experience, encouraged women to pursue spiritual mediocrity. By condemning self-assertion and demanding selfless love, Christian theology led to a whole catalogue of female sins: "triviality, distractability, and diffuseness; lack of an organizing center or focus; dependence on others for one's own self-definition; tolerance at the expense of standards of excellence; inability to respect the boundaries of privacy, sentimentality, gossipy sociability, and mistrust of reason—in short, underdevelopment or negation of the self" (Saiving, 1979).

Judith Plaskow (1980) built on this work in her study of two of the most influential male theologians in the twentieth century, contrasting their views of sin and grace with women's experience, in particular as it was given voice through Doris Lessing's heroine Martha Quest. Plaskow not only challenged whether traditional understandings of sin and grace are adequate to women's moral self-development, but opened the question of whether cultural definitions of femaleness accurately capture the meaning and content of women's experience. Plaskow doubts whether the tensions of transcendence versus immanence, and universality versus particularity, were the context of women's experience of their humanity rather than constructs of the male self. The emergence of such a line of questioning marked a qualitative divergence from Saiving. The attempt to describe and give value to women's experience so that it was not subsumed in the general category of authentic human experience would eventually undergird the new movements of women's spirituality.

The two impulses within feminist religion—the desire to claim women's full participation in humanity and their right to equal access to all roles in church and society, and efforts to make a distinctive women's voice heard in the religious world—were expressed in the debates over women's ordination and inclusive language. These two issues have dominated the struggles of Jewish and Christian women with male-controlled religious institutions.

THE STRUGGLE FOR ORDINATION

The demand for women's ordination has a long history. When nineteenth-century male religious leaders conceded women general spiritual equality with men, it became arguable whether this equality could be contained within a complementarity of roles and talents that told women that the rabbinate or ordained ministry was not their portion and vocation.

The debates surrounding women's ordination in Reform Judaism are a paradigm of the ambivalence of liberal religious bodies toward women's participation in religious authority. From its earliest days the Reform movement within Judaism has acknowledged the religious equality of women with men. In late nineteenth-century America, women attended the rabbinical seminary of Reform Judaism in Cincinnati at a time when access to ministerial studies for Christian women was rare. Yet, Martha Neumark's request for rabbinical ordination was turned down in 1921, even though the Central Conference of American Rabbis had agreed that women could not "justly be denied the privilege of ordination"(Umansky, 1979).

The same line of argument appears in the decisions of Christian bodies. Anglican bishops and high-ranking clerics of the Eastern Orthodox Church state that there are no "theological objections" to women's ordination yet, since it runs counter to the practice of their church, it is denied. Very often the debate over women's ordination has focused on the churches that do not (or did not until recently) ordain women. These are the older branches of Christianity with roots in Europe—the Roman Catholic Church, the Eastern Orthodox churches, and the Protestant churches founded during the Reformation. Consequently, the history of women ministers in churches that did ordain women prior to World War II and, in some cases, for over a century has been ignored.

The social profile of these churches is "sectarian" rather than "mainstream"; they are small bodies requiring high commitment and often strict conformity to the community's beliefs and practices. They tend to be of American origin or to have the bulk of their membership within the United States. Final authority is more likely to rest at the congregational level than with the church hierarchy. Recognition of ministerial leadership depends more on charismatic authority rather than on formal office. Such churches predominate in the Afro-American religious tradition. In contrast to the mainstream, tradition plays a minor role in many of these denominations for either theological argumentation or church practice. They are in many ways egalitarian but this is most frequently qualified in the case of gender.

In these churches women lay claim to spiritual gifts, often including the ability to preach, and exercise them in active leadership roles. In the nineteenth century two black women, Jarena Lee and Amanda Berry Smith, were among the most effective evangelists of their day. They were both members of the African Methodist Episcopal Church, founded by Richard Allen in response to racial segregation. The same Richard Allen refused to ordain Jarena Lee even when he became convinced of her preaching vocation. Ordination was also denied Amanda Berry Smith despite her international reputation as a revivalist preacher and missionary. On the other hand, the African Methodist Episcopal Zion Church ordained women as early as 1884.

The experiences of Jarena Lee and Amanda Berry Smith show that even though women in an Afro-American church are able successfully to use their ministerial abilities, there is resistance in such a church to the abolition of all gender distinctions in ministry. Most often this takes the form of barring women from a formally defined ministerial office even when they may already be performing its functions. Hence, in some Afro-American Pentecostal churches, the male ministers hold the title "preacher" but women ministers are called "teacher" although their tasks may be identical (Williams, 1974: 31). Usually the male "preachers" enjoy more prestige than the female "teachers" but not invariably so. In some denominations of the Afro-American Holiness movement there seems to be a genuine dual-sex system, with a parallel hierarchy of female ministers that is not subordinate to that of male ministers (Gilkes, 1986).

Women are most likely to attain leadership roles in newly emerged sectarian churches: Indeed, women are frequently their founders. This does not necessarily challenge gender roles in ministry since the situation of female authority can be perceived as an emergency: "There was no man around to do the work of the Lord." Sometimes women succeed a deceased husband in the pastorate of a church. Where women in a sectarian church are excluded from all functions perceived as ministerial, they may well try to exert an informal authority. Melvin D. William (1974) in his study of a black Pentecostal church in Pittsburgh described Sister Ulrich, who, in a church where women could not hold the title of either pastor or deacon, nevertheless became the most powerful member of the church after the pastor. The flexible structures of worship in a sectarian church permit women to take an active role even where ministry is formally denied them, as when the "exhortation" of a woman follows the sermon preached by the male minister. Still, one should not ignore the fact that such informal authority is contained within structures that prohibit women from the *recognized* roles of ministers.

The intertwined factors of socioeconomic class, social mobility, and racial group influence the perception and acceptance of women as ministers in sectarian churches. Afro-American women of the working class have always been part of the labor force out of necessity, and many Afro-American women of the middle and upper classes have worked outside the home in order to aid in the "uplift of the race." The experience of women as workers has made it easier for Afro-Americans to accept women as ministers. Yet, Afro-Americans and Afro-American churches were not immune to the ideology of domesticity (Willis, 1982). Racial uplift among better-educated Afro-Americans frequently entailed the desire to conform one's religious practices to those of the mainstream white churches. Social mobility, therefore, could mean the loss of leadership roles for women in the black churches.

The complexity of women's status in the Afro-American churches can be demonstrated by a comparison of attitudes toward women's ordination between black Methodist and black Pentecostal churches. The black Methodist churches are highly organized churches with membership drawn from better-educated and higher income groups than is the case for other Afro-American denominations. Over 90% of the male pastors in the black Methodist churches favor women's ordination. In contrast, only 10% of the male pastors of the Church of God in Christ, a black Pentecostal group first incorporated in 1897, accept women's ordination (Lincoln, 1983). The leaders of this long-established Pentecostal church retain more conventional attitudes about appropriate gender roles in ministry than do their counterparts in a black mainstream church, though it is not clear in which body women's actual roles are more powerful.

The experience of women increasingly being ordained in mainline Protestant churches bears many similarities to that of women in Afro-American denominations. There is a strong relation between women's presence in the professions in general and in the ordained ministry in particular. During World War II and the immediate postwar period, the numbers of women entering the professions, including the Protestant ministry, expanded, only to decline in the 1950s and early 1960s. There were one-quarter fewer women ministers in 1970 than there had been in 1950 (Carroll et al., 1981: 4). While some denominations, notably the United Presbyterians and the United Methodists, first decided to ordain women during the postwar era of the "feminine mystique," very few women were actually ordained. Many other denominations, such as the Episcopal Church, the Lutheran Church in America, and the American Lutheran Church, did not allow the ordination of women until the 1970s as women's presence in other male-dominated professions expanded.

In the mainline Protestant churches, acceptance of the *possibility* of women's ordination typically predates the large-scale entry of women into ministry or training for ministry. The small number of women in ministry prior to the emergence of the women's movement of the 1970s was due less to formal barriers than to the belief that few ministerial activities were congruent with women's role and character. Women ordained before 1970 often testify to their status as oddities in a male clerical world. Women were ordained only in exceptional circumstances; many served as overseas missionaries in areas where clerical manpower was stretched to the limit.

One of the areas of institutional strength for women was the missionary society. In many denominations, separate missionary societies organized by women and for women were established and took special responsibility for the recruitment and support of women missionaries. Conventional notions of gender distinction were turned into arguments for the autonomy of such groups. Supporters claimed that certain cultures only allowed women social contacts with other women, making female missionaries indispensable; further, because of the particular needs of their sex, women missionaries required the assistance of women's missionary organizations (see also Hagemann, 1974; Hill, 1985).

In some cases, women were also acceptable as ministers at home—in hospital chaplaincies; in charitable institutions, especially those devoted to the care of women or children; in positions where the conventional role of woman as nurturer could be seen as a professional asset. In contrast, women in parish ministry were rare. Most women engaged in full-time work for the church were not ordained. In the nineteenth century, a movement of deaconesses was founded by a Lutheran pastor and his wife in Germany, allowing unmarried women to work full time in the church's charitable organizations and often to live in community together. This model was adopted and adapted by other Protestant churches both in England and in America. Deaconesses were employed in church educational programs, the broad range of social welfare and evangelistic activities associated with the phrase "home mission," as well as in overseas missions. The training that these women received was often of poor quality until the middle of this century, when the professionalism of social work in the secular sphere raised standards for comparable occupations in the religious sector. Lack of ordination and education combined to lock these full-time women workers into positions subordinate to male clergy.

This background of women's ministry suggests that the willingness to ordain women in increasing numbers since the 1970s may not only reflect the impact of feminism on the perception of appropriate professional roles for women by Protestant church bodies, but also a desire to give a more feminine face to their pastoral care. Thus women ministers often find themselves confronted with conflicting expectations of professional performance: to be identical to their male colleagues yet provide a specifically female touch.

The reasons for women entering ministry are similar to those of women joining other professions. Women believe that they are able to obtain the required professional competence for ministry; they decide on ministry as a first or second career; they want to transform the sexist institution of the church by assuming a leadership role within it. There is a higher proportion of mature women (aged 29 and over) than men seeking ministerial training. Usually, these women have been engaged in voluntary church work for years before deciding that they are suited for full-time professional ministry. While some have combined voluntary church work with the role of homemaker, for the majority their previous experience of employment is not appreciably different from that of men seeking seminary training. Indeed, women candidates are more likely than male applicants to have had a first career with high status. One sample shows 59% of women in the age group 29 and over having had a career as professionals or business executives, compared to only 15% of the men (Carroll et al., 1981: 44-46, 67-72).

Women who decide to seek ministerial training typically have a record of high educational and career achievement, and would seem better-qualified than their male counterparts to compete in the academic setting of the seminary and the professional one of the pastorate. Yet only a third of women enter seminary with the primary goal of training for parish ministry. This is surprising since the Master of Divinity degree, the basic entry qualification for ordained ministry in most denominations, entails 3 years of study. In one study 73% of men had enrolled in seminaries with the intention of becoming parish ministers. In contrast, 60% of the women gave personal spiritual growth and faith development as a primary reason for attending seminary, as did only 35% of the men in the sample. Although women endorsed the goal of service to the church and world more often than did men as the primary reason for undergoing ministerial training, it is obvious that they also identified this aim more with personal fulfillment than with commitment to career.

Women leaving seminary do not have great difficulty in obtaining a first appointment. The difference between their prospects and those of their male counterparts lies in the type of appointment. Among the ministers serving in their first parish, studied by Carroll et al. (1981), 42% of the women were sole or senior pastors in their congregations, whereas 68% of the men held this position. This discrepancy in the levels of responsibility is intensified as clergy are called to their second, third, and later congregations. By the time male clergy are working in their third or later church, 92% are sole or senior pastors. The figure for women is 60%. The lower status of women on the clerical ladder is, of course, reflected in their salaries, which are appreciably lower than those of men at all points in the career. Women pastors are more likely to serve small congregations, in rural areas or small towns, with older and less wealthy members. They also tend to be interim pastors or serve congregations with declining numbers. In short, they find themselves in relatively unattractive ministerial positions (Carroll et al., 1981: 127-138), or as associate or assistant pastors replacing the female voluntary worker or deaconess as aide to the male minister.

Recent literature on women and ministry has focused on women as transforming a traditional male role. There is little evidence to suggest that women enter ministerial training and are ordained as clergy with this as their primary goal. However, there are many feminists among ordained women and feminist theology has had a major impact on the seminary curriculum in recent years. Even among those women clergy who do not consider changing the sexist nature of the church central to their ministry, very few are indifferent or hostile to feminism. Most women pastors think that female clergy do operate differently from male clergy, but with no less professional competence. A Congregational minister expressed the difference this way:

> By their very presence in ministry, women open up questions of vulnerability for those in the congregation. The unexpected, the unanticipated opens up queries not previously addressed with the same intensity. Seeing women in a role that has been traditionally viewed as male raises questions about many assumptions, attitudes, and presuppositions upon which people have built their lives and sometimes their faith. Women's tendency to be more vulnerable than men also readily opens the places of hurt and sensitivity in other person's lives [Gill, 1985: 99ff].

Women ministers and Christian feminists are divided on the question of whether the present church structures can recognize differences in women's ministry and, at the same time, grant it equality with the ministry of men.

The most radical and explicitly feminist movement to arise over the issue of women's ordination is within the Roman Catholic Church, where women are refused entry into the priesthood. Indeed, young girls are not even officially allowed to act as altar servers since this minor liturgical activity is intended to implant in the hearts of boys the desire to become priests, a choice forbidden to girls. In the Roman Catholic Church, arguments against women's ordination are primarily theological and only secondarily based on inappropriateness of priesthood to feminine nature and roles. The prohibition of women's ordination rests on two intertwined strands of argument. Jesus ordained his twelve disciples at the Last Supper; the twelve disciples were all men; therefore, Jesus intended to call only men to the priesthood. In the Eucharist the priest represents Christ; Christ in his human form of Jesus of Nazareth was male; therefore, the representation of Christ in the Eucharist requires a male priest.[1]

Faced with such inexorable patriarchal logic, Roman Catholic feminists have not been in great danger of being coopted into a male-dominated and hierarchical ministry. Rather, women's consciousness of their oppression has been heightened by the upheavals since the 1960s. Although Pope John XXIII's encyclical *Pacem in terris* condemned discrimination on the basis of sex, it continues unabated in the Roman Catholic Church. The Second Vatican Council led to a flowering of new theology, including a feminist theology that began with the work of the then Roman Catholic scholar, Mary Daly, and continues in the work of Rosemary Radford Ruether and Elizabeth Schüssler-Fiorenza. The contradictions within the Roman Catholic Church have led to revolutionary demands for change, as some women have gone beyond requesting women's ordination into the priesthood as it presently exists to a call for the dissolution of *all* hierarchical structures within their church and their replacement by democratically organized base communities (see Dwyer, 1980; Weaver, 1985: 109-144).

Lesbians remain excluded from the ministry even where ordination is possible otherwise. A few liberal—and numerically small—Protestant denominations such as the United Church of Christ and the Unitarian Universalists have formally opened ordination to homosexuals. However, since these denominations have a congregational structure of authority, which means that the local congregation chooses its pastor and ordination only occurs when the prospective minister has received a "call" from a local church, a lesbian is often faced with a frustrating search for a congregation that will accept her. In the 1970s discrimination against lesbians and gay men in the Christian churches led to the foundation of the Metropolitan Community Church, which because of its emphasis on the ministry to and of gay people draws its constituency from this group. There are ordained lesbians in the Metropolitan Community Church, although ironically they encounter the same sexist attitudes and practices from gay men within their church as women ministers do in the mainline Protestant denominations. Some congregations have formed separate women's churches within the Metropolitan Community Church, such as the De Los Flores group in Los Angeles.

Within Judaism, separate gay synagogues in which lesbians have been active have been established. The present rabbi of the gay/lesbian synagogue in Los Angeles, Beth Chayim Chadashim, is a woman. This synagogue was also the first to be admitted into the Union of American Hebrew Congregations, the association of Reformed synagogues (Maggid, 1982). Jewish lesbians have been able to seek ordination and religious leadership within their religious mainstream where this has been largely closed to Christian women.

Most major Protestant denominations remain hostile to the ordination of lesbians. For instance, at the 1984 general conference of the United Methodist Church, delegates passed a motion that demanded "fidelity in marriage and celibacy in singleness" from all ministers in a veiled attack on homosexual clergy. When the new bylaw appeared insufficient to bar gay men and lesbians from the ministry, the general conference passed a further motion that explicitly excludes practicing homosexuals. Nevertheless, in the United Methodist Church and other Protestant denominations there are many lesbian ministers who manage to keep their pastorates through the tolerance of their congregations and local church officials, or by the concealing their sexual orientation.

THE DEBATE OVER LANGUAGE

The second area in which feminism has had a major impact on churches and synagogues concerns the adoption of "inclusive language." In the religious context this phrase has come to mean not only the rejection of generically male terms to denote human beings, human attributes, and human experiences, but also the demand that God should be spoken of in either gender-neutral language or in ways that include female imagery. Both Christianity and Judaism stress that the God they worship transcends gender. As Rita Gross (1979: 170-172) pointed out in a Jewish context, clinging to male imagery of God and rejecting female imagery reveals that God is after all being understood according to a male-centered conception of humanity.

The effort to change the language in which the Christian churches address and refer to God drew widespread national attention with the publication of the *Inclusive Lectionary* in the fall of 1983 by the National Council of Churches. Mention of Jesus Christ as the "son of God" was replaced by "child of God," "Lord" by "Sovereign One," and God was addressed as "Our Mother" as well as "Our Father" in heaven. Although these changes were optional and some churches had already adopted such forms, the *Inclusive Lectionary* drew a barrage of criticism.

Resistance has been most severe in those churches that also opposed the ordination of women, and for much the same reasons. Arguments of tradition play a major role in the worship of older established churches because many liturgical forms have been inherited from the early centuries of Christianity and their use symbolizes the continuity of the church itself. A change in the language of the liturgy is equivalent to a transformation of identity. In the Episcopal Church, after a long struggle and an "irregular" ordination of women by a group of sympathetic bishops in Philadelphia in 1976, women have been able to enter the priesthood. Nonetheless, inclusive language is not widely employed in the liturgy. On the whole, Episcopal women priests wear the same liturgical vestments and say the same prayers as their male colleagues. Such patterns of worship are conscious demonstrations of the ancient origins of the church and unavoidably perpetuate its misogynist liturgical idioms.

The use of inclusive language has been widely reported and discussed, to little effect. The older male terms for God remain far more common than female or gender-neutral designations. Data from the General Social Survey of 1983, for example, indicates that more women than men thought of God in the image of male authority figures such as father, master, king, and judge. Educational attainment was more powerful than gender in accounting for a decline in the acceptance of male imagery for God. While 65% of women and 56% of men perceived "father" as a meaningful image for God, this was so for only 48% of those with a college degree, compared to 71% of those with less than a high school diploma. Only 28% of the women interviewed could conceive of God in terms of mother, but this was a higher proportion than among men. Women were in general more likely than men to envision God through human metaphors, as were people without a high school diploma (Roof and Roof, 1984).

Such resistance to inclusive language manifests the antifeminist structure of religious mentality in the Christian churches. As Nelle Morton (1985) has written, it is not the concepts, or the formal doctrines of God and humanity that control the behavior and attitudes of Christians as much as the deep structures of images that may even conflict with consciously adopted principles of the rational theological mind. The change from sexist to inclusive language makes evident the power of images. Female imagery is not equal in the religious imagination, and the opposition to it vents itself in inexplicable and often subtle hostility toward women in circumstances where their formal equality has been conceded (Morton, 1985: 20ff, 122-146).

FEMINIST THEOLOGY

The struggles over the ordination of women and inclusive language in the Christian and Jewish traditions have shaped the environment in which feminist theology has matured over the past two decades. Every area in the discipline of religion has been transformed by feminist scholarship. Feminist theology shares with women's studies in general the tension of a dual role in being both an academic discipline and an arm of the women's movement. Its practitioners must simultaneously investigate the construction of gender in the religious traditions and participate in the praxis and theory-building of religious feminism. The location of much of feminist theology in seminaries and divinity schools, where (women) ministers, are trained has prevented the isolation of academic feminist theological scholarship from the everyday reality of women working in religious institutions. At the same time, heavy professional and personal burdens are imposed on feminist theologians when their scholarly and political positions make it difficult to remain in their work place and also retain their original religious faith.

Mary Daly's journey from liberal Roman Catholic to post-Christian radical feminist epitomizes the transformations that the world of religious feminism has undergone. Her book *The Church and the Second Sex* (1968) marked the arrival of the second wave of feminism within the Christian churches and theology. In it she traced the development of misogynist teaching in Christianity and its underpinning in concepts of humanity and nature that defined woman as Other. As the title of her book suggests, she was heavily indebted to Simone de Beauvoir and, like her, advocated women's basic right to claim a self beyond sexual differentiation and through which women, on equal terms with men, could conduct their lives in search of transcendence.

Her book almost cost Mary Daly her employment at Jesuit-controlled Boston College. Although she was reinstated and promoted, she became increasingly alienated from the Roman Catholic Church and from her Christian feminist self. In *Beyond God the Father* (1973) and later books, Daly sought entry into a world of women's power and being through the discovery of women's language. For Daly, to be included within the God-language of the Christian tradition is to be interred in an irremediably patriarchal and necrophilic culture.

THE FEMINIST SPIRITUALITY MOVEMENTS

Mary Daly's work embodies the most innovative and radical trends in the development of feminist religion. There has been a shift of focus from the study and critique of the effect on women's lives of religious practices, beliefs, and communities to the study and celebration of women's lives themselves as a source of feminist spirituality. This has led to new forms of feminist theology and new feminist religious movements. Earlier, the work of Judith Plaskow was mentioned as emphasizing women's experience as the source of feminist theological reflection. Her close collaborator, Carol P. Christ (1980), drew attention to women's literature as revealing the patterns of women's spiritual quest and linked these explorations to other forms of contemporary women's art and to the creation of new women's rituals. Thus women's spirituality is not located in any defined religious activity or set of attitudes but is seen as permeating the whole of women's experience. Two salient and common features of the various movements of feminist spirituality are an affirmation of women's bodies and a profound sense of connection to nature.

Many of the movements of feminist spirituality use the image of the Goddess to direct revisioning of themselves. One does not worship the Goddess as one would a transcendent deity. The Goddess is not regarded as existing apart from human beings but rather as a symbol for "the divine within women and all that is female in the universe"(Budapest, 1979: 272). Sometimes the Goddess is perceived as distinct from the experience of an individual woman or group of women in the sense of being a source of power and protection. The world view of Goddess spirituality is nonetheless one of radical immanence: The Goddess sojourns within cosmic nature and women's/human bodies. Z. Budapest (1979), Starhawk (1982), and others base their image of the Goddess on their practice of feminist witchcraft. This is a conscious attempt to create a feminist spiritual identity through a religious history alternative to Christianity or Judaism. A genealogy is formed stretching through the women burned as witches in the sixteenth century to the remote past of prehistoric Europe and the ancient Near East (see Gimbutas, 1982; Spretnak, 1981; Stone, 1978). The existence of women-centered cultures in the ancient past (the "matriarchy thesis") is hotly debated both as to its historical factuality and its theoretical value to women's struggle in contemporary culture. The invocation of ancient goddesses such as Diana, Demeter, Isis, and Ishtar nevertheless has become a part of contemporary feminist ritual.

Christian feminist theology still inspires the majority of religious feminists, and its followers have the most access to intellectual and material sources because they are situated in seminaries and divinity schools. The movement is itself varied. There are *biblical feminists* who wish to maintain a positive relationship to traditional Christianity through reinterpreting its Scriptures as feminist in intent. Virginia Mollenkott, Letha Scanzoni, Nancy Hardesty, the Evangelical Women's Caucus, and the journal *Daughters of Sarah* can be taken as representative of this position.

At another point along the spectrum one finds the religious *socialist feminists*. This group is responsible for some of the major intellectual achievements of Christian feminists. Among their ranks are Rosemary Radford Ruether (a past chairperson of the Democratic Socialists of America), Beverly Wildung Harrison, Carter Heyward, and Claire Fischer. Even Goddess spirituality has had an impact on some areas of Christian feminism despite initial hostility, especially from the group of socialist feminists. Rosemary Radford Ruether included material on ancient Near Eastern Goddesses in her feminist theology reader, *Womanguides* (Ruether, 1985: 10-16, 44-51, 67ff, 113-117, 224-229), and reference to the Goddess is made in some Christian feminist rituals. Nonetheless, this reception of Goddess spirituality remains partial.

Jewish feminism has many features in common with Christian feminism: the struggle for women's ordination, the introduction of female images of God, the exploration of inclusive language in Jewish ritual, and the search for women's voices and experiences. Judaism cannot be subsumed under the dubious epithet "Judeo-Christian" because Judaism continued a vital and changing tradition after the close of the biblical period. A wealth of unique experiences and traditions gives Jewish feminism its own particular texture. A wider range of Jewish-born women affirm their Jewish identity than Christian-born women acknowledge their roots in the dominant religious culture. Jewish women cannot ignore their ancestry and resist identification with it as easily as can Christian-born women. Antisemitism in the women's movement and in religious feminism is a constant reminder to Jewish feminists, whether they are religious or not, that they have a different history, which they must interpret themselves or watch others distort it. Although some Jewish women have been reluctant to use words such as "theology" and "spirituality" to characterize their feminist reflection on religion because these words are rooted in the Christian tradition, a feminist rethinking of Judaism has taken place. Jewish feminist scholars have cooperated with Christian feminist theologians, and the development of the feminist study of Judaism has run parallel to that of Christianity.

BIBLICAL STUDIES

Every area in the discipline of religion has been transformed by feminist scholarship. Much of feminist theology has focused on the importance of religion for the cultural legitimation of patriarchy and on the task of recovering a usable past for religious feminists. Biblical studies have received much attention because the Bible has traditionally been accepted as normative for Christian identity. Bernadette Brooten's (1974, 1982) work on Jewish and Christian women in the ancient world is representative of the reconstruction of women's past; she questions the assumptions that have led male scholars to write women out of the historical record. She has shown that the apostle Junias in Paul's letter to the Romans (the most influential writing of the New Testament) was in fact a woman named Junia, and that women held titles of leadership in the ancient Jewish synagogue that only prejudice allows one to designate as "honorary" (Brooten, 1977: 141-144; 1982).

Christian biblical studies in this century have been dominated by the "problem of hermeneutics," that is, with the question of how a believer today can understand texts written from the presuppositions and imagination of a world so distant from our own. The problem is more severe and the sense of alienation deeper for feminists, whose investigations reveal these presuppositions and this imagination as patriarchal. The most important feminist contribution to an understanding of early Christianity and its biblical texts is Elisabeth Schüssler-Fiorenza's *In Memory of Her* (1984). Schüssler-Fiorenza chides other feminist theologians for trying to salvage biblical core that is free from patriarchy. Instead, she insists that feminists must concede that the biblical texts, even the most central ones, are "androcentric" (male-centered) but that the history and suffering of early Christian women demand that we simply do not abandon these texts to further patriarchal interpretation. Christian feminists are called to solidarity with their sisters of the past by reclaiming their history from behind the androcentric biblical texts. Schüssler-Fiorenza developed a "feminist critical hermeneutics of liberation" that acknowledges biblical authority in the experiences of women's sufferings and struggle, and not necessarily in the biblical texts themselves. Jesus' praxis, according to Schüssler-Fiorenza, founded a "discipleship of equals" between men and women. This discipleship of equals was minimalized, concealed, and distorted by the patriarchal forces in the early church who formed the Christian Scriptures as we know them. This patriarchal trend that came to dominate the Christian church was and is resisted by the *ekklesia* (church) of women, which is the model of the authentic church (Schüssler-Fiorenza, 1984).

Among the feminist scholars of the Hebrew Bible (the text known by Christians as the Old Testament) Phyllis Trible's work has reached a wide audience. Unlike Schüssler-Fiorenza, she emphasizes the literary nature of the biblical text and explores its narrative implications. This literary focus does not diminish her ability to expose the patriarchal character of biblical writings. While her earlier book *God and the Rhetoric of Sexuality* (1980) attempted to see key texts on human sexuality in the Hebrew Bible as not fully defined by patriarchal assumptions, her most recent work, *Texts of Terror* (1984), sees patriarchal violence against women occurring even within the literary structure of the text.

FEMINIST HISTORIOGRAPHY

Feminist scholars within and outside the discipline of religion have examined women's experiences in the historical development of Christianity and Judaism. Patristics, the study of the Christian leaders ("church fathers") who gave the new religion its definitive and patriarchal shape, has been a focus of feminist church history. Rosemary Radford Ruether, who published a respected monograph on Gregory of Nazianzus, later turned her patristic skills to uncovering the roots of Christian misogyny (1974, 1979). Elizabeth Clark has commented on and translated several of the patristic texts concerning women (1979, 1984). She has also (with Herbert Richardson) edited *Women and Religion* (1977), an invaluable collection of texts for the classroom.

Caroline Bynum's *Jesus as Mother* (1982) and Marilyn Massey's *The Feminine Soul* (1985) have made important methodological contributions to Christian feminist historiography. Bynum insisted that the prominence of feminine religious imagery in the spiritual experience of men, specifically twelfth-century Cistercian monks, implies nothing about their social attitudes toward women (Bynum, 1982: 110-169). Massey addressed the current feminist debate over "essentialism": Do women have distinctive qualities or does such a claim undermine the struggle for equality? Massey analyzes the development of the idea of a feminine soul in German moral and religious discourse of the late eighteenth and early nineteenth centuries, and discerns a subversion of its patriarchal invention. She asks, "What would happen if the representation of the feminine soul got out of hand, if it were wrenched free from systems of male thought and even from those male thinkers, who in a sense, conceived it?"(Massey, 1985: 172). Both these works, in their different ways, question the extent to which the construction of gender in Western religion, and indeed in culture generally, can ever include women, and also explore the ambiguous relationship of feminine images to real women.

The volume and breadth of feminist religious history is impressive. Ruether and Keller's three-volume work *Women and Religion in America* (1981) is exemplary in its recording of the religious lives of women of color, of Jewish women, and of women in sectarian movements as the substance of the religious texture of American society and not as loose strands. Such works as Ellen Umansky's (1983) study of the Jewish Englishwoman Lily Montagu, a leader in the movement of Liberal Judaism, and Clarissa Atkisson's (1983) monograph on the medieval mystic, Margery of Kempe, contribute to a body of research that makes the religious history of women integral to the study of women's history as a whole.

FEMINIST ETHICS

For all feminist theologians, the ethical dimension of religious experience is of crucial importance. Yet gaining a foothold for feminist ethics within the discipline of religious ethics has been an uphill task. Male ethical discourse in twentieth-century America, under the influence of Reinhold Niebuhr, has stressed political and economic doctrines. In developing a critique of individualism, Niebuhr and others relegated family and sexuality to the private sphere.

A group of socialist feminists have severely critiqued this dominant mode of thinking. Beverly Harrison's (1983, 1984, 1985) work has constantly explored the connection of sexuality and its control to the social order. Her starting point for ethics is the embodied and hence sexual character of human beings. She shares with Carter Heyward the view that correct relations between human beings are undergirded by passionate commitment of persons to one another (Heyward, 1984). Just as this "passion for justice" can and often does contain the erotic, so too do economic exploitation and political and social repression distort the expression of sexuality. Claire Fischer has for several years been working on a feminist theological analysis of work. She links spirtuality and labor, and deems this link necessary to overcome the sexual division of labor and the exploitation of working women if a Christian vision of a humane society is to be fulfilled.

From its inception, feminist ethics has proposed mutuality as the main normative category in the reconstruction of moral discourse and the evaluation of human behavior. Through it, feminists sought to apply the dictum that the personal is political to their confrontation with the dominant model of religious ethics (Ruether and Bianchi, 1976; Russell, 1979, 1981; Farley, 1977; Haney, 1980). Margaret Farley went to the crux of feminist thinking on mutuality when she wrote, "The kinds of changes that are needed in the patterns of relationship between women and men are changes which are finally constituted by a moral revolution. . . . We are talking about a revolution that must occur in the most intimate relations as well as the most public" (Farley, 1977: 70). Recently, attention has been given not only to mutuality (or lack of it) between women and men but also to mutuality between women. Since the appearance of Adrienne Rich's (1980) article "Compulsory Heterosexuality and Lesbian Existence," feminist moral discourse has examined the social and sexual implications of women's relations to one another for their lives (Raymond, 1986; Hunt, 1986). Raymond invented the term "gyn/affection" to characterize friendship between women, emphasizing that gyn/affection bonds women in political activity that allows them to be rooted in the world not as generic persons but as women.

In 1985 the reader in feminist ethics *Women's Consciousness, Women's Conscience* (Andolsen et al.) was published. This is a compendium of feminist thinking on the foundation of ethics as well as essays on issues such as violence against women, feminism and peace, and antisemitism in the women's movement, including important writings by black and Hispanic feminists.

PASTORAL COUNSELING

In the areas of psychology of religion and pastoral counseling, feminism has had a broad if somewhat diffuse effect. Pastoral counseling, in which humanistic approaches predominate, has been open to the insights of feminist therapy. Attention has centered on the specific problems that women bring to the pastoral counselor, such as their experience of domestic violence, a situation increasingly confronting the minister in the local congregation and the welfare agencies of religious bodies (Clarke, 1986).

Psychoanalytic theory has prompted feminist debates in the field of religion as elsewhere. One question is whether or not the explanation of the religious imagination in various psychoanalytic schools can aid women in their critique of patriarchal religion and help them to see beyond its mental constraints. Naomi Goldenberg assesses Jung's concentration on dreams and fantasy as indicative of a religious process within the individual independent of the external and conventional symbolism of religious institutions. The Jungian method, in her opinion, "may point to a source of religious iconography accessible to everyone, a source particularly appealing to those of us who are not entirely at home with orthodox creeds"(Goldenberg, 1979: 70). Judith van Herik has related the gender asymmetry in Freud's thought to his view of religion, especially the monotheisms of Judaism and Christianity, as psychic responses to the authority and murder of the primal father. Both Goldenberg and van Herik interpret psychoanalytic theory as a response to the crisis of patriarchal culture and its religion. Goldenberg looks to the Goddess imagery in feminist witchcraft as a psychic renewal of women and of human culture. Van Herik argues for the importance to feminist social theory of Freud's insight that, in the present culture, femininity is associated with fulfillment as opposed to the ideal of masculine development found in renunciation (van Herik, 1982: 194-200).

THE INFLUENCE OF FEMINIST THEOLOGY

Theology as a subdiscipline of religious studies has the character of normative and discursive reflection on the doctrines, history, liturgy, and symbols of a religious tradition. Feminists have redefined theology to include experiential and narrative elements. The experience of women is seen as normative for feminist theology, and women's stories as providing its content. Feminist theology, therefore, always has a broader meaning than the designation of one area of theological studies and is used for the intellectual products of religious feminism as a whole.

Nonetheless, the evolution of feminist theology in general has occurred in interaction with theology in the narrower sense. In the 1960s feminist theology emerged alongside black theology and Latin American liberation theology. Like them, it was joined to a social movement and criticized the dualistic framework of theological thinking, including the concept assumed to define the identity of theology itself: the distinction of church and world. Although feminist scholars had much to say about the traditional topics of theology— God, Christ, sin and redemption, and faith—its status as theology was defined because its reference was to the women's movement and women's religious experience and expression and not to the relationship of the church to the world. Alice Hagemann (1974) reports one reaction to her proposal to the faculty of the Harvard Divinity School in 1972 to create a Chair in Women's Studies. "We're here to train men for the Christian ministry. What does this proposal have to do with preaching the Gospel and bringing in the Kingdom?" (1974: 18).

Nonetheless, feminist theology has been able to claim a stake in the theological enterprise. Its critique of the dualism of systematic theology and of the exclusively male experience behind theological language has made inroads. Such critiques of patriarchal religion predominated in the early years, but from the outset feminist theologians intended more: a reconstruction of theology around a feminist core. This has come increasingly to fruition in such works as Rosemary Radford Ruether's book *Sexism and God-Talk* (1983) and Elisabeth Schüssler-Fiorenza's *In Memory of Her* (1984). *Sexism and God-Talk* displays the confidence that women have a historical tradition sufficiently researched to allow for interpretation, that women's experience is an adequate axiom and a necessary corrective for understanding the world, and that the goal of promoting or diminishing the full humanity of women is a valid critical principle for evaluating any system of religious ideas and practices (Ruether, 1983: 12-46).

While feminist theology has found a place among traditional schools of theology (Harvard Divinity School/Claremont Center for Process Studies, 1981), it also informs new critical models. Sharon Welch (1985) has utilized the methods of Michel Foucault to construct a feminist theology of liberation. She insists on the cherishing of human particularity in the face of the destructive power of universalizing discourse, as vested in the political, socioeconomic, and military institutions that threaten the survival of the planet. Welch develops a political epistemology in which liberation theologies embody the resurgence of "subjugated knowledges" against the normative self-universalization of the white patriarchal West (Welch, 1985).

RELIGIOUS FEMINISM

I have devoted so much space to a survey of the development of and present trends in feminist religious scholarship because feminist theology initiated and now sustains religious feminism to a degree that cannot be claimed for other types of feminist theory in other sectors of the women's movement. This does not mean that religious feminism is an unduly cerebral affair, but this background does have consequences for its social composition. Who considers herself a religious feminist? What is her social background in terms of level of education, race, social class, and sexual orientation?

In Educational Settings

The immediate constituency for feminist theology has been women in theological education. The survival and expansion of feminist theory in the academy has depended on the support and often militancy of women students. The Harvard Divinity School, despite its initial cool reception of Hagemann's proposal, under pressure from feminist students eventually established a program in women's studies in religion that has become the most extensive in the United States and for which a professorial chair is planned (but not yet funded). The proportion of women among theology students has more than tripled in a decade. In 1972 there were 3,358 women in theological education, or 10.2% of total enrollment. In 1983 the numbers had grown to 13,451, or 24.4% of the total enrollment (Taylor, 1984: 271). In some schools, women make up more than half of the student body. Recently a slight decrease has been noted in women's entry into some degree programs. The causes are unclear; in the case of Master of Divinity programs it may be disillusionment with the career prospects for women in ministry. If this trend continues it could be detrimental to the flourishing of feminist theology.

Feminist theologians have always been concerned about the reform of theological education.[2] For many years the Seminary Quarter at Grailville provided an opportunity for feminists to build an alternative education. In the fall of 1983, the Women's Theological Center in Boston enrolled its first students. This is a year-long residential program with the goal of helping women integrate feminist theological reflection with work they undertake in such settings as battered women's refuges. Although seminary credit is offered by the Women's Theological Center, it consciously recruits women from outside formal theological education. It also strongly emphasizes racial diversity and cross-cultural perspectives in the composition of its staff and students and in the programs it undertakes. In Los Angeles, the Immaculate Heart Center in 1984 instituted a Master of Arts degree in feminist spirituality. This consists of weekend courses taught by visiting feminist scholars. Its students come from a wide range of occupations—journalism, computer science, social work, homemaking, religious professions. Like the Women's Theological Center in Boston, the Immaculate Heart Center has a large proportion of women in the age groups above 40. The hallmark of feminist theological education is its intention to be nonhierarchical and praxis-oriented.

In Conferences, Journals, and Rituals

Other vehicles of religious feminism are conferences, journals, and rituals. Conferences have been a major impetus to the organization of religious feminism. The 1983 Woman Church meeting in Chicago was sponsored by the Women's Ordination Conference and other leading Roman Catholic organizations of laywomen and nuns. Twelve hundred women gathered to express not only their opposition to the present structures of the Roman Catholic church but to develop new forms of church life. In November, 1984, a conference took place in Los Angeles titled "Shekinah. Illuminating the Unwritten Scroll: Women's Spirituality and Jewish Tradition." It brought together leading feminist writers on Jewish law, culture, and liturgy. The conference acted to crystallize the consciousness of Jewish women that had already been evident in such activities as women's minyans (prayer groups) and the summer institutes of the progressive Havurah movement. After the conference, many participants continued to meet to coordinate existing projects and develop new ones. These two examples show how conferences function not solely, and often not primarily, for exchange of information but as opportunities to establish women's religous networks.

Because the ability of religious feminists to make connections with one another is a primary goal, conferences on religious feminism place a high priority on feminist process. Indeed, this often becomes a major focus when a conference attempts to bring women of various races, sexual orientations, and religions together. However, feminist process breaks down at conferences of religious feminists very much in the same way it has done in recent years at the annual meetings of the National Women's Studies Association meetings and often around the same issues—especially racism and anti-semitism. This was the experience of the facilitators of the process at the Women's Spirit Bonding conference at Grailville in July 1982.

Numerous religious feminist journals have come into existence (and in some cases gone out again) since the 1970s. *WomanSpirit, Lilith* (on Jewish feminist issues), and *Daughters of Sarah* (evangelical) are the most well known. Since 1985 an academic journal has been published under the title *Journal of Feminist Studies in Religion.*

Feminist ritual plays an important role in attracting women to feminist religious groups. Jewish and Goddess/Pagan feminist writers devote much attention to devising new rituals. In Goddess spirituality, the power-from-within, which is seen as the transformative life force in the individual and the community, is cultivated through ritual. Political action is therefore conceived in continuum with ritual. Starhawk (1952) has described several political actions into which she and others integrated the ritual of feminist witchcraft. Carrying out a blockade of a nuclear power plant or seeking healing from the violation of rape are situations in which women attempt to overcome their feelings of powerlessness and vulnerability through participation in feminist ritual. In women's centers, at women's music festivals, and at conferences, ritual has increasingly found a place.

In Judaism, unlike Christianity, ritual is not centered on a sacred place and is not the responsibility of a religious professional. The diffusion of ritual throughout Jewish life has prompted Jewish feminists to design new liturgies that honor women's experience, allow the female life cycle to be celebrated, and counteract the erasure of women from the Jewish memory solemnized in its major rituals. Women's gatherings to celebrate the New Moon (a holiday traditionally associated with women), ceremonies to mark the birth of a daughter, the rewriting of blessings and the Passover service encourage women's involvement in Jewish feminism. E.M. Broner, Aviva Cantor, and Marcia Falk are among those who have developed Jewish feminist rituals.

The Social Class Factor

The main channels of religious feminism (conferences and journals) attract largely educated women to the movement. Even feminist ritual does not draw, in terms of educational levels and social class, women from a significantly different constituency. Many religious feminists and feminist theologians do come from a working-class and/or poor family. I have already noted the prominent role played by socialist feminists in feminist theology. Although there are analyses of class in American and Western society by feminist theologians, there is to my knowledge no class analysis by a feminist theologian of religious feminism. There are only limited data from surveys conducted by religious feminist groups. *Daughters of Sarah,* a grassroots journal for Christian feminists who still identify very strongly with their religious tradition, published a study of its readership in 1985. In terms of family income and education, a large percentage belonged to the middle class: 41% had a family income above $30,000 and 70% had a family income of more than \$20,000; 54% held a graduate degree and a full 70% had done some graduate study (Daughters of Sarah, 1985).

Feminist theologians accept sadly that the direct impact of religious feminism has been largely restricted to the educated middle class. The same, of course, can be said of socialist feminism and in many but not all aspects of the women's movement in general. Yet it is not sufficient to invoke general reasons for the lack of participation of lesser educated and low income women in religious feminism. These women are present in American religious life, although not in positions of leadership and authority. One would expect that the emphasis of religious feminists on empowerment of those marginalized within the religious mainstream would have an appeal to other marginalized populations, but such is not the case. It is not only the intellectual medium of much religious feminist activity that inhibits the involvement of working-class and poor women, it is also the concentration on issues of concern primarily to well-educated, middle-class women.

The struggle for women's ordination has opened up the ministerial profession to relatively high status women, but working-class and poor women lack the educational and financial resources to train for the ministry (or for secular professions). There are also cultural barriers. I have already reported the results of a survey of religious language that showed that educational levels influenced most strongly whether one retained traditional religious language or not. The attention to language represents the more elaborate verbal codes with which middle-class women operate.

I am not trying to disparage or reduce the significance of the feminist campaigns for women's ordination or inclusive language. It is, however, the case that the most publicized concerns of religious feminists have not been those that working-class and poor women have perceived as directly relevant to their religious experience. On the other side, one must recognize that religious feminism and the resistance to it have had a profound indirect impact on the experience that all women have had of religion in the last two decades.

I have not found data on the attitudes of working-class and poor women to having a woman as a pastor. But women ministers in the mainline denominations are more likely than their male colleagues to be in congregations with a large membership of working-class and poor women. There are accounts written by women ministers of how they have reinvigorated congregations in poorer neighborhoods. Sometimes these accounts record the initial resentment of the congregation to a woman minister, taken as a token of the low esteem in which the church authorities hold a poorer congregation and of its limited financial ability to obtain the more desirable (male) pastors. It would seem that at the outset the relationship of a woman pastor to her female working-class and poor parishioners is ambiguous. But how is this ambiguity resolved? Is the woman pastor still seen as an inappropriate authority figure? Or does a relationship evolve according to the feminist ideal of the woman minister as an agent of empowerment for the less educated and poorer women with whom she works? These questions demand further investigation.

There are two areas today where religious feminists come into contact with working-class and poor women.[3] First, there are the shelters for battered women in which religious feminists work. Although physical abuse of women and children is not a prerogative of the working-class and the poor, places of refuge are utilized largely by lower income, less educated women. Judith Vaughan, who holds a Ph.D. in social ethics from the divinity school of the University of Chicago, is a sister in a Roman Catholic religious community and a cosignatory of the 1984 *New York Times* advertisement dissenting from the official Roman Catholic teaching on abortion. She has worked at the House of Ruth in Los Angeles, a shelter for battered women. She is an example of a considerable number of feminist theologians who prefer a praxis of social action and advocacy to an academic career.

The second area where religious feminists make contact with working-class women is in the labor movement, though the extent to which this has occurred is unclear. Working-class women active in the labor movement often do have strong religious beliefs and motivations for their involvement. This has been documented in the collection of oral histories of lower income women compiled by Fran Leeper Buss (1985). However, there is no indication that the religious outlook of the women, who record their lives in Buss's volume, has been touched by religious feminism. Mildred McEwen, who was active in the struggle for unionization at the J. P. Stevens textile plant in Montgomery, Alabama, spoke of the importance of religion to her:

> I enjoy watching the 700 Club with Pat Robertson, a preacher on TV. He's just a true, down-to-earth man. With us, you have a personal relationship with Christ; that's the only way you can be saved [Buss, 1985: 24].

Mildred McEwen's religious experience is shaped by the evangelical fundamentalism of the New Christian Right, perhaps the most virulently antifeminist segment of our population. Yet she does not voice any of the antifeminist positions of Pat Robertson and is eloquent in defending unions against the charge that they are anti-Christian, a common sentiment among evangelical fundamentalists. If religious feminism is to have a working-class constituency, then it is women such as Mildred McEwen who will organize it. What the issues of a working-class religious feminism will be and how they will be articulated cannot be even dimly outlined at present.

Women of Color

The representation of women of color in formal theological education has been limited. Blacks constitute 5.2% of the total enrollment of students in theological schools. Women make up 25% of the black students in professional degree programs, but of these 47.7% are concentrated in the less academically demanding 2-year programs (Baumgartner, 1985). The number of women of color among the feminist theologians is therefore small and most of those in academic theology are completing doctoral degrees or in junior faculty appointments. However, because of the long history of the black churches in America, and the prominent role women have played in them, blacks constitute the largest and most visible group of women of color in schools of theology. Black religious feminism emerged directly out of the black theology movement of the late 1960s and 1970s. M. Shawn Copeland, a Dominican nun, was one of the two staff members of the Black Theology Project, following the Theology in the Americas conference in Detroit in 1975 that brought Latin American liberation theologians into contact with black theologians and feminist theologians. Copeland was later active in the creation of the Women's Theological Center in Boston.

A collection of documents from the black theology movement, edited by Gayraud S. Wilmore and James H. Cone (1979), provided the first overall impression of a nascent movement. The essays in this volume by Frances Beale (1979), Theresa Hoover (1979), Pauli Murray (1979), Jacquelyn Grant (1979), and Alice Walker (1979) still provide a definitive statement of black religious feminism in its concern for the multiple social oppressions of black women. Jacquelyn Grant has devoted much of her attention to the history of black women in the ministry of the black churches and the theological implications of the acceptance or rejection of women's ministry by the black churches. She believes that the mission of the black churches—to preach freedom for the Afro-American people—can only be fulfilled when sexism is eradicated. In 1981, with a grant from the Lilly Foundation, she funded the study *Black Women in Church and Society* at the Interdenominational Theological Center in Atlanta. In the context of a black seminary she has organized meetings of Afro-American churchwomen designed to heighten their consciousness of gender issues in the church and of the significance of their own role within it. Black churchwomen have often been reluctant to identify their movement and efforts with feminism, which they perceive as dominated by white women. Nonetheless, Afro-American churchwomen have been in the vanguard in advocating radical social policy in the black churches. They have accumulated a fund of experience in women's religious leadership that can benefit religious feminism as a whole.

Pauli Murray brings an explicitly feminist commitment to the long-established role in the black community of the religious leader as social and political organizer. An attorney and a political activist who held several university teaching posts, she served on the Presidential Commission on the Status of Women. In 1977, at 66 years of age, she became the first black woman to be ordained by the Episcopal Church.

One of the themes of black feminist theology expressed by Alice Walker (1979) is the need for black women to recover the rich spirituality that was stifled in the lives and suffering of their foremothers. Women's artistic creativity, not allowed to come to fruition in the lives of so many Afro-American women, is viewed as the medium of black women's spirituality. Black folk culture is generally recognized as a medium for transmitting Afro-American religious experience, and black feminists have discerned in it a source of spiritual expression for black women. Katie Geneva Cannon (1985) has explored how Zora Neale Hurston gave black folklore a literary shape in which an ethic of black women could be articulated.

> Hurston and her female characters are Black women who learn to glean directives for living in the here-and-now. In their tested and tried existential realities, the majority of these women refuse to get caught up in the gaudy accoutrements of the middle-strata sham. Against the vicissitudes of labor exploitation, sex discrimination, and racial cruelties, they embrace an ingenuity which allows them to fashion a set of values on their own terms as well as to master, radicalize, and sometimes destroy pervasive negative orientations imposed by the larger society [Cannon, 1985: 44].

Because of the disparity between black and white women's experience, and the different emphasis of the black women's movement and white feminism, Alice Walker coined the word "womanist" to distinguish the black woman's perspective. Many black women theologians have endorsed Walker's shift in language. Nevertheless, white religious feminism and black "womanist" religion are parallel movements. Black and white women share much the same religious agenda but set their priorities differently. Black religious feminists have not insisted on inclusive language as fervently as have white women, yet Jacquelyn Grant and others have called for the end of the use of sexist language in the black churches.

Black feminist theology is at the moment located solidly within the Christian churches to which most black women still belong. Alongside the ardent commitment of Christian black women to their churches there is, if anything, a greater degree of religious diversity than among white women. There are the many Afro-American women who have joined the Black Muslims; there are black Jewish lesbians and black women who invoke the Goddess—frequently in the form of the Yoruba (West African) goddess Yemanya or other African female deities.

Much of what has been said of Afro-American women applies to women from other ethnic minorities. Other minorities form an even smaller percentage of the total enrollment of students in theological education than do blacks. Hispanics constitute 2.3% of theology students and Asian/Pacific Americans slightly less. The proportion of Hispanic and Asian/Pacific women studying for professional degrees and the percentage of them in the less academically demanding 2-year professional programs varies by only a bare margin from the corresponding figures for blacks. There may, however, be factors in the growth of women's theological education specific to particular ethnic groups.

The expansion of theological education among Hispanic women could be slowed down by the only recent and incomplete acceptance of the theological training of laywomen in the Roman Catholic Church in general and their limited opportunities for religious employment. The same observation is pertinent to Hispanic women in fundamentalist Protestant groups that in recent years have attracted many Hispanic members. The weak economic position of Afro-American women and the even lower income of Hispanic women places a larger proportion of women in these ethnic groups among those too poor to contemplate a theological education. Hispanic voices are nevertheless beginning to be heard among feminist theologians. Ada Maria Isai-Diaz and Yolanda Tarango have tried to make other feminists aware of the cultural barriers to the participation of Hispanic women in secular and religious feminism and of the alienation that Hispanic feminists feel because of a lack of recognition of their cultural identity by other feminists, and because of hostility toward feminism in the Hispanic movement (see Tarango and Isasi-Diaz, 1984: 85-88; Working Group of Racisim/Classism/Sexism, 1984; Isasi-Diaz, 1985).

Sexual Orientation

Lesbians have suffered discrimination, persecution, and even annihilation at the hands of a society that justifies its homophobia by appeal to the Bible. The close connection between religious ideology and the destruction of lesbian existence is cause for a distinctive anger among lesbians at a patriarchal religion that has supported the most vicious attacks against them. Not surprisingly many lesbians have left the Christian churches. Sally Gearhart, who for many years was active in the Lutheran and Methodist traditions, expressed the rejection of Christianity by lesbians who had been isolated, rendered invisible, and demeaned:

> We begin to see that the Christian church and the feminism to which we're feeling daily more connected are fundamentally incompatible. . . . We realize that no matter how hard we work to alter it, the church to be the church must continue its dehumanizing practices. It is the enemy of feminism and the enemy of women. For the church to "become" what it must in order to be humanized (womanized, Lesbianized), it will first of all have to commit unequivocal suicide [Gearhart, 1974].

Many Christian-born lesbians would agree with Gearhart's evaluation of the prospects of lesbian liberation in the church and, when they have sought a feminist spirituality, have looked for it in the post-Christian feminist philosophy of Mary Daly, feminist witchcraft, and Goddess religion. Jewish lesbians have tended rather to try to carve out room for themselves within

Judaism, having encountered antisemitism in post-Christian feminist spiritual-ity. The strength of Christianity among large sections of the Afro-American community has encouraged black Christian lesbians to remain in churches even when fear of discrimination and ridicule has forced them to hide their sexual orientation. The fear of losing their community and of encountering racism in groups dominated by white lesbians inhibits religious as well as other choices for lesbians of color.

Many lesbians of all races have remained in the Christian churches. Lesbians are present even in those denominations that are homophobic in their theology and in the social policies they advocate. There are women in the gay caucus of the conservative Evangelical Southern Baptists, and in 1983 the Conference of Catholic lesbians was formed. I have already discussed the severe difficulties that lesbians meet in seeking ordination to the ministry of most Christian denominations. Similar discrimination is suffered by lesbians who work in other church-related fields. Several lesbians have been fired from teaching in seminaries and in church-related colleges. In face of such repression, the number of feminist theologians who are openly lesbian is small. Carter Heyward, who is on the faculty of the Episcopal Divinity School in Cambridge, Massachusetts, has consistently integrated her lesbian experi-ence with her theological work (Heyward, 1985: 217-225; see also Heyward, 1984). A group of women at the 1983 annual meeting of the American Academy of Religion established a lesbian task force in the largest learned society in the field of religion. The formation of this group, which includes both lesbian and nonlesbian feminists, has led to the inclusion of sessions on lesbian-feminist issues at later meetings.

How a woman experiences her lesbian identity is influenced by her religious environment. Catholic lesbians such as Mary E. Hunt (1983) have argued that while the Roman Catholic Church has been hostile to lesbians it has provided settings in which women's friendships could flouish and be nurtured. The convent has been an alternative to heterosexual marriage for Roman Catholic women in which they could live in community with other women. The publication of *Lesbian Nuns: Breaking Silence* (Curb and Manahan, 1985) allowed lesbians who had left or who had remained within the convent to recount the variety of their experiences. The convent is an ambivalent setting for lesbian existence, both providing the opportunity for women's spiritual bonding and at the same time confining it within the mores of a heterosexist religion. Even more ambivalent is the public response to lesbians in the convent. Naiad Press, a lesbian-feminist publisher, sold the serial rights to *Lesbian Nuns* to *Penthouse* magazine without the permission of the volume's editors. The controversy that ensued highlighted the romanticization and sexual titillation that envelops women's religious community in Protestant-dominated American culture.

In Religious Orders

Women in religious orders and congregations are a microcosm of women's religious history and the current feminist impact on religion in North America.[4] Unlike nuns in Europe, where the model of a life of contemplation enclosed within the convent precincts has predominated, most American sisters have been active in society. Many new congregations of women religious were founded in the nineteenth century to care for the needs of an immigrant and poor Roman Catholic Church. American nuns established schools and hospitals and provided much of the social welfare for the Roman Catholic Church. Of all the women engaged in religious professions during the nineteenth and early twentieth centuries they were the most powerful and usually the best educated. Many headed large and thriving institutions, others taught in colleges founded by their own orders and congregations. They were disproportionately well represented among women with higher degrees (McEwen, 1978; Weaver, 1985: 71-108).

In the 1960s the Second Vatican Council introduced far-reaching reforms of the Roman Catholic Church. Nuns were in the vanguard of this reform movement and increasingly came into conflict with church authorities over their desire for change. The Immaculate Heart Center in Los Angeles is run by a religious community of women who were stripped of their official status as Roman Catholic nuns by the local archbishop in 1968. Feminism made an immediate impact on nuns because in the late 1960s they were generally open to new theological movements and many of them were pursuing higher theological degrees. Many of them undertook a major rethinking of their role in society, accompanied by a redirection of their resources. The exchange of the monastic habit for secular dress was an external sign of a much deeper transformation. Nuns became involved in radical politics and maintained and created educational institutions and social agencies in the poorest areas.

For black and Hispanic nuns, their religious communities provided them with educational opportunities and encouragement to become political and religious leaders. M. Shawn Copeland's role in the Black Theology Project has already been noted. She and another black Dominican nun, Jamie Phelps, have made important contributions to religious feminism among black women. Nuns of color have also organized themselves to fight against racism and sexism in the church. Yolanda Tarango is a member of Las Hermanas, a group of Hispanic religious feminists, both nuns and laywomen. She was also a participant in *Mujeres para el Dialogo,* an international feminist group convened during the meeting of the Latin American Bishop's Conference at Puebla in 1978, where the radical church movement associated with liberation theology was reconfirmed. The nuns of North America build a bridge between the Western women's movements and global feminism, as most of them belong to religious orders in which the majority of members are recruited from the Third World. Maria Augusta Neal, a nun and distinguished sociologist, is conducting a study of American nuns on the link between "altruism" and the "theology of letting go" seen in the nuns' radical politics, exemplified by adoption of nonhierarchical forms for organizing their own communal lives. A feminist community has been born in the bosom of patriarchy.

In the Third World

Feminist religion has Jewish, Goddess, and Christian forms. A religious feminist may be a minister, a homemaker, a professional woman, an academic, or a nun. She is usually well educated and is most likely to be white, middle class, and heterosexual. Women of color and lesbians are present but often feel alienated by the assumptions of the already existing mainstream of feminist religion. The majority of religiously active women in the United States are not part of religious feminism. From a worldwide perspective the impact of feminsism on the religious consciousness of women must be judged to be minimal. Yet it would be wrong to assume that religious feminism will remain restricted to a small elite segment of women in Western culture. Religious feminism already has a global dimension. There are Third World women among the feminist theologians such as Beatriz Couch (Argentina) and Mercy Amba Oduyoye (Nigeria). And feminism is not only a phenomenon in Western religious traditions. Since the publication of Nawal el Saadawi's *The Hidden Face of Eve*, the work of Islamic feminists has become increasingly known in the West (el Saadawi, 1980). Islamic feminism and the feminism of other Third World areas has a cultural and religious past. Already in 1927 the Egyptian Huda Sharawi articulated the sentiments of feminists who wish to stay faithful to a religious tradition.

> We, the Egyptian feminists, have a great respect for our religion.... In wanting to see it in its true spirit . . . we are doing more for it than those who submit themselves blindly to the customs that have deformed [Islam][Mina, 1981: 72].[5]

Women in Third World societies are examining the religious underpinnings of patriarchal culture. The spread of Christianity through Western missionary activity, although it brought some beneficial reforms to women in non-Western cultures, also cemented patriarchy in many areas by giving it new and universalized forms. The interaction of indigenous gender asymmetry and Western patriarchy has caused women in very diverse sociocultural settings to face similar practices and ideologies of discrimination. An African participant at the World Council of Churches' Conference in Sheffield, England, in 1981 expressed the need for sexual politics in the agenda of Third World women:

> I am told that racism and classism should be important to me because I'm from the Third World, and I am told that sexism is only personal and that it is really

an importation from the United States. Yet, I am also told by my African students that I am their first woman professor. Do I need a psychiatrist? Do I fight all three oppressions or just one? [Parvey, 1983: 7]

In resisting the homogenization of women's experiences into that of women of the dominant class or culture one must never assume that women in Third World countries or working-class or poor women and women of color in Western societies are genderless creatures. These women have not suspended exploring their sexuality or spirituality until their other oppressions have been abolished, although the representations of their search may not be readily accessible. Religious feminism, even in its Western white and middle-class form, makes us all aware that the control of spiritual resources, no less than that of material resources, shapes women's lives. Feminist religion attempts to prevent the spiritual reproduction of patriarchy and to place the powers of the religious imagination in women's hands.

NOTES

1. The official Roman Catholic position was reiterated in the Vatican's *Declaration on the Question of the Admission to the Ministerial Priesthood* made by the Sacred Congregation for the Doctrine of the Faith in October 1976. For a reprinting of this document and criticism of it, see Swidler and Swidler (1977) or Stuhlmueller (1978).

2. For discussions of a feminist approach to theological education see The Cornwall Collective (1980) and Cannon et al. (1985).

3. I am indebted to a conversation with Beverly Harrison for the suggestions that the movement for women's refuges and the labor movement might be areas where religious feminists and working-class women could make connection with each other.

4. In Roman Catholicism a distinction is made between religious orders (founded prior to the Council of Trent in the sixteenth century) and other religious communities founded later. Properly only members of the former can be designated nuns and this group makes up only about 2% of the women religious in the United States. In this article I am following popular usage and use the term "nun" for all women religious.

5. See also Haddad (1985) and Jayawardena (1986). Jayawardena deals extensively with the religious policies of reform movements in the Middle East and Asia during the nineteenth and early twentieth centuries and how these affected and were sponsored by women.

REFERENCES

ANDOLSEN, B. H., C. E. GUDORF, and M. D. PELLAUER [eds.] (1985) Women's Consciousness, Women's Conscience: A Reader in Feminist Ethics. Minneapolis: Winston.

ATKISSON, C. W. (1983) Mystic and Pilgrim: The "Book" and the World of Margery Kempe. Ithaca: Cornell University Press.

BAUMGAERTNER, W. L. [ed.] (n.d.) Fact Book on Theological Education. Vandalia, OH: Association of Theological Schools in the United States and Canada.

BEALE, F. (1979) "Double Jeopardy: To be black and female," pp. 368-378 in G. S. Wilmore and J. H. Cone (eds.) Black Theology: A Documentary History, 1966-1979. Maryknoll, NY: Orbis.

BROOTEN, B. (1977) "'Junia . . . outstanding among the apostles'(Romans 16:7)," in L. Swidler and A. Swidler (eds.) Woman Priests: A Catholic Commentary on the Vatican Declaration. New York: Paulist.

BROOTEN, B. (1982) Women Leaders in the Ancient Synagogue. Chico: Scholar's Press.

BUDAPEST, Z. E. (1979) "Self blessing ritual," in C. P. Christ and J. Plaskow (eds.) Womanspirit Rising: A Feminist Reader in Religion. San Francisco: Harper & Row.

BUSS, F. L. [ed.] (1985) Dignity: Lower Income Women Tell of Their Lives and Struggles. Ann Arbor: University of Michigan Press.

BYNUM, C. W. (1982) Jesus as Mother: Studies in the Spirituality of the High Middle Ages. Berkeley: University of California Press.

CANNON, K. G. (1985) "Resources for a constructive ethic in the life and work of Zora Neale Hurston." Journal of Feminist Studies in Religion 1: 44.

CANNON, K. G. and the Mudflower Collective (1985) God's Fierce Whimsy: Christian and Theological Education. New York: Pilgrim.

CARROLL, J. W., B. HARGROVE, and A. T. LUMMIS (1981) Women of the Cloth: A New Opportunity for the Churches. San Francisco: Harper & Row.

CHRIST, C. P. (1980) Diving Deep and Surfacing: Women Writers on Spiritual Quest. Boston: Beacon.

CLARK, E. A. (1979) Jerome, Chrysostom, and Friends: Essays and Translations. New York: Edwin Mellen.

CLARK, E. A. (1984) The Life of Melaina the Younger: Introduction, Translation and Commentary. New York: Edwin Mellen.

CLARK, E. A. and H. RICHARDSON (1977) Women and Religion: A Feminist Sourcebook of Christian Thought. San Francisco: Harper & Row.

CLARKE, R. L. (1986) Pastoral Care of Battered Women. Philadelphia: Westminster.

Cornwall Collective (1980) Your Daughters Shall Prophesy: Feminist Alternatives in Theological Edcation. New York: Pilgrim.

CURB, R. and N. MANAHAN [eds.] (1985) Lesbian Nuns: Breaking Silence. Tallahassee: Naiad.

DALY, M. (1968) The Church and the Second Sex. Boston: Beacon.

DALY, M. (1973) Beyond God the Father. Boston: Beacon.

Daughters of Sarah (1985) Vol. 11 (March/April).

DWYER, M. [ed.] (1980) New Woman, New Church, New Priestly Ministry: Proceedings of the Second Conference on the Ordination of Roman Catholic Women. Proceedings of the Women's Ordination Conference, Baltimore, MD, November 10-12, 1978.

EL SAADAWI, N. (1980) The Hidden Face of Eve. Women in the Arab World. Boston: Beacon.

FARLEY, M. (1977) "New patterns of relationship: Beginnings of a moral revolution," pp. 51-70 in W. Burghardt (ed.) Woman: New Dimensions. New York: Paulist.

GEARHART, S. (1974) "The miracle of lesbianism," in S. Gearhart and W. R. Johnson (eds.) Loving Women/Loving Men: Gay Liberation and the Church, San Francisco: Glide.

GILES, C. and N. RICHARDSON (1984) "Reflections on a process," pp. xxii-xxviii in J. Kalven and M. I. Buckley (ed.) Women's Spirit Bonding. New York: Pilgrim Press.

GILKES, C. T. (1986) "The roles of church and community mothers: Ambivalent American sexism or fragmented familyhood?" Journal of Feminist Studies in Religion 2: 42-59.

GILL, B. (1985) "A ministry of presence," in J. L. Weidman (ed.) Women Ministers. San Francisco: Harper & Row.

GIMBUTAS, M. (1982) The Goddesses and Gods of Old Europe, 6500-3500: Myths and Cult Images. Berkeley: University of California Press.

GOLDENBERG, N. R. (1979) Changing of the Gods: Feminism and the End of Traditional Religions. Boston: Beacon.

GRANT, J. (1979) "Black theology and the black woman," pp. 418-433 in G. W. Wilmore and J. H. Cone (eds.) Black Theology: A Documentary History, 1966-1979. Maryknoll, NY: Orbis.

GROSS, R. M. (1979) "Female God language in a Jewish context," in C. P. Christ and J. Plaskow (eds.) Womanspirit Rising: A Feminist Reader in Religion. San Francisco: Harper & Row.

HADDAD, Y. Y. (1985) "Islam, women and revolution in twentieth-century Arab thought," pp. 275-306 in Y. Y. Haddad and E. B. Findly (eds.) Women, Religion and Social Change. New York: SUNY Press.

HAGEMANN, A. L. (1974) "Women and missions: The cost of liberation," pp. 167-193 in A. L. Hagemann (ed.) Sexist Religion and Women in the Church: No More Silence! New York: Association Press.

HANEY, E. (1980) "What is feminist ethics? A proposal for continuing discussion." Journal of Religious Ethics 8.

HARRISON, B. W. (1983) Our Right to Choose: Toward a New Ethic of Abortion. Boston: Beacon.

HARRISON, B. W. (1984) "Human sexuality and mutuality," pp. 141-157 in J. L. Weidman (ed.) Christian Feminism: Visions of a New Humanity. San Francisco: Harper & Row.

HARRISON, B. W. (1985) Making the Connections: Essays in Feminist Social Ethics (C. S. Robb, ed.). Boston: Beacon.

Harvard Divinity School/Claremont Center for Process Studies (1981) Feminism and Process Thought: The Harvard Divinity School/Claremont Center for Process Studies Symposium Papers. Lewiston: Edwin Mellen.

HERIK, J. V. (1982) Freud on Femininity and Faith. Berkeley: University of California Press.

HEYWARD, C. (1982) The Redemption of God: A Theology of Mutual Relation. Washington, DC: University Press of America.

HEYWARD, C. (1984) Our Passion for Justice: Images of Power, Sexuality, and Liberation. New York: Pilgrim Press.

HILL, P. R. (1985) The World Their Household: The American Women's Foreign Mission Movement and Cultural Transformation, 1870-1920. Ann Arbor: University of Michigan Press.

HOOVER, T. (1979) "Black women and the churches: Triple jeopardy," pp. 377-388 in G. S. Wilmore and J. H. Cone (eds.) Black Theology: A Documentary History, 1966-1979. Maryknoll, NY: Orbis.

HUNT, M. E. (1983) "Lovingly lesbian: Toward a feminist theology of friendship," in R. Nugent (ed.) A Challenge to Love: Gay and Lesbian Catholics in the Church. New York: Crossroad.

HUNT, M. E. (1986) Fierce Tenderness. Minneapolis: Winston.

ISASI-DIAZ, A. M. (1985) "Toward an understanding of *feminismo Hispano* in the USA," pp. 51-61 in B. H. Andolsen et al. (eds.) Women's Consciousness, Women's Conscience: A Reader in Feminist Ethics. Minneapolis: Winston.

JAYAWARDENA, K. (1986) Feminism and Nationalism in the Third World. London: Zed.

LINCOLN, C. E. (1983) Report on attitudes of black pastors, presented at the annual meeting of the Society for the Scientific Study of Religion, Knoxville, TN, November 4-6.

MAGGID, A. (1982) "Lesbians in the international movement of Gay/Lesbian Jews," in E. T. Beck (ed.) Nice Jewish Girls: A Lesbian Anthology. Trumansburg: Crossing Press.

MASSEY, M. C. (1985) Feminine Soul: The Fate of an Ideal. Boston: Beacon.

McEWEN, M. (1978) The Role of the Nun in Nineteenth Century America. New York: Arno.

MINA, N. (1981) Women in Islam. Tradition and Transition in the Middle East. New York: Seaview.

MORTON, N. (1985) The Journey Is Home. Boston: Beacon.

MURRAY, P. (1979) "Black theology and feminist theology: A comparative view," pp. 398-417 in G. S. Wilmore and J. H. Cone (eds.) Black Theology: A Documentary History, 1966-1979. Maryknoll, NY: Orbis.

PARVEY, C. R. [eds] (1983) The Community of Women and Men in the Church: A Report of the World Council of Churches' Conference, Sheffield, England, 1981. Fortress: Philadelphia.

PLASKOW, J. (1980) Sex, Sin and Grace: Women's Experience and the Theologies of Reinhold Niebuhr and Paul Tillich. Washington, DC: University Press of America.

RAYMOND, J. (1986) A Passion for Friends: Toward a Philosophy of Female Affection. Boston: Beacon.

RICH, A. (1980) "Compulsory heterosexuality and lesbian existence." Signs 5: 631-660.

ROOF, W. C. and J. L. ROOF (1984) "Review of the polls: Images of God among Americans." Journal for the Scientific Study of Religion 23: 201-205.

RUETHER, R. R. (1974) "Misogynism and virginal feminism in the fathers of the church," pp. 150-183 in R. R. Ruether (ed.) Religion and Sexism: Images of Women in the Jewish and Christian Traditions. New York: Simon & Schuster.

RUETHER, R. R. (1976) From Machismo to Mutuality: Essays on Sexism and Woman-Man Liberation. New York: Paulist.

RUETHER, R. R. (1979) "Mothers of the church: Ascetic women in the late patristic age," pp. 72-98 in R. R. Ruether and E. McLaughlin (eds.) Women of Spirit: Female Leadership in the Jewish and Christian Traditions. New York: Simon & Schuster.

RUETHER, R. R. (1983) Sexism and God-Talk: Toward a Feminist Theology. Boston: Beacon.

RUETHER, R. R. (1985) Womanguides: Readings Toward a Feminist Theology. Boston: Beacon.

RUETHER, R. R. and R. S. KELLER (1981) Women and Religion in America (3 vols.). San Francisco: Harper & Row.

RUSSELL, L. M. (1979) The Future of Partnership. Philadelphia: Westminster.

RUSSELL, L. M. (1981) Growth in Partnership. Philadelphia: Westminster.

SAIVING, V. (1979) "The human situation: A feminine view," in C. P. Christ and J. Plaskow (eds.) Womanspirit Rising: A Feminist Reader in Religion. San Francisco: Harper & Row.

SCHÜSSLER-FIORENZA, E. (1984) In Memory of Her: A Feminist Theological Reconstruction of Christian Origins. New York: Crossroad.

SPRETNAK, C. (1981) Lost Goddesses of Early Greece: A Collection of Pre-Hellenic Myths. Boston: Beacon.

STONE, M. (1978) When God Was a Woman. New York: Harcourt Brace Jovanovich.

STUHLMUELLER, C. P. [ed.] (1978) Women and Priesthood: Future Directions. Collegeville: Liturgical Press.

SWIDLER, L. and A. SWIDLER [eds.] (1977) Women Priests: A Catholic Commentary on the Vatican Declaration. New York: Paulist.

TARANGO, Y. and A. M. ISASI-DIAZ (1984) "'Las Marias' of the feminist movement," pp. 85-88 in J. Kalven and M. I. Buckley (eds.) Women's Spirit Bonding. New York: Pilgrim Press.

TAYLOR, M. J. (1984) "Trends in seminary enrollment 1977-83," in C. H. Jacquet (ed.) Yearbook of American and Canadian Churches 1984. Nashville: Abingdon.

TRIBLE, P. (1980) God and the Rhetoric of Sexuality. Philadelphia: Fortress.

TRIBLE, P. (1984) Texts of Terror: Literary-Feminist Readings of Biblical Narratives. Philadelphia: Fortress.

STARHAWK (1982) Dreaming the Dark, Magic, Sex and Politics. Boston: Beacon.

UMANSKY, E. M. (1979) Women in Judaism: From the reform movement to contemporary Jewish religious feminism," pp. 338ff in R. Ruether and E. McLaughlin (eds.) Women of Spirit: Female Leadership in the Jewish and Christian Traditions. New York: Simon & Schuster.

UMANSKY, E. M. (1983) Lily Montagu and the Advancement of Liberal Judaism: From Visionary to Vocation. New York: Edwin Mellen.

WALKER, A. (1979) "In search of our mothers' gardens," pp. 434-442 in G. S. Wilmore and J. H. Cone (eds.) Black Theology: A Documentary History, 1966-1979. Maryknoll, NY: Orbis.

WEAVER, M. J (1985) New Catholic Women. A Contemporary Challenge to Traditional Religious Authority. San Francisco: Harper & Row.

WELCH, S. D. (1985) Communities of Resistance and Solidarity: A Feminist Theory of Liberation. Maryknoll: Orbis.

WILLIAMS, M. D. (1974) Community in a Black Pentecostal Church: An Anthropological Study. Pittsburgh: University of Pittsburgh Press.

WILLIS, D. W. (1982) "Womanhood and domesticity in the A.M.E. [African Methodist Episcopal] tradition: The influence of Daniel Alexander Payne," pp. 133-146 in D. W. Willis and R. Newman, Black Apostles at Home and Abroad. Boston: G. K. Hall.

WILMORE, G. S. and J. H. CONE (1979) Black Theology: A Documentary History, 1966-1979. Maryknoll, NY: Orbis.

Working Group on Racism/Classism/Sexism (1984) Transcript of the plenary discussion and the report from the conference, pp. 106-116, 130ff, in J. Kalven and M. I. Buckley (ed.) Women's Spirit Bonding. New York: Pilgrim Press.

16   The Women's Health Movement: A Critique of Medical Enterprise and the Position of Women

MARY K. ZIMMERMAN

Methods and conclusions formed by one half the race only must necessarily require revision as the other half of humanity rises into conscious responsibility.

—Elizabeth Blackwell, M.D. (1889)

In this chapter, we examine the women's health movement as a challenge to many of the assumptions and practices of mainstream modern medicine. In so doing, we not only learn about a significant health care development in its own right, but we also expand our understanding of the social nature of medical knowledge, institutions, and practice. The Women's Health Movement is not the only current challenge to modern medicine, but it is the most deeply rooted historically as well as the most analytically sophisticated. Catherine Reissman (1984) sees the women's health movement as exemplary of a broad critique of contemporary medicine that calls into question (1) "medicalization," the increasing tendency to apply medical definitions and control to phenomena not previously thought of as medical problems (Zola, 1972; Conrad and Schneider, 1980), (2) standard treatments that rely heavily on intervention and technology rather than prevention and self-care; and (3) typical medical power relations, which are highly asymmetric and where professional authority prevails with minimal reciprocity between doctor and patient and little involvement of family or friends. In addition, the feminist critique of medicine shows how the medical care system contributes to the control and maintenance of conventional status hierarchies and role relationships, mirroring and reproducing gender inequality in society.

Throughout history, human beings have developed numerous ways of interpreting and assigning meaning to diseases and other health problems. These definitions emerge from group interaction as members jointly construct their shared reality. The dominant system of medical knowledge and practice in the Western world today, deeply embedded in the institutions of our society and largely taken for granted, is an excellent example of such a "reality." We tend to see it as *the* reality rather than as only one of many possible ways of making sense of illness, disease, and health. Yet medicine is very much a product of socially constructed values, customs, and roles as well as their interpretations and reinterpretations. It is not the clear-cut, objective, scientific endeavor it is often thought to be (for an excellent analysis of this point see Mishler et al., 1981).

Thus, the women's health movement is important for its analysis of the contemporary medical care system, for the questions it raises about the nature of medical knowledge, and for its insights into how health care relationships and services affect the health and well-being of individuals. Furthermore, it is important to study because it shows medicine as an agent of social control with respect to key statuses and roles in society, such as those based on gender. We begin by exploring the viewpoint of the women's health movement—its basic assumptions and arguments—and how these ideas have developed historically. We then review its key strategies and issues, and close by considering these in relation to feminist theory and ideas about social change.

THE PERSPECTIVE OF
THE WOMEN'S HEALTH MOVEMENT

The women's health movement gathered momentum and became a recognizable force for social change along with the reemergence of the feminist movement in the late 1960s and early 1970s. It continued into the 1980s to provide serious challenges to central aspects of standard medical practice, such as the scientific objectivity of diagnosis and treatment, the economic exploitation of patients, and the efficacy and humaneness of the traditional doctor-patient relationship. The women's health movement offers an alternative perspective on health care values and beliefs. It also provides a system of direct services as an alternative to much mainstream health care, an extensive network of self-help groups, education and advocacy organizations, and women's clinics.

A fundamental assumption underlying the women's health movement is that women have not had ultimate control over their own bodies and their own health. With few exceptions, contemporary women live in social worlds where men occupy the vast majority of powerful, decision-making positions. Health policy, health legislation, health care planning and administration, health-related research, and the influential clinical roles that govern the creation of health knowledge and the delivery of health and medical services are all dominated by men or, more precisely, by male-centered thinking, whether from men or women. In addition, this androcentric system also controls the business and industrial corporations that heavily influence both environmental risks to human health and the nature of the technology developed to improve health. An important corollary assumption to the notion of male control is that men have many life experiences and interests unique from women's. Out of these distinctive experiences men develop interpretations of reality and agendas for action that serve male priorities. The preeminence of male-centered views means they also may be adopted by women.

From a feminist perspective, the belief systems and supporting institutions created and perpetuated through the dominance of one sex determine the health of the other in three basic ways. In terms of disease *etiology* or causation, women are affected by corporate and government environmental decisions that encourage (or prevent) exposure to risk and the development of disease (Doyal, 1983). These decisions, in turn, may lead to social policies designed to "protect" women but which at the same time segregate and exclude them (Randall, 1985). Dominant belief systems and institutions also affect women in terms of disease *diagnosis* by controlling which health problems are officially recognized and who ultimately is designated sick or healthy. Finally, they affect women in terms of medical *treatment*, by determining the nature of treatment regimens and rehabilitation programs as well as decisions regarding to whom these are applied. Since class and racial groups also are subject to conditions of dominance and exploitation, poor working- class women and women of color experience double or, frequently, triple jeopardy in such a system (Rodriguez-Trias, 1978; Wilkinson, 1980; Smith, 1982).

The lack of women's power relative to men in these critical areas is considered by feminists to be unjust, undesirable, and in need of change. On a more practical level, however, one can reasonably ask if it really has made a difference that men have been in control. If medicine is based on scientific fact and administered professionally, then how could gender matter? The response of the women's health movement is that gender *has* made a difference. Male dominance in the health system has jeopardized women through a pattern of actions that have been harmful rather than beneficial to women's health. It is important to point out that the feminist critique is based on the *impact* of these actions rather than their intent. Implicit in the perspective of the women's health movement is the belief that if women shared control, were more centrally involved in health decision making, and brought female-oriented perspectives to balance male views, there would be changes in the environment and in the structure of health care that would substantially improve the health of all persons.

As an example of the problems faced by women in a male-dominated medical system, let us look at the case of Thalidomide, a drug developed in the late 1950s by a German company which claimed that, among other uses, the drug was safe as a tranquilizer for pregnant women. By 1962, Thalidomide had been widely adopted in many Western countries, but not in the United States where it could be prescribed only on an experimental basis (Sunday

Times of London, 1979). By late 1961, reports began to surface that the drug caused severe birth defects as well as other health problems. Sherry Finkbine, an Arizona woman whose husband had brought the drug back from England and who had taken it in the early stages of pregnancy, read about the adverse effects. The bottle she had indicated only that the drug was a tranquilizer; the label did not give its name, nor any warnings. Aware of potential severe birth defects, Finkbine traced the drug to England, learned it was Thalidomide, and immediately contacted a local hospital to request therapeutic abortion. In 1962, however, abortion was illegal except in some states and under extremely restricted circumstances. Despite the likelihood that she would bear a severely—perhaps fatally—deformed child, and despite the fact that both she and her husband desired to terminate the pregnancy, their request was denied by the hospital and subsequently by the Arizona State Supreme Court. Sherry Finkbine eventually obtained a therapeutic abortion in Sweden, where the fetus was found to be grossly deformed (Finkbine, 1967).

This case illustrates many of the points of challenge that subsequently have been raised by the women's health movement. First, it raises the issue of an androcentric corporate world and the pharmaceutical industry, which actively and aggressively marketed a dangerous medication with assurances of safety. Second, it points to patriarchal governments that allowed women to be exposed to such dangerous health hazards. Third, it reveals a predominantly male medical establishment in Europe that failed to question or investigate the drug in depth, so that physicians prescribed it without reservation. A similar pattern appeared in the United States: Both the American Medical Association and the American press minimized the efforts of two respected women physicians to alert their profession and the public to the dangers of the drug (Ruzek, 1978).

Ultimately, the U.S. Food and Drug Administration (FDA) refused to approve Thalidomide due to the efforts of one woman, Dr. Frances Kelsey, who was placed in charge of the FDA review process for the drug. Under persistent pressure from drug companies, and despite the drug's widespread acceptance abroad, she raised serious questions about Thalidomide's effects on the fetus if taken by a pregnant women. Although the companies assured her that there was no problem in this regard, Kelsey refused to allow the drug to be openly marketed in the United States, a decision for which she later received a presidential citation. U.S. physicians, however, could and did give Thalidomide to their patients, many of whom gave birth to deformed babies (Sunday Times of London, 1979; Levin, 1980). It is estimated that as many as 10,000 children worldwide were affected by the drug (Persaud et al., 1985). Since most women who took it were unaware of what it was or of any dangers associated with it, the number of injured babies was undoubtedly greater than reported. Today, scientists recognize Thalidomide as one of the most powerful human teratogens in existence (Persaud et al., 1985).

The case of Thalidomide raises an additional issue, usually overlooked and of special concern to women. Children's health and the care of ill and disabled children is a responsibility assigned largely to mothers (Carpenter, 1980), even in families where there are two parents employed full-time (Northcott, 1983; Breslau, 1983). Thus the well-being of mother and child are intimately related. Although the greatest health risks from Thalidomide were for the fetus rather than the mother, reports from England, where more than 1,000 severely handicapped Thalidomide babies were born, have shown the devastating impact upon parents—suicide, permanent or long-term mental breakdown, divorce, and poverty. Largely neglected in most accounts is the particular anguish, time involvement, strain, and resulting life change for the major caretaker who was in almost all cases the mother (Sunday Times of London, 1979).

In sum, the policies of officials and professionals, most of whom were men, created a health risk, legitimated it, and imposed it on unsuspecting consumers, most of whom were women. This was done in the interest of profit within the competitive economic environment of capitalism. Furthermore, in the case of Sherry Finkbine, the medical treatment she preferred was refused due to the laws and local decisions of this same system. In England, where the damage to children and families was the most devastating, it took over a decade of struggle before victims were compensated (Sunday Times of London, 1979).

The Thalidomide example shows the potential consequences of a style of medical practice quick to intervene with drugs and other forms of technology in an environment where profit can outweigh human concern, and the particularly exploitive and harmful consequences for women who have little voice or direct power over their health care. It illustrates why the combined effects of overzealous medical intervention and the subordinate position of women in society constitute a key theme in the feminist critique of medicine.

An additional area of criticism not adequately dealt with in the Thalidomide example centers on the problem of medical diagnosis. The women's health movement directs attention not only to the origins and treatment of women's medical problems but also to the process by which these problems come to be defined as "medical" in the first place.

A Critical Perspective on the Diagnosis
of Women's Health Problems

Mainstream medicine, in the critical perspective, has constructed its scientific knowledge around prevailing male-centered cultural views of women's proper position. Diagnosis of medical problems and disease therefore can be used as an instrument of social control to keep women in their places. As the work of feminist historians demonstrates, medical authorities have claimed the right to define what a women is or should be since at least the nineteenth century (Elston, 1981).

Physiological signs and symptoms can be interpreted in any number of ways. Symptoms also can be experienced differently depending on how medical authorities react to them. Thus, in effect, the response of professionals can "create" diseases. Physicians do not create the actual physiological symptoms, but they negotiate and define which symptoms are important, which are to be disregarded, which should be treated, and which should not (for elaboration, see Mishler et al., 1981). In addition to organizing certain signs and symptoms into "diseases," physicians use these categories or *diagnoses* to designate people as sick or well. Once a person is diagnosed as sick, physicians then have the authority, through law and custom, to invade the person's body with drugs, surgery, or other manipulations that alter their anatomical and/or physiological condition. In some cases, these interventions may result in health improvement; in others, not.

Because of the totality of the power of diagnosis and the magnitude of its implications for individuals over whom it is exercised, critics of modern medicine—feminists in particular—have strongly questioned the validity of the knowledge on which diagnosis is based and through which intervention is justified.

Objectivity and Medical Knowledge

Activists in the women's health movement claim that medical knowledge is not objective, scientifically derived, or free of value judgments. The extent to which scientific knowledge can be influenced by and can reinforce societal values about women is illustrated in Herschberger's (1948) classic analysis of our common understanding of the basic biological act of conception:

> The outstanding device for entering opinion under the guise of objective fact . . . is consistently to animate one portion of a process and deanimate the other. The male cell acts, voluntarily, yet with a teleological sense of destiny, while the female reacts, involuntarily, taking her cues from him . . . the male sperm is by all odds the central character . . . who will make his own minute decision to swim toward the egg. The female egg is portrayed as the blushing bride, ignorant but desirable, who awaits arousal by the gallant male cell. The egg, like the human female, is receptive.

> In choice of terms the patriarchal biologist makes liberal use of the word *vestigial*, as applied to any organ in the female which is similar to an organ in the male but not quite like it. The uterus escapes being called a vestigial prostate because it bears sons, but the clitoris has never thrown off the label of vestigial penis.

> The patriarchal biologist employs *erection* in regard to male organs and *congestion* for female. Erection of tissue is equivalent to the filling of the local blood vessels, or congestion; but erection is too aggressive-sounding for women. Congestion . . . appears to scientists to be a more adequate characterization of female response [1948: 68-69].

Little has changed in recent years, as shown in the works of feminist scientists such as Estelle Ramey (1973), Ruth Hubbard (1981), and Ruth Bleier (1984, 1986).

The central criticism of medical diagnosis to develop out of the women's health movement is that physicians tend to view women's health problems, whatever their type, location, or symptoms, in terms of reproductive function. Thus cardiovascular problems, bone and skeletal disorders, cancer, skin problems, as well as emotional and psychiatric disorders—only to name a few—are first and foremost viewed as linked to or caused by female hormones. This preoccupation of physicians with the menopausal status of their patients has endured for over a century:

> Women are treated for diseases of the stomach, liver, kidneys, heart, lungs, etc.; yet, in most instances, these diseases will be found on due investigation, to be, in reality, no diseases at all, but merely the sympathetic reactions or the symptoms of one disease, namely, a disease of the womb [Dirix, 1869].

> A woman is a uterus surrounded by a supporting organism and a directing personality. In advancing this proposition I am neither facetious nor deprecatory of womankind. I am biologically objective [Galdston, 1958].

This reproductive-centered view also helps explain a seeming paradox in the feminist critique of medicine—that, on the one hand, physicians are all too willing to diagnose and intervene medically in health areas where women are unique in relation to men and, on the other, ignore or minimize women's problems in areas where men also have problems.

Viewing women in terms of their uniquely female reproductive functions has other serious implications. First, the underlying cause of a health problem may be masked if the physician thinks only of reproductive functions. If the reproductive system is *not* the source of the problem, then treatments directed there will be fruitless and, in fact, may be quite harmful (as in the use of estrogen therapy in mid-life or the current debate over progesterone as a remedy for "premenstrual syndrome").

A second implication of medical preoccupation with the female reproductive system is that, since this is a normal part of the the female body, if it also is considered to be a source of illness and disability then it follows that women are "normally abnormal" and, therefore, unfit (in comparison to men) for responsible, demanding, and authoritative roles in society. Such views have been used to support the exclusion of women from public life, thereby legitimating gender discrimination and inequality. The study of societal reaction to menstruation, for example, reveals it used as a basis for the separation of men and women and the exclusion of females from key societal activities in ancient Hebrew cultures and perhaps earlier (Delaney et al., 1977). In the nineteenth century also, physicians linked the common ailments of women to the vulnerability of their reproductive systems and actively campaigned against women who in various ways endeavored to enter public life (Haller and Haller, 1974; Barker-Benfield, 1976; Walsh, 1977, 1982). These physicians accepted the culturally predominant view that women should confine themselves to the domesticity of private households and avoid the public arenas of work and politics. Not only did physicians accept this view but they developed elaborate justifications for it with their theories, clinical opinions, and "scientific" facts. Moreover, it was clearly in their interest to do so. Medical theories and evidence were used to keep women from competing with men in many areas—not the least of which was the field of medicine itself—and ensured their supportive role in nurturing their families and maintaining domestic order.

The Social Construction of the "Abnormal Normal" Woman

As Bose (Chapter 10 in this volume) details, middle- and upper-middle-class women of the late 1800s were dramatically affected by the impact of the industrial revolution and the changes it created in the nature of work and domestic life. Women, who had produced domestic goods in physical proximity to the work of men, were now physically separated. Productive activity within the home was not considered "work" in the same sense as waged labor, and many middle- and upper-middle-class women were suddenly left with no clearly defined, active, meaningful, or productive roles. In light of contemporary views regarding the importance of such roles for mental and physical health, it does not seem surprising today to learn that many of these relatively affluent women were, in fact, the victims of a widespread epidemic:

> The woman grows pale and thin, eats little, but does not profit by it. Everything wearies her—to sew, to write, to read, to walk—and by and by the sofa or the bed is her only comfort. Every effort is paid for dearly, and she describes herself as aching and sore, as sleeping ill, and as needing constant stimulus and endless tonics. . . . If such a person is emotional she does not fail to become more so, and even the firmest women lose self-control at last under incessant feebleness [quoted in Ehrenreich and English, 1979].

This disease became a major target of physicians, who considered the underlying cause to be the excitation, atrophying, or otherwise pathological condition of the female reproductive system, a condition of which all women were considered to be at risk. Interestingly, the relative absence of such problems in working-class women was not considered problematic. Medical treatment varied from bed rest during the woman's menstrual period to a "rest cure" consisting of six weeks of total isolation and sensory deprivation (bed rest in dim light, no visitors, no reading or activity, bland foods, etc.) to various forms of sexual surgery including the removal of the clitoris or, more frequently, of the ovaries (Barker-Benfield, 1976; Duffin, 1978; Ehrenreich and English, 1979). In addition, doctors warned against women pursuing education or other "male" endeavors. Mental stimulation was considered harmful for reproductive function and future offspring and, therefore, a threat to the survival of the white upper classes. In the words of Dr. Horatio Storer of Harvard Medical School, a leading opponent of women's attempts to become physicians, menstruation was "temporary insanity" (Walsh, 1982).

To understand the enthusiasm of male physicians in diagnosing, treating, and theorizing about the "invalidism" of nineteenth-century women, we must remember that the physicians of the period were struggling for patients and for greater public acceptance (Starr, 1982). Surgery, then as now, was one means through which physicians could demonstrate their technical skills and therapeutic value. The symptomology of middle- and upper-class women as well as their ability to pay made them highly desirable patients for aspiring surgeons and gynecologists. In retrospect, there are numerous explanations for the symptoms experienced by these women, most notably the social ambiguity of their rapidly changing roles and the lack of opportunity for productive work either inside or outside the isolation of their homes. Other explanations include extremely constrictive clothing styles that, along with prevailing social norms, discouraged physical exercise (Mosher, 1923; Duffin, 1978). Affluent women of this era, for example, were expected to wear heavy garments over corsets that exerted an average of 21 pounds of pressure on internal organs (Ehrenreich and English, 1979). There also was drug addiction from the many tonics and patent medicines, easily obtainable over the counter and marketed specifically for these women (Stage, 1979). Such "medicines" often contained alcohol and/or opiates such as morphine and heroin (Duster, 1970). The notion of female frailty and sickness was seen as morbidly fashionable. To achieve this "ideal" some women went so far as to take arsenic (Haller and Haller, 1974).

The relative neglect of poor women and women of color in nineteenth-century theories of feminine frailty did not extend to surgical intervention. Access to medical care for the poor was inadequate, but there was no lack of willingness to intervene surgically when medical attention was given. In fact, poor and minority women have been particularly vulnerable to exploitation as subjects of medical experiments, often without their knowledge or consent (Levin, 1980). In the mid-1800s, Dr. J. Marion Sims, an aspiring physician who established his career treating the health problems of women and who was sometimes called "the father of gynecology," kept several black women slaves for the sole purpose of experimentation (Barker-Benfield, 1976). Sims tried various gynecologic surgeries on these women including, in the case of one, 30 separate operations within 4 years. And Dr. Sims was not an isolated case. In the 1960s, Dr. Joseph Goldzieher conducted a study to examine the reported side effects of oral contraceptive pills (Veatch, 1971). In his research, funded by an oral contraceptives manufacturer, Goldzieher used low income,

Hispanic women who came to a San Antonio clinic seeking contraceptives. Without even knowing they were participating in research, 76 women received placebos. Ten became pregnant. For the most part, the medical community ignored Goldzieher's experiment, refusing either to censure him or repudiate the study (Ruzek, 1978).

It is tempting to assume that these days and practices are past; however, from the perspective of the women's health movement, the legacy of nineteenth- century gynecology continues. High rates of hysterectomy and cesarean births raise questions about overuse of surgery. Hysterectomy rates in the United States, twice those in Britain, rose 25% between the mid 1960s and mid 1970s (Pearson and Clark, 1982; Sandberg et al., 1985) so that by age 65, 35% of all women have had a hysterectomy (Howe, 1984). Investigations have led researchers to conclude that many hysterectomies are unnecessary (Medical World News, 1981), "due as much to the practice style of physicians . . . as to gynecologic need" (Roos, 1984: 327). Cesarean rates have increased even more dramatically—from 5% of all deliveries in 1970 to 20% in 1983 (Taffel and Placek, 1985). The widespread use of hormones as treatment for various symptoms—many of which sound surprisingly similar to the female complaints of the nineteenth century—also echo the past. Evidence also can be found in the content of medical education (Campbell, 1974) and medical journals and texts (Scully and Bart, 1973; Zimmerman, 1977, 1981; Boston Women's Health Collective, 1984). While activist pressure and increased numbers of women medical students in the 1970s appear to have resulted in some changes, the impact has been neither fundamental nor necessarily feminist (Elston, 1981; Lorber, 1985). Exploitation of poor women and women of color continues in the United States and in many developing nations, with U.S. sponsorship (Ruzek, 1978; Levin, 1980).

Nor can we assume that the misguided theories and medical practices of the past were due solely to ignorance. As early as 1877, women physician-researchers conducted empirical studies concluding that menstruation posed little obstacle to work and social function (Jacobi, 1877; Mosher, 1923). Normal work routines with no restrictions were recommended along with proper exercise and better nutrition to deal with minor pain. Despite these data, menstruating women have been considered ill or functionally impaired throughout the twentieth century (Delaney et al., 1977).

The ideological bias in medical knowledge and physician behavior is particularly disturbing because of medicalization of social behaviors and physicians' readiness to expand their roles as experts (see Riessman, 1983). Gynecologists, for example, claim expertise about women that extends beyond reproductive and genital problems. In a 1970 text on adolescent behavior, the chairman of a medical school's department of obstetrics and gynecology writes,

A woman will always go after what she wants in a oblique manner, identifying with a secondary object and causing a tense situation. Only if a man is shrewd enough will he realize the woman really wants something other than what she claims she wants.

And, on the subject of marriage, we have the following:

> Woman, now that she has the power to control man's chance at biological immortality through children, must realize her power and the added responsibilities that come with it . . . confronted with a "new woman" the male may find himself torn between his home where he is no longer in authority and his work where he has no authority. . . . In contrast to this marriage where the roles are *misplaced*, let us consider the pattern of the *more ideal* marriage in which each partner accepts his *proper* role, *the male being dominant"* [Krantz, 1970: 277-278; emphasis added].

Even if, as some have claimed, medical educators' endorsements of inferiority and/or the subservience of women are decreasing, it must be remembered that many physicians practicing today were exposed to such material during their medical training and draw on it in communicating with patients, colleagues, and student physicians.

Given these characteristics of medical knowledge, as long as the conventional relationship between doctors and patients is characterized by a substantial power differential, so that the authority of the physician tends to prevail in most all medical consultations, the women's health movement is likely to continue to focus its critique on the quality of medical diagnosis and the ideological nature of medical knowledge.

THE ORIGINS OF
THE WOMEN'S HEALTH MOVEMENT

Differing male and female views on health and health care have existed for much of human history, even though these differences have gone largely unrecognized by scholars. They reflect the fact that men and women, while living in physical proximity, have lived in quite different social worlds. As a consequence, health problems perceived and experienced, as well as lay and professional reactions to them, have been gender specific. Women's unique experiences in childbearing account for some but by no means all of this variation.

Not only have men and women seen and been seen from distinct perspectives, but there is also historical evidence of conflict and activism surrounding women's health care in various periods (Marieskind, 1980). During the third century B.C., for example, women physicians and/or midwives in Greece lost their right to practice based on, among other things, the fact that they performed abortions. The prohibition reportedly ended when Greek women staged a public demonstration in order to gain acquittal for a popular gynecologist who had been arrested for practicing medicine under false pretenses when she disguised herself as a man. Contemporary writers, focusing on Western societies, suggest that gender conflict over the control of health care was heightened by the exclusion of women from universities, beginning in the eleventh and twelfth centuries, and the rise of professional medicine, which burgeoned in the eighteenth and nineteenth centuries (Lorber, 1984). In the fourteenth century, the Church decreed that any woman who healed without formal education was a witch and should be killed (Gage, 1980). During the witch-hunts of the fifteenth and sixteenth centuries, hostility and violence toward women healers resulted in thousands—possibly millions—of executions (Ehrenreich and English, 1979). Also during this period, King Henry V was petitioned to prevent all women from practicing medicine (Bowman and Allen, 1985).

By the early 1900s the gender shift in the provision of health care was nearly complete. Female healers and midwives, who for centuries routinely had cared for women (and many men), had been displaced by male physicians, many of whom campaigned to exclude women from formal medical training (Walsh, 1977; Osborne, 1984). This shift also meant a change in emphasis from natural, noninvasive procedures to the use of surgery, drugs, and other new technologies. In the United States, professional medicine developed as fee-for-service, a system often inaccessible to poor people. Though undocumented, women lay healers probably have continued as a source of health care for the poor. But the emphasis on women lay healers should not overshadow the fact that throughout the centuries a few privileged Western women consistently have managed to become "regular" physicians, practicing and serving on medical school faculties.

Little information is available on conflict and activism over women's health care in Eastern societies. Frequently the health care that existed for women was provided by other women due to strict religious and cultural norms that precluded attendance by men, regardless of professional status (Lovejoy, 1957).

In Western societies, male domination and gender-specific views have created the conditions for women's dissatisfaction and ultimate struggle for change. In this sense, the women's health movement did not begin in 1969 or 1971, but emerged out of the sociopolitical relationship between men and women that, in terms of health and health care, became accentuated with industrialization, the growth of technology, and the rise of "scientific" medicine in the nineteenth century.

Several recent sources trace the contemporary American women's health movement to the 1820s and 1830s and the then popular Ladies Physiological Societies (Marieskind, 1975; Fatt, 1978), an outgrowth of a broad-based "popular health movement," which emphasized demystifying medicine through self-awareness and self-knowledge, preventive measures, and acceptance of women as trained health practitioners. The popular health movement was opposed to interventionist techniques, the so-called heroic medicine of the time. This activism was different than today's in that challenging the traditional sphere of women was not the central issue. In fact, the domestic role of woman as wife and mother was emphasized by the physiological societies (Morantz, 1977). Women largely supported the idea that they were the "morally superior" sex and should be educated in proper health and hygiene for the benefit of their families.

Since some of the conditions for a full-scale social movement in the area of women's health had existed for decades, why did such a movement emerge only in the late 1960s and early 1970s? One possible answer is that although problems and grievances existed, the structural conditions were lacking. Specifically, organizational capabilities and opportunities for collective action were not effectively in place for women before the civil rights and student movements of the 1960s. Women were active participants in these movements, developing a heightened sensitivity to injustice and inequity and a growing belief in the rights of people—all people—to govern their own lives and destinies. They became increasingly aware of how they themselves were oppressed within these movements, at the same time that they were discovering their own capabilities. The public self-confidence of women activists as a group plus their concrete political experience stimulated the rebirth of feminism and, more specifically, the rise of the women's health movement (Ferree and Hess, 1985). Widespread concern for consumer control and more individual responsibility in health matters also contributed to these efforts.

A series of events in these years, including the Thalidomide scandal, thrust the grievances of women concerning the modern health system into sharper focus. It is important to underscore that these developments in themselves did not *cause* the women's health movement. The conditions for its development, as I have argued, were much more long-standing and dependent on long-term structural and institutional changes. Nevertheless, these more immediate events served as metaphors and rallying points for women's claims of injustice.

The legal availability of abortion is the issue commonly cited as pivotal in the development of feminist concern over health matters in the 1960s (Ruzek, 1978; Marieskind, 1980). Reproductive choice was seen as one of the most basic of all issues for women, based on the assumption that as long as the fundamental female functions of pregnancy and childbearing were outside the control of women, women would remain subservient. Lack of power in reproductive matters necessarily precludes women from control over their own lives, limiting their involvement in public life. Access to safe abortions was seen as essential for the empowerment of women; the prohibition of abortion was viewed as an attempt to perpetuate women's limited societal influence. As this issue generated increasing awareness of the lack of control women had over all aspects of their bodies and their health, the women's health movement's early focus on abortion, childbirth, birth control, hysterectomy, menopause, and sterilization was extended to other health concerns such as mental health, heart disease, cancer, diabetes, osteoporosis, eating disorders, and treatment of disability and impairment.

In the course of recognizing and examining this wide array of problems, similar patterns among them emerged. Because the corpus of medical knowledge had been developed with many built-in stereotypes and biases regarding women, the process of medical education had to be challenged. And, as it became clear that the relationship between doctor and patient and between male and female health workers paralleled the dominant-submissive pattern of relationships in the traditional patriarchal family, new forms of interaction within the health care context had to be developed.

STRATEGIES WITHIN
THE WOMEN'S HEALTH MOVEMENT

During the beginning phase of the women's health movement, from the early to mid-1970s, two organizational strategies emerged to realize the goals of this growing critique: self-help groups and political action organizations.

Self-Help

The most innovative of the two strategies was the concept of feminist self-help, eventually manifest in the existence of hundreds, perhaps thousands, of grass-roots self-help groups located throughout the United States (Ruzek, 1978; Gartner, 1985). Self-help both exemplified the aims of the movement and fueled its growth and development.

Feminist self-help groups appear on the surface to be the health equivalent of the feminist consciousness-raising groups of the late 1960's and early 1970's. The concept refers to any gathering of women who share common experiences, health care information, and skills. Usually these groups are small, with half a dozen to a dozen participants. Some groups focus on a particular subject such as fertility detection, breast examination, vaginal infection, or menopause, and have a finite time span of approximately 8 or 10 weeks. Other groups are broader in focus and continue indefinitely. The immediate purpose of the self-help group is for women to learn about themselves through mutual discussion and sharing information, including personal experiences. The most widely known of these groups is the Boston Women's Health Book Collective, whose efforts produced the popular health manual for women, *Our Bodies, Ourselves* (1984), first published in 1971.

Although the Boston group has received most public attention, California activists who founded the Los Angeles Feminist Women's Health Center in

1971 also have made a substantial contribution to the philosophical and organizational foundations of feminist self-help. Their procedures included self-performed pelvic examinations during which a woman could view her own cervix using a plastic speculum, a flashlight, and a mirror, as well as an early abortion procedure known as menstrual extraction. These techniques are described in the center's 1974 publication, *How to Stay Out of the Gynecologist's Office* (Federation of Feminist Women's Health Centers, 1981a), a clear statement of feminist self-help.

Similar views were shared by a self-help group in Chicago that, in 1969, organized to improve the situation of women seeking safe illegal abortions (Bart, 1981). Only a few states provided legal abortions in 1969 and Illinois was not among them. The Chicago women began by negotiating with area abortionists (men), offering them clients in exchange for feedback about the quality of their services and for allowing a percentage of free abortions for poor women. Eventually, the women learned to perform the abortion procedures themselves with medical results that compared favorably with licensed abortion facilities in New York and California. The illegal abortion collective, known as "Jane," operated until 1973, the year the U.S. Supreme Court legalized abortion.

The process of feminist self-help is now found in diverse areas such as cancer treatment, diabetes, and eating disorders (Osborne, 1984), carrying out the objectives of the women's health movement in a variety of ways. First, it is a reciprocal, participatory situation, nonhierarchical in principle, in stark contrast to the traditional dominance-passivity of most doctor-patient relationships. Second, its purpose is to help women learn about their bodies in a firsthand way without having to rely on the androcentric approaches frequently found in standard medical sources. Research has suggested that one reason patients are dominated and intimidated is that they lack requisite medical knowledge (Haug and Lavin, 1983). Viewing knowledge as power, self-help empowers women, providing them with expertise and a repertoire of questions so that they can be assertive and challenge mainstream medicine when necessary. Third, where women require medical treatment, the self-help method emphasizes noninterventionist, natural healing techniques—for example treating vaginal yeast infections with yogurt rather than antibiotics, or using exercise and massage instead of painkillers for menstrual cramps. To understand the significance of self-help within the women's health movement, let us consider each of these three contributions in greater detail.

Nonhierarchical organizational structure and equal participation among members is a theme expressed—though not easily achieved—throughout much of today's feminist movement. The ideological and practical significance of this objective is well exemplified in women's self-help groups. The elimination of a single authority or dominant leader ensures that women will not be cast in passive and dependent roles. It puts women in a position of active involvement where the norm is to talk, ask questions, and exchange information. In a nonthreatening group, self-help participants are able to reveal personal feelings and problems while being informed about the feelings and problems of others. Through mutual sharing, women learn that what they had thought was abnormal or a personal deficiency is really quite normal. Thus not only does the self-help group foster active participation, putting women into a position of control, but it also focuses on the critical area of medical "facts" and the task of separating reality from myth.

The nature of knowledge about women's bodies and health is another fundamental concern of the women's health movement, integrally related to the specific activities of self-help groups. The process through which the book *Our Bodies, Ourselves* (1984) evolved provides an example of this link. A 1969 Women's Liberation Conference in Boston on the topic of "Women and Their Bodies" resulted in a group that continued to meet regularly. Initially, these women had wanted to develop a list of "good doctors" as a reference for other women. As discussions progressed, so many complaints and issues were raised that it became impossible to compile such a list. Instead, participants began to share their grievances and to raise questions about what was myth and what was fact in the etiology, diagnosis, and treatment of many common female problems. Finally, they decided to find the answers themselves:

> Each took a topic such as birth control, natural child birth, masturbation, VD, abortion, post-partum depression or rape. They went to other women, they talked to nurses and doctors. They did research in medical texts and journals, where vital information is ordinarily kept inaccessible to the public. None had expertise in doing research or experience in any health-related field. However, they did trust they could find reliable information and learn the necessary research skills as they went. Each woman shared what she had learned in discussion with the rest of the group. From the very beginning, personal experience was integral to their analysis as it enabled them to develop a critique of the information and health care they were getting [Beckwith, 1985].

For this group, which ultimately became the Boston Women's Health Book Collective, what began with the idea of doing medical research from a feminist perspective evolved into one of the key information sources of the women's health movement.

The Los Angeles Feminist Women's Health Center can be considered the core of self-help activities within the women's health movement. In addition to participatory clinics, women there began to do their own research and writing early in the 1970s. Frustrated with the limitations of existing knowledge, they created their own, producing an extensive manuscript, of which three individual volumes had been published by 1986 (Federation of Feminist Women's Health Centers, 1981a, 1981b; Cassidy-Brinn et al., 1984). To illustrate what I mean by new knowledge, let us briefly consider one volume, *A New View of a Woman's Body* (Federation of Feminist Women's Health Centers, 1981b), and a chapter in it titled "The Clitoris: A Feminist Perspective."

For years, values and norms governing sexual activity came primarily from religious sources. In the nineteenth century, however, physicians in their struggle for professional credibility and control assumed the role of expert in defining appropriate as well as pathological sexual behavior. Yet since scientific grounding in sexual matters was quite limited, much of what was offered as medical advice or treatment amounted to little more than a reflection of dominant cultural views regarding gender, particularly the subordination of women. Once established as medical knowledge, these ideas and practices have proved resistant to change.

A key feminist issue in the area of human sexuality is orgasm. Physicians have defined women as frigid if they fail to achieve vaginal orgasm during coitus—even if they do so in other ways. Only in the 1960s did research identify the clitoris as the center of female sexual arousal (Masters and Johnson, 1966), better explaining how women's orgasms were achieved, contradicting the androcentric notion that orgasm without direct stimulation by the penis was abnormal. Building on this research, self-help activists such as the Los Angeles Feminist Women's Health Center thought women should thoroughly understand the structure and function of the clitoris. Such information, however, was missing from medical textbooks where there were cross-section illustrations of the penis, but none of the clitoris. The Los Angeles women conducted their own extensive study, showing what happened to the clitoris at each stage of orgasm in a series of very detailed drawings. Several key anatomical parts had never before been identified in the literature, so the women themselves had to give these parts names and explain their significance (for an excellent discussion of naming in relation to women's health, see Smith, 1975). The new findings also provide an alternative view of episiotomy during childbirth, in which the perineum is cut, since from the standpoint of this new knowledge the perineum can be viewed as part of the female sex organ.

The third way in which self-help embodies the aims of the women's health movement is through the direct provision of health care services to women by women, as in the activities of "Jane," the illegal abortion collective. While there are important quality reasons for a woman-to-woman approach, the fundamental basis for this strategy is *political*. In the words of Carol Downer, one of the principal founders of feminist self-help,

> In 1970 one of the first things we did was to get the idea of doing abortions ourselves. There was an illegal clinic here in town—abortion was legal in California at the time but it had to be done in a hospital, so this was illegal in the sense that it was a clinic setting and also because the man who started it was not a Doctor. . . . We had been referring women to him and so we thought, "Why are we making this man rich?" We thought, "Really, we should do this ourselves so that it would be *in the control of women.*" So, we learned how to do abortions. I think it was in that process that we became aware of how little we knew about our own bodies. It was such an electrifying experience to see how amazingly

simple the cervix was and to realize that here were women being put through humiliating, dangerous, degrading experiences—expensive—for such a basically simple kind of procedure [Downer, 1984].

From these comments it is clear that providing women with needed health services helps achieve the broader goal of empowering women to elevate their position and authority in society.

In 1971, the Los Angeles Feminist Health Center was raided by the police. Two women, including Carol Downer, were arrested. Downer was charged with practicing medicine without a license, stemming from her use of yogurt as a treatment for yeast infection. After a legal battle attracting national attention, she was acquitted.

For Downer, the self-help approach to women's health care is the taproot of the entire feminist movement, with the issue of who controls women's bodies and their lives the bottom line. For her, self-help activism is not an outgrowth or a subgroup of feminism. It *is* feminism. In her words,

> So, we switched to self-help. We thought that was a more fundamental thing— that the only way these things [exploitation of women] could survive was in ignorance, that as long as women stayed mystified about their bodies and alienated from each other then, of course, these things could happen. If we had the information, our reasoning was that women would become better consumers and devise more appropriate strategies for bringing about change. And I think that we were totally correct . . . it really has made us have a much more powerful voice because we really know what we are talking about [Downer, 1984].

It is not surprising that such criticism eventually evoked an editorial in an American Medical Association publication that asked, in a sarcastic and patronizing tone, what women patients wanted, why they were "questioning every procedure" and "insist[ing] on using natural childbirth, breast feeding, and diaphragms when modern medicine has provided them with much less bothersome and painless alternatives" (American Medical News, 1974).

Yet, by the early 1980s, the popularity of participatory self-help in the women's health care had declined due to several factors. Among these was the attempt by organized medicine to coopt self-help through endorsing health education, prevention, and an increase in an individual's sense of personal responsibility for her or his health (for excellent critiques of this trend, see Crawford, 1977; Millman, 1982). Another factor was that self-help is tedious, time-consuming, and requires a high degree of personal commitment. This fact is particularly well illustrated by the Los Angeles Women's experience in writing their next book (on menopause):

> In writing this book we studied hormones. How we did it was that we sat down, four of us, with a biology professor who was the husband of one of the women in the group and we just cracked the books. We read one book, the first few pages, a

very small book on endocrinology and every word we didn't know we wrote on an index card. By the time we had read just a few pages we had a stack of index cards like this, because when we looked up the definition we didn't understand the words in the definition so that added to our stack. So, we had this huge stack of cards and it went on like this for about four or five months. We met at least four or five days a week [Downer, 1984].

Clearly this type of research, as well as the participatory self-help approach in general, can prove difficult for women with urgent health needs and heavy time demands. This may well be one reason feminist self-help has appealed more to middle-class rather than to poor or working-class women (Marieskind, 1980; Ruzek, 1978).

Nonetheless, the concept of feminist self-help has produced approximately 100 women's health centers in the United States that offer direct health care services (Bruce, 1981). Most of these, like the Los Angeles Feminist Women's Health Center, focus on gynecological care such as pregnancy screening and counseling, birth control, pelvic and breast examinations, and abortion. Some clinics offer prenatal care with referrals for deliveries; others provide a full range of routine primary care. Consistent with the aims of the women's health movement and the three purposes of feminist self-help discussed above, these centers are characterized by a minimally hierarchical structure stressing the use of paraprofessional and lay health workers, the active involvement of clients, and a range of treatment options including natural, noninvasive methods (Marieskind, 1980; Bruce, 1981). These clinics also recognize the diverse circumstances and health needs of the poor, the disabled, lesbian women, single mothers, immigrant women, and women of color. Low fees and sliding fee scales are commonplace. As such, women's health centers provide an alternative for much mainstream ambulatory care.

Political Action Organizations

The other type of organizational structure adopted by the women's health movement has been the political action organization (see Ruzek, 1978). These groups have been mainly concerned with effecting political, legal, and institutional changes through activities such as public information campaigns, lobbying, community organizing, and mobilization. One of the most success-ful of these groups, with an international membership of several thousand, is California's Coalition for the Medical Rights of Women, founded in 1974. Coalition activities have been a powerful force in California politics and have affected national health policy in a number of ways. One of the coalition's early projects was to press for more stringent California standards for the regulation and labeling of drugs and medical devices. Once successful, these efforts in turn forced national manufacturers to comply—for example, by adding warning labels to over-the-counter drugs for pregnant women. The coalition's activities also have resulted in stronger regulations for intrauterine contraception devices (IUDs), the establishment of informed consent procedures for sterilization, and increased public and professional awareness of the medical and legal consequences of diethylstilbesterol (DES) exposure.

Another notable example of political action organizations within the women's health movement is the National Women's Health Network. Established in 1975 and located in Washington, D.C., where it closely monitors Congress and government agencies, the network functions primarily as an information clearinghouse and a consumer advocacy and lobbying group. Members have organized demonstrations, pressured governmental agencies, and testified at congressional hearings on behalf of such issues as national health insurance, examination of dangerous obstetrical practices, forced sterilization, and the elimination under the Medicaid program of federal funds for abortions.

Political action organizations rely on support from private donations as well as on volunteer help. Those that have survived have done so against significant odds and under constant financial pressure. As in the case of self-help, feminist commitment has been a key ingredient in the persistence of these organizations.

THEORETICAL ANALYSIS OF THE WOMEN'S HEALTH MOVEMENT

Stages of Development

Analysts of the women's health movement (for the United States, see Ruzek, 1978; for Britain, see Doyal, 1983) have linked it to other social movements in terms of change and development over time. Social movement theorists call this a "natural history" perspective.

Ruzek (1978) has discussed three stages of the movement's evolution in the United States. The first was a period of awareness-building or consciousness-raising in which an initial movement constituency took shape. This stage involved the dissemination of information as well as meetings and conferences where early participants considered and debated strategies for further action. A particularly sensitive issue during this period was the movement's position regarding hierarchical relationships such as the traditional one between doctor and patient, perceived by many as validating and perpetuating the oppression of women. As the movement developed its own organizations and clinics, the authority issue could not be avoided.

The second stage was one of policy determination as movement organizations expanded and utilized legislative and judicial means to effect change. Social movement theory suggests that at this stage movements tend to become formal and concerned with legitimacy. In the women's health movement, for example, clinics established during the first stage sought funding, licensing, and certification for health workers, while lobbying efforts required knowledgeable lobbyists and experts who could provide testimony. In the second stage, the movement began to specialize—that is, distinct groups emerged and worked relatively independently to pursue their own particular issues and agendas for change. In some cases, traditional forms of organization reemerged even though the issue of collective decision making versus a hierarchical model remained central.

The third stage, according to Ruzek, is an inevitable outcome of the second: "Successful social movements ultimately become institutionalized in some manner and enter a reform . . . stage of development" (Ruzek, 1978: 217). Specifically, movements become established interest groups in order to promote their newly legitimated causes. While this has been the case with some of the groups generated by the women's health movement, the full extent of this process is unclear. The fact that many "stage one" activities—self-help groups, alternative clinics, conferences, and education projects—have remained intact for nearly two decades, resisting mainstream institutional pressures, suggests that the "natural" evolution of the women's health movement may not be as inevitable as social movement theorists claim.

Writing about the women's health movement in Britain, Doyal (1983) has also identified three stages. The first stage, as in the United States, emphasized awareness and education. The second, however, while consistent with American developments in terms of a concern with policy development, was distinctive because in Britain feminists defended the *status quo* as embodied in the socialist principles of the National Health Service. The third stage has focused less on women's health care than on how societies create women's health problems and cause women's diseases. In Britain, as in the United States, the full development and implications of the third stage remain to be seen. Doyal points out that a social movement is not simply a homogeneous unit passing through distinctive stages. As social movements grow and expand and as subgroups differentiate, it becomes more and more difficult to refer to such a complex movement as a whole.

Theoretical Perspectives
Within the Women's Health Movement

The women's health movement and the broad array of organizations, groups, and programs that claim to serve the health care needs of women embody a wide range of philosophical emphases and perspectives. From the standpoint of the movement and its objectives, critical analysis of these different perspectives in terms of their assumptions about women and their programmatic consequences for gender equality is a fundamentally important task. As feminist theory, relatively young as an analytic tool, offers no single scheme entirely satisfactory for this purpose, this chapter presents several conceptual distinctions that could provide clarification and direction for further work.

Fee (1983) has distinguished "liberal" and "radical" feminists in relation to the women's health movement. She identifies as liberal those activists who primarily pursue activities designed to improve women's status through equal participation and equal access to societal resources, especially to the privileged and powerful positions typically occupied by men. Within the context of health care, liberals have focused on objectives such as increasing the proportion of women physicians, changing hospital procedures to reflect the needs of women, and establishing a range of community agencies and support groups responsive to women's health-related problems. The liberal position seeks remedies for past discrimination and exclusion, but does not question or attempt fundamental changes in the American political economy or its hierarchical structure. While many of these initiatives are undeniably of great value for individual women, they do not necessarily result in change for women as a group. Instead, such efforts validate and perpetuate the existing social structure, defining key positions as desirable. And, since the social structure is not considered problematic except for women's inequality, the liberal position makes it easier for the problems of women to be viewed as personal rather than social phenomena.

Radical feminists, according to Fee (1983), believe that equality can be achieved only by transforming existing social institutions and engaging in actions directly designed to do this. In contrast to liberals, therefore, radicals would not work toward an increase in the number of women becoming physicians as much as toward dismantling the conventional medical hierarchy; would not simply change specific hospital practices but also the process through which such policies are established; and would sponsor only those support programs and self-help groups that enhance the power of women, helping them to see their problems in relation to an oppressive social system rather than as personal failure or fate.

The value of Fee's distinction lies in its focus on social change. The flaw is that it confuses specific issues and actions (such as increasing the ranks of women physicians) with the strategic *intent* and *consequences* of these actions. The real value in using this distinction to analyze feminist social action should be the question of whether a program is being pursued for the sake of equal access and equal rights or for the purpose of changing the nature of society—whether, for example, women are being encouraged as physicians in order to share in the hierarchy or so that they can be in a position to change the hierarchy. The perspective of the women's health movement, as I have argued, is unified in its objective of societal change. The fact that the movement encompasses various philosophies and lines of action may well reflect differing levels of political awareness, analytic sophistication, and perceptions of how best to effect social change rather than expressions of simple support or rejection of the status quo. The critical test in analyses of feminist social action is not to assign labels to *issues* so much as to ask whether particular actions will reduce or reinforce existing gender inequality.

To illustrate such investigations, let us consider recent feminist analysis of self-help programs for two very different health problems—breast cancer recovery and weight control. Although feminist work has also examined questions of etiology and diagnosis for these conditions, self-help treatment approaches are especially revealing since they are typically placed outside the realm of critique, which is taken for granted as universally beneficial. The fact that such well-intended, individually helpful programs also can serve to perpetuate male dominance, as well as race and class interests, is testimony to the power of medicine as a mechanism of social control.

Self-help, as a generic concept, refers to people mutually helping themselves. It is critical for the feminist critique to examine whose interests are served by any given self-help group. Physicians and other mainstream health providers in recent years have initiated and sponsored self-help groups to accomplish their own medical goals. A recent report indicates that 47% of hospitals offer self-help programs to increase the effectiveness of hospital care (Salmon and Berliner, 1982). Such groups are vastly different from feminist self-help in content, process, and consequences (see Dean, 1986).

Of all the health-related fears and preoccupations of contemporary women, those associated with being overweight and with developing breast cancer undoubtedly head the list. Though the two conditions are vastly different, women experiencing them are similarly vulnerable to societal messages that define the social significance of each. Postmastectomy counseling as well as most weight reduction programs proceed from a set of androcentric assumptions about women, emphasizing physical attractiveness and sexual utility as opposed to overall health, independence, and productive activity. Therefore, programs designed and intended to benefit women may instead further victimize them, discourage them from taking control over their lives, and contribute to their disadvantaged position in society.

Audre Lorde (1980) has critically examined the "cancer establishment" in relation to the treatment of mastectomy patients. Mainstream medicine, according to Lorde, views recovery from breast cancer surgery as predominantly a *cosmetic* problem. Reach for Recovery, the self-help program of the American Cancer Society, plays a key role in promulgating this perspective, in cooperation with physicians and other health professionals. Begun in 1957 as a woman-to-woman volunteer organization providing emotional support to mastectomy patients, Reach for Recovery currently provides valuable personal service to more than two-thirds of all new mastectomy patients (Marieskind, 1980). From a feminist viewpoint, however, the underlying implications of Reach for Recovery's philosophy raise significant questions for the women's health movement. Immediately following Lorde's own mastectomy, a Reach for Recovery volunteer gave her a piece of lambswool to wear in place of her breast, assuming that it would be soon replaced with a prosthesis. When Lorde chose not to wear an artificial breast to the office of her cancer surgeon, she was chastised by the nurse who told her that not wearing it was "bad for the morale of the office."

The widespread emphasis placed on hiding the absence of a breast involves much more than insistence on a prosthesis. Lorde's analysis is both personal and penetratingly sociological, revealing not just feminist insight but also her reaction as a woman who is also black and lesbian. She points out that the social requirement to look "normal" leads women to spend large amounts of time, energy, and money on various ways of camouflaging their bodies, perpetuating societal attitudes toward women as decorative objects and impeding the process of successfully confronting cancer. As a result, women are vulnerable to commercial exploitation and also to what Lorde terms the next logical step of a depersonalizing and woman-devaluing culture—breast reconstruction through the insertion of silicone gel implants. Lorde presents evidence that some plastic surgeons have gone so far as to recommend that, in the interest of symmetry, both breasts should be removed and "reconstructed" at the same time. Ignored in the preoccupation with appearance is the effect of these further surgical interventions on cancer recurrence. Women themselves willingly participate in this process since they often view their bodies in terms of how they look and feel to others (for a discussion of how women's male-defined identity also affects *prevention* of breast cancer, see Finley, 1984). The fact that these consequences may be unintended does not lessen their impact:

> Prosthesis offers the empty comfort of "Nobody will know the difference." But it is that very difference I wish to affirm, because I have lived it, and survived it, and wish to share that strength with other women. If we are to translate the silence surrounding breast cancer into action—women with mastectomies must become visible to each other. For silence and invisibility go hand in hand with powerlessness. By accepting the mask of prosthesis [we] proclaim ourselves as insufficients dependent upon pretense [Lorde, 1980: 61].

Since self-help generally takes an interpersonal approach to solving health problems, it carries the risk of focusing so exclusively on individual change that the attribution of responsibility for health and well-being shifts from governments and health providers (where it has traditionally been located) to laypersons, so that the victims themselves are blamed for their own health problems (Kronenfeld, 1979). Placing responsibility on the individual increases the possibility of economic exploitation. Blaming the victim results in personal distress, low esteem, and withdrawal from social life, thus reinforcing existing patterns in women's illness and oppression (see Cole and Lejeune, 1972).

Chernin (1981) has observed that the United States is a society preoccupied with women's bodies, but where few women, fat or thin, feel comfortable with their own. Rather than questioning prevailing standards of thinness or examining their sources, most women devote a major portion of their personal resources, including billions of dollars each year, to trying to force their bodies to meet standards set by others. In some cases, the resulting alienation and antagonism toward one's own body develops into a life-threatening battle, as in anorexia nervosa (see Chernin, 1981; Freedman, 1986).

The current plethora of diet and weight-loss groups, composed predominantly of women, can be placed within the general category of self-help. Weight-loss groups view fatness as an individual problem. In studying such groups, Millman (1980) points out the compelling image of the "before and after," the notion of personal transformation in weight loss. Consistently, women are presented with the fantasy of a perfect, fulfilling life once they are slim, as if only fat is standing between them and their dreams. As in postmastectomy counseling, the processes of recovery and rehabilitation as well as the attainment of health define women in terms of decorative rather than productive, passive rather than active roles (Freedman, 1986).

The typical approach of weight-loss groups provides the conditions for further victimization of persons already blamed by a society hostile to fatness and fat people. If they are not successful in their weight loss—and numerous studies show that the vast majority are not (Chernin, 1981)—then the notion of fatness as a personal problem within the individual's control leaves participants perceiving themselves as chronic failures. Even if they do "succeed," they inevitably discover that most difficulties of daily life do not, in fact, vanish. When faced with continued problems, these women may experience severe distress. Such victimization is particularly exploitive for poor women among whom obesity is more prevalent than among the affluent (Van Itallie, 1985).

Millman (1980) concludes that diet and weight reduction programs contribute to gender inequality in two basic ways. First, the before-after fantasy of weight loss as a personal and social panacea is predicated on an assumption of passivity and dependence. Women change their looks in order to change their lives, neglecting the key aspect of oppression stemming from social structural arrangements. Second, the before-after fantasy leads to inaction because women tend to postpone major decisions until they are thin:

> In the end, the activity of postponing life is profoundly debilitating.... At first, the faith in transformation brings excitement, anticipation and great expectations. But when losing weight and starting to live are postponed—hopefulness turns into resignation and immobility—rather than give up the fantasy, we actually slow down and bring to a halt our life's effort itself [Millman, 1980: 244].

Clearly, powerlessness, exclusion, and lack of opportunity and fulfillment cannot be overcome through individualistic personal improvement strategies.

Although such programs may be beneficial for some, they lead others to give up. Most crucially, they do not address the institutional sources of women's oppression, an observation that Nancy Henley (1979) has made with regard to assertiveness training programs, another self-help strategy embraced by feminists.

STRATEGIES FOR CHANGE

The questioning and theoretical analysis stimulated by the women's health movement, as we have seen, include critical reexamination of the past as well as consideration of the problems and issues of today. This work has revealed that contemporary differences in theoretical perspective are not necessarily new. A long-standing point of difference among feminists concerns whether to emphasize women's uniqueness in relation to men or their similarities. Lorber (1984) calls this a maximalist-minimalist distinction. Monteiro (1984) refers to "women's culture" versus "equal rights" perspectives.

A historical illustration is Monteiro's (1984) comparative study of two famous women, both nineteenth-century pioneers in the field of health and medical care. Florence Nightingale (1820-1910) and Elizabeth Blackwell (1821-1910) had almost identical life spans as well as the common belief that increasing women's participation would improve the nature and quality of health care. Nightingale is remembered as the founder of modern nursing and a key figure in the development of public health, and Blackwell as a pioneer among women physicians. It is little known that each woman was an active feminist and that they knew each other well, debating the same problems and issues that still divide feminist women's health activists today.

The two women met in London when they were 30. Nightingale had won her family's consent to study nursing, provided she keep it secret, and within the next few years completed her nursing studies and also wrote a book on the subjugation of Victorian women. Blackwell, having graduated from medical school in the United States, was in London doing postgraduate work before returning to New York City where, with her sister Emily, a surgeon, she would in 1857 open a teaching hospital run entirely by women, the New York Infirmary for Women and Children. The following year, Blackwell returned to England to investigate establishing a similar hospital in England. She and Nightingale met and discussed the possibility of working together, agreeing on the need for such a hospital though not necessarily as a training place for women physicians.

Their disagreement reveals their very different views on the means to their common goals of empowering women and improving health and health care. According to Monteiro, Nightingale represented a "woman's culture" emphasis stressing homosocial bonds among women as well as the unique values characterizing their culture. Through the concept of nursing, she wanted to extend, rationalize (through education), and publicly legitimate women's traditional nurturing role.

In contrast, according to Monteiro, Blackwell took more of an "equal rights" emphasis, stressing female oppression and the ways in which women could overcome the exclusion and the constraints of male-dominated society (Monterio, 1984). In England, Blackwell wanted to open a small women's hospital in the country where she could surreptitiously educate women physicians. She envisioned a cooperative relationship with Nightingale such that the latter's proposed nursing curriculum would be a first-level of the medical school. Nightingale was adamantly opposed:

> Instead of wishing to see more doctors made by women joining what there are, I wish to see as few Doctors, either male or female, as possible for, mark you, the women have made no improvements—they have only tried to be "men"... they will not fail in getting their own livelihood, but they fail in doing good and improving therapeutics [quoted in Monteiro, 1984: 526].

In Nightingale's view, more women physicians would simply perpetuate a less than desirable status quo. Instead, she wanted nursing to change the structure of health and medical care. Despite such progressive ideas of structural change, Nightingale's overriding concern for the legitimacy and success of professional nursing led her to place her school squarely within establishment medicine, where it came under control of male physicians (see Freidson, 1970). Blackwell's approach, too, met with little success. It took a another century for women to break the barriers imposed by the male-dominated profession of medicine (see Walsh, 1977).

These developments have their contemporary analogues. Not only is "woman's culture" versus "equal rights" a persistent theme, but so too is the debate over "separatist" versus "integrationist" organizational strategies. As we can see in the experience of Blackwell and others who have attempted to effect change outside established institutions, separate female organizations are isolated and have relatively few resources with which to survive, much less pursue a program of societal challenge. On the other hand, as Nightingale's strategy reveals, the attempt to effect change within the establishment also is risky. In male-dominated structures, women's concerns are at low priority; they are left out of decision making, and their programs are coopted and politically diluted.

This does not mean that change is impossible. On the contrary, we can speculate, along with Monteiro, that had Nightingale and Blackwell been able to join forces in 1859 the position of women and their health and health care might have evolved differently. The fact that there are explanations for the disappointments of past efforts can be utilized constructively in new theoretical formulations and in future social action.

REFERENCES

American Medical News (1974) "And now the 'liberated' woman patient." October 7.

BARKER-BENFIELD, G. J. (1976) The Horrors of the Half-Known Life: Male Attitudes Toward Women and Sexuality in Nineteenth Century America. New York: Harper & Row.

BART, P. (1981) "Seizing the means of reproduction: An illegal feminist abortion collective—how and why it worked," in H. Roberts (ed.) Women, Health and Reproduction. Routledge & Kegan Paul.

BECKWITH, B. (1985) "Boston Women's Health Book Collective: Women empowering women." Women and Health 10, 1.

BLEIER, R. (1984) Science and Gender: A Critique of Biology and Its Theories on Women. New York: Pergamon.

BLEIER, R. [ed.] (1986) Feminist Approaches to Science. New York: Pergamon.

Boston Women's Health Book Collective (1984) The New Our Bodies, Ourselves. New York: Simon & Schuster.

BOWMAN, M. and D. ALLEN (1985) Stress and Women Physicians. New York: Springer-Verlag.

BRESLAU, N. (1983) "Care of disabled children and women's time use." Medical Care 21, 6.

BRUCE, J. (1981) "Women-oriented health care: New Hampshire Feminist Health Center." Studies in Family Planning 12, 10.

CAMPBELL, M. (1974) Why Would a Girl Go Into Medicine? Old Westbury, NY: Feminist Press.

CARPENTER, E. S. (1980) "Children's health care and the changing role of women." Medical Care 18.

CASSIDY-BRINN, G., F. HORNSTEIN, and C. DOWNER (1984) Women-Centered Pregnancy and Birth. Pittsburgh, PA: Cleis Press.

CHERNIN, K. (1981) The Obsession: Reflections on the Tyranny of Slenderness. New York: Harper & Row.

COLE, S. and R. LEJEUNE (1972) "Illness and the legitimation of failure." American Sociological Review 37.

CONRAD, P. and J. SCHNEIDER (1980) Deviance and Medicalization: From Badness to Sickness. St. Louis: C. V. Mosby.

CRAWFORD, R. (1977) "You are dangerous to your health: The ideology and politics of victim blaming." International Journal of Health Services, 7 (4).

DEAN, K. (1986) "Lay care in illness." Social Science and Medicine 22, 2.

DELANEY, J., M. J. LUPTON, and E. TOTH (1977) The Curse: A Cultural History of Menstruation. New York: Mentor.

DOYAL, L. (1983) "Women, health and the sexual division of labor: A case study of the women's health movement in Britain." International Journal of Health Sciences 13, 3.

DOWNER, C. (1984) Personal communication.

DUFFIN, L. (1978) "The cospicuous consumptive: Woman as an invalid," pp. 26-56 in S. Delamont and L. Duffin (eds.), The Nineteenth-Century Woman: Her Cultural and Physical World. New York: Barnes & Noble.

DUSTER, T. (1970) The Legislation of Morality: Laws, Drugs, and Moral Judgement. New York: Free Press.

EHRENREICH, B. and D. ENGLISH (1979) For Her Own Good: 150 Years of the Experts Advice to Women. Garden City, NY: Anchor/Doubleday.

ELSTON, M. A. (1981) "Medicine as 'old husbands' tales': The impact of feminism," pp. 189-211 in D. Spender (ed.) Men's Studies Modified. Oxford: Pergamon.

FATT, N. (1978) "Women's occupational health and the women's health movement." Preventive Medicine 7, 3.

Federation of Feminist Women's Health Centers (1981a) How to Stay Out of the Gynecologist's Office. Los Angeles: Women to Women.

Federation of Feminist Women's Health Centers (1981b) A New View of a Woman's Body. New York: Simon & Schuster.

FEE, E. (1983) "Women and health care: A comparison of theories," in E. Fee (ed.) Women and Health: The Politics of Sex in Medicine. Farmingdale, NY: Baywood.

FERREE, M. M. and B. HESS (1985) Controversy and Coalition: New Feminist Movement. Boston: G. K. Hall.

FINKBINE, S. (1967) "The lesser of two evils," in A. Guttmacher (ed.) The Case for Legalized Abortion Now. Berkeley: Diablo Press.

FINLEY, M. L. (1984) "Feminist perspectives on breast self examination: Dilemmas and paradoxes." Presented at the American Sociological Association meetings, San Antonio, TX, August.

FREEDMAN, R. (1986) Beauty Bound. Lexington, MA: Lexington Books.

FREIDSON, E. (1970) Profession of Medicine. New York: Harper & Row.

GAGE, M. J. (1980) Women, Church and State: The Original Exposé of Male Collaboration Against the Female Sex (1893). Watertown, MA: Persephone Press.

GARTNER, A. (1985) "A typology of women's self-help groups." Social Policy (Winter).

HALLER, J. S. and R. M. HALLER (1974) The Physician and Sexuality in Victorian America. Urbana: University of Illinois Press.

HAUG, M. and B. LAVIN (1983) Consumerism in Medicine: Challenging Physician Authority. Newbury Park, CA: Sage.

HENLEY, N. M. (1979) "Assertiveness training: Making the political personal." Presented at the Society for the Study of Social Problems Annual Meetings, Boston, August.

HERSCHBERGER, R. (1948) "Society writes biology," in Adam's Rib. Pellegrini and Cudahay.

HOWE, H. L. (1984) "Age-specific hysterectomy and oophorectomy prevalence rates and the risks for cancer of the reproductive system." American Journal of Public Health 74, 6.

HUBBARD, R. (1981) "The emperor doesn't wear any clothes: The impact of feminism on biology," in D. Spencer (ed.) Men's Studies Modified. Oxford: Pergamon.

HUBBARD, R., M. S. HENIFIN, and B. FRIED (1982) Biological Woman: The Convenient Myth: A Collection of Feminist Essays and a Comprehensive Bibliography. Cambridge, MA: Schenkman.

JACOBI, M. P. (1877) The Question of Rest for Women During Menstruation. New York: G. P. Putnam.

KRANTZ, K. E. (1970) "The matriarchal society," pp. 275-281 in J. P. Semmens and K. E. Krantz (eds.) The Adolescent Experience: A Counseling Guide to Social and Sexual Behavior. New York: Macmillan.

KRONENFELD, J. J. (1979) "Self care as a panacea for the ills of the health care system: An assessment." Social Science and Medicine 13A.

LEVIN, B. (1980) Women and Medicine. Metuchen, NJ: Scarecrow Press.

LORBER, J. (1985) "More women physicians: Will it mean more humane health care?" Social Policy (Summer).

LORBER, J. (1984) Women Physicians: Careers, Status, and Power. London: Tavistock.

LORDE, A. (1980) The Cancer Journals. Argyle, NY: Spinsters.

LOVEJOY, E. P. (1957) Women Doctors of the World. New York: Macmillan.

MARIESKIND, H. (1975) "The women's health movement." International Journal of Health Services 5, 2.

MARIESKIND, H. I. (1980) Women in the Health System: Patients, Providers and Programs. St. Louis: C.V. Mosby.

MASTERS, W. H. and V. E. JOHNSON (1966) Human Sexual Response. Boston: Little, Brown.

Medical World News (1981) "CDC calls 15% of hysterectomies 'questionable.'" December 7, p. 21.

MILLMAN, M. (1980) Such a Pretty Face: Being Fat in America. New York: Norton.

MILLMAN, M. (1982) "The ideology of self-care: Blaming the victims of illness," chap. 5 in A. W. Johnson et al. (eds.) Contemporary Health Services. Dover, MA: Auburn House.

MISHLER, E. G. et al. (1981) Social Contexts of Health, Illness and Patient Care. Cambridge: Cambridge University Press.

MONTEIRO, L. A. (1984) "On separate roads: Florence Nightingale and Elizabeth Blackwell." Signs 9, 3.

MORANTZ, R. M. (1977) "Making women modern: Middle-class women and health reform in 19th century America." Journal of Social History, 10 (Summer).

MOSHER, C. D. (1923) Woman's Physical Freedom. New York: Woman's Press.

NORTHCOTT, H. C. (1983) "Who stays home? Working parents and sick children." International Journal of Women's Studies 6, 5.

OSBORNE, K. (1984) "A feminist perspective on women and health," pp. 266-282 in A. Broome and L. Wallace (eds.) Psychology and Gynaecological Problems. London: Tavistock.

PEARSON, W. and M. L. CLARK (1982) "The mal(e) treatment of American women in gynecology and obstetrics." International Journal of Women's Studies 5, 4.

PERSAUD, T.V.N., A. E. CHUDLEY, and R. G. SKALKO (1985) Basic Concepts in Teratology. New York: Alan R. Liss.

RAMEY, E. R. (1973) "Sex hormones and executive ability." Annals of the New York Academy of Sciences 208: 237-245.

RANDALL, D. M. (1985) "Women in toxic work environments: A case study and examination of policy impact," pp. 259-281 in L. Larwood et al. (eds.), Women and Work: An Annual Review, Vol. 1. Newbury Park, CA: Sage.

REISSMAN, C. K. (1983) "Women and medicalization: A new perspective." Social Policy 14, 1.

REISSMAN, C. K. (1984) "The use of health services by the poor: Are there any promising models?" Social Policy 14, 4.

RODRIQUEZ-TRIAS, H. (1978) "Sterilization abuse." Women and Health 3, 3.

ROOS, N. P. (1984) "Hysterectomy: Variations in rates across small areas and across physicians' practices." American Journal of Public Health 74, 4.

RUZEK, S. (1978) The Women's Health Movement. New York: Praeger.

SALMON, J. W. and H. BERLINER (1982) "Self-care: Boot straps or hangman's noose?" Health and Medicine: Journal of the Health and Medicine Policy Research Group 1, 3.

SANDBERG, S. I. et al. (1985) "Elective hysterectomy: Benefits, risks and costs." Medical Care 23, 9.

SCULLY, D. (1980) Men Who Control Women's Health: The Miseducation of Obstetrician-Gynecologists. Boston: Hougton-Mifflin.

SCULLY, D. and P. BART (1973) "A funny thing happened on the way to the orifice: Woman in gynecology textbooks." American Journal of Sociology 28, 4.

SMITH, B. (1982) "Black women's health: Notes for a course," in R. Hubbard et al. (eds.) Biological Woman—The Convenient Myth. Cambridge, MA: Schenkman.

SMITH, D. E. (1975) "Women and psychiatry," in D. Smith and S. David (eds.) Women Look at Psychiatry. Vancouver: Press Gang.

STAGE, S. (1979) Female Complaints: Lydia Pinkham and the Business of Women's Medicine. New York: Norton.

STARR, P. (1982) The Social Transformation of American Medicine. New York: Basic Books.

Sunday Times of London (1979) Suffer the Children: The Story of Thalidomide. New York: Viking Press.

TAFFEL, S. and P. PLACEK (1985) "One-fifth of 1983 U.S. births of cesarean section." American Journal of Public Health 75, 2.

VAN ITALLIE, T. B. (1985) "Health implications of overweight and obesity in the United States." Annals of Internal Medicine 103.

VEATCH, R. M. (1971) "Experimental pregnancy: The ethical complexities of experimentation with oral contraceptives." Hastings Center Report 1 (June).

WALSH, M. R. (1977) Doctors Wanted: No Women Need Apply: Sexual Barriers in the Medical Profession, 1935-1975. New Haven: Yale University Press.

WALSH, M. R. (1982) "The quirls of a woman's brain," in R. Hubbard et al. (eds.), Biological Woman—The Convenient Myth. Cambridge, MA: Schenkman.

WILKINSON, D. Y. (1980) "Minority women: Social-cultural issues," in A. Broadsky and R. Hare-Mustin (eds.) Women and Psychotherapy. New York: Guilford Press.

ZIMMERMAN, M. K. (1977) Passage Through Abortion: The Personal and Social Reality of Women's Experiences. New York: Praeger.

ZIMMERMAN, M. K. (1981) "Psychosocial and emotional consequences of elective abortion: A literature review," in P. Sachdev (ed.) Abortion: Readings and Research. Toronto: Butterworths.

ZOLA, I. K. (1972) "Medicine as an institution of social control." Sociological Review 20, 4.

V

GENDER AND THE STATE

17 Feminist Legal Strategies: The Powers of Difference

AVA BARON
Rider College

FEMINISTS have always considered the law a key factor in creating, reproducing, and obscuring gender inequality. Feminists also have relied on law to relieve women's oppression and to improve women's social and economic positions. Nineteenth-century feminists, noting the egalitarian political rhetoric of the American Revolution and that neither the Declaration of Independence nor the Constitution made invidious distinctions based on sex, specifically denounced women's inferior legal status (Kerber, 1977; Flexner, 1975). These early feminists fought not only for the suffrage but for married women's property rights, rights to divorce and child custody, protection against male violence, and rights to reproductive control—with only partial success. For the new women's movement, therefore, expansion of women's legal rights is one crucial goal. Thus legal struggles in the areas of employment, family, and sexuality continue, although in different forms than in the past.

Given the historical relationship between women's political organizing and legal reform, it is not surprising that the rise of the women's movement in the 1960s stimulated the development of a body of literature on women and the law. Initially, much of this work was written by lawyers (Kanowitz, 1969; DeCrow, 1974). Research on women and law by sociologists or historians was limited to material on women and crime (Klein, 1973; Adler, 1975; Simon, 1975; Smart, 1977; Datesman and Scarpitti, 1980; Weisberg, 1982b; Leonard, 1982; Rafter and Stanko, 1982). Recently, however, research on women and law is developing at a rapid pace and includes a wide range of legal issues addressed from multiple perspectives and disciplines.

Three critical questions that have emerged in feminist debates will be

AUTHOR'S NOTE: I am grateful to Carole Turbin, Richard Butsch, Meredith Gould, Myra Marx Ferree, and Beth Hess for their helpful comments. This article was written in part while I was on research leave from Rider College and was a fellow at the Bunting Institute of Radcliffe College.

examined in this chapter. First, feminists seek to assess whether, and in what ways, women have benefitted from legal changes over the past two centuries. Has legal reform reduced gender inequality? Second, feminists need to decide whether the legal goals of freedom and protection are mutually exclusive. For example, can women obtain state protection against male sexual violence without this becoming paternalistic and resulting in further restrictions on women? Third, feminists must evaluate whether formal (legal) equality contradicts substantive (actual) equality. How should the law handle actual sex differences of sexuality and reproduction? These questions are interrelated and affect women's status in all areas of law. How they are answered will affect whether feminists continue their efforts to use the law in the struggle for gender equality, as well as the types of strategies they pursue.

The women's movement is at a critical juncture in developing legal strategies. Some feminists struggle to ward off right-wing attacks on recently won legal victories in the areas of reproductive rights and affirmative action. Others believe that legal change has not gone far enough; comparable worth and antipornography campaigns seek to use the law further to challenge patriarchy. Still others believe that law is too inherently masculinist and that feminists must explore other avenues for social change. Scholars disagree whether legal equality, even if achieved, would ensure actual gender equality.

The women's movement always has been ambivalent about law (Brophy and Smart, 1985: 1-20). Women's disagreement about antipornography legislation is a recent example. While feminists appear to agree that pornography is bad, they disagree about what, if anything, can be done about it. Most concur that the legal system is patriarchal—that is, law operates to reinforce male privilege and power—but disagree about what that means for feminist political action. Support for antipornography legislation hinges on the belief that women cannot wait for the law to become nonpatriarchal but must make it so. The opposition assumes that such laws will be ineffective and will provide the state with additional ammunition to use against women (see Sheffield, Chapter 6 in this volume). These debates suggest that feminists are still in the process of evaluating and developing not only a feminist theory of sexuality but a theory of the state and an understanding of the relationship between gender and law (Dworkin, 1981; Lederer, 1980; Griffin, 1981; Snitow et al., 1983; Burstyn, 1985).

In this chapter I first examine the premises shaping women's status under law. I then assess how U.S. law has shaped women's lives and the ways in which women have shaped legal reform in four areas: family law, male sexual violence, reproductive control, and employment. Finally, I consider some feminist alternatives.

I argue that law must be an important arena for feminist struggles, and that different and even contradictory legal and political strategies can be constructive if they are based on a clear-sighted assessment of previous successes and failures. Further, effective legal strategies to reduce gender inequality in our society require a uniquely feminist understanding and critique of law, a "feminist jurisprudence" (MacKinnon, 1982a, 1983; Olsen, 1984a; Polan, 1982; Rifkin, 1982; Wishik, 1985). This entails revealing the male world view that is substantively and procedurally embedded in law, while simultaneously infusing law with a feminist perspective and sense of justice (Elkins, 1983; Cole, 1984; Gilligan, 1982).

CHANGES IN THE LEGAL IDEOLOGY
OF SEXUAL INEQUALITY

The Decline of Coverture:
Has Legal Change Brought Equality?

The American woman's legal status was strongly influenced by the English common law's doctrine of coverture, under which a married woman's legal identity was submerged into that of her husband. As a result, a wife lost many legal rights she enjoyed as a single woman. A wife lost all legal title to her property. She could not execute contracts. Her husband could chastise her, rape her, and force her to stay in his home. The wife's recourse to divorce was extremely limited. Her husband had guardianship rights over the children (Kanowitz, 1969; Basch, 1982; Rabkin, 1980).

While the doctrine of coverture is no longer invoked directly, understanding women's common law status can help feminists evaluate the effectiveness of law in reducing gender inequality. Because this doctrine simultaneously restricted women's legal rights while claiming to provide protection, it highlights a similar contradiction in woman's current legal status as well as the dilemmas of using law to change gender relations.

Recent feminist debate on the impact of the common law on women's legal rights has led to the rediscovery of Mary Beard's (1946) challenges to the dominant feminist emphasis on women's subjection with its implication that woman's legal status had never changed and was therefore unchangeable. She argued that it was only with the development of Western capitalism that women were excluded from the exercise of power and that sex discrimination became pervasive. The nineteenth-century feminist movement, born during the period of diminished rights, assumed that such restrictions had always existed. Beard's critics argue that she failed to examine equity's limitations (Basch, 1982: 230). Research indicates that at least in some colonies women received little relief from equity law (Gampel, 1984).

The nineteenth-century enactment of the Married Women's Property Acts removed some of the common law restrictions on the legal rights of wives.[1] Feminists of the day, such as Elizabeth Cady Stanton, saw these acts as a victory—a result of pressure from the women's movement and a clear improvement of women's legal status. Unlike Stanton, current researchers conclude that the women's movement played a minor role in their passage and that the acts had limited impact on women's status (Thurman, 1966; Rabkin, 1980). Rather, contemporary scholars see these acts as growing out of efforts to codify and rationalize American law, to adjust debtor-creditor relations to a changing market economy (Friedman, 1971), to make the law conform to Jacksonian democratic principles, and to adapt the law to woman's changing economic and familial roles (Basch, 1982). In practice, neither the southern nor northern legislation increased women's control over their property or enhanced women's legal equality (Speth, 1982).

In sum, coverture has proved resilient. Although it no longer constitutes legal doctrine, its principles have been adapted to modern legal, economic, and social conditions. The development of industrial capitalism and the rise of the liberal state brought forth a new legal ideology of woman's status, building on the traditions and contradictions of the old.

The Rise of Dual Ideology:
Protectionism and Laissez-Faire

The nineteenth-century ideology of separate spheres—in which the public sphere of work was considered men's and the private world of family was women's—became the justification for sex-based laws. This was clearly articulated by the Supreme Court in *Bradwell v. Illinois* (U.S. 16 Wall 141, 1873), when the justices decided that admission to the legal profession was not one of women's "privileges and immunities" guaranteed by the Constitution. According to the Court, women's participation in the paid labor force could be legally restricted because "civil law, as well as nature herself has always recognized a wide difference in the respective spheres and destinies of man and woman." This legal ideology continued in modified forms through the 1960s (Taub and Schneider, 1982; Baron, 1981; Powers, 1979).

By contrast to the public sphere, the private sphere was divorced from legal regulation. Although the law restricted women's employment activities, it refused to protect them in the family. The principle of the sanctity of home was invoked to exclude marriage from contract law, while spousal immunity clauses exempted husbands from the criminal and civil liabilities applied to others. This laissez-faire approach to gender inequality in the family provided the appearance of neutrality but also concealed the ways in which the law legitimated and perpetuated patriarchal family relations (Smart, 1984; Olsen, 1983; Wishik, 1985). As MacKinnon (1983: 657) explains,

> The very place (home, body), relations (sexual), activities (intercourse and reproduction), and feelings (intimacy, selfhood) that feminism finds central to women's subjection form the core of privacy doctrine. But when women are segregated in private, one at a time, a law of privacy will tend to protect the right of men "to be let alone," to oppress us one at a time.

Legal reforms have failed to deal with women's needs and experiences because they have been premised on the public/private dichotomy. The freedom provided by the right to privacy (e.g., the basis for contraception and abortion legalization) conflicts with women's right to protection from harm (e.g., against male sexual violence, employment discrimination). In effect, the right to privacy and the right to protection are contradictory legal goals (Olsen, 1984a).

THE LIBERAL STATE
AND THE INEQUALITY OF WOMEN

Family Law

The family has long been identified by feminists as the locus of the oppression of women (Vogel, 1983; Hartmann, 1981). Family law reforms to improve women's status are based on the contradictory impulses of the liberal state's promise to provide equal rights and opportunities while upholding the gender hierarchy of the patriarchal family. The legal bifurcation of public and private spheres mediates this contradiction. The state also invokes the principles of the market (the public sphere) to legitimate its family (private sphere) policy. After the feudal restrictions of common law doctrine were removed, family law legitimated actual gender inequality by invoking laissez-faire doctrine. Similar to the inequality that remains in the market after the establishment of legal equality, this inequality in the family was considered to be natural and not the state's responsibility (Olsen, 1983). As both women's economic vulnerability and patriarchal gender relations in the family are revealed in an analysis of divorce laws, this section will focus on changes in women's right to obtain divorce, the economic consequences of divorce for women, and child custody provisions.

Availability of Divorce

Women's ability to obtain divorce in the colonies was extremely limited. Even in cases of husbands' desertion or adultery, judges were more likely to grant legal separation than divorce. The rise in women's divorce petitions and success in obtaining divorce during the eighteenth century (Cott, 1976) did not necessarily signify a trend toward equality (Kerber, 1980). Some communities liberalized divorce in order to reduce the economic burden on the community in cases where the husband had not fulfilled his obligation by allowing women to remarry and by removing the common law restrictions on married women's economic activities (Weisberg, 1982c), or in order to protect women from cruel or deserting husbands (Hindus and Withey, 1982; but see O'Neill, 1967).

The liberalization of divorce has followed an uneven historical course (Kerber, 1980; Salmon, 1979; Weisberg, 1982b; Hindus & Withey, 1982;

Glendon, 1980). But by the 1970s most states had passed some version of a no-fault law, which provides for divorce on the basis of marital breakdown without requiring that guilt of a spouse be established. Although divorce law reform was heralded as an avenue toward women's emancipation, and was fought for by women in the nineteenth and twentieth centuries, there is mounting evidence that women are not benefitting as expected from such reforms.

Economic Consequences of Divorce

Financially, husbands fare better under no-fault provisions than do wives (Bouton, 1984). The equal division of community property provision in California, for example, actually results in women receiving less than they traditionally would. Prior to no-fault, divorced women with children typically were awarded the family home; under no-fault it is more likely that the home will be sold and the proceeds divided. But the major problem is that equal division of property often refers only to tangible property and most families have little tangible property. Intangibles such as future earnings and career assets are exempted from the equal division requirement and typically remain with the husband (Weitzman, 1985).

In addition, under the no-fault system few women are granted spousal support (Bruch and Wikler, 1984). After the adoption of California's no-fault divorce law, even women divorcing after marriages of long duration in which they were fully committed to homemaking receive few support awards and then only minimal amounts. Child support awards, typically insufficient to cover actual costs, are diminished further by inflation and paternal noncompliance. For these reasons, divorced wives and their children experience rapid downward mobility, while divorced men experience an increase in their standard of living (Weitzman, 1985).

Thus equal treatment under the new divorce law generates greater economic inequality between men and women than under the prior statutes. Changes in divorce law have made women responsible for their own welfare, yet there have been inadequate changes in other areas, such as job training, employment, and wage equity. The combined effect of divorce provisions and discrimination in employment has been the increased "feminization of poverty."

Child Custody

A corollary to changes in the distribution of marital property has been change in child custody provisions. The "tender years" doctrine, which gave automatic preference to mothers in cases involving a minor child, is waning as it is increasingly viewed as a form of discrimination against fathers.

The tender years doctrine developed during the nineteenth century, when young children were likely to become economic dependents rather than contributors to the family income (Brown, 1981). In some respects, this doctrine represented an improvement over previous laws that gave the father custodial preference. The tender years doctrine at least defined women as responsible adults capable of heading families, while also enhancing women's power in the marriage since men stood to lose their children upon separation or divorce (Olsen, 1984b).

Despite these considerations, some feminists perceive the decline of the tender years doctrine as a step toward gender equality. Formerly, courts' power to label a woman an "unfit mother" reinforced social definitions of proper female traits, punishing women who did not accord with these standards. Careerism, lesbianism, or any other deviant sex role behaviors were used to deny women custody. Some also see the new child custody laws as encouraging fathers to participate in child care during the marriage by rewarding them with custody or joint custody upon divorce (Hunter and Polikoff, 1976; Polikoff, 1983).

In sum, although cloaked in notions of love and privacy, family law has justified men's domination of women, leading feminists to seek and welcome its reform. Yet divorce reform has exhibited contradictory tendencies: It supports and legitimates the patriarchal family while it also promotes women's independence and gender equality. The state has been unable to mediate successfully the conflicting premises of liberal capitalism and the patriarchal family.

Male Violence/Rape

Laws dealing with male sexual violence against women also highlight the dual problems of protection and privacy. This section explores the contradictions generated by the law's involvement in rape and wife beating on the one hand, and the individual and collective strategies women have developed to deal with male sexual violence on the other hand (see also Sheffield, Chapter 6 this volume).[2]

Some feminists view rape as violence against women, underscoring the difference between rape and so-called normal sexual relations. Susan Brownmiller (1975), for example, examines the displacement of violence onto sexuality revealed by rapes during riots, wars, pogroms, and revolutions. Rape laws symbolize women as men's property and provide a device to intimidate and control women and to deny their personhood (Griffin, 1977; Shafer and Frye, 1977; Peterson, 1977; Stanko, 1985; but see Schwendinger and Schwendinger, 1983). Others see rape as an expression of male sexuality and emphasize its similarity to normal sexual relations (Clark and Lewis, 1977; Atkinson, 1974; Russell, 1975).

Within patriarchal systems, however, sex and violence may be indistinguishable. The sexual marketplace is characterized by unequal bargaining power, making transactions between men and women potentially coercive in nature, but the legal system treats sexual intercourse as an interaction between equals. The law assumes that there are two distinct and mutually exclusive types of sexual relations: equal, consensual sexual intercourse and coercive sex imposed by a male aggressor on a female. However, sexual relations might more accurately be seen as on a continuum of consent and coercion (Olsen, 1984a; MacKinnon, 1983; Edwards, 1981).

The legal system regulates female sexuality and reproduction in accordance with a legal ideology about gender and sexuality (Foucault, 1978). Rape laws have assumed heterosexuality and female passivity, victimization, and masochism. Trial procedures and evidentiary requirements define the boundaries of correct sexuality. Evidence concerning a woman's past sexual conduct or her prior relation with the accused publicly disgraces a woman of sexual experience, provides a warning to all women, and reproduces sex-gender power relations.

Traditional rules of evidence in rape trials were premised on two misogynist images: woman as liar and as temptress. Fears of false rape charges and the belief that women wanted to be raped were the justifications for requiring corroborative evidence of the woman's testimony. By contrast, if a woman were robbed rather than raped such evidence would not have been necessary (Wigmore, 1934: 379; Tong, 1984: 98-104.).

Within the past two decades, most states have passed some form of rape reform legislation. From 1976 to 1979, 32 states amended their laws pertaining to sex offenses. Reforms have ranged from minor changes to major restructuring of legal definitions of sex offenses, rules of evidence, and sentencing. Revised rape statutes often define rape in sex-neutral terms, include acts other than penile-vaginal intercourse, and exclude the spousal exemption (Bienen, 1980).

Although women's groups lobbied for these reforms, some feminists are now questioning whether these changes meet their goals (Tong, 1984). Feminists' disagreement about the meaning of rape has generated debate about legal strategies. Two central issues are the consent requirements and women's responses to male violence as well as what these reveal about gender inequality and the social control of female sexuality.

Consent and Coercion

The starting point for legally proving rape is establishing that consent was not granted. Typically, this means demonstrating that the act exceeded the acceptable level of force for normal sexual behavior. Force itself is not proof of rape, since a certain degree of force is assumed to exist in normal sexual relations. Rape trials reveal that the legal definition of "normal" sex includes a high level of force (MacKinnon, 1983).

Lack of consent is operationalized in trials as demonstration that the women actively resisted immediate physical harm. Analysis of consent, then, turns on evidence of the victim's character, chastity, morality, and sexual history. Although recent reforms have eliminated the requirement to show resistance as proof of lack of consent, most rape statutes still require that the act be compelled by force, or threat of force, and be against the woman's will (Weiner, 1983).

In evaluating whether sufficient force was evident to meet the legal standard, courts adopt the perspective of the "reasonable man." The court decides if the defendant's behavior was reasonable by evaluating whether the amount of force used was sufficient to constitute compulsion and whether to believe a perpetrator's claims that he thought the woman consented.

While the reforms are a clear improvement over previous evidentiary requirements, feminists have identified two major problems with this approach. First, men and women may differ in what they consider reasonable; second, men and women may not communicate effectively in the sexual sphere (Weiner, 1983; MacKinnon, 1979, 1983). Built into the legal treatment of rape is a phallocentric bias. Because proof of a criminal act requires criminal intent (*mens rea*) the demonstration that rape has occurred turns on understanding the perpetrator's (man's) mental state, rather than the victim's (woman's). "Reasonable" behavior is defined by what the man understood, or what a "reasonable man" should have understood, at the time under those circumstances. Further, in our culture, a man may see coercive sexuality as seduction while a woman experiences it as rape.[3] Therefore, some feminists question whether consent is a meaningful concept at all (Clark and Lewis, 1977; MacKinnon, 1983).

The legal problem of determining what really happened assumes that there is a single underlying reality, and that this reality is the male view. The woman's experience of injury or violation is afforded no legitimacy (MacKinnon, 1983). Ironically then, a man could be acquitted for not understanding the woman's point of view!

Women's Resistance

An exclusive focus on male violence against women presents a one-dimensional portrait of women as victims who exercise little control over their lives. Yet recent feminist research demonstrates that women defend themselves against male violence in both collective and individual ways (Jones, 1985, 1980; Stanko, 1985; Schneider, 1982; Walkowitz, 1982; Schneider and Jordan, 1978; Taub and Schneider, 1982).

Women's collective responses to male violence have a long history. Women's organizations in the nineteenth century campaigned for victim support services, lobbied for legislative reform, and generally fought against women's oppression (Pleck, 1983). More recently, women also have brought (and won) class action suits against the police for not providing protection to abused wives (e.g., *Scott v. Hart,* Oakland, filed 1976; *State v. Wanrow,*

Washington Supreme Court, 88 Wash. 2d, 221, 559 P.2d 548, 1977; *Raguz v. Chandler,* Cleveland, 1975; *Bruno v. Codd,* New York City, 1977). These court victories help to change the official policy of noninvolvement as well as to raise public awareness about woman battering (Tong, 1984: 141-142; Gee, 1983). In the 1970s national attention focused on women's fighting back against male violence with the cases of Inez Garcia and Joan Little. Both had killed men who sexually assaulted them and both were acquitted on grounds of self-defense (Schneider and Jordan, 1978; Bochnak, 1981).

At the individual level, women who are isolated in the "privacy" of their homes sometimes respond to male violence by using deadly force in self-defense (Jones, 1980). Because a woman's use of force, particularly against her husband, contradicts gender expectations, she must again defend herself in court. As the law historically permitted wife abuse, judges and jurors may not see it as serious or life threatening. In fact, a history of victimization may further reduce the women's chances of success at trial by suggesting her compliance or complicity (Schneider, 1980: 629).

Even a courtroom victory for women in self-defense trials is problematic. Pleas of self-defense are often based on women's helplessness and physical weakness. Judges and jurors accept the reasonableness of a woman's use of deadly weapons because they also accept the argument that women lack sufficient physical strength to resist male attackers in other ways. But as only exceptional women fight back, they may receive the benefit of the stereotype of woman's weakness as a defense.[4] As long as a woman's right to defend herself rests on the perception that women are weak, women get off the hook only by putting themselves down (MacKinnon, 1982a).

Laws dealing with male sexual violence highlight the contradictions women confront in seeking legal protection in a juridical system premised on gender inequality. Feminists disagree over whether rape laws will alleviate male exploitation or increase the legal repression of women (Olsen, 1984a: 130). Recent reforms, while an improvement, continue to use men's sexuality and experience as the legal standard, while legal defense of women's resistance perpetuates views of women as weak.

Reproductive Control

Although the Supreme Court decisions in the early 1970s that relegalized abortion are often considered major victories for women, they did not grant women reproductive control (*Roe v. Wade,* 410 U.S. 113, 1973; *Dow v. Bolton,* 410 U.S. 179, 1973). These decisions were based on the same ideology that perpetuates gender inequality in other areas of law: the separation of public and private spheres. In addition, abortion reform was influenced by racist and classist ideologies. The exceptions and qualifications that later limited women's access to abortion (e.g., compulsory waiting periods, parental and spousal consent requirements, elimination of public funding) were consistent with the principles on which abortion legalization was justified. A woman's right to abortion remains in jeopardy because it was never firmly rooted in a woman's right to self-determination.

Privacy Rights Versus Women's Rights

Contrary to a common assumption, the relegalization of birth control in the past two decades did not legitimate a women's right to control her body. Contraception was legalized on the basis of the right of the couple to sexual privacy (*Griswold v. Connecticut*, 381 U.S. 479, 1965). The Planned Parenthood movement originally defined birth control as a family decision, not as a woman's right (Gordon, 1983). This focus on the family or couple ignored the hierarchy of decision making and inequality in the patriarchal family.

The Court granted a woman the right to choose an abortion on the basis of the right to privacy but made it clear that this right was not absolute. Therefore, the state did not need to demonstrate a compelling state interest in order to limit reproductive freedom, but merely to show an interest rationally related to some state objective. As in other areas of law, women's legal rights were defined and limited by their reproductive role.

Medical Control

Abortion rights did not mean a woman could do whatever she wished with her body. The Court's decisions distinguished between "therapeutic abortion," considered a medical necessity, and "elective abortion," deemed unnecessary, thus solidifying the separation of the issue of abortion from that of a woman's ability to control her body. In establishing this distinction and in empowering the physician to decide what constitutes "necessity," the Court negated the woman's perspective. In *Roe v. Wade* (410 U.S. 166, 1973), the Court declared that even during the first trimester "the abortion decision in all its aspects is inherently, and primarily a medical decision, and basic responsibility for it must rest with the physician." In other words, reproductive control was not given to women but to the largely male medical establishment. The legalization of abortion created an ideology that made it appear that a woman had reproductive freedom while at the same time denying her this freedom (Petchesky, 1984).

Class, Race, and Eugenics

The distinction between therapeutic and elective abortions was later used to justify eliminating federal funds for abortion. The Hyde Amendment in 1977 cut off most federal Medicaid funding for abortion services. The Court in 1980 (*Harris v. McRae*, 448 U.S. 297, 1981; Petchesky, 1984: 286-325) decided that federal funds could be denied for most abortion-related services. The

Court in essence has held that the right to choose an abortion does not entitle a woman to funds to secure that right, thus legitimating a class-divided fertility policy (Petchesky, 1984).

The state's interest in controlling the size and composition of the population has strongly influenced reproductive policies in the United States. Both the emergence of antiabortion laws in the nineteenth century and the relegalization of abortion were deeply rooted in classist and racist eugenics. Nineteenth-century lawmakers who were alarmed about the declining birthrate among white native-born Americans supported antiabortion laws,[5] as did doctors who were attempting to professionalize medical practice (Mohr, 1978).

Ironically, the Planned Parenthood movement in the 1930s and later in the 1960s relied on the medical profession and eugenicists to relegalize abortion. Fertility policy was defined in terms of state control over the racial, ethnic, and class composition of the population rather than in terms of women's self-determination (Gordon, 1983; Petchesky, 1984). Abortion relegalization, thus based on the seemingly contradictory premises of state population control and a laissez-faire "privacy" doctrine, resulted in reproductive policies that limit women's legal right to choose an abortion. Societal interests, medical decisions, and financial ability are allowed to set the parameters of women's reproductive control.

Work and Wage Earning/Protective Lesiglation

We have seen that the law defines women's legal rights in terms of their sexuality both in rape statutes and in reproductive policies (Cole, 1984; Williams, 1982; MacKinnon, 1983). However, sexuality and reproduction are also linked to employment policies, as the history of protective labor legislation reveals. By defining women's "very womanhood" in terms of their sexuality and reproductive functions, the law creates the illusion that women's unequal status is natural and inevitable. For example, in *Dothard v. Rawlinson* (433 U.S. 321, 1977), the Court argued that rape was part of a woman's "very womanhood." When the problem was thus conceived as resulting naturally from woman's sexual vulnerability, the obvious solution was to restrict women's employment opportunities.

Most feminists acknowledge that formal legal equality alone is inadequate to eliminate gender inequality. Some claim that achieving substantive (actual) equality requires legislation that acknowledges sex differences and provides different legal treatment for men and women (Hauserman, 1983); others argue that laws applying only to women are inherently discriminatory and necessarily restrict rather than protect women (Hill, 1979).

Special laws for women typically have been justified as benign or protective treatment (Cole, 1984; Kanowitz, 1969; Baer, 1978). Often, however, these laws enhance rather than eliminate sex discrimination and inequality, although it is not clear whether the negative consequences of these laws were deliberate or unintended (Baron, 1981; Erickson, 1982; Baer, 1978; Blewett, forthcoming; Kessler-Harris, 1982: 180-214). Regardless, the history of protective legislation reveals the ease with which such laws can be made restrictive.

Protective labor laws have perpetuated sex stereotypes and legitimated differential treatment of women workers. Based on the principle of protection, women were excluded from certain male-dominated occupations, either by direct prohibition or by employment terms that made women unequal labor market competitors (Hill, 1979; Baron, 1981). The constitutionality of protective legislation was established in 1908 in the case of *Muller v. Oregon* (208 U.S. 412), which justified placing women in a separate legal classification defined by their reproductive and social roles as mothers and wives. The Supreme Court based its decision on beliefs about the nature of women as documented by contemporary medical and social testimony rather than on precedent and legal argument.

According to the Court, women's right to contract was not inalienable, as it was for men, but should be granted only when it did not interfere with the interests of society. Employment law for men was based on the assumptions that the individual male employee could take care of himself and that state interference was an unjustified infringement on the male worker's liberty to contract his labor as he chose. The rationale for protective legislation was partially to aid women who were defined as inferior and inherently dependent on men, but also to protect their offspring; and, the Court argued, because all women are potential mothers, it was justifiable to place all women—not just pregnant women—in a separate legal classification (Baron, 1981).

Yet *Muller* assumed that women's interests and those of society were fused. That is, interest in women's health standards were identical with society's interest in the production of healthy offspring. The same argument has been used in recent labor legislation (Petchesky, 1979).

Based on the *Muller* principle that a woman's legal rights in the labor market may be restricted to accord with her reproductive function, current laws restrict access to jobs involving exposure to hazardous substances by women of childbearing age in the interest of protecting the fetus (Bell, 1979; Chavkin, 1979; Hill 1979). As a man's legal rights are not similarly determined by their reproductive function, such "protective" laws do not exist for them, and scant attention is given to the harm such substances may cause to men's reproductive systems and to their children. Not coincidentally, the jobs considered hazardous to the fetus and from which women are lawfully excluded are traditional male jobs; there has been little concern about protecting women from toxic substances in traditional female jobs, such as hairdressing (Wright, 1979).

The constitutionality of protective laws for women remained unquestioned until passage of the Equal Pay Act of 1963 and Title VII of the Civil Rights Act of 1964 (and its later amendments). Although Title VII prohibits discrimination on the basis of sex, the Supreme Court has not invalidated sex-based classification. *Muller* has been cited as binding precedent even in non-employment-related cases (Baron, 1981). Many believe an Equal Rights Amendment is required to overturn the *Muller* principle.

The argument against special legal treatment for women rests not only on the claim that it reinforces inequality and paternalism but also that it tends to obscure work place problems by dividing workers along lines of class and race as well as sex. For example, debates about protecting women from hazardous work substances mask the problem that such substances are dangerous for all workers. Similarly, provisions for special pregnancy leaves for women shift attention away from the general inadequacy of sick leave policies and focus it on the protection of women rather than workers generally (Williams, 1982: 196). The feminist argument for special treatment, on the other hand, is couched in terms of substantive rather than formal equality so that lack of legal protection for workers with special needs is seen as pseudo-neutrality (MacKinnon, 1979; Hauserman, 1983).

FRAMING FEMINIST ALTERNATIVES

Legal history teaches us that privacy rights and legal nonintervention do not necessarily provide the freedom to enjoy those rights but, rather, keep women isolated and victimized. Yet legal intervention in women's lives has often been paternalistic, restricting their freedom even further. Feminists are therefore in a quandary: It appears that women must choose between privacy and protection, freedom and security (Williams, 1982; Olsen, 1984a). But feminists disagree about what choice to make.

Gender-Neutral Laws as a Practical Strategy

Some feminists advocate gender-neutral laws as a way to win judicial (and other male-dominated) support for legal change. Because the position of the courts until the early 1970s had been that sex differences justified different legal treatment, the feminist legal strategy was to reduce differential legal treatment by minimizing perceived sex differences (Cole, 1984: 54). Supporting male plaintiffs, according to this approach, would help to challenge sex stereotypes and demonstrate that such stereotypes are limiting for both men and women. Therefore, cases were advanced by feminist lawyers in ways that also offered benefits to men. *In Weinberger v. Weisensfeld*, (420 U.S. 636, 1975), for example, feminist lawyers argued that the Social Security Act provision that gave benefits to surviving mothers but not fathers was a denial of equal protection to the working woman, her spouse, and their child, while the government argued that the discrimination was compensatory and therefore benign.

In some respects, this strategy was successful. In the 1970s, the Supreme Court began to repudiate the legal ideology of separate spheres. Legal equality came to mean sameness, and differences in the treatment of men and women based on overbroad generalizations were considered irrational products of sex stereotypes. In 1971, in *Reed v. Reed* (404 U.S. 71), for the first time in U.S. constitutional history the Supreme Court invalidated sex-based legislation on the grounds that it violated the equal protection clause of the 14th Amendment.

Yet this victory was limited. The standard of review used to determine whether a statute violated the 14th Amendment's guarantee of equal protection remained different for women than for other groups. Legislation differentiating on the basis of race or national origin was considered automatically suspect, and the Court required "rigorous review" and "strict scrutiny" of such legislation. In contrast, the standard of review adopted for sex discrimination cases was that there be a "rational relationship" between the legislation and some legitimate governmental objective. The burden of proof was on the individual to demonstrate that the law was unreasonable. Even the more stringent "substantial relationship" test, established in 1976 (*Craig v. Boren* 429 U.S. 190), is still considerably less restrictive than the criterion for a "suspect classification" (Freedman, 1983; Ginsburg, 1983).[6]

The argument that women were like men, combined with the use of male plaintiffs in sex discrimination suits, produced major changes in women's as well as men's legal rights, benefits, and obligations. For example, women gained equal access to benefits under military, social security, welfare, and worker's compensation programs; female children of divorce were granted child support for the same length of time as male children. Similarly, men received an equal right to social security child care allowance when their spouse dies, and child support and alimony became no longer exclusively the husband's responsibility (Williams, 1982). Noting the harmful consequences of sex discrimination for men, the Court acknowledged that sex discrimination might not always have benign results (Cole, 1984: 56).

However, this legal strategy had its limitations. Sex discrimination cases have been dominated by male plaintiffs and focused on men's rights. The Court, as Cole (1984: 37) explains, "has difficulty recognizing the wrongs women suffer, particularly when faced with 'protective' and 'benign' rationales for discrimination. When the contested treatment of women has an impact on men, however, the Court appears capable of perceiving the injustice." It is not surprising, therefore, that in a significant number of cases the Court has invalidated protective legislation for women because it caused harm to men, not women (Frug, 1979: 80). Despite the legal benefits women have gained, their need to rely on a male plaintiff to prove the wrongs of sex discrimination underscores the contradictions feminists face in using the law as a strategy to obtain gender equality.

The Need for Gender Considerations:
Problems with the "Similarly Situated" Test

Not all feminists agree with the gender-neutral legal approach. Arguments in favor of "genderless" laws, for example. ignore the imbalance of power between men and women (Cole, 1984: 67). The belief that men as much as women are hurt by sex discrimination (Kanowitz, 1981; Ringler, 1980) is simply erroneous; they have not been equal victims of sex discrimination. Critics of the gender-neutral strategy claim that basing legal decisions on this premise, and enlisting men's aid to the women's movement on the foundation of male self-interest, will do more harm than good to the women's cause by perpetuating men's lack of understanding of sexism (Olsen, 1984a; Ringler, 1980).

The current equal protection doctrine denies women substantive equality by upholding rules that are pseudo-neutral (e.g., medical disability plans that are purportedly neutral but exclude pregnancy). Measures to end gender inequality and women's subordination cannot be accomplished within a framework of neutral rules that are male formulated, reflect male needs, male concerns, and male experience (MacKinnon, 1983). The rigorous application of so-called gender-blind standards may be the best way to maintain *in*equality. Therefore, some feminists have argued that the Court should decide if laws are sex discriminatory on the basis of whether they systematically disadvantage women, not whether they are rational (MacKinnon, 1979; Olsen, 1984a; Hauserman, 1983).

The sameness (gender-neutral) approach fought for by feminists in the "first stage" of the women's movement, while increasing women's legal rights, has also brought the legal system and the feminist movement to a critical juncture. Equal employment cases in the 1970s simply required the Court to treat women like men. Now the legal system must deal with the "hard issues"—that is, the cases in which women are not like men (Williams, 1982). Interestingly, pregnancy/reproduction cases are the only area of sex discrimination not dominated by male plaintiffs (Cole, 1984). The sameness approach cannot work with issues of reproduction and sexuality; because women and men *are* biologically different, equality cannot mean sameness.

The controversy over pregnancy disability made this clear. The Court's strategy was to place pregnancy outside the class of phenomena giving rise to discrimination, and, in so doing, eliminated the need to review laws involving pregnancy with the "strict scrutiny" applied in other sex discrimination cases (Williams, 1982; Taub and Schneider, 1982; Scales, 1981). In other words, because there are biological differences between men and women, they are not similarly situated with regard to reproduction. As only women can become pregnant, the Court argued there could not be sex discrimination.

While claiming to reject traditional sex role stereotypes, the Court developed a new version of them, based on biological differences between men and women. The Court, however, tends to confuse the relationship between biological sex and gender, and to treat culturally determined differences as natural and immutable (Gould, 1979; Freedman, 1983: 944-947).

In response to the Court's refusal to recognize "pregnant persons" as a protected class, Congress in 1978 passed the Pregnancy Discrimination Act (PDA) defining discrimination on the basis of pregnancy, childbirth, and related medical conditions as sex discrimination. Under the PDA, pregnancy is to be treated *the same* as any other disability, thus invalidating some state statutes that had provided women with special treatment for pregnancy and maternity.[7]

Disagreement continues between those who favor special treatment for pregnancy, arguing that because it is a condition that does not affect men, special (and protective) laws are justified, and those who claim that the same rationale permitting special benefits allows pregnancy to be treated as "worse" than other conditions. It is also argued that the real issue is the lack of adequate safeguards and sick leave policies for all workers, so that special legislation deflects attention from these more general inadequacies (Williams, 1982). Many fear that special legislation for women is dangerous even in the short run and is likely to deteriorate into a new form of "detrimental protectionism" (Taub, 1980: 1691). Therefore, these critics only support gender neutral laws (Williams, 1982; Olsen, 1984a). The lesson from earlier legislation is that protection is at best, a double-edged sword.

Developing a Feminist Theory of Difference

The real issue may not be whether different treatment of men and women is justified, but what differences are recognized and who determines which differences matter (Rich, 1979: 125-155). As Cole (1984: 92) notes, women's difference as recognized in law has heretofore been defined by men in male terms:

> From the traditional male perspective, which insists on its own "objectivity", women's difference invites condescension and paternalism. By virtue of men's notions about "their difference," women have been excluded, silenced, demeaned, put on pedestals and placed in cages, objectified and acted upon, all in the name of "protection." When men, however, have failed to recognize women's differences, their definitions of equality and justice have been male-centered rather than generic. . . . In law, as in language, the generic has been defined and appropriated by men.

Feminists, then, face a dilemma. On the one hand, the male perspective that dominates the legal system recognizes women's difference in ways that perpetuate women's subordination, thereby turning special or benign legislation into paternalism. On the other hand, gender-neutral laws disregard substantive gender inequalities and actual sex differences. The result has been that women are allowed the same rights as men only when, measured against the male standard, women are judged to be men's equal—that is, the same as men, or, in the words of the Court, "similarly situated."

On this basis, the Court could ignore women's different relationship to pregnancy and childbearing by invoking an ideology premised on biological sex differences. Despite the rhetoric of equality, the Court allows discrimination by finding "real" differences that prevent women from being treated the same as men. In effect, the Court has used the language of equality to deny equality.

The women's movement in the 1960s challenged traditional gender roles and minimized sex differences. Women's unique qualities tended to be seen as those that defined women as inferior and impeded women's success. Recently, however, American feminism has acknowledged and even promoted women's difference from men (Rich, 1979; Eisenstein and Jardine, 1980; Gilligan, 1982). What is significant is not the fact of difference but of who defines difference. Women's ability to define their own difference is an expression and exercise of power and poses a potentially radical challenge to the established order (Marks and de Courtivron, 1980). As Hester Eisenstein (1980: xiii-xiv) explains, "If the naming of differences by the oppressor is replaced with, or at least challenged and contested by, the reclaiming of difference and of individuality by the hitherto oppressed, then a step has been taken along the road to liberation."

Feminist jurisprudence uses a model of equality that accounts for women's point of view without negating its difference. It demands that the law accommodate biological differences without perpetuating socially imposed "otherness" and the paternalism resulting from the male perspective on women's difference (Wishik, 1985; Cole, 1984). Some feminist alternatives already have been envisioned for rape (Olsen, 1984a; MacKinnon, 1983), sexual harassment (MacKinnon, 1979), pornography (Dworkin, 1981), and wage discrimination (Reskin and Hartmann, 1986).

Traditionally, legal reform emphasized the need for women's assimilation in order to obtain the same rights as men. The focus in employment, for example, was on eliminating the barriers to women's entry into traditional male jobs and on requiring women to receive equal compensation when they do the same work as men. The Equal Pay Act (1963) was of limited value because it did not address the real problem: the wage discrimination resulting from a sex-segregated labor market (Blumrosen, 1984; Treiman and Hartmann, 1981). Assimilation into existing social institutions is inadequate. If women are rewarded and protected only when they are like men, only exceptional women will gain while most women will continue to be exploited and subordinated.

By contrast, the concept of *comparable worth* supports rather than demeans women's difference; it rejects the premise that women's work is inherently worth less than men's and it recognizes that as long as women's work is devalued, job segregation will result in wage discrimination (Feldberg, 1984; Treiman and Hartmann, 1981; Remick, 1984; Kahn and Grune, 1982; Warren and Boone, 1984). But a serious problem with the comparable worth strategy is that it is most applicable to the employment situation of white women. For blacks, concerns for employment, for job stability, and for jobs with intrinsic value must be addressed before wage comparability can be meaningful (Scales-Trent, 1984). It is important that feminists develop strategies that account for differences among women as well as between women and men.

Do Women Lawyers Make a Difference?

Feminists trying to use the law for changing gender relations fear loss of their radical potential. By trying to undermine paternalistic notions of women's stereotyped difference, they risk assimilation. But to avoid assimilation (making women like men) and to offer affirmative definitions of women's differences is especially difficult within a legal system structured to exclude women's voices (Cole, 1984: 53).

On a basic level, the legal process is sexist because legal actors (legislators, lawyers, judges, police) are primarily male and have developed, interpreted, and enforced laws to serve their interests, whether consciously or not (DeCrow, 1974; Sachs and Wilson, 1978). In its extreme form, this view assumes that including female personnel in the legal system will bring about change (but see Smart, 1984: 16-23). A modified version of this argument emphasizes the need to have women included in the legal process in order to present a woman's point of view and thereby reduce the male bias in law. For example, sex discrimination cases involving an all male judiciary, male legal representation, and male plaintiffs yield decisions that pay little heed to women's perspectives, concerns, and experience (Cole, 1984).[8]

Until recently, women constituted only a small fraction of lawyers. Since the 1960s, the representation of women in the legal profession has quadrupled: from 3.3% in 1960 to 12% in 1980 (Epstein, 1981: 4-5). The proportion of female law students has increased even more dramatically. In 1965, 4% of all law students were women; by 1979, 32% were women (Fossum, 1983: 228); and in 1983, 43% (Statistical Abstracts, 1985: 151). Some believe that the increase in women as legal actors denotes an end to sex discrimination against women as law students and practitioners. Cynthia Epstein (1981), for example, argues that legal and normative changes since the 1960s paved the way for women's entrance into law schools and law firms.

Others point out that lawyering is becoming increasingly proletarianized as it is feminized. Like their male counterparts, women lawyers in large firms, corporate law departments, government offices, and law clinics find their professional autonomy eroded by an increasing number of bureaucratic procedures and rules, a more detailed division of labor, and a hierarchical authority structure. Yet even within this proletarianized bar, men and women are not given the same opportunities. In both the lower and the elite segments of legal work, women are more likely than men to be in the routinized sectors of the profession—sectors with lower pay and prestige, unconnected to promotion ladders (Baron, 1983; Kanter, 1978). Women's realization that legal education and practice have failed to fulfill their promise of equality provides another radical potential for change (Elkins, 1983).

To use the law as an effective strategy in the feminist struggle for gender equality requires changing the male perspective embedded in law; and, in turn, this requires women's voices. But women's voices are barely audible against the backdrop of patriarchal legal traditions, institutions, processes, and statutes. Adding women to a male legal process makes little difference unless it is connected to broader feminist struggles for social change.

Nonadversarial Alternatives

The women's movement has generally sought legal rights for women within the existing legal process, and over the past two decades the number of women litigants has increased dramatically.[9] There is no question of the effectiveness of the massive litigation efforts of the women's movement in gaining additional legal rights.

But there remains considerable doubt that the traditional legal process can eliminate gender inequality. Increasingly, women are seeking alternative forms for resolving disputes and attaining justice. Supporters of alternatives such as mediation believe that litigation can accomplish only limited social change. Because litigation incorporates male norms of hierarchy, combat, and adversary relations, it is thought to disempower women and reproduce gender inequality (Rifkin, 1984; Gould, 1983). The legal frame of reference for evaluating litigants' behavior remains the ideal of the "reasonable man." The litigator is taught to separate "facts" from "experience," and to focus on abstract legal rights.

Alternatives to litigation infuse decision making with concern for responsibility and for justice obtained through compromise rather than victory (Cole, 1984: 45-46). In contrast to litigation, which assumes an objective reality, mediation recognizes the existence of multiple viewpoints and realities. The feminist critique of litigation exposes how deeply the male viewpoint is embedded in both the substance and procedure of law, unmasking the illusion of neutrality and objectivity.

However, the practice of mediation does not necessarily alter structural patterns of gender inequality. In the social context of pervasive gender inequality, mediation may be detrimental to women because it assumes bargaining between equals. Under the rubric of willing compromise, mediation may unwittingly reproduce subordination. Research on the consequences of divorce mediation, for example, suggests that women fare less well financially than they do in divorce court. In some circumstances, women may be better off with formal court proceedings where they can obtain aggressive legal representation to protect their interests (Olsen, 1983: 1497, 1542). Thus mediation and litigation are equally incapable of yielding justice until broader social, economic and cultural changes occur.

OVERVIEW AND CONCLUSIONS

If feminists reject the legal process, they run the risk of denying women important legal safeguards. However, state involvement in women's lives has usually been paternalistic, and, as long as it is developed outside of a feminist perspective, women will be faced with the dilemma of choosing between freedom and protection. The feminist goal must be to create alternatives to the limited options of laissez-faire and paternalism (Smart, 1984: 224).

Unfortunately, our ability to envision alternatives has been narrowed by the tendency to see life as divided into separate spheres (Olsen, 1983: 1576). Legal rights in one sphere have been conceptualized without examining their implications in other areas. Antidiscrimination laws, for example, treat people as if they had no personal or familial obligations. They therefore fail to deal with discrimination resulting from women's disproportionate responsibilities for housework and child rearing. Emphasizing equality of opportunity for women in the work place then requires that women fit into a patriarchal work-place structure. As a result, women, but not men, must choose between family and career (Frug, 1979).

Similarly, the feminization of poverty has been the result of ignoring the connections between the two spheres. Many have noted that women's economic status declines upon divorce, but few have realized that this is not entirely a consequence of divorce law reform (but see Feldberg, 1984). Although women assume a disproportionate share of child support upon divorce, this increased economic responsibility would not result in poverty if women were not also forced to be economically independent heads of households while they work in a sex-segregated marketplace in which women are paid less than are men.

Feminist jurisprudence must desanctify the private sphere while also recognizing its importance for women's oppression. Too much emphasis has been placed on women's rights in the public sphere alone. A focus on women's formal equality of opportunity in employment is premised on the normative superiority of the public sphere over the private and thus perpetuates the primacy of the family for women (Powers, 1979: 86).

At the turn of this century, as women entered the labor force in larger numbers, the state attempted to circumvent the contradictions between equal opportunity in the labor market and the inequality of the patriarchal family by using the ideology of protectionism to justify sex-based laws. But the continued increase in the numbers of working mothers has created a crisis for both the patriarchal family and the liberal state: for the patriarchal family, because women's changing roles in the economy lead to changes in family life and increased reproductive freedom that threatens patriarchal power; for the state, because it has not been able to fulfill its promise of equal opportunity and simultaneously protect the patriarchal family (Eisenstein, 1981; Petchesky, 1984). The legal bifurcation of public and private spheres has increasingly failed to mediate the contradictions between capitalism and patriarchy.

A feminist jurisprudence also means uncovering the ways in which class, race, and gender biases are connected but obscured by law. Rape laws, for example, were used to control people of color as well as white women. Black slave women were systematically raped by white men, and black men were lynched on rape charges purportedly to protect white women. The myth that rape is more likely to be committed by a black man against a white woman persists (Davis, 1981; Tong, 1984). Even today, a black man is more likely than a white man to receive the death penalty for rape (Sherrill, 1983). This myth operates to perpetuate racism and to obscure the reality that it is men who rape women (MacKinnon, 1983: 646n). Wife abuse is also euphemistically called "spouse abuse" or "family violence," concealing that it is women who are battered. The new ideology of family violence centers on its classlessness and ignores the reality that poor women are confronted with quantitatively fewer economic resources in dealing with such violence (Fine, 1985: 381-408).

One lesson from the abortion legalization struggles is that feminist victories will be short-lived if the justifications for women's legal rights ignore the class and race issues inextricably bound up with gender. Abortion laws written and interpreted from a woman-centered viewpoint would have given women reproductive freedom. Legalization of birth control on the foundation of racist and classist eugenic rationales has resulted in increased population control rather than in women's reproductive freedom (Petchesky, 1984).

Despite the legal changes of the past two decades, or even previous two centuries, women still have not achieved social, economic, or legal equality. Indeed there is some indication that women's economic status has deteriorated over the past two decades (Stallard et al., 1983). Women's efforts to obtain legal rights have emphasized juridical equality as an end in itself rather than seeking the structural changes needed to achieve substantive equality. Rights, as Petchesky (1984: 7) states, "are by definition claims staked within a given order of things. They are demands for access for oneself, or for 'no admittance' to others; but they do not challenge the social structure, the social relations of production and reproduction." Wives' property rights as provided by the Married Women's Property Acts, for example, did little to democratize the family; and women's rights to obtain divorce did not deal with the patriarchal structure of marriage, the problem of wife beating, or the economic consequences of divorce (Olsen, 1983: 1538-1539).

Focusing on obtaining equal rights and equal opportunities through litigation tends to individualize women's problems. In this way, the law diverts feminist energies and resources and threatens to coopt the feminist struggle (Polan, 1982: 300). Feminists, therefore, are justifiably skeptical of turning to the law for justice. Nonetheless, legal reform can still be a useful feminist strategy (Smart, 1984: 15).

Women historically have achieved gains in the legal arena through concrete struggles. It is important to remember the lessons Mary Beard (1946) taught: If we reduce women to transhistorical victims of patriarchy, we run the risk of assuming that patriarchy is inevitable. Change has occurred and we should neither ignore it nor denigrate its significance for women's lives.

Yet change has not meant unilinear progress (Olsen, 1984a). Protective labor legislation, for example, was both a practical victory for working women in a number of female-dominated trades who obtained relief from harsh working conditions, as well as a practical defeat for women in male-dominated trades who were removed from their jobs. It was an ideological defeat for women since it justified sex-based legal classification, while also an ideological victory for workers generally who would benefit from the demise of the principle of laissez-faire in the law of employment. Similarly, the liberalization of divorce has benefited women by increasing their ability to escape from unhappy marriages. By easing divorce for men, at the same time, these reforms have reduced women's negotiating power in divorce settlements.

Given these contradictions, it is not surprising that the current women's movement remains deeply divided on whether and when to use law. The intensity of feminist debate over antipornography legislation is a case in point. But feminists need not agree on legal strategies to resolve the dilemmas before them. Given the historic resiliency of patriarchy, progress may require a variety of attacks from different angles, so dissension need not mean weakness (Marks and de Courtivron, 1980: 33; Cole, 1984). The quest for understanding women's difference requires a feminist discourse that cannot be confined within traditional male modes (Feral, 1980: 549). The many feminist strategies to confront women's legal dilemmas are welcome, and may be necessary. Realizing the potential embedded in law to subvert patriarchy demands that feminists both conceptualize alternatives that address women's problems and concerns, and continue to struggle for their voices to be heard—voices that today remain barely audible.

NOTES

1. Mississippi passed the first such act in 1839, followed by Maryland in 1843; later Maine, Massachusetts, Iowa, and New York passed similar laws. By the end of the Civil War 29 states had passed Married Women's Property Acts (Basch, 1982; Thurman, 1966; Speth, 1982).
2. Although a legal distinction is drawn between the battery of wives and marital rape, in

reality these forms of violence against women often occur together (Dobash and Dobash, 1979: 98-101; MacKinnon, 1983: 36n).

3. A proposed remedy for this is a negligence standard in ensuring consent that might encourage men to be more sensitive to potential ambiguities in sex communication (Weiner, 1983: 148, 150-157).

4. There are no systematic data available on the likelihood of a woman's acquittal for fighting back. Discussions of some cases are available (Bochnak, 1980; Jones, 1980, 1985; Schneider and Jordan, 1978).

5. The birthrate among native-born American women declined from 7 in 1800 to 3 in 1900. In the mid-nineteenth century married middle-class white Protestant women had the most abortions. According to some estimates 1 in 5 pregnancies ended in abortion (Mohr, 1978).

6. The first and only time the Court applied the strict scrutiny standard in a sex discrimination case was *Frontiero v. Richardson* (422 U.S. 677, 1973).

7. For example, the Montana law that forbade employers from firing women who became pregnant and further required them to provide reasonable maternity leave was invalidated (Williams, 1982).

8. Examples of such cases are *Schlesinger v. Ballard* (419 U.S. 498, 1975) and *Kahn v. Shevin* (416 U.S. 351, 1974).

9. The Women's Rights Project established in 1971 by the American Civil Liberties Union has worked toward establishing sex equality through litigation. *Reed v. Reed* (404 U.S. 71, 1971) was one of its first cases (Cowan, 1976).

REFERENCES

ADLER, F. (1975) Sisters in Crime: The Rise of the New Female Criminal. New York: McGraw-Hill.

ATKINS, S. and B. HOGGETT (1984) Women and the Law. Oxford: Basil Blackwell.

ATKINSON, T. (1974) Amazon Odyssey: The First Collection of Writings by the Political Pioneers of the Women's Movement. New York: Links Books.

BAER, J. (1978) The Chains of Protection: The Judicial Response to Women's Labor Legislation. Westport, CT: Greenwood.

BALKAN, S., R. BERGER, and J. SCHMIDT (1980) Crime and Deviance in America: A Critical Approach. Belmont, CA: Wadsworth.

BARON, A. (1981) "Protective labor legislation and the cult of domesticity." Journal of Family Issues 2 (March): 25-38.

BARON, A. (1983) "Feminization of the legal profession—progress or proletarianization?" Legal Studies Forum 7, 2-3: 330-357.

BASCH, N. (1979) "Invisible women: The legal fiction of marital unity in nineteenth-century America." Feminist Studies 5 (Summer): 346-366.

BASCH, N. (1982) In the Eyes of the Law: Women, Marriage, and Property in Nineteenth Century New York. Ithaca, NY: Cornell University Press.

BEARD, M. (1946) Woman as force in history: A study in traditions and realities. New York: Macmillan.

BELL, C. (1979) "Implementing safety and health regulations for women in the workplace." Feminist Studies 5 (Summer): 286-301.

BIENEN, L. (1980) "Rape III—National developments in rape reform legislation." Women's Rights Law Reporter 6, 3: 170-213.

BLEWETT, M. (forthcoming) Men, Women and Work: A Study of Class, Gender and Protest in the Nineteenth Century New England Shoe Industry. Urbana: University of Illinois Press.

BLUMROSEN, R. (1984) "Update: Wage discrimination revisited." Women's Rights Law Reporter 8 (Winter): 109-131.

BOCHNAK, E. [ed.] (1981) Women's Self-Defense Cases: Theory and Practice. Charlottesville, VA: Michie Co.

BONEPARTH, E. (1982) "Strategies for the eighties," pp. 296-312 in E. Boneparth (ed.) Women, Power and Policy. New York: Pergamon.

BOTTOMLEY, A. (1985) "What is happening to family law: A feminist critique of conciliation," pp. 162-187 in J. Brophy and C. Smart (eds.) Women in Law: Explorations in Law, Family and Sexuality. London: Routledge & Kegan Paul.

BOUTON, K. (1984) "Women and divorce: How the new law works against them." New York Magazine 8 (October): 34-41.

BROPHY, J. and C. SMART [eds.] (1985) Women in Law: Explorations in Law, Family and Sexuality. London: Routledge & Kegan Paul.

BROWN, C. (1981) "Mothers, fathers and children: From private to public patriarchy," pp. 239-267 in L. Sargent (ed.) Women and Revolution: A Discussion of the Unhappy Marriage of Marxism and Feminism. Boston: South End.

BROWNMILLER, S. (1975) Against Our Will: Men, Women and Rape. New York: Simon & Schuster.

BRUCH, C. S. (1976) "Property rights of de facto spouses including thoughts on the value of homemaker services." Family Law Quarterly 10: 101.

BRUCH, C. S. and N. J. WIKLER (1984) "Economic consequences of divorce as affected by the level of child and spousal support awards." Michigan Bar Journal 63 (June): 472-480.

BURSTYN, V. [ed.] (1985) Women Against Censorship. Manchester, NH: Salem House.

CHAVKIN, W. (1979) "Occupational hazards to reproduction: A review essay and annotated bibliography." Feminist Studies 5 (Summer): 310-325.

CHAVKIN, W. [ed.] (1984) Double Exposure: Women's Health Hazards on the Job and at Home. New York: Monthly Review Press.

CLARK, L. and D. LEWIS (1977) Rape: The Price of Coercive Sexuality. Toronto: Women's Press.

COLE, D. (1984) "Strategies of difference: Litigating for women's rights in a man's world." Law and Inequality: A Journal of Theory and Practice 2 (February): 33-96.

COTT, N. F. (1976) "Divorce and the changing status of women in eighteenth-century Massachusetts." William and Mary Quarterly 33 (3rd Series): 586-614.

COWAN, R. (1976) "Women's rights through litigation: An examination of the American Civil Liberties Union Women's Rights Project, 1971-76." Columbia Human Rights Law Review 8 (Spring/Summer): 373-412.

DATESMAN, S. and F. SCARPITTI [eds.] (1980) Women, Crime, and Justice. New York: Oxford University Press.

DAVIS, A. (1981) Women, Race and Class. New York: Random House.

DECROW, K. (1974) Sexist Justice. New York: Random House.

DENNY, M. (1983) "Recent developments in the law on sexual harassment: Whether they represent an advance or retreat may depend on the yardstick." Legal Studies Forum 7, 2-3: 160-173.

DOBASH, E. and R. DOBASH (1979) Violence Against Wives: A Case Against the Patriarchy. New York: Free Press.

DWORKIN, A. (1981) Pornography: Men Possessing Women. New York: Perigee.

EDWARDS, S. (1981) Female Sexuality and the Law: A Study of Constructs of Female Sexuality as They Inform Statute and Legal Procedure. Oxford: Martin Robertson & Co.

EISENBERG, S. E. and P. L. MICKLOW (1977) "The assaulted wife: 'Catch 22' revisited." Women's Rights Law Reporter 3: 138-161.

EISENSTEIN, H. (1980) "Introduction," pp. xv-xxiv in H. Eisenstein and A. Jardine (eds.) The Future of Difference. Boston: G. K. Hall.

EISENSTEIN, H. and A. JARDINE [eds.] (1980). The Future of Difference. Boston: G. K. Hall.

EISENSTEIN, Z. R. (1981) The Radical Future of Liberal Feminism. New York: Longman.

EISENSTEIN, Z. R. (1983) "Some comments on the patriarchal aspects of law." Legal Studies

Forum 7, 2-3: 317-324.

EISENSTEIN, Z. R. (1984) Feminism and Sexual Equality: Crisis in Liberal America. New York: Monthly Review Press.

ELKINS, J. R. (1983) "On the significance of women in legal education." Legal Studies Forum 7, 2-3: 290-316.

ELSHTAIN, J. B. (1974) "Moral woman and immoral man: A consideration of the public-private split and its political ramifications." Politics and Society 4, 4: 453-472.

EPSTEIN, C. (1981) Women and Law. New York: Basic Books.

ERICKSON, N. S. (1982) "Historical background of 'protective' legislation: *Muller v. Oregon*," pp. 155-186 in D. Kelly Weisberg (ed.) Women and the Law, Vol. 2. Cambridge, MA: Schenkman.

FELDBERG, R. L. (1984) "Comparable worth: Toward theory and practice in the United States." Signs 10 (Winter): 311-328.

FERAL, J. (1980) "The powers of difference," pp. 88-94 in H. Eisenstein and A. Jardine (eds.) The Future of Difference. Boston: G. K. Hall.

FINE, M. (1985) "Unearthing contradictions: An essay inspired by women and male violence (a commentary)." Feminist Studies 11 (Summer): 391-408.

FINEMAN, M. L. (1983) "Implementing equality: Ideology, contradiction and social change." Wisconsin Law Review 4: 789-886.

FLEXNER, E. (1975) Century of Struggle: The Women's Rights Movement in the United States (1959). Cambridge, MA: Harvard University Press.

FLICK, R. (1984) "Undermining the women's movement—the comparable worth debate: Can equality be measured by money." Human Rights 12 (Fall): 26-29, 51-53.

FOA, P. (1977) "What's wrong with rape?" pp. 347-359 in M. Vetterling-Braggin et al. (eds.) Feminism and Philosophy. Totowa, NJ: Rowman & Littlefield.

FOSSUM, D. (1983) "Law and the sexual integration of institutions: The case of American law schools." Legal Studies Forum 7, 2-3: 222-250.

FOUCAULT, M. (1978) The History of Sexuality, Vol. 1, An Introduction (R. Hurley, trans.). New York: Pantheon.

FREEDMAN, A. E. (1983) "Sex equality, sex difference and the Supreme Court." Yale Law Journal 92 (May): 913-968.

FRIEDMAN, L. M. (1971) A History of American Law. New York: Simon & Schuster.

FRUG, M. J. (1979) "Securing job equality for women: Labor market hostility to working mothers." Boston University Law Review 59 (January): 55-103.

GAMPEL, G. V. (1984) "The planter's wife revisited: Women, equity law, and the Chancery court in seventeenth-century Maryland," pp. 20-35 in B. J. Harris and J. K. McNamara (eds.) Women and the Structure of Society: Selected Research from the 5th Berkshire Conference on the History of Women. Durham, NC: Duke University Press.

GEE, P. W. (1983) "Ensuring police protection for battered women: The *Scott v. Hart* Suit." Signs 8 (Spring): 554-567.

GILLIGAN, C. (1982) In a Different Voice: Psychological Theory and Women's Development. Cambridge, MA: Harvard University Press.

GINSBURG, R. (1983) "The Burger Court's grapplings with sex discrimination," pp. 132-156 in V. Blasi (ed.) The Burger Court: The Counter-Revolution That Wasn't. New Haven, CT: Yale University Press.

GINSBURG, R. (1971) "Treatment of women by the law: Awakening consciousness in the law schools." Valpariso University Law Review 5: 480.

GINSBURG, R. (1976) "Women as full members of the club: An evolving American ideal." Human Rights 6 (Fall): 1-21.

GLEN, K. (1978) "Abortion in the Courts: A laywoman's historical guide to the new disaster area." Feminist Studies 4 (February): 1-26.

GLENDON, M. (1980) "Modern marriage law and its underlying assumption: The new marriage and the new property." Family Law Quarterly 13 (Winter): 441-460.

GORDON, L. (1983) Woman's Body, Woman's Right: A Social History of Birth Control (1976). New York: Penguin.

GOULD, M. (1979) "Sex, gender, and the need for legal clarity: The case of transsexualism." Valpariso University Law Review 13 (Spring): 423-450.

GOULD, M. (1983) "The paradox of teaching feminism and learning law." Legal Studies Forum 7, 2-3: 270-289.

GRIFFIN, S. (1977) "Rape: The all-American crime," pp. 313-332 in M. Vetterling-Braggin et al. (eds.) Feminism and Philosophy. Totowa, NJ: Rowman & Littlefield.

GRIFFIN, S. (1981) Pornography and Silence: Culture's Revenge Against Nature. New York: Harper & Row.

HARTMANN, H. (1981) "The family as the locus of gender, class, and political struggle: Example of housework." Signs 6 (Spring): 366-394.

HARTSOCK, N. (1980) "Difference and domination in the women's movement: The dialectic of theory and practice," pp. 157-188 in A. Swerdlow and H. Lessinger (eds.) Class, Race and Sex: The Dynamics of Control. Boston: G. K. Hall.

HAUSERMAN, N. (1983) "Sexual equality: An essay on the importance of recognizing difference." Legal Studies Forum 7, 2-3: 251-269.

HAYLER, B. (1979) "Review essay: Abortion." Signs 5 (Winter): 307-323.

HILL, A. (1979) "Protection of women workers and the courts: A legal case history." Feminist Studies 5 (Summer): 247-273.

HINDUS, M. S. and L. E. WITHEY (1982) "The law of husband and wife in nineteenth-century America," pp. 133-154 in D. K. Weisberg (ed.) Women and the Law, Vol. 2. Cambridge, MA: Schenkman.

HUCKLE, P. (1982) "The womb factor: Pregnancy policies and employment of women," pp. 144-161 in E. Boneparth (ed.) Women, Power and Policy. New York: Pergamon.

HUNTER, N. D. and N. D. POLIKOFF (1976) "Custody rights of lesbian mothers: Legal theory and litigation strategy." Buffalo Law Review 25 (Spring): 691-733.

JAGGAR, A. M. (1983) Feminist Politics and Human Nature. Totowa, NJ: Rowman & Allanheld.

JONES, A. (1980) Women Who Kill. New York: Holt, Rinehart & Winston.

JONES, A. (1985) Everyday Death: The Case of Bernadette Powell. New York: Holt, Rinehart & Winston.

KAHN, W. and J. GRUNE (1982) "Pay equity: Beyond equal work," pp. 75-89 in E. Boneparth (ed.) Women, Power and Policy. New York: Pergamon.

KANOWITZ, L. (1969) Woman and the Law: The Unfinished Revolution. Albuquerque: University of New Mexico Press.

KANOWITZ, L. (1980) "'Benign' sex discrimination: Its troubles and their cure." Hastings Law Journal 31: 1379-1429.

KANOWITZ, L. (1981) Equal Rights: The Male Stake. Albuquerque: University of New Mexico Press.

KANTER, R. M. (1978) "Reflections on women and the legal profession: A sociological perspective." Harvard Women's Law Journal 1: 1-17.

KAY, H. H. (1981) Sex Based Discrimination: Text, Cases and Materials. St. Paul, MN: West.

KERBER, L. K. (1977) "From the Declaration of Independence to the declaration of sentiments: The legal status of women in the early republic, 1776-1848." Human Rights 6 (Winter): 115-124.

KERBER, L. K. (1980) Women of the Republic: Intellect and Ideology in Revolutionary America. Chapel Hill: University of North Carolina Press.

KESSLER-HARRIS, A. (1982) Out to Work: A History of Wage-Earning Women in the United States. New York: Oxford University Press.

KING, K. and A. F. HOFFMAN (1984) "Comparable worth: A trade union issue." Women's Rights Law Reporter 8 (Winter): 95-107.

KLEIN, D. (1973) "The etiology of female crime: A review of the literature." Issues in Criminology 8 (Fall): 3-30.

LEDERER, L. [ed.] (1980) Take Back the Night: Women on Pornography. New York: William Morrow.

LEONARD, E. B. (1982) Women, Crime and Society: A Critique of Theoretical Criminology. New York: Longman.

LERMAN, L. G. (1984) "Mediation of wife abuse cases: The adverse impact of informal dispute resolution on women." Harvard Women's Law Journal 7 (Spring): 57-113.

LOH, W. (1981) "Q: What has reform of rape legislation wrought? A: Truth in criminal labeling." Journal of Social Issues 37, 4: 28-52.

LUKER, K. (1984) Abortion and the Politics of Motherhood. Berkeley: University of California Press.

MACKELLAR, J. (1975) Rape: The Bait and the Trap. New York: Crown Publishers.

MacKINNON, C. A. (1979) Sexual Harassment of Working Women: A Case of Sex Discrimination. New Haven, CT: Yale University Press.

MacKINNON, C. A. (1982a) "Towards feminist jurisprudence." Stanford Law Review, 34 (February): 703-737.

MacKINNON, C. A. (1982b) "Feminism, Marxism, method and the stae: An agenda for theory." Signs 7 (Spring): 515-544.

MacKINNON, C. A. (1983) "Feminism, Marxism, method, and the state: Toward feminist jurisprudence" Signs, 8 (Summer): 635-658.

MANN, P. (1984) "Pay equity in the courts: Myth v. reality." Women's rights Law Reporter 8 (Winter): 7-16.

MARKS, E. and I. DE COURTIVRON [eds.] (1980) New French Feminisms: An Anthology. Amherst: University of Massachusetts Press.

MARTIN, D. (1976) Battered Wives. San Francisco: Glide Publications.

MOHR, J. C. (1978) Abortion in America: The Origins and Evolution of National Policy. New York: Oxford University Press.

MORRIS, R. (1930) "Women's rights in early American law," pp. 126-200 in Studies in the History of American Law. New York: Columbia University Press.

O'NEILL, W. (1967) Divorce in Progressive America. New Haven, CT: Yale University Press.

OLSEN, F. (1983) "The family and the market: A study of ideology and legal reform." Harvard Law Review 96 (May): 1497-1578.

OLSEN, F. (1984a) "Statutory rape: A feminist critique of rights analysis." Texas Law Review 63 (November): 387-432.

OLSEN, F. (1984b) "The politics of family law." Law and Inequality, II (February): 1-20.

PETCHESKY, R. (1984) Abortion and Woman's Choice: The State, Sexuality and Reproductive Freedom. New York: Longman.

PETCHESKY, R. (1981) "Anti-abortion, anti-feminism, and the rise of the new right." Feminist Studies 7 (Summer): 206-246.

PETCHESKY, R. (1979) "Worker, reproductive hazards, and the politics of protection: An introduction." Feminist Studies 5 (Summer): 233-245.

PETERSON, S. R. (1977) "Coercion and rape: The state as a male protection racket," pp. 360-371 in M. Vetterling-Braggin et al. (eds.) Feminism and Philosophy. Totowa, NJ: Rowman & Littlefield.

PLECK, E. (1983) "Feminist responses to 'crimes against women,' 1868-1896." Signs 8 (Spring): 451-470.

POLAN, D. (1982) "Toward a theory of law and patriarchy," pp. 294-303 in D. Kairys (ed.) The Politics of Law: A Progressive Critique. New York: Pantheon.

POLIKOFF, N. (1982) "Why are mothers losing: A brief analysis of criteria used in child custody determinations." Women's Rights Law Reporter 7 (Spring): 235-243.

POLIKOFF, N. (1983) "Gender and child custody: Exploding the myth," in I. Diamond (ed.) Families, Politics and Public Policy: A Feminist Dialogue on Women and the State. New York: Longman.

POWERS, K. L. (1979) "Sex segregation and the ambivalent directions of sex discrimination laws." Wisconsin Law Review 1: 55-124.

RABKIN, P. A. (1980) Fathers to Daughters: The Legal Foundations of Female Emancipation. Westport, CT: Greenwood.

RAFTER, N. H. and E. Stanko [eds.] (1982) Women, Gender Roles, and Criminal Justice. Boston: Northeastern University Press.

REMICK, H. [ed.] (1984) Comparable Worth and Wage Discrimination. Philadelphia: Temple University Press.

RESKIN, B. F. and H. I. Hartmann [eds.] (1986) Women's Work, Men's Work: Sex Segregation on the Job. Washington, DC: National Academy Press.

RICH, A. (1979) On Lies, Secrets, and Silence: Selected Prose 1966-1978. New York: Norton.

RIFKIN, J. (1982) "Toward a theory of law and patriarchy," pp. 295-301 in P. Bierne and R. Quinney (eds.) Marxism and Law. New York: John Wiley.

RIFKIN, J. (1984) "Mediation from a feminist perspective: Promise and problems." Law and Inequality 2 (February): 21-32.

RIFKIN, J. and P. D'ERRICO (1983) "Response to Zillah Eisenstein." Legal Studies Forum 7, 2-3: 325-329.

RINGLER, S. M. (1980) "Sex equality: Not for women only." Catholic University Law Review 29: 427-460.

RUSSELL, D. (1974) The Politics of Rape: The Victim's Perspective. New York: Stein & Day.

RUSSELL, D. (1982) Rape in Marriage. New York: Macmillan.

SACHS, A. and J. H. WILSON (1978) Sexism and Law. New York: Free Press.

SALAAM, K. (1980) "Rape: A radical analysis from the African-American perspective," pp. 25-40 in Our Women Keep Our Skies from Falling. New Orleans: Nkombo.

SALMON, M. (1979) "Equality or submersion?: Feme covert status in early Pennsylvania," pp. 92-111 in C. R. Berkin and M. B. Norton (eds.) Women of America. Boston: Houghton Mifflin.

SALMON, M. (1980) "The property rights of women in early America: A comparative study." Ph.D dissertation, Bryn Mawr College.

SCALES, A. C. (1981) "Toward a feminist jurisprudence." Indiana Law Journal 56, 3: 375-444.

SCALES-TRENT, J. (1984) "Comparable worth: Is this a theory for black workers?" Women's Rights Law Reporter 8 (Winter): 51-58.

SCHECTER, S. (1982) Women and Male Violence: The Visions and Struggles of the Battered Women's Movement. Boston: South End.

SCHNEIDER, E. M. (1980) "Equal rights to trial for women: Sex bias in the law of self-defense." Harvard Civil Rights—Civil Liberties Law Review 15 (Winter): 623-647.

SCHNEIDER, E. M. and S. B. Jordan (1978) Representation of Women Who Defend Themselves in Response to Physical or Sexual Assault. New York: Center for Constitutional Rights.

SCHWENDINGER, J. and H. SCHWENDINGER (1983) Rape and Inequality. Newbury Park, CA: Sage.

SEARLE, E. (1982) "Merchet and women's property rights in medieval England," 45-68 in D. K. Weisberg (ed.) Women and the Law, Vol. 2. Cambridge, MA: Schenkman.

SHAFER, C. M. and M. FRYE (1977) "Rape and respect," pp. 333-346 in M. Vetterling-Braggin et al. (eds.) Feminism and Philosophy. Totowa, NJ: Rowman & Littlefield.

SHERRILL, R. (1983) "Death row on trial." New York Times Magazine, November 13, pp. 80-83.

SIMON, R. J. (1975) Women and Crime. Lexington, MA: D.C. Heath.

SMART, C. (1977) Women, Crime and Criminology: A Feminist Critique. London: Routledge & Kegan Paul.

SMART, C. (1984) The Ties That Bind: Law, Marriage and the Reproduction of Patriarchal Relations. London: Routledge & Kegan Paul.

SMART, C. and J. BROPHY (1985) "Locating law: A discussion of the place of law in feminist politics," pp. 1-20 in J. Brophy and C. Smart (eds.) Women in Law: Explorations in Law Family and Sexuality. London: Routledge & Kegan Paul.

SMART, C. and B. SMART [eds.] (1978) Women, Sexuality and Social Control. London: Routledge & Kegan Paul.

SNITOW, A., C. STANSELL, and S. THOMPSON [eds.] (1983) Powers of Desire: The Politics of Sexuality. New York: Monthly Review Press.

SPETH, L. E. (1982) "The Married Women's Property Acts, 1839-1965: Reform, reaction, or revolution?" pp. 69-92 in D. K. Weisberg (ed.) Women and the Law, Vol. 2. Cambridge, MA: Schenkman.

STALLARD, K., B. EHRENREICH, and H. SKLAR (1983) Poverty in the American Dream: Women and Children First. Boston: South End.

STANKO, E. A. (1985) Intimate Intrusions: Women's Experience of Male Violence. Boston Routledge & Kegan Paul.

TAUB, N. and E. SCHNEIDER (1982) "Perspectives on women's subordination and the role of law," pp. 117-139 in D. Kairys (ed.) The Politics of Law. New York: Pantheon.

TAUB, N. (1980) "Book review of Sexual Harassment of Working Women: A Case of Sex Discrimination, by Catherine A. MacKinnon." Columbia Law Review 80 (December): 1686-1695.

THURMAN, K. (1966) "The Married Women's Property Acts." LL.M dissertation, University of Wisconsin Law School.

TONG, R. (1984) Women, Sex and the Law. Totowa, NJ: Rowman & Allenheld.

TREIMAN D. and H. HARTMANN (1981) Women, Work, and Wages: Equal Pay for Jobs of Equal Value. Washington, DC: National Academy Press.

U.S. Bureau of the Census (1985) Statistical Abstracts of the U.S. Washington, D.C.: Government Printing Office.

VETTERLING-BRAGGIN, M., F. A. ELLISTON, and J. ENGLISH [eds.] (1977) Feminism and Philosophy. Totowa, NJ: Rowman & Littlefield.

VOGEL, L. (1983) Marxism and the Oppression of Women: Toward a Unitary Theory. New Brunswick, NJ: Rutgers University Press.

WALKOWITZ, J. R. (1982) "Jack the Ripper and the myth of male violence." Feminist Studies 8 (Fall): 543-574.

WARREN, B. and C. BOONE (1984) "*AFSCME v. State of Washington*: Title VII as a winning strategy to end wage discrimination." Women's Rights Law Reporter 8 (Winter): 17-49.

WEINER, R. D. (1983) "Shifting the communication burden: A meaningful consent standard in rape." Harvard Women's Law Journal 6: 143-161.

WEISBERG, D. K. (1982c) "Under great temptations here: Women and divorce law in Puritan Massachusetts," pp. 117-131 in D. K. Weisberg (ed.) Women and the Law, Vol. 2. Cambridge, MA: Schenkman.

WEISBERG, D. K. [ed.] (1982a) Women and the Law: The Social Historical Perspective, Vol. 1: Women and the Criminal Law. Cambridge, MA: Schenkman.

WEISBERG, D. K. [ed.] (1982b) Women and the Law: The Social Historical Perspective, Vol. 2: Property, Family and the Legal Profession. Cambridge, MA: Schenkman.

WEITZMAN, L. J. (1985) The Divorce Revolution: The Unexpected Social and Economic Consequences for Women and Children in America. New York: Free Press.

WIGMORE, J. H. (1934) Evidence. Boston: Little, Brown.

WILLIAMS, W. (1982) "The equality crisis: Some reflections on culture, courts, and feminism." Women's Rights Law Reporter 7 (Spring): 175-200.

WILSON, J. H. (1976) "The illusion of change: Women and the American Revolution," pp. 383-445 in A. F. Young (ed.) The American Revolution: Explorations in the History of American Radicalism. De Kalb: Northern Illinois University Press.

WISHIK, H. R. (1985) "To question everything: The inquiries of feminist jurisprudence." Berkeley Women's Law Journal 1 (Fall): 64-77.

WRIGHT, M. J. (1979) "Reproductive hazards and 'protective' discrimination." Feminist Studies 5 (Summer): 302-309.

ZIMMER, L. (1983) "The legal problem of implementing Title VII in the prisons." Legal Studies Forum 7, 2-3: 199-221.

18 Gender and Political Life: New Directions in Political Science

MARTHA ACKELSBERG
IRENE DIAMOND

A feminist tradition of thinking about the situation of women can be traced to the birth of the Englightenment in early modern Europe. The worldwide flowering of feminist theory, however, or what Elaine Marks and Estelle de Courtivron (1980) term "feminisms," is a distinctly late-twentieth-century phenomenon. It is only with the rebirth of a women's movement in the midst of the cultural and political tumult of the 1960s that feminisms emerged to challenge accepted canons and practices in virtually every sphere of life.

In recent decades, the dynamics of change in advanced capitalist nations have shifted to the cultural and psychic explosions produced by the high-speed communicative forms specific to late capitalism. Activist women in the Western world gained access to words and image-making in a way they had not during earlier women's movements. Consequently, these women were able to challenge knowledge-making and truth-making on a scale unprecedented in the history of rebellious movements. In the United States texts that ranged from Betty Friedan's best-seller *The Feminine Mystique*, to underground pamphlets such as "The Politics of Housework" and "The Myth of the Vaginal Orgasm," to government-funded reports on the status of women became crucial mechanisms for spreading the fires of creativity and self-awareness that both arose from, and in turn ignited, personal relationships and grass-roots political organizing.

In the midst of this whirlwind of movement, women who had their primary base in the academy struggled to create women's studies. They argued that what had counted as knowledge was based solely on male experience and that the resultant distortions and inaccuracies could be rectified only if women's voices were attended to.

What we wish to do here is to ask what has happened to our understandings of what we take politics to be, and of how we go about studying it, after more than a decade of the women's movement and the new scholarship on women. Since the field is a broad one, and we cannot hope to explore all of it—even in outline—in one brief chapter, we limit ourselves here to discussing some prominent trends and debates within the study of U.S. politics and political theory. We expect that the broader methodological questions we raise, however, will be relevant to political scientists (and social scientists) in a range of subfields.

In political science, as in virtually all other disciplines that have been subjected to sustained exploration and critique by feminist scholars, research and rethinking has taken three major forms: (1) critiques of conventional (male) views of women, as reflected both in the canon (classic texts of political philosophy) and in empirical studies of political participation and citizenship; (2) attempts to fill in the gaps and correct the misconceptions by "reading women in" to the existing bodies of literature and, more recently (3) exploring how a focus on women's experience may force us to transform the ways we theorize about politics, challenging conventional paradigms and understandings. While we will discuss these three sequentially, we do not mean to imply that the pattern of development has been a strictly linear one. In fact, research and writing continues on all three of these levels today.

CRITIQUES OF CANON AND CONVENTION

Empirical studies. Several different reviews of the literature on political behavior that appeared in the early 1970s pointed to the ways in which male behavior and male opinions came to define what was considered political. Building on populist and neo-marxist critiques of the pluralist perspective that dominated political science in the United States, feminist scholars such as Susan Bourque and Jean Grossholtz (1974), Jean Elshtain (1974), Lynn Iglitzin (1974), and Jane Jacquette (1974) argued that the equation of war/power issues with "politics" reduced conventionally female concerns to marginal status. Consequently, studies that claimed to find higher levels of political interest and efficacy among males than among females were biased at their core. These early studies raised many questions about the validity of earlier data regarding sex differences, demonstrating that these data were often based on unexamined stereotypes and sloppy research. Perhaps most drastically, they called into question accepted definitions of what constituted political life and analysis altogether.

Specifically, drawing on the work of feminist scholars in a variety of disciplines, they pointed to the power of conventional sex role expectations to constrain the possibilities of women's participation. The most widely explored example of the workings of conventional expectations was the so-called public-private split—the division of social life into a private/domestic domain (the purview of women), considered to be *outside* of "politics" properly understood, and a public/political domain (the purview of men/citizens), perceived as the appropriate focus of political/social analysis. Feminist scholars insisted that what went on in the private sphere was also political, and that political scientists ought to broaden their scope of study to incorporate a range of behaviors and concerns that has traditionally been relegated to that "private" (read: female) arena. Further, some began to point out the political nature of making the split at all.

With hindsight we can see that these early critiques reflected (and defined) the first stages of a debate about the significance of "difference" in the women's movement and in the academy. They pointed to the ways in which societal beliefs about differences between men and women were "naturalized" by political scientists—conceived as biological in origin—and (therefore) relegated to a place completely outside the realm of political analysis. Feminist critics insisted, instead, that many of the most salient differences between men and women were social constructs rather than natural phenomena, and that one of the tasks of a nonsexist political science would be to analyze their sources and their implications for politics. Aware of the political uses of difference (for example, as in the case of "separate but equal," which had been demonstrated not to be equal at all), feminists insisted that all claims of "difference" had to be justified, their political relevance demonstrated: that sex differences between women and men ought to be considered irrelevant to politics until proven otherwise (on the more general discussion of differences in the feminist movement and women's studies in this period see, for example, Eisenstein, 1980).

The political-philosophical canon. Feminist examinations of the classic texts of Western political philosophy revealed similar blindspots and misconceptions. The writings of Susan Moller Okin (1979), Arlene Saxonhouse (1984), Jean Elshtain (1974, 1981), Elizabeth Spelman (1982b, 1983) for example, explored the ways in which women were treated (or ignored) in the classic works of political theory and, ultimately, the sexist assumptions about women's nature that were central to the male canon.

Some examined the Greek classics, Plato and Aristotle, the "fathers" of political philosophy. Plato is often represented as the first feminist, the theorist who insisted (in Book V of *The Republic*) that differences between men and women were not relevant to their political capacities. But how were we to understand Plato's views on women in the context of the larger corpus of his work? Aristotle criticized Plato for, among other things, his egalitarian treatment of women and for the essentially nonpolitical nature of the polis. But the intense participation that Aristotle demanded for "citizens" excluded women; in fact, it depended on the existence of a group (including women, slaves, and many free-born men involved in "menial" occupations) that he considered "necessary conditions" but not integral parts of the political community. Aristotle inscribed into his political theory (and into the notion of political life that has prevailed in the West until today) a distinction between "public" and "private" spheres, defining the first as masculine, and the latter as feminine (and lesser). Early feminist critiques focused on this distinction and on its implications for contemporary political behavior and analysis.

Others turned to the social contract theorists, Hobbes, Locke, and Rousseau (see, for example, Okin, 1979; Flax, 1980; Pateman, 1975; Brennan and Pateman, 1979). What are we to make, they asked, of the fact that the state of nature—that essential birth-state of the democratic political community—is an all-male world? Are we to assume that these philosophers wrote in the "generic male" and that, therefore, women were present at the creation of political communities? Or are we to take their use (and the use of more recent contract theorists, such as John Rawls) of the term "man" to mean "male heads of households"—thus calling into question the otherwise egalitarian prepolitical state they described (see, for example, Okin, 1985)? What difference might our answers make to our understandings of what liberal social contract doctrines mean? What are the implications for our political communities? Similarly, how are we to read Rousseau? Do we take him to be the political egalitarian he appears to be in *The Social Contract*? or do we read that document in the light of *Emile*, in which he too seems to accept without question the separation of spheres and the relegation of women to an apolitical private domain? These and similar questions came to the fore as scholars began reading the classic texts with feminist eyes. Many remain unresolved; but they pose fundamental challenges to prefeminist readings of those texts and continue to suggest new directions for research and interpretation.

Both at the empirical and at the philosophical levels, then, feminist critics challenged the form and the definition of the division between public and private spheres. The new interpretations they offered derived in part from a recognition that the distinction relegated women, as a group, to a nonpolitical realm and, in part, from the feminist movement's insistence that "the personal is the political." While the emphases and approaches differed, these early feminist critiques seemed to agree on three fundamental premises: (1) The public and the private domains are integrally related; (2) the distinction between public and private is itself a political one, deserving of substantial explorations and analysis; (3) and the particular construction of each of the domains is political rather than "natural."

READING WOMEN INTO EXISTING LITERATURE

Spurred by the feminist critique of the conventional questions and modes of analysis in political science, particularly the invisibility within them of women as political actors, many feminist scholars attempted to adapt those analyses and models to incorporate what was termed "women's experience." While we shall argue in the next section that this attempt has in turn led to challenges to the paradigms themselves, here we explore some of the ways in which feminist scholarship has expanded the range of knowledge encompassed by those paradigms, by asking new questions and generating new data. We will consider three major trends: one that explores women as political actors; a second, which addresses women as objects of policy; and a third, which examines women's relationship to the welfare state.

Women as political actors. In a discipline that had largely defined politics as the study of voting, elections, and office-holding, it is not surprising that one starting place for critical reconstruction was in the study of women's electoral processes. These initial studies used traditional methods of behavioral analysis to document women's participation in the electorate, the parties, and public office. A key question that emerged centered on the striking difference between women's participation at the citizen level and their participation at the leadership level. Whereas the differences between women's and men's participation in such activities as voting and grass-roots campaign activities were relatively slight, the difference between women's and men's participation in elective offices was enormous—though greater for whites than blacks. In 1978, for example, when women held between 5% and 7% of all elective offices, black women held 12% of the offices held by blacks (Prestage, 1980: 243).

What accounted for the disparity between the two levels of activity? Why was it that for women, participation in citizen activities at the community level did not translate into public office? A variety of different explanations were offered, such as traditional sex role training, lack of professional credentials, prejudice on the part of party leaders, voter hostility, and difficulties in raising campaign funds. Though no one explanatory model emerged, the literature pointed to the complex ways in which women's political ambition was shaped, on the one hand, by the domestic division of labor and, on the other hand, by the gendered political opportunity structure (for overviews of this data see Amundsen, 1977; Baxter and Lansing, 1981; for more specific studies, Diamond, 1977; Clark et al., 1983, and Flammang, 1984).

In this first phase of critical reconstruction, recruitment was defined broadly and scholars tended to examine the recruitment process as a whole. More recently, as scholars have utilized more sophisticated methodological techniques, they have tended to focus their research on particular facets of the recruitment process, most especially the political opportunity structure. This phase of research has confirmed the earlier findings that male-dominated political parties are problematic for potential women candidates at the same time that it has refuted the idea that voter biases are a significant barrier (Flammang, 1984; Carroll, 1985). Interestingly, this newer research has also cast doubt on the widely held belief that women candidates have unusual difficulty raising funds. In 1980, for example, women congressional candidates had, on the average, smaller campaign chests than male candidates, but this difference was attributable to the fact that fewer of the women candidates were incumbents. While this research indicated that, among actual candidates, female nonincumbents were not disadvantaged in comparison with male nonincumbents, it also suggested that the belief that female candidates have difficulty raising funds still has an impact on the recruitment process (Uhlaner and Schlozman, 1986).

Research on women's participation in electoral politics has not been confined exclusively to barriers to participation, for the new interest in gender as a category of analysis coincided with a rapid increase in the number of women serving in state and local offices. Women are literally transforming the subject of study and, as a consequence, scholars have pursued a variety of new questions regarding the impact of women's presence. Policy agendas and coalition-formation have been considerably changed by women's activities, but there is considerable debate in the literature about whether women office-holders per se have had a distinctive impact on policy outcomes (Fowlkes, 1984). Some argue that party is still more important than gender, most especially when the issue is legislative voting. Others claim that women politicians and activists exhibit a politics of connectedness that is rooted in the gender division of labor (Flammang, 1984). Studies of local activism in black and white ethnic communities, for example, have suggested that women are often leaders in this context and their ability to work effectively depends on their rootedness, as women, in networks based on kinship, friendship or church membership (Gilkes, 1980, 1983; Susser, 1986). Since claims for a gendered politics of connectedness have been made in the context of local-level activities, it remains to be seen whether they hold at the national level, where the competitiveness of the recruitment process favors candidates who conform to male career patterns and women's movement activism is more likely to adhere to traditional interest-group norms.

This attention to gender in the study of electoral processes has not been confined to the study of political elites and activists. The question of a women's vote, or bloc vote, has gained considerable attention in recent years, most especially since the term "gender gap" first achieved popularity in the aftermath of the 1980 election. Indeed, with the emergence of the debate about the origins and meaning of the gender gap, scholars who heretofore had displayed little interest in studying electoral behavior became interested in analyzing and theorizing about this allegedly new political phenomenon.

The debate took off when 1980 exit polls indicated that only 47% of female voters supported Ronald Reagan, compared to 56% of men. This 9% spread in the voting choices of women and men was widely reported in the media. The difference was greatest for whites at the two extremes of the SES scale, but less among black voters, who are, in general, much more likely to vote Democratic (Miller, 1987).

The gap seemed to signal the arrival of the women's bloc vote that suffrage leaders had promised. Women's movement leaders, journalists, advisors to the major parties, and scholars all offered interpretations. Some argued that the gap was attributable to women's greater concern with the ERA, others for the importance of women's historic opposition to the use of military force, and still others pointed to women's greater dependence on social welfare spending that would be threatened by a Reagan presidency. Some argued that it was a fleeting phenomenon that was not really new, while others argued that it was a signal of a profound historical shift in consciousness (Piven, 1985). The differing interpretations have already spawned research on the politics of interpreting the gender gap (Mansbridge, 1985; Mueller, 1987), a line of research that is likely to contribute to additional political and methodological debate.

The best systematic research indicates that traditional women's rights issues such as the ERA and abortion are not particularly important in contributing to the gap (Mansbridge, 1985; Mueller, 1987), but this research does not address the question of how the organized women's movement may have sparked the gender consciousness that informs opinion formation and voter choice. The differences between women's and men's voting patterns are not nearly as great as those between blacks and whites, for example, and some analysts note that opinion differences between employed women and housewives are often greater than differences between women and men (Poole and Ziegler, 1985). Nonetheless, the fact that women have now become a numerical voting majority—in an era when polling has transformed the relationship between public opinion and democratic representation—suggests that attention to gender as a category of analysis in electoral studies is likely to form one basis of a new and growing body of research (e.g. Klein, 1984).

Women as objects of policy. An emerging and still-growing arena of concern for feminist political scientists has been that of public policy analysis. In recent years, the study of public policy has become a more legitimate arena of political inquiry, creating a space for scholars who want to examine how institutions handle the policy issues raised by the women's movement. This set of concerns has generated a wealth of descriptive research, including, for example, Boles (1979) on the struggle for the ERA; the Adams and Winston (1980) comparative volume on public policies that have an impact on working mothers; Stiehm (1981) on the integration of women into the U.S. Air Force Academy; the broadly focused edited volume of Boneparth (1982) on domestic and foreign policy; and Gelb and Palley's (1982) volume comparing the success of the U.S. women's movement in different policy arenas. For the most part, this body of research utilized traditional interest-group and policy analysis models to examine how institutions were responding to the range of policy concerns generated by contemporary feminist activism. Analysis was typically focused on discrete issues and generally assumed that the goals of the women's movement could be integrated into prevailing institutional structures.

Other recent work, such as Diamond's (1983) edited volume on public policies with respect to families and Petchesky's (1984) volume on abortion, moves away from traditional interest group models and draws more heavily on developments in feminist theory. Whereas the first phase of policy research often used the concepts of role equity and role change to explain policy debates, this newer body of work more typically utilizes structural models that presume the existence of some degree of gender, race, and class conflict. This newer phase of research is marked by its effort to link the study of contemporary public policy with historical analysis and the moral and philosophical concerns of traditional political theory. Through its insistence on investing public policy analysis with considerations of human nature, political transformation, and moral vision, this work lays much of the groundwork for feminist attempts to reconceptualize the possibilities of political life.

Women and the state. In recent years, social scientists from a variety of disciplines have turned attention to "the state." Rejecting both the liberal view of the state as merely the context for the play of (autonomous independent) interest groups, and the classical marxist view of the state as the "executive committee of the dominant class," theorists such as Theda Skocpol (1985) have argued that states must be seen as at least somewhat independent of the demands and interests of dominant social groups, and considered both as "organizations through which official collectivities may pursue distinctive goals" and as "configurations of organization and action that influence the meanings and methods of politics for all groups in society" (1985: 28). While the majority of social scientists exploring these new perspectives are not animated by specifically feminist questions, many feminists have been sparked by them to examine the role of the welfare state in defining and constraining women's lives. Feminist scholars have, in fact, gone beyond the formulations of many of these social scientists to explore not only the intervention of the state in the economy but also the state's role in organizing family life and sexuality.

The interrelationship among economy, family, and the state is clearly brought to the fore in contemporary feminist explorations of what has come to be known as the "feminization of poverty" (or the immiseration of women). Largely because of the sex segregation of the labor force, the subordination of women within the waged sector, sex role expectations that assign women the primary responsibility for child rearing, and divorce law reforms that have not taken adequate account of the subordinate status of women in the labor market, women are much more likely to be poor than are men. Thus those women and children living in female-headed households have a much greater chance of living in poverty than those living in male-headed households especially if they also belong to an ethnic or racial minority.

The "feminization of poverty," a term originally coined by sociologist Diana Pearce (1979), has been taken up by a variety of scholars and activists (see, for example, papers from the conference "Women and Structural Transformation," 1983; Piven and Ehrenreich, 1984; Sidel, 1986; Withorn and Lefkowitz, 1986). These studies point to the ways in which the uncontrolled functioning of the U.S. welfare state seems necessarily to generate high levels of poverty among women and have provided the grounds for claims that women ought to press the state to intervene actively in the economy on behalf of women and children (see also Freeman, 1980; Markusen, 1980; Eisenstein, 1984; Kamerman, 1984; Smith, 1984).

The debate here—which focuses on the question of whether the state can be used to advance women's interests, or whether it is experienced by women as yet another form of social control—is complex. For example, Piven and Cloward's *Regulating the Poor* (1976) has become a classic statement of the role of the welfare state in a system of social control. More recently, Piven has argued that the welfare state is an important arena for the empowerment of women. Drawing on the work of such "difference theorists" as Gilligan (1982) and Ruddick (1980), she argues for a "moral economy of domesticity" that is being transformed by the changes women are experiencing in the labor market and family life.

The erosion of the traditional family and women's deteriorating position in the labor market have concentrated women in the institutions of the welfare state, both as beneficiaries and as service providers. Nelson (1984) notes that women made up 65% of Medicare recipients, 62% of Social Security recipients, 81% of AFDC recipients, between 57% and 73% of food stamp recipients, and 70% to 80% of those receiving housing subsidies. On the other side, nearly a third of all employed women work in human services. Between 1960 and 1980 the growth of the social welfare economy accounted for 58% of the new jobs for black women and 39% of job gains for white women (Erie, Rein and Wiget, 1983: 103). Women of color are overrepresented among both recipients and providers of services and so could be expected to be at the forefront of efforts to resist cuts.

For Piven, the gender gap can be taken as evidence that women are demanding that their formerly private values be extended to the state (1985). In this view, the impoverishment of women (rooted in the restructuring of the economy and in transformations of traditional family structures) offers opportunities for consciousness-raising among women and for the development of coalitions among middle- and working-class women, labor unions, and members of poor and minority groups that can pressure the state for more comprehensive social programs (Piven, 1985).

In a somewhat similar vein, Zillah Eisenstein's recent writings have focused more directly on the (capitalist welfare) state. According to Eisenstein, the state is an active mediator between capitalism and patriarchy, which are characterized both as actors and as structures that constrain the actions of the state. These categories permit her to stress the ways in which the welfare state shapes women's position in the family and the economy. In her formulation, women are a *sex class* oppressed by both capitalism and patriarchy, but they have the potential to reach a feminist consciousness by experiencing the contradictions between capitalism and patriarchy in their experiences as working mothers. These women can then use the state (in pushing for the expansion of welfare state services) to challenge both capitalism and patriarchy (Eisenstein, 1984).

On the whole, arguments that the welfare state provides an arena for the empowerment of women have been made by scholars who have taken up the defense of the welfare state against dismemberment by Reaganomics and have placed a priority on electoral political organizing in the interests of women. As we have seen, these scholars have called attention to the ways in which state programs provide women with crucial economic supports. Another group of scholars we might term "state skeptics" have been less sanguine about state involvement in women's lives. These scholars' concerns have generally been animated less by tactical questions brought to the fore by contemporary political conflicts than by concern for the bureaucratic and disciplinary techniques that have accompanied state involvement and, specifically, their impact on women's family and sexual lives.

Wendy Saravasy (1986), for example, criticizes both the economism of the new feminist defense of the welfare state and its tendency to obscure class and racial differences among women. Instead of finding fault with earlier genera-tions of women activists who advocated protective legislation, Saravasy (1986) argues for the radical potential of a concept that created a language to talk about the special needs of women. Her criticism of the reformers, in contrast to those of Hartmann (1979) and Boris and Bardaglio (1983), for example, is that reformers did not take the protective legislation approach far enough. Saravasy's work is indicative of growing attention among scholars both to women as active participants in the historical processes that created the state and to the divisions among women regarding the appropriate goals of state programs.

Other state skeptics, such as Balbus (1982), Elshtain (1982, 1983, 1984), Ferguson (1984), and Diamond (1985) emphasize the bureaucratic and disciplinary techniques through which the contemporary welfare state organizes family life and sexuality. For Balbus (1982), the growth of the bureaucratic welfare state cannot be attributed merely to the reproduction requirements of a specifically capitalist mode of production. He argues that "a more complete comprehension of this growth demands an appreciation of the transformations in the form of childrearing that both underlie and are reinforced by it" (1982: 332). He speculates that more indulgent child rearing has intensified the child's early identification with an increasingly nurturant mother at the same time that suburbanization has increased the geographical and emotional distance between home and work place, and intensified the tendency toward father-absent families. "Into this breach steps the state. . . . This is the psychological transformation that underlies the transformation of the individual from citizen of the limited state to client of the unlimited state; therapeutic justice replaces the rule of law and the authority of the social worker" (1982: 332, 333).

Elshtain (1982, 1983, 1984) cautions feminists to attend to the fact that the bureaucratic techniques of the public world that standardize culture, ideas, and ideals are particularly deleterious to women. Rather than turning to the state for protection, she suggests women need to imbue the public arena with the "private" values of nurturing, caring, and love (1982, 1983; see also Ruddick, 1980). In her more recent writings (1984, for example) she draws on Michel Foucault's concept of disciplinary power to bolster her antistatist perspective. She contends that Foucault's analysis argues against the belief that improved social services necessarily widen people's options.

Foucault's insight that disciplinary power operates through mechanisms of enticement, regulation, surveillance, and classification offers a methodology that is increasingly used by feminist scholars exploring alternatives to neo-marxist interpretations of the state. For example, Diamond (1985; see also Diamond and Quinby, 1984; Ross and Rapp, 1981) argues that Foucault's approach to sexual discourse is particularly helpful in understanding the growth of the state's role in the organization of sexuality. She draws on his methodology to examine the problematic development of family planning programs and raises serious questions about whether programs advanced "on behalf of" women necessarily increase women's freedom.

Though Foucault's analysis lends itself to skepticism regarding reliance on the state, scholars who employ Foucault are not necessarily thoroughly antistate. Thus while Elshtain tends to make no distinction among state reform efforts, Ferguson (1984) calls for the evaluation of reforms on the basis of their ability to challenge the language and practice of bureaucratic capitalism. Indeed, what is particularly interesting to many feminists about Foucault's approaches to political organizing is his emphasis on local struggles.

TRANSFORMING THE PARADIGMS

In political science, as in a variety of other disciplines, feminist scholars have increasingly discovered that attempts to read women into the prevailing paradigms and modes of thinking ultimately call those paradigms themselves into question. While we cannot discuss here all the ways in which feminist scholarship calls on us to reconceptualize central categories of the discipline, in this final section we address how a focus on women's experience transforms the ways we think about politics by exploring two broad areas of the feminist reconstruction of political science: (1) attention to the theorizing of "difference" (both differences between men and women and differences among women); and (2) an examination of women's activism and participation, and its implications for the conceptualization of politics and democratic theory. As should be obvious from the previous discussion, we believe that feminist rethinking of the state (and in particular further explorations of the role of the state in organizing family, economy, and sexuality) also has the potential for major theoretical reconceptualization. It is our sense at this time, however, that—perhaps because of the close connections between these issues and public policy concerns—the reorganization of central categories of analysis in this arena has not yet taken place.

Theorizing "difference." The question of difference—differences between women and men and differences among women, based on culture, ethnicity, age, or class—frames much of the contemporary feminist debate and reconceptualization. We discuss here two arenas in which these issues have been raised: attention to issues of oppression and resistance, and the attempt to conceptualize a "feminist standpoint" or to "theorize difference." This discussion of difference then provides a backdrop to the exploration of feminist reconceptualizations of citizenship in the section to follow.

One important criticism of mainstream/pluralist views (from the perspectives of both black studies and women's studies) is that pluralist paradigms ignore or deny difference and diversity—or, at best, misrepresent their significance. To put it another way, the pluralist perspective fails to take seriously either people's own perceptions of their experiences or the larger context and meaning of oppression. These failures have a number of dimensions: (1) They pay insufficient attention to the nature and consequences of structured relationships of domination and subordination; (2) they lead observers to understand the situation of members of oppressed groups (if they notice them at all) almost entirely in function of the oppression; (3) they take differences in participation or power as necessary consequences of "cultural" or "gender" differences; and (4) they ignore the need that feminist and black studies scholars and activists have noted for members of oppressed groups to "find their own voice."

To fail to examine relationships of domination and subordination in society is to ignore the ways in which such structures affect people's sense of themselves. Feminist and black studies activists and scholars have spoken of the need for members of oppressed groups to find their voice, to articulate and act on their own understanding of their experiences (this is also, in somewhat simplified form, the essence of what we take much French feminist criticism to argue). Significantly, both for white women and for people of color, community seems crucial to the development of such an alternative perspective. Methodologically, then, getting a sense of what differential experience is, or has been, for different women (or members of different groups) in a polity may mean looking much more carefully at the (communal) context of people's lives rather than treating citizens as isolated individuals who come to "political" life with no prior ties.

The complexity implied by these perspectives becomes particularly actue when we turn to recent feminist attempts to theorize a "feminist standpoint" (a term introduced by Hartsock, 1983). The notion of a feminist standpoint has been developed in a variety of ways by political theorists and philosophers working out of (or in reaction to) the socialist feminist tradition who have tried to establish a material base for women's subordination. Their efforts are related, in varying ways, to the attempts of others to explore the nature, origins, and implications of a "woman's consciousness."

One could argue, in fact, that recent empirical findings of a gender gap between men and women have only heightened long-standing debate among feminists and others about the nature of those differences. Sociobiologists (for example, E. O. Wilson, Lionel Tiger, Joseph Sheper) have claimed that the source of these differences is genetic: Hormonal differences between men and women account for aggressive behavior in men and nurturant-conservative behavior in women. Some feminist "difference theorists"—most prominently Sara Ruddick (1980), Carol Gilligan (1982), Jane Flax (1980, 1983), Jean Elshtain (1982, 1983, 1984), Dorothy Dinnerstein (1976), Nancy Chodorow (1978), and Isaac Balbus (1982)—draw on object relations theory to locate the source of women's (political) consciousness in prevailing patterns of mothering; the fact that women are the primary caregivers to young people of both sexes creates a population of women who are attuned to caring, empathy, and nurturance, and a population of men whose primary concerns are separation and individuation. Others focus less on mothering and early childhood relations and more on the patterns of mutual support many women have developed through social and political struggle (Flammang, 1984; Ferguson, 1984; Dietz, 1985; Ackelsberg, 1983a, 1984) or on the relationships of domination and subordination that define and constrain the expression of women's personal and political selves (MacKinnon, 1982; Hartsock, 1983; Eisenstein, 1984).

These differing positions have important consequences for our conceptualization of political life. Most obviously, the sociobiological perspective perpetuates the "naturalizing" of sexual differences that earlier feminist criticism has taken to task, insisting that differences in attitudes and behaviors between men and women are rooted in biology and have, therefore, no independent political meaning (a perspective that might lead us to interpret women's apparent pacifism, for example, as merely an expression of a biological imperative, not to be taken seriously as a political perspective).

The consequences of the perspectives of the "difference theorists" are somewhat different. Some (for example, Balbus, 1982; Chodorow, 1978; Dinnerstein, 1976; Flax, 1980, 1983; and Gilligan, 1982) seem to suggest that, because of our patterns of mothering, men and women grow up as complements to one another rather than as complete beings in themselves. Consequently, neither is fully capable of functioning both as a responsible citizen (in the public sphere) and as a caring/nuturing parent/friend (in the private sphere). What is necessary, in this view, is a change in our family arrangements and child-rearing patterns so that both men and women "mother" and, consequently, boys and girls will learn to be both independent and nurturing, autonomous and caring. On the other hand, Jean Elshtain (1982, 1983, 1984) and Sara Ruddick (1980) argue that "maternal thinking" (described primarily as a consequence of women's experience as daughters and as mothers but also as a mode of thought, open to men and female nonmothers, that is distinguished by the way in which it connects reflections, emotion, and reason) is not only different from the prevailing instrumental-rationalist forms of political discourse but superior to them. In a sense, they reinforce an aspect of the traditional distinction between public and private spheres, but insist that modes of behavior from the private sphere are superior to those of the public. What is called for, according to this view, is a concerted effort to bring the nurturant perspectives of women into the public arena and to make politics more like "women's work" of love and care.

Others are wary of the attempt to retain the public-private dichotomy, even in its new guise. Some argue against giving priority to women's experience of nurturing, insisting that existing patterns of socialization create both men and women whose experience is "partial, incomplete, and distorted" (Ferguson, 1984: 170-171), and that familial relationships do not provide appropriate models for political behavior (Dietz, 1985; Ackelsberg, 1983a). These theorists suggest that we focus analyses on the kinds of collective action in which women have engaged and explore its implications for political life. Still others focus their analytical efforts on women's experience of subordination and the attempt to define the components of that subordination (see especially Hartsock, 1983; MacKinnon, 1982). These approaches are not mutually exclusive, of course. Nancy Hartsock's work, for example, draws heavily on the object relations theorists to define the nature and content of women's experience, but combines that approach with a variant of marxism in an attempt to describe a "liberating standpoint" that can be extrapolated from women's subordinate position.

Yet despite (or perhaps because of) the effort to take gender differences seriously—in the variety of ways in which they do so—many of these feminist theorists and activists are becoming aware that one price of these theoretical achievements may be obfuscation, or the virtual erasure, of the diversity of women's experience. Black women and working-class women from a variety of ethnic-cultural backgrounds have frequently expressed a wariness of both the feminist movement and of women's studies, which derived at least in part from concerns about the exclusive tendencies of a feminism evolved almost entirely from the experience of white, middle-class, Christian women. In recent years that debate has been taken up in print (see, for example, Spelman, 1981; Simons, 1979; Moraga and Anzaldua, 1981; Spelman and Lugones, 1983; Lewis, 1977; Joseph and Lewis, 1981; Hulls et al., 1982; Dill, 1983; Bulkin et al., 1984; Ackelsberg, 1983b), and many more white feminists have come to recognize the need to explore differences among women as seriously as they have taken differences between women and men. This literature not only challenges all attempts to define universalities in female experience but also suggests that the process of acknowledging diversity can be a source of creative and democratic resistance to existing structures of domination (Sawicki, 1986; Young, 1985; Lorde, 1984; Hooks, 1984).

Women's activism and democratic theory. New research on women's community activism has indicated that, both historically and in the contemporary period, women have been invölved in resistance movements in neighborhoods and communities, thus challenging the conventional notion of women as passive members of the polity, living their lives in the nonpolitical "private" sphere of the home (see, for example, Susser, 1982, 1986; Cockburn, 1977; Bookman and Morgen, 1986; Cameron, 1985). The historian Temma Kaplan (1982), who studied women's participation in popular uprisings in Spain in the early part of this century, argued that women developed a specifically female consciousness, which emerged out of their roles as caretakers of communities and households. She claimed that they developed a special sensitivity to quality of life issues, which accounted for their engagement in collective action.

Drawing on this work, others have argued that the split between the public and the private, community and work place—which has been accepted by pluralists, many neo-marxist critiques of pluralism, and even by feminist "difference theorists"—is undermined once we pay attention to the pattern of women's community activities. Women, especially poor women and women of color, cross those supposed boundaries continually in the process of carrying out their domestic duties. They are the ones who negotiate with landlords, markets, and agents of the state such as health care providers and welfare officers (Cockburn, 1977; Susser, 1986). They protest food prices, rent increases, inadequate health care and failures to provide decent education or safe streets (Hyman, 1980; Lawson and Barton, 1980; Rubin, 1972; Brightman, 1978; Bookman and Morgen, 1986). Moreover, in connecting public and private they draw on intricate networks of relationships (Flammang, 1984). Women—particularly women of ethnic and minority neighborhoods—do not enter the public arena as isolated individuals as liberal political theory presumes, but as people firmly grounded in networks of kin, church, or neighborhood (Ackelsberg, 1984; Gilkes, 1980, 1983).

The rootedness of women's political consciousness in connectedness provides an important challenge to traditional democratic theory, which has seen the key problem of politics as overcoming self-interest and creating allegiance to a larger community. While marxists have criticized that conceptualization, arguing that individualism must be transcended if true democracy and full personhood are to be achieved, the marxist paradigm insists instead that people deny connections to any community other than one based on class. But the networks on which many community activists draw are not simply class-based but are often nourished by religious, ethnic, and cultural ties (see also Kluger, 1975; Boyte, 1980; Boyte and Evans, 1982, 1984). The study of women's activism, then, leads us to challenge both the individualism of the pluralist paradigm and the priority of class in the marxist paradigm, suggesting that politics must be reconceptualized to take account of the reality of (and diverse bases for) community in women's lives—and in the lives of democratic citizens more generally.

It is this last point, in fact, that has opened new areas of thinking and led to some important attempts at reconceptualizing the very definitions of politics. Is politics, for example, to be understood as the study of power (in the sense of power over another, e.g. Dahl, 1957), or do we begin to explore politics as the study of communities—the relationships of communities to one another, and the activities of people to create, maintain, or undermine them? New feminist explorations raise many of these questions, elaborating the ways in which the activities of women (and many of the accomplishments of the women's movement, particularly the success of cooperatively structured organizations) both demonstrate the limitations of the conventional pluralist model and begin to offer more communalist alternatives (see, for example, Pateman, 1986, 1980; Mansbridge, 1980; Hartsock, 1983; Ferguson, 1984; Bulkin, 1981; Ackelsberg, 1986).

Finally, carrying to a new place some of the questions of difference first raised (though in another context) by earlier critical writings, feminist political scientists are beginning to address specifically the relationship of citizenship and difference. Pateman's recent work (1986) offers an interesting new perspective on the relationship between male-female differences and democratic theorizing. She argues that while many of the theorists of participatory democracy seem to have assumed that their theories apply equally to women and to men, in fact the notion of citizenship developed in them is encoded with a distinctly male bias. She challenges us to develop new ways of conceptualizing citizenship, to move beyond the unitary model of citizenship that has prevailed in democratic political thought (of both the liberal and participatory varieties) and to take seriously the relationships of connection that characterize many women's lives.

CONCLUDING REMARKS

In addition to the explorations of the themes of difference and public/private that have animated much contemporary feminist scholarship, and the range of approaches to the relationship of women and the state, another perspective that weaves through much of these debates is the question of discourse. Feminist scholars, many drawing on the insights offered by Michel Foucault, have urged us to develop new ways of thinking and speaking, which would avoid the instrumental rationalism central to the liberal paradigm. In challenging the exclusive tendencies of both conventional social scientific scholarship and much of the new feminist scholarship, feminist theorists have argued that it is necessary to transform both institutions and speech (see, for example, Ferguson, 1984: 155) and to incorporate into our models new ways of relating thought and emotion, reason and experience. One of the great wisdoms of contemporary feminist scholarship has been its exposition of the flight from bodily necessity that has riddled the Western tradition since its inception in ancient Greece. One of the challenges that the feminist critique poses is how we might create cultural and political institutions that live with, rather than flee from, the contingencies of the body (Diamond and Quinby, 1986; Diamond, 1985; Christ, 1986).

A variety of different feminist discourses converge in addressing this set of concerns. Thus ecofeminists (e.g. Griffin, 1978; King, 1981; 1983; Caldecott and Leland, 1983) question the ideologies of control that manifest themselves in attempts to control not only women but the earth itself, and suggest alternatively the need for developing new understandings of the relationship between human communities and the environment in which they are located. Anarchist feminists (e.g., Ferguson, 1984; Ehrlich, 1977; Kornegger, 1975; Ackelsberg and Addleson, 1986) question the ways in which the liberal political paradigm seems to necessarily include an acceptance of the need for domination and subordination, and suggest alternatively the value of building on cooperative networks and sustaining communities. Still others advocate rethinking our understandings of the state and of women's relationship to it in attempts to develop political communities that nurture rather than dominate (Elshtain, 1984) or in which women can truly become full citizens (Pateman, 1986; Dietz, 1985; Ackelsberg, 1986). And still others press us to look anew even at the feminist language of "the right to one's body," suggesting that, while it poses important challenges to male power over women and clearly articulates female subjectivity, it too is grounded in the psychology of instrumental rationalism (Diamond, 1986; Petchesky, 1984).

While none of these lines of thought has yet articulated a fully-developed alternative paradigm, they point us in important directions. First, they suggest that we may well be wrong to look for an alternative, all-inclusive paradigm. They point to the diversity of experience and the contextual nature of human relationships, suggesting that it may be more important for theories to note and acknowledge differences than to claim some ultimate homogeneity. Second, all question the instrumental rationalism that seems to lie at the core of much Western (political) thought. Not that they (or we) argue that rationalism must be replaced by some "feminine" irrationality; rather, that our understandings of reason and knowledge must be transformed, to take account of the connections between reason and emotion, thought and experience—perhaps the latest manifestation of the feminist debate about "the personal and the political."

REFERENCES

ACKELSBERG, M. A. (1983a) "'Sisters' or 'comrades'? The politics of friends and families," pp. 339-356 in I. Diamond (ed.) Families, Politics, and Public Policies. New York: Longman.

ACKELSBERG, M. A. (1983b) "Personal identities and collective visions: Reflections on being a Jew and a feminist." Smith College.

ACKELSBERG, M. A. (1984) "Women's collaborative activities and city life: Politics and policy," pp. 242-259 in J. Flammang (ed.) Political Women: Current Roles in State and Local Government. Newbury Park, CA: Sage.

ACKELSBERG, M. A. (1986) "Communities, resistance, and women's activism: Some implications for democratic theory," in A. Bookman and S. Morgen (eds.) Women and the Politics of Empowerment: Perspectives from the Workplace and the Community. Philadelphia: Temple University Press.

ACKELSBERG, M. A. and K. P. ADDLESON (1986) "Anarchist alternatives to competition," in H. Longino and V. Miner (eds.) Competition Among Women: Feminist Perspectives. New York: Feminist Press.

ADAMS, C. T. and K. T. WINSTON (1980) Women at Work: Public Policies in the United States, Sweden and China. New York: Longman.

AMUNDSEN, K. (1977) A New Look at the Silenced Majority. Englewood Cliffs, NJ: Prentice-Hall.

BALBUS, I. D. (1982) Marxism and Domination: A Neo-Hegelian, Feminist, Psychoanalytic Theory of Sexual, Political, and Technological Liberation. Princeton, NJ: Princeton University Press.

BAXTER, S. and M. LANSING (1981) Women and Politics: The Invisible Majority. Ann Arbor: University of Michigan Press.

BOLES, J. K. (1979) The Politics of the Equal Rights Amendment. New York: Longman.

BONEPARTH, E. [ed.] (1982) Women, Power and Policy. New York: Pergamon.

BOOKMAN, A. and S. MORGEN [eds.] (1986) "Introduction," Women and the Politics of Empowerment: Perspectives from the Workplace and the Community. Philadelphia: Temple University Press.

BORIS, E. and P. BARDAGLIO (1983) "The transformation of patriarchy: The historic role of the state, " in pp. 70-93 Irene Diamond (ed.) Families, Politics, and Public Policies. New York: Longman.

BOURQUE, S. C. and J. GROSSHOLTZ (1974) "Politics as unnatural practice: Political science looks at women's participation." Politics and Society 4, 2: 225-266.

BOYTE, H. (1980) The Backyard Revolution. Philadelphia: Temple University Press.

BOYTE, H. and S. EVANS (1982) "The radical uses of social spaces," Democracy (Fall): 55-66.

BOYTE, H. and S. EVANS (1984) "Strategies in search of America: Cultural radicalism, populism, and democratic culture." Socialist Review 75/76 (May-August): 73-102.

BRENNAN, T. and C. PATEMAN (1979) "Mere auxiliaries to the commonwealth: Women and the origins of liberalism." Political Studies 27, 2: 183-200.

BRIGHTMAN, C. (1978) "The women of Williamsburg," Working Papers (Jan/Feb.): 50-57.

BROWN, W. (1983) "Reproductive rights: A paradox for feminists," in Irene Diamond (ed.) Families, Politics, and Public Policies. New York: Longman.

BULKIN, E. (1981) Feminist Theory: Essays from Quest. New York: Longman.

BULKIN, E., M. B. PRATT, and B. SMITH (1984) Yours in Struggle: Three Feminist Perspectives on Anti-Semitism and Racism. New York: Long Haul Press.

CADE, T. [ed.] (1970) The Black Woman: An Anthology. New York: New American Library.

CAMERON, A. (1985) "Bread and roses revisited: Women's culture and working-class activism in the Lawrence strike of 1912," in R. Milkman (ed.) Women, Work and Protest: A Century of U.S. Women's Labor History. Boston: Routledge & Kegan Paul.

CARROLL, S. (1985) Women as Candidates in American Politics. Bloomington: Indiana University Press.

CHODOROW, N. (1978) The Reproduction of Mothering: Psychoanalysis and the Sociology of Gender. Berkeley: University of California Press.

CHRIST, C. (1987) "On finitude," pp. 213-227 in Laughter of Aphrodite: Reflections on Journey to the Goddness. San Francisco: Harper and Row.

COCKBURN, C. (1977) The Local State. London: Pluto Press.

DAHL, R. A. (1957) "The concept of power." Behavioral Science 2: 201-215.

DIAMOND, I. (1977) Sex Roles in the State House. New Haven: Yale University Press.

DIAMOND, I. [ed.] (1983) Families, Politics, and Public Policies. New York: Longman.

DIAMOND, I. (1985) "Knowledge, power and the body: Family planning in the American welfare state." Presented at the annual meeting of the Society for the Study of Social Problems.

DIAMOND, I. (1984) "Women and fertility: Notes toward the end of political economy." Presented at the annual meeting of the Western Political Science Association, Eugene, OR, March.

DIAMOND, I. and L. QUINBY (1986) "American feminism in the age of the body." Signs 10, 2: 119-125.

DIETZ, M. (1985) "Citizenship with a feminist face." Political Theory 13, 1: 19-37.

DILL, B. T. (1983) "Race, class, and gender: Prospects for an all-inclusive sisterhood." Feminist Studies 9, 1: 131-150.

DINNERSTEIN, D. (1976) The Mermaid and the Minotaur: Sexual Arrangements and Human Malaise. New York: Harper & Row.

EHRLICH, C. (1977) "Socialism, anarchism and feminism." Second Wave 5, 1: 29-35.

EISENSTEIN, H. (1980) "Introduction," pp. xvi-xvii in H. Eisenstein and A. Jardine (eds.) The Future of Difference. The Scholar and the Feminist, Vol. 1: Papers from the Barnard College Women's Center Conference. Boston: G. K. Hall.

EISENSTEIN, Z. (1984) Feminism and Sexual Equality: Crisis in Liberal America. New York: Monthly Review Press.

ELSHTAIN, J. (1974) "Moral women and immoral man." Politics and Society 4, 4: 453-473.

ELSHTAIN, J. (1981) Public Man, Private Woman: Women in Social and Political Thought.

ELSHTAIN J. (1982) "Feminism, family, and community." Dissent (Fall).

ELSHTAIN, J. (1983) "Antigone's daughters," in I. Diamond (ed.) Families, Politics, and Public Policies. New York: Longman.

ELSHTAIN, J. (1984) "Reclaiming the social-feminist citizen." Socialist Review 74: 21-27. Princeton, NJ: Princeton University Press.

ERIE, S. P., M. REIN, and B. WIGET (1983) "Women and the Reagan revolution: Thermidor for the social welfare economy," in pp. 94-119 Irene Diamond (ed.) Families, Politics, and Public Policies. New York: Longman.

EVANS, S. M. and H. C. BOYTE (1986) Free Spaces: The Sources of Democratic Change in America. New York: Harper and Row.

FERGUSON, K. E. (1984) The Feminist Case Against Bureaucracy. Philadelphia: Temple University Press.

FLAMMANG, J. [ed.] (1984) Political Women: Current Roles in State and Local Government. Newbury Park, CA: Sage.

FLAX, J. (1980) "Mother-daughter relationships: Psychodynamics, politics, and philosophy, " pp. 20-40 in H. Eisenstein and A. Jardine (eds.) The Future of Difference. The Scholar and the Feminist, Vol. 1: Papers from the Barnard College Women's Center Conference. Boston: G. K. Hall.

FLAX, J. (1983) "Political philosophy and the patriarchal unconscious: A psychoanalytic perspective on epistemology and metaphysics," pp. 245-81 in S. Harding and M. Hintikka (eds.) Discovering Reality: Feminist Perspectives on Epistemology, Metaphysics, Methodology, and Philosophy of Science. Dordrecht: D. Reidel.

FOWLKES, D. L. (1984) "Concepts of the 'political': White activists in Atlanta, "pp. 66-86 in J. Flammang (ed.) Political Women: Current Roles in State and Local Government. Newbury Park, CA: Sage.

FREEMAN, J. (1980) "Women and urban policy." Signs 5, 3 (suppl.): S4-21.

GELB, J. and M. L. PALLEY (1982) Women and Public Policies. Princeton, NJ: Princeton University Press.

GILKES, C. (1980) "'Holding back the ocean with a broom,' Black women and community work," pp. 217-231 in Rodgers-Rose (ed.) The Black Woman. Newbury Park, CA: Sage Publications.

GILKES C. (1983) "Going up for the oppressed: The career mobility of black women community workers." Journal of Social Issues, 39(3): 115-39.

GILLIGAN, C. (1982) In a Different Voice. Cambridge, MA: Harvard University Press.

GRIFFIN, S. (1978) Women and Nature: The Roaring Inside Her. New York: Harper and Row.

HARTMANN, H. (1979) "Capitalism, patriarchy, and job segregation by sex," pp. 206-247 in Z. Eisenstein (ed.) Capitalist Patriarchy and the Case for Socialist Feminism. New York: Monthly Review Press.

HARTSOCK, N.C.M. (1983) Money, Sex and Power. New York: Longman.

HILL, D. (1983) "Women, state legislators, and party voting on the ERA." Political Science Quarterly, 64(3): 718-33.

HOOKS, B. (1984) Feminist Theory: From Margin to Center. Boston: South End.

HULLS, G. T., P. B. SCOTT, and B. SMITH (1982) But Some of Us Are Brave: Black Women's Studies. New York: Feminist Press.

HYMAN, P. (1980) "Immigrant women and consumer protest: The New York City kosher meat boycott of 1902." American Jewish History 70: 91-105.

IGLITZIN, L. (1974) "The making of the apolitical woman: Femininity and sex stereotyping in girls," 25-36 in J. Jacquette (ed.) Women in Politics. New York: John Wiley.

JACQUETTE, J [ed.] (1974) Women in Politics. New York: John Wiley.

JOSEPH, G. I. and J. LEWIS (1981) Common Differences. Garden City, NY: Anchor/Doubleday.

KAMERMAN, S. B. (1984) "Women, children, and poverty: Public policies and female-headed families in industrialized countries." Signs 10, 2: 249-271.

KAPLAN, T. (1982) "Female consciousness and collective action: The case of Barcelona, 1910-1918." Signs 7, 3: 545-566.

KING, Y. (1981) "Feminism and the revolt of nature." Heresies 13: 12-16.

KING, Y. (1983) "Toward an ecological feminism and a feminist ecology," in Joan Rothschild (ed.) Machina Ex Dea. New York: Pergamon Press.

KLEIN, E. (1984) Gender Politics. Cambridge, MA: Harvard University Press.

KLUGER, R. (1975) Simple Justice: The History of Brown v. Board of Education and Black America's Struggle for Equality. New York: Alfred A. Knopf.

KORNEGGER, P. (1975) "Anarchism: The feminist connection." Second Wave 4, 1: 28-37.

LAWSON, R. and S. E. BARTON (1980) "Sex roles in social movements: A case study of the tenant movement in New York City." Signs (Winter): 230-47.

LEWIS, D. K. (1977) "A response to inequality: Black women, racism and sexism." Signs 3, 2: 339-361.

LORDE, A. (1984) Sister/Outsider. Trumansburg, NY: Crossing Press.

MACKINNON, C. (1982) "Feminism, Marxism, method, and the state: An agenda for theory." Signs 7, 3: 515-544.

MANSBRIDGE, J. (1980) Beyond Adversary Democracy. New York: Basic Books.

MANSBRIDGE, J. (1985) "Myth and reality: The ERA and the gender gap in the 1980 election." Public Opinion Quarterly 49, 2: 164-178.

MARKS, E. and I. DE COURTIVRON (1980) New French Feminisms: An Anthology. Amherst: University of Massachusetts Press.

MARKUSEN, A. R. (1980) "City spatial structure, women's household work, and national urban policy." Signs 5, 3 (Suppl.): S23-44.

MORAGA, C. and G. ANZALDUA [eds.] (1981) This Bridge Called My Back: Writings by Radical Women of Color. Watertown: Persephone Press.

MILLER, A. (1987) "Gender and the vote: 1984," in C. Mueller (ed.) The Politics of the Gender Gap. Newbury Park, CA: Sage Publications.

MUELLER, C. [ed.] (1987) The Politics of the Gender Gap. Newbury Park, Ca: Sage.

NELSON, B. (1984) "Women's poverty and women's citizenship: some political consequences of economic marginality." Signs 10(2): 209-231.

OKIN, S. M. (1979) Women in Western Political Thought. Princeton: Princeton University Press.

OKIN, S. M. (1985) "Justice and gender." Unpublished manuscript.

PATEMAN, C. (1975) "Sublimation and reification: Locke, Wolin, and the liberal democratic conception of the political." Politics and Society 5.

PATEMAN, C. (1980) "Women and consent." Political Theory 8, 2: 149-168.

PATEMAN, C. (1986) "Feminism and participatory democracy: Some reflections on sexual difference and citizenship." Unpublished manuscript.

PEARCE, D. (1979) "Women, work, and welfare: The feminization of poverty," pp. 103-124 in K. W. Feinstein (ed.) Working Women and Families. Newbury Park, CA: Sage.

PETCHESKY, R. (1984) Abortion and Women's Choice. New York: Longman.

PIVEN, F. F. (1984) "Women and the state: Ideology, power, and the welfare state." Socialist Review 74, 14, 2: 11-19.

PIVEN, F. F. (1985) "Women and the state: Ideology, power and the welfare state," pp. 265-287 in A. Rosse (eds.) Gender and the Life Course. Chicago: Aldine.

PIVEN, F. F. and R. CLOWARD (1976) Regulating the Poor. New York: Pantheon.

PIVEN, F. F. and R. CLOWARD (1982) The New Class War. New York: Pantheon.

PIVEN, F. F. and B. EHRENREICH (1984) "The persistence of poverty: 1. The feminization of poverty." Dissent (Spring): 162-170.

POOLE, K. and L. H. ZIEGLER (1985) Women, Public Opinion, and Politics. New York: Longman.

PRESTAGE, J. L. (1980) "Political behavior of American black women: An overview," pp. 233-45 in L. Rodgers-Rose (ed.) The Black Woman. Newbury Park, CA: Sage Publications.

ROSS, E. and R. RAPP (1981) "Sex and society: A research note from social history and anthropology." Comparative Studies in Society and History, XXIII (1).

RUBIN, L. (1972) Busing and backlash: White against White in an Urban School. Berkeley: University of California Press.

RUDDICK, S. (1980) "Maternal thinking." Feminist Studies 6, 2: 342-367.

SARAVASY, W. (1986) "Gender, race, class, and the contradictory legacy of the feminist welfare state founders." Presented at the annual meeting of the Western Political Science Association, Eugene, OR, March.

SAXONHOUSE, A. (1984) "Eros and the female in Greek political thought: An interpretation of Plato's *Symposium*." Political Theory 12, 1: pp. 5-27.

SIDEL, R. (1986) Women and Children Last: The Plight of Poor Women in Affluent America. New York: Viking.

SIMONS, M. A. (1979) "Racism and feminism: A schism in the sisterhood." Feminist Studies 5, 2: 384-401.

SKOCPOL, T. (1985) "Bringing the state back in: Strategies of analysis in current research," pp. 3-37 in P. B. Evans et al. (eds.) Bringing the State Back In. Cambridge, MA: Cambridge University Press.

SMITH, J. (1984) "The paradox of women's poverty: Wage-earning women and economic transformation." Signs 10, 2: 291-310.

SPELMAN, E. V. (1982a) "Theories of race and gender: The erasure of black women." Quest 5, 4: 36-62.

SPELMAN, E. V. (1982b) "Woman as body: Ancient and contemporary views." Feminist Studies 8, 1: 109-131.

SPELMAN, E. V. (1983) "Aristotle and the politicization of the soul," pp. 17-30 in S. Harding and M. Hintikka (eds.) Discovering Reality. Dordrecht: D. Reidel.

SPELMAN, E. V. and M. C. LUGONES (1983) "Have we got a theory for you! Feminist theory, cultural imperialism, and the demand for 'The Woman's Voice,'" Women's Studies International Forum, Hypatia 6 (6): 573-581.

STIEHM, J. (1981) Bring Me Men and Women. Berkeley: University of California Press.

SUSSER, I. B. (1982) Norman Street: Poverty and Politics in an Urban Neighborhood. New York: Oxford University Press.

SUSSER, I. B. (1986) "The participation of working class women in neighborhood movements: Brooklyn, New York," in A. Bookman and S. Morgen (eds.) Women and the Politics of Empowerment: Perspectives from the Workplace and the Community. Philadelphia: Temple University Press.

UHLANER, C. and K. SCHLOZMAN (1986)

WITHORN, A. and R. LEFKOWITZ [eds.] (1986) For Crying Out Loud: Women and Poverty in the United States. Boston: Pilgrim Press.

Women and Structural Transformation [conference] (1983) Rutgers University.

YOUNG, I. (1985) "The ideal of community and the politics of difference." Unpublished manuscript, Worchester Polytechnic Institute.

19 Feminists Thinking About War, Militarism, and Peace

CYNTHIA H. ENLOE
Clark University

THEORY AND THEORIZING:
WHO ARE THE "THEORISTS" OF MILITARISM?

In this chapter I want to ponder the question of what it means for women to "theorize" when the subject is state-sanctioned violence. All too frequently we tend to isolate theory, placing it in a separate or elevated category of human activity. Yet the reality is quite different; we search constantly for explanations, even if occasionally settling for shallow or parochial answers. Only a small part of all that explaining is shared, and an even smaller portion appears in books such as this, where it can be passed along, shelved, read again, debated, and perhaps even tested by practice.

When trying to make sense of the spread of military influence, it is especially important to look at the implications of theorizing as an activity, and not simply at the resulting theories. Living in militarized times makes it harder, yet more urgent, for women to collect the information needed to control our lives and to arrange that information so that it can explain women's condition in a number of increasingly interdependent, though unequal, societies.

Is it easier to go to the root of things when you are under extraordinary pressure or when you have the space to think? We know that women need resources—"a room of one's own"—to produce poetry, novels, and theory. But women need more than material resources and business connections in order to write and publish ideas. They need *physical security*. All the theorizing in this volume, for example, has been created because at least some women in some countries have the physical security required for devoting their energies to a project beyond day-to-day survival. Other women are less fortunate, unable to think about war and militarism because they lack a sense of elementary safety. Ironically, often the *more* a government is preoccupied with what it calls "national security," the *less* its women experience the physical security necessary for theorizing.

Thus we begin with the realization that those women in the world with the most pressing need to discover the underlying causes of war, militarism, and peace are precisely those with the least capacity to write down their thoughts, to have their words published and circulated among other women, at home or abroad. Societies in the grip of war or dominated by military regimes have not been very hospitable to women needing to print their ideas. To the contrary, women who question their own subordination are often perceived as "threats to national security." Millions of women—in nineteenth-century Turkey, the antebellum American South, 1960s Vietnam, and 1980s Guatemala and Lebanon—have indeed thought about why it is men who are the soldiers, why rape is so prevalent in wartime, why the very concept of a peaceful society is derogated by the use of feminine terms. That is, millions of women whose ideas never reach a book shelf have engaged in feminist theorizing.

In this chapter I will try to spell out some of the reasons why feminist theorizing about causes and effects—especially the causes—of militarism is paid so little attention in our era. I will then suggest several advantages to feminists of focusing on *militarization* as a social process, rather than on either war or peace, in our efforts to expose the way in which patriarchy promotes and sustains military values and military needs. Finally, I will draw some connections between theorizing by Third World women and by women in more industrialized countries, connections making it clear that we cannot get to the root of patriarchy's relationship to militarization unless we push to a level of analysis beyond the familiar political terrains of North America and Western Europe.

COMPETING THEORIES

Militarization poses a special problem for women seeking to be taken seriously because it has such wide-ranging effects on so many different groups that it evokes varied explanations. In addition, a woman's theorizing about militarism is often lightly dismissed, particularly if she is using feminist questions and concepts. A brief overview of the currently fashionable competing theories of militarization should illustrate the obstacles faced by feminist analysts.

The two principal nonfeminist theories are, first, that militarization is a logical consequence of *capitalism*, and second, that militarization is caused by the inherent inclinations of the *state* regardless of the nature of its economic system. Men and women who see capitalism as the moving force behind the military's expanding influence believe that government officials enhance the status, resources, and authority of the military in order to protect the interests of private enterprises at home and overseas (Melman, 1974; Kaldor, 1981;

Koisitnen, 1980). They conflate the interest of business with that of the nation. Thus it is in the boardroom rather than the war room that they believe the origins of wars, both hot and cold, will be found. These critics claim that the influence of major businesses with overseas investments is at the root of military interventionism, and that domestic armament industries dictate the development of weapons systems.

A corollary to this theory is the recognition that increasing numbers of workers in all the affected countries become dependent on military spending for their own livelihoods. The "military-industrial complex" therefore rests on a complex web of interdependency among four groups: government officials, "defense" contractors, unionized labor, and foreign government and military authorities. Although such "complexes" typically are described as characteristic of the United States, Great Britain, France, West Germany, Canada, and possibly Japan, they are also found today in less elaborate form in Argentina, Brazil, Israel, India, and South Africa (Anonymous, 1981; Ball and Leitenberg, 1983; Howard, 1983; Fischer, 1985; Ball, 1986; Nairn, 1986).

The capitalism-as-cause theorists take for granted that it is men who are the corporate executives, government officials, and the workers most involved in militarization. That is, they do not specifically investigate or try to explain this male predominance. As for women, their existence is acknowledged to the extent of occasionally noting their participation on the assembly lines that produce electronic weaponry. The theorists have not used this information to increase the power and utility of their paradigm; they have not taken *gender* into account in their explanatory scheme, which rests almost exclusively on economic factors.

Yet the capitalist-centered explanation is compelling in many respects. When a self-conscious feminist opens her morning paper and reads that in 1985 the average operating cost for a single American aircraft carrier (e.g., food for the crew, spare parts for the ship's 800 daily repairs, and the fuel to keep it in motion) is $490,410 *per day,* and this does not include wages or any share of the capital expenses of building the vessel, even her otherwise gender-sensitive thoughts might not turn immediately to concepts of masculinity or cultures of misogyny. She is more likely to wonder, "Who can be profiting from such incredible expenditures?" Theories about capitalism and the military-industrial complex have a surface simplicity and plausibility, especially for feminists familiar with that type of analysis in other sectors, even though women have been rendered invisible in these models.

The second set of explanations for militarization is based on the belief that once political power is organized into the formal centralized structure of the *state*, there is an inevitable tendency to expand the use of state-sanctioned force to ensure compliance within the society and to protect from outside assaults. States, by their very nature, it is argued, incline toward coercion in response to perceived threats. When public power is hierarchically structured and invested with vast material resources and symbolic centrality in the lives of citizens, militarization appears all but inevitable.

A subtheory within the statist approach focuses on the role of bureaucracy and bureaucrats, as the latter come to identify with their agencies' own parochial interests. The phenomenon of goal displacement not only affects government bureaus but the various branches of the military who fight among themselves for ever larger mandates and pieces of the budgetary pie, even if this ultimately weakens the nation's defense capabilities (Fitzgerald, 1972; Thompson and Smith, 1980; Adams, 1981; Bok, 1984; Klare, 1984; Talbott, 1985).

The lack of accountability of civilian civil servants, however, pales in comparison to the near secrecy with which the military can operate, even in a democracy. Not only is the military structurally isolated from the electoral process, but military officers and their civilian allies can rely on professional expertise to claim that "national security" should preclude oversight from government authorities, and certainly from the citizenry at large. In the case of the United States, a number of other recent cultural epiphenomena have been added to this mix—an upsurge in nationalism if not xenophobia, idolization of the violent avenger (the *Rambo* syndrome), and the tendency to confuse military technology with scientific rationality—to grant carte blanche for continued militarization (Edwards, 1985). In nondemocratic societies these oligarchical tendencies are even more pronounced, particularly when the military directly provides political leadership, as in Guatemala, or when the military is politicized, as in Iran or the Soviet Union (Valenta and Potter, 1984).

The appeal of statist and bureaucratic theories of militarization lies in their ability to explain parallel developments in countries with very different political and economic systems, and also to take the long historical view. According to this approach, we can understand why state elites have ruled by coercion and threat and have engaged in vast military enterprises long *before* the emergence of industrialism or capitalism. Yet these theories also take for granted the masculine character of state elites (even when the nominal ruler might be a woman). Statist theorizers do not perceive gender as an important variable, only the person's location in the hierarchy of power.

For a distinctly feminist analysis of power to be persuasive and valuable, therefore, its proponents must demonstrate that both capitalism-centered and state-centered theories are inaccurate, misleading, or at best, inadequate or incomplete. It must also go beyond a simple "impact-on" approach, that is, the taken-for-granted assumption that men are the natural actors under militarism so that women are considered only in terms of how militarism affects them, as if they were an off-stage chorus to a basically male drama. While we continue to insist that any discussion of how militarization transforms a society must include explicit descriptions of the changes in women's lives as well as men's, it is important that we recognize the impact-on approach as a *necessary* but *not sufficient* basis of analysis.

The next step would be a theory that explores how gender and, more specifically, the subjugation of women for the sake of sustaining male privilege—patriarchy—actually *causes* militarization and the wars that flow from it. For example, proponents of the modest impact-on approach do point out that women and men are *not* made economically dependent on weapons production in the same way (International Economic Conversion Conference, 1984; Wainwright, 1983; Plowshares, 1985). Women, as low paid workers and/or single mothers, will be less likely than working-class men to derive any benefit from increased military spending. But the implication of this reality rarely is spelled out: that if women—in the United States, Britain, West Germany, Brazil, and Israel, for example—can be shown to be affected by spiralling arms investments in ways different from the effects on men, then women's particular relationship to military-industrial complexes will have to be given serious attention by antimilitarists seeking their support.

But even such an impact-on analysis does not go deeply enough into the gendered quality of militarization. Harder questions will produce more radical answers than those suggested by this approach. Such questions are being asked today by the British and American women working in "conversion" campaigns aimed at dismantling the military-industrial structures of mutual admiration and dependence. Feminists in the conversion campaigns are asking why it is that so many male workers in ship, tank, and aircraft factories are so enamored of their jobs? And why are even those male union leaders who can see the wisdom of converting an industry from arms production to socially useful production nonetheless firmly entrenched in the belief that women workers are insignificant to military-industrial processes?

Such questions, often raised in anger over union strategy meetings in which women workers such as clerical staff and electronic assemblers are rendered invisible, have led to an emergent feminist analysis that argues that it is not capitalism or the state alone but *masculinity* that links the military and industry (Enloe, 1983a). Thus many male employees in weapons factories may be working against their own class-based interests because they perceive the making of fighter planes (or tanks or space lasers) as somehow more serious, more proper work for men than, say, the manufacture of buses or hospital equipment. The patriarchal assumption that they are really doing *men's work* reinforces militarization and the hegemony of the military-industrial complex in ways that may be crucial for the maintenance of such a militarizing alliance.

MASCULINITY MILITARIZED, MILITARISM MASCULINIZED

One of the most striking characteristics of militaries is that they are almost exclusively male. While we are learning more and more about the typically overlooked number of women who have served as soldiers, the military is portrayed, even by revisionist scholars, as an overwhelmingly male institution

(Keegan, 1977; Baker, 1982; Ellis, 1982; Terry, 1984; Enloe, 1983a). This is so for cultures and historical periods that otherwise share little in common. What, for example, is there about tenth-century China, nineteenth-century Britain, and late twentieth-century Kenya that produces state institutions for organized violence (i.e., militaries) dependent on maleness? Is there something, as suggested by Gailey (Chapter 1 in this volume), in the culture of statist societies that leads to organized violence in the service of male domination?

Militaries are composed of males as a result of quite self-conscious political policies, suggesting that state officials, themselves primarily male, create an explicit link between the presumed properties of maleness and the institutional needs of the military as an organization. It should also be noted that the boys and men who are typically recruited or pressed into service as foot soldiers or ships' crews are drawn from the relatively powerless strata of state societies— members of racial, ethnic, or religious minorities, peasants, poor urban dwellers. Yet, as with the elite males who serve as officers, they too are bound together by the threads of male camaraderie. In fact, nervous commanders often try to use the alleged common bonds of masculinity to reduce the all-too-obvious class and ethnic tensions among their troops (Enloe, 1980).

Feminists in different countries exploring such insights return again and again to examining the social construction of masculinity—that is, the creation and recreation of that package of assumptions, teachings, and expectations that serve as the standard for appropriate male behavior (Woolf, 1938; Trustram, 1984; Reardon, 1985; Bunster, 1986; Pierson, 1986; Isaksson, 1987). Both elite males and those without power have used these beliefs about masculinity to rationalize or normalize their involvement in the military. Indeed, the meanings attached to masculinity appear to be so firmly linked to compliance with military roles that it is often impossible to disentangle the two. According to one view, masculinity cannot be militarized because it is inherently militaristic in the first place (an argument that has its counterpart in current feminist debates between "essentialists" and "minimalists"). Only if we can say that masculinity has the capacity to be militarized over time can we then assert that there are conditions under which masculinity might be *non*militarized.

In the argument over how integral militarism is to masculinity, or vice versa, each side has ample evidence on which to draw. For instance, if masculinity is essentially based on its conceptual distinctiveness from femininity (i.e., dependent on the "otherness" of femininity) then it is not difficult to explain how militarism takes root in societies and eras so vastly different from one another. Feminist anthropologists (see Gailey, Chapter 1 in this volume) have shown that virtually all state-organized societies are characterized by ideological categories that clearly separate "masculine" from "feminine" roles and attributes.

Conversely, there are those who believe that, while tightly interwoven at certain times and in certain cultures, masculinity and militarism are nonetheless analytically separate. That is, that each of these ideological constructs has its own distinct history. For example, it is not all that easy to induce young males to enlist in their country's army. In many cases it is also necessary to subject recruits to intensive socialization into the role of soldier. Also, masculine beliefs in their "raw" civilian form are not always appropriate to military requirements. At the very least, emergent ideas of manliness must be honed by the military experience (e.g., "We turn boys into men"; Trustram, 1984; Pierson, 1986). In other words, according to the separate development argument, if masculinity as a social construct were identical to militarism, no state would risk its legitimacy with harsh conscription laws, and military institutions would not require extended "basic training." If masculinity were inherently militaristic, each would be redundant.

Even accepting the argument that masculinity and militarism are not isomorphic, we can explore how and why they have become so intimately entwined. Currently most analyses of this question come from a few societies, such as ancient Athens, Britain in the nineteenth and twentieth centuries, and Germany, the United States, and Japan among contemporary nations. While such states are characterized by gender-dualistic ideologies, the ways in which masculinity perpetuates militarism will vary from one culture to another. For example, Japanese antimilitarist feminists have noted differences in the social construction of masculinity between Japan and Germany or the United States. The Japanese model of masculine behavior eschews the more flamboyant aspects of the "John Wayne" prototype and appears on the surface to support a "softer" version of masculinity, including the legitimation of a man's wish to be "mothered" by his wife (Ikegame, 1984). Possibly, militarist strains in Japanese masculinity are less strong than in other cultures, or simply harder to detect, not only among the government's military promoters but also among the men who dominate the Japanese peace movement. In any event, Japanese feminists are confronted with different problems from American and Western European women in explaining their country's current rearmament drive, as well as in dealing with men in various peace organizations.

Such cross-cultural caveats warn us that no theory of the links between masculinity and militarism will be complete without hypotheses that can be tested on a range of societies. Were the men and women of Vietnam mobilized for the war against France and then the United States by notions of femininity complementing masculinity in ways that were identical to those prompting American and French women and men to support their government's military priorities? Do Vietnamese, French, and American drill sergeants draw on the same ideological assumptions about what constitutes a "real man"?

These may seem to be politically outrageous questions to pose, for clearly the military and the state were themselves in different relationship to each other in colonizing than in colonized societies. In addition, soldiers acting in immediate defense of their own homes may draw on different aspects of masculinity than do those who see themselves defending national interests at a distance. The former could be expected to show greater protectiveness; the latter, domination. Did men in the South Vietnamese army act out of the same cultural "pool" of notions of masculinity as did North Vietnamese soldiers, but with a different political agenda? An examination of how American military advisors related to their Vietnamese counterparts might shed light on the question of cross-cultural variations in masculinity; was misogyny sufficient to generate bonds of trust across so many differences; or did the American advisors tend to treat the Vietnamese as sexual as well as cultural subordinates (e.g., disparaging the ARVN as soldiers because of their small stature and less ferocious displays of maleness)?

WOMEN, THE MILITARY, AND THE MYSTIQUE OF COMBAT

The focus on masculinity has also shed fresh light on the centrality of "combat" in military mythology, a matter of some importance as increasing numbers of women have recently entered the U.S. military. In 1984 there were approximately 200,000 women in the active duty forces, constituting almost 10% of the total uniformed force. The Marine Corps has the lowest percentage; the Air Force the highest (U.S. Department of Defense, 1985).

Sexist and racist ideologies and structures interact in the process of militarization as they do in so many other societal processes. Consequently, feminist theorizing about both the causes and consequences of increasing militaristic influences need to include explicit explanations for how and why militarization uses and affects women from different—and usually unequal—ethnic and racial groups. For instance, the startling fact that by 1985, black women composed 42% of all enlisted (nonofficer) women in the United States Army—that is, *four* times their proportion of all American women—suggests that the U.S. military's appeal to or claim on women is far from race neutral.

It may well be that the militarization of American society in the 1980s is increasing the vulnerability of precisely those women who are most precariously positioned in the economic system, enhancing the appeal of the military's offers of shelter, health benefits for children, and a steady income. There is no evidence that black women join the U.S. military in disproportionate numbers because they are more militaristic than other women in their attitudes and beliefs. It would also be analytically dangerous to assume that race operates autonomously, that is, to presume that American black men and women voluntarily enlist out of identical economic needs or ideological outlooks. It is far more useful theoretically to see racism and sexism as analytically separate but intimately related, for men and women of all racial groups in any society, as they are affected by, or try to control, that society's military apparatus (Enloe, 1983a, 1985; Enloe and Jordan, 1985.)

Such increases in the number of women in the military have had little effect on the relative power of male and female officers. Because of restrictions on combat duty, few women are on career ladders that will lead to the upper echelons of the military. Yet despite a growing reliance on female recruits, who are typically better educated than male personnel, resistance to women in combat roles remains firm. Indeed, the vision of "American girls being drafted and sent to 'war' was a powerful counter-argument to the proposed Equal Rights Amendment" (National Organization for Women, 1981). Quite aside from the fact that promotion to most of the highest military ranks requires combat experience (thus giving the military command a vested interest in having wars), some analysts propose that combat per se is at the core of masculine uniqueness, so that sharing this experience with women would diminish their identity as masculine creatures (Goldman, 1982; Chapkis, 1982, 1985; Rogan, 1982; Devilbiss, 1985; Yuval-Davis, 1985).

Yet in reality, combat is messy in its definition, as in its practice. "Combat" has been continually redefined by those who guard its precincts. Despite cultural and historical differences, male elites have guarded this inner sanctum against feminization. Even men who have never held a gun will insist that women are just not as "naturally" fit for combat as are men. Remembering the ancient Greek elite's ideological assumptions, some scholars suggest that combat offers men the hope of immortality; that is, human frailty could be transcended by acts of heroism possible only in military combat (Hartsock, 1983). The presumption that only masculine people partake of combat preserves the patriarchal state by justifying the rule of men, as only they will have the requisite courage and honor.

Every modern military has an official definition of combat, but it differs country by country, and government by government, according to the cultural definitions of femininity, the official perception of contemporary weaponry and battlefield tactics, and the military's own need for and shortage of "manpower." Not even among the 16 NATO allies is there a uniform definition of combat or a standard policy regarding women soldiers' participation in this slippery thing called "combat." In 1983, the U.S. Army tried to expand the definition, arguing that technological and tactical advances in warfare had made it imperative now to include *carpenters, interior electricians,* and *plumbers* as combat roles, thus closed to women. But by 1983, a politically skilled women's lobby within the Defense Department and Congress had emerged, capable of rolling back the Army's expansive new definition so that at least carpenter jobs were excepted. Interior electricians and plumbers, however, are now officially designated as combat roles, open only to male personnel, denying women access to yet another set of craft skills.

This 1983-1984 example of the bureaucratic process raises a serious issue for feminist theorists. Is the ability of women lobbyists operating within military and legislative offices to modify one of the male military elite's desired policies to be taken as evidence of a *de*masculinization of the military? Perhaps this limited but new experience of political success should be held up as proof that militarization—using society's resources to maximize military strength—can be analytically separated from masculinization. Or can the lobbyist's partial success be more accurately interpreted as evidence of cooptation into the militarizing political process, demonstrating how women can be persuaded that women's best interests are served by pressing for ever larger roles within the military establishment? To weigh these theoretical alternatives, we must refine the concept of cooptation, for only when cooptation can be accurately monitored and measured can we determine whether or not seemingly successful political organization by women on behalf of extending women's opportunities reinforces or diminishes the underlying structures of militarization (Minerva, 1985, 1986).

The interplay among socially constructed notions of combat, public life, and masculinity that sustains patriarchy is a dynamic structure that sometimes requires great effort to keep in place. the examples of societies where insurgent militaries challenge the state are instructive in this regard. As most insurgencies today involve popularly based groups struggling against dictatorial regimes, a shortage of resources (both money and people) forces male leaders of the insurrection to permit women to assume roles that in more conventional circumstances would be defined as combat. Accepting such roles has not been difficult for women who have become politicized in part by their marginalization in the existing political order. But we do not know if combat then loses its special relationship to masculinity or if women are simply perceived as symbolic males (see Gailey, Chapter 1 in this volume). In the case of Nicaragua, it is interesting to note that when the Sandinistas were the insurgents, there were many women in their ranks. But today, seven years after the new state's creation, while women account for a major proportion of militia members, they have been exempted by the Sandinista regime from military conscription (Seager and Olson, 1986). This exemption suggests that as insurgent forces become more statist, they also move toward reassertion of the masculinist character of their militaries. Yet among the armed forces seeking to overthrow the Sandinista government today, there are no women—only U.S. advisors, former members of the military, and very young men impressed into service (Enloe, 1985).

MILITARISM, WAR, AND PEACE:
WHY MAKE DISTINCTIONS?

Of all forms of state-organized violence, it is war—the most concentrated and seemingly contained experience of violence—that has provided the most urgent context for theorizing. Some wars have been more fruitful than others in providing women with the impetus and resources for thinking about the connections between state violence and gender hierarchies. Yet a focus on wars can also distort, leading to the perception that intense militarization can "open doors" to women. We are only now discovering how American, Canadian, European, Soviet, and Japanese women experienced the two world wars in this century, as feminist scholars embark on the reconstruction of the past from below, from the diaries and oral histories of ordinary people (Anderson, 1981; Hartman, 1982; Enloe, 1983a; Campbell, 1984; Cambridge Women's Peace Collective, 1984; Honey, 1984; Koonz, 1987; Pierson, 1986.)

The recent revival of interest in "Rosie the Riveter," the mythical woman factory worker of World War II, has reawakened a classic debate among feminists: Does war reinforce the dominance of men and masculine conceptions of virtue and worth, or, paradoxically, undermine these bases of patriarchy? Further, is the state so powerful that it can contain all the contradictory forces let loose by total mobilization? These questions surfaced in 1914 when suffragists split over supporting the national government's war policy, and they remain unanswered today (Wiltsher, 1985; Isaksson, 1987).

Do wars benefit women? According to one school of thought, patriarchal societies have an inherent proclivity toward war because of the supreme value placed on control and the assumption of a natural male tendency toward displays of physical force. Warfare, therefore, periodically confirms male superiority over all females and over men from more vulnerable societies. Conversely, it can be argued that the growth of industrial states and the magnitude of their weaponry means that interpatriarchal wars can be fought only under those conditions of total mobilization that would blur the line between public and private, masculine and feminine, as the efforts of all would be required.

That wartime can be a "window of opportunity" has been illustrated by the passage of women's suffrage following their support for the war effort, by the changes in women's self-concept in World War I, and by the large number of women who remained in the labor force following World War II. In both periods, moreover, certain jobs previously closed to women were opened "for the duration" but never again totally shut. Yet it also has been argued that such changes have been relatively cosmetic; that the basic structures of dominance have not been challenged; and in any event, short of total war, radical changes are highly unlikely (Milkman, 1982; Campbell, 1984; Pierson, 1986).

In part, different interpretations of Rosie the Riveter reflect a deeper dispute over the consciousness and manipulative capacity of patriarchal state elites. Feminists who see wars as an opportunity for challenging gender relationships do not believe that the ruling elite, even when equipped with all the powers of the state, is powerful enough to control the social and ideological contradictions activated by total warfare. These feminists recognize that efforts can be made by an alliance of male business executives, labor leaders, and government officials to keep women war workers from mastering masculinized skills, and that emotional blackmail can be used to convince women to retreat to their kitchens or to low paid "women's jobs" when the war is over and the "boys" come home to claim their jobs. They also acknowledge that empty-headed sex symbols will replace the images of strong women that filled the movie screens and women's magazines. But these feminists contend that, despite all such attempts to restore the status quo ante, expectations of women and men will have been irrevocably changed by their wartime experiences, and women will not suddenly lose their hard won skills or their new sense of public place. The genie cannot be so easily stuffed into its patriarchal bottle, nor the bitten apple be made whole. The patriarchal state is powerful but not omnipotent. Its very need to wage total war leads to a weakening of the male privilege it is designed to protect.

A less sanguine view of the possibilities for change is based on monitoring the situation decades after the war has ended. Rather than being impressed that women gained access to shipbuilding jobs during the war, these analysts would point to the fact that such jobs were being *de*skilled at precisely the time that women were allowed to take them. Further, these critics note that continued race and gender stratification of war work serves to divide and thus weaken women's collective strength. In this view, far from liberating women, the wartime experience only demonstrates the extent to which women's lives were controlled by male elites.

Thus far the theoretical debate over the potential liberating effects of wartime has centered on twentieth-century world wars—especially as experienced in the most industrialized societies. Consequently, feminist theories about militarization are derived solely from World War I and II, and may fail to appreciate the strains in patriarchal societies under "normal" tendencies toward increasing militarization. In the 1980s there appears to be a lessened interest in wars than in a host of other military actions affecting our daily lives, even when there is no officially declared state of hostility. Without the visible manifestations of wartime, it is extremely difficult to make visible the deeper insinuating process of militarization.

There exists both a theoretical dependency and a tension between war and militarism. Militarization—the ways in which militarism is spread—is a social process; it occurs in time and space, and requires an explanation. What is distinctive about feminist theorizing on militarization is that it posits gender—that is, social constructions of masculinity and femininity—as a critical factor in the construction and perpetuation, and therefore the possible reversal, of that process. Possibly, the feminist approach would also show how militarization differs from other gendered social processes.

Feminists who believe that it is war, and not the apparently diffuse processes of militarization, that demands explanation are understandably impatient with analyses that tend to blur into other seemingly less life-threatening processes (Thompson, 1983). At least most wars have recognizable beginnings and endings, making them susceptible to systematic analysis. Yet it can be argued that wars do not occur without prior militarization, nor do they end with the signing of a peace treaty. When the war is over, it is still women who relinquish their freedom and who are expected to repair the damage done to militarized sons, husbands, and lovers. In the defeated country, other women may be drawn into prostitution to service the sexual needs of soldiers of occupation. In this latter view, the conventional phrase "postwar era" and the historiography on which it rests appear less like peace and more like militarization in postwar camouflage.

PEACE: IS IT THE ABSENCE OF WAR?

Peace is commonly juxtaposed with war. Indeed, the dichotomy has been so widely assumed as obvious, logical, and true that peace has gotten the short end of the theoretical discussion, as if all one needed to do were to determine the causes of war, eliminate them, and *voila,* produce peace. In this formulation, peace is discussed as if it were a static condition—the absence of overt state-sponsored hostilities. In reality, peace is also a process; it must be able to reproduce itself. In addition, peace has lacked adequate theoretical attention from patriarchal intellectuals because it has been defined in negative, often feminine terms. When war is seen as active, heroic, and masculine, peace becomes merely the absence of all these stirring qualities. Thus social processes such as capital formation, state-building, and war have great aesthetic appeal when male scholars select topics on which to focus their energies, even in the cause of criticizing such processes (Caldecott and Leland, 1983; Enloe, 1984; Brock-Utne, 1985; Frontiers, 1985; Helicon Nine, 1985; Wiltsher, 1985).

Feminist thinking about peace, however, is not necessarily locked into the war-versus-peace dichotomy. Perhaps because feminists start from the conditions of women's lives, and because they see how many forms violence, unhappiness, and distress can take, they often define peace as women's achievement of control over their own lives. They also apprehend that any such achievement is fragile and tentative unless processes are created to reproduce it. For example, a Kenyan woman might argue that the opposite of peace is oppression, not war, and that we must explain oppression if we are ever to imagine, much less realize, genuine peace (Feminism and Non-Violence Study Group, 1983; Connexions, 1984; Wolf, 1984; di Leonardo, 1985; Elshtain and Tobias, 1987).

But to view oppression as the sole obstacle to real peace may obscure the analytical importance of militarism. For instance, British feminists within the Owenite Socialist movement in the 1830s and 1840s were addressing members of a society governed by an imperial state, speaking to women and men whose political leaders were militarizing economic, ethnic, and gender relations within Britain and its colonies. Yet the Owenite feminist women did not think about state armies or the government's claim to need to recruit and arm such globally ambitious military forces. In these women's theoretical framework, the "war zone" was not India, Africa, or the Caribbean, but the domestic household in Britain itself. Lack of peace, they argued, lay in the oppressive structures of patriarchal marriage (Taylor, 1984). Although this recently rediscovered analysis of marriage is among the most provocative and useful ever produced by women, it remains limited by its failure to discuss the role of militarism and its relationship to local and overseas patriarchal oppressions. For them, the opposite of peace was not militarism but marriage (and other contributors to this volume might agree).

This essentially theoretical debate over just what is the opposite of peace and what are the basic barriers to achieving peace is reflected in the current argument among women activists over how to maximize scarce resources in order to produce effective social change. If one believes that militarization is the basic obstacle to peace, then a woman in a violent marriage would be urged to attend a rally against escalating military spending, by drawing the causal links between her husband's abusive behavior and the wider militaristic culture that legitimates all forms of violence (Cook and Kirk, 1983; Harford and Hopkins, 1984).

By contrast, a feminist working in a local battered woman's shelter— especially one who has also spent time at one of the women's peace camps— would likely rely on a rather different set of connections to help the same woman decide where to spend her energies. In this latter view, militarization is a surface symptom of more basic assumptions in the culture about marriage, property, reproduction, and heterosexuality—all of which are essential to the maintenance of male privilege and the permission for interpersonal violence on which such dominance often rests. Therefore, one would urge the antimilitarist activist to enlist in the struggle against wife abuse, on the grounds that stopping legitimized oppression in personal relationships is the most "theoretically efficient" way to end militarism (Breaching the Peace, 1983; Enloe, 1984).

We must make clear the practical and theoretical links between heterosexist domination and the military's exploitation of women, however complex these links and however many other issues claim our energies and resources. Second, rather than imagining that war and peace are opposites, we must clarify the ways in which "peacetime" conditions under which American and European women currently live actually foster the wartime conditions faced by women in Afghanistan, South Africa, El Salvador, and Nicaragua.

WHY MILITARIZATION?

Analyses of the causes and consequences of militarization begin with an understanding that it is not simply synonomous with war nor is it the sole antithesis of peace. One theoretical strength of militarization as a concept is that it is not subject to patriarchal historiography in the same way as the concept of war is. Women must always struggle against the ways in which historians have used their own conceptual tools to divide and explain social change. Perhaps nowhere is this caveat more necessary than in the definition of a war. When did it start, when did it end, and how can one tell? A Sri Lankan feminist in the 1980s, for example, may accurately conclude that her government is waging war on its Tamil community, with serious consequences for women in all the country's ethnic groups, even though no established Sri Lankan male historian will call it a war. Similarly, American and Japanese women would be misled if they believed that the intensely militarized gender relations of World War II were simply reversed on the day in 1945 that the Emperor announced his nation's surrender. One must look several decades beyond the technical cessation of hostilities. In contrast to the apparently limited definition of war, the concept of militarization is far less amenable to the markers of mainstream historiography, so that its temporal diffuseness becomes its feminist theoretical strength.

Second, militarization casts a theoretical spotlight on a convergence of social processes—cultural, economic, and political. It is a concept that assumes something is happening *over time* to relations among women, among men, and between women and men. As a process rather than an event, militarization becomes analytically compatible with other processes examined by feminists, such as oppression, industrialization, colonization, division of labor, reproduction, liberation, and sexual harassment.

Third, the concept of militarization permits the investigation of ideological change. We can monitor ideas of masculinity and femininity over years and generations to see how presumptions about masculinity are either bolstered or challenged by other ideological constructs such as authority, nationhood, enemy, sexual pleasure, and the state. This is not to say that all analysts of militarization give sufficient attention to its ideological dimensions; some treat it merely as a technological process; others simply as a diplomatic process; and still others as an economic process (McClintock, 1985; Young and Phillips, 1986). But since militarization can be explained only by specifying its causes in one society over time, one is prompted to watch for *any* changes in the culture. Changes in a society's dominant beliefs and values can be charted as *reflections* of other militarizing transformations or as a *precondition* of other changes. For instance, do technological and managerial advances undermine the conventional notions of male honor and bravery? And does this in turn make it harder to sustain popularly based militarism among both women and men?

Finally, militarization is especially valuable for theory because it encourages rather than suppresses cross-cultural dialogue. North American and Western European women have drawn their questions and hunches mainly from *wars,* especially those experienced firsthand. American women, for instance, will use the Rosie the Riveter myth to explore the state's ideological manipulations of women's family and work expectations, but remain relatively ignorant of how the Argentine government exploited notions of "motherhood" to secure support for its war with Britain over the Malvinas (Falkland) Islands. Similarly, North American and European feminists failed to develop conceptualizations of sexual property and women's responses to them in Vietnam during that country's wars against France, the United States, and now Kampuchea. Instead, Western feminists examined only how "wives" and "sweethearts" in their own societies were socially constructed during World War II, and attempted to generalize from these essentially parochial observations to global statements about war and militarism.

THIRD WORLD WOMEN AND MILITARIZATION

In the 1980s some of the most lively theorizing about state-sanctioned violence comes from Third World women in the Philippines, South Korea, Puerto Rico, Thailand, Chile, and Guatemala, and the major concept that anchors their diverse explanations is *militarization* (Thitsa, 1980; Connexions, 1984). Women in countries whose governments are not formally at "war" or whose lands have not been "officially" invaded can, nonetheless, employ the concept of militarization to clarify the profoundly distorting transformations caused by the dominance of militaristic values and military needs. For example, Filipina and South Korean women have revealed how military bases used by American troops are gendered in ways that oppress women, many of whom find employment as barmaids and prostitutes. In these countries, the morale of a foreign military's male soldiers is maintained by the evocation of racism as well as sexism (Enloe, 1983a, 1985). For Guatemalan and Chilean feminists, *rape* is identified as a central process in militarizing their societies, tracing the links between their own soldiers' sexual assaults and the allegedly "ungendered" national security doctrines of their American allies (Bunster, 1986; Burgos-Debray, 1985).

The work of Third World women underscores the need to look beyond formal military institutions for an explanation of militarization. Indian feminists, for example, have described how popular acceptance of their government's violence ultimately depends on the continued legitimation of patriarchal family beliefs and structures (Vanita, 1985). Although militarization waxes and wanes (India's high point in recent years being the period of emergency under Indira Gandhi), so long as patriarchal family traditions reinforce male dominance in the private sphere, and so long as men can convince Indian women that they are protected only within the confines of the household, the seeds for militarization in that country remain alive.

Other Third World feminists focus less on the patriarchal family and more on the male-dominated work place to draw the connection between militarization and the oppression of women. Many Filipina and South Asian women are acutely aware of how their countries have been militarized through the development of seemingly nonmilitary sectors such as the garment and electronics industries, and the direct exploitation of women through "sex tourism" (Villariba, 1983; Enloe, 1983b).

When Western feminists realize how germane these Third World theoretical discussions are to their own concerns, studies of the relationships among women, men, and war will give as much prominence to the militarization of Victorian society as they do now to the influence of gender on the waging of the two twentieth-century world wars. We might learn how gender became a state weapon for expanding the British Empire, seeing how the cult of domesticity and the simultaneous yet contradictory mobilization of women and children for capitalist industrial production were in part militarizing processes. The mill girl, the middle-class home-bound wife, and the prostitute were all necessary to British imperialism—symbolizing the rewards of empire, justifying colonizing myths, making profitable the manufacture of raw materials from the colonies, or serving to maintain the morale and sense of manliness of Her Majesty's troops (Liddle and Joshi, 1985).

Thus far we have more elaborate theories about how nineteenth-century Western capitalist industrialization depended on male privilege and the oppression of women than we have theories about how gender was used to enhance the simultaneous militarization. Filipina theorist-activists propose by implication that these two historical processes cannot be—then or now— explained only in parallel, but must be understood as they support or contradict one another (Villariba, 1983; Grassroots, 1986). Analyses of how hierarchies of gender promote capitalist industrialization should also consider militarization. Conversely, feminist theorizing about militarization, war, and peace must examine such phenomena as Victorian notions of "public" and "private," domesticity, the sexual division of labor, and the concept of the "fallen woman"—all of which have been used by state officials as tools to expand military influence and values throughout a "civilian" society.

CONCLUSION: THEORIZING IN DARK TIMES

Our own historical period may rank as the most thoroughly militarized in history; more people in more societies are dependent on or controlled by the military and military priorities—that is, are militarized—than at any previous time. This makes our theoretical task more critical than ever. Military expenditures, militaristic values, and military authority now influence the flow of foreign trade and determine which countries will or will not receive agricultural assistance. They shape the design and marketing of children's toys and games and of adult fashions and entertainments. Military definitions of progress and security dominate the economic fate of entire geographic regions. The military's ways of doing business open or shut access to information and technology for entire social groups. Finally, military mythologies of valor and safety influence the senses of self-esteem and well-being of millions of people. Yet the very breadth and depth of militarization in so many countries make it difficult to develop unambiguously *feminist* theories of militarization.

Feminist theorizing is distinctive insofar as it reveals how much of social practice depends on manipulations of gender. Sometimes, the variety of ways in which military policies and values affect all of us make it appear foolish or arrogant to assign causal priority to the social construction of gender. The very darkness of our times, whether measured in megatonnage of nuclear explosives or numbers of people in refugee camps, tempts us to dilute our distinctly feminist approach. Although it appears that the spread of military beliefs and influence cannot be sustained unless fueled by the hierarchical arrangements of gender (i.e., patriarchy), we may hesitate to press the issue in a group that has come together out of quite different concerns about militarization.

The composition of the antimilitarism campaign is often extremely diverse: men and women who see a threat to democracy in the government's use of force to quell popular protest; aboriginal people who fear the escalating demand for the uranium deposits under their already scarce lands; mothers alarmed over the conscription of their sons; parents desperate to locate "disappeared" children; workers opposed to their employers' growing dependence on military contracts; citizens alarmed over the government's willingness to lease land for foreign bases; and men who feel that their own male honor is violated by soldiers who rape their wives and daughters.

The ripple effects of militarization are so far-reaching that it is tempting to think that feminist explanations can provide only *part* of the answer. Some women may also wish to avoid *elementalism* (or "essentialism")—the proposition that males are biologically inclined toward support of state-sanctioned violence, and, conversely, that females are inherently peaceful. This is an argument that has informed feminist theory on a number of issues, as seen in several other chapters of this book. Although elementalism has great surface plausibility, it is an argument that has been used against women as a rationalization for male dominance in the public, if not private, sphere. The elementalist position could also shrink the potential base for antimilitarist organizing, concomitantly enhancing the power of the state and its repressive apparatus. Finally, militarization has so many guises, such global reach, and is so dangerous that even a woman convinced of its roots in the social constructions of femininity and masculinity, if not biological maleness, may soften her analysis for fear of fragmenting the already "out-gunned" forces of antimilitarism.

Feminist theorizing about militarization, therefore, is quite different from theorizing on other social processes. When we try to make sense of rape or the sexual division of labor, we confront enormously difficult political tasks, but at least we start with an understanding that women are the losers in social systems shaped by heterosexism and misogyny. At various times and for different reasons, feminists have claimed that violence against women, or, less directly, the sexual division of labor in gender, "hurts" men as well as women and that men should therefore join the struggle against patriarchy. This echoes the argument that has long divided socialist women and other feminists. Starvation and apartheid, for example, affect all members of the society, so that a gendered analysis may well fragment resistance. Nonetheless, in the case of militarization, women have become the principal agents of challenge because it is they who have the most to gain from collective action.

Militarization, in contrast to other forms of gender oppression, really does injure men, literally as well as figuratively—on the battlefield, in jail cells, and as objects of forced conscription. Thus men are relatively easy to mobilize as allies in antimilitarist campaigns but, at the same time, difficult to convince of the need for a feminist analysis of what causes and perpetuates militarization. To overcome these very real theory-in-action dilemmas, feminists must demonstrate exactly what is lost, analytically and strategically, when gender considerations are left out of the explanation. At the very least, we must show convincingly that if the social constructions of femininity and masculinity are ignored or trivialized, we will fail to grasp why people's lives have become increasingly dominated by military values and agendas, and our subsequent actions will fail to reverse these trends.

If soldiers, generals, national security elites, jingoistic journalists, refugees, defense contractors and their employees, wartime rape victims, weapons engineers, and their spouses are all analyzed as if they are ungendered persons—as if they could as easily be women as men—the resultant theoretical understanding of militarization will be fundamentally flawed. Finally, and most radically, a feminist analysis implicates patriarchy—not just the capitalist military-industrial complex, and not just the hierarchical state—as the root cause of militarism. It is this patriarchal structure of privilege and control that must be dismantled if we are to be rid, once and for all, of militarism. A radical feminist theory of militarization should be able to show that as long as patriarchal assumptions about masculinity and femininity shape people's beliefs and identities, and their relationships with one another, militarization, however temporarily stanched, only lies dormant, capable of rising again and again.

REFERENCES

ADAMS, G. (1981) The Iron Triangle: Politics of Defense Contracting. New York: Council on Economic Priorities.

ANDERSON, K. (1981) Wartime Women. Westport, CT: Greenwood.
ANONYMOUS (1981) "Indian defense forces and arms production." Bulletin of Concerned Asian Scholars 13, 1: 53-57.
BAKER, M. (1984) Nam. Berkeley, CA: Berkeley Books.
BALL, N. (1986) "Security expenditures and economic growth in developing countries," in Pugwash Annals 1985. London: Macmillan.
BALL, N. and M. LEITENBERG (eds.) (1983) The Structure of the Defense Industries: An International Survey. London: Croom Helm.
BOK, S. (1984) Secrets. New York: Vintage.
Breaching the Peace (1983) London: Onlywoman Press.
BROCK-UTNE, B. (1985) Educating for Peace: A Feminist Perspective. Oxford: Pergamon.
BUNSTER, X. (1986) "Surviving beyond fear: Women and torture in Latin America," in J. Nash and H. Safa (eds.) Women and Change in Latin America. South Hadely, MA: Bergen & Garvey.
BURGOS-DEBRAY [ed.] (1985) I, Rigoberta Menchu: An Indian Woman in Guatemala. London: Verso.
CALDECOTT, L. and S. LELAND [eds.] (1983) Reclaim the Earth. London: Women's Press.
Cambridge Women's Peace Collective (1984) My Country is the Whole World: An Anthology of Women's Work on Peace and War. London: Pandora Press.
CAMPBELL, D. (1984) Women at War with America. Cambridge, MA: Harvard University Press.
CHAPKIS, W. (1982) Loaded Questions: Women in Militaries. Washington, DC: Transnational Institute/Institute for Policy Studies.
Connexions (1984) Special issue of "Women and Militarism," 2 (Winter).
COOK, A. and G. KIRK (1983) Greenham Women Everywhere. Boston: South End.
DEVILBISS, M. C. (1985) "Gender integration and unit development." Armed Forces and Society 2, 4: 523-552.
DILEONARDO, M. (1985) "Morals, mothers, militarism: Antimilitarism and feminist theory." Feminist Studies 2, 3: 599-618.
EDWARDS, P. N. (1985) Technologies of the Mind: Computers, Power, Psychology and World War II. Working Paper 2 (December). Santa Cruz: University of California, Silicon Valley Research Group.
ELLIS, J. (1982) The Sharp End of War: The Fighting Man in World War II. London: Corgi Books.
ELSHTAIN, J. and S. TOBIAS [eds.] (1987) Thinking About Women, Militarism and War. New York: Littlefield, Adams.
ENLOE, C. H. (1980) Ethnic Soldiers: State Security in Divided Societies. Athens: University of Georgia Press.
ENLOE, C. H. (1983a) Does Khaki Become You? The Militarization of Women's Lives. Boston: South End.
ENLOE, C. H. (1983b) "Women textile workers in the militarization of Southeast Asia," pp. 407-425 in J. Nash and M. P. Fernandez-Kelly (eds.) Women, Men and the International Division of Labor. New York: SUNY Press.
ENLOE, C. H. (1984) "On common ground: Peace movement dilemmas." Women's Review of Books 1, 12: 3-5.
ENLOE, C. H. (1985a) "Bananas, bases & patriarchy: Feminist questions about the militarization of Central America." Radical America 19, 4: 16-17.
ENLOE, C. H. (1985b) "Black women in the U.S. military." Sojourner (November): 16-17.
ENLOE, C. H. and H. JORDON (1985) "Black women in the military." Minerva 3, 4: 108-116.
Feminism and Non-Violence Study Group (1983) Piecing It Together: Feminism and Non-Violence. Devon: Westwood Ho.
FISCHER, G. [ed.] (1985) Armament, Disarmament, Human Rights, Disarmament. Paris V.

FITZGERALD, A. E. (1972) The High Price of Waste. New York: Norton.

Frontiers (1985) Special issue on "Women and Peace," 8, 2.

GOLDMAN, N. G. [ed.] (1982) Female Soldiers—Combatants or Non-Combatants? Westport, CT: Greenwood.

Grassroots International (1986) Special issue on "Women and Change," 2, 1.

HARFORD, B. and S. HOPKINS [eds.] (1984) Greenham Common: Women at the Wire. London: Women's Press.

HARTMAN, S. M. (1982) The Home Front and Beyond. Boston: Twayne Publishers.

HARTSOCK, N. (1983) Sexuality and Politics: The Barracks Community in Western Political Thought. New York: Longman.

Helicon Nine (1985) "Special Peace Issue," 12-13 (Summer).

HONEY, M. (1984) Creating Rosie the Riveter: Class, Gender and Propaganda During World War II. Amherst, University of Massachusetts Press.

HOWARD, E. (1983) "Israel: The sorcerer's apprentice." MERIP Reports 112 (February): 16-25.

IKEGAME, M. (1984) Sisters of the Sun: Japanese Women Today. London: Change International Reports—Women and Society.

International Economic Conversion Conference (1984) Proceedings, Chestnut Hill, Boston College, MA.

ISAKSSON, E. [ed.] (1987) Women and Military Systems. Brighton, England: Wheatsheat Books.

JONES, L. [ed.] (1983) Keeping the Peace. London: Women's Press.

KAHN, K. (1985) "Gender ideology and the disarmament movement." Resist Newsletter 180 (December).

KALDOR, M. (1981) The Baroque Arsenal. New York: Hill & Wang.

KEEGAN, J. (1977) The Face of Battle. New York: Vintage.

KLARE, M. (1984) American Arms Supermarket. Austin: University of Texas Press.

KOISITNEN, P. (1980) The Military Industrial Complex: An Historical Perspective. New York: Praeger.

KOONZ, C. (1987) Mothers in the Fatherland. New York: St. Martin's.

LIDDLE, J. and R. JOSHI (1985) "Gender and imperialism in British India." Economic and Political Weekly, New Delhi 20, 43 (October 26).

McCLINTOCK, M. (1985) The American Connection: El Salvador and Guatemala, Vols. 1 and 2. London: Zed.

MELMAN, S. (1974) The Permanent War Economy. New York: Simon & Schuster.

MILKMAN, R. (1982) "Redefining women's work: The sexual division of labor in the auto industry during World War II." Feminist Studies 8, 2: 337-372.

Minerva (1985-1986) Quarterly Report on Women and the Military. Vol. 3, nos. 2-3; Vol. 4, no. 1.

NAIRN, A. (1986) "South Africa's war machine." Multinational Monitor, April 15, pp. 8-11.

National Organization for Women, Legal Defense and Educational Fund (1981, March) Amicus curea brief.

PIERSON, R. (1986) "They're Still Women, After All": The Second World War and Canadian Womanhood. Toronto: McClelland Steward.

Plowshares (1985) Special issue on "Women and Economic Conversion," 10, 3.

Puget Sound Women's Peace Camp (1985) We Are Ordinary Women. Seattle, WA: Seal Press.

REARDON, B. (1985) Sexism and the War System. New York: Teachers College Press.

ROGAN, H. (1982) Mixed Company. Boston: Beacon.

SEAGER, J. and A. OLSON (1986) Women in the World: An International Atlas. New York: Simon and Schuster.

STEIHM, J. (1981) Bring Me Men and Women: Mandated Change in the U.S. Air Force Academy. Berkeley: University of California Press.

STEIHM, J. (1985) "The generations of U.S. enlisted women." Signs 2, 1: 155-175.

TALBOTT, S. (1985) Deadly Gambits. New York: Vintage.

TAYLOR, B. (1984) Eve and the New Jerusalem. New York: Pantheon.

TERRY, W. (1984) Bloods: An Oral History of the Vietnam War by Black Veterans. New York: Ballantine.

THITSA, K. (1980) Providence and Prostitution: Image and Reality for Women in Buddhist Thailand. London: Change International Reports—Women and Society.

THOMPSON, D. [ed.] Over Our Dead Bodies. London: Virago.

THOMPSON, E. P. and D. SMITH [eds.] Protest and Survive. London: Penguin.

TRUSTHAM, M. (1984) Marriage and the Victorian Army at Home. Cambridge: Cambridge University Press.

U.S. Department of Defense (1984) Equal Opportunity Office Report. Washington, DC: Government Printing Office.

VALENTA, J. and W. POTTER [eds.] Soviet Decision Making for National Security. Boston: Allen & Unwin.

VANITA, R. (1985) "The 1984 elections: United we fall—into the trap of manipulators." Manushi: A Journal About Women & Society, New Delhi, 26.

VILLARIBA, M. C. (1983) The Philippines: Canvass of Women in Crisis. London: Change-International Reports on Women.

WAINWRIGHT, H. (1983) "The women who wire up the weapons," in D. Thompson (ed.) Over Our Dead Bodies. London: Virago.

WILTSHER, A. (1985) The Most Dangerous Women: Feminist Peace Campaigners of the Great War. London: Pandora.

WOLF, C. (1984) Cassandra. London: Virago.

WOOLF, V. (1938) Three Guineas. New York: Harcourt Brace Jovanovitch.

YOUNG, A. and D. PHILLIPS [eds.] (1986) Militarization in the Non-Hispanic Caribbean. Boulder, CO: Lynne Rienner Publishers.

YUVAL-DAVIS, N. (1985) "Front and rear: The sexual divisions of labor in the Israeli army." Feminist Studies 2, 3: 649-676.

INDEX

Abbott, E. 271
Abidjan (Ivory Coast), 220.
    See also Africa
Abortion, 21, 154, 164-67,
    430, 445, 452-53, 454-55,
    456, 458, 510; historical
    perspective on, 165-66;
    ideologies concerning,
    166; and law, 483-84, 485,
    495. See also Repro-
    duction, *Roe v. Wade*
Abortion Law Reform Act
    (1967, British), 409
Ackelsberg, Martha, 28, 29,
    515, 517, 518, 519
Aclla, 57, See also Inca
Adam, B. 135
Adams, C. T., 510
Adams, G., 529
Addams, Jane, 72, 134
Addelson, K. P., 135, 519
Addis Ababa (Ethiopia),
    220,See also Africa
Adler, C., 183
Adler, F., 474
Adler, T. F., 85
AFDC. See Aid to Families
    with Dependent
    Children
Affirmative Action, 283, 334
Afghanistan, 539
Africa, 36, 37, 40, 51, 60, 57-
    58, 59, 63 (n.2), 216, 218,
    220, 221, 223, 224, 226,
    229, 232, 233, 246, 432,
    528, 531, 538, 539
African Methodist Episcopal
    Church, 411
African Methodist Episcopal
    Zion Church, 411
Afro-American Holiness
    movement, 411
Afro-American Pentecostal
    Churches, 411, 412
Afro-Americans, 26-27, 270,
    359, 373; religious tradi-
    tion of, 26-27, 411-412,
    431-32, 433. See also
    Blacks, Black women
    Race, Women of color

Aggression, 32, 39, 41-43,
    45; men and women com-
    pared, 75-76, 543
Aid to Families with Depen-
    dent Children (AFDC),
    302, 398, 512
Ajzen, I., 105
Alaya, F., 75
Alexander, S., 69
Allan, J. M., 71
Allegier, E. R., 124
Allen, D., 453
Allen, Richard, 411
Allen, P. G., 128
Allport, Gordon W., 110,
    112 (n.6)
Almquist, E.M., 281
Altman, D., 132, 146
Amatniek, J. C., 86
Ambivalence, 14, 331; and
    family, 358; towards
    housework, 338, 339
American Academy of Reli-
    gion, 434
American Cancer Society,
    464
American Federation of
    Labor (AFL), 275, 279
American Lutheran Church,
    412
American Medical Associa-
    tion (AMA), 445, 459
American Telephone & Tele-
    graph (AT&T), 289
American Revolution, 474
Amin, S., 51, 220
Amram, F., 79, 84, 86
Amundsen, K., 508
Ancient Greece, 60, 452-53,
    519, 534
Anderson, B., 312
Anderson, E. G., 71
Anderson, K., 274, 536
Anderson, M. 350, 369
Anderson, R. E., 393
Andolsen, B. H., 424
Andrews, B. W., 211 (n.1)
Androcentrism, 20, 25, 40-
    41, 78, 127, 131, 142, 148,
    349, 421, 443-44, 445, 456,

458, 464, 476. See also
    Sex Bias
Androgyny, 96, 105. See also
    Femininity, Masculinity,
    Traits
Anglicans, 409, 410. See also
    Episcopal Church
Annastasi, Anne, 75
Anorexia nervosa, 465
Another Voice (1975, Kanter
    and Millman), 9, 10
Anthropology, 33, 53. See
    also Social sciences
Antifeminism, 18, 20, 71, 146,
    348
Antimilitarism. See Pacifism,
    Peace, Militarism
Anzaldua, G., 517
Apartheid, 246, 544
Applebaum, E., 329, 330
Ardener, S., 74
Arditti, R., 260
Ardrey, R., 39
Argentina, 234, 528, 541
Aries, P., 369
Aristotle, 506
Arizona State Supreme
    Court, 445
Arizpe, L., 217, 227, 228,
    233, 234, 235
Arnheim, R., 192
Arnold, E., 73
Arrow, K., 300
Asch, Adrienne, 166
Ashmore, R. D., 100, 101,
    102, 108
Asia, 35-36, 37, 41, 44, 47,
    48, 54, 216, 219, 220, 221,
    223, 224, 225, 226, 229,
    230, 231, 232, 233, 274,
    281, 331, 397, 453, 527,
    532, 533, 536, 540, 541
Asian-American women, 274,
    281, 373. See also Minor-
    ity women, Women of
    color
Asian-Americans, 281, 370,
    371, 373. See also Asia,
    Asian-American women,
    Race

Martha Ackelsberg teaches urban politics and political theory in the Government Department at Smith College. She has written a variety of articles on changing family structures and their implications for political life, on women's political activism, and on the Spanish anarchist movement—all exploring the theme of community and diversity. She is currently at work on a book about the Spanish anarchist women's organization *Mujeres Libres*.

Ava Baron is Professor of Sociology at Rider College. She studied sociology and law at New York University and received her Ph.D. in 1981. She has written articles on protective labor legislation; women lawyers; and gender, work, and technology in the sewing and printing industries. Currently she is completing a book entitle, *Men's Work and the Woman Question: The Transformation of Gender and Work in the Printing Industry, 1850-1920.*

Bettina Berch, an economic historian, taught courses on women and the economy at Barnard College for the proverbial seven years. She wrote a textbook on the subject, *The Endless Day: The Political Economy of Women and Work.* Then she was fired. (Postfeminist institutions may have that bad habit of shooting the messenger.) She continues her research on women and high technology, housework history, and labor history, and has just finished the biography of the iconoclast American designer and political activist, Elizabeth Hawes.

Christine E. Bose is Associate Professor of Sociology at the State University of New York at Albany, where she also served as director of the Women's Studies Program from 1978 through 1981. She holds a joint appointment in the Department of Puerto Rican, Latin American and Caribbean Studies. She has published in the areas of occupational prestige, gender and status attainment, women's home and paid employment at the turn of the century, and the social impact of household technology. She is the author of *Jobs and Gender: A Study of Occupational Prestige* (Praeger, 1985) and has coedited two books: one with Glenna Spitz, *Ingredients for Women's Employment Policy* (SUNY Press, 1987) and the other with the Women and Work Research Group titled *Hidden Aspects of Women's Work* (Praeger, 1987). She is currently engaged in a research project on Hispanic women's employment in the contemporary United States.

Sheila Briggs is Assistant Professor in the School of Religion at the University of Southern California. She teaches women's and black studies in the field of systematic and historical theology.

Muriel G. Cantor earned her Ph.D. in sociology from the University of California, Los Angeles, in 1969 and now is a Professor in the Sociology Department at American University, Washington, D.C. She has published several books and reports as well as many articles and book reviews in the areas of mass communications, work and occupations, and the sociology of women. Her latest book (with Sandra Ball-Rokeach), *Media, Audience, and Social Structure,* was published in 1986, and her book *The Soap Opera* (with Suzanne Pingree) in 1983. She has been teaching courses on women and gender since 1972 and created a minor in women's studies at American University in 1981.

Penelope Ciancanelli is Assistant Professor of Accounting at Baruch College, City University of New York. She has written on social accounting systems and the construction of gender. Her current writing is concerned with the social impact of financial accounting systems. While a graduate student, she helped create programs in class and gender in the Economics Department at the New School for Social Research and in the Metropolitan Studies Program at New York University.

Kay Deaux is Professor of Psychology at the Graduate School and University Center of the City University of New York. Her primary scholarly interest concerns issues of gender, and she has done extensive gender-relevant research in both laboratory and field settings. She is the author of two books in this area, *The Behavior of Women and Men* and *Women of Steel* (the latter coauthored with Joseph C. Ullman). She has fellow status in the American Psychological Association, in the American Association for the Advancement of Science, and has twice been a resident fellow at the Center for Advanced Study in the Behavioral Sciences. Most recently, she was named the 1988 recipient of the Carolyn Wood Sherif Memorial Lectureship, awarded by the American Psychological Association's division of the psychology of women.

Irene Diamond received her Ph.D. in politics from Princeton University. She is the editor of *Families, Politics, and Public Policy: A Feminist Dialogue on Women and the State* (Longman, 1983), author of *Sex Roles in the State House* (Yale University Press, 1977), and coeditor with Lee Quinby of the collection *Feminisim and Foucault: Reflections on Resistance* (Northeastern University Press, 1987). She is active in the American Green Movement and is Associate Professor of Political Science at the University of Oregon. She is also working on a book titled *Women and Fertility: The Political and Spiritual Promise of Ecofeminism.*

Paula England is Associate Professor of Sociology and Political Economy at the University of Texas, Dallas. She is coauthor (with George Farkas) of

Households, Employment and Gender: A Social, Economic, and Demographic View (Aldine, 1986). She testified before the U.S. Civil Rights Commission at its 1984 hearings on comparable worth, and has served as an expert witness in Title VII litigation.

Cynthia H. Enloe is currently Professor and Chair of Government and formerly Director of Women's Studies at Clark University in Worcester, Massachusetts. She and Joni Seager are the North American editors for *Women's Studies International Forum*. Among her recent books are *Does Khaki Become You? The Militarization of Women's Lives* (1983), and *Of Common Cloth: Women in the Global Textile Industry* with Wendy Chapkis (1983). She is currently working on a book (to be published by Pandora Press) exploring women's experiences of colonialism, international economies, and foreign policy.

Myra Marx Ferree is Professor of Sociology at the University of Connecticut and former Director of the Women's Studies Program there. She has also been a Visiting Professor of Women's Studies and Social Sciences at the University of Frankfurt, West Germany. Her research interests are focused on women and work, especially concerning working-class women, and on feminist attitudes and organizations. With Beth B. Hess she has coauthored *Controversy and Coalition: The New Feminist Movement* (G. K. Hall, 1985). Her recent work includes a comparison of the West German and American women's movements and a study of women's discontent with the divison of household labor.

Christine Ward Gailey is an Assistant Professor in the Sociology and Anthropology Department at Northeastern University, Boston. She is the author of *Kinship to Kingship: Gender Hierarchy and State Formation in the Tongan Islands* (University of Texas Press, 1987). Several of her articles on state formation and gender have appeared in anthropology journals in both the United States and Canada. Gailey received her doctorate from the New School for Social Research in New York (1981). She is currently working on a book on state origins.

Evelyn Nakano Glenn is Professor of Sociology and Women's Studies at the State University of New York, Binghamton. Her research and writing focus on women's work, both in the household and in the labor market. She is especially interested in issues of technology and racial stratification of women's work, and has published widely on impacts of office automation, racially ethnic women, and domestic service. Her most recent publication is *Issei, Nisei, Warbride*, a sociohistorical study of Japanese-American women domestic workers.

Meredith Gould is a sociologist at New Jersey's Department of Higher Education, where she manages the Business/Humanities Project.

Beth B. Hess, a graduate of Radcliffe College and Rutgers University, is currently Professor of Sociology at County College of Morris, Randolph, New Jersey. She has authored or coauthored a number of textbooks in social gerontology and sociology: *Aging and Old Age,* with Elizabeth Markson (Macmillan); three editions of *Growing Old in America* (Transaction); and three editions of *Sociology,* with Elizabeth Markson and Peter Stein (Macmillan). Her earlier collaboration with Myra Marx Ferree led to the publication of *Controversy and Coalition: The New Feminist Movement* (G. K. Hall, 1985). She has also authored numerous journal articles and book chapters on friendship, older women, family relations in older life, poverty, and the impact of public policy on women and the elderly. In addition to her writing, she has been active in professional organizations and currently serves as President of Sociologists for Women in Society, and Association for Humanist Sociology, and the Eastern Sociological Society.

Mary E. Kite is an Assistant Professor of Psychology at Ball State University in Muncie, Indiana. Her research interests are in the area of gender stereotyping: in particular, she has investigated the role that gender plays in the stereotyping of various subgroups such as homosexuals, members of various nationalities, and the elderly.

Helena Z. Lopata was born in Poland and came to America during World War II. She obtained her Ph.D. in sociology from the University of Chicago in 1954 and is now Professor of Sociology and Director, Center for the Comparative Study of Social Roles, Loyola University of Chicago. Some of her published works include *Occupation: Housewife; Widowhood in an American City; Polish Americans: Status Competition in an Ethnic Community; Women as Widows: Support Systems; City Women: Work, Jobs, Occupations, Careers, Volume 1—America, Volume 2—Chicago* (with Debra Barnewolt and Cheryl Allyn Miller); and *Widows and Dependent Wives: From Social Problem to Federal Policy* (with Henry Brehm). She is now researching changes in the homes, neighborhoods, and suburbs around Chicago where she initially interviewed in 1956.

Lori McCreary is an Economic Analyst with the City of Dallas and a Ph.D. candidate in the Political Economy Program at the University of Texas, Dallas. Her interests include race and ethnic relations, urban labor markets, and gender.

Barbara Katz Rothman is Associate Professor of Sociology, Baruch College and the Graduate Center, City University of New York. She is author of *In Labor: Women and Power in the Birthplace,* published in paperback as *Giving Birth,* and *The Tentative Pregnancy: Prenatal Diagnosis and the Future of Motherhood.* She is currently working on a book to be published by W. W. Norton & Co., on the changing ideology of motherhood.

Janet Sayers, author of *Biological Politics: Feminist and Anti-Feminist Perspectives* (1982) and of *Sexual Contradictions: Psychology, Psychoanalysis, and Feminism* (1986), teaches women's studies, social work, and social psychology at the University of Kent, Canterbury, England.

Beth E. Schneider received her Ph.D. in 1981 from the University of Massachusetts, Amherst, and is currently Associate Professor of Sociology at the University of California, Santa Barbara. She has written extensively on the dimensions, relationships, and consequences of the sexualization of the work place and on the experiences of heterosexual and lesbian women at work. She currently serves as the Chair of the Sexual Behavior Division of the Society for the Study of Social Problems. Her new research focuses on political generations among women and the development of political consciousness in women's relationship to the contemporary feminist movement.

Carole J. Sheffield is Associate Professor of Political Science and Women's Studies at William Patterson College of New Jersey. She is the author of "Sexual Terrorism" (in *Women: A Feminist Perspective,* 1984). She has lectured widely on feminism and male violence against women. She was a founding member of the college's women's studies program and for that program teaches courses on politics and sex, and on racism and sexism in a changing America (a course required of all students). Her current research interest is in the forms of implied violence and intimidation against women that have not yet been recognized or studied.

Susan Tiano is Assistant Professor of Sociology and the Associate Director of Academic Programs for the Latin American Institute at the University of New Mexcio. After receiving her Ph.D. from Brown University, she served as Director of the Office of Women in International Development at Michigan State University. She is coauthor of *Women on the U.S.-Mexico Border: Responses to Change* (Allen & Unwin, 1987).

Mary K. Zimmerman has been actively involved with the study of gender since teaching her first course on the sociology of women in 1972. She currently is Associate Professor of Health Services Administration and Sociology at the University of Kansas, where she teaches courses in medical sociology, health research methods, and women's health issues. She is the author of *Passage Through Abortion: The Personal and Social Reality of Women's Experiences* (Praeger, 1977) and a number of research articles examining women's work-related and reproductive health issues.

NOTES

NOTES